WITHDRAWN

Symbols and Society

FOURTEENTH SYMPOSIUM
OF THE
CONFERENCE ON SCIENCE,
PHILOSOPHY AND RELIGION

THE PAPERS included in this volume were prepared for the fourteenth meeting of the Conference on Science, Philosophy and Religion in Their Relation to the Democratic Way of Life, which was held at Harvard University on August 30, 31, and September 1, and 2, 1954. Each paper represents only the opinion of the individual author.

SYMBOLS and SOCIETY

FOURTEENTH SYMPOSIUM
OF THE CONFERENCE ON SCIENCE,
PHILOSOPHY AND RELIGION

Edited by

LYMAN·BRYSON
PROFESSOR EMERITUS OF EDUCATION
TEACHERS COLLEGE, COLUMBIA UNIVERSITY

LOUIS FINKELSTEIN
CHANCELLOR, THE JEWISH THEOLOGICAL SEMINARY OF AMERICA

HUDSON HOAGLAND
EXECUTIVE DIRECTOR, WORCESTER FOUNDATION FOR EXPERIMENTAL BIOLOGY

R. M. MACIVER
LIEBER PROFESSOR EMERITUS OF POLITICAL PHILOSOPHY AND SOCIOLOGY,
COLUMBIA UNIVERSITY

COOPER SQUARE PUBLISHERS, INC.

New York   1964

By unanimous vote of the
Conference membership on September 4, 1952,
this book
is gratefully dedicated to

PHILIPP G. FRANK,

who has through his teaching,
his writing, his participation in the Conference,
and his example, contributed magnificently to
the integration and advancement of knowledge.

Preface

These papers were prepared for and discussed at the Fourteenth Conference on Science, Philosophy and Religion, held at Harvard University from August 30 to September 2, 1954.

The First Conference on Science, Philosophy and Religion Lecture was presented by Harlow Shapley on August 30th. The editors are especially pleased that this notable address, "Galaxies and Their Human Worth," is included in this volume.

As indicated in the program, papers had been expected from Henry D. Aiken, Irving Lorge, and Richard P. McKeon. However, these men were prevented from completing their manuscripts for publication.

During the academic year 1953–1954, Lyman Bryson conducted at The Institute for Religious and Social Studies in New York a faculty seminar on Symbolism. The editors appreciate the opportunity to include in this symposium the material prepared by Thomas Ritchie Adam, Lyman Bryson, and William Y. Tindall for this seminar.

The Conference volumes are listed on page vi.

The oral proceedings of the sessions were recorded, and although it has not been possible thus far to arrange for their publication, the stenotype report is available at the Conference offices to qualified students.

The editors express their deep gratitude to all who participated in the Conference program, to those who attended the sessions, to the authors of comments, and above all to the original writers, whose work formed the basis of the Conference meetings and the substance of this volume. In particular they record their indebtedness to the officers and staff of Harvard University where the working sessions were held. They again wish to thank Jessica Feingold for her indispensable help in every phase of the Conference program.

The participants in the meetings of 1954; and the authors of papers and comments are listed on pages 581 to 592. A report on the Conference as a whole is given in Appendix V.

PUBLICATIONS OF THE CONFERENCE ON SCIENCE, PHILOSOPHY AND RELIGION

Science, Philosophy and Religion, A Symposium, 1941. (The papers prepared for the meetings held in New York City on September 9, 10, and 11, 1940). Out of print.

Science, Philosophy and Religion, Second Symposium, 1942. (The papers prepared for the meetings held in New York City on September 8, 9, 10, and 11, 1941.)

Science, Philosophy and Religion, Third Symposium, 1943. (The papers prepared for the meetings held in New York City on August 27, 28, 29, 30, and 31, 1942.) Out of print.

Approaches to World Peace, Fourth Symposium, 1944. (The papers prepared for the meetings held in New York City on September 9, 10, 11, 12, and 13, 1943.) Out of print.

Approaches to National Unity, Fifth Symposium, 1945. (The papers prepared for the meetings held in New York City on September 7, 8, 9, 10, and 11, 1944.) Out of print.

Approaches to Group Understanding, Sixth Symposium, 1947. (The papers prepared for the meetings held in New York City on August 23, 24, 25, 26, and 27, 1945.)

Conflicts of Power in Modern Culture, Seventh Symposium, 1947. (The papers prepared for the meetings held in Chicago on September 9, 10, and 11, 1946.) Out of print.

Learning and World Peace, Eighth Symposium, 1948. (The papers prepared for the meetings held in Philadelphia on September 7, 8, 9, and 10, 1947.)

Goals for American Education, Ninth Symposium, 1950. (The papers prepared for the meetings held in New York City on September 7, 8, 9, and 10, 1948.)

Perspectives on a Troubled Decade: Science, Philosophy and Religion, 1939–1949, Tenth Symposium, 1950. (The papers prepared for the meetings held in New York City on September 6, 7, 8, and 9, 1949.)

Foundations of World Organization: A Political and Cultural Appraisal, Eleventh Symposium, 1952. (The papers prepared for the meetings held in New York City on September 5, 6, 7, and 8, 1950.)

Freedom and Authority in Our Time, Twelfth Symposium, 1953. (The papers prepared for the meetings held in New York City on September 4, 5, 6, and 7, 1951.)

Symbols and Values: An Initial Study, Thirteenth Symposium, 1954. (The papers prepared for the meetings held in New York City on September 2, 3, 4, and 5, 1952.)

Table of Contents

ix

APPENDICES

I. Bars, Cafés, Sports, Tobacco, Fast Religion Fact
Institutions and their Energy, Water, Heat, Sanitation

II. Early Establishment of Community and Racial Aspects:
Human Dimensions

III. Analysis and Evaluation: Human Resources 95

IV. Composition by N. L. Assumption 239

V. Relation to this Community: its Scientific, Philosophy, and its
Religion 279

Conclusion: Bewitched and Sense 366

References

Reference: Conference on Human Biology ... of I.D.A., W. A.D.
.... past annual jr. Conference .... and + 1975 485

Index
.... 509

CHAPTER I

The Physical Universe as a Symbol

By PHILIPP G. FRANK

WHILE THE PICTURE of the physical world that has been developed by physical science has undergone radical changes since the times of Plato, Aristotle, and Saint Thomas, the picture outlined by Thomistic philosophy has not changed. The foundations of the Thomistic doctrine on science have been and are today: firstly, the doctrine that every material body in the commonsense meaning of this word consists actually of "prime matter" and "substantial form," and, secondly, the doctrine that the laws of nature are not only uniformities but "genuine laws" which are imposed by a lawgiver.

In close connection with these doctrines is the general feature of Thomistic philosophy of science that has been described by a representative of this school as an "analogy of being in the vertical dimension," according to which all physical phenomena are analogous to the phenomena exhibited by living organisms. This is an analogy to commonsense experience, for the main constituents of our commonsense experience are the behavior of simple mechanisms and the familiar rules about the behavior of our fellow men. All this amounts to the doctrine that our physical universe that can be understood according to physical science by a search for physical laws, causal or statistical ones, is, from the viewpoint of the philosopher, operated for certain purposes "for a common good," as Thomistic philosophers say. The universe is not regarded as a dead machine but as a society of living beings which is somehow similar to human society and can be used as an ideal of how human society should operate. This means that all physical phenomena can be interpreted not only by the traditional laws of physics but also by moral laws.

This interpretation of the physical universe as a moral universe started in antiquity in the writings of Plato and was continued strongly in medieval philosophy, with particular lucidity in the work of Saint Thomas. It is easy to understand that in medieval poetry this moral

I

interpretation of the physical universe was a favorite topic. The most famous example of this physicomoral world picture is Dante's *Divine Comedy,* where the physical universe is interpreted as consisting of Hell, Purgatory, and Paradise, or, in other words, as a place where rewards and punishments are dished out according to the moral merits of human beings. The great American philosopher, George Santayana, in his "Essay on Dante," provided a particularly lucid and instructive presentation of the medieval idea about the physical universe. Santayana directs our attention to the fact that the mere distinction between "prime matter" and "substantial form" introduces a moral element into the physical world. The natural lines of cleavage were obliterated, and, as Santayana writes, "moral lines of cleavage" were substituted for them. "Nature was a compound of ideal purposes and inert matter, or a compound of evil matter and perfect form. . . . Evil was identified with matter."

This doctrine has infiltrated a great many philosophical interpretations of science. Even in our twentieth century, quite a few philosophers and philosophically inclined scientists have extolled Rutherford's "Theory of the Atom," because the largest part of the atom is empty and only very tiny pieces of matter (nucleus and electrons) have remained. Like the followers of the medieval philosophers, these contemporary authors believe that by reducing the quantity of matter in the physical universe the world has been purged from evil. For Dante, as Santayana writes, "moral distinctions are displayed in the order of creation. The creator himself was a poet producing allegories. The material world was a parable which he built out in space in order to be enacted." The idea of medieval philosophy, Christian, as well as Jewish and Moslem, was that the purpose of nature was to produce "the good," and the physical laws were symbols by which the moral laws are revealed to man.

In order to put all this in the right perspective, we must remember that this conception of physical laws by no means originated in medieval Scholastics but had its origin far back in antiquity. Santayana pointed out that this moral interpretation of physical phenomena was with particular lucidity presented by Plato in his dialogue *Phaedo.* Socrates, the spokesman of Plato in the dialogue, complains about the way in which some philosophers (in our language, the scientists) claim to have explained the features of our physical universe, whether the earth is round or flat, how the earth is supported at its place, etc. These philosophers disappointed him because they tried to explain everything by what we would call today causal or physical laws, while he expected them to prove that the actual physical universe is "the best" in the moral sense of the word. According to Santayana, this Platonic philosophy, later the basis of medieval thought, said bluntly: "the world is a work of reason. It must be interpreted as we interpret the actions of a man, by its motives." In order to learn how precisely Plato rejected what we today call causal or physical explanations, we may quote some sentences from the Platonic dialogue *Phaedo*.

Socrates says:

> I imagined that he (the philosopher Anaxagoras) would tell me whether the earth is flat or round; and whichever was true he would proceed to show the nature of the best and show that this was best; and if he said that the earth was in the center of the universe he would further explain that this position was the best, and I should be satisfied with the explanation given and not want other sort of cause. . . . What expectations I had formed and how grievously was I disappointed! As I proceeded, I found my philosopher altogether forsaking reason . . . but having recourse to air and ether and water and other eccentricities.

It is illuminating to note that the Platonic Socrates calls all physical causes "eccentricities," in contrast to the explanation by purposes.

However, we can go back much further if we want to find examples for the symbolic role of the physical universe. We are all accustomed to relax every seventh day of the week, and a great many of us every sixth and seventh day. The root of this habit is a theory of the Old Testament about the way our physical universe originated. The Hebrew cosmology has been interpreted through the ages as a rule of human conduct that has not outlived its validity today.

Among liberal theologians it has become a habit to say that the Bible is not a textbook of physical science but a guide to moral behavior. However, it would be more nearly correct to say that the Bible is a textbook of physical science which teaches science in a form which has lost much of its technological value but kept, to a high degree, its social value. From a careful study of the Book of Genesis, we can easily learn that even the Law of Causality itself was interpreted by the writers of the Old Testament as an incentive for moral conduct. After the great Flood, God says to Noah: "I established my Covenant with you and the waters shall never again become a flood to destroy all flesh . . . while the earth remains, seedtime and harvest, cold, heat, summer and winter, day and night shall not cease."

If we remember the scientific meaning of the Law of Causality, we can say that God pledged after the Flood that the Law of Causality will remain valid eternally, unless man would behave in such an immoral way that God would punish him by abolishing causality. God behaves like a constitutional king who proclaims a constitution and promises not to violate it except in case of emergency.

The fact that in the Bible the Law of Causality is regarded as a reward for the good conduct of man, becomes clear from some passages in the Talmud, a commentary to the Old Testament which contains the oral Jewish tradition: "When the Holy One, blessed be He, created the first man, He made him lord above everything, the cow obeyed the plowman and the furrow obeyed the plowman. Adam having sinned, they rose up against him: the cow no longer obeyed the plowman, nor did the furrow obey the plowman. With Noah, they quieted down." It is instructive to note that the reaction of the cow to man, a law of animal psychology, is treated on an equal footing with the reaction of the furrow to the plow, a physical law. In the same way, the laws that governed the motion of liquids served moral purposes. The Talmud continues: "Before Noah, the waters used to rise twice a day, once at morning prayer, and once at evening prayer, and they used to flood the dead in their graves. With Noah, the waters quieted down." If we consider instead of the ancient Hebrew world picture Copernicus's picture of the physical world, we read in his main book: "The sun is sitting on a royal throne, rules the family of stars moving around it." The planetary system is described by the analogy with the system of government in the monarchy. We have to remember that this analogy was used by Copernicus for the purpose of bolstering his heliocentric system. "The condition of immobility," wrote Copernicus, "is considered more noble and divine than the condition of change and instability, which therefore is more fitting to the earth than the universe."

All these examples lead up to the general conception of the physical universe as analogous to a human society by which this universe becomes a useful symbol for encouraging a desirable way of life. E. Topitsch gave to this conception the name of "sociocosmic" universe. He collected from a great many sources material from which we learn that this conception prevailed not only among Hebrews and Greeks but also in China, India, and Mesopotamia. "The whole world," Topitsch sums up these examples, "is conceived as a state, a city or a well-ordered household, and the regularities of nature correspond to the rules that govern civil life."[1]

From this conception it became possible to derive what should be regarded as a "natural" or "ideal" structure of human society: the structure that corresponded to the structure of the physical universe. By the same argument, the history of mankind was also regarded as determined by the motions of the stars. According to the original idea of astrology, the stars did not determine the life of individual persons but only historic events. Obviously the life of kings belongs in this sphere; but the sale of "horoscopes" to indiscriminate individuals belongs in a decayed phase of astrology.

Werner Jaeger, in his book on Aristotle, stresses the close correspondence between the Greek ideas in astronomy and their ideas about the moral order in the city-state. "The human laws should be obeyed," as Topitsch summarizes Jaeger, "because, and insofar as they were a part of the rules governing the cosmos which became, by this reflection, the pattern of the right order in society, the metaphysical foundation of the city-state morality."

However, it would be a great mistake to believe that this symbolic use of the physical universe has been abandoned in our scientific century. When atomic physics abandoned strict determinism as the supreme law for the motions of the smallest particles, this has been used as a symbol for the freedom of human actions. We have only to look into the book of one of the most prominent American lawyers and philosophers of law, *Fate and Freedom* by Jerome N. Frank, to learn the moral conclusions which have been drawn from the "non-deterministic" character of the physical world picture that has prevailed in the twentieth century.

The philosophy of Dialectical Materialism which has become the official doctrine of all Marxist groups, has made continuous efforts to shape the picture of the physical world in such a way that the laws of human behavior would be derived from physical laws by way of "dialectics." The laws of "dialectics" have been construed as the most general principles which are equally valid for physical and social phenomena. The most palpable of these principles is the "transition from quantity into quality." If a property increases quantitively more and more, a point will

[1]E. Topitsch, "Society, Technology and Philosophical Reasoning," *Philosophy of Science,* vol. 21, no. 4, 1954.

come when the property undergoes a change in quality. The most famous example in physics is the heating of water. As its temperature increases more and more, the water remains unchanged in quality; it remains water. But, at the boiling point, water is converted into a body of changed quality, the vapor of water. The physicist would not see in this presentation of the boiling process a great help to advancement in the theory of heat. But, Friedrich Engels, the main collaborator of Karl Marx, already had pointed out that this presentation shows clearly the analogy between the physical universe and social behavior. If, in a human society, the accumulation of the means of production (capital, machinery, etc.) increases, the character of the society changes only quantitatively; the society remains qualitatively a society of private owners. But, if we apply the physical theory in its dialectical presentation, we can expect, that after great quantitative changes, great accumulations of capital in few private hands, there will be a qualitative change by which the means of production will be taken out of private hands and will become the property of the community.

The prediction of the coming collectivization of private property derives, in the Marxist philosophy, its strength and reliability from the fact that it is derived from a sound understanding of the laws governing the physical universe. If we look "understandingly" at physical phenomena such as evaporation, we immediately feel, according to Dialectical Materialism, how properties like temperature are increasing quantitatively more and more without experiencing any qualitative change, until the accumulated drive toward a qualitative change eventually becomes so strong that it frees itself in a sudden jump. The necessity of a social revolution manifests itself, according to Dialectical Materialism, to everyone who attempts to have a real understanding of the origin of changes in the physical world.

If we analyze this conception of the physical universe as a symbol for rules of human behavior, we run into some difficulties which are evident to anybody who has done some "hard thinking" in the logic and epistemology of science. As we have pointed out, the picture of the physical world that is accepted at a certain period serves, in a symbolic way, as a source from which rules for human behavior can be derived. The shortest way of presenting these rules is to say that the physical universe can be interpreted as an ideal human society; every real human society attempts to come as close as possible to this ideal, and this approach becomes the rule of its moral behavior.

If we describe this situation as a whole, we easily note that, first, our picture of the physical universe is created by the human mind as an image of our actual human society; but that, second, once this image is firmly established, it becomes an example by which human society is guided in its attempt to become an ideal society. This, however, is a clear example of circular thought; man creates the universe as an image of his own social organization, and then shapes his organization according to the image that he has himself created. It is logically clear that by this procedure no feasible rule for human behavior can be derived. Topitsch writes in the paper quoted above: "I tried to show that these procedures generally lead into purely analytical propositions which are either eternal truths because they are tautologies and disguised definitions, or eternal problems because they are self-contradictions." Historically, of course, the idea of the physical universe as a symbol for human society has had a great influence upon human behavior, because, at every individual moment of history, man has an individual picture of the universe; practically, the complete chain of reasoning is not conscious to man when he has to make a decision.

Comment by Stewart G. Cole:

In your paper you raise the question whether the physical universe is also "a moral universe." Historically you have presented several classical traditions illustrating how the spokesmen for these viewpoints have resorted to the principle of analogy to substantiate their particular claims for belief in a moral or a divinely governed universe. Toward the end of your essay you point out rather convincingly the inherent weakness of the method of analogy as a procedure leading man from the consideration of secondary causes (scientific) to the affirmation of primary causes (philosophical or religious) with respect to the nature and behavior of the cosmos.

This paper renders an important service to our Conference and issues a challenge to scientists, philosophers, and religionists to discover a more substantial intellectual foundation for their faith in "a moral universe," if they believe that the physical world really does care for the human family. Have I failed, by chance, to discover in your closely reasoned paper a clue to your own approach to this basic issue, from which there is no escape in man's struggle to make his peace with the physical world?

The Physical Universe as a Symbol

CHAPTER II

The Queen as Political Symbol in the British Commonwealth

By THOMAS RITCHIE ADAM

THE BRITISH COMMONWEALTH of Nations has undertaken a curious experiment in political association. It has dispensed unobtrusively and almost surreptitiously with the façade of legal sovereignty that once bound its component parts into the semblance of a political community. Though the bond of a common allegiance had ceased to denote political subordination of one part to another, it was assumed until very recent times to be indispensable in terms of formal structure. India's determination to become a Republic while remaining within the Commonwealth forced a reexamination of the nature of Commonwealth association. The last vestige of authority in the form of an almost fictional sovereignty was dropped overboard, and the concept of a free association of peoples joined together in the recognition of a common symbol took its place.

This resurgence of symbolism as an effective political tie seems unique since the decay of the Holy Roman Empire. As the experiment is no more than a few years old, it is, of course, impossible to prognosticate its success or failure. It would seem worthwhile, however, to examine what is meant by the use of a symbol as a serious political tie between free peoples. The constituent document binding the member nations to this novel concept reads in part:

> The Governments of the United Kingdom, Canada, New Zealand, Australia, South Africa, India, Pakistan and Ceylon, whose countries are united as Members of the British Commonwealth of Nations and owe a common allegiance to the Crown, which is also the *symbol* of their free association . . .
>
> The Government of India has however declared and affirmed India's desire to continue her full membership of the Commonwealth of Nations and her acceptance of The King as the *symbol* of the free associ-

9

ation of its independent member nations and as such the Head of the Commonwealth.[1]

India's insistence on the concept of the Monarch rather than the Office may be held to bind the other Commonwealth members who accepted India's declaration. Prime Minister Nehru explained this decision on the grounds that India had ceased to owe allegiance to the Crown but had agreed that the Monarch would be recognized as a symbol of free association.[2] By this declaration the Monarch as Head of the Commonwealth, is distinguished from the Crown acting as the source of legal sovereignty in member nations.

As matters stand today, the British Commonwealth of Nations has no Sovereign. It certainly lacks a political Administration, nor can it boast as an entity of representative bodies. Even the unifying factor of common principles of Law and Justice has vanished with the renunciation of the Privy Council as a Court of Appeal from the High Courts of the Dominions. There is not even a body of treaties between the component nations that might spell out some obligation of continuing association. In terms of formal organization, there would seem to be little more than some casual memoranda.

The best authoritative description of the Commonwealth relationship remains that given by the Imperial Conference of 1926:

> They are autonomous communities within the British Empire, equal in status, in no way subordinate one to another in any aspect of their domestic or external affairs but united by a common allegiance to the Crown and freely associated as Members of the British Commonwealth of Nations.

A commentary on this declaration added: "It (the Commonwealth) depends essentially, if not formally, on positive ideals. Free institutions are its life blood. Free cooperation is its instrument." As "common allegiance to the Crown" has ceased to be an essential element since 1949, "free association" alone seems to remain. This has stripped the last shadow of legal framework from the institution. The term, political, then, must be used without reference to law, government, or sovereignty, if the Commonwealth is to be named a political association. In a broad

[1]Commonwealth Prime Ministers' Meeting, 1949, *Final Communiqué*, 27 April, 1949, author's italics.
[2]Jawaharlal Nehru, "Speech to the Indian Constituent Assembly," 16 May, 1949, *Indian Constituent Assembly Debates,* vol. 8, pp. 2–10.

sense, however, the objectives of Commonwealth association lie within political fields. For the purpose of this paper, politics will be taken to include more than law, government, or sovereignty, and any instrument that is used to hold peoples together in common action will be considered a political instrument. In this sense a symbol may be a political instrumentality even though it is not a means of government or a product of law.[3]

The Character of Free Association. Free association is a novel political concept. In political theory all association within a state is conditioned by law through either positive or permissive rules. Association among sovereign states is determined by the analogous concept of international law, normally in the form of treaties, conventions, or other forms of international legislation. The Commonwealth is not a sovereign state and has no domestic law. The constituent member states of the Commonwealth are not bound together by any system of treaties. The manner of association, therefore, lies outside obligatory forms. It exists as planned cooperation of peoples through their governments beyond the demands of law. In political theory this might be treated as supporting the doctrine of philosophic anarchism, particularly the views of Kropotkin.[4]

In practice this association consists of a network of voluntary but customary consultation between political institutions on all levels from the heads of governments to subordinate parts of the bureaucracy. The extent of this consultative system is seldom realized. A recent book requires four hundred pages for a concise description.[5]

The effective strength of this cooperation is a matter of historical opinion. In the twentieth century the widely scattered constituent elements appear to have achieved a remarkable unity of policy through several wars and troubled intervals of peace.

Factors Involved in Free Association. Government agencies of inde-

[3]Prime Minister Nehru has expressed this perhaps even more obscurely than the writer:

> In this particular declaration nothing very much is said about the position of the King, except that he will be a symbol. It has been made perfectly clear—it was made perfectly clear—that the King has no functions at all. He has a certain status. The Commonwealth itself, as such, is not a body, if I may say so; it has no organization through which to function and the King also can have no function.

Indian Constituent Assembly Debates, vol. 8, pp. 2–10.

[4]Prince Petr Aleksteevich Kropotkin, *Mutual Aid,* W. Heinemann, London, 1904.

[5]Heather J. Harvey, *Consultation and Co-operation in the Commonwealth,* Oxford University Press, London, 1952.

pendent, sovereign states act as the instruments of cooperation. It may be argued that they do so principally for reasons of convenience, a convenience that has proved itself as an historical fact. This would reduce free association to an internal administrative device of modern bureaucracy. The attitudes and feelings of the peoples concerned would not be an important factor.

All the members of the Commonwealth, however, have representative systems of government under varying degrees of democratic control. It is unlikely that even one of the governments concerned could afford to commit itself to a policymaking or administrative system not rooted in popular favor or understanding. It is almost impossible that all the governments concerned could follow this course over any period of time without serious internal challenge.

It may be accepted, then, that the several peoples partake actively in the process of free association. The question remains whether this participation requires any institutional formulation. A vague, unorganized sentiment, a *participation mystique,* could be assumed. Sorel's[6] concept of the social myth creating a *solidarité* that provided a practical path to mass action could perhaps be extended to the wideflung segments of Imperial Britain. The touching faith of Kropotkin in man's passion for cooperation with his fellows whenever a loophole is provided by hostile authority, might be offered in further argument.

Unorganized, instinctive, or traditional sentiment, however, is a very weak peg on which to hang the massive, concrete fact of Commonwealth cooperation. Institutional forms exist as a focus for Commonwealth sentiment among the masses of the several states. It is worth examining whether one or more of these institutions may possess effective force in determining political attitudes outside the normal channels of lawmaking, law enforcement, and general administration.

Standards of what might constitute effective force might be listed as follows:

(a) Power to influence public opinion in terms either of positive political policies or as a negative check on governmental practices.

(b) Recognition as a binding convention by political power groups and institutions.

(c) Methods of expression which can be understood at the individual

[6]Georges Sorel, *Reflections on Violence,* translated by T. E. Hulme, P. Smith, New York, 1941.

level and are flexible enough to be adapted to changing circumstances.

(d) Continuity in historical time so as to become part of the traditional or educational environment.

The Monarch as a Method of Association. The Queen possesses institutional form. As living wearer of the Crown she is the repository of legal sovereignty in all the member states, except India. This, however, is primarily a domestic matter in each country. Its value as an associational tie is questionable. The degree to which the masses in the component states understand legal sovereignty or allow it to affect their attitudes cannot be readily ascertained. Fortunately, the Monarch has an institutional character outside that of the Crown. She (or He) is a Corporation Sole in English Law. This may be brashly translated as a Family Holding Company to pass on nongovernmental property or, what is perhaps more important, Family or Dynastic prestige. It is the institutional Monarch, not the institutional Crown, who is the Head of the Commonwealth.

The governmental heads of all the member states transact certain types of official business directly with the Monarch without passing through United Kingdom governmental channels. These matters, principally in relation to foreign affairs and the granting of honors, are submitted to the Queen personally or through a Governor General by the head of the government concerned. The binding convention is that Her Majesty will always accept the advice of her overseas ministers as fully as that of her domestic ministers. This does not prevent the Monarch discussing the questions raised at unknown length or in terms that are never made public. She is in a position, as the recipient of the confidences of all her other ministers, to correlate policies and to advise from an altitude above party politics or particular nationalisms. She is a carefully nurtured, multinational personality almost unique in training and outlook. The secret doubts, of, say, the executive of New Zealand, as to how some aspect of their foreign policy might be viewed in some other portion of the Commonwealth can perhaps be tested out in discussions with the Queen. In all respect, one might say that the Monarch has been trained as an interCommonwealth guinea pig. Her symbolic status as Head of the Commonwealth is not pure mystique. Underlying it is a discipline of training and environment which particularizes the Commonwealth sentiment into the viewpoint of a living person.

It is possible, therefore, that the political symbol of an abstract idea does not merely represent that idea but literally embodies it, in so far as it may be given physical form.

Each Dominion Prime Minister may have his own personal philosophy of the nature of the Commonwealth that he would defend to the death against any or all of his peers among the other Commonwealth Ministers. Sooner or later, however, he must test his views against the concrete reality of the Monarch's reaction. In this way a certain common element, or perhaps limiting factor affects the right of equal and sovereign governments to stress their own views.

It appears something of a paradox that in this case the political symbol is a concrete, limited reality that serves ultimately to define the abstract idea.

Association of Peoples. The former concept of the Commonwealth that it was composed of peoples separated by the Seven Seas but united by common language, a common system of law, and the same sort of common loyalty to the Crown, is no longer valid. It is questionable if it was ever accurate. Canada and South Africa have always had a bilingual culture with Common Law and Roman Law holding equal place.

The common outlook among all the peoples of the Commonwealth appears to have deeper roots.

Patterns of social thought based on the continuity of institutional forms are widespread among all Commonwealth peoples. English institutional forms provided the dominant basis for a great part of the development of Commonwealth culture. Even in India the literate class is still an offshoot of the English educational system. Nehru has admitted this frankly:

> Now the House knows that inevitably during the past century and more all kinds of contact have arisen between England and this country, many of them were bad, very bad, and we have struggled throughout our lives to put an end to them. Many of them were not so bad, many of them may be good, and many of them, good or bad, irrespective of what they may be, are there. Here I am the potent example of these contacts, speaking in the Honourable House in the English language. . . . The fact remains that we are functioning here under certain rules and regulations for which the model has been the British Constitution. These laws which exist today have been largely forged by them. . . . Largely our educational apparatus has been influenced. Largely our military apparatus has

been influenced by these considerations and we have grown up naturally as something rather like the British Army.[7]

One of the clearest examples of common institutional traditions throughout the Commonwealth is the prevalence of Parliamentary democracy.

> We are not just democracies in the British Commonwealth. We have a special sort of democracy which is almost unique to us. This is a Parliamentary democracy which was discovered and elaborated in this country and which has spread to all the other countries of the Commonwealth. . . . The consequence is that all the statesmen of the Commonwealth speak the same political language.[8]

These common roots of basic social institutions do not prevent the development of great diversities fostered by new circumstances under strange skies.

A dichotomy between the old and the new way of life constantly bedevils individuals in Commonwealth lands. Parliamentary democracy, military subordination to the civil authority, are abstractions hard to grasp even for the better educated members of the community. Radical change often appears as a concrete device appealing to common sense.

On the side of tradition, however, the Queen provides a personification of many of the old forms. Parliamentary democracy (in its British form) is entangled with a certain ritual behavior toward the Monarch (as India may soon discover). An executive or legislature cheating on the rules generally find the position dramatized on the level of individual understanding by the charge of wrong behavior to the Queen's personal representative, the Governor General.

The military system of subordination rests on the Officer Corps of the Commonwealth Armies holding their commissions from their respective Governors General. Their loyalty is to neither a legislative body nor to a political executive, but to the Monarch personally. The Armed Services throughout the Commonwealth, as in England, are apolitical.

Individual Commonwealth citizens, then, largely determine the amount of institutional continuity they believe desirable in terms of their feelings toward the Queen. Conservative peoples, such as the New Zea-

---

[7] "Speech to the Indian Constituent Assembly," 16 May, 1949, *op. cit.*

[8] "Speech of the Secretary of State for Commonwealth Relations to the Royal Empire Society," 12 October, 1950. *United Empire,* vol. XLI, no. 6, pp. 333–335.

landers, might be expected to, and in fact do, demonstrate an intense sentiment toward Her Majesty. On the other hand, Afrikaners have a shrewd conviction that the Queen remains the principal obstacle to Afrikaner domination in South Africa.

> As far as South Africa is concerned, there have always been two schools of thought, not only in recent years, but for years and generations, namely, the republican idea on the one hand and the other conception on the other hand, that we must be linked up with a nation overseas. We have failed to reconcile these two standpoints and we will not and cannot succeed in reconciling them.[9]

The Queen, then, throughout the Commonwealth affords a personification of certain traditional institutional forms held more or less in common. As a living person and not an abstract idea the Queen is well within the comprehension of the masses. The personal attitude of an individual within the Commonwealth toward Her Majesty can and does influence a line of action to be taken in concrete political and social situations.

Personification of an institutional complex may be held to be an effective means of mass communication influencing individual action.

In this connection the political symbol would seem to the mass mind to be the reality while the abstract idea served as the representation.

Parliamentary democracy does not rest on fundamental law. Written Constitutions, such as those of Canada and Australia, serve to spell out the political structure, to allocate governmental powers. They do not, however, as in the United States create the mystique of a Supreme Law, the ultimate guardian of the rights of the individual as a social being. In British eyes all laws are but pale reflections of the idea of Justice which itself is the inexpressible essence of social union. David Hume's words still summarize the British viewpoint.

> Justice is certainly approved of, for no other reason than because it has a tendency to the public good; and the public good is indifferent to us except so far as sympathy interests us in it. We must presume the like with regard to all the other virtues which have a like tendency to the public good. They must derive all their merit from our sympathy with those who reap any advantage from them, as the virtues which have a

[9]"Speech of Prime Minister Malan to the South African House of Assembly," 11 May, 1949, *South Africa House of Assembly Debates*, vol. 68, coll. 5551–5565.

tendency to the good of the person possessed of them derive their merit from our sympathy for him.[10]

The idea of limited government in Commonwealth countries is bound up with the observance of political conventions. To the large majority of the peoples these conventions are little known or understood. The sanctions behind them, however, consist of a strong popular sentiment in favor of certain social patterns held to lie beyond the right of political government to overturn.

The Queen as Personification of the Family Tie. The Family in all Commonwealth countries is held to be an inviolate social pattern. Political government is considered limited in its power to disrupt this tie. It is not, however, limited by law but by sentiment. In order that sentiment may have effective force it must be canalized in definite, positive terms. There must be a concrete idea as to what constitutes the family tie, in terms of its attributes and rights as against the political order.

Since the reign of Victoria, the monarchy has constituted itself into a Royal Family that has served as a personification of the family tie, common to the whole Commonwealth. The concretion of the idea into a living group has afforded sharp definitions, comprehensible to the masses. It would be a bold government in any part of the Commonwealth (outside Asia) that would attempt to change divorce, the rights of women, the privacy of the home, in any way that contrasted sharply with the practices of the Royal Family itself.

The value placed throughout the modern Commonwealth on the Monarch's symbolization of the Family may be illustrated by the remarks of the Canadian Prime Minister on the occasion of the abdication of Edward VIII.

> The one question upon which we really had to express an opinion was whether or not we could as a government undertake the responsibility of introducing to this parliament a bill to make possible a morganatic marriage. We felt that no government in Canada would for one moment think of assuming that responsibility any more than in any of the other Dominions of the British Empire or in the United Kingdom itself.[11]

[10]*Hume's Moral and Political Philosophy,* edited by Henry D. Aiken, Hafner Publishing Company, New York, 1948, p. 167.
[11]*Canada House of Commons Debates,* 1937, vol. 1, coll. 37–68.

In her personification of the Family, the Queen is permitted greater freedom for positive action than in almost any other role. She can speak for herself by herself without the intermediary of any Minister. The well known Christmas tableau of the Monarch talking from her home to all the homes in the Commonwealth is an effective act of mass communication beyond the reach of political governments.

During her recent tour the Queen enunciated dogma well within her royal prerogative: "But woman's paramount duty will always be in the home and toward her family, where the virtues that make for human welfare and happiness have their origin."[12] This may sound harmlessly platitudinous, but a Commonwealth government that sought, say, to conscript women for the armed services in time of peace might find public sentiment sharpened and fortified against them by the royal proclamation on the rights of the family.

Again the personification of the social concept provides the political symbol. It is the symbol in this case that serves as the concrete standard that enables practical judgments to be formed in individual minds.

The Social Order. Professor Lasswell[13] suggests "shared respect, shared rectitude, and shared affection," as important integrating factors in a social order. A common outlook that would bind Commonwealth peoples in terms of action must clearly be based on definite standards of social worthiness. Great diversity might be expected in view of the geographical, economic, and historical differences among Commonwealth countries. Political power, wealth, hereditary claims might compete with each other as a measure of social value. The Monarch, however, sets a pattern in her own person and that of her personal representatives, the Governors General. The highest social prestige, with all the trappings of pomp and ceremony, are accorded in all Commonwealth countries to the Queen's representatives. The marks of social distinction, honors, and decorations flow from the Queen. Though political Ministers actually decide rewards, they must keep within the bounds of recommendations suitable for the Queen to grant.

In a negative sense this hinders the rise of particular oligarchies, aristocracies, or ruling classes among the separate Commonwealth peoples.

---

[12]"Speech of Queen Elizabeth II," Brisbane, March 17, 1954, reported in *New York Herald Tribune,* March 18, 1954.

[13]Harold D. Lasswell, *The World Revolution of our Time,* Stanford University Press, Stanford, 1951.

The actual wielders of social power must conform to the general pattern to receive the tokens of social prestige. In the positive sense social recognition is linked to a concept of detached service, modeled on the Monarchy itself. Hume's view of the functional nature of social prestige applies in the Commonwealth situation:

> I believe most people, at first sight, will be inclined to ascribe our esteem of the rich to self-interest and the prospect of advantage. But as it is certain that our esteem or deference extends beyond any advantage to ourselves, it is evident that that sentiment must proceed from a sympathy with those who are dependent on the person we esteem and respect and who have an immediate connection with him. We consider him as a person capable of contributing to the happiness or enjoyment of his fellow creatures whose sentiments with regard to him we naturally embrace. And this consideration will serve to justify my hypothesis in preferring the third principle to the other two, and ascribing our esteem of the rich to a sympathy with the pleasure and advantage which they themselves receive from their possessions. For as even the other two principles cannot operate to a due extent, or account for all the phenomena without having recourse to a sympathy of one kind or other, it is much more natural to choose that sympathy which is immediate and direct than that which is remote and indirect. To which we may add that where the riches or power are very great, and render the person considerable and important in the world, the esteem attending them may in part be ascribed to another source, distinct from these three, *viz.,* their interesting the mind by a prospect of the multitude and importance of their consequences, though in order to account for the operation of this principle, we must also have recourse to *sympathy,* as we have observed in the preceding section.[14]

This shrewd speculation from a prepsychological era has perhaps been given some substance from the modern phenomenon of the Hollywood personality. The influence exercised by these almost fictitious personages over the manners and morals of a continent can hardly be explained by the logic of self-advantage. Direct participation in the glamor and greatness of mighty affairs seems possible through a sympathetic bond between millions of nonentities and a conspicuous personage.

In British lands the Monarch is peculiarly fitted to stimulate this bond because her magnificence is displayed in ritual terms of direct appeal to the imagination and hallowed by tradition. While elected representatives

[14]*Hume's Moral and Political Philosophy, op. cit.,* p. 166.

provide a means of participation in that area of political association ruled by self-interest and material necessities, the more stimulating aspects of the social bond based on the emotions and the spirit require different representation. Sympathy focused on a living individual has survived as an effective bond of union, despite the rigorous scrutiny of the Enlightenment.

Shared affection is a more difficult concept. Peoples are, however, sometimes united in terms of a common fear or in admiration of a bully, as in Mussolini's Italy. The prevalent sentiment in the Commonwealth swings the other way toward a faintly mawkish feeling directed to the person of the Queen as an admirable young woman and mother. The depth or significance of this sentiment cannot be adequately measured. It does, however, create in the masses of the peoples concerned an understanding that political association can be linked with human affection and is not invariably a matter of power or crude self-interest.

The attributes of social respect and affection may be fairly described as representing the feelings of Commonwealth peoples about the person of the Queen. Social prestige could often be described in Commonwealth countries as "worthy of being honored by the Queen." This would imply that the Queen as a symbol is the measure of practical standards. The abstract ideas draw their sustenance from their relation to a living person in actual situations.

The Queen as Exemplar. When the Queen's position as political symbol is examined in totality it resembles that of an exemplar. Specially trained and conditioned for her task, the Queen embodies in the pattern of her behavior standards of conduct recognized as common to all Commonwealth peoples. Free association is possible because these standards have been given concrete form by a generally accepted authority. A common outlook in terms of basic social and traditional attitudes holds the center of the Commonwealth stage in the form of the dramatic pageantry of the Royal Family.

To some extent this singular Commonwealth bond represents a reverse side of the medal presented by the emotional antipathy that at the moment divides the Communist from the nonCommunist world. This antipathy appears to go beyond the material necessities of the situation, involving millions of people in an emotional revulsion to one another perhaps positively harmful to their immediate self-interests. It is a fair assumption, in view of present day facts, that political theory based on narrow concepts of law, authority, and economics has disregarded some vital factor in human association. This neglected element might prove to be Hume's idea of sympathy as a motivating force in mass action. Any exploration of this thesis should start with an examination of the values and meanings of political symbols in the modern world. Are they merely forms of shorthand, reminders of established faiths, or do they possess independent powers of their own to unite or disrupt peoples? The management of symbols, which may eventually prove essential to all purposeful political association will depend upon a true assessment of their character.

If the United States is taken as an example, the most obvious symbol of our Union is the Constitution itself. A theory of political symbols that holds them mere representations of beliefs might consider the actual document to be the true and effective symbol. Learning its history, memorizing its words, understanding its concepts would then provide common feelings for a united people. To the British mind this viewpoint would seem arid and meaningless, robbed of the essence of human sympathy. The Union to come alive in British terms would need to be given the attributes of actual life. To peoples for whom the separation of Crown and Monarch is the most casual of miracles this would mean little difficulty. The Supreme Court, for all its imperfections, is demonstrably alive. In human terms, as everyone knows, it is the Constitution from day to day. As a political symbol of Union it can be easily divorced from political government in terms of authority, administration, or lawmaking. Best of all, it is the worthiest exemplar of how one should think and feel about the ideal of Union when one's mind is divorced from self-interest and powerseeking. Besides it possesses emotional content and can be loved or hated.

The British use of the political symbol as a central force in political association could be extended then beyond the historical character of the Monarch. It represents to some degree an antiauthoritarian view of human society. People cling together at least in part because they are in sympathy with each other. Institutions to survive and grow must provide adequate channels for this sympathy, as well as for the more pedestrian ordering of affairs. The most effective center of mass sympathy is a living person who serves as an exemplar in some one aspect of life common to all. Limitations are probably as important as capacities. Should the living symbol seek to exemplify too wide an area of individual life, the appeal might be drastically curtailed to a handful of fanatics. The more removed the person of the exemplar from everyday life, the stronger the attraction for the masses who have only occasional need to think such high thoughts or essay such proud deeds. Of course the exemplification must be meaningful in terms of great affairs, or the symbol ceases to be political and sinks to the level of a Hollywood fantasy.

The British Commonwealth's revival of the symbol as an instrument of political association beyond Law or Force, may be merely a restatement of a principle long operative in Chinese political philosophy. The Emperor as a living exemplar, responsible through his personal behavior for maintaining public standards of morality, was a favorite device in Chinese history. The Emperor, like the Queen, ruled through being, not doing. The *Tao Teh Ching* comments:

> He who in dealing with the empire regards his high rank as though it were his body is the best person to be entrusted with rule; he who in dealing with the empire loves his subjects as one should love one's body is the best person to whom one can commit the Empire.[15]

Colonial Peoples. This paper has dealt solely with member nations of the Commonwealth. Colonial peoples though not member states are a part of the present Commonwealth. The value of the symbolism of the Queen in the present colonial system has been very little explored. It is possible to speculate that by providing continuity to the custom of chieftainship in a time of transition, the Queen may be a powerful political symbol in some colonial lands. There are other possibilities, such as the embodiment of the ideas of racial or cultural equality through common subjection of all peoples to the single Monarch. The materials for evaluation, however, are not easy to obtain, and the topic is raised merely to explain that it has not been attempted.

[15] Arthur Waley, *The Way and Its Power*, Houghton, Boston, 1942, p. 157.

CHAPTER III

Symbols of Political Community

By KARL W. DEUTSCH

SYMBOLS OF international politics are often studied for two purposes: to find out what can be learned from their observation, and what can be accomplished by their control. In the first case, we study symbols as possible indicators of political change; in the second, we study them as possible "regulators"—a term of Quincy Wright's—or instruments of manipulation of political developments.[1]

Symbols as Indicators

Viewed as indicators, political symbols and their statistical distribution can tell us something about the flow of messages between political groups and organizations, such as states, countries, regions, peoples, special interest groups, or particular institutions, such as governments, foreign offices, legislatures, newspapers, and other media of mass communication or control. Such flows of messages can tell us something, in turn, about the distribution of attention of the individuals, groups, and organizations concerned. By noting which symbols are frequently associated with each other, we may learn something about the context in which political messages are perceived, remembered, and recalled on later occasions. Thus they help us understand political meaning and political perception at different times and in different communities.

New political symbols may be created, and may become associated with old or new patterns of political behavior. Political information, like all other information, may be remembered or recorded piecemeal by individuals or organizations. It may be dissociated into smaller patterns; and these smaller patterns may later on be recombined to new configurations which had not been received as messages before, and which may never have existed until they were now for the first time put together.

---

[1] *Cf.* Quincy Wright, Introduction, Ithiel de Sola Pool, *Symbols of Internationalism,* Stanford University Press, Stanford, 1951, p. 2.

Such new configurations of symbols may themselves be completed patterns, readily available for application to decisions about political behavior. Or they may undergo a process of strategic simplification in which they may be stripped of nonessential features for their new employment, and in which they may thus lose all obvious traces of their combinatorial origin. The simplified cross of the Crusaders, the white cross of Switzerland, the crescent-shaped sword of Islam, the simplified world map that serves as emblem of the United Nations—all these are symbols of this kind.

Political symbols, like all symbols, are orders to recall something from memory.[2] In this respect, they have several functions: 1) they *denote* or designate some particular group, region, event, behavior pattern, or the like, or they designate a bundle of such memories which are to be recalled together as if they formed part of one concept or unit (such as "Frenchman" or "Western Europe" or "United Nations"); 2) they *connote* a number of other memories which are to be recalled in less vivid detail and associated less rigidly than the memories that fall within the denotation, but which are still effective in modifying the denoted concept and its effects on further associating, thinking, and "decisionmaking" (such as the connotations, "valorous" or "unstable," respectively, when added to the symbol, "Frenchmen"); 3) they *represent* a particular combination of denotative and connotative meanings for at least three different contexts: a) the universe of memories of the speaker or the source of the symbol; b) the universe of the audience, intended or unintended, by whom the message is received; c) the general cultural and social context which may be common to the source and the audience of the symbol, but which may nevertheless differ to some extent from the private universe of memories of either.

The distribution of the flows of political messages, the speed, precision, and economy of effort with which they are understood and responded to, and the experience of reward and satisfaction by which these processes of communication are accompanied, together form a significant indication of the presence or absence of political community among the groups, countries, or peoples among whom they occur. From them we may gain indications of the unity or diversity of the memory pools of the groups and individuals participating in the process; of the mutual compatibility

[2]For an excellent discussion of "signs" and "symbols," see Susanne K. Langer, *Philosophy in a New Key,* New American Library, New York, 1948.

of their major political values; and of the mutual compatibility and responsiveness of the political decision systems and control processes by which they regulate their behavior.[3]

"Independence" and "Security" as Political Symbols

Apart from the context of these processes of social and political communication, such powerful political symbols as "independence" and "security" cannot be understood. Men have been willing to fight and die for their independence and security, that is, for the independence and security of the group of which they formed a part or with whom they had come to identify themselves. But the terms, "independence" and "security," could tell neither them nor us just whose independence is to be defended, from whom, and for what purpose.[4]

Within the context of communication, however, the meaning of these symbols can be perhaps more readily discerned. Independence and security are terms that symbolize the freedom and protection of the self from the nonself, and the nonself can be distinguished from the self in terms of communication and responsiveness. Neurophysiologists have noted that patients who lose sensation in or control over a limb of their own body tend to perceive this limb as alien, as not part of the self.[5] In a somewhat similar manner, we may think perhaps of political independence as *independence from an unresponsive political community or political decision system.* We wish to be independent from any governments, coun-

---

[3]For a more detailed exposition of this approach, as well as for a number of qualifications, see Karl W. Deutsch, *Political Community at the International Level: Problems of Definition and Measurement,* Doubleday & Company, New York, 1954, pp. 46–64. See also Quincy Wright, *A Study of War,* University of Chicago Press, Chicago, 1942, vol. II, pp. 970–986, 1240–1260, 1278, 1286.

[4]"Perhaps the most to be said," Quincy Wright told an earlier meeting of this Conference, "is that a nationalist has identified himself with a group, larger than the local community and smaller than the world, which he regards as sharing some social and political characteristics with himself and as in some way different from other similar human groups. It also implies that he is prepared to support policies which he regards as in the interest of that group. It is clear, however, that nationalism neither defines those interests nor the group that is supposed to have them." Quincy Wright, "Symbols of Nationalism and Internationalism," *Symbols and Values: An Initial Study,* Conference on Science, Philosophy and Religion, New York, 1954, Chapter XXVI, pp. 390–391.

[5]I am indebted to Warren S. MacCulloch for this point. For a related approach, see also Herbert A. Simon, *Administrative Behavior: A Study of Decision-Making Processes in Administrative Organization,* The Macmillan Company, New York, 1947, pp. 154–171, 198–219.

tries, or groups of people who do not respond adequately to our messages and to our needs. We wish to be secure from those who might infringe upon our own political autonomy, that is, from those who might hinder or overburden or disrupt the chains and channels of communication and decisionmaking by means of which we control our own behavior and the behavior of the group and the environment that have been linked to us by effective processes of communication and control, with such satisfactory results in terms of our own personal memories, habits, and values, that we have come to include them into the "we-group" and the "we" symbols with whom we identify ourselves. Unions or alliances of countries or peoples which lead to such experiences of successful joint adaptation of behavior and mutual responsiveness, followed by significant joint rewards or satisfaction for the politically important groups among the participants, and by expectations for similar or greater rewards in the future, are likely to leave them with favorable memories and with a desire to see the union or alliance continued or renewed.

Virginians between 1763 and 1790 thus did not desire, by and large, independence from, or security against, Pennsylvanians with whom their frontiersmen were beginning to share the settlement of the Ohio Valley. Rather in the course of the events leading to the American Revolution, the perception of England as part of the political self of colonists in Virginia faded, and the perception of Pennsylvanians, New Yorkers, and New Englanders as allies, associates, and eventually as part of a new political self which preserved the symbol, "Virginia," but linked it ever more closely with a new symbol—"Americans"—came to take its place. Has there occurred any comparable change in our own time, let us say during the past thirty or fifty years, involving a shift in prominence between the symbols of the various nation-states, on the one hand, and the symbols of internationalism, or of regional political integration, such as in Western Europe, on the other?

Recent Trends in National and International Symbols

In order to seek an answer to this question, it may be well to summarize and compare the results of a number of recent research undertakings, at the risk that the data from some of them may be familiar to some readers. It is in the comparison of the findings of the different surveys that the present summary may possibly be found useful.

Among the conclusions of a survey of symbols of nationalism and internationalism in the "prestige papers" of five major countries between 1890 and 1949, carried out by Ithiel de Sola Pool and others, are the following:

> In interaction this world certainly has become one. The whole world has become responsive to events everywhere, or, more accurately, to events in the same main centers of policy formation. . . . There is . . . a remarkable degree of reciprocity in the attitudes of states toward each other. . . . Somehow in this interdependent world the attitudes of the elite in one state come to be known and returned by the elite of other states . . .
>
> Attention to international organizations set in after the first World War and has increased since . . . (Except for Russia), the trend toward increased attention to international organizations seems general.
>
> Other types of international political terminology may be showing somewhat less vitality. . . . Except for *Izvestia,* the greatest emphasis on those symbols which are commonly used for talking about the instrumentalities and principles of international relations, seems to have been in the period between the world wars. . . . The sharpening of conflicts and the growth of a certain cynicism may partly account for the recent decline in these terms. . . .
>
> While the world community may be increasingly tightly knit as far as interaction is concerned, it is certainly not becoming more unified in attitude. On the contrary, hostility is growing, and lines are becoming more sharply polarized between friends and enemies. . . . The total picture is that of an increasingly bipolar world.[6]

This suggestion of a bipolar consolidation of the world into two closely knit camps may require careful qualification. The long term study just cited found evidence for the persistent failure of any integration between Germany and France; throughout the half century covered by this survey, these two countries remained most unfriendly to each other. The percentage of unfavorable judgments between them, out of all judgments of one country by the prestige newspaper of the other, averaged ninety per cent, as compared to slightly above seventy per cent between Russia and Britain, and Russia and the United States. For the period as a whole,

[6]Pool, *op. cit.,* pp. 60–63. Reprinted with the permission of the author and of the publishers, Stanford University Press. Copyright 1951 by the Board of Trustees of Leland Stanford Junior University. Published under a grant from the Carnegie Corporation, New York.

Pool's figures also suggest that Germany remained far more unpopular internationally than Russia or any other of the countries surveyed, *i.e.,* the United States, Britain, and France.[7]

If one computes not merely the "psychic distance" in terms of unfavorable mutual judgments between any two countries, but computes the psychic distances or frequencies of unfavorable mutual judgments for any possible three-country coalition among the powers surveyed in Pool's study, one can rank the ten possible three-country coalitions among these five powers in increasing order of internal dissension or mutual hostility among the partners. This computation shows that only one of the ten possible coalitions, that between the United States, Britain, and France, would unite countries which during the past half-century average less than fifty per cent unfavorable judgments of one another; the exact sum of percentages of unfavorable judgments for these three countries is 115 out of a possible maximum of 300. (The latter figure would mean that the three countries attaining it had all judged each other unfavorable all the time.) The other three coalitions not including Russia are the United States-Britain-Germany, with an index of mutual hostility of 202; Britain-France-Germany, with a hostility index of 211; and the United States-France-Germany, with such an index of 216. In these three coalitions the chances of mutually unfavorable judgments among the partners tended to be somewhat better than two to one. Somewhat less handicapped by traditional animosities in their prestige papers appear the combinations of the United States-Britain-Russia with an index of 176; Britain-France-Russia with 177; and the United States-France-Russia, with 184. The first two of these coalitions correspond to actual though temporary alliances in World War II and World War I, respectively. The three-country coalitions which include Germany, on the other hand, appear to have little if any precedent in history; and the three-country combinations which include Germany and Russia are at the bottom of the rank list of mutual psychological acceptability (or at the top of the rank list of mutual dislikes) with indices ranging from 242 to 249.[8]

[7]*Ibid.,* pp. 15–19.

[8]The full list follows: United States-Britain-France, 115; United States-Britain-Russia, 176; Britain-France-Russia, 177; United States-France-Russia, 184; United States-Britain-Germany, 202; Britain-France-Germany, 211; United States-France-Germany, 216; United States-Russia-Germany, 242; Britain-Russia-Germany, 244; France-Russia-Germany, 249. The indices of mutual hostility within each coalition were computed from data in Pool, *loc. cit.* It may be noted that the only coalition which contains no English-speaking country ranks at the bottom of the entire list, and the chances for mutual recriminations among its members would be five to one.

The quantitative study of symbols by Pool and associates, from which the data for this argument were drawn, is confirmed to a large extent by an independent study by Frank L. Klingberg, based on a survey of opinions of experts in international affairs in 1938–1939. The extreme psychic distance between Germany and France is conspicuous in Klingberg's model, as well as in Quincy Wright's separate estimate in July, 1939. Pool's, Wright's, and Klingberg's studies[9] suggest that the alienation between France and Germany persisted regardless, to some extent, of political changes in Germany, and of the changes in French ability and willingness to fight the Germans. The absence of any major psychological rapprochement between France and Germany in the years after World War II seems further confirmed by the results of the Unesco surveys of public opinion in a number of European countries, studied by William Buchanan and Hadley Cantril;[10] and it appears further confirmed to some extent by the conspicuous French lack of interest in "social," "personal," or "human interest" news from Germany, as shown by the survey of the flow of international news in 1952–1953, conducted by the International Press Institute.[11]

A survey in trends in international trade in Western Europe between 1880 and 1952 suggests that Germany and France may have become more estranged from each other in economic terms during much of that period. In 1880, Germany and France had an average share of 9.4% in each other's imports and exports. This share fell to 9.1% in 1913; to 7.3% in 1928; and to 5.5% in 1937. It had recovered somewhat from this low point by 1952, when it rose to 6.6%, that is, to a level roughly one-third below that of 1880. The same trend is found in the average share of their total foreign mail which each of the two countries sent to the other. This average percentage was 15.2% in 1888. By 1913 it had fallen to 12.3%; by 1928 to 5.3%; and in 1937 it dropped to 3.7%. After the Second World War it recovered slightly to 4.4%, that is, to about one-third of its pre-World War I level between 1888 and 1913. These trends in German-French mail communications contrast strongly with mail communi-

[9]Frank L. Klingberg, "Studies in the Measurement of the Relations among Sovereign States," *Psychometrika*, vol. VI, 1941, pp. 335–352; "Studies in the Measurement of the Relations among Sovereign States," Thesis, University of Chicago Library, 1939; Quincy Wright, *A Study of War*, University of Chicago Press, Chicago, 1942, vol. II, app. XL, pp. 1466–1471; Pool, *op. cit.*, pp. 15–19, 26–29.

[10]William Buchanan and Hadley Cantril, *How Nations See Each Other: A Study in Public Opinion*, University of Illinois Press, Urbana, 1953, pp. 45–55.

[11]*Cf. The Flow of the News: A Study by the International Press Institute*, International Press Institute, Zurich, 1953, pp. 20–21, 25, 131–134, 140–141, 143, 146–148, 259.

cation trends among certain countries among whom community appears to have grown. Thus the average percentage of their total foreign mail which the Scandinavian countries—Sweden, Norway, Denmark, and after 1913, Finland—each sent to the others was 31.1% in 1888. It declined only slightly to 29.3% in 1913 and remained at the same level in 1928, but it rose above the 1888 figure to 31.4% in 1937, and further to 39.1% in 1949. Similarly, the percentage of her total foreign mail which Ireland sent to the United Kingdom rose from 77.5% in 1928 to 78.3% in 1937 and 83.3% in 1949.[12]

If one accords some weight to the well known view of Ernest Renan that a national community is the result of a "plebiscite of everyday life," then data of this kind may deserve serious consideration also in gauging the prospects of supranational political communities. Taken together, the evidence of these surveys may convey an indication of the deepseated psychological and material obstacles in the way of Western European Union and of any effective realization of current plans for European Defense Community.

Beyond the confines of Western Europe the trends toward a bipolar world, noted by Pool, have to contend with the recent great increase in the prominence of the symbols of local nationalism and local or regional political activity in such countries as India, China, Indonesia, the Arab countries, and generally the nonwhite areas of the world. In many of these regions, political attention seems likely to remain concentrated largely on local and national issues rather than upon the claims and counterclaims of the two distant contending giants, the United States and the

[12]Sources of trade data: Great Britain, Board of Trade, *Statistical Abstract for the Principal and Other Foreign Countries, 1873–1883*, London, 1885, W. Page, editor, *Commerce and Industry*, Constable, London, 1919; League of Nations, *Memorandum on Balance of Payments and Foreign Trade Balances, 1911–1925*, vol. II, Geneva, 1927; League of Nations, *Memorandum on International Trade and Balances of Payments, 1926–1928*, vol. III, *Trade Statistics of Sixty-Four Countries*, Geneva, 1930; League of Nations, *International Trade Statistics, 1938*, Geneva, 1939; United Nations, *Yearbook of International Trade Statistics, 1952*, New York, 1953. Sources of mail data: Universal Postal Union, Bureau International, *Relevé des tableaux statistiques du service postal international (Réception)*, 1887, Berne, 1889; *(Expédition) 1888*, Berne, 1890; *(Expédition) 1913*, Berne, 1915, *(Expédition) 1928*, Berne, 1930; *Statistique générale du service postal (Réception), 1913*, Berne, 1915; *Statistique générale du service postal, 1928*, Berne, 1930, p. 16, col. 65; *Statistique générale du service postal international, 1937*, Berne, 1939; *Statistique complète des services postaux, 1949*, Berne, 1951; *Statistique des expéditions dans le service postal international, 1949*, Berne, 1951. Computations from both trade and mail data were carried out by Mrs. Johanna Lederer at the Center for Research on World Political Institutions, Princeton University, and by the author.

Union of Soviet Socialist Republics, and the membership of these "new" countries in the Free World implies precisely their unwillingness to accept too close ideological or political implementation from any agency or power outside their own territory. Indeed, it does not seem clear whether the two contending superpowers of today have greatly increased their traditionally limited abilities to keep large coalitions of countries together, nor is it clear whether the many smaller and middle sized countries of today are easier or harder to keep in line.

There is some evidence, though not conclusive, pointing to the latter possibility. The progress of modern technology has perhaps done more to facilitate the mutual interaction and impact among governments than it has done to equip these governments to deal with its burdens. We have mechanized the transmission of information, but not the process of listening to it; we can use machines to reproduce symbols in vast numbers, but we get little help from machines in understanding them. By increasing our opportunities for domestic, as well as foreign contacts, we have increased the burdens on our attention; and the political decision systems of modern governments may sometimes be so near to being overloaded with urgent business, foreign and domestic, that they may end up by devoting a smaller rather than a larger share of their attention to foreign countries and to international affairs.

Data on recent shifts in the proportion of domestic to foreign mail suggest the possibility of such a shift of our attention. During the past forty years, the proportion of domestic to foreign mail has been increasing in most of the countries of the world for which we have data; in many countries it is now about twice as high as it was before the First World War.[13] There has been a somewhat similar, though smaller, increase in the proportion of domestic national income (as indicated by gross national product) and foreign trade (as indicated by the sum of imports and exports), with the result that foreign trade over the past twenty-five years, at least, has been forming a decreasing share in the national income of many countries. Thus in the United States in about 1951 the ratio of domestic mail to foreign mail was about seventy to one; the ratio of gross national product (minus exports) to total foreign trade was about ten to one; the ratio of domestic to foreign text material in a

[13]Computations for fifty countries were carried out at the Center for Research on World Political Institutions at Princeton University, based on data from the Universal Postal Union from 1887 to 1951, with results to be published in due course.

representative sample of ninety-three newspapers in 1952–1953 was about eleven to one.[14] Earlier experiments have indicated that there is a close connection between the extent of a newspaper reader's previous contacts with persons and places mentioned in a news story and the likelihood of his actually reading it. According to data by Wilbur Schramm, about three out of four potential readers actually read news stories dealing with their community, but not with anyone they knew personally; one in five read stories about a place which he knew well, though outside his community; and only about one in seven read stories about persons and places which he did not know well.[15] If this is so, a growth or decline in the absolute or relative frequency of personal contacts through travel, trade, and mails, across national boundaries might be linked to readership interest in foreign news, and conceivably to interest in international affairs.

At present [summer, 1954], the evidence is by no means conclusive; but the 1952–1953 survey by the International Press Institute has some interesting data on this point. About one-sixth of local news published in American newspapers was actually read; and so was about one-seventh of national news; but only somewhat less than one-eighth of international news published was actually read,[16] so that the ratio of domestic to foreign news actually read would be closer to fourteen to one. Foreign news was more likely to be read when the word, "American" or "U.S." was included in the headline.[17] When asked in the spring of 1953, "Would you like to have your newspaper reduce the amount of local news or national news in order to give you more foreign news?", only eight per cent of the respondents said that they would, and seventy-eight per cent said they would not.[18]

Taken together, data of the kind cited in the last few paragraphs may serve as a group of indices of domestic or national self-preoccupation. There is some evidence that such indices tend to be higher the greater the population, area, wealth, literacy, and perhaps general domestic social and political activity of a country. Compared with other countries in

[14]*The Flow of the News,* unpublished studies, Center for Research on World Political Institutions, Princeton University, p. 219.

[15]Wilbur Schramm, "The Nature of News," in W. Schramm, editor, *Mass Communications,* University of Illinois Press, Urbana, 1949, pp. 299–300.

[16]*The Flow of the News,* pp. 62–63.

[17]*Ibid.,* pp. 63, 66.

[18]Fourteen per cent expressed no opinion. *Ibid.,* p. 58.

these terms, the self-preoccupation of the United States public would appear, if anything, slightly lower than might seem "normal" for a country of its size, wealth, resources, and domestic level of activity.

This, however, is just the salient point. High and rising levels of national self-preoccupation may be normal for most countries in the world at this particular stage in its development, leaving only limited resources for attention and action to international symbols, messages, and problems.[19] Further data on the increase or decrease of self-reference symbols in political communications (such as an increase or decrease of the symbols, "French" and "France," in the French press) would be of interest in this connection.[20] If such a general increase should turn out to be the case, it might indicate an increase in the difficulty of insuring sufficient mutual attention and responsiveness on the part of the political elites and politically relevant strata of different states to make any international or supranational political integration practicable.

As regards particular countries, Pool's study found:

> Attention to international organizations . . . (like) attention to foreign states . . . has most markedly increased in the *New York Times,* which, since the end of the controversy over joining the League, had reflected American isolationism by giving relatively little attention to these instrumentalities. While America has been abandoning isolationism, Russia has been adopting it, and in her recent symbol flow devotes very little attention to international organization.[21]

In a related study of the most frequently used political symbols, Pool found for the *New York Times* among other changes a decline of attention to the symbols TARIFFS and FREE TRADE; for the London *Times,* among other trends, an increase in the symbols of PATRIOTISM; and for *Izvestia* he found: "The words that have increased most in attention from the 1920's to the recent period are, in order, FATHERLAND, COLLECTIVISM, and PATRIOTISM."[22]

After World War II, according to Pool's figures, Russian attention to international political symbols remained significantly higher than it had

[19]Unpublished studies, Center for Research on World Political Institutions.

[20]In Pool's count of the distribution of geographic symbols, such "self-references" were specifically excluded. See Pool, *op. cit.,* pp. 37–39.

[21]*Ibid.,* p. 61.

[22]Ithiel de Sola Pool, *The "Prestige Papers": A Survey of Their Editorials,* Stanford University Press, Stanford, 1952, pp. 76, 80–81.

been in the 1930's, but somewhat lower than it had been in the 1920's, and much lower than it had been in the "prestige paper" of Tsarist Russia, *Novoe Vremia,* before the First World War.[23]

These findings of a rising trend of national self-preoccupation in Russia appear confirmed by the sharply rising ratios of domestic to foreign mail in that country, from about seventeen to one in 1928 to almost ninety-six to one—a world record, so far as we could find—in 1937; no further data on mail volumes for Russia appear to have been published by the Universal Postal Union since the latter year, but there is reason to think that the Russian ratio of domestic to foreign mail may have risen even above this record level.[24]

A similar trend in the ratio of Russian gross national product to total foreign trade has long been obvious. From these and similar indications it seems plausible that an ambitious Russian Communist might advance his career most effectively by spending most of his time and attention on Russian internal affairs, and very little on international politics. Political decisionmakers in Russia—and perhaps in time in China—may thus share to a particularly high degree a common problem of government in all highly self-preoccupied countries: the problem that a high interest and competence in international affairs may become inversely related to a policymaker's chances of success in the domestic contest for popularity and power. If these processes should continue unchecked in Russia or in any other large country, they might eventually produce incompetence in international politics by natural selection, and thus promote the eventual disintegration of any international coalition of which such a country formed a part.

Some Trends in the United States

The comforting finding of a long run trend in the United States away from isolationism, which was suggested by the count of symbols in the *New York Times,* appears to require some qualification in the light of some of the findings of the Princeton study. The ratio of domestic to foreign mail in the United States rose from about twenty-five to one in 1880 to about twenty-eight to one in 1928, and to almost sixty-five to one in 1951. The ratio of United States domestic national income to total foreign trade rose from less than five to one in 1879 to about seven to one

[23]Pool, *Symbols of Internationalism,* p. 41, table 8.
[24]Unpublished studies, Center for Research on World Political Institutions.

in 1890 and 1913, and to almost twelve to one in 1950 and about eleven to one in 1951.[25] A few other indicators, such as the ratios of immigrants to total population, the study of foreign languages—with enrolments in high school language courses dropping to almost one half between the early 1930's and the late 1940's, despite the increase in high school enrolments generally[26]—the conspicuous decline of the proportion of references to foreign research in American scientific publications between 1890 and 1954,[27] all these likewise seem to qualify the finding of the symbol studies.

To this should perhaps be added the consideration that the *New York Times* is perhaps not quite as representative of the thinking of the political elite of the United States as are the London *Times* or *Izvestia*, or as was *Le Temps*, for their respective countries. American political decisionmaking is less concentrated in New York than French, British, or Russian decisionmaking are concentrated at Paris, London, or Moscow. There is no single close knit political elite in the United States, and the constitutional separation between legislative and executive further tends to keep most members of the Senate and the House of Representatives more interested in domestic political affairs than in international relations. A trend away from isolationism in terms of a change in the distribution of editorial attention of the *New York Times* may thus tell us more of the attitudes of an important segment of American public opinion, and perhaps of a major part of the executive branch of the government, than it would tell us about any change in the attitudes of Congress or of the American electorate as a whole.[28]

[25]Unpublished studies, Center for Research on World Political Institutions.

[26]*PMLA: Publications of the Modern Language Association,* vol. 68, no. 5, December, 1953, p. xi. The editors of PMLA reported a drop of fifty-two per cent in enrolment in high school foreign language courses in the period 1934–1949, and an estimated drop of forty-three per cent in foreign language entrance requirements by American colleges in the period 1936–1953. (*Ibid.*) The increased enrolment in foreign language courses at Berlitz Schools, reported in the same issue (p. xiv) would not seem to have been large enough to reverse this trend.

[27]Karl W. Deutsch, George Klein, J. J. Baker, and associates, "Is Science Becoming Less International?", Massachusetts Institute of Technology, June, 1954, multigraphed.

[28]Pool has been careful to point out this particular character of the *New York Times:* "The *New York Times* was most independent (of all the 'prestige papers'), having favored tariff reductions all through the 1920's and having advocated international cooperation even when the administrations, under pressure, had to give allegiance to isolationism. In these respects it was probably closer to the views of our career diplomats than was official policy . . . ," Pool, *The "Prestige Papers,"* p. 5. For an important treatment of the broader subject of decisionmaking, see also Richard C. Snyder, H. W. Bruck, and Burton Sapin, *Decision-Making as an Approach to the Study of Inter-*

Perhaps the search for quantitative indicators of any American trend toward or away from isolationism are most likely to confirm something that has been intuitively familiar to many observers: that we are facing in the United States a multiplicity of contradictory trends in public opinion, and that even a major trend toward international involvement still leaves many of the trends toward greater national self-preoccupation unimpaired, just as any temporary upsurge of nationalistic or isolationist sentiment would continue to clash with political and social processes making for greater involvement in international affairs. Under these conditions it is perhaps to be expected that our foreign policy resembles less the consistent expression of a single clearcut trend, and more a collection of persistent contradictions. We favor increased trade with the free world but will not lower tariffs; we seek security through hydrogen bombs and long range bombing planes but are unwilling to spend corresponding sums on the defense of our own big cities; we ask our diplomats to maintain a worldwide system of alliances but expect them to make few or no major concessions to the views of our allies; we take pride in the position of the United States in the United Nations, but many of our patriots protest against the display of the United Nations flag or the use of Unesco material in our public schools. Many contradictions of this kind may continue to characterize our politics for some time to come, for they may be the visible expression of larger and deeper contradictory processes in our national development. As we come to understand better these contradictory trends within our own national political community, we may learn how to control them and keep them in safe bounds, so as to avoid international commitments that go beyond our capabilities of political self-control, and so as to learn to play an ever more effective part in building a stable political community among the world's free countries.

Symbols as Instruments of Political Change or Control

If the study of symbols as indicators of international communication can tell us something about the difficulty of this task, the study of symbols as "regulators" or instruments of political control may tell us something about what could be accomplished toward its fulfilment with their

---

national Politics, Foreign Policy Analysis Series, no. 3, Foreign Policy Analysis Project, Organizational Behavior Section, Princeton University, Princeton, 1954, especially pp. 54–67.

aid. What can symbols do in furthering or hindering the integration of political communities?

Politics is the making and unmaking of enforceable commands. A political community is a group of persons among whom certain commands are backed by a significant probability of enforcement, as well as by a significant probability of voluntary or habitual compliance even without supervision. Such a political community usually becomes established by a process of social learning, in which enforcement probabilities and compliance habits may mutually reinforce each other. The specific study of politics involves under this aspect the study of the ways in which changes in the enforcement patterns of society—legislative, administrative, military, and the like—may accelerate, retard, or otherwise influence these broader processes of social learning.

It is characteristic of these processes of social learning, however, that they may change the boundaries of the political community within which they first developed. Such changes may involve the size of the political community, the interplay of enforcement probabilities and compliance habits within it, and the range of its functions—that is, the range of tasks that are put before the government of the political community by the changing expectations of its own population, or by the changing requirements of the survival of this political unit in its historical and political environment. What can symbols do to influence these processes of change? What can they do, in particular, to influence the processes by which several smaller political communities merge into a larger one; or by which a larger political community becomes divided into small sovereign units; or by which several sovereign states establish a pluralistic political community—such as the British Commonwealth of Nations, or the only partly formalized community of Scandinavian states—within which their populations may securely expect only peaceful and legitimate changes by processes of mutual communication, accommodation, and responsiveness?

Historical processes of this kind have been studied by a team of historians and political scientists at the Center for Research on World Political Institutions at Princeton University.[29]

The areas and cases covered by this study are: 1) The British Isles, in-

[29]Karl W. Deutsch, S. A. Burrell, R. A. Kann, M. du P. Lee, Jr., M. Lichterman, R. Lindgren, F. Loewenheim, and Richard Van Wagenen, *Political Community: Historical Experiences and Contemporary Problems of International Organization,* in preparation.

cluding the unification of England, the Union with Wales, the Union with Scotland, the Union with Ireland, and the dissolution of the latter; 2) the United States, including the secession of the Thirteen Colonies, their Confederation and later Federal Union, the failure of their envisaged union with Canada, the temporary disruption of the United States in the War between the States, and the reunion that followed it; 3) the development of the Swiss Confederation; 4) the unification of Italy; 5) the unification of Germany; 6) the development and eventual disruption of the Austro-Hungarian Empire; 7) the Swedish-Norwegian Union and its dissolution. Among them, it is hoped, these cases may include a sufficient variety of political, economic, social, and historical conditions to throw at least some light on the processes of political integration and disintegration in political communities in the general area of Western culture. Since some of this work is still in progress, only very tentative and preliminary results can be indicated here, in so far as they may bear on our problem of the role of symbols in the processes of political union or secession.

The first impression to emerge from a study of these cases was that of the *multiplicity* of unifying symbols in cases of successful union, or even of a successful pluralistic political community. Such political symbols can be divided into six broad categories: 1) abstract symbols, such as words, ideas, slogans, works of literature, or songs; 2) pictorial symbols, such as colors, flags, statues, relics, historic objects, buildings, animals, flowers, and the like; 3) personal symbols, such as heroes, kings, leaders, saints, prophets, or poets; 4) symbolic places, such as capital cities, historic sites, national shrines, centers of pilgrimage, battlefields, tombs of martyrs, or places of scenic beauty or grandeur; 5) symbolic organizations or institutions, such as congresses, church synods, political parties, legislatures, law courts, universities, bureaucratic or military organizations, in so far as any of these acquire symbolic functions in addition to their primary activities; 6) religious symbols—this is a category that cuts across the other five in many instances, but it is perhaps not exhausted by them. The potential usefulness of this tedious enumeration rests perhaps in this: when one lists the cases of successful and unsuccessful political integration, it turns out that in the successful cases one finds effective common symbols not in just one or two, but in five and often all six of these categories. There seems to be no case among those surveyed where a single unifying symbol showed overwhelming power. Rather it seems to have been the multiplicity of integrative symbols, their mutual interrelatedness and mutual reinforcement, that seem to have been most effective in promoting political integration.

The second impression that emerges from a study of these cases is the importance of the relatedness of the effective political symbols to the previously acquired memories of the communities to whom they appeal. Successful symbols, it appears, were only partly new; the "Union Jack" combined the old crosses of Saint George and Saint Andrew, the old symbols of England and Scotland; the red, white, and blue of the flag of the United States repeated the red, white, and blue of the flag of Britain; the ancient sign of the cross reappeared in the new flag of the Swiss Confederation. The same was true of abstract symbols: Scotsmen in 1638 united around the Covenant to defend "the King and the true religion," although within a short time they found themselves defending their "true religion," Presbyterianism, against their king, and eventually were instrumental in Charles I's capture, and indirectly in his beheading at Whitehall. Most of the successful political unions, monarchic as well as republican, were solicitous of the existing symbols, habits, and institutions of the smaller units.

A third impression is one of the limited effectiveness of symbols, and even of groups or systems of symbols, in and by themselves. The integrated symbol systems of the American Revolution, or of the nineteenth century German nationalism, were apparently far more powerful than any one symbol by itself; yet even these symbol systems had to correspond to the past memories and present life situations of the populations whom they were to move. Benjamin Franklin pleaded in vain with the citizens of Montreal to throw in their lot with the Americans; and further to the east most of the "Yankees of Nova Scotia" failed to join their New England cousins in the revolution. The appeal of German nationalism, powerful in Schleswig, proved powerless in German-speaking Switzerland and even, to a large extent and to the embarrassment of German nationalists, in German-speaking and German-ruled Alsace between 1871 and 1918. In all these cases, it appears, the life experiences and expectations of the populations concerned did much to decide the relative power or impotence of the political symbols addressed to them.

Taken together, these impressions suggest a paradox in regard to symbols of interdenominational or international unity. The more all inclusive such symbols are intended to be, the fewer may be the specific

memories and habits of specific people to whom they can appeal. Moreover, most of the successful symbols offer to those who accept them a
better opinion of themselves. They may do this indirectly, by first casting them down as "Little Englanders" or "miserable sinners," as the
case may be, but they offer them the eventual prospect of salvation into
the ranks of the saved souls or good patriots, with consequent superiority
over those who have remained in darkness. Political unions, too, benefit
from this appeal of prestige, implicit as well as overt, and it is striking
to note how sometimes the greatest reluctance to enter upon a wholehearted union is shown by the group which is the most popular or pres-
tigeful among its prospective members. In this manner it was the English
Parliament that was most reluctant to accept Anglo-Scottish Union between 1603 and 1707, and the present day reluctance of many French
leaders to accept Western European Union, or the reluctance of some
midwestern leaders of opinion in the United States to consider closer
American integration into an Atlantic community, may well be strength-
ened—in addition to many other factors—by only partly conscious considerations of prestige.

This leads us to the consideration of the familiar pessimistic claim that
political unity essentially requires an excluded out-group that can be
despised or feared, and thus used to keep the members of the newly
built larger in-group together. Our data do not support this claim. Successful unions have been brought about in which considerations of excluded out-groups played little or no significant role. Such a union was
the successful union between England and Wales; the successful acceptance of the Reformation and equality before the law for the Welsh appear to have been the dominant consideration, and the notion of excluding the Papacy from Wales appears to have had little importance for the
Welshmen of that time. Inclusiveness rather than exclusiveness appears
stressed in many of the symbols of the American Revolution. "Life, Liberty, and the pursuit of Happiness" are not exclusivistic symbols, nor is
the "decent respect for the opinions of mankind" that is explicitly avowed
at the beginning of the Declaration of Independence. It is the symbols,
"men," "human," and "mankind," that loom prominently in that document, and so does the reference to the Creator by Whom all men have
been endowed with inalienable rights. The theme is echoed in the line
of the song, *"My country, 'tis of thee"*: ". . . let all that breathe partake . . . ," and it is echoed again in the humility of Abraham Lincoln's

statements on equality in the Lincoln-Douglas debates, in his Second Inaugural Address, and in his image of America at Gettysburg as "a new nation, conceived in liberty and dedicated to the proposition that all men are created equal." That these inclusive symbols have been conspicuously successful, perhaps few will care to deny. Any new fashion to strike the symbols, "men," "people," and "human," from the future utterances of American statesmen, and to put exclusively references to "America" and "Americans" in their place, would itself represent a major departure from the American tradition.

In the Old World, too, the political appeal of the Swiss Confederation during its formative centuries appears to have been inclusive rather than the opposite. New cities and peasant communities continued to join the Confederacy, Basel and Appenzell only at the beginning of the sixteenth century, Geneva even later. Like America, Switzerland appealed to a principle and to a way of life, and the openended symbols which expressed it were highly successful.

If we think today of the few symbols of the emerging world community, we find again that the inclusive symbols appear to have more life in them. The International Red Cross, the United Nations, Unesco, the United Nations Children's Emergency Fund, the World Health Organization, all these aim in principle and spirit to include eventually all mankind rather than a select clientele of approved nations. The human symbols of a possible world community—men as different as Albert Schweitzer, Frank Laubach, Albert Einstein, and the late Mahatma Gandhi—all have exemplified inclusiveness rather than exclusion in their lives.

In any case, however, the community of all mankind may be far away, and the building of regional communities among at least some of the world's free countries may be the next step to be faced. Here, too, perhaps, we may find again, as could be found in a study of past cases of political integration, that the fate of a political community seems to depend less on the unattractiveness of the states and peoples who have remained outside it, and more on the positive attractions that men may find within it. Such a community may have to absorb many of the symbols of traditions of its constituent units by a process of partial incorporation. It may have to invent many new symbols, of many kinds, with the aim of bringing about their mutual reinforcement. In so doing, it would not be enough to merge or combine merely the symbols of community.

Before common symbols can move men, they must have common or complementary memories and experiences to which these symbols can appeal; and the common symbols of any new international community may require a broadening stream of international communication, mutual attentiveness, and actual cooperation among the participating countries.

It is not enough to arrange for the international exchange of benefits, British inventions such as penicillin, radar, and jet engines for the United States, or American methods of mass production for Britain; it is essential that these benefits should be perceived as coming from the other country. The organization of symbols involves the organization of perception and of memory. Each gain toward integration in terms of perceiving and remembering experiences and symbols conducive to a greater sense of community, will make easier the reception of additional unifying symbols, and enhance their effect; each successfully established symbol of this kind, in turn, would make easier additional steps in communication and action toward more community. The actual existence of joint benefits and joint rewards for the participants would be essential for the success of such a development, and perhaps even more important if we are to go by the evidence of the cases studied, would be the continuing perception of these benefits and the common expectation of joint benefits to come.

Once a community has grown among several formerly separate political units through this process of rewarded social learning, it may grow beyond any short range expectation of reward, and it may prove able to withstand great shocks and strains. Men are willing to suffer and die for that which they have learned to love; but they must first have learned to love it. A people, Saint Augustine wrote many years ago, is a community of rational beings united in the object of their love. These words might still suggest a fairly realistic approach to the problem of building a community among nations.

Comment by John H. E. Fried:

Do universal symbols suffer from a lack of "anti"-content?

One of the most important findings, reported by Karl W. Deutsch, of the study project of the Center for Research on World Political Institutions at Princeton University ("Political Community: Historical Experiences and Contemporary Problems of International Organization") concerns what he calls "the familiar pessimistic claim that political unity essentially requires an excluded antigroup that can be despised and feared, and thus used to keep the members of the newly built larger in-group together."

He reports that the data collected by that group of political scientists and historians "do *not* support this claim. Successful unions *have* been brought about in which considerations of excluded out-groups played little or no significant role." He stresses, very rightly, for example, the *inclusive* character of "many of the symbols of the American Revolution" (italics mine).

Yet, the proponents of that "pessimistic claim"[30] could still point out that unions, federations, confederations, and alliances are not universal. While the establishment of the United States of America was the outstanding example in modern history of a new union with no offensive purposes and an inclusive, universalist ideology, and while there have been other unions, leagues, and blocs which had no offensive purposes, it cannot be denied that there have been others which either had such purposes or which caused the formation of counteragglomerations and thereby indirectly led to controversy and war.

The point to be made here, is that the formation of a union (using the term in the widest sense) between previously separate political units, or of a "regional community," is essentially different from the creation of an international or universal community. The former can still harness the symbols, values, and "memories" which have developed *on the unit basis*—they may be political, linguistic, economic, religious, geographic, dynastic, etc. The international community, in turn, must—if we exclude World Government, without discussing its desirability and possibility, as practically unobtainable for the foreseeable future—include *diversities* in these respects. More than that, the international community, and its symbols, must not only include but assure diversities. And yet, it must be built on symbols, values, and expectations which transcend these diversities, which are large enough to embrace the diversities, which allow them to exist "under" these symbols; and which are strong enough to keep within bounds the frictions inevitably resulting from the continuance of those diversities, just as, for example, the individual nation-state must keep within bounds its own, opposing political parties. The universal symbol must do *more* than, as Deutsch says, "denote or designate some *particular* group, region, event, behavior pattern, and the like" (italics added); it must denote or designate, at least potentially, the whole human community.

Hence, the question would still be whether these symbols would be handicapped by the fact that by definition they cannot rely on the cohesion which, according to "the familiar pessimistic claim," results from the very antagonism to, or from, other groups. These schools must be rather skeptical about the "life expectancy" of any international or supranational symbol which lacks the cement of "otherness" they posit as required, for the universal symbol is distinguished by the fact that it does *not* discriminate—even while it must make distinctions inherent in its contents.

It is submitted that this *combination of nondiscrimination* (*nonhostility*) *with firm insistence on its own essentials*, is, indeed, capable of engendering a great deal of cohesion. For, while the international community and its symbols do not rely on pressure from, or against, out-*groups* (and do most definitely not stipulate a *character indelibilis* for the "outcasts"), they sublimate aggressivity against out-*groups* into negativity toward "out-*ideas*."

The basic principles of the United Nations furnish a good illustration. They are universal in the sense that they are also binding on any *non*member. Article 2 of the

---

[30]*E.g.*, J. Dollard, "Hostility and Fear in Social Life," in Newcomb & Hartley, *Readings in Social Psychology*, Henry Holt & Company, New York, 1947. In a brief but succinct discussion, Solomon E. Asch, *Social Psychology*, Prentice Hall, New York, 1952, pp. 329-331, traces the view that "hostility to other groups is a condition of peace within the group" to William Graham Sumner and shows its relation to theories of Hobbes, Darwin, and Freud.

Charter sets forth the Principles (with a capital *P*) of the United Nations (respect for the sovereign equality of all members: settlement of international disputes by peaceful means; refraining from the threat or use of force, etc.) and then declares that the Organization

> shall *ensure* that states which are *not* members of the United Nations act in accordance with these Principles so far as may be necessary for the maintenance of international peace and security.[31]

In fact, the United Nations, *because* of its claim of universality for its essential principles, is conceived in the Charter as an *exclusive club*. Membership is restricted to peaceloving nations. This meant, for the time being, exclusion of the Axis Powers—which, however, like any other nonmembers, are expected to conform to the essential principles of the United Nations. If, as we just saw, "the Organization is *directed* [*ratione* 'shall ensure'] to see that nonmember states do not threaten or breach the peace"[32] this applies, without discrimination, also to the former Axis Powers, as long as they are not members. In addition, Article 107 of the Charter permits members to take action against former Axis Powers which would not be permissible against other nations, whether members or not:

> Nothing in the present Charter shall invalidate or preclude action, in relation to any State which during the Second World War has been an enemy of any signatory to the present Charter, taken or authorized as a result of that war by the Governments having responsibility for such action.

In simpler language, this means that the Big Five (which are the governments "having responsibility for any special action against any former Axis Power") may, for example, occupy or authorize the occupation of territory of any former Axis Power.[33] These provisions, again, do *not* put the former Axis Powers beyond the pale of the principles of the United Nations but were to permit the liquidation of the Second World War. Otherwise, *e.g.,* the occupation of Germany and Japan would have been illegal under the Charter. Such measures were, however, considered necessary, not as breaches of the United Nations principles, but in order to extinguish the *anti*United Nations ideologies and institutions of the Axis, and thus to pave the way for the *inclusion* of those nations in the Organization. Concerning matters *not* related to World War II, all member states are, *vis-à-vis* the former Axis Powers, bound by the limitations of the Charter.

To conclude, it has often and rightly been said that universal institutions must have "teeth" in them. Their symbols can, and must, emanate firmness. Realistically, the

---

[31]Article 2, 6. The *Report to the President* [of the United States of America] *on the Results of the San Francisco Conference* comments: "Such action by the Organization [as authorized in the just quoted Article 2, 6 to *ensure* the respect of nonmembers to the essential principles of the United Nations] is, *of course,* an essential condition for the preservation of the general peace of the world. At San Francisco this principle was unanimously adopted. . . . At the background of the thought of many delegates was the action by Germany and Japan, exmembers of the League, who menaced the peace until finally they wrought havoc throughout the world" (Department of State Publication 2349, Conference Series 71, p. 42, italics added).

[32]*Ibid.*

[33]In addition, at the San Francisco Conference, "on the proposal of the U.S. Delegate, the [Technical] Committee voted unanimously to insert in its report an understanding that the enemy states in this war shall not have the right of recourse to the Security Council or the General Assembly until the Security Council grants them this right" (*ibid.,* p. 164).

Charter of the United Nations contemplates as an ultimate resort, military action on behalf of the United Nations. The extremely important point is that such military action can, by its essence, never be dictated by aggressiveness but results from *opposition* to it. The actions and attitudes required to uphold universal symbols, allow, then, for the sublimation of hostility drives; and even the proponents of the "familiar pessimistic claim" agree that it is possible to sublimate the aggressiveness which, they maintain, holds groups together.[34] Looking at the strength and obstinacy of *anti*universal symbols and trends, the danger that the universal institutions and symbols would become "soft," is exceedingly remote.

The long tradition of universalism

In order to appraise the acceptability of the inclusive symbols of the international community, we have to take into account the tradition and appeal of such universalist symbols as "mankind," "brotherhood," "natural law," "universality of science," etc., and, above all, "peace." (Who could count, *e.g.,* the antiwar references in the literature of the peoples of the world?) In order to become aware of the true extent of their tradition and appeal, we should, incidentally, refrain from setting their beginnings at the chronological date of their *formulation* as ethical principles, religious postulates, or legal norms. For, on the one hand, unless we are smug, we must admit that the *formulations* have by no means meant their general acceptance, even in theory.[35] On the other hand, these ideas have not been alien to peoples, and philosophical and religious systems that have not partaken in the development of the West. When Voltaire located the kindly and wise people of his Eldorado in a remote region, he followed the fashion

[34]Here is an example of a catalogue of legitimate outlets for aggression: "In our society, we are allowed, for example, a limited right to compete for direct goals as by business manipulations, courtship, or sport. We may, also, kill in wartime, defensively, of course; and we have limited rights to derogate others, such as children by adults, women by men, those who cannot get work by those who cannot give it, and some politicians by other politicians" (Dollard, *op. cit.,* p. 472). Since there is so much room for choice, we may still stand a good chance of excluding those outlets which the author by clear implication decries; we could well "settle" on ever continued competition, *e.g.,* in courtship or sport, or the derogation of some politicians by other politicians.

[35]Filmer S. C. Northrop, in Chapter IV of this book, "Linguistic Symbols and Legal Norms," points to the "novel moral ideal" of the Roman law "that no rule for ordering personal or social conduct is truly moral unless any human being whatever can be substituted for an instance of the rule," and states that "prior to the philosophers of ancient Greek mathematical physics and the Stoic Romans the idea of moral man being universal man had not been conceived even as an ideal." Northrop mentions, to prove this, the Laws of Manu which applied different legal penalties for identical offenses according to the caste of the offender (pp. 59–60). Yet, how recently has slavery been abolished in the Western Hemisphere! Legal inequalities persist everywhere to a certain degree, in spite of the movement from Status to Contract, and also outside the Law of Contract. Differences are based on citizenship, ethnic origin, race, sex, etc. Some are considered as undesirable, others are generally accepted because they tally with the *mores* of the respective community. The latter type of inequalities—those which are generally accepted—are more interesting for the present discussion. For, while the universalist symbols are intrinsically opposed to them, those inequalities, as long as they are not being "exported" and remain on the lower level of the autonomy of the smaller communities, do not seriously threaten the essential tenets of universalism.

of his day, but to some extent the reports of travelers, anthropologists, and missionaries agree with him. Any static society is self-centered, and the isolation of community from community was imposed by the state of technology before it was posited as an ideological *desideratum*. Isolationism, in the present connotation of the term, is anachronistic when there is no isolation to which it is concomitant.

The universality of democracy

It is true, however, that the doctrines of "democracy" lend themselves naturally, and with particular ease, to their expansion into universalism. In fact, such expansion is inherent in them, as was, for example, so clearly realized at the time of the American and French Revolutions. If this is so, a *mutual fertilization* of democratic particularist, and democratic universalist symbols and institutions is possible, and should receive attention. To be more concrete, there is, for example, insufficient awareness of the concrete advantages of a constructive international policy for the domestic scene. A greater awareness of the interaction between domestic and "foreign" (!) policies would increase the general interest in the latter.

Since the symbols and values of a democratic world community are identical with those of the democratic community on a national, state, or township level, the citizens of a democracy should be particularly receptive to the symbols and values of the world community: they "fit" with their established ways. This writer happened to visit the Netherlands at the time when Indonesia, with the help of the United Nations, had just gained independence from the Netherlands. The Dutch East Indies had been by far the largest Dutch colonial possession and this development was difficult to accept. There was some open criticism of the United Nations, and of the attitude of certain of its members. But there was, to my knowledge, no outburst, and nobody even suggested that the Netherlands should quit the United Nations, or the like. The attitude was truly democratic, which implies, among other things, a fine sense for prestige, and the realization that it is no disgrace to lose, if the rules of the game which one had accepted, were adhered to.

The understanding that "my team cannot always win," is at the core of civilized existence. To the degree to which loyalty to universal symbols and values increases, the pain of "losing" diminishes, because the "defeat" can be experienced as an affirmation of the higher principle. This, again, is true of democracy at home. We do not kill the judge who has announced a judgment against us.

Yet, it may be asked, how typical was, for example, the admittedly admirable test of the Dutch people in the Indonesian case. It is true that the problem we are faced with is *not the weakness of universal symbols*,[36] but the *fear of their clash with group symbols, e.g.,* national symbols. In this sense, the discussion as to whether and when the United Nations flag may be shown together with the national flag, and whether it may be hoisted lower or higher or on the same level, is revealing. As national symbols are highly charged with emotions, any fear lest they be weakened, leads to emotional reactions. It must immediately be admitted that if the fear were justified, the antagonism against the universal symbols would be justified. The question, then, is whether the fear is justified, and here is a most fruitful field for the social sciences.

Characteristically, and paradoxically, manipulators of public opinion often see a need, especially in time of stress, of strengthening the community symbols by universal symbols. Frequently, they actually borrow or adapt them for their purposes—which is en-

---

[36]It is, in a way, heartening to see that a razor blade manufacturer has to be prevented from registering a trade mark, "United Nations razor blades." (The example is fictitious but analogous to real occurrences.)

tirely desirable and legitimate, and the highest compliment that can be paid to the force of the universal symbols. ("God—the universal God!—is on the side of my fatherland.") But while the reference to universal symbols, as many experiences show, strengthens the community symbols, it casts doubt in extreme cases into the hearts of those who feel bound to both. This happens most dramatically in times of greatest tension, namely, war, when universal symbols are invoked most heavily to bolster the national symbols. "How can my Church bless my weapons with which to kill the children of the same God—while the same Church blesses the weapons on the enemy side which are to kill me and my family?" Of course, when there is no war, the dilemma can be dissolved, if the two categories of symbols do not endanger or exclude each other.

Conceivably, such remembrances as the centuries old fight between State and Church have conditioned Western man to a fallacious monism in questions of loyalty to general symbols. It can be stated with only a little oversimplification that, *e.g.,* to posit a dilemma between loyalty of the United States citizen to the United States of America and his support of the United Nations, is not much different from saying that an inhabitant of New York City has to be loyal *either* to New York City or *to* the State of New York. I choose this random example because so far there has been no debate between the United Nations and the United States of America nearly as acrimonious as the controversy between the State and the City regarding New York City finances.

Dilemmas are possible. But every person and group stands in multiple relations to other persons and groups, and the circles of loyalties, duties, and affinities frequently overlap. Every man has to face competing demands from his family and his career, or from his parents and his children, etc. Such dilemmas are not easy of solution. But the one solution which is unacceptable to society, is to sacrifice one duty in favor of another, to throw one overboard. In fact, society can be defined, in this sense, as the sum-total of pressures, taboos, and sanctions which tend to guarantee the perpetual coexistence of different loyalties, duties, and affinities, *all of which* are essential, *although* at times some may come into conflict with others.

In the international community, these preserving forces are weaker than they are in the national community. The danger is increased by the fact that the relative strength of universal symbols *while there is no conflict* may conceal the possibility of their being thrown overboard, even if conflict is only *feared,* and not real. The fact cannot be overlooked that man, just as he makes and craves symbols, is at times ready to unmake them. To destroy the authority as expressed in symbols, yields a near patricidal, obscene pleasure-pain—a burst of feelings of omnipotence which, as soon as it is burned out, creates an equally dangerous need for retrogression, and thus for refuge in atavistic symbols and actions. Such an outbreak may conceivably lead to an aggressiveness and chauvinism more dangerous than the prior isolationism.

The symbols of "independence" and "security"

Political symbols, apart from their function of designating, as Deutsch says, "a bundle of *memories,"* also designate a bundle of *expectations.* Sometimes, the memories are more important, and sometimes the expectations. Frequently, they combine. The mixture varies from symbol to symbol and, within the same symbol, in time and place. Furthermore, both the memories and the expectations which one and the same symbol is to designate, can be variegated. The latter point is of great significance. The combinatory quality of symbols is one of their secrets, and source of their strength; in turn, it makes their effects difficult to predict.

All of these considerations enter into the understanding of the complicated symbol, "security," to which Deutsch refers. How much security is security? According to banking rules for loans, 120% security is not secure. The risk must always be smaller than the security. How much smaller? How probable must the risk be to require securing against it? In the field of international affairs, the obtainable security is always relative, as the factors which determine both the risk and the safety margin, are bound to be uncertain. The architect of a house knows formulas and data to calculate, and assure against, the risks of fire, gale, and perhaps earthquake. The architect of foreign policy is in a more difficult situation. This is implied in Deutsch's statement that "we wish to be secure from those who might infringe upon our own political autonomy."

The problem is hidden in the term, "might." Whether they "might" infringe and under what circumstances, and under what circumstances they might not, cannot be answered with certainty. The search for "full" security would imply the possibility of creating at the present time a system where nobody could, or would infringe upon anybody else. Assuming this were obtainable *for* that *moment,* it would no longer be true for the next moment, because we cannot command the ever changing variables, economic, political, social, military, technological, etc., to stand still. And what does the term, "infringe," mean? Is the dumping of export goods an infringement? The erection of traffic barriers? The denial of entry visas? The erection of military bases? The extension of military training periods? Discourtesy against an ambassador? Calumnies in the press? Alienation of allies?

Security is, thus, never static but always in process.

In this process, the constantly necessary judging of risks will, as Deutsch indicates, very much take into account the trends in national and international symbols. I also agree with Deutsch's methodology of closely linking the symbol, "security," with the symbol, "independence" (and the latter with the symbol, "allies"). Not only is "security" a dialectic concept in the sense that at one point more security becomes less security; independence and security, if we take both terms, as we must, in their widest sense, also decrease and increase inversely to each other. Even the mightiest nation, in order to be secure, will have to take measures (and to persuade other nations to allow, or participate in measures) which will make it in various ways more dependent on other nations, and on many factors over which it has no control. The "we" group to which Deutsch refers is actually an *"interdependence" group.* As long as there is little reliance on universal symbols, that "interdependence" group is constantly dependent on the "they" group which is again an "interdependence" group, and in turn dependent on *our* interdependence group.

What, then, is the difference between the two groups? As Deutsch indicates, the "we" symbols which designate "our" group, are symbols which permit of a higher degree of tolerance and confidence.

Does this beg the question? Does it boil down to the tautology that one is friendly to friends, and cool to adversaries—or that the definition of a friend is somebody to whom one is friendly? Not quite. The analysis shows the relativity of the friend-foe relation, a relativity which is obscured by the way our language says "country *A is* a close friend," and "country *B is* a doubtful friend," etc. What comes first, is the expectation of friendship. To those from whom friendship is expected, every nation is very much more tolerant than to others. The "we" group is not a group where frictions and disagreements are absent; but where there is a readiness either to disregard them, or to compromise them and, in any case, to handle them in such a way that they do not become a "danger."

This would be simple if the categories, "friends, allies, enemies," were permanently defined. They are not. History abounds with examples where friends become enemies, and *vice versa,* almost literally from one day to the next. And what is so astounding is the comparative ease with which the transition is accomplished. Hence, the question remains: what determines what? Does a nation or group belong to the "we" community because friction and disagreement can easily be straightened out, or can they be easily straightened out because the "friend" symbol is affixed to them? And when is the symbol taken away from them?

How much the "we" group extends, and whether such shifts happen, will—in the atomic age more than ever—determine our destiny. The outcome will largely be determined by the strength and vitality of the universal, cooperativist symbols.

The sudden emergence of international symbols

In this context, it is interesting to observe that in the field of international relations, symbols are relatively *easy* to create. Just as different wines need different periods of time for aging, different symbols appear to require different lengths of time to become potent. Looking only at recent history, we have but to think of such symbols as, *e.g.,* "Munich," "Fifth Column," or "Pearl Harbor." It would be instructive to find out why, for example, the small village of Lidice became at once the international symbol for Nazi brutality, although before and after the Nazis committed similar acts on a much larger scale.

One of the remarkable illustrations of an event which almost overnight grew into a symbol, was the battle of Dienbienphu in IndoChina in the spring of 1954. It seems only a partial explanation, to say that the strength of the new symbol was due to the intensity of the preexisting symbols with which it was connected ("aggression," "Communist threat," etc.). The interesting thing was that these preexisting symbols suddenly derived strength from the addition of an ingredient, Dienbienphu, which in and of itself evoked *no* memories. Yet the new symbol almost became the starting point for a major military operation on the part of the United States of America. History knows of similar cases, such as the Fashoda crisis which almost led to war between France and Great Britain, or Emperor William II's *Panther-Sprung* to Tangier that almost made a European war erupt several years before the crisis of Sarajevo did in 1914. In a sense, the two latter examples are more illustrative of the symbolmaking capacity of some events, because these two crises developed in an atmosphere much less explosive than that of the spring of 1954.

Evidently, the term, "crisis," in international relations has a meaning different from that, *e.g.,* in medicine, or the "breaking point" of a metal. The rules which govern the carrying capacity of an iron bridge, are different from those governing the "crises" and "breaking points" in international politics (if, indeed, there are rules here). In the latter field, an added "pound" of weight may have a breaking effect which a different "ton" of weight may not have.

Also, the weight of the symbol may change rather quickly—that is, an event may exhaust, or lose, its symbolic significance. The intensity of a symbol at any given time does not allow predictions as to its durability. It is probably safe to predict that within a relatively short time, "Dienbienphu" will have lost any symbolic quality in the popular mind.

It appears permissible to state, as a preliminary working hypothesis, that under certain constellations, events on the international scene may suddenly develop a symbolic character with potentially sweeping consequences, "out of proportion" to the event itself. I realize, of course, that the phrase, "under certain constellations," begs the question of why and when this is so. I am unable to suggest an answer—except for believing that it does not suffice to say that the modern mass media have made it comparatively easy for the manipulators of public opinion to "make" and "unmake" symbols. I submit only that the question is of extraordinary scientific and practical portent.

Flexibility of international symbols

Leaving the "comet" symbols for the more lasting ones, we notice that, as symbols of the international community become more widely accepted, their *contents become less clearly defined*. They will mean different things to different people, especially as it becomes "the proper thing" to accept them, because they confer prestige. In a controversy, either side will claim to be true to the common principles, and accuse the other side of violating them. This is in itself not *necessarily* bad, the smile of the cynic notwithstanding. The more universal a symbol, the less can we reasonably expect it ever to have exactly the same meaning to all who accept it.

As the thought patterns and images of most persons are locally determined, even sophisticated individuals may inadvertently color the universal symbols they accept; and consider this to be "natural." In other words, they will assume that the wider symbol *A* includes, "of course," the narrower symbols *B, C,* and *D*. The millions who connect "Christmas" with "snow flakes," "illuminated trees," and "gifts," easily forget that there are other millions who celebrate Christmas in the hot season, do not illuminate trees, and do not even exchange gifts on the occasion.[37]

The task of the academic disciplines concerned, is to study with the greatest possible detachment the reasons for the differences in the interpretation of universal symbols, and the degree of unity behind these differences. The task is difficult because there is bound to be disagreement as to what parts of the contents of universal symbols are essential, and what parts are peripheral. Only children will think that Christmas is no longer Christmas without presents. But scholars will disagree whether, *e.g.,* the United Nations can guarantee peace without military enforcement machinery. But it can be said of the symbols of the international community that the degree of divergence of the claims made by invoking the same symbol is (if the reference to the symbol is not in bad faith)[38] an indicator of the vitality of the symbol. As long as contending factions refer to a common symbol, its intrinsically unifying force has still a chance to assert itself.

For example, that the United Nations has survived the tensions of these years, is one of the few encouraging facts of this troubled era. This is probably due in no small measure to the "width" of the symbol, "United Nations," which, *e.g.,* allows it to stand for stability *and* for change. With every universal symbol, there will always be efforts by the adherents of one of its "meanings" to impose it on others; the symbol, in order to be universal, must allow for discussion, and for endeavors to gain adherents to

[37]A story is told at the United Nations of a representative of a Western country who, at the height of the Palestinian crisis, invited Jewish and Arab leaders to his chambers, and when all were seated, opened the meeting with the words, "Gentlemen, let's try and settle this matter as good Christians." Clearly, the speaker intended to appeal to the spirit of tolerance, fairness, and peace, and postulated their acceptance as universal. At the same time, he connected, or identified, them with Christianity. If he limited these virtues to Christianity, he unintentionally revealed an exclusive attitude, claiming a superiority for his own religion and inviting the members of the other faiths to abide by its precepts to solve their problem. If he intended to appeal to religiosity without excluding Judaism and Mohammedanism, he was revealingly inept in his choice of words.

[38]Hypocrisy is the compliment which vice pays to virtue. But the juggling of commonly accepted symbols can have fatal consequences. To quote one illustration, Hitler's strategy of cloaking his aggressive and expansionist designs against Germany's neighbors by invoking the "right to self-determination" confused Western public opinion and even statesmen during the crucial period when, without this confusion, it might still have been possible to call his bluff and through firmness to avoid World War II.

different interpretations. The history of all successful symbols has shown that their success depended largely on their flexibility. We have only to think of the ever changing interpretation of the United States Constitution—changes which left the symbol, "United States Constitution," unimpaired.

Interplay of political symbols, and difficulty of predicting the results

Political symbols are as potent as they are difficult to manipulate[39] and difficult to predict in their effects. Symbols may be "vague"—they perhaps are so by their essence —and yet they have a logic all their own. Their commutability and compatibility, and the consequences of their commutation and combination are often unexpected. Mistakes in predictions are probably due to erroneous assumptions as to their mutual hierarchy in the minds of their adherents. Closer inspection then indicates that seemingly suppressed, dividing symbols had gained ascendency although opposite symbols continued to be held. Let us take, as examples, the readiness of "France" to put up military resistance against "Germany" in the two world wars.

Prior to August, 1914, despite the coolness of FrancoGerman relations referred to by Deutsch, many (perhaps the majority of) French and German workers (who would have to do the fighting in the mass armies) thought that their supranational "solidarity" would prevent war between the two countries. That solidarity was one of the strongest symbols of the labor movement in France and Germany at the period. However, when the war came—in their language, "when the warmongers finally succeeded in their sinister plans to take the workers to the slaughter-house"—the symbols, "fatherland," "danger to our families," etc., proved to be stronger. But the story does not end here. Within two years, the internationalist and solidarity feelings and the antagonism against their ideological adversaries at home, gained the upper hand in a sector of the German Social Democratic Party. This led to a lasting split within the party, with historic consequences. In 1939, Hitler represented a more serious threat to France than did the Kaiser's Germany, and Nazism was unpalatable to the majority of Frenchmen. Yet, as events showed, their will to fight was much less than it had been in 1914. In turn, a substantial number of the traditionally military and nationalistic circles in France who had been considered as safely wedded to the symbols of *"patrie," "gloire,"* and the like, were so much imbued with the antidemocratic authoritarianism symbolized by Hitler, and the French domestic political symbols of the period, such as "Popular Front," were so obnoxious to them (*plutôt Hitler que Léon Blum*) that Marshal Pétain became the head of a collaborationist puppet government. The attraction of the Hitler symbol had turned these men into what Pertinax called the gravediggers of France. But this again was not the end. Relatively many of the men who had shown little fighting spirit before, became *maquis* fighters although the situation had become much more difficult, *e.g.,* they knew they would be executed or tortured when captured, a risk they did not run when falling into the hands of the Germans as prisoners-of-war during regular warfare. The population at large hated the Doriot's even more than they hated the Nazi invaders. The symbols of French patriotism reasserted themselves. After the war, Pétain was condemned as traitor; but at that moment, the symbolic character of his rank reasserted itself contrariwise: characteristically, he was not executed, as was, *e.g.,* his Prime Minister, Laval, to whom the nimbus of Pétain's military rank was not available. A

[39]One thing that probably can safely be stated is that slogans cannot be inflated into symbols. Synthetic symbols are contradictions in terms. They are like the wheels of a car which are not entirely parallel. The driver does not even notice the deficiency while the car goes slowly; but in the situation which matters, when he goes into high speed, the car may break apart.

closer analysis would probably reveal an even more intricate interplay of different supranational and national symbols contributing to the French-German relations in these two periods.

From whatever angle we look at political symbols, particularist and universal, we find that the problems they pose are among the most challenging and important with which the social sciences have to deal.

Comment by Jiri Kolaja:

Karl W. Deutsch supports his thesis of a rather increasing concern with domestic affairs as compared to foreign affairs by several interesting data from the field of mail, foreign news publication, reading interest, etc. As he explains modern nationalism mainly in terms of relatively decreased communication and lack of shared symbols, world community seems far off. However, one factor should be brought into the picture before final judgment. There has been a tremendous increase in personal contacts between people from distant countries. Simultaneously, psychological space, if this ambiguous term may be used, could often be considered smaller as a result of progress in transportation. If a traveler can tell in New York a story that happened to him yesterday in Paris, our cultural norms of time and space are due to be adjusted accordingly. The past century lacked this perception of simultaneity of our lives all over the world. For example, in romantic Czechoslovak poetry from the past century, foreign countries were described often as "distant," "far away," "foggy," etc. In general, distance was perceived in terms of a rather diffused past or future. Modern poetry, on the contrary, tends more to perceive the simultaneity of events happening in Singapore, Prague, Chicago, etc. The simultaneity aspect can be used as "an inclusive symbol," speaking in Deutsch's terms. The fact of the cyclical nature of time endured inevitably by all of us, lends itself to the inclusive function of the symbols that we need so badly. On the contrary, the category of space-locale seems to serve more the exclusive, particularistic use of symbols.

Professor Deutsch's reply:

I appreciate Jiri Kolaja's highly pertinent comment. It seems true that distant places are mentioned far more often nowadays in news dispatches, as well as in poetry and other literature, and that they are usually mentioned in contexts suggesting simultaneous happenings and immediate contacts. This frequent and urgent appearance of foreign symbols in our press and literature, however, does not automatically make for realistic images of the countries and peoples for which they stand. Foreign place names may serve as new labels for homemade preconceptions. An American historian, Daniel J. Boorstin, has recently suggested that many American images of Europe have been of this kind.[40] The frequency, therefore, with which we recall incomplete images from memory is not necessarily a substitute for more frequent and careful attention to the incoming messages from the countries and peoples to which these images refer.

This leads to a second point. Even if we were to assume that any relative increase in literary references to foreign countries corresponds to an increase in our actual political and social attention to their populations, we still should have to ask whether such an increase in our attention to foreign affairs has been large enough to keep pace with

[40]*Cf.* Daniel J. Boorstin, "American Nationalism and the Image of Europe, 1914–1945," The University of Chicago, Department of History, 1954, multigraphed; to appear as a chapter in the *L'Europe du XIXe et du XXe siècles: Problèmes et interprétations historiques,* edited by Pierre Renouvin, Franz Schnabel, *et al.,* Marzorati, Milan.

the contemporaneous increase in our international involvements and responsibilities. It is difficult, of course, to form any quantitative estimate of the extent to which our international involvements have increased during the past thirty years. An article by Senator John F. Kennedy of Massachusetts suggests that the relative share of international affairs in our national legislation may have increased about fourfold. "In 1925," he writes, "only one Act of Congress in twenty-five had any direct relationship to international relations, and that was generally inconsequential. Today, at least one of every six or seven enacted bills are of tremendous worldwide concern."[41] Senator Kennedy's statement obviously is not to be taken as a precise measurement of the relevant dimensions of our problem, but it does suggest that the claims of international affairs on the attention and decisionmaking capabilities of our Senators threaten to outrun by far the international information available to their constituents, or the time and attention which their voters at home have been devoting to these matters. If so, we might become, in David Riesman's terms, increasingly "other-directed" as individuals and in domestic politics, while remaining predominantly "inner-directed" as a nation and in our dealings with other governments and peoples. This, in turn, might have important effects on our ability to hold together any stable coalition of free countries. The problem of international communication and community is thus a complex one for the United States, as it is for other nations, but it is immediate and real; and the data and questions offered by Kolaja may well help us further toward its better understanding.

Comment by Daniel Lerner:

Karl W. Deutsch makes good use of the symbol studies by Lasswell, Pool, and myself to confront propositions that have emerged from his own studies. His survey of "Symbols as Indicators" is illuminating. The briefer section on "Symbols as Instruments" perforce covers much ground rapidly, hence readers may bypass one point of capital importance for action. Deutsch reminds us that the key symbol of our historic documents is "human" and not "American," world-inclusive not national-exclusivist. He further adds: "Any new fashion to strike the symbols MEN, PEOPLE, HUMAN from the future utterances of American statesmen, and to put exclusively references to AMERICA and AMERICANS in their place, would itself represent a major departure from the American tradition."

This suggests a proper inference from the data on symbol usage which I reported to the Thirteenth Conference in these terms:

> In the postwar years, a new shift appears to be developing in American usage—the tendency to *identify* Democracy with America. This leads to the new definition that Democracy *is* whatever America does. This represents a dangerous parochialization of our key symbol . . . at a time when the demand is for rousing symbols of expansive and cosmopolitan appeal. . . . The diverse peoples of the world will hardly be elated by the news that Democracy and Americanism are coterminous.[42]

Deutsch's action-oriented restatement of these facts might well become the opening sentence of a current guide for publicists. It would help those Americans "who speak for man" by reinforcing their conviction that the high moral tone goes more appropriately with the symbols of humanity than with the harsh accents of conspicuous "Americanism."

---

[41]John F. Kennedy, "Foreign Policy and the People," *The New York Times Magazine,* August 8, 1954, p. 28.

[42]Daniel Lerner, "Symbol and Act in Propaganda," *Symbols and Values: An Initial Study,* Chapter XXV, p. 380.

Professor Deutsch's reply:

Daniel Lerner's point impressed me at the time that he contributed his paper to the Thirteenth Conference, and it was one of the factors which increased my interest in watching self-reference symbols and communications as possible indicators of political behavior. A similar scrutiny of French and German political value symbols for the possible presence or absence of self-referent associations (*e.g.*, "civilization is what Frenchmen are accustomed to" or "justice is what Germans desire") might be one of the many potential applications of Lerner's approach.

CHAPTER IV

Linguistic Symbols and Legal Norms

By F. S. C. NORTHROP

UNDESCRIBED EXPERIENCE came first. Expressed experience, and hence language, came afterward. Before one can express, there must be something to be expressed.

But one can give expression to experience in many modes. Language may refer not so much to experience itself as to the effect of experience upon the perceiver, as in the words "Ouch!" or "Damn it!" Because of its problematic character, experience may raise queries. Thus arises the interrogatory mode. In the present inquiry we shall restrict ourselves, however, to language in the indicative mode, *i.e.,* to the character which language takes on in its attempt to express experience itself, including the experiencer.

With respect to experience in the indicative mode, two components are to be noted. One component is experience in itself in its all embracing entirety as given with immediacy. The other component is the factor in human knowledge which is inferred from, but not contained in, immediate experience. Elsewhere the writer has termed these two components the "esthetic component" and the "theoretic component" respectively.[1]

These two components of experience in its indicative mode are important for any analysis of language, since the type of linguistic symbolism best suited to convey the one is quite different from that most appropriate for the other. Moreover, the type of ethical and legal norms of cultures, handling experience in one or the other or both of these two different ways, differ correspondingly. Hence the connection between linguistic symbols and ethical and legal norms.

To make the foregoing conclusions evident several things are necessary. It must be realized that we approach culture and symbolism at the end of a lengthy historical tradition which is the product of the converg-

[1]F. S. C. Northrop, *The Meeting of East and West,* The Macmillan Company, New York, 1946.

ing of many cultures. This means that our symbolism is of necessity a mixed symbolism, even perhaps, as the sequel will suggest, a bastard symbolism, due to the fact that a given cultural language devised to convey experience in one indicative mode found itself forced, due to outside influences, to convey experience in the other indicative mode for which it was in many ways ill fitted.

It becomes necessary, therefore, if confusion and linguistic corruption of the diverse esthetic and theoretic components of knowledge are to be avoided, to separate out from the complexity of our present linguistically expressed experience the immediately experienced factor, *i.e.,* the esthetic component, from the theoretically inferred factor, *i.e.,* the theoretic component. Having done this, we should then be able to determine the two different types of linguistic symbols most appropriate for each.

To this end let us consider the following example: one directly senses within the all embracing continuum of immediacy a specific, differentiated color. To this immediately experienced datum in the esthetic component of knowledge, convention, in the English language, has assigned the word "blue." Consider with care precisely how "blue" in this sense gets its meaning. Clearly the entire meaning of the word is given by a datum in the all embracing immediacy of experience, which itself is immediately experienced. Yellow, red, pain, and pleasure are other examples of this type of symbol. Such a symbol we have called a concept by intuition, where by intuition is meant something not mediated to the knower through something else, but given immediately after the manner of a specific, particular, immediately sensed blue.

Consider now, by way of contrast, an electromagnetic wave traveling in vacuo with a speed of 186,000 miles a second and with a wave length of 4,862 angstroms. To this wave with this specific wave length, the English language also assigns the word "blue." Clearly, however, "blue" in the latter sense has a fundamentally different meaning and designates a quite different object from "blue" in the former sense. Neither the wave with a speed of 186,000 miles per second nor its wave length is immediately experienced after the manner in which the sensed color in the all embracing continuum of immediacy is directly inspected. In other words, "blue" in the sense of the electromagnetic wave is an object of knowledge inferred from but not contained in the all embracing immediacy of experience. It is, in short, a factor in the theoretic component of knowledge.

But if the symbol "blue" in the sense of the concept of the electromagnetic wave refers to something which is not directly inspected in the all embracing immediacy of experience, how then is this symbol given meaning in an unambiguous way? Clearly this concept cannot gain its meaning by the method of pointing or sensing or immediately apprehending after the manner in which the concept of "blue" which is a concept by intuition gains its meaning. The answer is that the concept of "blue" in the sense of the electromagnetic wave with a specific wave length obtains its meaning only through the construction by some scientist of an axiomatically constructed, deductively formulated theory in which the entity, *i.e.,* the wave with its specific wave length, functions as a variable, satisfying a certain type of formally defined order or relatedness. Because "blue" in the sense of the electromagnetic wave depends upon a set of deductively formulated postulates for its meaning, it is appropriate to call it, or any other concept knowable in whole or in part in this way, a concept by postulation.

One of the tragically unfortunate weaknesses of present education is that the same word "blue" is used in the conventional, commonsense English language for these two fundamentally different types of concepts, referring to radically different objects for their meanings and that the reader is not made aware, nor is the English language appropriate or adequate to make him aware, of the radical difference in the method to be used to obtain the meaning of the one concept as compared with the meaning of the other. In fact, as the sequel will show, ordinary language whether it be English, French, German, Sanskrit, or Chinese, is ill fitted to convey the meaning of any concept by postulation.

Moreover, and this is the point of essential importance for the present inquiry, there is a fundamental difference between the relation of the object to the symbol in the case of a concept by intuition as compared with a concept by postulation. In the instance of "blue" in the sense of the ineffable sensed color, the symbol *qua* symbol says nothing. If one did not have with immediacy the experience of an instance of blue, the symbol "blue" would be a meaningless set of marks. Thus in the case of this type of symbol one gets what it means when one throws the symbol away. In fact, what the symbol means cannot be said symbolically. The symbol instead is merely a conventional pointer which can be thrown away the minute the immediately experienced object of its pointing is found.

In the case of any symbol which is a concept by postulation, referring to inferred objects that cannot be directly inspected, such as an electromagnetic wave of a specified wave length, the relation of the symbol to its object is the exact converse of the relation of the symbol "blue" which is a concept by intuition to the sensed datum which is its object. Since electromagnetic waves, traveling at 186,000 miles per second are not directly inspected, to throw away the symbol "blue," in the sense of the number for the electromagnetic wave length, is to be left with nothing. Without the language, this object cannot be known. In short, whereas the objective referents of symbols which are concepts by intuition cannot be said and can only be pointed at by their symbols, those of concepts by postulation can be said but cannot be pointed at symbolically.

Also the sensed datum "blue" can be known in its full meaning quite apart from its sensed relations to other factors; the knowing of its relations to other things is not an essential part of the knowing of it. However, in the case of the wave length, or any other object of a concept by postulation, its relatedness to everything else is of the essence. An electromagnetic wave is only knowable through the specific systematically and postulationally constructed mathematical relatedness, with specified formal properties, which it alone satisfies. Consequently the language, the only exact language, for indicating such inferred objects within human experience is the language of mathematics and more particularly the logic of relations.

The ordinary prose of the ordinary languages, as studied by the traditional linguists, is quite inadequate to convey knowledge of inferred entities in the theoretic component of knowledge. In fact ordinary language, because of its two-termed, noun-verb grammar and subject-predicate way of thinking about everything, tends to corrupt this way of knowing experience in its indicative mode. Furthermore, Whitehead has given cogent reasons for believing that the ordinary languages of commonsense usage, upon which linguists have concentrated their attention, corrupt every dimension of experience—the esthetic, the religious, the psychological, and the social—just as much as they distort and corrupt the knowledge of mathematical physics.[2] If the relatedness of expe-

[2]Alfred North Whitehead, *The Concept of Nature,* Cambridge University Press, London, 1920, and *Dialogues of Alfred North Whitehead* as recorded by Lucien Price, Atlantic-Little, Brown, Boston, 1954.

rience, even of esthetic experience, is a many-termed relatedness, this is the case. And if it be the case, our traditional linguistic habits have distorted and corrupted all our esthetic, moral, religious, and social judgments. Again one sees the essential connection between language and ethical and legal norms.

This becomes evident in a concrete way when one compares the symbolism of mathematical physics with that of ordinary language with respect to the ethical implications of each. In mathematical physics individual entities are not regarded as truly known unless the universal laws, *i.e.,* the complex relations which define their properties and which they satisfy, are specified. This means that a truly known individual, even a truly known man, is always an entity which in its essential nature is an instance of a universal law. Directly experienced man is of a quite different character, as the ethics and the legal procedures of cultures which have never discovered the mathematical physicist's way of knowing, clearly demonstrate. In all such cultures, where only the ordinary languages are used, moral man is always inductively observed, family and tribal man. Never, in the social norms for ordering human relations, is he conceived as universal man. Thus the notion that color of skin or family connection or tribe has nothing to do with the norms of a moral society is in fact foreign to peoples and cultures which have not discovered the way of knowing individuals by means of the linguistic universalism of deductively formulated mathematical physics, a mode of knowing which occurred first with the ancient Greeks.

It was this way of knowing, passing over through Greek philosophy into Roman law, which gave rise to the Western law of contract and to the novel moral ideal that no rule for ordering personal or social conduct is truly moral unless any human being whatever can be substituted for an instance of the rule. Then, for the first time, moral and political man was broken loose from Roman, Greek, Hebrew, Arab, Hindu, or Chinese family and tribal man. And even with the Romans, the break was made largely as an ideal and only in part in fact. The point to be noted, however, is that prior to the philosophers of ancient Greek mathematical physics and the Stoic Romans the idea of moral man being universal man had not been conceived even as an ideal. In the case of Hinduism and its Laws of Manu, this is unequivocally clear. Different legal penalties are applied for identical offenses according to the caste to which one belongs and a higher moral quality is assigned to the patriarchal families descended from Manu than any other patriarchal families in the Hindu-Aryan community.

Sir Henry S. Maine has described this difference between 1) the ethics and law throughout the entire world before the Stoic Romans created Western legal science and 2) the ethics and law afterward as "a movement from Status to Contract."[3] The law of status is the type of ethics and law that goes with a symbolism which restricts its reference to experience in the indicative mode, to experience as conceived in terms of common sense, substantial persons, and things as given in naive commonsense observation in the ordinary man's language. Since such an excessively inductive and naive way of knowing restricts knowable reality to the *status quo,* the ethical and legal norms of such a linguistic symbolism have nothing to which to refer but to the *status quo.* In the *status quo* as immediately experienced men are not identical; they have different colors of skin. To treat them, therefore, as equal is to be untrue to their essential nature. It is not an accident that the Sanskrit word for caste is the Sanskrit word for color.

Moreover, even with respect to families with the same color of skin, different families, as naively observed, have different ancestors. Thus there are tribal differences as well as color differences. To act, therefore, as if all tribes are equal, is to act contrary to what is the case. Moreover, one of the tribes must in fact lead. In Hindu-Aryan society this was the tribe of Manu. Hence their privileged position morally and socially in Hindu Indian culture.

Even in societies, such as the Confucian Chinese, in which one tribe did not enjoy ascendancy over all other tribes and families, the law of status approach to human nature of a linguistic symbolism, restricting itself to naive experience, reveals families' ties to be given with immediacy as stronger than other social ties. Hence people in such societies concluded that to treat sons in other families under the same legal or moral rules which one applies to sons in one's own family is again to falsify human nature. In short, filial piety, or family loyalty, becomes the highest social morality and nepotism, instead of being the vice it is in a society guided by the ethics of a law of contract, becomes instead the highest social virtue.

Historically the ethics of the law of status society, with its linguistic

[3] Sir Henry S. Maine, *Ancient Law,* John Murray, London, 1908, p. 151.

symbolism, which roots all symbolic meaning in experience as given in naive observation, came first, and the law of contract society with its concept of moral man as universal man and its deductively formulated, mathematical symbolism, which finds its empirical meaning in the theoretical component of knowledge which is inferred from but not contained in immediate experience, arose afterward. Moreover, it was discovered first by the ancient Greeks who founded deductively formulated and indirectly verified mathematical physics. It is because this new way of arriving at symbolic meaning passed over through classical Greek philosophy to the Stoic Romans who created Western legal science, that the ethics of the law of status with its moral attachment to family and to tribe was transformed into the ethics of the law of contract according to which moral man is universal man.

Seen from the linguistic point of view, this epochmaking ethical transformation centers in the shift from 1) the symbolism of commonsense language, which finds meanings for entities like a particular blue, a particular pain, a particular pleasure, a particular naively observed table or naively observed family, apart from the relation of these entities to one another to other entities, to 2) the more complex syntactical symbolism of mathematics in which the entities are meaningless by themselves and are meaningful only in terms of the formal properties of the postulationally constructed relations which they satisfy. In law and social morality, this permits the construction of utopias. The ideal is freed from the actuality of the naively observed *status quo*. The moral and the ideal is released also from the restrictive emotional ties between parents and children and from the commonplace objects that are naively observed. At the same time the utopian constructions, illustrated in the Western world's ideologies and political constitutions, express actuality—the actuality, however, of inferred rather than naively observed reality.

The exceedingly syntactical symbolism of mathematics and the revolutionary personal and social ethics of the law of contract, which it generates, have their limitations, however, as well as their unique assets. They cannot convey the syntactically inexpressible. This means that they cannot convey the elementary objects of immediate experience which have to be experienced to be known and which cannot be said. "Blue" in the sense of the experienced color is such a factor. Anything known with immediacy has this character of being inexpressible. The entire continuum of immediacy cannot be said. In its ineffability it has to be experienced to be known. This is why Oriental linguistic symbolism has to use words like "Om," "Nirvana," or "Such-ness" to designate it. The point to note about such symbols is that they are devoid of syntax. They merely point, they do not relate, nor do they say. If you do not know, apart from them, what they mean, then such symbols are for you meaningless.

These considerations explain why the philosophy of traditional Western mathematical physics and the ethics of Western constitutional societies with their attention upon mathematical symbolism and upon abstract, dry, and technical legally formulated constitutions and statutes have tended to leave modern Western man starved emotionally with respect to esthetic immediacy. For the latter type of experience—that component of indicative knowledge which is immediate—the early pictographical symbolisms of the Sind Valley or the Chinese civilizations with their lesser elements of syntax were the ideal symbolisms. Such a symbolism shows rather than says. This is why the Chinese symbolism, even with its additional syntactical elements going beyond the initial pictograms, and Chinese thought, expressing itself through Chinese symbolism, move on the concrete esthetic surface of things and, as Lin Yutang says, "always remains on the periphery of the visible world," and have a "dislike of abstract terms."[4] This does not mean that by sufficient additions and qualifications the Chinese symbolism cannot express syntactical ideas. The Japanese linguistic additions to the Chinese symbolism do exactly this. But they do it only by pointing to the syntactical meanings rather than embodying them exactly as English grammar points at and talks about the much more subtle syntactical meanings of mathematical language without actually embodying them.

By using enough ordinary English words and introducing sufficient definitions to give them precise meanings, other than their commonsense meanings, it is possible for a person who knows mathematical logic or mathematics to express the theories of mathematical physics with almost 100 per cent accuracy in ordinary English prose. But what such complex technical English prose does cumbersomely in an indirect and roundabout manner, thereby causing its superficial readers to criticize its writers as unnecessarily pedantic, mathematical symbolism can say directly and literally and elegantly with the utmost beauty and economy. As Wittgenstein has noted of the form of the perfect language of mathe-

[4] Lin Yutang, *My Country and My People,* John Day Company, New York, 1939, p. 83.

matics, the relatedness of the symbols is identical with the relatedness of the objects symbolized. Where the same thing is said by the circumlocutions of English prose, this isomorphism of symbols and symbolic objects is not present.[5]

We arrive, therefore, at the following important conclusions: for the factor in human knowledge in the indicative mode which is inferred from immediate experience but not immediately apprehended in it and which hence can be known only through linguistic expression, the symbolism of mathematics and mathematical logic is the ideal symbolism; whereas for that component of human knowledge which is knowable with immediacy, the pictograph symbolism with its lesser emphasis on syntax is the ideal form of expression and to each type of symbolism there is a corresponding ethics.

This conclusion has one important corollary. The present languages of the linguists and the humanists are bastard symbolisms corrupting both modes of knowing and both types of the good life. Ordinary language has too much grammar and syntax in it to convey esthetic immediacy in all of its ineffable subtlety and richness, thereby leaving the warmhearted mediational ethics of emotive esthetic immediacy unexpressed, while at the same time not possessing sufficient syntactical complexity to convey the inferred theoretic component of man and nature. More than this, the partial syntax which ordinary language introduces, due to its subject-predicate form, actually falsifies the meager portion of the relatedness of things which it attempts to convey.

This is probably the reason why the morality of our humanists is so conventionally dull and so sterile and ineffective before the moral needs and demands of the contemporary world. This suggests that it is our humanists, due to their worship and propagation of an inadequate symbolism unfitted for either mode of indicative knowing, who have let us down morally. In any event we must move away 1) by means of existential, scientific, and philosophical thinking and by impressionistic art to esthetic immediacy, on the one hand, and 2) by means of training in the logic of relations to an adequate syntactical symbolism, on the other hand, with the aim in the end of combining both in a harmonious synthesis. When this occurs, the humanists will measure up to their responsibilities, and mankind will have its symbolically expressed values in

[5]Ludwig Wittgenstein, *Tractatus Logico-Philosophicus*, Kegan Paul, Trench, Truebner & Company, Ltd., London, 1922.

accord with the richness of human experience in both modes of indicative knowledge.

Comment by Robert E. Bass:

Countless billions of plants and animals have flourished during the vast stretches of geological time. Countless billions of organisms are spread over the face of this planet. Naturalists have distinguished enormous numbers of different kinds of plants and animals.[6] They are united by similarities in function and structure and can be ordered in a few superclasses (or *"phyla"*) and in groups within groups.[7]

Imagine a human body, or a redwood tree, or a bacillus, think of any animal or plant! The energy current passing through them is a property they have in common.[8] Each has some way to release chemical energy for a variety of processes, some common to all, and some suited to the needs of particular organisms. Among these functions are growth, rebuilding of injured tissues, heat regulation, locomotion, and reproduction.

In plant and animal structures a particular kind of basic unit can be found, the *cell,* in which, among other components, nucleus and cytoplasma can be distinguished. Processes in which *cells* function are necessary for processes pertaining to the whole plant or animal, for instance, for growth and reproduction. The cell is a unit of structure and function,[9] one kind of unit in billions of different plants and animals.

In organisms chemical processes go on, forming a class of great complexity, yet showing unity: stored chemical energy is released. Part of this energy becomes available for work within the cells.

What is the source of this energy? Some types of organisms use atmospheric carbon dioxide for their supply of carbon. Particularly photosynthesis in green plants performs this feat. In all its complexity this class of processes shows unity: carbon compounds rich in chemical energy are built.

The two classes form one whole: one group of processes helps to capture and the other to release chemical energy.

Radiant energy from the sun is converted into chemical energy and stored in carbon compounds, due to green-plant photosynthesis. Part of this chemical energy is subsequently used for work in the cells. The *sun* is the grand source of this energy.

Stars differ from each other in many ways, f.i., by their state of motion, their mass, size, color, spectral type, and luminosity. Yet countless billions of heavenly objects are united by a common property: they radiate energy, including *light*. Human eyes can receive this kind of radiation, and we become conscious of the stars.

Also *lines* of the same sort have been found in the spectra of the sun and the stars, including extremely remote ones, and in the spectra of substances on earth. The same elements occur again and again in the sidereal universe.

The stars we can see widely apart, the globular clusters of stars, the faintly shining band of the milky way, some luminous nebulae, and some dark clouds are in a special group: our galactic system.[10] There are, however, systems outside this one.[11] Some of

[6]A. F. Shull, *Evolution,* McGraw-Hill Publishing Company, New York, 1951, p. 24.

[7]*Cf.,* f. i., T. I. Storer, *General Zoology,* McGraw-Hill Publishing Company, New York, Toronto, London, 1951, Chap. 11. Shull, *op. cit.,* chap. 2.

[8]"Fuer alle Lebewesen ist ein nie fehlendes Kennzeichen der Energiestrom," Wilhelm Ostwald, quoted from S. A. Waksman, *Principles of Soil Microbiology,* Williams & Wilkins Company, Baltimore, 1932, p. 351.

[9]*Cf.,* f. i., Storer, *op. cit.,* p. 48.

[10]*Cf.* Harlow Shapley, *Galaxies,* The Blakiston Company, Philadelphia, Toronto, 1947.

[11]This fact was confirmed by E. Hubble in 1924 on the basis of Shapley's discovery

these exterior systems are spheroidal, and some have irregular shapes as have the Magellanic clouds. Another form is that of a colossal flattened spiral, including core and spiral arms, for instance, the great spiral in Andromeda. Photographs taken with the 100-inch reflector have shown stars in the outer parts of this exterior system.[12] The luminous core is also made up of stars, as was first concluded from theory involving observations of its spectrum and luminosity. Later separate stars in the nucleus were also photographed.[13] Photographs have also shown individual stars in the big Magellanic cloud and in other exterior systems of irregular shape, also in some exterior spheroidal systems. Astronomy subsumes all these systems, including our own, under one grand class: *galaxies*. The Magellan-type, spheroidal and spiral forms are held to be different stages in galactic evolution.[14] In some cases the systems were found to form groups in space, so-called clusters of galaxies. Within a sphere of radius 2,000,-000,000 light years there are perhaps 2,000,000,000 galaxies,[15] and one of them is our system! In our galaxy there are many thousand millions of stars, and one of them is our sun! Unity is found in the world of stars and galaxies. On earth and everywhere nature is subject to law and order.

In the endeavor to discover physical laws, the scientist makes up a world picture; but, as Planck points out, "the world picture of physics is a conceptual structure, arbitrary to a certain degree."[16] He calls this world picture a human artifact.[17] Also in Einstein's view the concepts of mathematical physics are, in a way, free inventions of the human mind. Yet these concepts and the theories that use them should be suited to the physical world,[18] and, therefore, deductions from the theories should be open to tests by observation.

From Kepler science learned the laws of planetary orbits; and Galileo found the laws of falling bodies. Yet Newton's law of gravity is the basis of a theory from which both kinds of laws can be deduced. Solar and lunar eclipses occur at the predicted times. The theory describes the paths of comets. Discovery of the law permitted the prediction of a new phenomenon: attraction between heavy masses situated on the earth.[19] Newton suggested the idea that even the stars are subject to the law of gravity; thus modern astronomy uses the law for determining the masses of double stars.

One law helps to describe phenomena of enormous scope and complexity, including facts that did not even seem to be related.

Einstein attempted to trace connections between more phenomena, to find unity in an even greater complex.

---

of the relation between period and luminosity of the cepheid variables. *Cf.*, f. i., H. R. Baker, *Astronomy*, D. Van Nostrand Company, Toronto, New York, London, 1950, p. 491. Shapley gives "A Survey of the Inner Metagalaxy" in *The American Scientist*, vol. 39, 1951, p. 610.

[12]E. Hubble, 1924.

[13]W. Baade, *cf.* Baker, *op. cit.*, p. 484.

[14]According to Shapley, it is probable that galaxies develop from Magellan-types to spiral forms and then to spheroidal shapes. *Cf.* Shapley, *Galaxies*, p. 217.

[15]This number is taken from Shapley's surveys and estimates which will probably be published in a forthcoming Harvard Observatory Monograph. (Personal communication, 1952, from Shapley.)

[16]Max Planck, *A Scientific Autobiography*, Philosophical Library, New York, 1949, p. 128.

[17]*Ibid.*, p. 145.

[18]Albert Einstein, *The Meaning of Relativity*, Princeton University Press, Princeton, 1950, p. 2.

[19]Henry Cavendish, 1798.

In the entire sphere of physics, theorists try to propound simple ideas that fit the multitude of facts. Advancing theory has shown unity on a more universal scale. Confirmation of physical theories has led to results in harmony with the view: simplicity is at the root of the complexity of nature.

Classical physics endeavors to find laws that permit us to predict the state of a physical system at any time, if initial and boundary conditions for the system are known.

Yet nature shows another feature, unity of basically different character. When we throw a stone, gravity forces it to fall back on the earth. Gravity could possibly make the planets fall into the sun. Some comets, on the other hand, visit our solar system, and, in spite of gravity, leave it for all time. The law of gravity alone does not say whether the earth will circle around its central star throughout the eons, or will fall into its flames, or will fly away from its light and warmth forever. In order to keep the earth in its stable orbit near the sun, certain *conditions* must prevail in conjunction with the law of gravity, yet not contained in the law itself. In fact, such additional conditions are fulfilled; thus the earth maintains its nearly circular path close to its central star. The planetary system is a *unit,* fit for continued existence.

For plants, animals, and men water is of unique importance. The greater part of the earth is covered with water. Hydrogen is the one of its chemical constituents. Hydrogen occurs throughout the world of stars and galaxies. Hydrogen is the basic chemical element. Its atom is made up of a nucleus and an electron. Quantum mechanics attempts to describe this system. The nucleus attracts the electron, yet the system does not collapse: the electron remains outside the nucleus.[20] The atom is fit for continued existence, it is one whole, a unit.

Now consider the great variety of chemical elements which we find in the stars, in the earth's crust, in the bodies of humans or of tiny microbes: order of peculiar kind prevails in the array, known as the periodic table. A first principle of physics, in quantum mechanics known as the antisymmetry principle,[21] points to unity in the overwhelming complexity of the chemical elements!

The world of life shows the features of organization. Through its roots a plant receives water and minerals from the soil. Organs for assimilating atmospheric carbon dioxide are in the leaves of green plants. The atmosphere receives this gas from many processes: efflux from volcanoes; gas exchange from oceans, lakes, and rivers; decay of plant and animal tissue and of waste due to the agency of microorganisms; combustions; and exhalations from plants, animals, and men. The green plant returns oxygen to the atmosphere. Without this oxygen supply we could not breathe. And all these processes are instrumental for the maintenance of life as a whole on this planet.

By virtue of the structure and function of the reproductive systems, a plant species can maintain its continued existence. But the particular species is not isolated. It lives in interaction with other species and with the physical world. Winds carry pollen. Bees, driven by their instinct for gathering food, carry pollen from flower to flower and are thus instrumental in the reproduction of other species.

Physical nature and the world of life together show the traits of unity. The sun radiates light required for the photosynthesis in plants. The soil supplies the necessary water. The sun, the soil and its water and minerals, the atmospheric gases, the green plants, and the other organisms are members of a *whole* which is fit for continued existence. We recognize units: single organisms; species of organisms; life on this planet

[20]*Cf.* E. U. Condon and P. M. Morse, *Quantum Mechanics,* McGraw-Hill Publishing Company, New York and London, 1929, p. 57.

[21]*Cf.* Henry Margenau, "The Exclusion Principle and its Philosophical Importance," *Philosophy of Science,* vol. XI, 1944, p. 187.

as a whole, in interaction with physical nature. From one unit we progress to the next, more universal unit.

Highly ordered, highly differentiated forms gradually come forward. From the bud the blossom unfolds. Individual organisms develop before and after birth. Species and genera develop. And as we know younger and older people living together, so we find stars and galaxies in different states that are interpreted as states of evolution. In all spheres we find development.

In his paper F. S. C. Northrop raises important problems. He compares the symbolism of ordinary language with that of mathematical physics. In ordinary language "blue" means an immediate experience, a sensation. In Northrop's classification the symbol "blue" denotes a concept by intuition. In a certain conceptual scheme, in the world picture of mathematical physics, we do not deal with this sensation, we deal with rays made up of electromagnetic waves of certain mathematical properties. Wave length is one of these properties. If the symbol "blue" is then assigned to the waves themselves, the same symbol is used, a) for a sensation, b) for one physical link in a causal chain leading to that sensation. The same symbol is then used for a concept by intuition and for a concept by postulation.[22]

We may, however, keep psychology and physics apart by the use of a different symbolism. Then we call the ray a "link in a causal chain leading to the sensation blue," and keep the symbol "blue" for our immediate experience. We may retain the entire mathematical description of the waves, including the wave length; we still keep the essentials of the mathematical theory of waves. Ordinary language calls the sky "blue," and a leaf "green." It assigns the color to the *object. We,* however, experience the color "green" under suitable conditions: when we look at a leaf which is irradiated by daylight and thus emits certain characteristic waves, the leaf, the waves it emits, and our sensation "green" are links in one causal chain.

Northrop compares the symbolism of sense experience with the symbolism of mathematical physics. These symbolisms refer to different attempts to gain knowledge, a) by such immediate sense experience as seeing, or hearing, b) by means of theoretical science, based on schemes of abstract concepts; "electromagnetic wave" is an example of such a concept. Northrop further considers *social norms.* He classes them in the following manner: a) social norms in which a man is held subject to different standards of conduct, according to his color, skin, family, or tribe. Here the same offense is judged differently according to a man's status. The author then goes on to discuss social norms in which man is treated as "universal" man; the same standards of conduct are here required of all. Northrop searches for connections between man's attempts to gain knowledge and man's social norms.

Are the falling of a stone or the motion of a planet *singular* events? In mathematical physics they are treated as instances of the universal law of gravity. In ethics individual man is an instance of "universal" man, subject to universal laws of ethical conduct. *Universality* is an idea common to both kinds of lawfulness.

We have surveyed some features of the atom, of the planets, stars, and galaxies, and of the earth with its great world of life. We find nature subject to law and order, a universe in which individuals are members of wholes, a world of living creatures in dependence on each other and the environment; we see how the existence and well-being of one group is necessary for the existence and well-being of another group. We find unity as a fact. Yet in our hearts the ideal arises: unity in *our* sphere of actions. We want the good. With our conscience we have to examine our emotions, thoughts, and

---

[22]F. S. C. Northrop, *The Logic of the Sciences and the Humanities,* The Macmillan Company, New York, 1948, chap. V, p. 77.

actions. We have to distinguish between right and wrong. We have the choice between unity and discord; ours is the decision to follow the road to higher stages of development: it is up to us to recognize goodness, mutual help, charity as universal law.

Comment by Hajime Nakamura:

F. S. C. Northrop's distinction between "a concept by intuition" and "a concept by postulation" reminds us of the similar distinction given by Dharmakirti, an Indian philosopher (7th century A.D.), although I think the former was not influenced by the latter. Pure sensation (*pratyaksa*) in Dharmakirti's interpretation means a moment of pure, undifferentiated, ineffable sensation, whereas conceptual knowledge (*kalpanā*) acquired through the process of inference is to be associated with verbal expression.[23]

The notion "that a truly known individual, even a truly known man, is always an entity which in its essential nature is an instance of a universal law," which the professor stresses, can be found in the concept of *"dharma"* held chiefly by Buddhists and Jains.

The professor says that "prior to the philosophers of ancient Greek mathematical physics and the Stoic Romans the idea of moral man being universal man had not been conceived even as an ideal." His opinion about Hindu law is quite all right. But I would like to take the liberty of mentioning the thought of equality of all men held by early Buddhists. The Buddha wished to discard all the discriminations between the castes in his day. He said that difference between men is only nominal.[24] "What has been designated as 'name' and 'family' in the world is only a term, what has been designated here and there is understood by common consent."[25]

This is evidenced by Megasthenes (*c.* 300 B.C.), a *Greek* ambassador to India, who said:

> Of several remarkable customs existing among the Indians, there is one prescribed by their ancient philosophers which one may regard as truly admirable: for the law ordains that no one among them shall, under any circumstances, be a slave, but that, enjoying freedom, they shall respect the *equal right* (*isotēs*) to it which all possess for those, they thought, who have learned neither to domineer over nor to cringe to others will attain the life best adapted for all vicissitudes of lot.[26]

On the contrary the Greek and Roman societies were, as is well known, established upon the institution of slavery.

Professor Northrop's reply:

Hajime Nakamura suggests that the well known Oriental philosophical distinction between concepts referring to immediately apprehended factors and concepts referring to inferred objects is identical with the distinction made in this paper and other writings between a concept by intuition which obtains its meaning from factors that are immediately apprehendable and a concept by postulation which requires an axiomatically constructed set of postulates in a specific deductively formulated theory for its specifica-

---

[23]I hope the reader will refer to the following works: Th. Stcherbatsky, *Buddhist Logic*, Leningrad, 1930–1932, 2 vols., and *La théorie de la connaissance et la logique chez les bouddhistes tardifs, traduit par* T. de Manziorly *et* P. Masson-Oursel, Paris, 1926; Satkari Mookerjee, *The Buddhist Philosophy of Universal Flux*, Calcutta, 1935.

[24]*Suttanipāta* 602–611.

[25]*Ibid.*, 648, *cf.*, *Sacred Books of the East*, translated in part by F. Max Mueller, vol. X, pp. 111 f., 116; M. Winternitz, *History of Indian Literature*, University of Calcutta, Calcutta, 1933, vol. II, pp. 47 f.; T. W. Rhys Davids, *Indian Buddhism*, Hibbert Lecture, pp. 51–63, and so on.

[26]Diodorus II, 39,5. J. W. McCrindle, *Ancient India as Described by Megasthenes and Arrian*, Truebner & Company, Calcutta, etc., 1877, p. 40.

tion. His suggestion fails to distinguish two fundamentally different kinds of inferred objects: 1) Those defined in terms of sensed qualities which are capable of immediate apprehension, even though the object so defined is not of the moment immediately apprehended, *e.g.*, an atom of fire defined as hot and dry, where hot and dry are predicates capable of being directly sensed in some instance, if not in the inferred instance; and 2) those satisfying the formally constructed axioms of a deductively formulated theory in which no sensed predicates whatever enter into the axiomatically constructed conceptual meaning, *e.g.*, the scientific concept of the electron in the axiomatically formulated electromagnetic theory of Lorenz. Only an inferred entity of the latter type instances a concept by postulation. The classical Hindu, Buddhist, and Confucian philosophers had the former, but not the latter, type of inferred entity. Hence, they did not have concepts by postulation in the sense in which I define such a concept.

Consider now the statement in this paper which Nakamura quotes to the effect that "prior to the philosophers of ancient Greek mathematical physics and the Stoic Romans the idea of moral man being universal man had not been conceived even as an ideal." Considered thus out of context, I agree completely with what Nakamura says about it. In fact the interested reader will find this very point made in my Presidential Address before the American Philosophical Association entitled, "The Philosophy of Natural Science and Comparative Law."[27] In that paper three, rather than two, types of procedure for settling disputes between men are treated. One of these three ways derives from the nominalistic theory that each dispute is unique, of Confucianism, the Nirvana concept of Buddhism, and the Brahman concept of nondualistic Vedanta Hinduism. Because, in all these three theories, each individual person and each individual dispute between any two persons or any two groups of persons is unique, it becomes immoral to settle disputes by recourse to determinate legal norms or codes, as this treats different men as alike rather than each as unique. Instead, determinate legal norms and codes are regarded as evil or a second best, only to be resorted to when mediation between the disputants fails.

My paper left this Oriental mediational type of legal procedure out of account, because, as its title indicated, it restricted itself to legal norms; that is, to those societies having determinate legal codes for settling disputes. Sir Henry S. Maine and others have made it clear that such legal norms fall into but two types—namely, the law of status and the law of contract. Pulled, therefore, out of context, the comment which Nakamura makes on the aforementioned quotation from my paper is correct; kept within the context of the paper, where it refers explicitly to the ethics of a law of status and the ethics of a law of contract, the quotation is correct, I believe, as it stands.

Comment by Joshua Whatmough:

Why does expressed experience come before expressed direction, *i.e.*, the imperative, which is directed to the future, toward a goal? The indicative (with its event-splitting, *i.e.*, tenses; or attitudes, *i.e.*, aspects and moods other than the indicative) is derivative (by contrast) and similarly its meaning so far as that it also is a goal-directed activity.

"Radically different objects" (p. 57): or radically different expression? This is crucial. Is it maintained that ordinary language tells us nothing? Or that we can know language, but nothing else?

An "exact" language (p. 58) is built upon ordinary language (historically), it is acquired through ordinary language (learning), and usually needs exegesis in ordinary language (*e.g.*, legal language, the Scriptures, or a liturgy). Scientific language (includ-

[27] *Proceedings and Addresses of the American Philosophical Association, 1952–1953,* September, 1953, vol. XXVI, pp. 5–25, inc.

ing that of Linguistics) has been called parasitic (a better term than bastard): this is true only by etymological definition. That is, special languages feed upon ordinary language, without which they die (the process has been compared with entropy). A rigorous language (*i.e.,* a logic) sooner or later comes to this end (so that a new logic is created, as is happening in our own day wherever Aristotelian logic is rejected).

"Ordinary" language is a status (the convergence of comparative, historical, descriptive, and now statistical and mathematical linguistics on this point is convincing), a metastable equilibrium, that maintains itself by a process of selective variation.

But it also lags; the reason that ordinary English prose cannot cope with modern physics is that it needs new (linguistic or grammatical) categories—tense, aspect, mood, case, number, and the rest are not adequate to do the task.

The ineffable cannot be said, *i.e.,* it is negative. This is not a criticism of "ineffable"; but it is unreasonable to criticize language for *not* saying what *cannot* be said!

Professor Northrop's reply:

Joshua Whatmough's first query concerning my paper raises the question of the imperative. This question goes beyond the paper which restricted itself to linguistic symbols in the indicative mode. Whatmough suggests also that my paper is unreasonable because it "criticize[s] language for *not* saying what *cannot* be said." Quite the contrary. The paper distinguishes a language which points but cannot say from a language which literally says but does not point. My criticism of ordinary language is that it has too much grammar and syntax in it to be an ideal language for pointing and not enough relational syntax in it to express adequately the portion of experience which extends beyond immediacy and hence can only be said and cannot be pointed at.

Comment by Howard L. Parsons:

The problem for morality, according to Northrop, is that 1) the classical Western theoretical ethics "cannot convey the elementary objects of immediate experience" and so "leaves modern Western man starved emotionally," and 2) the language expressing the esthetic component is restricted to the immediately and naively given, to status, to substantial persons, etc. Moreover, the present languages of the humanists are "bastard symbolisms corrupting both modes of knowing." Can we have a "harmonious synthesis" of the values of the two types of languages expressing the two modes of experience? Can we combine the comprehensive universalism of mathematical theory with the unique pungency of immediate qualitative experience?

The solution offered to these two problems depends on the concepts of experience and knowing with which one begins. Consequently, the solution suggested below will be different from Northrop's in so far as it is derived from concepts of experience and knowing different from his.

Let us begin with a proposition which Northrop himself sometimes seems to accept in his explanation of the "undifferentiated esthetic continuum": that the primary, immediate mode of experience is *feeling*—the continuing, gross, more or less undifferentiated, unitary perception of elements in a context of events; Whitehead's prehension. Inherent or potential in this apperceptive matrix lies a mass of qualities and relations (structures) which, when events and organism conjoin in a certain way, emerge into direct awareness, but which, for practical purposes, may be disentangled, discriminated, related, and lifted out by the perceiving person. Many if not all of the structures of science are refinements, extrapolations, inferences, etc., of these experiential qualities and relations, as the qualities of art are enhancements, omissions, clarifications, etc., of the qualities of preanalytic experience. Both science and art, in short, are symbolic abstractions from this matrix of immediately experienced qualities and relations.

The discriminating and relating of both quality and relation derive their character and value, in large part, by reference to the life of feeling. Feeling (or "quality") in turn is a function of the interaction of organism and environing events. The color blue, as H. N. Wieman says, is a "conjunction" of many events moving like strands through time—light rays, eyes, organism, empty space, etc.[28] Visual sensation, to take the example used by Northrop, is a mode of feeling; whether vivid or faint, expressive or evocative, it is always embedded in a context of events and a matrix of feelings. While the specific meanings of colors may vary, their esthetic character remains constant. Also, a particular blue image possesses instrumental value only as it disposes the person to act so as to have some consummate, conjunctive quality of feeling—the taste of the plum, or the felt cold of the lake water.

Similarly, a theoretical structure or an "idea" derives its status and value for persons via feeling. We distinguish one idea from another, as Hume says, by its "feel"; and the objects, values, commands, or concepts signified by ideas—the consequences or "meanings" of ideas—are possessed and appraised by means of some feeling-response. "Common sense" (not in Northrop's meaning of the term) is this capacity common to most men to feel or "sense" (in the broad sense) the qualitative shadings and shiftings of their world, the rise and the fall, the power and the pulsation, of events. This basic gyroscopic "sense" is the source of all affective thinking, whether it be nontechnical, esthetic, scientific, or philosophical. It is the starting point, testing ground, and landing field of all flights of thought. It is, as Dewey says in his essay, "Qualitative Thought," "the background, the thread, and the directive clue in what we do expressly think of." Thinking that is not cemented to events by the cohesion of human feeling will become trivial and brittle and peripheral to the deepest forces and concerns of human living, and, like the abstractions of many postwar physicists and biologists, will pursue its isolated way, uncontrolled by those concerns and eventually destructive of them.

As I interpret him, Northrop wants to know how this breach between the theoretic and the esthetic components may be healed. According to his concept of experience, the ethical and legal norms of naive observation and commonsense language—laws of individuals, status, family, and tribe—are particularized and concrete, but excessively narrow; whereas the deductively formulated laws of contract—which postulate a social rule in which "any human being whatever can be substituted for an instance of the rule"—are "universal" but are incapable of expressing the qualities of immediately experienced persons or situations. Moreover, we should add, precisely because these "universal" legal and ethical codes are postulated, utopian, and inferred, as Northrop himself says, they cannot be free of arbitrariness, and hence, as mathematicians have shown of all empirical hypotheses, cannot be "necessary" or *a priori*. So far as they purport to refer to actual men, they cannot be absolutely true; but if they do not refer to actual men, then of what use are they? When, on the other hand, we take refuge in the naive substantivism of common sense, we find ourselves a far cry from any genuine universalism.

The difficulty of finding a universal norm for human conduct inheres, I think, in Northrop's assumption that all (or most) structures in science and philosophy are inferred and lie in a noumenal realm beyond the empirical observation exemplified in sense perception. Northrop seems to prejudice the case for a "harmonious synthesis" when from the beginning he puts asunder structure and feeling. Yet it was William James who pointed out that we *feel* certain relations: we have "a feeling of *and,* a feeling of *if,* a feeling of *but,* a feeling of *by.* . . ." Does it seem a violation of our experience to regard such feelings as lying on a continuum with our sensations and emotions, and

[28]Henry N. Wieman, *The Directive in History*, Beacon Press, Boston, 1953, p. 15.

to consider the shifting, dynamic context of events wherein we are immersed, as the rich storehouse, the potential, the tap root, or the fountainhead out of which the relatively superficial sensations are evoked and differentiated?[29]

So we feel structures. What, then, are their origin and locus? Whether some structures exist prior to any human experience of them whatsoever is, to say the least, a question difficult to settle with any degree of philosophical or scientific consensus today. What is contended here is that we dimly and half-consciously perceive some structures of events before we specify those structures by means of language. Children sense the presence and character of chairs long before they can give a "realistic" definition of the term "chair," as philosophers sense the presence of realities about which they find it difficult to talk intelligibly. I cannot believe that this difficulty of philosophers is due to some professional deficiency, such as aphasia, or that it is due to sheer delusion. Some philosophers, not counting many recent ones, have acknowledged this difficulty as a real one: Plato, Aquinas, Whitehead, and even Wittgenstein.

Fortunately it may happen that after some time the blind mind of the philosopher is opened and illuminated, and his inarticulate tongue is loosed, so that he finds a language for at least partially specifying the structure of events which he has been given to see. In such a case, he does not "invent" the structure—he does not even construct the verbal side of the structure—nor would it be accurate to say that he "discovers" this structure which, like the North Star in daylight, has been eternally and fixedly hovering over him but has not been, for want of inspiration, apprehended. Rather, as a set of many events, including the minded organism, converge and form a "conjunction," the mind and its ideas (specifications of structured events) are transformed and a new feeling and thought emerges. The new structure and new quality are fused into one partless, coalescent perception. But almost as soon as a scientist undergoes this transformation of mind issuing in a new perception, he ordinarily and automatically shakes off the initial spell and thrill of creative discovery (recorded for us by the great scientists) and forsakes romance for the laborious days of precision work. He abstracts out the barren structure, devoid of the distractions of quality. The artist, by contrast, will sponsor and nurture that first fine careless rapture of quality, letting the structure fade away into background and lend whatever order is required for his work. Thus, the creative transformation of the mind is the source of both quality and structure (as perceived), and they are created together.

On this view, structures are ingredient in qualities, not superimposed on them or correlated at a distance with them. Consequently, structures created in the emergent conjunction of events may confront us with the same arbitrariness and finality as do the qualities of sense. We may take intrinsic delight in the fluid water colors of the sunset, and at the same time feel the force of time and the dimly sensed but overwhelming structure of fate and death. Whitehead remarks that there is a kind of absoluteness in the taste of a lump of sugar; there is a kindred absoluteness in our spontaneous love of freedom, in our hatred of enslavement, in the beauty of holiness, in the rockbottom, "stubborn and irreducible" character of events, in the vast, overruling grandeurs of nature, in the heavy imperatives laid on by history and by life itself. Such experiences are experiences of structures which are organic to our feelings and inextricable from our direct awareness. They are not hypothetical constructs. They are not even rarefied idealizations of what is had with richness and potency in the immediacy of experience. They are

[29]See F. S. C. Northrop, *The Meeting of East and West*, The Macmillan Company, New York, 1946, p. 343, where Northrop describes this esthetic continuum as "the great mother of creation."

the foundations of our world as we feel it. It is philosophy's task to express them. Science is concerned with less permanent and less pervasive structures; its ultimate aims are prediction, manipulation, and control of structures. Bent on conscious contrivance and action, it cannot be acutely aware of what events are doing to it in the way of transforming it. Only in its deepest and most contemplative reaches—as in the pure, unmanipulative mysticism of an Einstein's meditations—does science touch upon the structures sought by philosophy.

Philosophy thus finds a way between the transient and local particularities of ordinary perception, and the idealized, barren, perfected, nonempirical, syntactical notions of the utopians. The first are born of the carnival, the second of the cloister and laboratory. Both are abstractions, distillations drawn off the full stream and tide of creation; and both represent partial perspectives upon life and the good of life. But is it possible to be concrete and at the same time universal? Is it possible to lay hold of a universal structure which is not a construct of the imagination but is an existential structure delivered unto us through the depth of feeling and identified by the specifications of the discriminating mind?

Eastern philosophies, such as Zen, admit the existence of such a concrete reality but explicitly shun any attempt to specify its structure lest it thereby be arbitrarily confined within the forms of the human understanding. Western philosophies, whether supernaturalistic, naturalistic, or positivistic, have tended to deny that such a concrete, qualitatively felt universal exists, and have resorted to postulations in order to establish a universal good. But it is just as hard to unknot the enigma of a speechless mysticism, as it is to apply the provincialism of an elementalistic, commonsense ethics, or to respect a Platonism which reduces the individual to a mere instancing of a general rule.

With what, then, are we left? With the common fact of our concrete existence; with this particular experience here and now, a funding of thought and feeling in the unity of creation. This felt particularizing, as Hugh Miller says, is "the sole necessity known to us."[30] In the full concreteness of his being, every man, perhaps every creature, experiences the fact of particularity: his individuality is a unique synthesis of his unique situation. To be is to perceive, to perceive particularity. More nearly accurately, what is perceived when we turn our attention upon our most naive and immediate experience is a particularizing and pluralizing process, a process of creation—a process in which the events of the world are welded into one, and in which the apperceptive mass, the feelings and structures of the mind, are continuously transformed "into something rich and strange."

Does this creative process exhibit a structure common to all men, East and West? Some Western naturalists, following a line similar to the antiHegelianism of Kierkegaard but repudiating his impatience with description, maintain that there is such a common structure. With respect to Northrop's question, "Can we combine theoretic universalism with esthetic immediacy," their answer is *Yes*. Only the rational-empirical fact of a particularizing but universal creativity, they say, can avoid the trap of tribalism, the babels and wars of fanatic utopias, and the impotence of mysticism. The person who can live in the keeping of this deepest and most concrete reality will never be "starved emotionally"; indeed, his cup will run over and he will never thirst again. Like Ramakrishna he will be able to experience the universal creative power within a multiplicity of forms. On the other hand, he will be freed from the compulsive narrowness of naive common sense, taking or leaving the objects of sense perception as creativity demands. But Northrop, I think, is unnecessarily harsh with the humanists and ethicists whose

[30]Hugh Miller, *The Community of Man,* The Macmillan Company, New York, 1949, p. 11.

formulations fail to satisfy the emotional needs of modern Western man. The joy of creation is not likely to be communicated by symbols, whether "bastard" or legitimate, unless the interpreter of the symbols has had an experience that will permit him to respond with the feeling of creation. Great poets need great audiences; and great poets are not apt to arise, except in response to the demands of great audiences.

There remains to be answered Northrop's other question: "Can the language of morality synthesize theory and esthetic immediacy?" The structures specified by science and philosophy will always call for a language which is special, definite, unambiguous, and austerely precise, and which, therefore, does not, as languages of the arts can, express the qualitative resonance and complexity of the esthetic side of experience. But this is all the more reason why scientists and philosophers should strive to direct their inquiry toward the discovery of structures which facilitate the creative vivifying, widening, deepening, and refining of the life of feeling. The good of human living is just the ferment of this juice: the creative transformation of feeling: the innovating and integrating of new feeling-responses, within persons and cultures, between persons, and between cultures. When the feelings of a person are not directed by the structures of science and philosophy, he may readily, in an industrialized culture, forfeit those dynamic conjunctions, that vital network of delicate arteries and vessels tying him to the great aorta of life and feeling. He may sink into some urban niche of anonymity, or lose contact with reality by passing into one of the more noticeable and less tolerated forms of pathology. Even the "well adjusted" person has lost touch with reality if the structures of his own mind and family and place of work do not direct him in the ways of creative fulfilment. On the other side, science and philosophy which are not fed by the unifying and sympathetic force of feeling will become, at best, private and autistic playthings, and, at worst, empty vanities, delusional systems of symbols, and tools of destruction.

The division of labor which is inevitable among the different discourses need not divide the laborers if they are informed and impelled by a common task. Even so, no humanist, however wise, however multilingual, can express all that there is to be expressed in all the modes. Some failure must always infect the attempts of the scientist and the artist to communicate. They live in different universes of discourse; the space between those two universes may be bridged, but it cannot be obliterated. Their experiences are incommensurable, and the language of one cannot be translated into the language of the other. Yet there is a partial remedy for this dualism, for while their languages differ they do live in the same eventful universe of feeling, thought, and action. Science and philosophy, as Northrop suggests, may become more "existential," concerning themselves with those structures which are most intimate to man's values; and art may become less "impressionistic" and "abstract," dabbling in trivialities, and more deeply intuitive of the inner feelings and coercive structures of all men. Thus, by referring in a direct or adumbrative way to the structure of the creative source of good, art today, like the great art of the past, may acquire some of the comprehensiveness of science and the depth of philosophy. Correspondingly, science and philosophy, by directing their efforts to an ampler perspective upon this generative root of quality, may gather unto their otherwise barren skeletal structures the flesh and blood of vital feeling until those dry bones shall rise again and walk as companions with men in the streets; they will become, as in past ages of faith (which were the great ages of inquiry), seekers and servants, in heart and mind, of the directive and destiny of human living. If science is not permitted to intrude poetic meanings into its disinfected discourse, philosophy, so far as it differs from science, may signify the ever present but partially unspeakable qualities and structures of our common life. In doing so it will receive from and send back to its culture the reverberations and overtones in meaning and feeling which cannot be explicitly expressed but which bind the culture together by a kind of unspoken rhythm and sympathetic vibration.

Except for a rare mutation among their ranks, philosophers will express the temper and tempo of their time. The method of philosophy is, in Whitehead's phrase, "sheer display." Philosophers express what is impressed upon them, what they are permitted to perceive. They are caught in the currents of their culture; they discern banks and shoals, surfaces and depths, as their mates teach their eyes to discern; and their symbols are their only sounding and navigation devices. Their vision may transcend the narrow scope of their companions or the befogging mists of their surroundings; in such cases, if they are not prophets without honor, they may pilot their culture into a new watercourse, open another vista, and become agents in the transformation of their cultures.

But the task of leadership falls on all. The speakers of diverse tongues must recognize that symbols are means, and that there are many means to the common goal of the good life. Also, scientists, philosophers, artists, religious leaders, and ordinary men must recognize that their various symbolisms spring from a common source of creation, and that these symbolisms should therefore properly serve that source by inquiry, celebration, faith, and work. When they do so, then the current confusion of tongues may be transmuted into an orchestrated harmony and a paean of human hope and joy.

Professor Northrop's reply:

Howard L. Parsons's rich comment on my paper deserves a lengthy reply. Space permits reference but to one point. Parsons suggests that the problem of combining the immediately experienced factor in human knowledge and discourse with the axiomatic and universalized inferred factor centers in ". . . Northrop's assumption that all (or most) structures in science and philosophy are inferred and lie in a noumenal realm beyond the empirical observation exemplified in sense perception . . . ," adding, ". . . Northrop seems to prejudice the case for a 'harmonious synthesis' when from the beginning he puts asunder structure and feeling." Parsons then adds that William James ". . . pointed out that we *feel* certain relations. . . ." I agree completely with James and Parsons that the immediately apprehended factor in experience, which I term the "esthetic component," contains relational factors as well as *relata*. The fact that the entities in the inferred component of experience, which I term the "theoretic component," are known only through the axiomatically constructed relations which they satisfy, does not mean, as he has inferred, that I deny the existence of immediately felt relational factors in the esthetic component of experience. The latter type of relations are, however, existential and nominalistic in character. Furthermore, they cannot be said in any set of postulates but must be experienced to be known. Thus the problem of relating the immediately apprehended and the inferred factors in human knowledge and of finding an adequate complex symbolism for doing this does not center in any failure of mine to appreciate and recognize the existence of immediately felt relations. The difficulty arises because their presence is recognized; not because it has been ignored. The fact is that immediately sensed relatedness is not isomorphic with the axiomatically constructed relatedness. Furthermore, the ethical norms expressed in the law of status of the one contradict the more universal ethical norms codified in the law of contract of the other. Put in the form of indicative scientific knowledge, the immediately felt relatedness of the esthetic component of experience is not isomorphic with the axiomatically constructed relatedness of the theoretic component.

The reader must not suppose, moreover, that this is merely an academic question.

Every Asian and African society in the world today is wrestling with the problem of incorporating Western law of contract—constitutions and norms which break moral man loose from family and clan and tribe—while at the same time preserving their African or Asian cultural values and ways which are rooted in the intuitively felt relations of parents to children of a traditional society whose highest determinate ethical loyalties are to the family rather than to the larger constitutionally guided interfamily national or international community.

Comment by Mordecai M. Kaplan:

The distinction that F. S. C. Northrop draws between the "esthetic component" and the "theocratic component" of experience corresponds to the traditional distinction between qualitative experience and quantitative experience. The "blue" which is "a datum in the all embracing immediacy of experience" is a qualitative experience. The "blue" which designates a wave length of 4,862 angstroms is a quantitative experience. Instead of deploring, we should rather welcome, the fact that the same symbol "blue" is used in both senses, for that has enabled man to enlarge the scope of his control over experience. The knowledge of coincidence of particular qualitative experience with particular quantitative experience is the source of man's ability to manipulate the conditions of his life. That does not mean, however, that we can afford to reduce qualitative to quantitative experience. Such reductionism is fatal to the functioning of human values.

Qualitative experience differs from quantitative in one highly significant respect: the former is anthropocentric and subjective, the latter is noncentric and objective. Hence, they are mutually incommensurate. That should put us on our guard against the ambiguity of the concept "universal," which may be used either in a qualitative or in a quantitative sense. In a quantitative sense, the term "universal" denotes that which exists ubiquitously in space or time. In a qualitative sense, the term "universal" is equivalent to the Platonic notion of the "ideal," or to the Aristotelian notion of the "perfect" or to more recent notions like "the norm" or the "ought." All of these equivalents express universality because *all* things are what they are to the extent that they reflect or have a share in those equivalents.

The difference between "universal" in a qualitative and "universal" in a quantitative sense underlies the difference between ancient and modern science. A "universal law" to Plato meant a principle that defined the perfection of a thing. A "universal law," to Newton, meant a fact which was true at all times and places. When we say that the more universal a human being is the more individual he is, we do not use "universal" in a quantitative or mathematical, but in a valuational, qualitative, or anthropocentric sense. In the latter sense, "universal" refers to those qualities which belong to the "perfect" man. Such a man probably has never existed nor will exist, but essentially, nonspatially, and nontemporally, he always abides in the mind of God (that is a symbolic way of saying that perfection is not to be found in nature). "Man in the image of God" is the ancient mythical way of stating that fact.

On the other hand, when Northrop affirms that a "truly known individual, even a truly known man, is always an entity which in its essential nature is an instance of universal law," he evidently refers to "universal law" not in the "Platonic" but in the "Newtonian" sense. If that is the case, then what is true of an individual thing is not *necessarily* true of man. What makes man man can only be that which has meaning for man *as* man. To have such meaning, it must necessarily be a value and not a quantity. Quantity denatures man; it robs him of his humanity.

Universal man is not one who is neither black nor white, or who is neither Jew nor Christian, neither American nor French, etc. One can hardly subscribe to the principle that "no rule for ordering personal or social conduct is truly moral unless any human being whatever can be substituted for an instance of the rule." In the first place, the moral rules that apply to mature human beings do not apply to immature ones. The obligations and responsibilities to one's kith and kin are different from those to total strangers. "Charity begins at home" is not an immoral principle. It is just as "universal" as "thou shalt love thy neighbor as thyself." The "universal" to which the various cultures seek to live up in their ethics and legal procedures is that which they regard as the perfect human type.

A people's conception of what is the perfect human type is determined by two factors: a) the extent to which the inertia of the unconscious experience of a people operates in its culture, and b) the extent to which that people has had the opportunity to enlarge the horizon of its experience. With these facts in mind, we are bound to interpret differently from the way Northrop does the distinction which Sir Henry S. Maine drew between the preStoical and the Stoical approach to ethics and law.

In the first place, even Sir Henry could not have meant that status has been completely replaced by contract law. Were that the case, inheritance laws should long ago have been abolished, nor would it have been necessary for the United States Supreme Court to reckon with the need of introducing *gradually* the changes required by its decision on segregation in public schools. The experience of the Roman government with its subject peoples opened its eyes to the untenability of the assumption that all foreigners were of a lower human order, particularly if they could be conquered in war. When an Epictetus becomes a slave, that assumption turns out to be ridiculous. Lacking that kind of experience, even an Aristotle could nonchalantly write off all foreigners as destined for slavery. On the other hand, the ancient Hebrews who during the first part of their stay in Egypt had experienced what it meant to be welcomed as sojourners, arrived at the principle "thou shalt love the sojourner as thyself" (Leviticus 19, 34). In reviewing the recent book *Through Malan's Africa* by Robert St. John, John Burkham says that the author "feels that this long isolated country has had insufficient contact with political and sociological advances made elsewhere; hence its official doctrine of white supremacy at this midpoint in the twentieth century."

From the standpoint of "universal man," in the qualitative sense as the perfect or ideal man, it seems to me that the Hebraic civilization very consciously arrived at it ahead of both the Greeks and the Romans. Even a superficial reading of the biblical myth of the beginnings of the human race reveals that Adam and Eve were at first the ideal types of man and woman. Their names, in the original Hebrew, are meant to indicate this fact. It was only as mankind fell away from that ideal type of man for whom God had created the world, that God is represented as having selected Abraham to be the founder of a people that would be representative of humanity, by living up to the perfect type that God had expected Adam, *i.e.,* the whole of mankind, would prove to be. But the entire burden in the rest of the Bible seems to be that "the chosen people" has never lived up to the divine expectation. The great Prophets, however, were certain that God's will could not remain permanently frustrated. They were certain that a time—at the end of days—was bound to come, when the "chosen people" would repent, and, by setting an example to the rest of mankind, would draw it within the orbit of human perfection. Then universal man would come to his own.

Professor Northrop's reply:

Mordecai M. Kaplan raises many important points with which I am in considerable agreement. First let me say that I do not deplore the use of the same symbol "blue" in two different senses; but I agree with him in welcoming it, providing that the symbolic rules of ordinary language do not obscure the two quite diverse types of meaning. Second, it is to be doubted that the distinction between the esthetic and theoretic components corresponds to that between qualitative and quantitative experience. There is an intuitive meaning for quantity as well as axiomatically constructed number theory. Thus quantity applies as much to the esthetic component as it does to the theoretic. Kaplan's comments on Plato seem to me to ignore the mathematical and quantitative factor in Plato's theory of universals. In any event, there was a concept of the universal, in what Kaplan terms the "Newtonian" sense, in the Stoic Romans, if not in Plato and Aristotle, and certainly it appears again in Kant's categorical imperative.

If my paper gave the impression that Sir Henry S. Maine or I believe that "status has been completely replaced by contract law," then it is certainly misleading. Both clearly are still with us. As my paper noted, "the break [from status toward contract] was made largely as an ideal and only in part in fact." I agree also with Kaplan that an adequate social ethics must pay attention to the existentially felt differences between men, as well as to the universal element in human nature.

Comment by Jiri Kolaja:

The concept of the particular statusbound man with a corresponding pictograph symbolism which is characterized by lesser emphasis on syntax, as well as its counterpart concept of the universal contractbound man with a deductively formulated mathematical symbolism, represent two types of society usually termed as *Gemeinschaft* and *Gesellschaft*. The trend leading from status to contract, from the traditional to rational relationship has been, however, counteracted by an increasing desire for the preservation or reinvigoration of the community in Josiah Royce's sense. However, the new community can no longer escape the context of the whole world. Thus, a combination of esthetic immediacy (esthetic component) with universal inference (theoretic component) is required. It seems that this need is partially met by a relatively new system of communication—the motion picture. For example, a shot of a European woman in juxtaposition with a Chinese woman may establish a general, universal relationship. And, yet, both shots are esthetically immediate, and because of their wealth of qualities nearly overwhelming. Thus, by editing a motion picture a producer may relate objects usually far unrelated without depriving them simultaneously of their immediate context. In a verbal communication, for example, a poem, a word, or sentence actualizes within the new context only a part of their meanings. On the contrary, a film shot is semantically more self-sufficient. Even if a series of shots generalizes, especially when helped by spoken commentary, the single shots tend to preserve their esthetic immediacy. Thus a combination of sound and picture realizes partially the requirement for both the immediate particular community and the inferred universal world.

Professor Northrop's reply:

Jiri Kolaja adds an important factor when he notes the value of the motion picture to acquaint different peoples in an intuitively felt way with their diverse norms and values. By means of the motion picture, if properly directed, the beholder can feel the experience of seeing another culture from the native people's standpoint. The difficult problem arises, however, of finding the two different techniques for conveying in intuitive terms 1) the values of a people who root their social norms in nonintuitive axiomatically constructed and codified principles, and 2) the values of a people who derive their social norms from immediately felt man and nature. The solution of this problem depends, I believe, on a more intense study of the two types of symbols noted in my paper and the specification of the photographic techniques appropriate for each.

CHAPTER V

Circles of Prestige

By LYMAN BRYSON

THE PURPOSE OF this essay is to describe what I believe to be the processes by which publicity for one's name has become the chief prestige symbol in American life. It is intended as observation and analysis,
not as moralizing; adjectives of value will be excluded as far as that is
possible. If there is some modest indulgence in value judgment at the
end, it will be labelled. American life is thought of here as a phase of
Western industrial culture, in which European trends have developed
more swiftly because of more generous resources, a larger scale in operations and fewer impediments in the form of feudal remnants either of
ideals or institutions. The major pattern only is under observation, without regard for the numerous minor deviate patterns which are the
source of our creative energies and also without mention of the deposit
of older enduring valuès. If anyone doubts that name-publicity has become the chief prestige-symbol in American life he may be able nevertheless to follow the analysis part way and apply the description in measured terms.

By name-publicity, I mean the appearance of one's name, real or professional, in public print, or its sound on the broadcast air, the pervading
evidence that one's name has arrived and that the public is taking notice. To say that this is the predominant American prestige-symbol is to
say that it is sought for and enjoyed as the fruit of achievement, that to
enjoy it by accident or personal favor is good luck not bad, that it plays a
bright part in the dreams of youth.

Like any other dominant value, name-publicity can be the motive for
heroic, as well as for comic behavior. Any major trait of a culture is
likely to have both its heroic and its comic aspects. Many of its manifestations lie so deep in assumptions that they are never noticed.

At the heroic end of the spectrum of action which is motivated by
desire for name-publicity is loyal service to the reputation, rather than
to the program of an institution. Still beyond that is vigorous action on

behalf of a person who has been "unjustly" deprived of credit for an achievement or a good deed. Many a wife, or mother, or grownup child, in America now, will resent with generous bitterness a mistake in public opinion which deprives a loved one of the "honor" due him for his work or his talents. We need to examine both the concept of justice here and the concept of honor. The semantic evidence in these matters is always tricky but it is not wholly irrelevant. Unless public notice is a value, unless name-publicity is a prestige-symbol, then there can be no injustice in anyone's being deprived of it, no matter what foul or forceful means were used to deprive him. It is not "unjust" to take away from anyone a worthless thing. To disguise name-publicity with the label "credit" does not change its character.

When seeing one's name or picture in print is called an "honor," Americans are indicating a similar evaluation. Shakespeare's character called his purse trash but wanted to protect his "good name," he might have called it his honor. But he did not mean public display. As was still more obvious in the values of the eighteenth century, honor for a man meant the right and the willingness to resent an insult with a weapon. A woman's honor was her chastity. Now honor means benefits given by public opinion in smaller or larger circles, rewards, the gains of reputation.

At the other end of the spectrum is seen the comic, the type called the "ham." The derisive word is often used to cry down a troublemaker who deserves sharper adjectives; modest hamming is only a small infringement of the best American taste. A ham is a person who wants to be admired by persons whom he does not know. This means, of course, that he is not asking questions regarding the standards of these strangers who applaud him, nor in fact caring much for their reasons. Merely being noticed is achievement. The ham is a comic character but he is not a type who can be traced back through literature. The pretentious man is comic in all civilizations because the artists can show a gap between what he is and what he pretends to be. So also are the too ambitious social climber, the befooled lover, the stupid clown, the rigid fanatic, and the others. But not the ham. There are reasons for this which ought to be evident as we go on. A comic character has to be institutionally possible; being merely humanly possible will not earn him a place in literature.

Prestige-symbols, of course, exist in all cultures and in a complex culture, like that of America today, with many groups within groups and many deviant forces, they exercise their fascinations in various ways, sometimes in competition with each other. In saying that name-publicity is dominant in America now, I mean that it counts for most, above and beyond all the other signs of reputation which can be observed in small and special aggregations of persons. It is the predominant symbol of public interest in the most extended public world.

Enjoyment of prestige-symbols is a public sign of reputation and reputation is public approval, granted for one reason or another. Achievement is one means of getting a reputation and enjoying prestige-symbols and other gains but it is not a prerequisite. Some persons have name-publicity without achieving anything, even anything evil, although the possession of the symbols may bring them some of the rewards which more logically acquired reputations bring to others. A good example is a person who makes a career out of letting the public in on the secrets of a personal life such as having a hermaphrodite body changed by surgery into a female body. And, obversely, someone whose achievement is of substantial usefulness to society may fail, for accidental reasons or because malice has intervened, to get the reputation he deserves.

We are using the word reputation to mean the public awareness of some person's position. Position is access to the rewards of achievement that are socially conferred. These usages are not unusual but we must, in social analysis, restrict common words to precise signification, if we are to make any precise statements. A person has a reputation when his position is generally known, he has a position if he has received or is receiving some of the gains which a society or a group confers on achievement or on some semblance of achievement. Neither reputation nor position need be founded on merit but they are what merit "deserves" according to the mores of the society.

The rewards of achievement, or the gain, can be divided into two kinds. We can call one "content," the other, "prestige-symbol." Content is mostly money and power but there are other tangibles of preferment and privilege. Prestige-symbols are the principal intangible gain. These two kinds of gain are independent; that is, a position may bring more or less of content with more or less of prestige, but they are not irrelevant. The success myth of American society implies that both kinds of gain are generously conferred on any hero or heroine.

It is quite important to distinguish between what is called prestige, that is, the possession of socially accredited symbols of reputation, from leadership of any kind, and also from the various kinds of power. Power is listed with the tangible gains or content of reputation. We do not need to pause for sharper definitions of the various different kinds of power, but it must be noted that they are all thought of here in culturefree terms. That is, we mean to separate theoretically what cannot be separated in experience, power in its material simplicity from power imbued with the prestige meanings which cultural evaluations confer. Power in this sense means food, not dining. It means sex as access, not ritualistic and humane forms of personal belonging. Nothing human can ever be so inhuman, of course, but the proportions of simple power and prestige elements change. We owe to Remy de Gourmont the idea that the degree of civilization in any society is measured by the extent to which any naked action is clothed with ritual and added values, "sophisticated" in his term. This is to say in other words that the content may be lessened although prestige is being enhanced.

Even when considered in this abstract form, however, power may be simple or naked power (dependent on actual or potential force) or it may be "authority" (institutional power backed by actual or potential force and public acceptance) or "influence" (without force). The smaller the group, the more there can be of simple power; that is, personal dominance by brute strength. We do not call the psychic dominance of one person over another person, in face-to-face contacts, a form of power in our scheme because reputation is not therein involved.

General Theory of Prestige Circles

To describe what has happened in America as name-publicity has gained its present dominance and become the form of prestige-symbol which means most to most Americans, it is necessary to have a general theory of prestige, even though crude, and also to examine some historical examples of transformation. The general theory proffered here can be stated in these terms: every person lives in concentric circles of potential reputation. At least three of these must be described. Every person lives in a first circle, or circles, which are small groups of face-to-face confrontations and contacts. This kind of central circle is the "small-group." Many persons live in more than one small-group.

In any small-group there may be some persons who have reputations which extend, as if along a radius, into the next larger circle which surrounds the small-group.

This next larger circle can be called a "special-world." It is the circle which includes all the persons who would accord or deny reputations for professional or other special achievements not implied in the small-group contacts. These special-worlds often exist actively, filled with passions of triumph and defeat, although their existence is not noticed by members of the same society who do not belong. I remember a charming sketch of two white wings discussing a third street sweeper. One remarks: "Did you ever think Bill was really very good in corners?" In my own memory is registered the mild shock of discovering, when I first by accident became director of a science museum, that museum directing was a special-world. It had its organs of publicity and fame, its rivalries, its gossip, and its glory. I had never even imagined that such a world existed until I fell into it.

Many special-world groups are, of course, less esoteric. Everyone takes it for granted that men who are engaged in the same business have good and evil opinions of one another which are very different from the opinions they hold of mankind in general. The residue of these opinions is a special-group reputation.

Position in a small-group does not much affect a reputation in a special-world. Reputation in the special-world, however, often leads to reputation in the next, the largest of the circles, which we can call the "public-world." This is one circle surrounding all the others; here are the heroes, the villains, and the comics of the public mind.

In the public-world, we are far removed from the warmth and immediacy of small-group contacts. *Esprit de corps* has gone with the smaller solidarities. Competition is more brutal and more admired. Persons who have reputations in the public-world, such as the politicians and entertainers who make up the largest part of its population, are well known to many consumers of reputations who have never seen them in the flesh, spoken to them, or exchanged any other kind of communication. They are known as pictures on screens or in print, as voices, as loosely coagulated presences in print. Their fellow citizens to whom they are known are called consumers of reputation rather than admirers because reputations may be either favorable or adverse; they are still reputations and still bring gains.

Many of the reputations which reach out into the public-world from special-worlds are based on achievement of substantial value. In fact, such reputations are much more likely to be based on achievement than those which are made entirely and *de novo* in the public-world. To illustrate, we can say that a man who bases a political career, which is a struggle for prestige-symbols and other gains in the public-world, on his reputation as a lawyer among lawyers, is trying to extend his earned special-world reputation into the wider circle and has something more than public approval to back his claims. On the other hand, a pretty girl who is put into a motion picture before she has a reputation, and thus demands a reputation in the public-world before she has earned any other kind is the more likely to suffer or gain by the caprices of popular judgment or accident. The important point for our purpose is that this lucky girl, if she is lucky, will, in the near future, get at least as much gain from her reputation, in the form of prestige-symbols, as will the lawyer who earned his chance in a narrower, more exacting competition. They will both get name-publicity.

We can now go back and take a closer look at the constituents of these groups and relations among them. Regarding the innermost, the small-groups, to which all persons must belong in any society because they comprise the most intimate relations, we note that members of complex societies belong to many. In simple social organizations, there are fewer social classifications. It is true, of course, that primitive systems of blood and possible marriage relationships are often complicated to a degree which bewilders and fascinates the inspecting anthropologist. But, otherwise, there are only a few sex and age and rudimentary occupational associations which provide the structure of the interpersonal business of living. As societies become elaborate they become also more tolerant, except for the highly artificial and unstable "monolithic" societies of modern revolutionary states. In most modern societies, especially in America, there are many varieties of personal loyalty patterns which may be found among those who associate superficially as members of the same society but distribute their personal associations in various ways.

The ideal of being judged "by one's own conscience" is a survival from the aristocratic age of "honor," with its disdain for public opinion. Whether or not it represents an ethical standard higher than the scramble for notice which is more customary in our time, is a serious question which should be discussed, but not here. In fact, to repeat a warning, we are not approving or defending any of the judgments on which positions are founded, reputations earned, gains collected in circles of various extent. Nor are we remarking on the fact that prestige-symbols, as "empty" gains, may be fought for with as much ambition and passion as are the concrete gains, the content of money and power and tangible preferments. The small-group gains are probably heaviest in content and least important as prestige. In the closest relations it is impossible to distinguish usefully between prestige which demands and affection which gives. But it is also true that in the small-groups, the qualities and achievements of the holder of a reputation position are more fully known than in larger circles. The qualities and achievements are either approved, or admired, or else they engender fears. This does not mean that judgments in small-groups are more likely to be valid than the more impersonal elements in wider reputations; the accepted myth that we know best those we know most, to the contrary notwithstanding. They may be based on mistaken admirations, that is, on admirations for qualities not really possessed by the admired one; or based on unfounded fears. They are probably warmer and that gives us the feeling that they are nearer truth.

The boundary line between the small-group and the special-group is dim and the line between the special-group and the public-world is still more difficult to draw cleanly. This is because membership in the special-world brings to the holder of a reputation there some enjoyment of the symbols of prestige which dominate the public-world and which the managers of the organs of general publicity often extend to those who are eminent in the special-group. These publicists need material for exploitation. The makeup of a modern newspaper reflects this fact. Any one of the marriages of a famous movie actress may be described on the front page, which shows that she lives in the public-world with all the involved penalties and privileges; the marriage of the daughter of a middle class professional or business man will be described in the "society" columns. Or, in a similar fashion, a change in the control of a great insurance company or a railroad, a deal big enough to be of interest in the public-world, will be noticed on the front page; a new vice president of an ordinary, large scale business will get his picture in the "business" columns.

We have remarked that position in the small-group does not lead to reputation in the special-world as readily as position in the special-world leads to a wider reputation in the outermost circle of the public-world. The small-group is knit together, or organized nervously, by face-to-face contacts. This means that control by naked power is more possible there but it also means that competition may be softened by affection or pity. Many kinds of achievement which are acknowledged and rewarded in the small-group are impossible in larger circles. This, it may be remarked in passing, has been the cause of a factor in current social changes. Feminism, in America, has been the embattled resentment of women and their friends against confining their abilities to work in the small-groups. In face-to-face relations, women have been powerful in all societies and all systems. Feminists have wanted them admitted to competition for gains in the larger circles and also seem to want—this is weakened by its inescapable vagueness—recognition in wider circles for achievements in small-groups.

Also, some of the ambiguities of the "group dynamics" method in managing associated action come from the mistake of applying small-group procedures to events in larger circles where prestige-symbols begin to play a part. Even John Dewey's famous theory of five steps in thought, if taken as a description of social action, is weakened by this mistake.

At the same time, we should guard against taking too seriously the folk myth that the possession of the prestige-symbols of the public-world deprive one completely of the satisfactions of the small-group or person-to-person living. The fact that it is a folk myth does not prove it either right or wrong but does dangerously infect thought: the folk myth is a natural development in an equalitarian country like America. Royal families, such as are left in European countries, are generally regarded by Americans as very nice people who might be normal and happy if they were not by duty bound to reign. This can be seen in deft comedy in a motion picture such as "Roman Holiday," as well as in the response of Americans generally to the pictures of Elizabeth II being crowned, or to visits by a Greek Queen and King. The folk myth, as usual, is a half truth.

The facts are, in so far as observation is possible in these difficult precincts, that great figures in the public-world may have happy personal relations in what is left of their small-group lives if they are unusually intelligent and reasonably lucky. This residual truth which is useful for our purposes is that they have to struggle much harder to attain such primitive enjoyments than do the men and women and children who do not carry the great prestige-symbols. The famous cinema blonde, desired by all men, may discover that the single exception is her husband.

There is still more to be said on this level of analysis, however, about the relation between the small-groups to which even kings and tycoons must belong at home, and the public-world where being a king or a tycoon or a cinematically exposed blonde is greatness. Although the reputation in the public-world does reflect back into the small-group, making success there more difficult, it is also diminished at home because reputations in which there are highly artificial elements tend to lose their glitter seen closeup. Folklore is full of proverbs on the point: familiarity breeds contempt, is only the most brutal of the sayings. It is to counteract this effect that professional public relations experts in America so often bend their efforts toward establishing that their client is "a human being after all," thus arguing that if you knew him in a small-group you would not despise him for being only human but love him because he was, after all, just like yourself.

However, the influence which runs in the opposite direction, that is, from small-group relations to public-world behavior, is likely to be underestimated. For example, a great publisher who appears to his rivals and his staff to care only for money and power, may risk both in a crusade for righteousness because he wants the respect of some of the people he dines with. This kind of action may be confused with a sacrifice of money and power, content, that is, for prestige gains, and in any real instance it might be very difficult to extricate from each the motives involved. For our purposes there is no need to do so, but it is important to take into account the fact that great decisions are often made for what seem, in the public-world, like trivial reasons. This is related to the more extensive fact, so sharply noted by Chesterfield in advising his son toward a successful life, that accident and caprice, as well as private motives, enter into great matters. Chesterfield, in fact, makes the failure to see the effect of small-group and personal influences on public-world behavior the mark of an outside observer (*Letter* of December 5, 1749):

> Such closet politicians never fail to assign the deepest motives for the most trifling actions, instead of often ascribing the greatest actions to the most trifling causes, in which they would be much seldomer mistaken. They read and write of kings, heroes and statesmen, as never doing anything but upon the deepest principles of sound policy. But those who see and observe kings, heroes and statesmen, discover that

they have headaches, indigestion, humours and passions, just like other people; every one of which determine their wills in defiance of their reasons.[1]

There are subtle and heretofore unobserved effects of public crisis, however, in the relations between the influences of experience in the different groups where any individual simultaneously finds himself. We can make only tentative statements about these phenomena, in anticipation of study by more penetrating techniques than we now possess. But it would appear that the feeling of crisis, no matter how much or how little justified by events, will increase the effect of small-group influences on all kinds of public-world behavior. This shows itself in the fact that public figures of all kinds will act, in real or imagined crises, more obviously than in calmer times on basic "natural" motives, which is the same as saying that they will act more on small-group feelings and ideals. Small-group motives do not change so much in time and place, in cultural transformations, as do public-world motivations. Responses to or desire for prestige-symbols are almost wholly the product of cultural training. The kind of leadership known as charismatic is leadership by a person with whom large numbers of others can identify themselves in a small-group intimacy with a transcendent mystical respect.

Transformations in History

With these notes on a theory in mind, we can consider with equal brevity the several pertinent historical transformations, hoping again to instigate more searching studies. A quite rational and helpful history of Western civilization could probably be written mostly in terms of the shifting hierarchies of prestige and the shifting of occupations, callings, sexes, generations, and kinds of achievement up and down the scale. Our purpose is to contrast name-publicity, which is the contemporary American desire, with the symbols which it supplanted.

In England and in France, to take two countries whose history is familiar, the prestige-symbol in the eighteenth century was not name-publicity but family-name. They are wholly different. The family-name symbol was, and wherever it feebly continues, still is, an inheritance from feudalism. In the feudal organization, loyalty (outside the Church) was more

[1] *Lord Chesterfield's Letters*, vol. I, edited by Lord Mahon, Bentley, London, 1845–1853, p. 367.

to a hierarchy of persons than to an impersonal institution. The person-ages were themselves, strictly speaking, formalized into institutions, but to follow this would take us too far afield, as would also any discussion of the probability that the Church outlasted feudalism because it was a hierarchy of forms, not of men.

Pertinent to our inquiry is the fact that family-name had a halo of inevitability, backed by assumptions stronger than any serving similar purposes in contemporary America. It was assumed that family-name, a status-symbol, could be acquired only by birth, that it implied ancestry of a certain certainty, "noble" blood, in the organic phrase. But when a man whose biological origins were obscure commanded attention, he was given a family-name by public opinion, much as public opinion today confers our prestige-symbol, publicity. The only effective public opinion, of course, was the throne and its controlling support; its deci-sions were final. If the king, speaking for this group, called a man a duke, he was a duke and his descendants, from that moment had noble blood, whatever might be said by envious peers.

This, I would say, makes family-name as logically a gain from reputa-tion as is the differently conferred and less durable symbol now used in the United States. The fact that it was inherited more firmly and effectively gives it a character which we are required to scrutinize but it does not defeat the analogy. Inheritance works also, feebly, in the modern American system; the daughter of a movie actress and an Asiatic playboy will be given a certain degree of prestige before she has time to grow up and either earn or destroy it. Obviously, persons are much more mobile in the modern system; it took decisive military or fiscal eminence, not momentary flash power, to get a title in England or France in the eighteenth century. Family-name was a much more brutally dominant prestige-symbol than anything tolerated in an equalitarian society. Americans give privileges often without deference and this is not entirely because we have forgotten our manners. The effective causes are tangled in the records. We do know that in England the rise of industry brought in new forms of wealth and new ways of getting rich; consequently, new kinds of men acquired titles. This allied real content, that is, money and power, effectively with the family-name symbols. In America other guerdons had to be accepted in place of suddenly discovered "noble blood."

We could move more surely among the facts if we could be sure that we had a good test of the dominance of any prestige-symbol. Contemporaries are not entirely trustworthy in this, any more than they are in other historical judgments, because they take for granted most of what we would like to make explicit. The whole mythmaking process, as Malinowski has shown,[2] tends to confirm the holy inevitability of status-equations and all the beneficiaries of a system are happy to agree. This applies fully to the Americans of today; it might help them to ferret out the hermetic assumptions in their own standards if they examined more of those of other times and places.

The American colonies did not fix the British system in their own manners in the century and a half of colonial dependence, and the Revolution set in motion counter influences of emotioncharged force. What might have happened, if George III had been better advised, can be guessed at by looking at Canada where there is a sometimes uneasy mixture of the American independence with the British tradition.

Provisionally, when we embark on historical comparisons we can take as a test of dominance the extent to which a prestige-symbol is manipulated in exchanges and rivalries for content, that is, what manipulative relations exist between the prestige-symbol and such tangibles as money and power. In eighteenth century England, money and power were constantly used in manipulating family-name prominence; in modern America money and power are used to manipulate name-publicity.

It was a story told me by a friend which first crystallized my growing understanding of the role played in modern America by name-publicity. His tale was a complaint against an injustice. He had been robbed of "credit." Anyone who accepted the current standards of American life, and who believed he was telling the whole story, would have had to agree that he had been misused. He had, as a skilled producer in the communications industry, turned a dubious assignment into a triumph. Whereupon, the superiors in his company who had been quite willing to have him billed as sole agent when the outcome was doubtful, and had led him to believe that he would be published to the world as sole genius of writing, production, and direction, moved in without apology and distributed the higher credits among themselves. They left him a meager byline fame.

This is a clear case of manipulation. Power, which is here the em-

[2]Bronislaw Malinowski, *Myth in Primitive Psychology*, W. W. Norton & Company, Inc., New York, 1926.

ployer's combination of money and emotional coercion, was used to acquire, shamelessly, the prestige-symbol. It would not be difficult to find examples in which, working in the contrary direction, the symbol coerced money and was used as power to acquire a tangible gain.

The prestige-symbol can be accepted as a substitute for content. It can be used to buy or coerce content. Or, content in the form of money or power or other tangibles can be used to force the granting of the prestige-symbol. These manipulations are roughly the same in any society.

For example, in eighteenth century England and much more in the nineteenth century, a man who got possession of large wealth from banking or transportation or brokerage or more adventurous enterprises could found a "noble" family with title, landed estate, and all appurtenances. *Per contra,* a duke might be a formidable rival in any economic struggle big enough and sanctified enough to tempt a duke. It is true, of course, that these matters were seldom as crudely set up as I have made them. They are concealed by the passage of time, as when the second or third generation of a great enterpriser assumes all the prerogatives and prestige of the founder's achievement. Balances shift between gains in content and gains in prestige when any symbol is dominant and we must keep in mind that all gains, even tangible content, are charged with emotion. One who possesses any of the rewards of socially valued achievement is likely to believe he has a moral right to all the others.

These are the typical manipulations of ambitious men and they show the standing of a prestige value in a social system. It is often said, as if it were a final judgment, that men "really" want money and power and the tangible rewards of achievement or luck. This is true, but it does not follow, as is assumed, that men want prestige-symbols only as tools of manipulation whereby the tangible content can be obtained. Did a man who spent a fortune to get a title want only a bigger fortune, which he thought the title might enable him to get? Is the man who uses his power to take a prestige-symbol away from a weaker man wasting his power? Or is he using it to get what is for him a valued object? The manipulations, as was said, are worked both ways: prestige to get tangible contents; tangible contents to buy or capture prestige. The proportions of these two kinds of gains which will please men of different temperaments and different biographies cannot be calculated. Both kinds of gain are imbued with emotion; each kind seems to its possessor to confer a moral claim to more.

To see the manipulations in any social system allows one to measure the dominance of the symbols. In France, as contrasted with England, the manipulations between family-names and contents did not develop on the same scale. Rich and powerful men did not buy titles with the same ruthless rationality. After the abolition of the monarchy in the nineteenth century, the "noble" families lost the public opinion to which they could appeal for recognition in the form of prestige so, concurrently, the existing aristocracy declined. It might be said, superficially at least, that France, although its monarchy was abolished, made a less effective transition from family-name prestige than did England, where the monarchy and titles persist and where new noble families are still being founded by royal decree. The illogicality of England's mixed prestige-symbols would be presumably unpleasant to the French mind, but in fact the French mixture of the new and the older system is bewildering.

It is useful to caution those who discuss these problems, over and over, against the mistake of confusing the symbols of prestige with the achievement for which the prestige is conferred. The kinds of achievement may vary; the special reputations with more or less competent judges will vary also. The prestige-symbols we are discussing are common coin. They are the same, no matter who possesses them and no matter how they are earned. It is specially useful to keep the exact meanings of all these words in mind when we try to compare different nations and different historical periods in this rough fashion.

Prestige Changes in America

Turning back to America, we can recall that the first European immigrants into the wilderness brought hierarchies and symbols with them. The Spaniards of the South and Southwest who came to convert the Indians and get rich, the adventurers and outcasts of Virginia who came to get a new start, the patroons of the Hudson Valley, and the Puritans of New England who sought a free field for a new theocracy, these kinds of Europeans did not expect to be new kinds of Americans. What they all discovered, in the processes that were to make Americans of their descendants, was that the family-name symbols were less effective in the new conditions. Both the difficulties and the opportunities of living here gave an overpowering influence to the more tangible content of reputation from the beginning, and after the Jacksonian Revolution the agrarian strength from the West, which came close to being sheer power and money content without symbolic decoration, blanked out the prestige-systems of Virginia and New England and New York. The War between the States completed that work.

For a period of about seventy years, from 1830 to the turn of the century, the economic preoccupations of the Americans gave them a crude simplicity of standards. A society restlessly on the make will not, it seems, set up prestige-symbols of general dominance apart from the ostentatious possession of the material contents of success. The little islands of social and intellectual and spiritual discrimination which existed all through this time were picturesque and some literature came out of them. Since this is an attempt at something like a scientific analysis, the writer is not bound to say whether Ralph Waldo Emerson and Nathaniel Hawthorne of Concord, Massachusetts, were more or less significant phenomena than Jim Fiske, for we are speaking only of the reputations men enjoyed during their lifetimes and of the signs by which public acknowledgment of achievement was shown. In these terms, there were, in fact, no symbols generally current in American life at the beginning of our industrial development. There was no royalty and no court, so there was no public opinion of the feudal or aristocratic sort which conferred prestige-symbols in eighteenth century England. Family-name could not well be established in a country where there was no "noble blood," because there were no labels to proclaim it.

It is easy to make the mistake of thinking that there was, in these early and in the Western moving pioneer societies, no gentility, no refinement, no civilized balances of taste and judgment, no quest for the elusive grails that are not measured in money and power. The spiritual side of American pioneer life is the side which later American sentimentalists have conspicuously failed to see. Only in very modern writers does it begin to get sensitive notice. But refinements and spiritual threads, running heroically through physically crude existence, are not the source for the kind of general prestige-symbol we are looking for, nor for any other kind of generally accepted signs of public approval. One can doubt that they have ever been anywhere, with the possible exception of Athens in a few brief disintegrating years. Public approval for high standards in intellectual and artistic achievement has usually elsewhere been conferred by a royal court or a surrogate thereof.

It would be difficult to discern any one prestige-symbol that dominated America in the great boom. I mean to include in this a much longer period than is usually embraced in any ordinary boom and recession rhythm; American history was one boom with intermittent and sometimes painful pauses, from 1870 to 1914. The economy breathed with a kind of second wind after the War between the States, because as a matter of fact that war, if all its moral meaning and its tragedy are disregarded, was a recession of unusual costliness, caused by the resistance of the Southern slave economy, antiquated and doomed of its own weakness, against the natural drive of industrialism.

Other huge and prolonged booms of this kind might be found in history but there are no easily found records to indicate when they happened. The combination in the United States was practically unique. There were these factors: an ample supply of industrial skills and technical lore imported from Britain where the Industrial Revolution had gone on just long enough to have found solutions for most problems of beginning industry; next, and as a result of the same historical chance, an ample supply of capital also imported from Britain; next, an ample supply of crude labor as needed, imported from Britain, Ireland, and the European continent; next, an ample supply of all the raw materials needed for industry as then developed; and lastly a great single market.

In achieving its own leadership in the generations just before the American boom, Britain had only a small helping of these same kinds of advantage. Industrial techniques were mostly invented by her own enterprisers. Labor was supplied by the abandonment of submarginal agriculture and by the rapid growth in population which industry made possible. The imported capital came from Holland, in vaguely measured amounts. The market was the world. The British record may possibly show more of human greatness than the American; in quantity it is comparatively meager. These are hardy generalizations, I know, and one is ready to have them flatly denied. No matter. The important point for this report is that, whether unique or not, the American achievement, for about seventy years, was colossal. And in a society in which the dynamism is so powerful and the changes so incessant, social approvals do not settle into patterns as stably and discernibly as in slower times. In the two great halves of the great boom, before and after the War between the States, money and power were practically interchangeable and this included political power.

In crudely corrupt countries, such as the United States was through-out most of this period, it is taken for granted that political skills will win wealth and that wealth has, in its own right, a voice in politics. Wealth, allied to political power, exercised as direct and practically ir-resistible a control over the lives of Americans as had been enjoyed in aristocratic times by those whose gains in money and power were la-belled with the prestige-symbol, family-name.

A general prestige-symbol of this kind was needed in American so-ciety, it seems, when money and political power began to be separated. The new prestige-symbol became possible when modern agencies of publicity were invented.

Money, by itself, ceased to be a sufficient symbol when its possession and ostentatious use were no longer admired. Riches, richly displayed, continued to be envied for a long time after that but wealth and virtue, wealth and greatness, wealth and happiness, ceased to be natural cou-plings in American thought when it became profitable for journalists and politicians to tell in public what most people already knew.

It is easy to make this seem too simple, however. The life of the first J. Pierpont Morgan, which began in 1837 and ended in 1912, spans the period. Morgan was never a corrupt character; he was far too regal in temper and too tremendous in personal power to care about pilferings. Aside from a few minor and quite possibly innocent scandals in his financial youth, he made a career out of good judgment, audacity, and personal influence. He was powerful enough to pull the country out of a panic twice, almost wholly by his own judgment and courage. There were men with more money but he showed more than any other how money itself can be a prestige-symbol.

This was the time when Veblen's wry satiric strictures on conspicuous spending were, temporarily, true of American ways. Morgan was, how-ever, the man in whose career, symbolically and actually, money was clearly separated from political power. Morgan was shocked when Theodore Roosevelt attacked his financing combines without first call-ing him in and allowing him to agree to make legal rearrangements. He thought of himself as not above the law, but above political attack. He did not perceive that Roosevelt was putting into bold action a new the-ory of politics, the dramatization of political action as a fight against wealth, not as creative business but as entrenched privilege, an attack by politicians as friends of the poor. Theodore Roosevelt was innocent of

Marxism; but he and the muckrakers invented or discovered, or put into dramatic form, a pseudoMarxist version of American history which has not been abandoned by politicians in either party since.

When wealth is only a tangible advantage and not a desirable symbol, and political power is ostensibly in conflict with it, and in the meantime great new engines of prestige-conferring machinery are coming into play, a new form of prestige-structure will be raised. The process was interrupted and obscured by two world wars, much as the big boom was interrupted by the War between the States. Military rank became for a while the dominant prestige-symbol and this affected many other con-current kinds of change. The growing rebellion of women against being confined to small-group reputations, which had been showing itself in a fight for the vote, and also for public office and for freedom in the sec-ondary levels of business achievement, showed its current form in the rush of women into military service. Women had always done most of the hard work and suffered serious privations and most of the anxieties in all wars; but in small-group action and for small-group rewards. Now they wore uniforms, got rank, and moved into the special-world compe-titions. At the same time, of course, manners were relaxed and women also began to smoke and drink in public, dress as nakedly or naturally as they pleased, and otherwise reject customary restraints. This did not, perhaps, directly contribute to the changes in prestige-factors; it did make it more useful to have new prestige-symbols which would apply as well to women as to men. No one at that time, perhaps, foresaw the moral atmosphere after the Second World War when women in the entertainment world would be famous for anatomical peculiarities.

I am carefully avoiding any use of cause and effect terms in this sketchy summary; what was cause and what was effect is obscure and probably insignificant. The new kind of prestige-symbol was useful; the new agencies for conferring prestige, at the behest of public opinion, were invented and were utilized. The interrelation between public opin-ion and the communications agencies is far too complex to be gone into here. Whether pictures and print and electronic sounds make public opinion, serve public opinion, or engage in a kind of chain reaction to and with public opinion—these alternatives do not affect our under-standing of the result.

It would be the kind of mistake indulged in generously by moral and esthetic critics of the "mass" media of communication to fail to take into account the fact that the mechanical, as well as the economic, structure of all agencies of mass communication makes them greedy of facts and fancies that can be expanded into reputations. They want "front page personalities" whether or not any living human beings deserve such honor. In this, the various agencies differ as to methods of exploitation but not as to need.

We can take as a primary example the daily newspaper. In spite of inroads by electronic devices, the daily newspapers are still the chief source for most people of information on current events. The broadcasters may beat them to public attention in meager statements of flash events and compete seriously in the analysis of significance. Also, television may make still pictures less exciting. The news magazines, too, offer a different kind of rivalry. But it is not yet evident that all these kinds of competition make the newspaper less necessary. The economic problems which have reduced the number of dailies so drastically are not our business at the moment.

What are the newspapers? They are agencies for merchandising novelty. Novelty and significance are not the same thing; many significant facts have no novelty or no eyecatching value. Many novel and momentarily exciting facts have no significance. It is unfair to the newspapers to ask them to keep events in proportion and what we get—thanks to their enterprise and skill—is a generous dose of what can be called news. To publish, on the front page of a newspaper, the picture of the most important personage in the country, on every day of the year, would not be news. We should discover, if we had any means of selecting such a face, that it did not change and the picture would soon be a postage stamp design—not an eyecatcher.

What the editors want is valid professional excuses for printing new faces, as many as possible, or old faces in new and surprising scenery. Their method may be as vulgar as to trick J. P. Morgan into getting snapped while he holds a midget on his knee at a Congressional hearing, as trivially human as showing a hole in Adlai Stevenson's shoe while he campaigns for the Presidency, as strange a combination of banality and touching honesty as Mr. Hoover fishing, or as lethal as an investigating Senator. A new face in an old setting, or an old face surprised. One can not deny all significance to these scenes; that is not our point. But significance is not the criterion by which they were chosen.

Consequently, if there are no worthy subjects, the space is filled with subjects even less significant and name-publicity is conferred on miscellaneous men and women and children, as if the newspapers had a stock of labels designating greatness which they were bound to use up somehow and would stick on anyone handy. This is what we, the consumers, buy.

In spite of differences in their techniques of appeal and the psychological differences among their consumers, all agencies of public communication are alike in this. Their disdainful largesse may be handed out capriciously and accidentally at first; if anyone stays in the pictures, he must earn further prestige. Continuing reputation may be earned by achievement, by misfortune, by vulgarity, which in a person of established reputation is a fascinating spectacle, or by manipulations already referred to. If there is any steady correlation to be observed, or guessed at, it is the positive probability that men of substantial achievement will earn more evidences of prestige in the long run than will the light and lucky.

This high geared demand for new names to attach reputations to is related to the serious problems of mass communications in recruiting talent. Just as radio and television producers are required by the periodic regularity of their shows to use inferior scripts and worn out ideas, since they produce more shows than the natural flow of talent justifies, so news editors are required to confer reputation, involving prestige-symbols at least and possibly content also, on far more persons than "deserve" such rewards, as not enough persons are known to have the true combination of achievement and exploitable "news" color. It is also a factor in the behavior of managers of news media that reputations have most news interest when they are in the buildup or the inevitably succeeding takedown phase. Plateaus are monotonous in all kinds of experience.

Critics and moralists condemn these practices, in most cases, without taking the trouble to find out much about the practical problems involved, assuming that harried producers are without taste or honesty because they are, in truth, without stables full of geniuses. We are always in danger of making similar judgments on newspapers for putting before our jaded eyes so many pictures of persons we do not much care to know and telling us "human" stories about personages whose humanness could well be ignored. In this they are somewhat manipulated, of course, by the public relations experts who translate content (money and power) into prestige (name-publicity) for their clients, individual, personal, or institutional, but it would be more nearly accurate to think of these public relations experts as middlemen in a business in which the newspapers and other agencies are eager customers.

Another good example of the general habit of judging all modern events in terms of old institutions and older ideas, is the fact that Americans speak of the instability of reputations in their own world as an evil. They have inherited faith in stability, or "permanence," from the older world where the system of family-name prestige made stability not only a desired element in prestige, as it would be in any system, but necessary. Family-name could not be a prestige-symbol unless it was possessed by a family line as well as by a family group.

Name-publicity is an ephemeral symbol for many reasons, some of which have been indicated, but for the American equalitarian society it is an advantage to have prestige shortlived. The gospel of equality has not meant in any society a devotion to permanent equality of position. The passion for equality can be regarded only with ironic doubt, unless it is seen that the passion is real and lambent when it inspires a man to equal the gains of others. It is negative. It is the sentiment, "I am as good as anybody," or more often, "I am as good as he is." It does not, as political doctrine, generally mean, "He is as good as I am." In fact, that high sentiment marks not the equalitarian but the superior person.

Americans, like others who have built equality into their habitual political evaluations, making it, as De Tocqueville said, the greatest of their values, are no more confused about it than others have been. They would probably be uneasy if told that their sentiment is negative, a correction of claims to superiority rather than a denial of admissions of inferiority. This is not important. But it is of great importance that we, in trying to understand the American situation, see that it stimulates effort to have all reputations subject to change. No one in the present name-publicity atmosphere is *hors de combat* or secure. So all small ambitions can be kept alive. This is related to the already mentioned vulgarity of reducing all famous personages to "human" dimensions. This serves both to reassure the presently humble that no one is safely in a niche above him, and that the humble cannot safely be kept down. An observer might say that whereas Napoleon hoped that every soldier in his army would carry a marshal's baton in his knapsack, just in case, every American has ready a toothy smile for a news photographer should one come along.

None of the facts and guesses set forth here is changed by the additional fact that name-publicity in the American prestige-hierarchy does not give lasting or deep satisfaction to most of those on whom it is conferred. Sentimentality, which is part of the sympathetic pattern of American idealism, leads many Americans, and especially some popular writers, to harbor both a judgment that the things of "the world" are trivial and also a hope that these trivialities may be shared by everyone.

The lack of deep contentment, or indeed of anything but boredom relieved by excitement, which can be observed in the lives of many famous persons in America today may be the result of the precariousness of the guerdons we are describing. The head that wears the crown of public notice so obviously wobbles. But there may be deeper reasons. The tangible gains, the content rather than the prestige-symbols of reputation, may well prove on possession to be less than had been expected. This would probably not poison possession, unless there was also a constant doubt of worthiness in those who truly deserved what real gains they got; matched by the suspicion that something was not being delivered according to promises, in those who deserve little. It is evidently of the nature of these joys to disillusion and dismay anyone capable of truth and to satisfy only the paranoid politician or the self-adoring entertainer. There is no very convincing evidence that other prestige symbols, in other times and places, were more solidly gratifying; their relative permanence may well have led to boredom when it did not lead to resentment.

It may properly be said, with the caution that this may be a value judgment and thus suspect in an objective description, that the greatest disadvantage in the present American prestige-system is the kind of behavior it induces in those who feel themselves growing dim in the public eye. It is not our business to compare it with the kind of sycophancy toward the monarch or higher nobles which once plagued the noble whose family position was endangered. He was not as vulnerable, as is, for example, the movie star, or the Senator, although he could not, unless greatly talented, do much to enhance his position except by pleasing the "public opinion" of the throne. The person in the limelight in American society, unless he is greatly gifted, may, after he has become a great man, sink to antics to get public attention which would have revolted him before he had prestige to protect. Unless he is a self-deluded fool, he may well question the validity of his position, but adulation, or American equivalents in public notice, can easily dim the judgment while it whets the appetite. One can see this sometimes in popular writers, still more in popular lecturers in America, who slowly disintegrate morally as they distort more and more of their own minds to keep up the incoming fodder of praise. This may even be true of one who, by rare chance, gets to be famous for a genuine contribution to clarity or depth of public understanding. He discovers the fact, no more often evident in America probably than elsewhere, but true, that "if you make people think they are thinking they will love you but if you make them think they will hate you" (Fred Rodell).

These statements are no doubt infected with valuation. They do not, I think, discredit the observations on present American conditions, or the sketches of history. As part of the process by which America is being transformed, the symbols of prestige have changed.

CHAPTER VI

Symbols and Images in the Constitution of Society

By ALBERT SALOMON

"À travers une forêt de symboles"
Baudelaire

I

THE SOCIAL SCIENTIST approaches the question of symbols in a perspective which is distinguished from the concerns of the philosopher and those of the theologian. The philosopher will attack the problem of symbols as the genuine problem of philosophy and state that the categories are the symbols of the scope of the human mind. Ernst Cassirer has made a genuinely pioneering effort in the field from his early illuminating studies on the categories of substance and function to his crowning work, *The Philosophy of the Symbolic Forms.* This book opened up a new field of inquiry into epistemology and the types of philosophizing. The student of religion undertakes the study of symbols as an investigation into the continuous efforts made by the theologians to comprehend the all embracing mystery of the whole in the historical religions.

The philosopher and theologian take for granted the reality of ideas and the absolute Being of the Divine which come into being in the process of history. They oppose the true Being of the mind and spirit to the ceaseless Becoming of social action. They maintain in a truly Platonic spirit that the symbolic forms of the mind and spirit are the very reality.

The student of the social sciences, however, will start with the hypothesis that all societies in action establish their own worlds through the acts of the formation of a plurality of symbol patterns. Such symbols are the living and concrete images of meaningful wholes. In other words, the sociologist presupposes the creative reality of the historical process of society. Religions, arts, and philosophies are different modes of realizing society's need for meaning, certainty, and security.

Men produce and select symbols in social action. Everything in the orbit of nature and in the realm of the collective mind can become relevant to the creation of symbols. Groups impose symbolic significance on words, events, objects, documents, and persons, according to their specific requirements in their historical and social context. Societies continuously change their symbolic forms and indicate the processes of transformation by the withdrawal from traditional to new and revolutionary symbols. Symbolconstructing and -destroying activities are fundamental to the foundations and transformations of human societies. It is of primary importance to the social scientist to analyze the structure of the ideal images and of their symbolic value in the continuous change of history.

Symbols are signs of a unique nature. They are living and concretized ideas of meanings which unite the members of a group on the various levels of their existence. Such meanings refer to the diverse experiences of all human societies. First, basic are the experiences of death and sex which circumscribe man's relations to nature and to a spiritual universe. Men respond to such fundamental shocks by creating the symbols of eternal and divine beings beyond time and space which deserve to be feared and loved. Secondly, basic are the experiences of passing time and of the eternity of institutions which require symbolic manifestations of the duration and continuity of the various collective organizations, such as clan, family, state, and church. Thirdly, basic are the experiences of belonging, of being a member of a group as against other groups. Here arise the symbols of all social, political and professional organizations. These symbols create the integration of a society, they consolidate the bonds between finite men and infinite meaning in which humans participate. Symbols secure the knowledge of man's position in the universe, they illuminate his place in the divine creation, they make articulate his role in the concrete time of history and in the organization of social groups. They demonstrate the conquest of time and space in monuments and in the representative institutions of family, army, state, and church.

In an age of total revolution and in the rise of an atheistic theology, even the revolutionary groups are compelled to build up the symbols of their belief in the absolute meaning of their radical action. The cults of the French Revolution, the Tomb of Lenin, and the worship of the *Fuehrer* testify to the truth of the statement.

Men live, indeed, in a forest of symbols which comprehends the various strata and modes of meaningful existence. Human societies construct symbols which express their position in the "Larger Whole"—the religious symbols, they establish symbols of their political and social organization such as the symbols that represent the two aspects of the state— the military and legal. They express the continuity and duration of clans and families in their collective recollections, in the worship of ancestors, and in the tradition of their ideal images. Societies continue the symbolic patterns of the professions and of the universities—products of a pre-industrial world in an age of industrialism.

In the formation of symbols, societies demonstrate the constructive power of the human mind and of collective affections. In these acts, men succeed in penetrating and illuminating the labyrinth of life. Human groupings control and organize their lives by building up forms and patterns of significance which enable men to transcend the unintelligibility of destiny and to discover meaning in the irrationalities of life.

It remains the grandeur of the human collectivity that mankind never ceases to interpret the uninterpretable, to find meaning in the meaningless and still to erect symbolic forms in the jungle of social action.

The problem of the Conference is primarily a sociological one, if the philosophical and theological approaches are met with. Durkheim has clearly seen the central question of our inquiry. Throughout his works, he has pointed out the integrating function of the Collective Conscience and its significance in the formation of religious and social symbols. In the *Elementary Forms of the Religious Life* Durkheim developed the profound thesis that the primitives do not know a division of labor which recognizes autonomous spheres of political, economic, and social life. All life is religious. Religion is the frame of reference in which all modes of conduct take place. The religious symbols comprehend all the requirements of social action and establish the authority which society exerts over its members. It was a profound insight into the depth structure of social life to state that humans live and act under the direction and guidance of divine meanings as visible in the symbols of the sacred.

Durkheim erred in assuming that the religious commands functioned only to secure the authority of society. He concluded that religion was merely a prescientific manifestation of authority within society.

Such scientific imperialism was and still is the characteristic feature of the conflict between the sciences and philosophy. Durkheim attempted to make the social process the common denominator of the manifestations of the human mind. This thesis includes religion as a necessary pattern which secures meaning, controls behavior, and assumes the final authority on human action. The conclusion is that society is the very foundation of all human activities.[1]

Durkheim's concept of society should be more closely scrutinized. Society means to Durkheim the autonomous functioning of the social and economic process, beyond the pale of political institutions. Durkheim was deeply concerned with the reconstruction of a moral theory on a scientific basis for modern lay societies. Durkheim's *Division of Labor in Society* indicates conspicuously the limitations of his definition. In this early book, the author points out the process of society as abstracted and independent from the complex dynamics of history. He shows the progress of mankind from primitive groups to individualized functional societies. Durkheim maintains in this context that the two antagonistic patterns of law which he dubs the "repressive" and the "retributive" types of legal norms are the symbols of the social transformation.

This is a fundamental mistake. No economic and technological society is in a position to establish symbols. Symbols refer to the objective significance of acts, objects, events, and ideal images which represent a living and concrete pattern for the context of a social whole. Economic processes, however, remain in various degrees subjective and have no symbolic connotation, except in a medieval corporate or modern totalitarian society.

For this reason the patterns of law are symbols of the political society which secures peace and the proportionate distribution of justice.

In the context of our problems, it is necessary to redefine the concept of society. Societies are all processes which have unity and structure in social action. They attempt to realize human goods for their members. Such a definition includes religious, social, and political institutions of the historical world. It is also valid for the world of the primitives, if we assume that here the religious and political processes merge and remain one and indivisible.

No society is capable of establishing symbols with the exception of political and religious institutions which comprehend the totality of hu-

---

[1]This intellectual trespassing of a scientific discipline on the grounds of philosophy is rightly called sociologism and has its corresponding features in Jung's psychologism and Dilthey's historicism.

man life. There remains the question of the interdependence or autonomy of political and religious symbols. As mentioned before, Durkheim had developed the illuminating idea that religious institutions set the pattern for all moral and social obligations of human conduct. The thesis is not restricted to the world of the primitives. In all human societies, including the atheistic revolutionary ones, the religious beliefs or pseudo-theological maxims condition the contents of all political norms and principles of rights and duties. They are and remain the frame of reference which determines the scope of human obligations in their social relationships.

It is important to keep in mind the interdependence of political and religious symbols, because men are inclined to regard legal and military symbols as autonomous. We forget that flags are blessed by the religious authorities; that chaplains of the armed forces have an important function to fulfil; and that judges enjoy social honors because they establish peace through the norms of equity. Peace is the concern of religion and of the body politic. Religion is an institution which secures man's understanding of and participation in a larger whole. In acts of piety men find peace, in spite of the terrors of the world.

The body politic is an institution which organizes and maintains outer and inner peace for its citizen. Its symbols of Justice and Power, of Belonging and Unity, are interrelated with those of the Sacred. Man is a symbolcreating animal. Religious and political institutions and their subdivisions require symbols to visualize the ideal reality of collective affections and of collective consciousness. Among the social institutions, the family and the clan are most relevant to the construction of symbols and ideal images. The Scottish and Irish clan organization, the Jewish family traditions survive because of their collective recollections and the traditions of ideal images which symbolize the chain of identity in the passing time. These primary groups point out clearly that all societal relationships are based on trust and faith. Trust and faith are "vague things." For this reason the strength and duration of all face-to-face organizations depend on the formation of symbols which illuminate the sense of belonging, raise the pride of uniqueness and the awareness of distance to other groups.

Similarly, the medieval traditions of the universities and of the professions as the symbolic incorporations of the spirit of Learning and of its application have endured. In the contemporary world, the universities and professions still carry on the symbols of their outstanding place in the community.[2]

Religious institutions exist on various levels of social life. There are the great historical religions and their ecclesiastical institutions. Apart from this, there are remnants of earlier religious symbols—*i.e.*, folklore, proverbs, and superstitions.[3]

The symbols of life and death as elaborated by all primitive and pagan societies have been eliminated by the establishment of the Christian religion. But it is interesting to note that they were not lost. They found a residual life in the fairy tales, the folk ways, the proverbs, and superstitions of the people who officially turned Christian. In the oral traditions of the illiterate people, the symbols of the past gods turned into the images of good and evil spirits which favored the good people and angered the bad. We learn more about the old symbolic forms and the beliefs in the symbolic significance of natural phenomena and human acts from the works of the Grimms on language and from Bezold's analysis of the survival of the pagan gods in the Christian world than from philosophy or from theology.[4]

The symbols of life and death, of fertility, and of ancestor worship mark the relationship of man to the basic forces of vitality and time, of self-realization and of decline. They belong to the area of religious symbols concerned with the meaning of human constructivity and frustration alike.

All societal relationships, regardless of their specific contents, such as the family, the political, and religious communities, are united and continually reunited by the mutual recognition of the symbols which represent their will to unity, duration, and meaningfulness.

It is interesting to reflect on the fact that from the dawn of history to

[2]The founders of the old European universities have ruled that in the procession at the academic functions the theologians march first and all the other branches of learning follow in the sequence of the times of their origins. In the modern secular universities the social scientists march first.

[3]Erwin Rhode, *Psyche,* J. C. B. Mohr (Paul Siebeck), Tuebingen, 1910, Jane Ellen Harrison, *Prolegomena to the Study of Greek Religion,* The University Press, Cambridge, England, 1922.

[4]Jacob and Wilhelm Grimm, *Woerterbuch, Deutsche Rechtsaltertuemer,* In der Dieterichsche Buchhandlung, Goettingen, 1854; Friederich von Bezold, *Das Fortleben der antiken Goetter im mittelalterlichen Humanismus,* Kurt Schroeder, Bonn and Leipzig, 1922.

the age of total revolution, it was common practice to leave untouched the symbolical patterns of the ruler and the ruled in a critical analysis of social and political conflicts. The ruler was the symbol of moral perfection as the people were the symbol of good and well meaning service. Only the ministers of princes and demagogues among the people stirred up unrest and caused conflict and revolution.

The ruler and the ruled are symbols of their mutual cooperation and recognition.[5] Such symbols are perennial in all institutions which express a meaning of life for the community. The social scientist looks at the problem from the point of view of the reciprocal relationships of recognizing and recognized parts of the social whole. The sociologist asks, what do symbols look like in the routine of everyday life? Men express their trust and faith in a family organization, in a political or religious community through the symbolic images which they hold of society.

The symbol of the august position of rulers is made a social concern in the images which diverse classes hold of their superiors. It is a true sociological thesis that it is scientifically possible to predict social conflict and catastrophes according to the changing images of the ruler-ruled relationships in the decisive social organizations.

It is a well known theory in social philosophy and sociology that all classes of society conceive of various parts of their social worlds in terms of normative or average social images or counterimages. It is a tradition which advances from Montaigne and Montesquieu to Max Scheler and Robert K. Merton.

In Montesquieu's profound and charming *Persian Letters* the problem is squarely stated. All strata of society have a philosophy of life which consists of a comprehensive imagery of all social, national, international groupings at home and abroad. Such images result from the processes of education to which men are subject from kindergarten to clubs and professional and social controls. All images and counterimages have a positive or negative connotation according to the prevailing systems of social preferences. In a militaristic society (*i.e.,* pre1914 Prussia) the

[5]In particular, during the age of the *Staendestaat,* the solemn inauguration of the new ruler was symbol of the basic mutuality between the ruler and the ruled. First, the future king took the oath that he was going to protect and defend the peace of the realm and the liberties of the estates. Then the representatives swore their allegiance and loyalty as long as he kept his oath. In the oath of Aragon the estates conclude: *"Et si no, no."* This is an unforgettable symbol of the theory of contract.

lower middle class high school teacher, not very high in rank on the civil service ladder, could ridicule and poke fun at the business man and merchant, while exalting the officer and the bureaucrat.

It is a fundamental assumption of the sociologist that societies function merely because men live on their prejudices, *i.e.,* on the images and counterimages of the various social classes and agencies as seen from their own social position. Scheler has rightly elaborated on the scope and range of social imagery on which men live.[6] He maintained that there are not only class images, but that there are professional and occupational, national and spiritual, international and ideal images, which attract or destroy the allegiances and loyalties of the various groups of society.

The Ruler and the Judge, the Hero and the Saint are symbols of the potentialities of human perfection. They work in social action as normative images which establish meaning for the life of man in society. Montesquieu has been fully aware of the fact that the classification of human beings into specific patterns of social imagery has two aspects. First, the invention and construction of such social images makes life easy. The manipulation of social images establishes what might be called, metaphorically, the map which articulates the various areas of social topography. Such guidance and tools of orientation make it possible for members of society to believe that they live in not a jungle, but in a well organized and good society. Secondly, Montesquieu and Paul Valéry have seen very clearly the implications of such social imagery as a fictitious scheme of true human reality. How can one be oneself? How can one be a human being if there are merely social images and sociological categories for classifying people? Is our concrete individuality the true existence and society a fiction? Or is society the very reality and the individual merely an illusion?

II

In the context of the problem, it is a basic issue to reflect on the fact that there are conspicuously two antagonistic notions of society which imply different approaches to the problem of symbols and images. All thinkers who take the concrete individual as the true reality will conclude that society is a structure of art, that the collective process is fiction

[6]Max Scheler, *Schriften aus dem Nachlass,* Der Neue Geist Verlag, Berlin, 1933.

as against the true state of nature. Hobbes and Mandeville, Tarde and Simmel, and all individualistic sociologists in their company, explain society and its organized order as a realm of fiction, the area of symbolic coercion.

There is an author whose works are not considered relevant to the social scientist—Goethe. He has, however, made a considerable contribution to the problem of the role of symbols in the constitution of society. Goethe began to study society when the French Revolution drew his attention to the problems of coexistence with, for, and against one another. At the same time, he entered into the scientific treatment of nature. In the merging of such different reflections, he found a new starting point which had never been taken before. He rejected the traditional alternative of nature or art. He maintained that society is something independent and moving by its own dynamics. Society transforms continuously elements of nature and art for its own purposes. The dual character of society never ceased to fascinate Goethe. He had been taught that society is the very reality of ideal human standards in the frame of a plurality of reciprocal relationships. As a student, he had discovered that the true reality of human action was to be found beneath and beyond the social establishments—in the dark labyrinth of the human passions. It is remarkable that Goethe described the nature of society in almost the same contrasting terms which he coined when giving a phenomenological description of the Demonic. The Demonic is the realm between God and nature in man. Society is the area between nature and art. Society unites necessity and accident, purpose and drift, just as the Demonic comprehends the coincident opposites of the inevitable and of the contingent, of the beneficial and of the destructive.

Both, society and the Demonic, are ambiguous in their very nature. This ambiguity is a fundamental trait of the human constitution which indicates man's basic polarity. It is interesting to note that Goethe applies his favorite metaphor of the woof and warp in describing the dualistic dynamics of society. Men as members of society are subject to the symbols of peace, law, and social conventions, they are supposed to conform to the ideal images and normative examples which society has constructed for its own protection. This set of symbolic patterns is the control of society over its members, it is an abstraction from the very reality of the concrete person which endeavors to realize its individual self. Society is fiction, illusion, *"Schein."*

It is indicative of Goethe's individualistic position that he considered the study of the Roman Carnival[7] the most appropriate subject-matter for achieving a completely objective analysis of the structure of society. Goethe stated in 1789 in the *Annals* that it was his intention to present the Roman Carnival as the social phenomenon *per se*. Such it is because it is spontaneous and not prescribed by the authorities. The Carnival is the true topic of all formal sociologies because it is unadulterated by the subjective interests of groups and individuals.

Goethe's critical approach toward society was determined by his experience of the never ceasing conflict between the expanding individual and the rigid controls which society imposed upon its members, regardless of the spontaneity and power of the single human being. For this reason society was fiction. Its symbols and normative images were coercive fiction. Life in general was a never ending play in which every human being was forced to participate in a variety of roles. All members of society took part in a variety of shows which made it indispensable to have a great number of masks available. There are the masks of authority and representation, disguising and idealizing poor human creatures. There are the masks of power, wealth, and prestige, symbolizing the true social forces. There are the masks of the professions and the symbolic images of the preindustrial classes. There are the masks of the beggar and of the jester as the symbols of homelessness, poverty, and solitude.

The masks are the symbols of the all absorbing coercion which society exerts upon its members. They are the demonstration of the duality and ambiguity of human life. How far do people identify themselves completely with their various masks and roles? Is the human being conforming with the requirements of society without reservation, escape, or revolt? It is Goethe's contention that the collectivity conditions the individual completely and shoves him while he believes himself to be pushing. The requirements of society are expressed in the symbols of decorum, of conformity, of social conventions beyond the pale of the legal, political, and religious institutions. The plurality of symbols establishes a universe which illuminates the fiction of harmony, peace, and beauty.

Goethe's view of society as reflected in the selection of the Roman Carnival, as the pattern of collective existence, develops the thesis that

[7]The description of the Roman Carnival in *Italienische Reise,* Johann Wolfgang von Goethe, *Werke, Jubilaeumsausgabe Cotta,* vol. 29, *Annalen,* vol. 30.

society is something in between nature and art. It is the world of the *Schein*. (Actually, the term challenges all translations: it is shining light, appearance, illusion, fiction, duplicity, and ambiguity. It is beauty as its climax.) According to Goethe, there are three powers which control the world: wisdom, force, and *Schein*. The functions of wisdom and force are conspicuous. What is the significance of *Schein*? *Schein* is the sum-total of all ideal images and symbols which direct, guide, and give meaning to social conduct. The notion receives its proper meaning in the frame of Goethe's philosophy of nature. The genesis of Goethe's conception of *Schein* as a basic sociological category can be traced back to his earliest philosophical essay, the *Fragment ueber die Natur* (1781–1782).[8]

In this significant statement of his philosophical conviction, Goethe declared that all life, including human life, is nothing but the expression of a universal creativeness of nature. Nature holds within itself guilt and gain, happiness and misfortune, soul and spirit. In a passage written in 1828, Goethe confirmed that his youthful essay remained an adequate expression of his philosophical and religious views. The essay contains the following statement: "Nature takes pleasure in illusion. She punishes like a harsh tyrant him who destroys it in himself and others. She presses him to her heart who obeys her trustingly."

Illusion is a constructive and beneficial constituent of the organization of social action. It enables men to reach for the impossible in order to accomplish the possible. At the same time it enables men to endure the vicissitudes of life and to hope for a new beginning. Illusion is the trust in the truth of symbolic meanings. It is the very foundation of social conduct. The truth of *Schein* and the *Schein* of truth is the secret of the ambiguity of man's living in the world of society.

Faust curses all constructive forces which men display in establishing the fictitious symbols of the social good as guides to the peace of society. He curses all ideal images as illusions which brighten our everyday life and help us to endure our sorrows. Faust lays bare the self-deceptive mechanism of the soul which manipulates the symbols of the good and meaningful life. He condemns all illusions and fictitious principles which Goethe regarded as the fundamentals of the constitution of society.

The symbols which secure the continuity and duration of society could be called "creative illusions" in Goethe's sense. The term could be

[8]*Ibid.*, vol. 39.

defined as indicating the protecting, guiding, and controlling functions of those symbolic patterns and ideal images which maintain and secure the process of social action. Representation is a creative illusion because it makes possible the division of labor in society and the organization of all social institutions. All representations are symbolic because the representatives are *Schein* as compared to their concrete human reality. All foundations of society are based on acts of mutual recognition and made articulate in the reciprocal images of rulers and ruled.

It is part of Goethe's philosophy of life to be aware of the ambiguity of all patterns of *Schein,* of the dual aspects of all illusions. The possibilities of creative illusions imply the contrasting patterns of corrupted illusions. Illusions are corrupted when men sever relationships between their social roles and their implied social functions, when they wear the masks without playing the roles. Goethe has given several illustrations of such behavior patterns in his literary works. The scenes at the emperor's court in the second part of *Faust* take place in the world of corrupt illusions. Here the masks of the carnival merge with the symbolic images of authority, wealth, and power to the all embracing fiction of illusion and to the illusion of life as a process of the carnival.

Nobody has felt the pressure of society's requirements and its fictitious coercion more strongly than Goethe. Nobody has submitted more resolutely to its commandments and to the illusions of decorum than the mature Goethe—perhaps to the detriment of his life. There is an unforgettable document which illuminates such precarious subjection with its disastrous consequences for a human being. His daughter-in-law had opened her heart to the old man in a letter which described the purgatory of her marriage. Goethe's son was an alcoholic, he beat his wife, and had numerous adulterous relationships. Goethe answered her: "I need not tell you how deeply I sympathize with you. You cannot tell me how greatly you suffer. Let us therefore pretend to one another."

Pretending is an act of dissimulation. It is an attitude of submission to the symbols of social peace which should be described as legal and social conventions. If human beings hide their suffering to maintain the illusion of domestic happiness, they recognize the truth of fiction and renounce the truth of their own lives. Goethe called such behavior resignation. It is the withdrawal from a fight for human integrity for the sake of an esthetic attitude which is the illusion of harmony and peace. In one of the *Maskenzuege,* Goethe makes Mephistopheles say: "It is said that dissimulation is a great vice. Yet we live by dissimulation." Pretending and dissimulation are the negative illusions of the fictitious order of society. Goethe's theory of *Schein* as the symbolic fiction of society is a great contribution to social theory, just because it derives from the individualistic approach of a thinker and poet to whom the world was full of positive and negative symbols.

III

There is, however, a conception of society which is antagonistic to the individualistic approach. The discipline of sociology as an empirical science has its *raison d'être* in the assumption that society is the sum-total of collective consciousness and of collective affections. The sociologist sees the individual as part of a whole. He regards the individual as conditioned and indoctrinated by the system of preferences and of goods which appear as a plurality of symbols to the members of society.

It has been the lasting merit of French sociology, of Durkheim and of his disciples, in particular, of Mauss and Halbwachs, to have set the pattern for the scientific treatment of the diverse collective representations such as collective affections, collective recollections, collective consciousnesses. Their hypothesis is of the greatest relevance for the explanation and interpretation of the symbolic patterns which unite, integrate, and construct the seals of meaning for human acting and suffering.

Durkheim's analysis of the social significance of religious symbols has been the foundation on which his disciples have erected a most complex scientific construction.

Durkheim's students and friends formed a team which extended, refined, and reformed the master's original position. In their cooperation with philosophers, physiologists, and psychologists, they discovered the range of social effects on all aspects of life, from ways of walking and speaking to the act of earning one's living and to the spiritual conditions of body, mind, and soul. In such comprehensive enterprise, they invented a new term, *"la situation sociale totale."*[9] The term rejects critically

[9]Marcel Mauss, *Sociologie et Anthropologie*, Presses universitaires de France, Paris, 1950, pp. 147, 329, and compare his definition of *"Faits sociaux totaux,"* p. 274:

> They are all inclusive. All actions are at the same time legal, economic, religious, even esthetic and morphological. They belong to private and public law and include moral evaluations of all sorts and obligations which refer to all social classes, clans, and families. They are religious as prohibiting or commanding certain behavior patterns by cults and magic. They are economical, for the notions of value, luxury, utility, expenses . . . are present.

Durkheim's idea of sociologism. It suggests that the social process is not an invariable. The new concept emphasizes that society is the result of the plurality of interacting collective representations which condition the social fabric and are conditioned by all organic and institutional forces of human life. The total social phenomenon comprehends the religious and the legal, the political and the economic forms of interdependent relationships. It includes all those modes of acting, speaking, moving, and playing which display the range and control of collective principles. All human activities have their purpose, follow a pattern, and establish the symbol of meaning in their achievements and failures. For this reason the life of a people, chiefly of an archaic or primitive people, is controlled by an almost impenetrable forest of symbols which regulate the behavior of society in its domestic and intertribal relationships. The disciples of Durkheim have described and explained the diverse possibilities of collective representations, such as the representations of death, of loyalty, of time and eternity; or the representations of exchange.[10]

They were primarily concerned with the symbol systems in all kinds of society because they set the patterns of conduct which the members of all groups took for granted and as imperative. In the primitive and archaic societies the symbolic forms have an integrating reality and express affections which are in contrast to the fictitious symbols of coercion which prevail in individualistic societies. It is logical and necessary that all authors, mentioned above, were attracted to an analysis of the religious symbols as the most crucial and most comprehensive among the collective representations.

Marcel Mauss and Robert Hertz have given much attention and did considerable research in order to verify Durkheim's notion of *Homo Duplex*. The concept is of primary importance to Durkheim. It indicates the basic duality of man, who is a unique individual and a *socius*. A *socius* is a human being as an agent and functionary of a group, regardless of his personal goals. As members of society, men live in the frame of normative symbols which direct and order their lives without considering the desires and possibilities of the individuals. But men are more and less than *socii*. Human being is a living and concrete totality of an

---

[10]Maurice Halbwachs, *Les Cadres Sociaux de la Mémoire*, F. Alcan, Paris, 1925, 2nd edition, 1952; *La Mémoire Collective*, Presses universitaires de France, Paris, 1950; *Les Causes du Suicide*, F. Alcan, Paris, 1951; Robert Hertz, *Mélanges de Sociologie Réligieuse et Folklore*, F. Alcan, Paris, 1926; Mauss, *op. cit.*

individual potency which desires to expand and to realize itself within or beyond the established symbols of peace, law, and social conventions. Georg Simmel often defined human being as the strange phenomenon which is life and more than life.[11] This formulation might be taken as a definition of Durkheim's *Homo Duplex*. Man as an organic being desires to unfold his vitality and power against all established institutions. Man as a member of society shares in the collective representations, affections, and value attitudes of the diverse groups of which he is a member. This dualism is lasting and cannot be eliminated. It is expressed religiously in the antagonism of the Sacred and Profane, a dualism which dominates the spiritual world of the primitives. It extends even to the primitives' social organizations.

The two phratries which constitute the structure of a primitive tribe are distinguished reciprocally as the sacred and the profane. This antagonism is necessary for the survival of the group. For such a divided tribe elaborates the first pattern of the division of labor. It separates the vital-social from the religious-symbolic functions. Such division is the precondition for its functioning and duration. In the development of these early societies, the fundamental dualism is replaced by a hierarchy of castes and classes, of which the one is noble, sacred, and in charge of all ruling functions, while the other is profane and committed to labor and toil. The social polarity is always a reflex of and result of the religious polarity. This human and spiritual dualism is the necessary presupposition for the variety of symbolic forms which control directly the lives of the primitive and archaic people and indirectly the attitudes of historical societies.

I will select the two most important cases which illustrate the all pervading symbolism in the world of the primitives. The one deals with the symbolism of the body, the other with the symbolic forces inherent in the earliest forms of contract or exchange. The law of polarity has first been applied to the human body. The sexual dualism has received its positive and negative significance. The male part is the symbol of potency, strength, fortitude, while the female symbolizes the weak, the tricky, and the evil.

The primitives went still farther. They have ascribed religious and

[11]Georg Simmel, *Lebensanschauung, Vier metaphysische Kapitel*, Duncken & Humbolt, Munich and Leipzig, 1919; *Fragmente und Aufsaetze*, Drei Masken Verlag, Munich, 1923.

symbolic relevance to certain organs and to their location. The differentiation between the positive or negative meanings of the right and the left hand, or rather the conditions for the preeminence of the right hand, are one of the lasting symbolic constructions of the archaic world. The student of religion and of society needs to be a philologist and inquire into the meanings and the history of words. In all IndoEuropean languages the terms which name the right and the left have received symbolic connotations. The right hand and arm were considered to be the lucky, the blessed, the side closest to the Divine. The left hand was regarded as unfortunate, exposed and attractive to evil spirits. The Maori and many other Pacific peoples took it for granted that the right is the side of life and force, while the left is the side of weakness and death. Such symbolic interpretations are frequently extended to the directions of space. There are many instances in the mythology of the Indo-European peoples in which early societies have connected the right side with the East and South as the good and lucky regions, while they regarded the West and North as unfortunate and fateful.[12]

Throughout the world, the right hand is the symbol of righteousness and dexterity in the literal and symbolic senses. The right is the hand which takes the oath, which affirms a promise, which seals the bond of marriage. The left hand is always connected with the principle of evil, of bad luck, and of demonic spirits. Whoever has lived with people who were brought up in the traditions of superstitions and old folkways, will know that these old archaic beliefs still survive.

In all rural parts of Europe, the peasant population has been much closer to primitive societies than to their contemporary urban and industrial surroundings. Their folkways, their modes of conduct, their ways of life, their festivals, from the celebration of birth to the tremendous dinners at funerals, were the uninterrupted continuity of primitive attitudes and beliefs.

I remember very vividly a fellow soldier during the First World War. He came from a rural and Catholic part of Southern Germany. He told me how his folks swear. They raise the right hand for the oath; at the same time they bring their left hand in the corresponding position down-

---

[12]Hertz, *op. cit.*, pp. 110 ff., p. 43:

In the Christian representation of the Crucification, the sun shines on the region located at the right side of the cross where the New Church triumphs. The moon sheds its pale light on the left side of the robber and the Fallen Synagogue.

ward. Thus they can conduct and kill every oath they want to. It was meant to be good advice.

How can we explain the symbolic significance which the traditions have ascribed to the preeminence of the right? Neither the slight asymmetry of the organism nor the determinations of space can explain the symbol system which sanctifies the right hand. The only valid explanation can be derived from the structure of the collective consciousness. The collective consciousness is a dynamic process, the dialectics of which are called polarity. The universal polarity of thinking has its symbolic image in the *Homo Duplex* who makes it imperative to divide the All in the fundamental antagonisms of the Sacred and of the Profane. For this reason the primitive societies have sanctified the right and abhorred the left side. These traditions still survive in the usages and mores of modern society.

The analysis of the preeminence of the right hand is a model case of investigation into the symbol structure of the interdependent layers of society. The disciples of Durkheim, in particular Marcel Mauss, have made a great contribution to the scientific penetration and explanation of the functions of symbols. They have carried forward our knowledge of human attitudes and our insights into the complex structure of social facts, the totality of which they have stressed.

Marcel Mauss's[13] great essay on the gift is of primary importance to the student of symbolism. All exchanges between groups, clans, and individuals are not the manipulation of objects. All objects are related to the giver and to his spirit which is again a manifestation of one or several totems. Every present requires the return and the exchange of gifts. Such mutual presents are, of course, required by the social imperatives, such as honor, prestige, wealth of individual and of clan. The main postulate, however, demands that the fiction of spontaneous and voluntary giving be maintained. These gifts are simultaneously political, legal, and economic acts. As such they symbolize the moral standards of the respective groups and their just and peaceful minds. But they are still more. They are the solemn symbols of the spiritual context in which the various groups live. They represent the balance and harmony of the moral world as the fundamental aspect of the meaning of the universe. Its peace and tranquillity would be greatly disturbed, if the giver would not have re-

---

[13]Mauss, *Sociologie et Anthropologie,* pp. 145–330. An American translation of the essay on the gift was published by the Free Press in 1954.

ceived a present in exchange, or if the receiver would not have accepted a gift with gratitude and humility.

Mauss has developed a theory of the three obligations which prevail in all primitive and archaic societies and still survive in the contemporary world in the books of etiquette. The three postulates demonstrate the symbolic relevance of moral conduct. The first norm obliges men to return the received presents and never to keep them. Such behavior is not offensive. On the contrary, it displays the highest respect for the spirits and totems of the giver, for men should not deprive objects and their spirits of their frame of belonging. The second command orders the noble and rich, the chieftains and the powerful clans to make presents—*noblesse oblige*. The third rule requests men to receive gifts graciously and in the spirit of mutual recognition. The complete theory of the various aspects of exchange, the ethics of giving, of receiving, and of reciprocating is the foundation of all forthcoming patterns of contract. Its symbols indicate that social life is possible only on the basis of trust and friendship. Trust and friendship, however, do presuppose principles of peace and equity as securing a final meaning of the larger whole.

Mauss's studies verify the thesis that the diverse reciprocities which make up the social fabric find their ultimate significance in religious symbols which refer to the meaning of unity, peace, and correspondences.

Such study in symbolism is not an ivory tower concern. Mauss explicitly stated that his investigations in the patterns of total presentations, although describing the oldest system of law and economy, resulted in the discovery of the foundations of the ethics of exchange. These archaic worlds still teach the modern sociologist a lesson. They demonstrate that economic relationships are not autonomous, but refer to a code of morals. Like his master Durkheim, Mauss regarded the contemporary unleashed industrial process as in need of moral principles of orientation such as prevailed in the preindustrial worlds. In the archaic worlds[14] the economy is still full of religious symbols. Money has still its magic connotation and is tied up with the clan and the single individual. Diverse

---

[14]Mauss, *op. cit.*, p. 265:

Ainsi, d'un bout à l'autre de l'évolution humaine, il n'y a pas deux sagesses. Qu'on adopte donc comme principe de notre vie ce qui a toujours été un principe et le sera toujours: sortir de soi, donner librement et obligatoirement; on ne risque pas de se tromper. . . . Donne autant que tu prends, tout sera très bien.

economic activities, such as marketing and bargaining, are surrounded with solemn rituals and myths. Life is still total, a unified context of meaning in a plurality of human activities on all levels of the Profane and of the Sacred. Not one single power has yet established its autonomy and exploded the integrity and significance of the whole. According to Mauss, these studies on archaic societies should have their impact on his contemporaries. They offer explicit advice to the modern unregulated and autonomous process of a technological and industrial society. They suggest to the modern world that it would be imperative to include and to insert the expanding economic process in a structure of norms and their symbolic manifestations in order to maintain a frame to which all human activities could be referred.

In a completely different way and indirectly, Maurice Halbwachs has dealt with the symbols of society in the description and analysis of the Collective Recollections in time and space.[15]

He made the valuable distinction between historical collective recollections and the plurality of collective memories as materialized in the living traditions of families, clans, professions, regional groups, etc. Historical recollections change continuously according to the versatile interests and the diverse systems of value as applied by the historians. For this reason historical symbols appear and disappear in conformity with the prevailing traditions and preferences. Historical symbols can be of two different types, dates and images. Victories or defeats, the dates of revolutionary discoveries and inventions, Hiroshima or Compiègnes, Lexington and Gettysburg are such symbolic events for nations and for mankind, as indicating crucial transformations in mankind's journey.

Apart from dates, historical recollections construct and preserve the images of historical persons as symbols of national or human greatness or wickedness. Washington and Lincoln, Attila and Hitler, Socrates and Montaigne, Protagoras and Aretino, are symbolic images of the antagonistic human possibilities within and beyond national boundaries.

Collective recollections, in contrast to historical recollections, refer to the lasting identity of a group or society in spite of their external changes. It is even possible to define collective recollections as a social

[15]Maurice Halbwachs, *Les Cadres Sociaux de La Mémoire; La Mémoire Collective; La Topographie Légendaire des Évangiles en Terre Sainté, Etude de Mémoire Collective,* Presses universitaires de France, Paris, 1941.

institution in its inner dynamics. Collective memories are realized in images, meetings, and monuments which are symbols of man's power to conquer time. Being mindful and loyal, to recall and not to forget are preconditions for man's qualifications of constructing symbols which transcend the process of time. The acts of remembering are complex phenomena. They unite intellectual, emotional, and imaginary elements, and move toward an ideal of eternity, immortality, and objectivity beyond the flux of time. This is exactly the function of symbolic images, gatherings, and documents. They evidence the constructive forces of man to realize the polarity in the acts of objectifying himself. In all political and religious institutions the individual members pass away while the organized group is lasting. It is this phenomenon which is the precondition for all symbols of duration and eternity. All families and clans as they still prevail in the organization of Scottish, Irish, and Jewish societies, have carefully preserved and cultivated the symbols of their belonging together: they remain true to the images of their ancestors, they recognize the authority of their traditions as symbols of their duration, in spite of all transformations and changes in the social worlds. The contemporary human being is easily inclined to ridicule the spirit of traditionalism. This is his privilege. It should be noted, however, that all strong and constructive groups or societies are those which carry on the traditions of their fathers and respect the symbols of their common recollections. They enable men to face and to control problems as they arise in their contemporary world.

It is of utmost relevance to the problem of collective recollections to distinguish between two different symbolic manifestations as they refer to time and space. Both are equally important, both refer to different modes of thought and of affections. There are memories which are centered around places, monuments, *i.e.*, the symbolic significance of space. There are recollections which find their symbolic manifestations in the time process. Such distinction points toward a fundamental differentiation. There are obviously two antagonistic ways of symbolic thinking: the utopian and the messianic. The one refers to the control of space as the meaning of rational perfection, the messianic thought assumes the unfolding of meaning in the process of time.[16] We might distinguish two types of categories, wish-space and wish-time conceptions.

[16]Abraham J. Heschel, *The Sabbath*, Farrar, Straus & Young, New York, 1951, has made a remarkable contribution to the time element in Jewish thinking.

IV

There remains still another area of investigation which the sociologist is obliged to analyze and to explain. If it is taken for granted that societies live in a pluralistic universe of symbols, it should be added immediately that such a universe is not static, but a dynamic process. All symbols are living forms of collective representations and subject to continuous transformations, destructions, and reconstructions. All societies are integrated unities of a variety of reciprocal relationships. All reciprocal relationships consist of the mutual cooperation of give and take, of superordination and subordination. Such mutuality is maintained when the interacting parts recognize each other as meaningful and functional processes in a common field of social action. Such mutual recognition finds expression in the symbolic images on which all societies live. As mentioned before, all classes have certain images of themselves and of the other classes in their field of social action. These symbols are subject to the vicissitudes of changing collective affections. Normative social images change as the result of inner or outer causes. Their transformation into counterimages can be manipulated for diverse purposes. The symbols themselves can be used as instruments for attaining certain goals.

Symbols can be activated as images in a frame of reference in order to divert, discipline, and control human souls. In the spiritual revolution which is called Counter-Reformation, a new and revolutionary social psychological technique was developed. It manipulated the symbols of faith in order to stir the imagination and to direct the will toward accomplishing a character type of self-control and self-determination within a spiritual community.

Loyola's Spiritual Exercises are a revolutionary effort. Although Loyola did continue some patterns of the medieval exercises and copied some famous passages by Ludolf of Saxony and Thomas à Kempis, his little book is a radical transformation in the world of piety and spiritual contemplation. The medieval treatises of spiritual exercises should help the individual to exercise by himself. It was the general pattern of mystical piety to dedicate one's soul to a complete contemplation in order to come close to the cognition of the Divine. In psychological terms, the mystical contemplation is a procedure in which the pious concentrates his attention on certain complexes of perception. He penetrates such perceptions with specific affections which produce the act of vision or cognition. All such techniques are applied by the individual mystic for his own perfection.

Loyola has created a new and revolutionary type of spiritual exercise. First, he opposed the traditional ideal of spiritual contemplation. He offered instead a new postulate of a spiritual character in action. He intended to educate the bodies, minds, and souls of men in such a way as to enable them to find their own place of service within the Church Militant as laymen or clerks. Secondly, he introduced a societal relationship in the act of exercising. Human beings should not be left alone, but directed and guided in the most responsible reflections on their place in God's world and in the Church Militant. According to Loyola, the radical transformation of the function of Exercises was accompanied by a no less revolutionary procedure. He introduced a relationship between master and disciple, officer and soldier in the practice of contemplation.

This reformation was revolutionary, because Loyola keenly attacked the psychological problems of social relationships. All previous types of mystics, the philosophical and the Quietistic thinkers, were concerned only to elaborate techniques of individual psychology. Loyola inaugurated a new era. His treatise disclosed the possibilities of social psychology. It showed how to manipulate human minds by working on their imagination and will. Loyola had learned and experienced that the concentration of our imagination on the symbols and images of the religious verities will when wisely directed, produce profound changes in human character.

Loyola himself compared such social psychological techniques to the gymnastics of the body. These are spiritual gymnastics because they train the student to produce at will the imagination of certain symbols and images which imply certain affections. Loyola went even farther. He was aware of the fact there is a profound connection between physiology and spirituality in the act of prayer. He stated the causal relationship between the right modes of breathing and the true ways of praying. His interest in social psychological techniques was based on a very strong conviction. Loyola has frequently stated his opinion that the usual patterns of intellectual indoctrination in matters spiritual and moral will never affect human beings profoundly. For this reason his own revolutionary methods start from the assumption that a master of exercises has to condition all five senses of the disciple at the same time in order to achieve his complete loyalty and dedication. To give an illustration, there should be a rather dim light in the room in which the student listens to the officer's voice which comes from another place. In each case the master should consider the position of the trainee, whether kneeling, lying on the floor, or sitting, is the most appropriate way for his concentration. In the light of such physiological and psychological preparations, the exercises of the first two weeks receive their significance. They are focused around the principle of manipulating the symbols and images of the religious traditions in order to produce an attitude toward self, world, and God. The theme of the first week is the sinfulness of man. The master of exercises directs the reflection of the trainee to the symbols of the eternal verities, such as the angels, the one angel who was sent to hell, the damned, the fallen Adam, who were all condemned for one sin. In contrast to them, the master of exercises makes the student regard his own continuous sinfulness. In Loyola's technique the imagination of the trainee is turned to reconstruct his sins in the minutest details in space and time. Sins are actions and omissions alike. Loyola knows very well that they result from passions and inertia. Loyola forces the student to visualize the never ceasing process of our many sins and at the same time to be conscious of the absolute horror of each single one. Such visual reconstruction of one's life as a symbol of Adam's nature, the continuous comparisons with the images of the angels and of the damned, create the feeling of human futility. This procedure brings about the shock of being dangerously close to the abyss and far removed from God's grace.

The repetition of the first and second Meditations in the third and fourth Meditations betrays Loyola's deep psychological insight. He was conscious of the fact that it was necessary to repeat the same procedures again and again in order completely to penetrate the senses, the imagination, and the reflection. Another psychological device is conspicuous in the general organization of the book. All Meditations are surrounded by prayers. The prayers preceding the Meditations should prepare and open the mind. The prayers following the Meditations should prevent despair. The second week begins with two symbolic stories. The first contains a detailed topography of the holy places where Jesus spent his youth and began to preach; the second parable tells the story of a king who summons his subjects to follow him in a war against the Infidels. Loyola does not hide the symbolic meaning of this story. It would be a disgrace to reject a request of our temporal king to fight the heathens, how much more should we be ashamed not to follow Christ, when He orders us to fight under His banner for the victory of the spirit and for the good?

These Meditations correspond to those of the first week. At the first week's Meditation the trainee became aware of his sinfulness. In the second week he becomes aware of the boundless grace of God. In these Meditations Loyola describes as a great poet the idyll of Jesus's youth, His wanderings, and His entrance into the Temple. The chief Meditations in the second week deal with the symbolic presentation of the decision which God has offered to man in the person of Christ. They reconstruct the famous images which Thomas à Kempis had conceived in his *Imitatio*. These are the images of the two antagonistic camps in the world. On the one side, Satan gathers those who are seduced by his promises that they will be able to gain wealth and power and to satisfy their lusts. On the other side, Christ displays His banner, calling all those who are willing to follow and serve Him, taking poverty, humiliation, and degradation as their lot. Such symbolic images of the alternatives in the world are applied in order to achieve a nonmystical goal. The goal can be described as the formation of a spiritual character type with the iron discipline of a soldier. Such character structure is a necessary postulate for all those who want to serve God and His Holy Church in all ways of social action.

Loyola is a great revolutionary in the religious and psychological fields. One cannot overestimate the radicalism of his new techniques. They open up vast perspectives for the manipulating of individuals and groups.[17]

Loyola laid the foundations for all social psychological techniques as they developed in the process of social action. He first recognized the reality of the *"situation sociale totale"* which the French sociologists have conceived in scientific terms. Loyola knew by experience and the minutest observations of himself and of others that the physiological, psychological, and social conditions of people have great importance for their spiritual health. He was fully aware of the fact that a well trained director and officer could apply such knowledge for molding human minds and controlling men's characters in order to make them fit for

[17]Henri Delacroix, *Les grands mystiques Chrétiens*, F. Alcan, Paris, 1938; Heinrich Boehmer, *Loyola und die deutsche Mystik*, 1921, translated by Paul Zeller Stradach, *The Jesuits: an historical study*, The Castle Press, Philadelphia, 1928.

situations of combat and endurance. His knowledge implied his techniques. The medieval mystic had contemplated the symbols of the eternal verities of religion. Loyola made them the instruments of his spiritual training.

This revolutionary change set the pattern for techniques which were applied in political and social action. All revolutionary groups secularized Loyola's procedure. They transformed the traditional symbols and images of authority, prestige, and greatness into counterimages or caricatures of the former.

The phenomenon of revolution displays the most conspicuous evidence for the intertwined relationship between symbols and images. In all monarchies, the authority and dignity of the regime rest with the respect and the recognition which the people pay to the king and queen as the symbols of their unity.

As soon as such affections are gone, the basis of political authority is jeopardized. When the king and the queen are no longer considered as the images of the good and noble life, but as subject to and practising vulgar desires regardless of their position, the foundations of the state are shaken. For the people do not tolerate being deprived of the lofty and ideal images of the rulers which they carry in their minds and affections.

Perhaps the most impressive case which verifies this thesis is Goethe's prediction of the revolution in 1785 on the occasion of the Necklace Affair. He reported later on that his friends believed him almost mad when he was shocked by the scandal to such an extent that he foresaw the debacle of the revolution.[18] This anticipation was completely justified. The symbol of majesty was polluted and attacked when the image of the queen was abused for and in a criminal action. Goethe was deeply aware of the fact that no regime—whatever its constitution—can endure when the representative rulers, the symbols of its unity, dignity, and meaning, are left to the contempt and ridicule of the people.

It is not an accident that in the prehistory of all revolutions, from the Necklace Affair to the Rasputin case, the immoral and undignified conduct of the queens was a primary condition for destroying traditional loyalties. In all societies, radical intellectuals have been successful in debunking the symbolic authority of rulers and ruling classes by demonstrating the abyss between the symbolic requirements of the highest posi-

[18]Goethe, *Werke Jubilaeumsausgabe,* vol. 9. p. 378, vol. 30, p. 7.

tions and the actual behavior of their representatives. In all revolutions, the parties of opposition have made the illicit or perverted sex relationships of the elite a subject of attack and of attractive propaganda.

It is a general feature of rising revolutionary attitudes to destroy traditional beliefs in the symbols and images of authority, power, and law. The sociologist who analyzes the continuous transformations in the formation and critical reexamination of social images is capable of predicting quite accurately the trends toward social integration or disintegration. In the fifty years which preceded the French and the Russian Revolutions, one can observe in the minutest details how the respected symbols of the fatherly king, the patriarchal nobleman, and the benevolent and fair judge were turned into counterimages. The king became the heartless tyrant, the exploiting aristocrat was considered a bird of prey, the oppressing lord was regarded as a hawk. From the French to the Bolshevik Revolutions, such transformation of the symbols and of their social images indicated the inner destruction of the symbols of political unity and integration.

I have attempted to give a survey of the various aspects in which symbols and images appear to the social scientist. It is the implicit thesis of such review that society as the sum-total of collective representations, affections, and recollections has its own symbolconstructing powers which are different from the works of the philosopher. Different they are because they are manifestations of the totality of human efforts to create living and concrete images as symbols of duration, meaning, and eternity in time. For this reason all these constructions take place within the political and religious institutions. The philosopher's symbols refer to a different universe of discourse.

There remains, however, a grave question which should be the concern of the contemporary human being who tries to find the interpretation of his own precarious situation.

Do we not live in a world in which the integrating power of symbols is shrinking rapidly, in which the "vague things" of symbolic images are disregarded, while mankind is merely interested in precision and certainty?

The rapid development of a technological and scientific mass society has revolutionized the intellectual and emotional attitudes in all human relationships. Men live on stereotypes and uniform patterns of behavior and have renounced the penetration of the whole by symbols and ideal images because they are not scientifically valid. Paul Valéry predicted this development twenty-five years ago.

The scientifism of the contemporary world is the reappearance of a new state of barbarism. Such it is because the men of learning have become technicians, engineers, and experts in all fields of knowledge. They do not refer their work any longer to the "vague things" which the symbols of their professions express. The academic professor is no longer a "professor." He is no longer the ideal image or the symbol of man's participating in a larger whole. He is no longer an example of enlightened *Humanitas* and the normative image of wisdom and of the love of it. Professors are just experts, and the result of this trend is the situation of the Tower of Babel. We all speak a variety of languages, but we do not understand one another. This is a symbol of the scientific age.

Symbols are necessary constructs of the mind which includes intelligence and affections alike. Love and sympathy are positive modes of cognition. Are such patterns of human orientation still possible in a world which is totally dedicated to quantitative methods?

> Une société qui aurait éliminée tout ce qui est vague et irrattionel pour s'en remettre au mesurable et vérifiable, pourrait-elle subsister? Le problème existe et nous presse. Toute l'ère moderne montre un accroissement continu de la précision. Tout ce qui n'est pas sensible, ne peut pas devenir précis, et retarde en quelque sorte sur le reste. . . .[19]

Comment by Mordecai M. Kaplan:

1) I find it difficult to accept the "division of labor" which Albert Salomon introduces into the study of symbols between the "student of religion" and "the student of the social sciences." Why should the student of religion have to confine himself, in the study of symbols, to the "efforts of theologians" in dealing with "historical religions"? Why may he not approach religion in the same spirit as the social scientist? Those "efforts of theologians" constitute a relatively insignificant portion of religion, as it functions in human life. One who does no more than study those "efforts" hardly deserves to be called "a student of religion." He is merely a theologian.

2) It is apparent that Salomon does not deal with symbols in general, but only with group symbols. Like all other symbols, group symbols are a means of communication. But what they communicate has to do with the group as a whole. The purpose of such communication is not to convey information of fact concerning the group but to arouse the emotions and activate the will in one's relation to the group. It is, therefore, questionable whether "traffic lights," which are signs rather than symbols, and even the "Eternal Light" in so far as it is a symbol of eternity and does not, as such, refer to the group, belong to the discussion.

3) Durkheim's contribution to the sociology of religion is to be found in his *Elementary Forms of Religious Experience,* which is by far more relevant to the subject

[19]Paul Valéry, *Variété,* vol. II, Gallimard, Paris, 1930. p. 60.

of symbolism than his *Division of Labor in Society*. It is difficult to understand why the former book is not even mentioned. I do not have the book before me, and it is a long time since I read it, and therefore what I say about it may be mistaken. But I am almost certain that Durkheim's thesis in that book is not, as Salomon maintains that "the religious institutions set a pattern for all moral and social obligations," but that the impact on the human mind of the group's wants, hopes, fears, joys, sorrows, inhibitions, and satisfactions is such as to give rise to all the religious, social, economic, and political manifestations within the group. Transferred to the area of highly sophisticated society that thesis would be tantamount to saying the opposite of what Salomon ascribes to Durkheim, namely, that "the moral and social obligations of human conduct" set the pattern for religion as well as for the other forms of group behavior. It is because Durkheim considers as products of group life all human self-expression, including even the categories of logic, to say nothing of religion, that he is justly charged with "sociologism."

4) One misses in the use of the term religion in this discussion, any attempt to distinguish different types, like the religion of magic, of morale, of ethics, of salvation. The fact that those different types exist as strands interwoven into the actual religion of most men, does not exempt the social scientist from the need of recognizing their different motivations, as well as the different types of symbols by which they are transmitted from one generation to the next and communicated to contemporaries. Likewise one expects to find in a discussion of symbols, the chief function of which is *conscious* communication, some reference to the role of the conscious, and to the fact that magic, which is the source of much of the group symbolism, arises during the preconscious, or at best during the protoconscious stage of society.

Magic that is free from considerations of morale, ethics, or salvation belongs, as a rule, to the protoconscious stage. It arises out of a kind of reflex psychic activity with no awareness of purpose. Such, however, is the inertia of human conduct that the magical practices persist long after man has become self-conscious, and has the ability to contemplate an action before and after it is performed. Even then he is not always able to localize causes and effects. He continues to engage in his magical practices, all the while blaming himself when they fail to bring about the desired results. He does not discontinue them, even when he realizes that they are intrinsically ineffective. That is also true of others in his group. Their heightened consciousness, however, impels them to find some reason for their continuing their magical practices. As a rule, they assume that some deity had ordered that they be performed. That is the way men explain the compulsive feeling that drives them as a group to do something for which they see no special purpose.

The deity, however, to be worthy of worship cannot be regarded as arbitrary. As a deity he is concerned in the welfare of the group. In place, therefore, of the original function of the magical practice, which was to attain some kind of potency, some new function is ascribed to it. It is said to be a means of heightening the prestige of the group (the equivalent of morale), improving its character, or enabling it to achieve salvation (immortality and bliss). It is then that the magical practice is *transformed* into a religious symbol. Its purpose then is not directly to obtain potency, but, *qua* symbol, to communicate the group feeling which leads to the conduct necessary to achieve any of the foregoing truly religious purposes.

That is the time when there arises a group awareness, and when the group comes to be endowed with cosmic significance, with holiness, immortality, or other attributes whereby it is apotheosized. It is then that the group becomes an *ecclesia*, a *kenesset*, or a church. Even in this stage of socioreligious development, symbols may retain their original magical character by functioning as sacraments, and symbolic persons, their magical potency by being regarded as possessing *charisma*. In addition to all this, magical practices which have not become symbols may survive as a form of desiccated magic, like avoidance of the number thirteen, or knocking on wood. That is analogous to the functioning of the unconscious long after man has achieved the conscious.

Had Salomon reckoned with the distinction between magic and symbol, he would not have so readily adopted Baudelaire's phrase, *forêt de symboles,* as marking the life "chiefly of an archaic or primitive people." Symbols belong to the highly *civilized* stage of a people. An archaic or primitive people is dominated by active magic. A flag at the head of an army is a symbol, but the Ark which was carried at the head of the Israelites in the Wilderness was a vessel of magic. It possessed a kind of "sacred electricity," which later shocked Uzziah to death. The leader of a group is, in primitive society, not a symbol but a charismatic person endowed with magical power. That survived in the belief that the "King's touch" could heal. That, however, does not mean that "magic" and "symbol" can be used interchangeably as Salomon seems to do. That confusion leads him to use as illustrations what he terms the "symbolisms of the body." Actually it is the magic of the body that he describes. The case of the folk of rural Germany is not a matter of one *symbol* counteracting another, but one type of potency (the left arm) cancelling out the other type of potency (the right arm). Magic, it must be remembered, deals with potency, but symbols deal with communication.

That distinction places Loyola's contribution to the technique of individual and group control in the proper light. His technique does not come under the rubric of magic. It was based on intuitive sociopsychological knowledge. He was aware of the effect of group symbols on the will and emotions of those who were exposed to them. His discovery, therefore, consists in realizing, first, that religion is not essentially a process of ideation but of feeling and acting, and, secondly, that the only way to communicate emotions that move to action is to use group symbols and group symbolic actions.

5) The view of society, which Goethe formed on the basis of what he observed of the Roman Carnival, is relevant to the discussion of group symbols. But that view is far from having scientific value, even though it might serve as a theme for excellent poetry. It should not be at all surprising that his "works are not considered relevant to the social scientist." The formula which he derives from the "Roman Carnival" conception of society that "three powers which control the world are wisdom, force, and *Schein* (illusion)" cannot be taken seriously. By "the world" Goethe, no doubt, means human society. Unless he intended to pack into the term "wisdom" not only all truth but also all goodness, not only knowledge, foresight, prudence, but also fear, hatred, kindness, love, trust, and hope, he certainly overlooked many of the most important forces that govern society.

Moreover, Goethe's conception of *Schein* as one of "the three powers which control the world" is altogether untenable. In his very attempt to make it sound plausible by distinguishing between "creative" and "corrupting" illusions, he proves all the more how untenable it is. That distinction takes us beyond illusion and into the area of reality. Creativity and corruption are facts and not illusions. They determine, and not the illusions, whether there shall or shall not be a world. Wisdom controls the world; force controls the world, but *Schein* or illusion puts the world beyond control or nullifies whatever control wisdom exercises.

It is hardly possible that Salomon would have us accept Goethe's conception of society, and infer that symbols are "masks" which create the illusions necessary to "control the world." Such a conception of social symbols is not only false; it is dangerous. It plays into the hands of all reactionaries who fear the truth, which is the antithesis of illusion. From that point of view, they might well reason that, since ignorance, which is the mother of illusion, is bliss, why allow the spread of knowledge, particularly among the masses? It might extinguish their ignorance. On the contrary, pile on the symbols as much as one can. Before long they will cease to be symbols and become magic, and men will achieve the bliss of ignorance that "passeth understanding."

Professor Salomon's reply:

1) It was my assignment as expressed in the title to deal with the plurality of symbol-constructing forces in the process of society and to disregard the systematization of symbolic forms as achieved by the philosopher and the theologian.

2) I tried to describe the scope of my topic in the introduction and to establish the thesis that only religious and political groups and their diverse subdivisions such as clan, family, army, professions, construct symbols.

3) I have criticized Durkheim for attempting to turn patterns of law into symbols of the economic society in the age of industrialism.

4) You will see that I did not neglect Durkheim's basic thesis on religion, although I did not directly quote *The Elementary Forms of the Religious Life.* I recognized the validity of his theory that primitive societies construct a religious frame of reference from which they derive all social obligations. But I have also criticized him for having identified "The Larger Whole" with the authority of society (my note on sociologism).

5) It was not my assignment to deal with religions, specifically, but rather with the general process of society. The process of social action can be seen by the sociologist in two different ways. He can assume that the individual is the very reality, and society a construction of art. Or he can start from the hypothesis that the Collective Conscience is the true reality and the individual its agent. Both positions imply specific forms of symbolism.

There is a pattern of individualistic sociology which is represented by Hobbes, Tarde, Simmel, and Dupréel. Goethe might be added to this group of social thinkers.

I have selected Goethe's social theory, because he attempted to give a broader definition and conception of society than the other authors.

As far as Goethe's analysis of society is concerned, he saw clearly the grim conflicts between the expanding forces of the individual and the requirements of society as symbolized in laws, conventions, and social roles. These roles secure the external peace and the superficial harmony of society.

I have pointed out that this theory of coercive illusion was disastrous to all who subjected themselves to it, and I have strongly emphasized what Goethe's subjection to such symbols implied for the truth of his own life.

6) The second part of my paper deals with the sociological perspective which has been developed by Durkheim and his school who presuppose the true reality of the Collective Conscience. In their analyses of the *"Situation Sociale Totale,"* they discovered the plurality of symbols which control the lives of all societies, primitive and historical alike. I have tried to make this point clear in my paper, and I have adopted Baudelaire's phrase in reference to the whole topic, including primitive and civilized societies. It is the *motto* of the *whole* paper.

7) As a student of Marcel Mauss and René Hubert, I did not see any reason why it was necessary to distinguish between magic and religion in the context of my paper. I am dealing with symbolic forms, while magic deals with techniques of coercing the divinities, not with the establishment of a context of meaning.

8) The polarity of the body and the theory of the *Homo Duplex* as described by Hertz, Mauss, and Durkheim, present a genuinely symbolic pattern of the unity in duality in a universe of meaning. This is not magic.

Mordecai M. Kaplan is, however, correct in dubbing magic the personal souvenir which I mentioned. It is a case of the degradation and corruption of a genuine symbolism to a pattern of popular magic. All genuine symbols are exposed to such deterioration. Erasmus gives overwhelming material for this process in the *Colloquies*.

9) In the third part of my paper, I dealt with the manipulation of symbols in spiritual and political revolutions. I am greatly concerned with demonstrating that the sociologist can contribute to a scientific prediction of the social process by analyzing the changes and transformations in the Images and Counterimages which the various groups of society have of one another. The student of revolutions is able to state in scientific terms the growth of a revolutionary state of mind in the establishment of extreme alternatives.

10) In the last section, I suggested a topic for a new Conference: what are the prospects of the symbolic forms in an age of rapidly expanding technology and of quantitative methods.

CHAPTER VII

Symbol, Reality and Society

By ALFRED SCHUTZ

> Do not interpretations belong to God?
>
> Genesis 40.8

Contents

I) *Introductory Remarks*

1) *Some controversial points in the present discussion of signs and symbols*

Present day discussion of the problem of symbolic reference shows several bewildering features.

a) There is first a group of terms, such as "mark," "indication," "sign," "symbol," etc., which, in spite of the efforts of the best minds, seem to resist any attempt toward a precise definition. The customary distinction between natural and conventional signs makes it possible to subsume under these terms phenomena as different as the halo around the moon indicating rain, the footprint of an animal, the ringing of a buzzer, a traffic light, characters used in musical notation, gestures of approval, and so on. The term "symbol" is used for designating no less heterogeneous phenomena: names or linguistic expressions are considered as symbols, but also the lion is called the symbol of courage, the circle a symbol of eternity, the cross a Christian symbol of salvation, the flåg a symbol of a nation, the letter *O* a symbol of oxygen, *Moby Dick* or Kafka's *The Trial* a symbol of the human condition. But even more: according to some authors the formation of a scientific theory, the rain-dance of the Zunis, the role of the Queen in the British Commonwealth can be denoted by the term "symbol."

b) Secondly, if there seems to be some agreement that man, in the words of Cassirer, is an *"animal symbolicum,"* there is no agreement whatsoever about where the process called symbolization starts in human thinking. Some authors, such as A. N. Whitehead in his book on *Symbolism*[1] as well as in *Process and Reality,*[2] see the origin of symbolic reference in perception, namely, in the integration of percepta in the mode of presentational immediacy with percepta in the mode of causal efficacy in our commonsense perception. Charles Morris in his book *Signs, Language and Behavior*[3] defines a sign (and he uses this term as a more general one) as something that directs behavior with respect to something that is not at the moment a stimulus. The particular event or object, such as a sound or a mark, that functions as a sign is called the sign-vehicle; the organism, for which something is a sign, the inter-preter; anything that would permit the completion of the response se-quence to which the interpreter is disposed because of a sign, its deno-tatum; and the conditions under which the sign denotes, its significatum. If the sign is produced by its interpreter and acts as substitute for some other sign with which it is synonymous, it is called a symbol, otherwise a signal.

To C. J. Ducasse[4] a sign-relation is not independent of the mind but essentially psychological in character. Interpretation is a kind of mental event, consisting in this, that consciousness of something causes us to become conscious of something else. Interpretanda are either signs or symbols. A sign proper begets an opinion or leads us to assert a proposi-tion, whereas a symbol merely leads the mind to think of something else without a proposition.

[1]Alfred North Whitehead, *Symbolism, its Meaning and Effect* (Barbour Page Lectures, University of Virginia), The Macmillan Company, New York, 1927, chap. I.
[2]Alfred North Whitehead, *Process and Reality, An Essay in Cosmology* (Gifford Lectures), The Macmillan Company, New York, 1929, part II, chap. VIII.
[3]Charles W. Morris, *Signs, Language and Behavior,* Prentice Hall, New York, 1946, pp. 345 ff.
[4]C. J. Ducasse in two articles, "Symbols, Signs and Signals," *Journal of Symbolic Logic,* vol. IV, 1939, and "Some Comments on C. W. Morris' 'Foundations of the Theory of Signs,'" *Philosophy and Phenomenological Research,* vol. III, 1942, pp. 43 ff.

John Wild[5] criticizes the theories of both Morris and Ducasse for interpreting sign-relations as causes and not as objects of knowledge. Both have disregarded the fact that a natural sign (for example, "Smoke is a sign of fire") is *really* connected with its signatum irrespective of its effect on us; on the other hand, there are certain natural signs, such as concepts and imaginative images, which are formal signs, that is, their whole nature is to signify, to specify the noetic faculty by something other than themselves. Formal signs are *nothing but* signs, whereas it is characteristic for the other natural signs, called instrumental signs, that their whole being is not exhausted in their signifying function. (Smoke is certainly more than a sign of fire.) Arbitrary signs, in contrast to natural ones, are not "really" connected with what they signify. Wild's general definition of the nature of the sign-relation is that a sign is anything capable of manifesting something other than itself as an object to the knowing faculty.

Ernst Cassirer[6] distinguishes signs (or signals), which are operators and part of the physical world of being, from symbols, which are designators and part of the human world of meaning. The former, even when understood and used as signals, have, nevertheless, a sort of physical or substantial being, whereas symbols have only functional value. Signs or signals are related to the thing to which they refer in a fixed and unique way, whereas the human symbol is not rigid and inflexible, but mobile. To Susanne K. Langer,[7] who follows Cassirer's theories to a considerable extent, a sign indicates the existence—past, present, or future—of a thing, event, or condition. Signs are proxies for their objects, which they announce to the subjects, and the sign-relation is, thus, a triadic one: subject, sign, and object. Symbols, however, are vehicles for the *conception* of objects; it is the conception and not the things that symbols directly "mean." For this reason, any symbolic function requires four terms: subject, symbol, conception, and object, it being understood that not the act of conceiving but what is conceived enters into the meaning pattern. Like Cassirer, Mrs. Langer considers the name as the simplest type of

---

[5]John Wild, "Introduction to the Phenomenology of Signs," *Philosophy and Phenomenological Research*, vol. VIII, 1947, pp. 217 ff. See also Ducasse's rejoinder in the same issue.

[6]Ernst Cassirer, *An Essay on Man*, Yale University Press, New Haven, 1944, pp. 32–35.

[7]Susanne K. Langer, *Philosophy in a New Key*, Harvard University Press, Cambridge, 1942, now also as Penguin Book, Penguin Books, Inc., New York, 1942, chap. 2–4.

symbol for the thing named and calls this complex relationship the denotation of the symbol, whereas the more direct relationship of the symbol to the associated conceptions it conveys is called its connotation. It seems that Mrs. Langer in her last book, *Feeling and Form*,[8] has extended her definition of "symbol." A symbol is now any device whereby we are enabled to make an abstraction.[9]

The preceding summary of a few theories concerned with the problem of significative or symbolic reference, although dealing merely with some samples of proposed approaches, is bewildering enough and strongly suggests that the difficulties of finding a unified approach are not of a mere terminological nature. A brief examination of two additional groups of controversial problems reinforces this suspicion.

c) As we have seen, most of the writers deal with the (real or psychological) relationship between sign and signatum or symbol and meaning. However, it is controversial whether the relationship between the two members of the pair is reversible or not. According to Whitehead the mere fact that a common element underlies both terms within which the symbolic reference is established does not in itself decide which shall be symbol and which meaning. There are no components of experience which are only symbols or only meanings. Symbolic reference holds between two components in a complex experience, each capable of direct recognition. The more usual symbolic reference is from the less primitive component as symbol to the more primitive one as meaning.[10] According to Mrs. Langer, if it were not for the subject or interpretant, sign and object would be interchangeable. Thunder may just as well be a sign that there has been lightning, as lightning may signify that there will be thunder. In themselves they are merely correlated. It is only where one is perceptible and the other (harder or impossible to perceive) is *interesting* that we actually have a case of *signification belonging to a term*.[11] According to Wild, we take that member of the pair as a sign which is better known to us than its signatum and, therefore, *as a sign,* dissimilar to it. The footprint of the animal is more knowable than the animal. However, the sign may really signify the signatum when neither the one nor the other is actually known. Signs are discovered, not made.[12]

[8]Susanne K. Langer, *Feeling and Form*, Charles Scribner's Sons, New York, 1953.
[9]*Ibid.*, p. xi.
[10]Whitehead, *Symbolism, its Meaning and Effect*, p. 10.
[11]Langer, *Philosophy in a New Key*, Penguin edition, p. 47.
[12]Wild, *loc. cit.*, pp. 227–230.

Yet in spite of these authors who defend the thesis of the interchange-ability of signs with their signatum (at least with respect to "natural" signs), commonsense thinking refuses to admit that fire may be a sign for smoke, pain the sign for moaning, the physical object the sign of the concept. The dilemma becomes especially complicated as soon as language is taken into consideration. The problem was clearly stated by Aristotle in the beginning of *De Interpretatione* (16a4 ff.): "Spoken words are the symbols (Aristotle uses here the term *'symbola'*) of mental experience and written words are the symbols of spoken words. Just as all men do not have the same writing, so all men do not have the same speech sounds, but the mental experiences (*'pathēmata tēs psychēs'*) which these directly symbolize (here Aristotle does not use as before the term *'symbolon'* but *'semeion,'* that is, sign) are the same for all as also are those things of which our experiences are the images (*homoiomata*)." We have here the rather complicated relationship: physical event (sound or penstrokes on paper) denoting the thing named, connoting the conception referred to. These are most certainly irreversible relations. The same holds good for all symbolic references of a higher order.

d) Another controversial question is that of the intersubjective character of signs in the broadest sense. For the purpose of the present discussion we wish to disregard the behavioristic thesis so ingeniously defended by George H. Mead, Charles Morris, and others. We are, therefore, not concerned with the signal functions of certain signs, nor with the—otherwise eminently interesting—problem of so-called animal language. We follow Aristotle's statement that "a name is a sound significant by convention (*kata synthēkēn*)" (*De Interpretatione*, 16a19). Aristotle explains that this limitation is necessary because nothing is by nature a name, it is only so when it becomes a symbol (16a26 f.). And he adds that inarticulate sounds, such as those which brutes produce, are significant, yet none of these constitutes a name (*onoma*). According to Aristotle, therefore, language and artificial signs in general are matters of conventions. But the concept of convention presupposes the existence of society and also the possibility of some communication with the help of which the "convention" can be established.

Our question is now a more general one: does this statement hold good also for other than linguistic signs? Or for all signs other than natural ones? Or even perhaps for the latter? Or still more generally:

if it is true, as it is widely believed, that any sign or symbol-relation involves at least three terms, of which one is the subject of the interpreter, is this interpreter tacitly assumed to have already established communication with his fellow man so that the sign or symbol-relation is from the outset a public one? Or, are sign or symbol-relations possible within the private psychological or spiritual life of the lonely individual? If so, to what extent can they be shared? Are my fantasies, my dreams, and the symbolic system involved therein also capable of socialization? Does artistic creation, religious experience, philosophizing presuppose intersubjectivity? If, on the other hand, there are private and public symbols, does a particular sociocultural environment influence the structure of either or both of them and to what extent? Is it not possible that what is a sign or a symbol for one individual or one group has no significative or symbolic meaning to another? Moreover, can intersubjectivity as such, society and community as such, be experienced otherwise than by the use of a symbol? Then, is it the symbol which creates society and community, or is the symbol a creation of society imposed upon the individual? Or is this interrelationship between society and the system of symbols a process of such kind that symbols, or at least some of them, originate in society and, once established, influence in turn the structure of society itself?

2) *Plan of the following investigation*

This group of problems will be the particular concern of the present paper, although it would, of course, be futile to hope to do more than arrive at a highly incomplete catalogue of open questions. But even this modest task cannot be accomplished without some preparatory work which we propose to perform in three steps.

Our first step will be concerned with the question how it happens that in ordinary language, as well as in philosophical discussion, so many heterogeneous ideas are clustered around a set of terms (sign, symbol, mark, indication, etc.) aimed at denoting the significative or symbolic reference. If we encounter a synonymy of such extent we have, of course, the duty of determining as clearly and unequivocally as possible the meaning of each term used in the discussion. Nearly all the writers on this topic have made such an attempt, but as our introductory remarks have shown, without arriving at any consensus. Yet there is a second task involved, namely, to try to find the ground of such a state of affairs, that is, the basic features common to the various conceptualizations; moreover, if this can be done, to demonstrate (by sketching a kind of typology of their possible interpretations) that many controversial views defended by various writers result from the application of different schemes of interpretation to the same basic phenomenon which is, we believe, the phenomenon of appresentation studied by Husserl. His teachings will be connected with Bergson's theory of multiple orders. It is hoped that this discussion will help us to establish certain principles governing all kinds of sign and symbol-relations which might be helpful for the discussion of more concrete problems.

Our second step will deal with the investigation of the motives which lead a man to the use and development of significative and symbolic relations in order to obtain knowledge of the world he lives in, of his fellow men, and of himself. In a very sketchy way we will have to deal in this section with certain basic problems of philosophical anthropology, namely, the place of man in a cosmos which transcends his existence, but within which he has to find his bearings. Signs and symbols, so we propose to show, are among the means by which man tries to come to terms with his manifold experiences of transcendency. We will have to describe how the perceptible world actually given to the individual at any moment of his biographical existence carries its open horizons of space and time which transcend the actual Here and Now; and we will have to show how the communicative common environment originates in the comprehension of fellow men, how society transcends in still another sense the individual's actual experiences.

We submit that a specific form of appresentational relations—called marks, indications, signs—corresponds to each of these particular transcendencies. They all have in common the fact that they are experienced within the reality of everyday life. But this is not the only reality in which man lives. There are other transcendencies beyond those mentioned so far. In a third step we will, starting from a theory proposed by William James, briefly consider the multiple realities, or "subuniverses," such as the world of religion, of art, and of science, that can only be experienced in a particular form of appresentation for which we reserve the term symbol. We will study the function of the symbolic relation on some of these various levels of reality and as means for interconnecting one level with another. For we will find that the world of everyday life, the commonsense world, has a paramount position among the various provinces of reality, since only within it does communication with our fellow men become possible. But the commonsense world is from the outset a sociocultural world, and the many questions connected with the intersubjectivity of the symbolic relations originate within it, are determined by it, and find their solution within it.

II) *Appresentation as the General Form of Significative and Symbolic Relations*

1) *Husserl's Concept of Appresentation*

If we try to find the common denominator of the various theories on significative and symbolic relations studied in the previous section, we may say that the object, fact, or event called sign or symbol refers to something other than itself. Smoke is a physical thing given to our sensory perception. It can be seen and smelled and chemically analyzed. But if we take smoke not as a mere physical object, but as an indication of fire, then we take it as manifesting something other than itself. Calling smoke the sign and the indicated fire the signatum, as some of our authors do, we may say that both form a pair.

Husserl, in the later period of his life,[13] studied the general phenomenon of pairing or coupling which is, according to him, a general feature of our consciousness. It is a form of passive synthesis which is commonly called association. It is beyond the scope of this paper to embark upon a presentation of the phenomenological interpretation of association. We restrict ourselves to the discussion of that particular form of pairing or coupling, which Husserl calls "appresentation" or "analogical apperception." The most primitive case of a coupling or pairing association is characterized by the fact that two or more data are intuitively given in the unity of consciousness, which, by this very

[13]Edmund Husserl, *Cartesianische Meditationen* (*Husserliana* I), Nijhoff, Haag, 1950 (French Version, "*Méditations Cartésiennes,*" Colin, Paris, 1931), especially V. *Méditation,* sec. 49–54; see also *Ideen II* (*Husserliana* IV), Nijhoff, Haag, 1952, esp. sec. 44–47, sec. 50 (with supplement p. 410), sec. 51. esp. p. 198. See also Marvin Farber, *The Foundation of Phenomenology,* Harvard University Press, Cambridge, 1943, pp. 529 ff., esp. p. 532.

reason, constitutes two distinct phenomena as a unity, regardless of whether or not they are attended to.

Let us take as an illustration our perception of an object of the outer world. We may say that in immediate apperception the thing is perceived as this or that object, perspectively shortened and adumbrated, etc. Here it is, in copresence with us, and through acts of immediate intuition we intuit the object as a "self." Yet, strictly speaking, if we apperceive an object of the outer world, then that which we really see in our visual perception is merely the frontside of the object. But this perception of the visible frontside of the object involves an apperception by analogy of the unseen backside, an apperception which, to be sure, is a more or less empty anticipation of what we might perceive if we turned the object around or if we walked around the object. This anticipation is based on our past experiences of normal objects of this kind. From the apperception of the frontside we believe that this object is a wooden cube of red color, and we expect that the unseen backside will be of the same shape, color, and material. But it is quite possible that our anticipation will be disappointed. It may turn out that the unseen backside is deformed, of iron, and blue. Nevertheless the unseen side will have *some* shape, *some* color, and consist of *some* material. At any rate, we may say that the frontside, which is apperceived in immediacy or given to us in presentation, appresents the unseen backside in an analogical way, which, however, does not mean by way of an *inference* by analogy. The appresenting term, that which is present in immediate apperception, is coupled or paired with the appresented term.

This is, however, just an example in order to make the problem of appresentation understandable. In his *Logical Investigation* VI (sec. 14 f. and 26)[14] and in the first volume of his *Ideas* (sec. 43)[15] Husserl has already shown that all significative relations are special cases of this form of analogical apperception or appresentation which is based upon the general phenomenon of pairing or coupling. To be sure, in these earlier writings Husserl's terminology was a somewhat different one. But he states quite clearly that if we perceive an object of the outer world as a self, no apprehension on a higher level, that is, no appre-

[14]Edmund Husserl, *Logische Untersuchungen*, vol. II, part II, Niemayer, Halle, 2nd ed., 1920; see Farber, *op. cit.*, pp. 410–415, and 430 f.

[15]Edmund Husserl, *Ideas*, vol. I, translated by Boyce Gibson, The Macmillan Company, New York, 1931, pp. 135 f.

sentational references are built up on the basis of this apprehending act of intuition. On the other hand, in the case of a significative relation, we have the appresenting object as perceived in the intuitive field, but we are not directed toward it, but through the medium of a secondary apprehension or a *"fundiertes Auffassen"* toward something else which is indicated or, in Husserl's later terminology, appresented by the first object. Thus, by appresentation, we experience intuitively something as indicating or depicting significantly something else.

Experience by appresentation has its particular style of confirmation: each appresentation carries along its particular appresented horizons, which refer to further fulfilling and confirming experiences, to systems of well ordered indications, including new potentially confirmable syntheses and new nonintuitive anticipations.

This is, however, only half the story. So far we have tacitly presupposed that appresentation requires copresence of the appresenting with the appresented member of the pair. This, however, is just a special case of a more general situation. In his study *Experience and Judgment* (secs. 34–43)[16] Husserl has shown that a passive synthesis of pairing is also possible between an actual perception and a recollection, between a perception and a fantasm (*fictum*), and thus between actual and potential experiences, between the apprehension of facts and possibilities. The passive synthesis of association here involved brings it about that the apprehension of a present element of a previously constituted pair "wakens" or "calls forth" the appresented element, it being immaterial whether one or the other is a perception, a recollection, a fantasm, or a fictum. All this happens, in principle, in pure passivity without any active interference of the mind. To give an example: the present percept "wakens" submerged recollections which then "start rising," whether or not we want them to do so. And, even further, according to Husserl, any active remembering takes place on the basis of an associative wakening that had occurred previously. In general, by the functioning of the passive synthesis a unity of intuition is constituted not only between perceptions and recollections, but also between perceptions and fantasms.

So far Husserl. It seems to us that Husserl's theory of appresentation covers all cases of significative and symbolic references dealt with by

[16]Edmund Husserl, *Erfahrung und Urteil,* edited by L. Landgrebe, Acadamia Verlag Buchhandlung, Prague, 1939, pp. 174–223.

the various authors discussed before. In all these cases an object, fact, or event is not experienced as a "self," but as standing for another object which is not given in immediacy to the experiencing subject. The appresenting member "wakens" or "calls for" or "evokes" the appresented one. The latter may be either a physical event, fact, or object which, however, is not perceivable to the subject in immediacy, or something spiritual or immaterial; it may be real in the sense of commonsense reality, or a fantasm; it may be simultaneous with the appresenting one or precede or follow it, or it may even be timeless. These appresentational relations may occur on various levels: an appresented object may in turn appresent another one, there are signs of signs, and symbols of symbols, etc. Moreover, the appresenting immediate experience need by no means consist in the perception of the physical object: it may be a recollection, a fantasm, a dream, etc.

2) *The various orders involved in the appresentational situation*

We have, however, to go a step further. So far we have directed our attention merely to the pair formed by the appresenting and the appresented object, as if neither were interconnected with other objects. There is, however, neither in immediate nor in analogical apprehension such a thing as an isolated object of which I could have an isolated experience. Each object is an object within a field; each experience carries along its horizon; both belong to an order of a particular style. The physical object, for example, is interconnected with all the other objects of Nature, present, past, and future, by spatial, temporal, and causal relations, whose sum-total constitutes the order of physical Nature. A mathematical object, say, an equilateral triangle, refers to all the axioms and theorems, by which this mathematical object is defined and to all the theorems, etc., which are based on the concepts of triangularity and equilaterality, of a regular polygon, or of a geometrical figure in general. The same holds good for any kind of object and our experiences of it. There is even an order of our fantasms and an intrinsic order of our dreams which separates them from all the other realms, and constitutes them as a finite province of meaning.

We will have to revert to this problem later on (Section VI of this paper). For the time being we have to consider that in the relationship of coupling either member of the pair is merely one object within an order which includes other objects pertaining to the same realm. If the appresenting object is a physical thing of nature, then it is connected with all the other physical objects, events, and occurrences within the realm of nature. And, in a like manner, there is also an interrelationship between the appresented objects and other objects pertaining to the same order as the appresented one.

We are, consequently, led to the conclusion that in any appresentational reference a relationship between several orders is involved. This is obvious if the appresenting object is a physical thing (say, a flag), whereas the appresented object belongs to another realm (the republic for which it stands). But brief deliberation will show that there are also several orders involved if both the appresenting and the appresented objects belong to the *same* realm, say, if both are physical things of the outer world. Smoke and fire are both physical things, perceptible by our senses. But being paired with the unseen fire, that is, in its appresentational reference, the physical thing "smoke" is not interpreted as this or that perceived object in the intuitive field toward which we are directed, but as a carrier or vehicle or medium of a secondary apprehension which is directed toward something else, namely, the fire indicated by the smoke. Thus, we find in this simple relation several orders involved. But even this is not enough. In higher forms of appresentational references I may know that an object refers appresentationally to another one, but either without knowing the nature of this appresentational reference, that is, the context established by it, or (even if I know the context) without being able to establish the synthesis of pairing the appresenting objects with the particular appresented one. I find, for example, in a catalogue of a bookseller some items marked with an "*." I know that the character "*" is generally used as reference to a footnote. But there is no footnote and I am at a loss as to what this sign means. Or I may recognize certain patterns of inkstrokes on paper as Chinese ideograms or as Gregg shorthand, without being capable of reading them. Appresentational references of a higher degree also presuppose, therefore, a knowledge of the order within which the pairing itself occurs.

In general, we may state that in any appresentational situation the following four orders are involved:

a) the order of objects to which the immediately apperceived object belongs if experienced as a self, disregarding any appresentational references. We shall call this order the *"apperceptual scheme."*

b) the order of objects to which the immediately apperceived object belongs if taken not as a self but as a member of an appresentational pair, thus referring to something other than itself. We shall call this order the *"appresentational scheme."*

c) the order of objects to which the appresented member of the pair belongs which is apperceived in a merely analogical manner. We shall call this order the *"referential scheme."*

d) the order to which the particular appresentational reference itself belongs, that is, the particular type of pairing or context by which the appresenting member is connected with the appresented one, or, more generally, the relationship which prevails between the appresentational and the referential scheme. We shall call this order the *"contextual or interpretational scheme."*

Now in describing an appresentational relationship we may take any of these orders as our home base, as our starting point, as our system of reference, or, to use the term of Husserl, we may "live in" any of these orders. Of course, we may at any time substitute one system of reference for another and, in the natural attitudes of daily life, we indeed continuously do so. But while we attend to one of these schemes as the basic order, the other schemes seem to be characterized by arbitrariness, contingency, or even by a want or absence of order.

3) *Bergson's theory of concurring orders*

Bergson has studied the problem of the absence of order in a famous section of his *Creative Evolution* entitled: *"Les deux ordres et le désordre"* ("The two orders and the disorder").[17] We are here not concerned with the particular nature of the two orders established in the system of Bergson's philosophy, namely, the spontaneous order of life *versus* the automatic order of the intellect. We are, however, much interested in his interpretation of the relationship between several coexisting orders. Bergson starts from the examination of the notion of disorder and comes to the conclusion that what we call "disorder" is merely the want or absence of a particular kind of order we expected and to which any other order appears just a contingent arrangement. This can be illustrated by the use we make in daily life of the notion of disorder. What do we mean if we enter a bedroom and say, "it is in disorder"? The position of each object can be explained by the auto-

[17]Henri Bergson, *Evolution créatrice*, Alcan, Paris, chap. III, pp. 238–244, and 252–258.

matic movements of the persons who inhabited this room or by the efficient causes, whatever they may be, which put each piece of furniture or clothing, etc., in its place. All this occurs strictly in accordance with the order of physical causality. But we are simply not interested in this kind of order if we expected to find a tidy room. What we expected to find is the human orderliness of appropriate, although arbitrary, arrangements of things in the room. If, on the other hand, we imagine Chaos, we have in mind a state in the world of physical nature which is not subject to the laws of physics but in which events emerge and disappear in an arbitrary way. In this case we apply to the world of nature the principles of human (and this is arbitrary) order, replacing *"l'ordre automatique"* by *"l'ordre volu."* Absence of order in the sense of absence of *any kind of order at all* is, therefore, says Bergson, a meaningless expression, and refers only to the fact that an expected *particular* kind of order is wanting. Yet, this implies that another kind of order, irreducible to the former, prevails. One order is, however, necessarily contingent with reference to the other. And Bergson comes to the conclusion that the geometrical order is merely the suppression of the spontaneous order, a suppression required by certain necessities of our practical life.

4) *Application of Bergson's theory to some controversial opinions concerning signs and symbols*

Let us apply Bergson's findings to our problem of the various schemes of orders involved in the appresentational reference. We stated that we may interpret the appresentational relation by taking either the apperceptual, appresentational, referential, or contextual scheme as a system of reference. In doing so the selected system of reference becomes the prototype of order. Seen from it, all the other schemes have seemingly the character of arbitrariness and mere contingency. This is important in several respects if applied to the particular appresentational forms generally referred to by the terms "signs" and "symbols." It explains also certain controversial theories proposed for the solution of the problems involved.

It is the common opinion of nearly all otherwise highly dissident authors that all sign- or symbol-relations are of at least a triadic character, involving not only the sign or symbol and the object for which it stands, but also the mind of the interpreter (or the interpretant's thought) for whom the significative or symbolic relation exists. Now it is obvious that not only the philosopher, who tries to describe the sign-symbol relation, but also the interpreter, who lives in it, has a certain, although limited, freedom to select one of the schemes as a basic system of reference for interpreting the significative or symbolic relation. This becomes of particular importance if the Bergsonian idea of the relativity of systems of orders is taken into account. It leads to the conclusion that what is sign or symbol for one individual (or, as we will later see, for one social group) might be without any significance for another.

Furthermore, we pointed out that several authors are of the opinion that the relationship between sign and signatum is principally reversible. It follows from Bergson's interpretation of the relativity of several orders that the question of which member of the pair is taken as a sign and which as a signatum depends first upon the decision of whether the appresentational or the referential scheme is taken as system of reference, and second upon the particular contextual scheme by which the appresentational scheme is related to the others.

Moreover, Bergson's theory seems to explain the customary distinction between natural and arbitrary (or conventional) signs. This distinction implies that a particular scheme was chosen as system of reference, as a prototype of the appresentational relationship. The so-called "real relation" underlying natural signs consists in the fact that both, sign and signatum, are events within the physical world of nature. The same apperceptual scheme, then, is actually applicable to the sign and potentially to the signatum. Or in other words, those authors who—and rightly—see that a triadic relationship including the interpreter has to be established, hold that in the case of natural signs the appresentational scheme coincides with the referential one, whereas the interpretational scheme is merely taken for granted. In the case of arbitrary signs, however, the interpretational scheme has to be taken as a basic system of reference.

Finally, those authors who maintain that all conceptualizations are as such already symbols or signs and those who believe that in addition imaginative images have to be considered as signs, take the referential scheme as the basic system, and interpret the paired elements belonging to the apperceptual scheme in terms of context.

The preceding all too condensed remarks try to show that the prevailing confusion in dealing with the group of phenomena designated by terms such as signs and symbols, is not entirely of a terminological origin. It emanates, at least partially, from the possibility of choosing either the apperceptual or the appresentational, the referential or even the interpretational scheme involved as a basic order from which the others have to be explained. But the interpreter having once made a decision to consider one of those schemes as the archetype of order, sees the other schemes as merely contingent, arbitrary arrangements, or as wanting in all order. This is at least one of the reasons why it is generally maintained that signs and symbol-relationships are essentially ambiguous.

5) *The principles governing structural changes of appresentational relations*

Another reason for the essential ambiguity of appresentational relations consists in the fact that higher forms of appresentational references are especially subject to an internal structural change. Without entering into all the implications involved here, we want to mention three principles by which this internal structural change is governed.

A) *The principle of the relative irrelevance of the vehicle*

This principle means that an appresented object X, which was originally paired with an appresenting object A, might enter a new pairing with an object B, which will henceforth appresent X. The new vehicle B, if apprehended (remembered, fantasied) in copresence will "waken" or "call forth" in the mind of the experiencing subject the same appresented object X which formerly was paired with the original vehicle A. This principle explains several otherwise bewildering phenomena:

a) The meaning of a scientific paper is independent of whether it is printed in this or that typographical style, written in typescript or longhand, or read aloud to an audience. To the patriot the meaning of his national anthem remains unchanged whether it is sung in any particular key or played on any particular instrument.

b) The possibility of substituting one vehicle for another is one pre-requisite—but only one—for translating the same appresentational con-tent—at least to a certain extent—from one sign system to another one (London, Londres; two, *deux, duo, zwei,* etc.)[18]

c) If the pairing of the appresented object *X* with the new vehicle *B* takes place, two cases are possible:

i) *either* the original appresenting vehicle *A* is preserved and con-tinues beside the new one (*B*) in its appresentational functions. Then both the former (*A*) and the new vehicle (*B*) will become *"synonyms"* in the broadest, not merely linguistic, sense of this term. Both will evoke the same appresented object *X* (ship—vessel; leap—jump; but also 10 and ten, MDCCCCLIV and 1954, *Fer* and iron, etc.);

ii) *or* the appresented object *X* may become detached from the orig-inally appresenting one (*A*) with which it formed a pair, in which case the original appresentational reference may become obfuscated or entirely forgotten. If this happens the former vehicle ceases to "waken" the appresented object: although it might be preserved in a more or less ritualistic way, it loses its significance. For example, many *surahs* of the Koran begin with a number of disconnected letters of the Arabic alphabet, whose significance is no longer understood.

B) *The principle of variability of the appresentational meaning*

The same situation prevails here as in i, but the appresentational meaning changes with the substitution of *A* by *B* although the ap-presented object *X* remains the same. Husserl[19] has already shown and Ogden and Richards[20] came to the same result, namely, that, for in-stance, several proper names may have different meanings but name the same object. The Commander in Chief of the Allied Armies on D Day, 1944, the author of the book *Crusade in Europe,* the actual President of the United States, are all proper names denoting Dwight D. Eisenhower, but each appresentational reference is a different one.

---

[18]Husserl, *Logische Untersuchungen,* vol. I, sec. 12; Farber, *loc. cit.,* p. 229.
[19]*Ibid.,* "The victor of Jena" and "the one who was defeated at Waterloo."
[20]C. K. Ogden and I. A. Richards, *The Meaning of Meaning,* Kegan Paul, London, 1946, p. 92: "The King of England" and "the owner of Buckingham Palace."

The expressions, "an equilateral triangle" and an "equiangular triangle," denote the same geometrical figure but have different appresentational meanings. The same situation refers to relations such as $A>B$ and $B<A$, and although in terms of geography and transportation, of milestones and signposts, the road which connects Paris and Chartres is identical, regardless of whether we follow it in one direction or the other, Péguy,[21] to whom Chartres is the symbol of French Catholicism, has to deny that the road leading to Chartres can be termed identical with the road leading away from it.

C) *The principle of figurative transference*

This principle is the opposite of the principle of the relative irrelevance of the vehicle: an appresenting object A, originally paired with the appresented object X, enters into a new pairing with an appresented object Y, eventually also with a third object Z, etc. Again two cases are possible:

    a) *either* the original appresentational reference $(A\text{-}X)$ is preserved and continues to coexist with the new one $(A\text{-}Y)$. One single appresenting object (A) may then appresent two or more objects $(X, Y, \ldots)$. This is the origin of any form of tropes in the broadest, not merely linguistic, sense and of the figurative use of the originally appresented object. This case is of particular importance: on the one hand, it leads to the equivocal use of the appresenting term $A;$ on the other hand it makes the construction of higher levels of appresentational relations possible.

    b) *or* the original appresentational reference $(A\text{-}X)$ is obfuscated or entirely forgotten, and merely the new one $(A\text{-}Y)$ preserved: this is the phenomenon of the "shift of meaning," well known to all students of signs or symbols in whatever form. For example, the circle, but also the serpent rolled into a circle, becomes a symbol of eternity because, like eternity, it has no beginning and no end.

The three principles just discussed will prove to be useful if applied to more concrete problems. In order to prepare their study we will now pass to our second step, the investigation of the motives which lead men to the use and development of symbolic relations.

[21]Charles Péguy, *Note conjointe sur la philosophie bergsonienne et la philosophie cartésienne,* Gallimard, Paris, 1935, pp. 312 ff.

III) *The World Within My Reach and Its Dimensions, Marks, and Indications*

1) *The world within my actual and potential reach and the manipulatory sphere*

We start our analysis with the description of the situation in which I find myself within the world at any moment of my everyday life, intentionally disregarding at this level the existence of fellow men and of society. Through my natural attitude I take this world for granted as my reality. I have to understand it to the extent necessary to come to terms with it, to act within it and upon it, and to carry out my projects at hand. In this sense the world is given to my experience and to my interpretation. This interpretation is based upon a stock of my previous experiences which in the form of "knowledge at hand" functions as a scheme of reference. To this knowledge at hand belongs also my knowledge that the world I live in is not a mere aggregate of colored spots, incoherent noises, centers of warm and cold, but a world of well circumscribed objects with definite qualities, objects among which I move, which resist me, and upon which I may act. From the outset these objects are experienced in their typicality:[22] as mountains and stones, trees and animals, and, more specifically, as birds and fishes and snakes.

This world as experienced through my natural attitude is the scene and also the object of my actions. I have to dominate it and change it in order to carry out my purposes. My bodily movements—kinesthetic, locomotive, operative—gear, so to speak, into the world, modifying or changing its objects and their mutual interrelationship. On the other hand, these objects offer resistance to my acts, which I have either to overcome or to which I have to yield. In this sense it may be correctly said that a pragmatic motive governs my natural attitude in daily life.

In this attitude I experience the world as organized in space and time around myself as a center. The place my body occupies at a certain moment within this world, my actual "Here" is the starting point from

[22]See Husserl, *Erfahrung und Urteil*, sec. 18–22; see also Alfred Schutz, "Common-sense and Scientific Interpretation of Human Action," *Philosophy and Phenomenological Research*, vol. XIV, 1953, pp. 1–38, esp. pp. 5 f.; also "Language, Language-disturbances, and the Texture of Mind," *Social Research*, vol. 17, 1950, esp. pp. 384–390.

which I take my bearing in space. It is, so to speak, the center *"O"* of a system of coordinates which determines certain dimensions of orientation in the surrounding field and the distances and perspectives of the objects therein: they are above or underneath, before or behind, right or left, nearer or farther. And, in a similar way, my actual *"Now"* is the origin of all the time-perspectives under which I organize the events within the world, such as the categories of fore and aft, past and future, simultaneity and succession, sooner or later, etc.

This sector of the world of perceived and perceptible objects at whose center I am shall be called *the world within my actual reach,* which includes, thus, the objects within the scope of my view and the range of my hearing. Inside this field within my reach there is a region of things which I can manipulate. (It is hoped that this highly sketchy characterization will be sufficient for the purpose of this paper. The problem involved is more complicated, especially at a time when by the possibility of using long range rockets the manipulatory sphere may be extended beyond the world within my reach. The spreading of the manipulatory sphere is perhaps one of the outstanding characteristics of the actual state of Western civilization.)

The manipulatory sphere[23] is the region open to my immediate interference which I can modify either directly by movements of my body or with the help of artificial extensions of my body, that is, by tools and instruments in the broadest sense of this term. The manipulatory zone is that portion of the outer world upon which I can actually act. In a certain sense it might be said that the part of the world within my reach which does not belong to the manipulatory zone transcends it: it constitutes the zone of my potential manipulations or, as we prefer to call it, of my potential working acts.[24] Of course, these realms have no rigid frontiers; to each belong specific halos and open horizons, and there are even "enclaves" within "foreign territory." It is also clear that this whole system "world within my actual reach," including the manipulatory area, undergoes changes by any of my locomotions; by displacing my body I shift the center *O* of my system of coordinates to

[23]It is the great merit of G. H. Mead to have shown that the "manipulatory area" constitutes the core of reality. See his *Philosophy of the Present,* Open Court Publishing Company, Chicago, 1932, pp. 124 ff.; *The Philosophy of the Act,* University of Chicago Press, Chicago, 1938, pp. 103–106, 121 ff., 151 f., 190–192, 196–197, 282–284.

[24]Regarding the concept of "working," see Alfred Schutz, "On Multiple Realities," *Philosophy and Phenomenological Research,* vol. V, 1945, pp. 533–576, esp. pp. 549 ff.

O', and this alone changes all the numbers (coordinates) pertaining to this system.

2) *Marks*

I experience the world within my actual reach as an element or phase of my unique biographical situation, and this involves a transcending of the Here and Now to which it belongs. To my unique biographical situation pertain, among many other things, my recollections of the world within my reach in the past but no longer within it since I moved from There to Here, and my anticipations of a world to come within my reach and which I must move from Here to another There in order to bring it into my reach. I know or assume that, disregarding technical obstacles and other limitations, such as the principal irretrievability of the past, I can bring my recollected world back into my actual reach if I return to whence I came (*world within restorable reach*); I expect also to find it substantially the same (although, perhaps, changed) as I had experienced it while it was within my actual reach; and I know or assume also that what is now within my actual reach will go out of my reach when I move away but will be, in principle, restorable if I later return.

The latter case is to me of an eminently practical interest. I expect that what is now within my actual reach will go out of my reach but will later on come into my actual reach again, and, especially, I anticipate that what is now in my manipulatory sphere will reenter it later and require my interference or will interfere with me. Therefore I have to be sure that I shall then find my bearings within it and come to terms with it as I can now while it is within my control. This presupposes that I shall be able to recognize those elements which I now find relevant in the world within my actual reach, especially within the manipulatory zone, and which (I assume by a general idealization, called the idealization of "I can do it again" by Husserl)[25] will prove relevant also when I return later on. I am, thus, *motivated* to single out and to *mark* certain objects. When I return I expect these marks to be useful as "subjective reminders" or "mnemonic devices" (Wild's terms).[26] It is immaterial whether such a mnemonic device consists of the breaking of the branch of a tree or the selecting of a particular

---

[25]Edmund Husserl, *Formale und transcendentale Logik*, Niemayer, Halle, 1929, sec. 74, p. 167.
[26]Wild, *op. cit.*, p. 224.

landmark to mark the trail to the waterhole. A bookmark at the page where I stopped reading or underlining certain passages of this volume or pencilstrokes on the margin are also marks or subjective reminders. What counts is merely that all these marks, themselves objects of the outer world, will from now on be intuited not as mere "selves" in the pure apperceptual scheme. They entered for me, the interpreter, into an appresentational reference. The broken branch of the tree is more than just that. It became a mark for the location of the waterhole, or, if you prefer, a signal for me to turn left. In its appresentational function, which originates in the interpretational scheme bestowed upon it by me, the broken branch is now paired with its referential meaning: "Way to the waterhole."

This mark which functions as a subjective reminder is one of the simplest forms of the appresentational relationship; it is detached from any intersubjective context. The inherently arbitrary character of my selecting certain objects as "marks" should be emphasized. The mark has "nothing to do" with what it should remind me of, both are in an interpretational context merely because such a context was established by me. According to the principle of the relative irrelevance of the vehicle, I may replace the broken branch by a stonepile, according to the principle of figurative transference, I may dedicate this stonepile to a naiad, etc.

Wild[27] sees a characteristic distinction between marks or mnemonic devices and signs in the fact that a sign might be misconstrued or misinterpreted, whereas we cannot be "misreminded" by a reminder. I cannot agree with this statement. Rereading a book I had read as a student, I find several marks on the margin whose meaning I no longer understand. Even more, I am uncertain why I found the marked passage of special interest. Why did I put a button into my pocket this morning? I tried to recall something but what it was I can no longer tell.

3) *Indications*

We mentioned before the stock of knowledge at hand as an element of my biographical situation. This stock of knowledge is by no means homogeneous. William James[28] has already distinguished between

[27] *Ibid.*

[28] William James, *Principles of Psychology,* Henry Holt & Company, New York, 1890, vol. I, p. 221.

"knowledge about" and "knowledge of acquaintance." There are, more-over, zones of blind belief and ignorance. The structuration of my stock of knowledge at hand is determined by the fact that I am not *equally* interested in all the strata of the world within my reach. The selective function of interest organizes the world for me in strata of major and minor relevance. From the world within my actual or potential reach are selected as primarily important, those facts, objects, and events which actually are or will become possible ends or means, possible obstacles or conditions for the realization of my projects, or which are or will become dangerous or enjoyable or otherwise relevant to me.

Certain facts, objects, and events are known to me as being inter-related in a more or less typical way, but my knowledge of the particular kind of interrelatedness might be rather vague or even lack transparency. If I know that event B usually appears simultaneously or precedes or follows event A, then I take this as a manifestation of a typical and plausible relationship existing between A and B, although I know nothing of the nature of this relationship. Until further notice I simply expect or take it for granted that any future recurrence of an event of type A will be connected in typically the same way with a preceding, concomitant, or subsequent recurrence of an event of type B. I may then apprehend A not as an object, fact, or event standing for itself, but standing for something else, namely, referring to the past, present or future appearance of B. Here again we have a form of pairing by appresentation which most authors subsume under the concept of sign. We prefer to reserve the term "sign" for other purposes and to call the appresentational relationship under scrutiny *indication*.

Husserl[29] has characterized this relationship of indication (*"Anzeichen"*) as follows: an object, fact, or event (A), actually perceptible to me, may be experienced as related to another past, present, or future fact or event (B), actually not perceptible to me, in such a way, that my conviction of the existence of the former (A) is experienced by me as an *opaque* motive for my conviction for, assumption of, or belief in the past, present, or future existence of the latter (B). This motivation constitutes for me a pairing between the indicating (A) and the indicated (B) elements. The indicating member of the pair is not only a

---

[29]Husserl, *Logische Untersuchungen I,* vol. II/1, sec. 1–4, esp. p. 27; Farber, *op. cit.,* p. 222.

"witness" for the indicated one, it does not only point to it, but it suggests the assumption that the other member exists, has existed, or will exist. Again the indicating member is not perceived as a "self," that is, merely in the apperceptual scheme, but as "wakening" or "calling forth" appresentationally the indicated one. It is, however, important that the particular nature of the motivational connection remain opaque. If there is clear and sufficient insight into the nature of the connection between the two elements, we have to deal not with the referential relation of indication but with the inferential one of *proof*. The qualification contained in the last statement eliminates, therefore, the possibility of calling the footprint of a tiger (recognized as such) an indication or "sign" of his presence in the locality. But the halo around the moon indicates coming rain, the smoke fire, a certain formation of the surface oil in the subsoil, a certain pigmentation of the face Addison's disease, the position of a needle on the dial of my car an empty gas tank, etc.

The relationship of indication as described covers most of the phenomena generally subsumed under the category of "natural signs." The knowledge of indications is of eminent importance from the practical point of view, because it helps the individual transcend the world within his actual reach by relating elements within it to elements outside it. The relation of indication is again an appresentational category which does not necessarily presuppose intersubjectivity.

IV) *The Intersubjective World and Its Appresentational Relations: Signs*

1) *The world of everyday life is from the outset an intersubjective one*

Marks and indications are, as we have seen, forms of appresentational relations which can be explained by the pragmatic motive governing the individual in his endeavor to come to terms with the world within his reach. These forms of appresentational references do not necessarily presuppose the existence of fellow men and the possibility of communicating with them, although they may—and indeed do—also function within the intersubjective context. So far we have analyzed the world within my reach and its dimensions by abstaining from any reference to intersubjectivity, as if I found myself in the natural attitude alone within the world of daily life.

Yet the world of my daily life is by no means my private world but is from the outset an intersubjective one, shared with my fellow men, experienced and interpreted by others; in brief, it is a world common to all of us. The unique biographical situation in which I find myself within the world at any moment of my existence is only to a very small extent of my own making. I find myself always within an historically given world which, as a world of nature as well as a sociocultural world, had existed before my birth and which will continue to exist after my death. This means that this world is not only mine but also my fellow men's environment; moreover, these fellow men are elements of my own situation, as I am of theirs. Acting upon the others and acted upon by them, I know of this mutual relationship, and this knowledge also implies that they, the others, experience the common world in a way substantially similar to mine. They, too, find themselves in a unique biographical situation within a world which is, like mine, structured in terms of actual and potential reach, grouped around their actual Here and Now at the center in the same dimensions and directions of space and time, an historically given world of nature, society, and culture, etc.

It would, of course, far surpass the purpose of the present study to enter into a detailed phenomenological analysis of the constitution of intersubjectivity. And inasmuch as we are here merely concerned with an analysis of the commonsense experience of the world in daily life, it would be sufficient to state that man takes for granted the bodily existence of fellow men, their conscious life, the possibility of intercommunication, and the historical givenness of social organization and culture, just as he takes for granted the world of nature into which he was born.

Yet having to study the appresentational relations involved in various aspects of intersubjectivity and especially in communication, we cannot forego indicating a few implications of the topic and clarifying the notion of a social world taken for granted. This, however, can be done only step by step, and we start with some brief remarks on the foundation of the relationship between the I and the other—or, as modern sociologists[30] call it, between ego and alter—without, in this section, taking into

[30]For example, Talcott Parsons and Edward A. Shils in their monograph, "Values, Motives, and Systems of Actions" in *Toward a General Theory of Action,* edited by Parsons and Shils, Harvard University Press, Cambridge, 1951, pp. 55 f.

account the fact that the world into which I was born already contained social and political organizations of a most diversified nature and that I as well as others are members of such organizations, having a particular role, status, and function within them. We intend, therefore, to consider first the appresentational references by which we obtain knowledge of another's mind, then the structuration of the commonsense world as shared with the fellow man and its inherent transcendencies, before we turn to the study of comprehension, manifestation, and communication, and of the appresentational relations upon which they are founded: the signs.

2) *Our knowledge of the other mind is itself based on appresentational references*

To discuss the age old problem of our knowledge of other minds is not within the framework of this paper; nor can we sum up the highly controversial opinions on this subject proposed by outstanding thinkers of various philosophical schools. It seems, however, that behaviorists and existentialists, logical positivists and phenomenologists agree, if we disregard the phenomenon of telepathy, that knowledge of another's mind is possible only through the intermediary of events occurring on or produced by another's body. This is, in Husserl's terminology, an outstanding case of appresentational reference. According to him,[31] the other is from the outset given to me as both a material object with its position in space and a subject with its psychological life. His body, like all other material objects, is given to my original perception or, as Husserl says, in originary presence. His psychological life, however, is not given to me in originary presence but only in copresence; it is not presented, but appresented. By the mere continuous visual perception of the other's body and its movements, a system of appresentations, of well ordered indications of his psychological life and his experiences is constituted, and here, says Husserl, is the origin of the various forms of the systems of signs, or expressions, and finally of language. The physical object "the other's body," events occurring on this body, and his bodily movements are apprehended as expressing the other's "spiritual I" toward whose motivational meaning-context I am directed. So-called "empathy" in the

---

[31]Husserl, *Cartesianische Meditationen V*, sec. 50 ff., *Ideen II*, sec. 43–50; see also Alfred Schutz, "Discussion of Edmund Husserl's Ideas Vol. II," *Philosophy and Phenomenological Research*, XIII, 1953, pp. 394–413, esp. 404 ff.

other person is nothing but that form of appresentational apprehension which grasps this meaning.

According to Husserl, this situation may also prevail with respect to what is generally called cultural objects. A book is an outer object, a material thing. I see it as it appears to me, here on my desk, to my right, etc., but reading it I am not directed toward it as an outer object but toward the meaning of what is written therein: I "live in its meaning" by comprehending it. The same holds good for a tool, a house, a theater, a temple, a machine, etc. The spiritual meaning of all these objects is appresentationally apperceived as being founded upon the actually appearing object which is not apprehended as such but as expressing its meaning. And if we listen to somebody, we do not experience the meaning of what he says as something connected with the words in an external way. We take the words apprehensively as expressing their meaning, and we live in their meaning by comprehending what the other means and the thought he expresses.[32] To be sure, everyone has only his own experiences given in originary presence. But by the intermediary of events in the outer world, occurring on or brought about by the other's body, especially by linguistic expressions in the broadest sense, I may comprehend the other by appresentation; by mutual understanding and consent a *communicative common environment is thus established,* within which the subjects reciprocally motivate one another in their mental activities.

This analysis of Husserl is modeled after one specific intersubjective relationship, namely, that which sociologists call the "face-to-face relationship."[33] In such a relationship both partners share time and space, perceiving one another, etc. It is, moreover, supposed that the mutual appresentational comprehension of events in the other's mind leads immediately to communication. All these assumptions, however, require some elaboration.

We begin with the characterization of the tacitly presupposed idealizations upon which the establishment of a "communicative common environment" in the face-to-face relationship is founded.

[32]Edmund Husserl, *"Vom Ursprung der Geometrie,"* edited by E. Fink, *Revue Internationale de Philosophie,* 1939, p. 210.

[33]The term was coined by Charles H. Cooley, *Social Organization,* Scribner, New York, 1909, chap. III–V, but used in a different sense. We designate by it merely a purely formal aspect of social relationship.

3) *The general thesis of the reciprocity of perspective*[34]

a) *The idealization of the interchangeability of standpoints*

The sector of the world within my actual reach is centered around my Here, and the center of the world within the actual reach of my fellow man around his, which is, seen from my Here, a There. Both sectors may partially overlap, and some of the objects, facts, and events in the outer world may be in mine as well as my fellow man's actual reach, and even within his and my manipulatory zone. Nevertheless, such an object, fact, or event will have a different appearance as to direction, distance, perspective, adumbration, etc., seen from the center of my coordinates, called Here, than from his, called There. Now it is a basic axiom of any interpretation of the common world and its objects that these various coexisting systems of coordinates can be transformed one into the other; I take it for granted, and I assume my fellow man does the same, that I and my fellow man would have typically the same experiences of the common world if we changed places, thus transforming my Here into his, and his—now to me a There—into mine.

b) *The idealization of the congruency of the systems of relevances*

Each of us, as has been stated before, finds himself in a unique bio-graphically determined situation, and for this very reason my and my fellow man's purpose at hand and our systems of relevances originating in such a purpose must necessarily differ. Yet, as another basic axiom, I take it for granted until counterevidence is offered—and assume my fellow man does the same—that the differences originating in our private systems of relevances can be disregarded for the purpose at hand and that I and he, that *"We"* interpret the actually or potentially common objects, facts, and events in an "empirically identical" manner, *i.e.,* sufficient for all practical purposes.

This general thesis of the reciprocity of perspectives which involves idealizations by which—to use Whitehead's terminology—typifying constructs of objects of thought supersede the thought objects of my and

---

[34]This subsection 3 closely follows my aforementioned article, "Commonsense and Scientific Interpretation of Human Action," *loc. cit.,* p. 7.

my fellow man's private experience[35] is the presupposition for a world of common objects and therewith for communication. To give an example: we both see the "same" flying bird in spite of the difference of our spatial position, sex, age, and the fact that you want to shoot it and I just to enjoy it.

4) *The transcendence of the other's world*

So far we have dealt only with the face-to-face relationship in which a sector of the world is both in my and my fellow man's actual reach. To be precise, the world within my actual reach overlaps that within his reach but necessarily there are zones within my actual reach which are not within his, and *vice versa*. Facing another, for example, I see things unseen by him and he sees things unseen by me. The same holds good for our manipulatory spheres. This stone placed between us is within my manipulatory sphere but not within his.

In this sense, the world of another transcends mine. But it is a corollary of the idealization of the interchangeability of standpoints (above, 3a) that the world within actual reach of another is also within my attainable (potential) reach and *vice versa*. Within certain limits (to point them out would lead us too far afield) even the world within another's restorable reach and that within his anticipated one is within my potential reach (a potentiality of the second degree, so to speak) and *vice versa*.

The world of another transcends mine, however, in still another sense. In order to understand the particular form of this transcendence, we have first to consider the predominant function of the face-to-face relationship for the constitution of the social world. Only in it is another's body within my actual reach and mine within his; only in it do we experience one another in our individual uniqueness. While the face-to-face relationship lasts we are mutually involved in one another's biographical situation: we are growing older together. We have indeed a common environment and common experiences of the events within it: I and you, *We* see the flying bird. And this occurrence of the bird's flight as an event in outer (public) time is simultaneous with our perceiving it, which is an event in our inner (private) time. The two fluxes of inner

<hr />

[35]Alfred North Whitehead, *The Organization of Thought*, Williams & Norgate, London, 1917, now partly republished in *The Aims of Education*, Mentor Books, New York, 1949, see p. 110 of this edition.

time, yours and mine, become synchronous with the event in outer time (bird's flight) and therewith one with the other. This will be of special importance for our study of events in the outer world which serve as vehicles for communication, namely, significant gestures and language.

Nevertheless, another's existence transcends mine as mine does his. We have in common only a small section of our biographies. Moreover, either of us enters the relationship with only a part of his personality (Simmel) or, as some modern sociologists express it, by assuming a particular social role. And, finally, as the other's system of relevances is founded in his unique biographical situation, it cannot be congruent with mine: it cannot be brought within my reach, although it can be understood by me.

And there is a third kind of transcendence involved, but a transcendence which surpasses not only mine but also the other's world: the We-relation itself, although originating in the mutual biographical involvement, transcends the existence of either of the consociates in the realm of everyday life. It belongs to finite province of meaning other than that of the reality of everyday life and can be grasped only by symbolization. This statement anticipates a set of problems which we are not yet prepared to approach.

We have, however, to indicate that the face-to-face relationship characterized so far is only one, although the most central, dimension of the social world. If we compare it with the world within my actual reach, we can also find dimensions in the social world comparable to the various forms of the world within my potential reach. There is the world of my contemporaries, with whom I am not biographically involved in a face-to-face relationship, but with whom I have in common a sector of time which makes it possible for me to act upon them as they may act upon me within a communicative environment of mutual motivation. (In primitive societies in which the souls of the deceased are supposed to participate in the social life of the group, the dead are deemed to be contemporaries.) There is the world of my predecessors, upon whom I cannot act but whose past actions and their outcome are open to my interpretation and may influence my own actions; and there is the world of my successors of whom no experience is possible, but toward whom I may orient my actions in more or less empty anticipation. It is characteristic of all the dimensions of the social world other than the face-to-face relation that I cannot grasp my fellow men as unique individuals but only experience their typical behavior, their typical pattern of motives and attitudes in increasing anonymity.

We cannot enter here into a detailed discussion of these various dimensions of the social world. But it is indispensable to keep the underlying problems in mind in order to analyze correctly certain issues connected with communication and the appresentational apperception of society.

5) *Comprehension, manifestation, signs, communication*

It is true that, as Husserl stated, any comprehension of the other's thought—always disregarding telepathy—requires as vehicle, carrier, or medium the apprehension of an object, fact, or event in the outer world, which, however, is not apprehended as a self in the mere apperceptual scheme but appresentationally as expressing cogitations of a fellow man. The term "cogitation" is here used in the broadest Cartesian sense, denoting feelings, volitions, emotions, etc. We propose, for the purpose of this paper, to use the term *"sign"* for designating objects, facts, or events in the outer world, whose apprehension appresents to an interpreter cogitations of a fellow man. This definition needs some explanation.

a) *Comprehension*

The objects, facts, and events which are interpreted as signs must directly or indirectly refer to another's bodily existence. In the simplest case, that of a face-to-face relationship, another's body, events occurring on his body (blushing, smiling), including bodily movements (wincing, beckoning), activities performed by it (talking, walking, manipulating things) are capable of being apprehended by the interpreter as signs. If there is no face-to-face relationship, but distance in space or time, we have to keep in mind

> i) that apprehension does not necessarily presuppose actual perception, but that the appresenting member of the appresentational pair may also be a recollection or even a fantasm; I remember (or: I can imagine) the facial expression of my friend when he learned (or will learn) some sad news. I can even fantasy a sad looking centaur.

ii) that the result or product of another's activity refers to the action from which it resulted and, thus, can function as a sign for his cogitations;

iii) that the principle of the relative irrelevance of the vehicle is applicable. (The printed lecture refers to the talk of the lecturer.)

b) *Manifestation*

That an object, fact, or event in the outer world is interpreted as a sign for a fellow man's cogitation does not necessarily presuppose

i) that the other meant to manifest his cogitation by this sign, even less that he did so with communicative intent. An involuntary facial expression, a furtive glance, blushing, trembling, the other's gait, in brief, any physiognomical event can be interpreted as a sign for a fellow man's cogitation. A certain hesitation in the other's voice can convince me that he lies although he tries to hide that he does. The letter writer wants to convey the content of a message, but the graphologist disregards the content and takes the handwriting as such, that is, the static result of the unintentional gestures performed by the writer, as signs.

ii) If the sign was meant to function in a communicative context, the interpreter was not necessarily intended to be the addressee.

iii) It is, moreover, not necessarily presupposed that the two partners of a communicative sign-relation are known to each other (example: whoever erected this signpost wanted to show any passerby the direction).

c) *Types of signs*

In his excellent book, *Der Aufbau der Sprache,*[36] Bruno Snell developed a theory of three basic forms of bodily movement which, according to him, have corollaries in different kinds of sounds, words, morphological elements, the syntactical structure of Western languages, forms of literature, and even in types of philosophy. He distinguishes purposive, expressive, and mimetic movements (*Zweck-, Ausdrucks-, und Nachahmungsbewegungen*). The first category, the purposive movements, may consist in gestures, such as nodding, pointing, beckon-

[36]Bruno Snell, *Der Aufbau der Sprache,* Claassen Verlag, Hamburg, 1952, chap. I and II.

ing, but also talking; the second, the expressive movements, are exterior-
izations of inner experiences, primarily without purposive intent; the
spatial-temporal differentiation of movements, according to high and
low, wide and narrow, fast and slow, gives certain gestures their expressive meaning; the third category, the mimetic gesture, imitates or represents another being with whom the actor identifies himself. The animal
and fertility dances, well known to the anthropologist,[37] are examples.
Snell also points out that the pure purposive gesture reveals expressive
characteristics, for example, in the pitch and speed of the voice in talking, and that all three types of gesture can be used for communicative
purposes (for example, expressive ones by the actor on the stage, mimetic
ones by the pantomimist). According to Snell, the purposive gesture indicates what the performer wants, the expressive gesture what he feels,
and the mimetic gesture what he is or what he pretends to be.

The expressive and mimetic gestures (or, in our terminology, signs)
are of particular importance as foundations of higher appresentational
forms, namely, symbols. Communication as such is based foremost on
purposive signs, as the communicator has at least the intention of making himself understandable to the addressee if not to induce him to react
appropriately. But certain requirements have to be fulfilled to make
communication possible.

d) *Communication proper*

i) The sign used in communication is always a sign addressed to an
individual or anonymous interpreter. It originates within the actual manipulatory sphere of the communicator, and the interpreter apprehends it as an object, fact, or event in the world within
his reach. However, the conditions mentioned above (under a,
i–iii) apply to this situation. Consequently, it is not necessary that
the interpreter's world within his reach overlap spatially the
manipulatory sphere of the communicator (telephone, television),
nor that the production of the sign occur simultaneously with its
interpretation (Egyptian papyrus, monuments), nor that the
same physical object or event used by the communicator as carrier
of the communication be apprehended by the interpreter (prin-

[37] A highly interesting discussion in Curt Sachs, *World History of the Dance*, Seven Arts
Publishers, New York, 1952, chap. 2, pp. 49–138.

ciple of the relative irrelevance of the vehicle). In more complicated cases of communication, which cannot be studied here, any number of human beings or mechanical devices might be inserted into the communicatory process between the original communicator and the interpreter. The main point of importance for the following is the insight that communication requires under all circumstances and events in the outer world, produced by the communicator, and events in the outer world apprehensible by the interpreter. In other words, *communication can occur only within the reality of the outer world,* and this is one of the main reasons why this world, as we will see very soon, has the character of *paramount reality.* Even the voices which the schizophrenic believes he hears are hallucinated as *voices,* and refer, therefore, to events within the outer world.

ii) The sign used in communication is always preinterpreted by the communicator in terms of its expected interpretation by the addressee. To be understood the communicator has, before producing the sign, to anticipate the apperceptual, appresentational, and referential scheme under which the interpreter will subsume it. The communicator has, therefore, as it were, to perform a rehearsal of the expected interpretation and to establish such a context between his cogitations and the communicative sign that the interpreter, guided by the appresentational scheme he will apply to the latter, will find the former an element of the related referential scheme. This context, as we have seen (section II, 2, d, of this paper) is, however, nothing else than the interpretational scheme itself. In other words, communication presupposes that the interpretational scheme which the communicator relates and that which the interpreter will relate to the communicative sign in question will *substantially* coincide.

iii) The italicized qualification is important. Strictly speaking, a full identity of both interpretational schemes, that of the communicator and that of the interpreter, is, at least in the commonsense world of everyday life, impossible. The interpretational scheme is closely determined by the biographical situation and the system of relevances originating therein. If there were no other differences between the biographical situations of the communicator and that of the interpreter, then at least the "Here" of either one is a

"There" to the other. This fact alone sets insurmountable limits for a fully successful communication in the ideal sense. But, of course, communication might be and indeed is highly successful for many good and useful purposes and may reach an optimum in highly formalized and standardized languages such as in technical terminology. These considerations, seemingly of a highly theoretical nature, have important practical consequences: successful communication is possible only between persons, social groups, nations, etc., who share a substantially similar system of relevances. The greater the differences between their system of relevances, the fewer the chances for the success of the communication. Complete disparity of the systems of relevances makes the establishment of a universe of discourse entirely impossible.

iv) To be successful, any communicative process must, therefore, involve a set of common abstractions or standardizations. We mentioned under 3, b, of this section the idealization of the congruency of the system of relevances which leads to the superseding of the thought objects of private experience by typifying constructs of public objects of thought. Typification is indeed that form of abstraction which leads to the more or less standardized, yet more or less vague, conceptualization of commonsense thinking and to the necessary ambiguity of the terms of the ordinary vernacular. This is because our experience, even in what Husserl calls the prepredicative sphere, is organized from the outset under certain types. The small child who learns his mother tongue is at an early age capable of recognizing an animal as a dog or a bird or a fish, an element of his surroundings as a stone or a tree or a mountain, a piece of furniture as a table or a chair. But, as a glance in the dictionary shows, these are the terms most difficult to define in ordinary language. Most of the communicative signs are language signs, so the typification required for sufficient standardization is provided by the vocabulary and the syntactical structure of the ordinary vernacular of the mother tongue. We will revert to this problem later on.

e) *Language, pictorial, expressive, and mimetic presentation*

The structure of language as a set of signs combinable under syntactical rules, its function as a vehicle of discursive (propositional) thinking, its power not only to name things but also to express relations among them, not only to build propositions but also to formulate relations among propositions—all this has been described so carefully and extensively in recent literature that for our purpose it is unnecessary to enter into this subject.

Here we simply want to indicate that it is of the essence of language that normally any linguistic communication involves a time process; a speech is built up by sentences, a sentence by the step by step articulation of successive elements (polythetically, as Husserl[38] calls it), whereas the meaning of the sentence or the speech can be projected by the speaker and grasped by the listener in one single ray (monothetically). The stream of articulating cogitations of the speaker is thus simultaneous with the outer event of producing the sounds of the speech and the perceiving of the latter simultaneously with the comprehending cogitations of the listener. Speech is, therefore, one of the intersubjective time-processes—others are making music together, dancing together, making love together—by which the two fluxes of inner time, that of the speaker and that of the listener, become synchronous one with the other and both with an event in outer time. The reading of a written communication establishes in the same sense a quasisimultaneity between the events within the inner time of the writer and that of the reader.

Visual presentations, however, as Mrs. Langer has correctly shown,[39] are structurally different by their nondiscursive character. They are not composed of elements having independent meanings, that is, they have no vocabulary. They cannot be defined in terms of other signs as can discursive signs. Their primary function is that of conceptualizing the flux of sensations. Mrs. Langer sees the appresentational relationship of a pictorial presentation founded in the fact that the proportion of parts, their position, and relative dimension correspond to our conception of the depicted object. That is the reason we recognize the same house in a photograph, a painting, a pencil sketch, an architect's elevation drawing, and a builder's diagram. To Husserl,[40] the characteristic of the picture (in contradistinction to all other signs) consists in the fact that the picture is related to the depicted thing by similarity, whereas most of the other signs (disregarding, for example, onomatopoeia) have no content

[38]Husserl, *Ideen I*, sec. 118, 119.
[39]Langer, *Philosophy in a New Key*, pp. 55 ff. and 77 ff.
[40]Husserl, *Logische Untersuchungen VI*, vol. II/2, sec. 14; *Ideen I*, sec. 111; see also Farber, *loc. cit.*, pp. 410–414.

in common with that which is signified. (That is the reason many authors emphasize the "arbitrariness" of linguistic signs.) Nevertheless, the appresentational relationship prevails also in pictorial presentations, although sometimes in a rather complicated way of interconnected levels. Looking, for instance, at Duerer's print, "The Knight, Death, and The Devil," we distinguish first—as we would say, in the apperceptual scheme—the print as such, this thing in the portfolio; second, still in the apperceptual scheme, the black lines on paper as small colorless figures; third, these figures are *appresented* as "depicted realities" as they appear in the picture, "the knight of flesh and blood" of whom, as Husserl states, we are aware in his quasibeing, which is a "neutrality modification" of being.[41] Here Husserl stops, but we could and have to continue to follow the appresentational process further. These three figures, the knight, death, and the devil, as appresented in the neutrality modification of their quasibeing, appresent, in turn, in an appresentation of the second degree, so to speak, a meaningful context, and it is especially this meaning which Duerer wanted to convey to the beholder: the knight between death and the devil teaches us something about the condition of man between two supernatural forces. This is the *symbolic* appresentation, to which we must turn in the next section.

Communication by expressive and mimetic gestures has so far not found the attention it deserves from students of semantics. Examples for the former are gestures of greeting, paying respect, applauding, showing disapproval, gestures of surrender, of paying honor, etc. The latter combine features of the pictorial presentation, namely, similarity with the depicted object, with the time-structure of speech. Even a kind of mimetic vocabulary can be developed, as, for instance, in the highly standardized use of the fan by the Japanese *Kabuki* dancer.

6) *World within reach and world of everyday life*

It is the main thesis of this paper that appresentational references are means of coming to terms with transcendent experiences of various kinds. In an earlier part (4) of this section we have briefly characterized the transcending character of my experiences of the other and his world. Our analysis of the various forms of signs and communication has shown that the appresentational references characterized by these terms

[41]Husserl, *Ideen I*, sec. 111.

again have the function of overcoming a transcendent experience, namely, that of the other and his world. Through the use of signs the communicative system permits me to become aware, to a certain extent, of another's cogitations and, under particular conditions even to bring the flux of my inner time in perfect simultaneity with his. But as we have seen, fully successful communication is, nevertheless, unattainable. There still remains an inaccessible zone of the other's private life which transcends my possible experience.

The commonsense praxis of everyday life, however, solves this problem to such an extent that for nearly all good and useful purposes we can establish communication with our fellow men and come to terms with them. We have already mentioned briefly that this is possible only if the communicative process is based on a set of typifications, abstractions, and standardizations, and we referred briefly to the fundamental role of the vernacular of the mother tongue in establishing this basis. A later section (VII) of the present paper will have more on this point. Here, however, we wish to clarify some basic features, simply taken for granted by commonsense thinking of everyday life, upon which the possibility of communication is founded. They are in a certain sense an amplification of the general thesis of the reciprocity of perspectives analyzed in part 3 of this section.

The term "taken for granted," used before, has perhaps to be defined. It means to accept until further notice our knowledge of certain states of affairs as unquestionably plausible. Of course, at any time that which seemed to be hitherto unquestionable might be put in question. Commonsense thinking simply takes for granted, until counterevidence appears, not only the world of physical objects but also the sociocultural world into which we are born and in which we grow up. This world of everyday life is indeed the unquestioned but always questionable matrix within which all our inquiries start and end. Dewey[42] saw this in full clarity when he described the process of inquiry as the task of transforming in a controlled or directed manner indeterminate situations encountered or emerging within this matrix into "warranted assertibility."

Reverting to our particular problem, I take for granted until counterevidence appears, not only the bodily existence of my fellow man but also the fact that his conscious life has substantially the same structure as my

---

[42]John Dewey, *Logic, the Theory of Inquiry,* Henry Holt & Company, New York, 1938, part I, esp. pp. 19–20, and chap. III, *passim.*

own and, furthermore, that to a certain extent I can apperceive analogically through appresentational references my fellow man's cogitations (for example, the motives for his actions) as he can mine. Moreover, I take it for granted that certain objects, facts, and events within our common social environment have for him the same appresentational significances as for me, which significances transform mere things in the outer world into so-called cultural objects.

Until counterevidence is offered, I take it for granted that the various apperceptual, appresentational, referential, and contextual schemes accepted and approved as typically relevant by my social environment are also relevant for my own unique biographical situation and that of my fellow man within the world of everyday life. This means:

a) *with respect to the apperceptual scheme* that normally our apperception of objects, facts, or events of the outer world are guided by the system of typical relevances prevailing within our social environment and that a particular motive has to originate in the personal biographical situation of each of us in order to evoke our interest in the uniqueness, in the atypicality, of a particular object, fact, or event, or in its particular aspects;

b) *with respect to the appresentational scheme* that we both, my fellow man and I, take for granted the typical way in our sociocultural environment by which immediately apperceived objects, facts, or events in the outer world are apprehended not as "selves," but appresentationally, namely, as standing for something else, that is, as "wakening," "calling forth," or "evoking" appresentational references.

c) *with respect to the interpretational scheme* that in the case of communication the other (as communicator or addressee) will apply the same appresentational scheme to the appresentational references involved in the communication as I will. If, for instance, communication occurs through the medium of the vernacular of ordinary language, I take it for granted that others who express themselves in this idiom mean by the linguistic expression they use substantially the same thing that I understand them to mean, and *vice versa*.

If the term "world of everyday life" or "reality of everyday life" does not merely designate the world of nature as experienced by me but also the sociocultural world in which I live, then it becomes clear that this world does not coincide with the world of outer objects, facts, and events. To be sure, it includes those outer objects, facts, and events which are within my actual reach and those which are within the several zones of my potential reach (comprising those within actual and potential reach of my fellow men). It includes, however, in addition, all the appresentational functions of such objects, facts, or events which transform things into cultural objects, human bodies into fellow men, their bodily movements into actions or significant gestures, waves of sound into speech, etc. The world of everyday life is thus permeated by appresentational references which are simply taken for granted and among which I carry on my practical activities—my working activities, as we have referred to them before[43]—in terms of commonsense thinking. But all these appresentational references still belong to the finite province of meaning, called the reality of everyday life. Nevertheless, nothing has to be changed in our thesis that all appresentational references are means of coming to terms with experiences of transcendences. This we have tried to show with respect to the appresentational references studied so far, namely, marks, indications, and signs. All the transcendences they helped to come to terms with themselves belong to what we have now characterized as the reality of everyday life. As transcendences—of my actual Here and Now, of the Other, of the Other's world, etc.—they were still immanent to the commonsense world of my everyday life, coconstituting the situation in which I find myself placed in this world.

But there are experiences which transcend the finite province of meaning of the world of everyday life so that they refer to other finite provinces of meaning, to other realities, or, to use the term coined by William James,[44] to other subuniverses, such as the world of scientific theory, of arts, of religion, of politics, but also of fantasms and dreams. And there is again a group of appresentational references, called symbols, with whose help man tries to apprehend these transcendent phenomena in a way analogous to our perceptible world. We turn now to the study of these symbols and the problem of multiple realities.

V) *The Transcendence of Nature and Society: Symbols*

1) *The experience of this transcendence*

I find myself in my everyday life within a world not of my own making. I know this fact, and this knowledge itself belongs to my biographical situation. There is, first, my knowledge that Nature transcends the

---

[43]See footnote 24.

[44]James, *Principles of Psychology,* vol. II, chap. 21; also sec. VI of the present paper.

reality of my everyday life both in time and in space. In time, the world of Nature existed before my birth and will continue to exist after my death. It existed before man appeared on earth and will probably survive mankind. In space, the world within my actual reach carries along the open infinite horizons of my world in potential reach, but to my experiences of these horizons belongs the conviction that each world within potential reach, once transformed into actual reach, will again be surrounded by new horizons, and so on. Within the world in my reach there are, moreover, certain objects, such as the heavenly bodies, which I cannot bring within my manipulatory sphere, and there are events within my manipulatory area, such as the tides, which I cannot bring within my control.

I know, furthermore, that in a similar way the social world transcends the reality of my everyday life. I was born into a preorganized social world which will survive me, a world shared from the outset with fellow men who are organized in groups, a world which has its particular open horizons in time, in space, and also in what sociologists call social distance. In time, there is the infinite chain of generations which overlap one another; my clan refers to other clans, my tribe to other tribes, and they are enemies or friends, speaking the same or another language, but they are always organized in their particular social form and living their particular way of life. My actual social environment refers always to a horizon of potential social environments, and we may speak of a transcendent infinity of the social world as we speak of a transcendent infinity of the natural one.

I experience both of these transcendences, that of Nature and that of Society, as being imposed upon me in a double sense: on the one hand, I find myself at any moment of my existence as being within nature and within society; both are permanently coconstitutive elements of my biographical situation and are, therefore, experienced as inescapably belonging to it. On the other hand, they constitute the framework within which alone I have the freedom of my potentialities, and this means they prescribe the scope of all possibilities for defining my situation. In this sense, they are not elements of my situation, but determinations of it. In the first sense, I may—even more, I have to—take them for granted. In the second sense, I have to come to terms with them. But in either sense, I have to understand the natural and the social world in spite of their transcendences, in terms of an order of things and events.

From the outset I know also that any human being experiences the same imposed transcendences of Nature and of Society, although he experiences them in individual perspectives and with individual adumbrations. But the order of Nature and of Society is common to all mankind. It furnishes to everyone the setting of the cycle of his individual life, of birth, aging, death, health and sickness, hopes and fears. Each of us participates in the recurrent rhythm of nature; to each of us the movements of sun and moon and stars, the change between day and night, and the cycle of the seasons are elements of his situation. Each of us is a member of the group into which he was born or which he has joined and which continues to exist if some of its members die and others enter into it. Everywhere there will be systems of kinship, age groups and sex groups, differentiations according to occupations, and an organization of power and command which leads to the categories of social status and prestige. But in the commonsense thinking of everyday life we simply know that Nature and Society represent some kind of order; yet the essence of this order as such is unknowable to us. It reveals itself merely in images by analogical apprehending. But the images, once constituted, are taken for granted, and so are the transcendences to which they refer.

How is this possible? "The miracle of all miracles is that the genuine miracles become to us an everyday occurrence," says Lessing's Nathan. This is so because we find in our sociocultural environment itself socially approved systems offering answers for our quest for the unknowable transcendences. Devices are developed to apprehend the disquieting phenomena transcending the world of everyday life in a way analogous to the familiar phenomena within it. This is done by the creation of appresentational references of a higher order, which shall be called *symbols* in contradistinction to the terms "marks," "indications," "signs," used so far.

2) *Symbolization*

a) *Definition*

A symbol can be defined in first approximation as an appresentational reference of a higher order in which the appresenting member of the pair is an object, fact, or event within the reality of our daily life, whereas the other appresented member of the pair refers to an idea which transcends our experience of everyday life.[4]

This definition corresponds substantially to the notion of symbol as developed by Karl Jaspers in the third volume of his *Philosophie,*[46] from which we give the following freely translated quotation, omitting certain references to Jaspers's particular philosophical position:

> We speak of meaning in the sense of sign and image, of simile, allegory, and metaphor. The main difference between meaning within the world and of metaphysical meaning consists in the criterion of whether in the relationship between the image and that which it represents the latter itself could be apprehended as an objectivity, or whether the image is an image for something that is not accessible in any other way; that is to say, whether that which is expressed in the image could also be stated or demonstrated in a direct way, or whether it exists for us merely in so far as it exists in the image. Only in the latter case should we speak of a symbol. . . . The symbol cannot be interpreted except by other symbols. The understanding of a symbol does not, therefore, consist in grasping its significance in a rational way but in experiencing it existentially in the symbolic intention as this unique reference to something transcendent that vanishes at the limiting point.

b) *Genesis of the symbolic appresentation*

We have now to study the problem of the constitution of the appresentational pairing which might function as a symbol. How is it possible that an object, event, or fact within the reality of our daily life is coupled with an idea which transcends our experience of our everyday life? This problem can be approached on two different levels. There are first sets of appresentational references which are universal and can be used for symbolization because they are rooted in the human condition. It is a problem of philosophical anthropology to study these sets of appresentational references. Secondly, the particular forms of symbolic systems as developed by the various cultures in different periods might be investigated. This is the problem of cultural anthropology and of the history of ideas. We have to restrict ourselves here to fugitive remarks describing some items of the first group, illustrating them by example, belonging to the second.

[45] This definition will be restated in the following sec. VI, 3.
[46] Karl Jaspers, *Philosophie,* Julius Springer, Berlin, 1932, vol. 3, *"Metaphysik,"* chap. 1, p. 16.

As to the latter, we prefer for reasons we shall mention briefly, not to take our examples from the world of our present Western culture. The latter has developed several systems of symbols such as science, art, religion, politics, and philosophy, some of which will be characterized in the next section. We have, however, to consider that the coexistence of several symbolic systems which are merely loosely, if at all, connected one with another, is the special feature of our own historical situation and the result of our attempt to develop an interpretation of the cosmos in terms of the positive methods of the natural sciences. We take the world as defined by the mathematical natural sciences as the archetype of an ideal order of symbolic references and are inclined to explain all the other symbolic systems as derivations from it or at least as subordinated to it. Whitehead in his book *Science and the Modern World*[47] has rightly stated that Galileo's discoveries and Newton's laws of motion established the fundamental concept of the *"ideally isolated system"* which is essential to scientific theory so that science would be impossible without it. Whitehead explains that

> the isolated system is not a solipsistic system, apart from which there would be nonentity. It is isolated as within the universe. This means that there are truths respecting this system, which require reference only to the remainder of things by way of a uniform systematic scheme of relationships.

On the other hand, many investigations of modern anthropologists, sociologists, mythologists, philologists, political scientists, and historians[48] have shown that in other cultures and even in earlier periods of our own culture man experienced nature, society, and himself as equally participating in and determined by the order of the cosmos. As an illustration of this point of view, in contrast to that expressed in the quotation from Whitehead, we refer to the following passage from Ernst Cassirer's *An Essay on Man*[49] which illuminates the relationship between men, society, and nature in mythical experience and shows why any element in one of these orders may become a symbol, appresentationally referring to the corresponding element in that of the other orders:

[47] Alfred North Whitehead, *Science and the Modern World*, The Macmillan Company, New York, 1925, now also available as Pelican-Mentor Book (New American Library), New York, 1949, p. 47 of the latter edition.

[48] We refer to the writings of Émile Durkheim, Lucien Lévy-Bruhl, Marcel Mauss, Marcel Granet, Bronislaw Malinowski, Ernst Cassirer, Bruno Snell, Alois Dempf, Arnold J. Toynbee, and Eric Voegelin.

[49] Cassirer, *An Essay on Man*, pp. 83–86.

To mythical and religious feeling nature becomes one great society, *the society of life*. Man is not endowed with outstanding rank in this society. . . . Life possesses the same religious dignity in its humblest and highest forms. Men and animals, animals and plants are all on the same level. . . . And we find the same principle—that of the solidarity and unbroken unity of life—if we pass from space to time. It holds not only in the order of simultaneity but also in the order of succession. The generations of men form a unique and uninterrupted chain. The former stages of life are preserved by reincarnation. . . . Even totemism expresses this deep conviction of a community of all living beings—a community that must be preserved and reinforced by the constant effort of man, by the strict performance of magical rites and religious observances.

And Cassirer endorses Robertson Smith's statement (*Lectures on the Religion of the Semites*):

The indissoluble bond that unites men to their god is the same bond of blood-fellowship which in early society is the one binding link between man and man, and the one sacred principle of moral obligation.

An example of the full integration of the symbolic interrelation called by Cassirer the society of life can be found in classic Chinese thought. According to the French Sinologue Marcel Granet,[50] there is in classical Chinese literature a unity of structure between the microcosm—man—and the macrocosm—the universe—and the structure of the universe is explained by the structure of society. All these structures are dominated by two fundamental principles: first, the position of the Male and the Female, the positive and the negative, the *Yang* and the *Yin;* and second, the opposition between the chief and the vassal in the hierarchical structure of society. Based on these principles, etiquette prescribes and regulates meticulously all details of the everyday life world.

We shall try now to show by a few examples how universal symbols originate in the general human condition. As stated before, man considers himself as a center *O* of a system of coordinates under which he groups the objects of his environment in terms of "above and underneath," "before and behind," "right and left." Now, for every man an element of the underneath is the earth and of the above the sky. The

[50]Marcel Granet, *Études Sociologiques sur la Chine,* Presses universitaires de France, Paris, 1953, p. 268; see also Marcel Granet, *La Pensée chinoise,* Albin Michel, Paris, 1934, *passim.*

earth is common to men and animals; it is the procreator of vegetative life, the provider of food. The sky is the place where the celestial bodies appear and disappear, but also the place from which rain comes, without which no fertility of the earth is possible. The head, the carrier of the main sense organs and the organ of breathing and speech, is on the upper part of the human body, and the digestive organs and that of procreation in the lower part. The connection of all these phenomena makes the spatial dimension "above and below" the starting point of a set of symbolic appresentations. In Chinese thought, for example, the head symbolizes the sky (and so does the roof of the house) whereas the feet (the floor) symbolize earth. But since the sky has to send rain in order to fertilize the earth, the sky is also to Chinese thought the male principle, the positive principle, *Yang,* and earth the negative, female *Yin.* And this symbolism of higher-lower has its correlate in Chinese medicine, music, dance, social hierarchy, etiquette, all of which are correlated and can be brought into symbolic appresentational reference one with the other.[51] There is also a symbolism of the directions before-behind, things which are faced or have to be faced and are thus visible, and those which are not and therefore possibly dangerous, and also of right and left.[52]

Sun, moon, and stars rise and set for all men in opposite directions which are to everyone "marks" for finding his bearings. But the four cardinal points of the compass so ascertained have also their symbolic connotations, because they are connected with the change between day and night, light and darkness, being awake and asleep, the visible and the invisible, the coming-to-be and the passing-away. The life cycle of men—birth, childhood, adolescence, manhood, old age, death—has its analogy in the cycle of the seasons and the cycle of vegetative and animal life which is equally important for farming, fishing, and animal husbandry, and is in turn correlated to the motions of the heavenly bodies. Again a set of correlations is established which permits the appresentational pairing of its elements in the form of symbols. The social organization with its hierarchies of rulers and subordinates, chiefs and vassals, has its correlate in the hierarchy of the heavenly bodies. Thus, the cosmos, the individual, and the community form a unit and are equally subject to the universal forces which govern all events. Man has to

[51]*Ibid.*
[52]See the highly interesting article by Granet, *"La droite et la gauche en Chine,"* *Études sociologiques,* pp. 261–278.

understand these forces and, because he cannot dominate them, to conjure them or to appease them. To do so is, however, not the business of the isolated individual, it is the concern of the whole community and its organization.

The symbolic forms in which the forces of the universe of nature as well as of society are appresented (*mana, orenda, manitu, Yin* and *Yang,* deities of various kinds and hierarchies, etc.) are as manifold as the symbols appresenting them (expressive, purposive, or mimetic gestures, linguistic or pictorial presentations, charms, spells, magical or religious rites, ceremonies). The symbols of myths have the particular function of justifying and vouching for the truth and validity of the order established by the other symbolic systems (Malinowski).[53]

At this level the world of the sacred and that of the profane are closely interrelated. Studying the origin of the names of deities in Greek mythology, Bruno Snell comes to the following result:

> Everything that is active is originally conceived as a deity. Many things carry the name of a deity which will later on be designated by an abstract term. Not only what is active in nature, such as the sun, the cloud, the lightning, the earth, the tree, the river, is to the primeval mind a divine being, but also everything that acts within man, within the individual (such as love, fighting spirit, prudence) as well as within the community (such as peace, war, law, fortune, injustice, and all forms of disaster). . . . The question whether the sun was experienced first as a thing and thereafter interpreted in the mythical way, or whether first the noun denoting the thing or the name of the deity existed, is as wrongly put as the question whether the river or the river-god existed first. The acting phenomena of nature are just divine. . . . It is meaningless to ask whether Eros was first a god or the emotion of love, since the emotion of love is apprehended as an intervention of the deity.[54]

As to the role of the symbol (in the sense used in this paper) in human society and political organizations, we want finally to quote Eric Voegelin who sums up the results of his four volume study on the history of political ideas in his book, *The New Science of Politics,* as follows:

> Human society is not merely a fact, or an event, in the external world to be studied by an observer like a natural phenomenon. Though it has

[53]Bronislaw Malinowski, *Magic, Science, and Religion,* Doubleday & Company, New York, 1954, pp. 100 f.
[54]Snell, *op. cit.,* pp. 160 f.

externality as one of its important components, it is as a whole a little world, a cosmion, illuminated with meaning from within by the human beings who continuously create and bear it as the mode and condition of their self-realization. It is illuminated through an elaborate symbolism, in various degrees of compactness and differentiation—from rite, through myth, to theory—and this symbolism illuminates it with meaning in so far as the symbols make the internal structure of such a cosmion, the relations between its members and groups of members, as well as its existence as a whole, transparent for the mystery of human existence. The self-illumination of society through symbols is an integral part of social reality, and one may even say, its essential part, for through such symbolization the members of a society experience it as more than an accident or a convenience; they experience it as of their human essence. And, inversely, the symbols express the experience that man is fully man by virtue of his participation in a whole which transcends his particular existence.[55]

We think that our definition of the symbol as an appresentational reference of a higher order is not only compatible with, but also corroborated by the findings of the thinkers just discussed. It might be helpful to show this in some detail.

We shall not attempt the hopeless task of outlining the manifold forms in which the experiences of the transcendences involved are appresented in the great symbolic systems of the sciences, the various branches of philosophy, the arts, mythology, religions, politics, etc. Nor do we intend to show the innumerable symbolic references to the transcendences of the real world in the life of the social group or even of the individual (for, whereas signs refer by definition to the intersubjective situation, a symbol may, and frequently does, remain outside of communication). The great themes of all symbolizations can themselves only be expressed in symbols. To outline them would require a complete encyclopedia of the philosophic sciences in the Hegelian manner. In each of these spheres—or, as we shall call them, finite provinces of meaning—the symbolic appresentations are formed according to the cognitive style characteristic of this province. Hence, we restrict ourselves to some remarks concerning the particular features of appresentational references involved in any symbol situation.

[55]Eric Voegelin, *The New Science of Politics, An Introduction* (Charles R. Walgreen Foundation Lectures), The University of Chicago Press, Chicago, 1952, p. 27.

c) *The particularities of the symbolic appresentation*

First, we have to understand that symbolization is an appresentational reference of a higher order, that is, based on preformed appresentational references, such as marks, indications, signs, or even symbols. Jacob, awakened from his dream of the ladder in which God revealed Himself to him (Genesis, 28, 10–25), took the stone that he had put for his pillow and set it up for a pillar and poured oil upon the top of it, vowing that this stone shall be God's house. "Surely," he said, "the Lord is in this place; and I knew it not." The irruption of the transcendent experience into the world of everyday life, which transforms it and gives each element of it an appresentational significance ("the Lord is in this Place"), which it did not have before ("I knew it not"), has hardly been told in a more dramatic way. The stone becomes the pillow, the pillow a pillar, the pillar God's house. Another example can be found in Husserl's analysis of Duerer's print, "The Knight, Death, and The Devil," previously mentioned.

Second, we have to consider that on each level of a series of appresentational references the three principles pointed out in an earlier section of the present paper (II, 5) may become operative: each of the appresenting vehicles may be replaced by another, each appresentational meaning may undergo a series of variations, and the principle of figurative transference pervades the whole appresentational structure. All this explains the essential ambiguity of the symbol, the vagueness of the transcendent experiences appresented by it, and the difficulty of translating their meaning into discursive terms of more or less precise denotations. This is exactly that particularity of the symbol which Jaspers has in mind when he speaks of the vanishing of the transcendent at the limiting point. To him the transcendent manifests itself in ciphers, and it is man's existential problem to decode the cryptography of the symbols.[56]

Third, we have to remember our explanations of the four orders involved in any appresentational reference, which we called the apperceptual, the appresentational, the referential, and the interpretational or contextual scheme. The complicated internal structure of the symbolic relationship implies that all of these schemes enter each of the various appresentational levels involved, and that on each of these levels one of

[56]Jaspers, *op. cit.,* vol. III, chap. 4.

these schemes may be selected as the archetype of the order, from which the other orders appear as merely arbitrary and contingent. But, and this point has to be emphasized, the Bergsonian problem of order refers also to the interrelationship prevailing among the various layers of appresentational references, and here the identity, or at least similarity, of the *interpretational scheme* is of the highest importance for the establishment of a universe of discourse between the interpreters. Various interpreters of a symbolic structure may accept the same referential scheme, yet apply different appresentational schemes to the apperceptual configurations. The history of sects and heresies in all religions is an example of this statement: both the *Homoiousian* and the *Homoousian* believe in the Trinity, but the former holds that the three Divine Persons are neither identical nor different in substance, but similar, whereas the latter maintains their consubstantiality. The same holds good for parties and factions in political organizations which believe equally in the basic law of the country but differ as to its interpretation.

It is, however, also possible that the *appresentational* aspect is taken as a prototype of order with the consequence that various referential schemes which are frequently inconsistent, are connected with the same symbolic structure; also, it is possible that the *referential* scheme, once constituted, becomes, so to speak, autonomous, *i.e.,* independent of the appresentational scheme, which seems, then, merely contingent or lacking any order. In the latter case, the symbols are reinterpreted and understood without reference to the originally appresenting elements.

Finally, we have to recall that each object of our immediate or analogical apprehension is an object within a field, referring to other objects of the same experiential style. There is an intrinsic order of our perceptions of outer objects, or of so-called inner experiences, of fantasms, and even of dreams, which separates them from all other realms and constitutes them, according to our formulation, as a separate province of meaning. Here again we have within limits the freedom to select one of these realms as our system of reference, that is, to "live" in one of these orders or, to bestow upon one of them the accent of reality. We have, then, several concurrent and competing orders of reality—that of our everyday life, that of the world of our fantasy, of art, of science, etc., among which the first is paramount, because only within it is communication possible. Because of its importance for understanding the symbolic structure, this problem of multiple realities deserves to be considered briefly.

VI) *On Multiple Realities*

1) *William James's subuniverses; finite provinces of meaning*

In a famous chapter of his *Principles of Psychology*[57] William James shows that there are several, probably an infinite number of orders of realities, each with its special and separate style of existence. James calls them "subuniverses," and mentions as examples the world of senses or physical things (as the paramount reality), the world of science, the world of ideal relations, the worlds of mythology and religion, the world of "idols of the tribe," the various worlds of individual opinions, and the world of sheer madness and vagary. "Each world *whilst it is attended to* is real after its own fashion; only the reality lapses with the attention." Reality means simply relation to our emotional and active life; whatever excites and stimulates our interest is real. Our primitive impulse is to affirm immediately the reality of all that is conceived, as long as it remains uncontradicted. ". . . All propositions, whether attributive or existential, are believed through the very fact of being conceived, unless they clash with other propositions believed at the same time, by affirming that their terms are the same with the terms of these other propositions."[58]

Many other examples could be quoted. The play world of the little girl, as long as it is undisturbed, is her reality. She is indeed the mother, and her doll her child. Only from the point of view of the reality of the outer world is the knight in Duerer's print a pictorial presentation in the neutrality modification. In the world of art, that is, in this case, of pictorial imagination, knight, death, and devil have "real" existence as entities within the realm of artistic fantasy. While the play lasts, Hamlet is to us *really* Hamlet and not Laurence Olivier "acting the part of" or "representing" Hamlet.

The ingenious theory of William James has, of course, to be detached from its psychological setting and analyzed for its many implications. We have made such an attempt elsewhere.[59] In this paper we prefer to

---

[57]James, *op. cit.*, vol. II, chap. 21.

[58]*Ibid.*, pp. 293, 290.

[59]Schutz, "On Multiple Realities." Some of the following passages, esp. 4, are borrowed from this paper.

speak of finite provinces of meaning upon which we bestow the accent of reality, instead of subuniverses as does William James. By this change of terminology we emphasize that it is the meaning of our experiences, and not the ontological structure of the objects, which constitutes reality. Each province of meaning—the paramount world of real objects and events into which we can gear by our actions, the world of imaginings and fantasms, such as the play world of the child, the world of the insane, but also the world of art, the world of dreams, the world of scientific contemplation—has its particular cognitive style. It is this particular style of a set of our experiences which constitutes them as a finite province of meaning. All experiences within each of these worlds are, with respect to this cognitive style, consistent in themselves and compatible with one another (although not compatible with the meaning of everyday life). Moreover, each of these finite provinces of meaning is, among other things, characterized by a specific tension of consciousness (from full awakeness in the reality of everyday life to sleep in the world of dreams), by a specific time-perspective, by a specific form of experiencing oneself, and, finally, by a specific form of sociality.

2) *The paramount reality*

William James rightly calls the subuniverse of senses, of physical things, the paramount reality. But we prefer to take as a paramount reality the finite province of meaning which we have called the reality of our everyday life. In an earlier section (IV, 6) we pointed out that the reality of our everyday life which our commonsense thinking takes for granted includes not only the physical objects, facts, and events within our actual and potential reach perceived as such in the mere apperceptual scheme, but also appresentational references of a lower order by which the physical objects of nature are transformed into socio-cultural objects. But since these appresentations of a lower order also have objects, facts, or events of the outer world as their appresenting member, we believe that our definition is compatible with that of James. We can also agree with Santayana[60] that "the spirit can never possess, much less communicate, ideas without a material endowment and a material occasion":

[60]George Santayana, *Dominations and Powers,* Charles Scribner's Sons, New York, 1951, p. 146.

The tongue must move; the audible conventional word must come to the lips and reach a ready ear; the hands with tools or plans in them must intervene to carry the project out.

The outer world of everyday life is a paramount reality:

a) because we always participate in it, even during our dreams, by means of our bodies, which are themselves things in the outer world;

b) because the outer objects delimit our free possibilities of action by offering resistance which requires effort to overcome, if it can be overcome;

c) because it is that realm into which we can gear by our bodily activities and, hence, which we can change or transform;

d) because—and this is just a corollary to the preceding points—within this realm, and only within this realm, we can communicate with our fellow men and thus establish a "common comprehensive environment" in the sense of Husserl.[61]

The preceding characteristics of the reality of everyday life do not mean, however, that other finite provinces of meaning are incapable of socialization. To be sure, there are certainly finite provinces of meaning which cannot be intersubjectively shared, such as my dreams or even my daydreams. There are others, such as the play world of children, which permit intersubjective participation and even interaction in terms of the shared fantasms. In the world of religious experiences there is, on the one hand, the lonely vision of the mystic or of the prophet and, on the other hand, the community service—there are lonely prayers and prayers offered by the congregation.

It is not our aim here to develop a typology of the forms of socialization in the various finite provinces of meaning. But we wish to emphasize that in all cases in which such an intersubjective participation in one of these provinces takes place, the existence of "a material occasion or a material endowment" is presupposed. In other words, communication occurs by objects, facts, or events pertaining to the paramount reality of the senses, of the outer world, which are, however, appresentationally apperceived.

This holds good also for symbolic appresentations, in so far as they are communicated or designed to be communicable. But there is, nevertheless, a main feature by which symbolic appresentations are distinguished

[61]Husserl, *Ideen II,* sec. 50 and 51.

from all the other appresentational relations, and a brief consideration of this situation gives us the opportunity to restate our definition of the symbol.

3) *The definition of symbol restated*

All appresentational references, as we have emphasized, are characterized by a specific transcendence of the appresented object in relation to the actual "Here and Now" of the interpreter. But with the exception of the symbolic appresentation, the three terms of the appresentational relation—the appresenting and the appresented members of the pair and the interpreter—pertain to the same level of reality, namely, the paramount reality of everyday life. The symbolic reference, however, is characterized by the fact that it transcends the finite province of meaning of everyday life so that only the appresenting member of the related pair pertains to it, whereas the appresented member has its reality in another finite province of meaning, or, in James's terminology, in another sub-universe. We can, therefore, redefine the symbolic relationship as an appresentational relationship between entities belonging to at least two finite provinces of meaning so that the appresenting symbol is an element of the paramount reality of everyday life. (We say "at least two" because there are many combinations such as religious art, etc., which cannot be investigated within this paper.)

4) *The transition from the paramount reality to other finite provinces of meaning, experienced through a shock*[62]

The world of everyday life is taken for granted by our commonsense thinking and thus receives the accent of reality as long as our practical experiences prove the unity and congruity of this world as valid. Even more, this reality seems to us to be the natural one, and we are not ready to abandon our attitude toward it without having experienced a specific shock which compels us to break through the limits of these "finite" provinces of meaning and to shift the accent of reality to another one.

To be sure, these experiences of shock befall us frequently in the midst of daily life; they themselves pertain to its reality. Within a single day or

[62]See footnote 57.

even hour I may run through several such shock experiences of various kinds. Some instances are: the inner transformation we endure if the curtain in the theater rises as a transition to the world of the stage play; the radical change in our attitude if, before a painting, we permit our visual field to be limited by what is within the frame as a passage into the pictorial world; or falling asleep as a leap into the world of dreams. But also religious experience in all its varieties—for example, Kierkegaard's experience of the "instant" as the leap into the religious sphere—is such a shock, as well as the decision of the scientist to replace all passionate participation in the affairs of "this world" by a distinterested contemplative attitude.

On the other hand, we have to emphasize that consistency and compatibility of experiences with respect to their peculiar cognitive style subsist merely within the borders of the particular province of meaning to which these experiences belong and upon which I have bestowed the accent of reality. By no means will that which is compatible within the province of meaning P be also compatible within the province of meaning Q. On the contrary, seen from P, which is supposed to be real, Q and all the experiences belonging to it would appear as merely fictitious, inconsistent, and incompatible, and *vice versa*. We have here again an application of Bergson's problem of several coexisting orders.

We want to illustrate this point by briefly discussing the "fictitiousness" of the world of everyday life as seen from the symbolic system pervading other provinces of meaning upon which the accent of reality has been bestowed. Our first example takes the world of physical theory as a system of reference, our second the world of poetry.

5) *The concept of finite provinces of meaning illustrated by symbols in science and poetry*

As to the finite province of meaning called science, we recall the statement by Whitehead that the creation of an "ideally isolated system" was the necessary prerequisite of the development of the modern natural sciences. The realm of nature with which the theory of physics deals is such an ideally isolated system, and the phenomena of nature in the commonsense experience of everyday life have been, by a process of abstractions, generalizations, and idealizations, entirely transformed into such a system. "Every physical theory," says Philipp G. Frank in his

"Foundations of Physics,"[63] "consists of three kinds of statements: equations between physical quantities (relations between symbols), logical rules, and semantical rules (operational definitions)." And he closes his monograph in a rather ironical vein with the statement:

> Words like "matter" and "mind" are left (namely, by the theoretical physicist) to the language of everyday life where they have their legitimate place and are understood by the famous "man in the street" unambiguously.[64]

And Hermann Weyl in his *Philosophy of Mathematics and Natural Science* sums up his criticism of Brouwer's "idealism" in mathematical thinking as follows:

> It cannot be denied that the theoretical desire, incomprehensible from the merely phenomenal point of view, is alive in us which urges us towards totality. Mathematics shows that with particular clarity; but it also teaches us that that desire can be fulfilled on one condition only, namely, that we are satisfied with the symbol and renounce the mystical error of expecting the transcendent ever to fall within the lighted circle of our intuition.[65]

And in explaining the methodological principles of physics as "the distillation of the objective world capable only of representation in symbols, from what is immediately given in intuition," Weyl gives the following illustration:

> Whereas for Huyghens colors were "in reality" oscillations of the ether, they now appear merely as mathematical functions of periodic character depending on four variables that as coordinates represent the medium of space time. What remains is ultimately a *symbolic construction* of exactly the same kind as that which Hilbert carries through in mathematics.[66]

These statements show clearly that scientific theory is a finite province of meaning, using symbols appresenting realities within this realm and operating them—and, of course, justly so—on the principle that their

---

[63]Philipp G. Frank, "Foundations of Physics," *International Encyclopedia of Unified Sciences,* University of Chicago Press, Chicago, 1946, vol. I, no. 7, p. 73.

[64]*Ibid.,* p. 76.

[65]Hermann Weyl, *Philosophy of Mathematics and Natural Science,* Princeton University Press, Princeton, 1949, p. 60.

[66]*Ibid.,* p. 113.

validity and usefulness is independent of any reference to the common-sense thinking of everyday life and *its* realities.

As a second illustration we turn now to a brief consideration of symbols in poetry. T. S. Eliot in his famous essay on Dante states:

> Genuine poetry can communicate before it is understood. . . . Words have associations, and the group of words in associations have associations, which is a kind of local self-consciousness, because they are the growth of a particular civilization. . . . I do not recommend, in first reading the first canto of the Inferno, worrying about the identity of the Leopard, the Lion, or the She-Wolf. It is really better at the start not to know or care what they do mean. What we should consider is not so much the meaning of the images but the reversed processes, that which leads a man having an idea to express in images. . . . Dante's is a visual imagination. . . . He lived in an age in which men still saw visions. . . . We have nothing but dreams and we have forgotten that seeing visions—a practice now relegated to the aberrant and uneducated—was once a more significant, interesting, and disciplined kind of dreaming.[67]

And Goethe, commenting in his *"Maerchen"* of the golden snake (*Unterhaltungen deutscher Ausgewanderter*) which combines highly symbolic elements that were during his lifetime already interpreted by various writers in the most controversial way, wrote on May 27, 1796, to Wilhelm von Humboldt: "Es war freilich schwer, zugleich *bedeutend* und *deutungslos* zu sein" ("It was rather difficult to be at the same time significant [relevant, important—all the three meanings are involved in the German *"bedeutend"*] but without interpretation [or not interpretable—both meanings are involved in *"deutungslos"*]).

Both statements, that of T. S. Eliot and that of Goethe, show the poet's insight into the fact that within the finite province of meaning of the work of art the interrelationship of the symbols as such is the essence of the poetic content and that it is unnecessary and may even be harmful to look for the referential scheme which the appresenting elements of the symbolic relationship would symbolize, if they were indeed objects of the world of daily life. But their connection with these objects has been cut off; the use of the appresenting elements is just a means of communication; whereas poetry communicates by using ordinary language, the ideas symbolized by this language are real entities within the finite province of poetical meaning. They have turned, to use a term of Jaspers,

---

[67] T. S. Eliot, *Selected Essays, 1917–1932*, Harcourt, Brace & Company, 1932, pp. 199–241, 200, 201, 204.

into "ciphers" for transcendent experiences to be understood by those who have the existential key to them. And in this sense, and only in this sense, Jaspers says: "The symbol establishes communion without communication."[68]

VII) *Symbol and Society*

We are now prepared to answer at least two of the questions with which we started: to what extent are significative and symbolic appresentations dependent upon the sociocultural environment? How is intersubjectivity as such and how are social groups experienced by significative and symbolic appresentations?

1) *The dependence of appresentational references on the social environment*

The first question deals with the main problem of any sociology of knowledge that does not misunderstand its task. To answer it we start again from our experience of the reality of everyday life which, as a sociocultural world, is permeated by appresentational reference. When in section III we developed the concepts of marks and indications, we assumed for the sake of clearer presentation that a supposedly insulated individual has to "map out" the world within his reach. In truth, man finds himself from the outset in surroundings already "mapped out" for him by others, *i.e.,* "premarked," "preindicated," "presignified," and even "presymbolized." Thus, his biographical situation in everyday life is always an historical one because it is constituted by the sociocultural process which had led to the actual configuration of this environment. Hence, only a small fraction of man's stock of knowledge at hand originates in his own individual experience. The greater portion of his knowledge is *socially derived,* handed down to him by his parents and teachers as his social heritage. It consists of a set of systems of relevant typifications, of typical solutions for typical practical and theoretical problems, of typical precepts for typical behavior, including the pertinent system of appresentational references. All this knowledge is taken for granted beyond question by the respective social group and is thus *"socially approved* knowledge." This concept comes very near to what Max

<hr/>

[68]Jaspers, *op. cit.,* vol. III, p. 26: *"Das Symbol stiftet Gemeinschaft ohne Kommunikation."*

Scheler called the *"relativ natuerliche Weltanschauung"* (relative natural conception of the world)[69] prevailing in a social group and also
Sumner's[70] classical theory of the folkways of the in-group which are
taken by its members as the only right, good, and efficient way of life.

Socially approved knowledge consists, thus, of a set of recipes designed
to help each member of the group to define his situation in the reality of
everyday life in a typical way. It is entirely irrelevant for a description of
a world taken for granted by a particular society whether the socially
approved and derived knowledge is indeed true knowledge. All elements of such knowledge, including appresentational references of any
kind, if *believed* to be true are real components of the "definition of the
situation" by the members of the group. The "definition of the situation"
refers to the so-called "Thomas theorem" well known to sociologists: "If
men define situations as real, they are real in their consequences."[71] Applied to our problem and translated into our terminology this means: if
an appresentational relationship is socially approved, then the appresented object, fact, or event is believed beyond question to be in its
typicality an element of the world taken for granted.

In the process of transmitting socially approved knowledge the learning of the vernacular of the mother tongue has a particularly important
function. The native language can be taken as a set of references which,
in accordance with the relative natural conception of the world as approved by the linguistic community, have predetermined what features
of the world are worthy of being expressed, and therewith what qualities
of these features and what relations among them deserve attention, and
what typifications, conceptualizations, abstractions, generalizations, and
idealizations are relevant for achieving typical results by typical means.
Not only the vocabulary but also the morphology and the syntax of any
vernacular reflects the socially approved relevance system of the lin-

[69]Max Scheler, *Die Wissensformen und die Gesellschaft, Probleme einer Sociologie des
Wissens,* Leipzig, 1926, pp. 58 ff. *Cf.* Howard Becker and Hellmuth Dahlke, "Max
Scheler's Sociology of Knowledge," *Philosophy and Phenomenological Research,* 1942,
vol. II, pp. 310–322, esp. 315.

[70]William Graham Sumner, *Folkways; A Study of the Sociological Importance of
Manners, Customs, Mores, and Morals,* Guin, New York, 1906, esp. chap. I.

[71]It was first developed by William Isaac Thomas in his book, *The Child in America:
Behavior Problems and Programs,* Knopf, New York, 1928, p. 572. See also W. I. Thomas,
Social Behavior and Personality, edited by E. K. Volkart, Social Science Research Council,
New York, 1951, pp. 14 and 80 f.; the term "Thomas Theorem" was coined by Robert K.
Merton, *Social Theory and Social Structure,* Free Press, Glencoe, 1949, p. 179.

guistic group. If, for example, the Arabian language has several hundred nouns for denoting various kinds of camels but none for the general concept "camel"; if in certain North American Indian languages the simple notion, "I see a man," cannot be expressed without indicating by prefixes, suffixes, and interfixes whether this man stands or sits or walks, whether he is visible to the speaker or to the auditors; if the Greek language has developed morphological particularities such as the dual number, the optative mood, the aorist tense, and the medium voice of the verb; if the French language, so eminently suited to express philosophical thoughts, has for both "consciousness" and "conscience" a single term, namely, *"conscience"*—then all these facts reveal the relative natural conception of the world approved by the respective linguistic groups.

On the other hand, the determination of what is worthwhile and what is necessary to communicate depends on the typical, practical, and theoretical problems which have to be solved, and these will be different for men and women, for the young and for the old, for the hunter and for the fisherman, and in general, for the various social roles assumed by the members of the group. Each kind of activity has its particular relevance aspects for the performer and requires a set of particular technical terms. This is because our knowledge is *socially distributed;* each of us has precise and distinct knowledge only about that particular field in which he is an expert. Among experts a certain technical knowledge is taken for granted, but exactly this technical knowledge is inaccessible to the layman. Some things can be supposed as well known and self-explanatory and others as needing an explanation, depending upon whether I talk to a person of my sex, age, and occupation, or to somebody not sharing with me this common situation within society, or whether I talk to a member of my family, a neighbor, or to a stranger, to a partner or a nonparticipant in a particular venture, etc.

William James[72] has already observed that a language does not merely consist in the content of an ideally complete dictionary and an ideally complete and arranged grammar. The dictionary gives us only the kernel of the meaning of the words which are surrounded by "fringes." We may add that these fringes are of various kinds: those originating in a particular personal use by the speaker, others originating in the context of the speech in which the term is used, still others depending upon the

[72]James, *op. cit.,* vol. I, pp. 281 f.

addressee of my speech, or the situation in which the speech occurs, or the purpose of the communication, and, finally, upon the problem at hand to be solved. What has been stated about language holds good in general for appresentational references of all kinds. In communication or in social intercourse each appresentational reference, if socially approved, constitutes merely the kernel around which fringes of the kind described are attached.

But all this already presupposes an existing typification of social relations, of social forms of intercommunication, of social stratification taken for granted by the group, and therefore socially approved by it. This whole system of types under which any social group experiences itself has to be learned by a process of acculturation. The same holds for the various marks and indications for the position, status, role, and prestige each individual occupies or has within the stratification of the group. In order to find my bearings within the social group, I have to know the different ways of dressing and behaving, the manifold insignia, emblems, tools, etc., which are considered by the group as indicating social status and are therefore socially approved as relevant. They indicate also the typical behavior, actions, and motives which I may expect from a chief, a medicine man, a priest, a hunter, a married woman, a young girl, etc. In a word, I have to learn the typical social roles and the typical expectations of the behavior of the incumbents of such roles, in order to assume the appropriate corresponding role and the appropriate corresponding behavior expected to be approved by the social group.[73] At the same time, I have to learn the typical distribution of knowledge prevailing in this group, and this involves knowledge of the appresentational, referential, and interpretive schemes which each of the subgroups takes for granted and applies to its respective appresentational reference. All this knowledge is, in turn, of course, socially derived.

Let us focus and summarize our findings. We may say that in terms of the relevance system the following are all socially determined: first,

[73]Readers familiar with Parsons's and Shil's monograph quoted in footnote 30 will recognize in this statement an allusion to their theory of "role-expectancies." Although the approach of the present paper differs from these authors' in several respects, their treatment of a common system of symbols as a precondition of the reciprocity or complementarity of role expectations is compatible with the view here suggested. Cf., *f.e., op. cit.,* pp. 105, 162 f., 166; see also Talcott Parsons, *The Social System,* Free Press, Glencoe, 1951, esp. chap. IX, "Expressive Symbols and the Social System." Of course, Parsons's notion of "symbol" is not the same as that of this paper.

the unquestioned matrix within which any inquiry starts;[74] second, the elements of knowledge which have to be considered as socially approved and which might, therefore, be taken for granted (here we would add that those elements which might become problematic are traced out by the social situation); third, which procedures (with respect to signs and symbols)—practical, magical, political, religious, poetical, scientific, etc. —are appropriate for dealing with the problem involved; fourth, the typical conditions under which a problem can be considered as solved and the conditions under which an inquiry may be broken off and the results incorporated into the stock of knowledge taken for granted. This is of particular importance for symbolic references to myths and to rituals. If the successful connecting of a problem at hand with a socially approved symbol is considered as its typical solution, then the appresentational relationship thus established may continue to function as an appresenting element of other and higher symbolizations which might be founded on the problem deemed typically solved.

2) *The symbolic appresentation of society*

In an earlier section (IV, 4) we described briefly the various dimensions of the social world grouped around the central face-to-face relationship between consociates. Only in the We-relation, so we stated, can consociates by their mutual biographical involvement experience one another as unique individuals. In all the other dimensions of the social world—that of contemporaries, predecessors, and successors—a fellow man is not experienced in his individual uniqueness but in terms of his typical behavior-patterns, typical motives, and typical attitudes, and in various degrees of anonymity. In social situations of everyday life relations pertaining to all these dimensions are frequently intertwined. If in a face-to-face relationship with a friend I discuss a magazine article dealing with the attitude of the President and Congress toward the admission of China to the United Nations, I am in a relationship not only with the perhaps anonymous contemporary writer of the article but also with the contemporary individual or collective actors on the social scene designated by the terms "President," "Congress," "China," "United Nations"; and as my friend and I discussed this topic as citizens of the United States of 1954, we do so in an historical situation which is at least

[74]See footnote 42.

codetermined by the performances of our predecessors. And we have also in mind the impact which the decisions now to be taken might have on our successors, the future generations. All these notions are understandable to us as unclarified terms of commonsense thinking, because their meaning is taken for granted within our sociocultural environment. How is this possible?

We submit that in commonsense thinking we experience the social world on two levels of appresentational references:

i) We apprehend *individual* fellow men and their cogitations as realities within the world of everyday life. They are within our actual or potential reach, and we share or could share with them through communication a common comprehensive environment. To be sure, we can apprehend these individual fellow men and their cogitations only analogically through the system of appresentational references described in section IV, 4, and in this sense the world of the other transcends mine; but this is an "immanent transcendence" still within the reality of our daily life. Consequently, both members of the appresentational relation through which we apprehend this transcendency belong to the same finite province of meaning, the paramount reality.

ii) Social collectivities and institutionalized relations, however, are as such not entities within the province of meaning of everyday reality but constructs of commonsense thinking which have their reality in another subuniverse, perhaps that which William James called the subuniverse of ideal relations. For this very reason, we can apprehend them only symbolically; but the symbols appresenting them themselves pertain to the paramount reality and motivate our actions within it. This statement requires some comment.

We may start with the most obvious case, our experience of the social collectivity. Strictly speaking, we all are in the situation of Crainquebille, in the story by Anatole France, to whom government is just a grouchy old man behind a counter. To us government is represented by individuals: Congressmen, judges, tax collectors, soldiers, policemen, public servants, perhaps the President or the Queen or the *Fuehrer*. The political cartoonist shows us Uncle Sam conversing with John Bull and Marianne, or even the globe looking with a bewildered face at a hydrogen bomb which shows its teeth. The reason for this rude symbolism is, however, deeply rooted.

We mentioned before (IV, 4) that the We-relation as such transcends the existence of either consociate within the paramount reality and can be appresented only by symbolization. My friend is to me and I am to him an element of the reality of everyday life. But our friendship surpasses our individual situation within the finite province of meaning of the paramount reality. Since our notion of the We-relation is a purely formal one which refers to face-to-face situations of all degrees of intimacy and remoteness, the symbols by which such relations are appresented are of a great variety. Its appresenting member is always the common situation as defined by the participants, namely, that which they use, experience, enjoy, or endure together. A joint interest makes them partners, and the idea of *partnership* is perhaps the most general term for the appresented We-relation. (*We* are buddies, lovers, fellow sufferers, etc.)

The symbols become more discernible the more the social relationship is stabilized and institutionalized. The dwelling place of the family gets the appresentational meaning "home" which is protected by deities such as the *lares* and *penates*. The hearth is more than the fireplace, matrimony and wedlock are the ceremonial (or even sacramental) and legal symbols for marriage, a neighborhood is much more than an ecological concept.

All these examples refer, however, to social relations which can be brought within actual reach. This is the type of groups which Cooley[75] had in mind when he introduced the highly equivocal concept of primary group, and justifies the interest of modern sociologists in so-called small groups defined, for example, by Homans as

> a number of persons who are few enough so that every person may communicate with all the others not at second hand through other people but face-to-face.[76]

The situation is, however, different if the group is larger and a face-to-face relation cannot be established. Max Weber, who founded his theory on interpreting the social world in terms of the subjective meaning of the individual actor, is perfectly consistent in maintaining

> that it is *only* the existence of the probability that, corresponding to a certain given subjective meaning complex, a certain type of action will

[75]See footnote 33.

[76]George C. Homans, *The Human Group*, Harcourt, Brace & Company, New York, 1950, p. 1.

take place, which constitutes the "existence" of the social relationship. Thus that a "friendship" or a "state" exists or has existed means this and only this: that we, the observers, judge that there is or has been a probability that on the basis of certain kinds of known subjective attitudes of certain individuals there will result in the average sense a certain specific type of action.[77]

But this statement is itself a construct by the social scientist and, therefore, does not belong to the commonsense thinking of man within everyday life. He experiences the social and political organization by specific appresentations which Eric Voegelin has carefully analyzed in the book from which in section V, 2, b, we cited a characteristic quotation. According to this author, a political society as a cosmion illuminated from within

> has its internal meaning, but this realm exists tangibly in the external world in human beings who have bodies and through their bodies participate in the organic and inorganic externality of the world.

Representation, for example, may be taken in the elemental sense of external institutions (for example, members of the legislative assembly hold their membership by virtue of popular election) or in the existential sense,[78] meaning that political societies in order to be capable of action must have such an external structure as will enable some of its members —the ruler, sovereign, government, prince—to find habitual obedience to the acts of command. In other words,

> a political society comes into existence when it articulates itself and produces a representative.

But that is not all. We have, in addition, to distinguish

> between the representation of society by its articulated representatives and a second relation in which *society itself becomes the representative of something beyond itself, of a transcending reality.* . . . All the early empires understood themselves as representatives of the cosmic order . . . the great ceremonies of the empire represent the rhythms of the cosmos; festivals and sacrifices are a cosmic liturgy, a symbolic participation of the cosmion in the cosmos; and the ruler himself represents society,

[77]Max Weber, *Wirtschaft und Gesellschaft,* translated as *Theory of Economic and Social Organisation* by A. M. Henderson and T. Parsons, Oxford Press, New York, 1947, p. 119.

[78]See footnote 55. Voegelin, *op. cit.,* pp. 31, 34, 37, 49, 54 (italics mine).

because on earth he represents the transcendent power which maintains cosmic order.

Voegelin's book brings abundant illustrations for this "self-interpretation" of the group which he contrasts with the interpretation of the same symbols by the theorist. We cannot enter here into this fascinating topic. We merely want to add that the symbolic appresentations by which the in-group interprets itself have their counterpart in the interpretations of the same symbols by the out-group or out-groups. However, those interpretations will be necessarily different from that of the in-group, because the system of relevances of both groups (and the respective apperceptual, appresentational, and referential schemes taken as systems of reference for interpreting the "order" so created) cannot coincide. A wide field of concrete investigations is open here for the social scientist, investigations which are important not only from the theoretical but also from the practical point of view; for the manipulating of symbols, whether for persuasion or propaganda, requires at least a clarification of their intrinsic structure.

VIII) *Concluding Remarks*

We have seen that man is indeed an *"animal symbolicum,"* if we understand under this term his need and also his capacity to come to terms, with the help of appresentational relations, with the various transcendences surpassing his actual Here and Now. The analysis of these transcendences—from those going beyond the limits of the world within his actual reach to those transgressing the paramount reality of everyday life—is a major task of any philosophical anthropology. At the same time, the clarification of the categories of commonsense thinking within everyday life is indispensable for the proper foundation of all the social sciences. As far as symbols in the narrower sense are concerned, the fact that they transcend the realm of the paramount reality tends not to exclude, but rather to encourage the investigations of symbolic functions and forms within the social world by the empirical social sciences in accordance with the rules governing the concept and theory formation of these sciences.[79] The philosophical problem involved, however, was stated by Goethe with unsurpassable clarity:

[79]Alfred Schutz, "Concept and Theory Formation in the Social Sciences," *Journal of Philosophy*, vol. LI, 1954, pp. 257–273.

Das ist die wahre Symbolik, wo das Besondere das Allgemeinere repraesentiert, nicht als Traum und Schatten, sondern als lebendig-augenblickliche Offenbarung des Unerforschlichen.

(True symbolism is where the particular represents the general, not as a dream and a shadow, but as a vivid instantaneous revelation of that which cannot be explored.)[80]

Comment by Charles Morris:

Alfred Schutz's paper is a welcome addition to the literature of contemporary semiotic, since there are few basic discussions in this field written from the standpoint of phenomenology. His paper helps to fill this gap.

Since it would be impossible adequately to assess this approach without comparing it to other approaches, I will raise only two related queries internal to the paper itself. Both center around the term "transcendence." For the most part the term "transcendence" is linked with the term "experience" (as in the phrase "transcendent experiences"), but at times this is not so (as in the phrase "an inaccessible zone of the other's private life which transcends my possible experience"). It seems to me that an unnoticed passage back and forth from *experience of transcendence* to *transcendence of experience* obscures the argument at a number of crucial points.

Connected with this is the question of the relation of transcendence to marks, indications, signs, and symbols (*i.e.,* to "appresentational relations"). Does the experience of transcendence come first and exist independently of appresentational relations, or is the experience of transcendence simply the experience of appresentational relations? I do not see that this last possibility is excluded by the analysis given by the paper. But unless it is, then the "main thesis" of the paper (that "appresentational references are means of coming to terms with transcendent experiences of various kinds") is on insecure ground. And if in the thesis "transcendent experiences" were taken to mean "transcendences of experience," then it would be difficult to see the sense in which the approach is phenomenological.

Professor Schutz's reply:

I am extremely grateful for Charles Morris's critical remarks which are entirely to the point. The relationship between transcendence and experience is indeed at the core of my argument and I admit frankly that my presentation of this crucial problem is by no means satisfactory. I should be glad if I had merely to plead guilty of linguistic imprecision in using the term "transcendent experience" equivocally. Unfortunately, the problems involved are far more complicated. To investigate them thoroughly would require a paper of at least equal length on the phenomenological theory of constitution. Morris's admirably concise questions give me at least the welcome opportunity to characterize the underlying complications in a very rough and sketchy way.

Morris finds that an unnoticed passage back and forth from experience of transcendence to transcendence of experience obscures the argument of my paper at a number of crucial points. I hope that my paper shows that there are several levels of experience. Each of them may be selected as the basic system of reference and in relation to it the others appear as transcendences. Thus, for example, the world within my potential (restorable and attainable) reach transcends the world within my actual reach, once selected as basic system of reference; the intersubjective sociocultural world that of physical things; the various "subuniverses" of science, art, religion, etc., the paramount reality of the world of everyday life. In brief, transcendences of this kind are experienced on each level, and man has to come to terms with them by appresentational references.

[80]Johann Wolfgang von Goethe, *Aus Kunst und Altertum,* 1826.

So far, however, I have merely dealt with the experience *of* transcendence. But this is only half the story. It is one of the basic findings of phenomenological analysis that there is no such thing as a readymade cleancut isolated experience. Each actual experience carries with it its inner and outer horizons, which are more or less empty; each experience is from the outset "thematic" within a marginal field. For instance, the actual perception of an object of the outer world in its particular perspective and adumbration refers, first, to a horizon of potential aspects of the same object in different perspectives and adumbrations, and, secondly, to other objects constituting its environment. Some of these experiences are not actualized, but merely anticipated as possible actualizations. In this sense it could be said that any experience (*e.g.,* a sensory one) transcends itself if, not otherwise, then by its reference to its open horizons. In this respect phenomenological analysis meets with certain (although unclarified) basic tenets of *Gestalt* psychology, with William James's concept of "fringes," with Whitehead's theory of the principle of aggregation (that is, the transformation of the various sense-presentations into thought-objects of perception), and with certain points of G. E. Moore's analysis of commonsense experience.

I submit, therefore, that the "passage back and forth from experience of transcendence to transcendence of experience" is deeply rooted in the structure of the activities of the mind, the outcome of which is generally called experience.

The second query of Morris is, I hope, also answered by what precedes. He asks: "Does the experience of transcendence come first and exist independently of appresentation, or is the experience of transcendence simply the experience of appresentational relations?"

As to the second part of this question, my answer is emphatically in the negative. To be sure, man can come to terms with experiences of transcendences only by means of appresentational references. But this implies neither that the experiences of transcendence are simply the experiences of appresentational references, nor that there are not appresentational references of a different kind. As to the first part of this question, it seems to me that the problem of whether the experience of transcendence comes first, loses its meaning in the light of the already given outline of the concatenation of experience and transcendence, let alone the highly equivocal meaning of the term "comes first."

CHAPTER VIII

Symbolism and the Education of Man

By ROBERT ULICH

Let it be a word, a proposition, a book, a man, a fellowship, or whatever you please: as soon as it is proposed to make it serve as limit, in such a way that the limit is not itself again dialectical, we have superstition and narrowness of spirit. There always lurks some such concern in a man, at the same time indolent and anxious, a wish to lay hold of something so really fixed that it can exclude all dialectics; but this desire is an expression of cowardice, and is deceitfulness toward the divine.[1]

Toute chose dont on peut se faire une idée nette perd de sa force de prestige et de sa résonance dans l'esprit.[2]

I

According to the Greek dictionaries the word *"symbolon"* indicates all that which serves as a token for something that cannot be immediately shown or provided; *e.g.,* a contract concerning future financial obligations is called "symbolon"; a symbolon is also the signal or portent of natural events; it may also be a sign by which a person can establish his identity, or distant persons can recognize their messages.[3] Thus, since the symbolon was conceived of as the representation of the important, yet not existing in concrete actuality, it could also denote the invisible appearing in the visible, the abstract in the real, and the transcendent in the world of immanence. The symbolon became the bridge between the two banks of the seen and the unseen which flank the river of human existence.

When the Greek term—if I am not mistaken, mainly through theological channels—entered into the development of our multifarious West-

---

[1]Sören Kierkegaard, *Concluding Unscientific Postscript,* translated by D. F. Swenson and W. Lowrie, Princeton University Press, Princeton, 1944, book I, chap. 11, par. 2, p. 35 n.

[2]Paul Valéry, "Fonction et Mystère de L'Académie" in, *Regards sur le Monde Actuel,* Gallimard, Paris, 34th edition, 1945, p. 292.

[3]On the philology of the word "symbolon" see Max Schlesinger, *Geschichte des Symbols,* L. Simion Nf., Berlin, 1912, pp. 7–34 (contains extensive bibliography).

ern civilization, its scope widened with the increasing wealth of human experience. According to modern English dictionaries "symbol" is "that which suggests something else by reason of relationship," or "a visible sign of something invisible." Consequently, it could apply to a picture, a national flag, the Christian cross, and Hitler's *Hakenkreuz*. We have a "philosophy of symbolic forms" as we have various forms of "symbolism" in the fine arts and an enormous amount of symbolic suggestion in modern propaganda and advertising.

In an ultimate sense, all human language is a form of symbolism, so is mathematics, and so are our various systems of script and musical notation. Thus Herbert Spencer is correct when he says in his *First Principles* (2nd part, chap. XXIV, par. 194):

> The interpretation of all phenomena in terms of matter, motion and force is nothing more than the reduction of our complex symbols of thought to the simplest symbols; and when the equation has been brought to its lowest terms, the symbols remain symbols still.

Even the perceptions that connect us with the outer world, are symbolic. They are so in a twofold sense: first, they symbolize to us the object (which we never see or feel at once in its essence and totality); second, they symbolize previous elements in our mental life. The words "house" or "table" represent not only this house or that table, but a synthesis between a specified perception and a complex interaction of those inner phenomena to which—to mention only one among many—Kant devotes the "transcendental doctrine of elements" in his *Critique of Pure Reason*.[4]

[4]For literature on the topic of Symbolism see:

Ernst Bloch, *Geist der Utopie*, P. Cassierer, Berlin, 1923, and *Freiheit und Ordnung: Abriss der Sozial-Utopien*, Aurora Verlag, New York, 1946.

Ernst Cassirer, *The Philosophy of Symbolic Forms*, translated by R. Manheim, preface by C. W. Hendel, Yale University Press, New Haven, 1953.

H. F. Dunbar, *Symbolism in Medieval Thought and Its Consummation in the Divine Comedy*, Yale University Press, New Haven, 1929.

C. G. Jung, *Aion: Untersuchungen zur Symbolgeschichte*, Rascher, Zurich, 1951.

A. E. M. Katzenellenbogen, *Allegories of the Virtues and Vices in Medieval Art*, The Warburg Institute, London, 1939.

Ludwig Klages, *Der Geist als Widersacher der Seele*, especially 3rd Band, 2nd Teil, J. A. Barth, Leipzig, 1932.

Susanne K. Langer, *Philosophy in a New Key; A Study in the Symbolism of Reason, Rite and Art*, Harvard University Press, Cambridge, Massachusetts, 1942.

Max Schlesinger, *Geschichte des Symbols: Ein Versuch*, L. Simion Nf., Berlin, 1912. The most comprehensive special work on symbolism known to me.

Since that which means too much means eventually nothing, the term symbol has lost all semantic usefulness, unless it is precisely defined. However, regarding the meaning of "symbol" and especially of "symbolism" the educated layman is probably influenced most of all by our spiritual tradition and would tell us that the term in question refers primarily to the aspirational and artistic domains of human culture. If he is a Catholic, the holy water is the symbol of ceremonial purity; if he is a Lutheran Protestant, the iron cock on the steeple of his church may remind him of Peter's betrayal of Christ; if interested in foreign cultures, he may read a description of the overwhelming wealth of symbolism in a Buddhist temple or an Indian dance.

This realm of what I may call "aspirational symbolism" is of greatest significance for human culture and its understanding in that it expresses the eternal conflict in man's destiny between the finite and the infinite, and the relative and the absolute, which is part of man's destiny. Before the greatest, men become silent. They are disturbed by the chatter of voices and the pallor of concepts; yet they desire to be united exactly by their common sense of the noiseless, unspeakable, sublime, and perhaps unachievable. Symbols fulfil this purpose. They are expressions of man's loneliness as well as of his desire for belonging and community. The silence of the Quakers is one of mankind's greatest symbolic acts.

Of this group of symbols I wish here to emphasize one particular function. Whenever man in his finiteness and fallibility is confronted with the infinite, he is thrown into a situation of polarity. On the one hand, he is overwhelmed by the feeling of distance between that which is and that which is beyond; on the other hand, the beyond works in him as a voice of judgment and a spur. Human life is forever confronted with the unachievable. But if this were not the case, it would have remained in the low regions of a merely vegetative life.

II

Needless to say, the unachievable is in itself of no worth. If someone constructed a symbol for his desire to walk physically on clouds, or to

---

Alfred North Whitehead, *Symbolism, Its Meaning and Effect,* The Macmillan Company, New York, 1927.
Needless to say, almost all books on esthetics contain chapters and references to symbolism, and so do many books on religion and anthropology.

live without food and sleep, we would think of calling a psychiatrist. That which is beyond reach and attainment must be something worth striving for, it must give him the sense of goal and direction; and, though beyond fulfilment, it must fill him with the conviction that the ideal may wait for him and be spiritually nearer than the things nearby. In this way man recognizes that human life is ever self-transcendent, and that the achievable is but the foreground before the ever present, yet immense landscape of ultimate reality.

Symbols indicative of this situation are to be found in all important activities of the human race.

1) Of those belonging to the *religious* sphere we have already spoken. The ever present, yet ever evasive is, for my feeling, most beautifully expressed in Lao Tse's symbol of the Tao, or the Way toward Truth.

> That which cannot be seen is formless. That which cannot be heard is noiseless. That which cannot be touched is bodiless. These three cannot be examined in detail, for they really constitute one indivisible whole.
>
> This indivisible whole (Truth) does not appear bright when viewed at the summit, or dark when viewed at the nadir. It is imperceptible and indescribable. It is always changing, and reverting to the state of Nothingness. It is formless, shapeless, vague and indefinite. Facing it, one cannot see its head; pursuing it, one cannot see its tail. Abide by the primordial Truth, and the States of today can be ruled. Know the primary conditions, and you know the principles of Truth.[5]

In the Judaic and Islamic traditions the recognition of the Divine as the utter Beyond is so strong that they forbid its artistic representation. Man must not make "graven images," not only because the Absolute may lose its intangibleness and be dragged down into the area of idols competing against each other, but also because man may lose the feeling of fearful, yet exalting distance between the Perfect and the frailty of all that is human. Also Buddhism and Christianity are pervaded by the idea of the *Deus Ineffabilis*. Yet, both not only permit images, but often look with indulgence, if not with favor, at their veneration. Thus, while some cults and places of worship may invoke in us a sense of sublime wonder and elevation, at others we may have embarrassing doubts

[5]Lao Tzyy, *The Works of . . . Truth and Nature Popularly Known as Daw-Der-Jing, . . .* edited and translated by Cheng Lin, The World Book Company (Ancient Chinese Classics Series), Yonkers, New York, 1949?, p. 40.

whether we find ourselves still in a transcendental-monotheistic, or in a magic-polytheistic culture.

2) Still more than in religion, it is in the political sphere that there emerges the danger of fusion between symbols of infinite transcendence and symbols of human immanence and self-satisfaction. As a matter of fact, one may doubt whether this sphere with its preoccupation with power and success is capable of driving man beyond his material environment. Yet, for some French knight the *oriflamme* or *aurea flamma,* coming originally from the famous abbey of Saint Denis, may have been not merely a palladium or a national emblem which, in itself, often has an aspirational and educational value. The sacred symbol may have reminded him that the life of the warrior and his nation is neither in the hands of men alone, nor exclusively for them, but under and for the light of God. In this case the political would have combined with the religious —a frequent mixture, the value of which depends on whether the first or the second gains priority.

If André Maurois speaks of his country as *"le pays des croisades et des cathédrales, de Jeanne d'Arc et de saint Louis,"*[6] does he speak merely of human achievement and use events of transcendent, if not transcendental character, for enhancing *"la gloire de la patrie,"* or does he speak of a great, yet never fulfilled vision? Similarly, mixed sentiments are to be found in every advanced civilization. No doubt the concept of liberty, as expressed by the Founding Fathers of this country, was something to be fought for in the immediate realm of political reality; on the other hand, it also was conceived of as an ideal ever pointing forward and giving direction to action but never fully achieved. In spite of the aversion to religious dogmatism, "liberty" in the mind of Jefferson rang a religious, as well as a political note. The same was the case with the ideals of the French revolution during their formative period. For the Englishman the "crown" is neither an object of jewelry nor merely a sign of power, but, as the symbolism of the Coronation shows, also an appeal. The question of the future is whether the modern national state becomes the end in itself, like the Church under the Inquisition, or whether it will understand itself as a part of the "objective *Geist"* or as an instrument working under the judgment of human conscience which should transcend all instruments and institutions. If the latter is the case,

[6]André Maurois, *Histoire de la France,* Dom. Wapler, Paris, 1947, p. 212.

human history is but in its beginning; if the first happens, then we are already at the end of the road. The future will be self-destruction.[7]

We have now for the first time a political symbol without a national territory behind it, namely, the flag of the United Nations. We all know that the complete political unity of mankind is an unachievable ideal; it can only be striven for. But the striving has always been the only safeguard of mankind.

3) Naturally, as in religion and politics, there always have been symbols of the infinite and undefinable also in the intellectual and moral spheres. The Greek symbol of wisdom appears still in Hegel's profound word that a culture arrives at its deepest insights when the "owls of Athene" begin their evening flight. The "Tower of Wisdom" is a standard picture in medieval florilegia; medieval fantasy created the *"Gral"* which was for Wolfram von Eschenbach the analogy to the supernatural mysterium of the Eucharist and the symbol of knightly education. The "cardinal virtues" have inspired Andrea Pisano's symbolic representation on one of the doors at the Baptisterio of Florence.

And just as the art of the great cathedrals and their symbolic sculpture has mystical and at the same time aspirational significance, so there works a certain mystique also in famous universities and learned institutions. The definable and already attained constantly point toward the undefinable and not yet achieved.

Of the Académie Française Paul Valéry says:

> We are that which we believe to be and that which others believe that we are. No one, not even we ourselves is able to define it precisely. The singular characteristic of the *Académie* is its undefinableness. If it were not of that kind its glory would not be what one says it is. Everything of which one can form a neat concept loses its power of prestige and its resonance in the minds of men. . . .

---

[7]I leave it to the reader to decide under which category of political symbolism he wishes to place some sentences in President Eisenhower's Address to the Nation on "Multiplicity of Fears." See *New York Times,* April 6, 1954, p. 16c.

> To have a free, peaceful and prosperous world we must be ever stronger. We must be ever stronger not only in the things I've mentioned, but particularly in the spiritual things. . . .
> But we do not have to be hysterical. We can stand up and hold up our heads and say "America is the greatest force that God has ever allowed to sit on His Footstool."
> As such it is up to us to lead this world to a peaceful secure existence. And I assure you we can do it.

Therefore a certain mystery surrounds the Academy, which is essential for its understanding.[8]

III

When the symbolic image is venerated by the faithful as an object in itself, supposed to bring the sacred and ideal down to earth, to radiate healing power, or to do damage to the enemy, it has changed from a symbol into a magic contrivance and is then of little or no educational value. The fact that the *oriflamme* fell in disgrace after the defeat at Agincourt in 1415 indicates that for most Frenchmen it had not been a transcendental symbol, which, like the cross for the true Christian, can never be defeated, but a charm. When the French revolutionaries forgot that the terms *liberté, fraternité,* and *egalité* are symbols of moral postulates the full realization of which lies always in the future, but tried to enforce them upon their fellow men, they erected the guillotine rather than the kingdom of man. *Fraternité ou la mort* means terrorism as much as the Inquisitional concept of *nulla salus extra ecclesiam*. When the American citizen hears from political chauvinists that there is only one right way of living, namely, the American, his instincts may be flattered, but actually he hears not a democratic voice. For such a voice, in all love for the country, would also speak of the relativity of all human institutions and the unachieved hopes in this as well as in other nations. To set one's country in the place of the Absolute endangers both the country and its true ideals.

Does it follow from this premise that only a society of "transcendental" (not to be confused with "transcendent") or "supranatural" character can be productive of aspirational symbolism, whereas a so-called "naturalist" society cannot?

As a matter of fact, we find in many books on religious and moral problems the assertion that exclusively the former kind of society is capable of creating the symbols and cults which, through reminding man of the perfect and unachievable as the judge above, motivate him at the same time to strive for ever higher ideals.

[8]Paul Valéry, *Regards sur le Monde Actuel*, Gallimard, Paris, 1945, p. 292. Translated by author. One could write an interesting essay on the symbolism in the seal of Harvard University. What are the reasons behind the fact that in some periods it contained the word, *Veritas*, in combination with the words, *Pro Christo et Ecclesia*, and in other periods only the first of the two mottos?

This contradistinction between supranaturalism as rich and naturalism (then easily identified with materialism) as barren of edifying symbolism seems to have a certain historic justification. One thinks of medieval Christianity with its rituals, processions, and cathedrals, and contrasts with it our time of supposedly jejune and dreary "rationalism" and "mechanization."

Yet, this distinction is built on a confusion of ill defined terms; in addition, it is often not without ulterior motives. It commits the same error as the conclusion of rationalists of the superficial brand, from Comte de Volny of the eighteenth century to certain "dialectic materialists" and dogmatic "experimentalists" of our time, who proclaim that religion, because from their point of view identical with anti-empiricism and superstition, has been nothing but a retarding element in human history and education.

We generally believe we know what the terms "supranaturalism" and "transcendentalism" intend to convey: the source of life and mind is not in nature, but "beyond." But that phrase has no sense unless one defines what one means by "life," "mind," and especially by "nature." Certainly, if they mean nothing but mechanically directed or self-ordering, compounds of "matter"—whatever "matter" may mean—then the poor "naturalist" is doomed to live in a world without inspiration, chances, transcendent symbols, and ideals. But who advocates such a position in regard to human civilization? In contrast, if by "nature" is meant a constantly developing cosmos, an emerging and dynamic universe with that mysterious and inextricable mixture of what we humans call "matter" and "mind," what would prevent the "naturalist" from living in a profound feeling of ever occurring self-transcendence?

For the supranaturalist Christian of the Middle Ages fate was anchored in God. He was the fountain of human blessedness and salvation. Thus, the wheel as the image of human destiny, is pictured in medieval manuscripts as being turned by God. But the more "naturalist" Renaissance humanist, for whom the factors of chance, individual decision, and exposure entered into the interpretation of human life, who, in other words, was no longer a "transcendentalist" of the traditional kind, there still existed the man-transcendent idea of destiny. But now the wheel was turned by the capricious lady *Fortuna;* or it was replaced by the symbol of the sailboat with man steering but nevertheless never sure whether he could catch the right wind into the canvas.

And where do we find a more profound feeling for the wonder of life and the moral mission of humanity, in some of the typical Sunday sermons with their anthropomorphical tendencies, or in the following letter which the Prussian "atheist" and Voltarian, King Frederick II, wrote in 1762 to the pious Princess Amalie of Prussia?

> You have relations to Heaven which I do not have. Therefore you may know whether and how your eternal father-in-law looks on us with favor or disfavor. I live as a poor mortal who does not know a dog in Paradise, and in my ignorance I receive joyfully the good and suffer patiently the disagreeable that occur to me. Permit me nevertheless that a poor layman directs your attention at some difficulties which originate at the bottom of your doctrine. The pagans pictured fortune to be blind because mostly she is unjust; her qualities were caprice and fickleness, which is a correct observation. If now you put divine providence in place of fortune then you are bound to charge this divine providence with all its little injustices which the pagans attributed to their *fortuna*. This however, in my opinion, would be a kind of sacrilege. I feel a profound reverence for the Divine and, for this reason, guard against ascribing to it an unjust and wavering attitude which one would condemn with the humblest mortal. Hence, my dear sister, I believe that the omnipotent and benevolent Ground of Being cares not in the least for our human affairs. Rather I think that whatever happens must first be attributed to us and to the necessary effects of uncalculable causes. And I bow silently before the sacred Ultimate, confessing my ignorance about its ways which, in its divine wisdom, it has not deigned to reveal to me.
>
> Goodbye, my dear bride of Christ. If you think I lack in the right faith, please do not decide to burn me at the stake. And though you consider me a great heretic, believe nevertheless that I love you with a feeling of true affection.[9]

Thus, why should more humane and humanistic ideals, even if they have sometimes grown out of an anti-supranaturalist attitude, have less transcendent and inspiring power than transcendental symbols? On the contrary, humane ideals and their expressions may encourage man to include in the orbit of his dreams responsibilities that otherwise would be neglected. Truly, the rationalist, humanist, and naturalist have to guard themselves against the danger of overestimating the power of man and

[9] Translated by the author from *Deutsche Geisteswelt*, Herausgegeben von Hermann Noack, Bd. I: *Von Luther bis Hegel*, Holle Verlag, Darmstadt, 1953, p. 104.

thus becoming irrealistic rather than realistic. On the other hand, the supernaturalist and religious should protect themselves against two seemingly opposite dangers, namely, mistaking their manmade symbols for the language of God, or placing the infinite and unachievable so far into the sphere of the utter beyond that its affinity with all that is human becomes lost, and with it the incentive to strive and the hope that there is a relation between human endeavor and progress. There is such a danger in some forms of modern Protestant neoorthodoxy. Not without justification have men who fought against human poverty suspected a certain transcendentalism as providing "opium" rather than health for the people. Thus, if one reads today that political ideals, because world-immanent and naturalist, tend to create fetishes, one might also remember that the same was the case with transcendental symbols. Totalitarianism, as an attempt to present the infinite as finite, the unachievable as achieved, the partial as the whole, and the fallible as infallible, is apparently a temptation to which men have succumbed in ecclesiastical as well as in secular environments. There is no other salvation from man but man's belief that the truth is always larger.

The symbol alone does not justify the crusade. The holy may turn into a cruelty. There were pious crusaders with the cross on their armor who had not more respect for the lives of the "infidels" than had the Nazi generals with the swastika on their decorations for the lives of their political and racial enemies. Hitler also spoke of a new religion and of a thousand years necessary for achieving the impossible; also he demanded sacrifice. And many Russian Communists never concealed from themselves and others their conviction that their own generation, and even later ones, would have to suffer for the goal of the world revolution. I remember pathetic figures among Russian and German students who believed in Communism or National Socialism as salvation from man's corruption with the same vigor that the Seventh Day Adventists believe in the truth of their gospel. And there were visitors from the United States and other countries who believed both the Communists and the Nazis—believed because they felt a deep urge to believe; they were probably more ready to give themselves to something of great dimension than those who ridicule or persecute them. It would have been better for them and the whole of mankind if there had been less symbolism, but more rationality.

Hence, if we may be permitted to speak of humanly productive or humanly destructive symbols, the criterion cannot lie in the distinction between supranatural and natural, transrational and rational, or transcendental and world-immanent.

All these attitudes can contain the notion of the greatness that transcends the immediate; all of them can evoke an inner passion which is hard to differentiate from the religious. And in all of them lurks the danger of the perversion of the sublime into the diabolic, of the inspirational into the demonic, and of the devotional into the murderous.

Symbols may help man toward the vision of the great and the holy. However, the creative impulse lies not in the symbols themselves but in the sensitiveness of man to higher and universal values. And when, on the one hand, we admit that the communalizing quality of symbols may elevate the mediocre person for a while above his ordinariness, it may, on the other hand, excite his false pride, his fanaticism, and his tendency to surrender his individual responsibility to the lure of the moment. For such is the greatness as well as the danger in all collectivizing agents.

IV

As a matter of fact, the realm of the symbolic may be gradually limited from two sides without any harm to human progress.

First, empirical research and increasing knowledge will encroach on the kind of pseudomysticism and pseudosymbolism that enjoys human ignorance and insecurity because they provide a chance to relate supposedly inexplicable events to "divine will" or the working of miracles. Up to the time of Franklin lightning was a sign of the wrath of God. Even in our so-called technical era similar superstitions have not yet entirely disappeared. Yet, without doubt the greatest force against mystical symbolism has been exact science, with its reliance on the functional symbols of numbers and geometrical signs, rather than on the inherent quality of things and the poetic charm of metaphors, though the first pioneers of the symbolism of mathematics were at the same time also lovers of mystical symbolism. (As a matter of fact, this seemingly paradoxical phenomenon would deserve a special phenomenological analysis.) Second, critical research and intellectual honesty may teach man that it is better to confess his ignorance and to look, as it were, straight into the impenetrable eyes of the infinite, than to resort to the foreground of symbols. Indeed, the retreat from unsolved problems into the fog of mystery has often prevented mankind from lifting itself onto the level of courageous reasoning and self-education. Only a few symbols may still be great enough for men trained to think and, consequently, also willing to acknowledge the limits of their thinking. As far as I know there are very few symbols in Kant's language. The image of the "starry heaven" at the end of his *Critique of Practical Reason* was more a metaphor for the inner order that he divined in the natural and moral cosmos than a genuine symbol.

But where, then, is to be found the criterion which distinguishes between the angel and the devil?

The criterion lies in the fact that the truly great symbol, as well as the truly great ideal, is inclusive rather than exclusive, universal rather than restricted, embracing rather than rejecting. The symbol of the cross may have been abused a thousand times, yet in its essence it contains the idea of the salvation of mankind, irrespective of "blood" and "soil." The verbal symbols of "equality" and "liberty" are intended to liberate not only the French and Americans but humanity as a whole. Even the "gentleman ideal," originally restricted to a privileged group of Englishmen, has since the seventeenth century gradually developed not into an ideal of conduct restricted to a particular class or nation, but into a general human ideal.

But here again, we are in a logical trap. For if we use the test of inclusiveness, we have certainly to eliminate Hitler's National Socialism; but we can hardly eliminate Communism with its strong Socialist and world-embracing attitude. But we dislike Communism not only because we find ourselves in an international entanglement with Russia, but because it is, in too many respects, opposed to our ethical ideas.

Therefore, in addition to the criteria of transcendence and inclusiveness in regard to our group of symbols, we have to search for another and more valid criterion. This criterion lies in the use of the *means* by which men try to materialize their vision. If the end justifies the means, *i.e.,* if the ideality of the goal allows the seeker to idealize even the most dirty and bloody path, then it makes no difference whether there flies on the banner the cross, or the star of David, or the hammer and sickle.

These considerations lead us out of the restricted area of symbolism into another realm of discourse, namely, the ethical. Indeed, ultimately the symbols of the infinite and ideal have to be described by the same categories as the ethical. The ethical, too, is transcendent, it points toward ever receding goals, it tends to be comprehensive. But, in addition, it includes in its judgment the means by which the goal is to be approximated. Furthermore, if one believes, as I do, that in the final analysis the ethical and the rational converge, or that in an ultimate sense the *summum bonum* and the *summum verum* are the same, then one would have to add a further criterion by asking the question, "Does the challenge of the symbol not only remind man of transcendence, inclusiveness, and morality in regard to both ends and means, but does it also encourage him to use and emphasize his rational capacity to the utmost?"

V

But if the language of symbolism can be replaced by other forms of expression, why do we have symbols? Why do we take them so seriously? Are they perhaps merely decorative elements which block rather than open man's view toward the infinite? Would the wealth of logical, ethical, and educational concepts and precepts, of philosophical and religious wisdom, as it has developed in the course of centuries, not suffice to make man better if he *wanted and strove* to be better? If not, symbols make no difference.

Here we leave the area of the theoretical and enter the realm of the practical.

Pure wisdom and ethical principles might suffice for some, but certainly not for the majority of human beings for whom the invisible and ideal needs some semblance in the realm of appearances. Symbols not only satisfy the esthetic and communal sense in man; they also relieve tension; they help the person as well as its society to maintain themselves in the uncertainty of existence between finiteness and infinity. Though, in their tendency to make themselves absolute, they lead man downward, in pointing beyond the achieved toward the unachieved, they lead him upward. It is with the symbolic, as it is with the romantic. The romantic is dangerous. But take it away, and life becomes an ocean of boredom.

Whatever the value or nonvalue of symbols may be, they are a highly favored medium of a majority of men in their dialogues with each other and the otherwise too distant infinite. The disappearance of the symbolic would in those many persons who are not used to abstractions weaken the sense of inspiring imagination. In stricter reference to education, conceived now as a device for molding the minds of the young, the question would be, "To what degree is a certain amount of symbols necessary to arouse in the youth of a nation, as well as in its teachers, a vivid sense of the inspiring influence of the ideal worthy to strive at, though beyond achievement?"

This question may cause a smile on the lips of many modern teachers and psychologists.

The present, and in some ways natural, trend in education is that effort follows interest and that interest cannot develop unless there is a feeling that the goal in sight is not too distant and difficult. Consequently, eliminate the unachievable as much as possible, for it generates only a sense of frustration and with it a lessening of interest and effort. To a large degree, this argument is correct, at least as far as we are concerned with the acquisition of definite skills and forms of knowledge. We know of early failures in languages and mathematics with their permanent effect on a person's whole life. More often than not this consequence could have been avoided if a gradual introduction and encouragement had been preferred to the frightening picture of the impossible. But even within the usual sphere of learning the situation is not so simple. For certain people, young and old, there may be stimulation in the sense of the difficult and the realization that mankind as a whole is constantly confronted with its challenge. First failure has often been the beginning of lasting success. It may help one to face life more courageously and thus to arrive finally at heights which otherwise would have been judged too distant. The sense of the unachievable lifts the level of the achievable; its absence lowers the standard.

This is so for the following reasons:

1) The formation of a lasting purpose in the life of a well endowed individual comes not always from the immediately tangible, but from a goal known to be in the realm of the ideal. This very capacity of inspiration distinguishes the individual of high quality from the mediocre person. It is a dangerous mistake if under the influence of a misunderstood "pragmatism" every goal that is not "immanent," "instrumental," "functional," or "experimental," is considered extraneous to the learning process, subject to the danger of dogmatism and fixation, and therefore a hindrance to cultural progress. It is the very mark of great human visions that they transcend the powers of individual man, perhaps even

of humanity as a whole. So does Socrates's vision of harmony which is behind his symbol of Eros, or the god of Love.

> He who under the influence of true love rising upward from these tangible and perishable beauties begins to see that beauty absolute, is not far from the end. And the true order of going or being led by another to the things of love, is to use the beauties of earth as steps along which he mounts upwards for the sake of that other beauty, going from one to two, and from two to all fair forms, and from fair forms to fair actions, and from fair actions to fair notions, until from fair notions he arrives at the notion of absolute beauty, and at last knows what the essence of beauty is.[10]

And so does Saint Paul's vision of the *imitatio Christi:*

> Not as though I had already attained, either were already perfect: but I follow after, if that I may apprehend that for which also I am apprehended of Christ Jesus.[11]

It is a mistake to think that every idea or ideal must first be fully defined in order to work productively in a person's life and mind. Though I know of nothing more dangerous than a certain modern antirationalism that pictures the logical desire in man as the adversary of life and action, it is just as dangerous to assume that only that is "understood" which is logically fully analyzed and empirically proved. All our great conceptual and ethical syntheses, from the idea of truth to the idea of justice and human brotherhood are somehow "utopian," "no-man's lands," as it were, between the human and the absolute in their inconceivable wholeness. We grasp the great by a fusion of many of our mental faculties. This fusion may sometimes lead to confusion, but it is at the same time the condition of civilization.

In his *Adventures of Ideas,* Whitehead speaks of "the idea of the intellectual and moral grandeur of the human soul" and describes it as "a hidden driving force, haunting humanity, and ever appearing in specialized guises as compulsory on action by reason of its appeal to the uneasy conscience of the age."[12]

[10]Plato, *The Symposium, The Works of Plato: translated into English with analyses and introductions,* B. Jowett, The Dial Press, New York, vol. 3, p. 342.
[11]*Philippians,* iii, 12.
[12]Alfred North Whitehead, *Adventures of Ideas,* The Macmillan Company, New York, 1933, p. 19.

2) Great symbols provide not only the possibility of lasting purpose and of high aspiration, they also provide a feeling which, in the complicated dialectic of life, is as necessary as the sense of happiness and fulfilment, namely, the feeling of suffering under the curse of imperfection and incompleteness. Every sound human strives for some kind of satisfaction. If he did not do so, he would be sick. On the other hand, a life that thinks of nothing but satisfaction is also bound to be sick. When we translate today the Aristotelian *"eudaimonia,"* which means "to live in the company of a good daimon," and Thomas Aquinas's similarly symbolic term, *"felicitas,"* by our worn out word "happiness," we give them a hedonistic flavor. "Blessedness" would be better.

That which Whitehead calls the "hidden driving force, haunting humanity," is in biblical language "the groaning of the creation" or the idea of "sin" as the eternal thorn and sting in the life of man. The saint is the one who feels the tension between sin and purity more than others, and for this very reason he becomes a saint. This means in Whitehead's secular language that:

> The ultimate motive power, alike in science, in morality, and in religion, is the sense of value, the sense of importance. It takes the various forms of wonder, of curiosity, of reverence, of worship, of tumultuous desire for merging personality in something beyond itself. This sense of value imposes on life incredible labors, and apart from it life sinks back into the passivity of lower types.[13]

And it may well be that for keeping alive this painful sense of unachievable greatness we need great symbols.

VI

These considerations may help us to arrive at a more comprehensive understanding of the complexity of the educational process than is generally prevailing.

Modern psychology of education is primarily interested in the learning process. We hear of the conditioned response, of motivation, of tension and tension release, effort and reward, transfer of training, and the law of effect. Animal experiments are used in order to explain the learning

[13]Alfred North Whitehead, *Aims of Education and Other Essays,* The Macmillan Company, New York, 1929, pp. 62–63.

behavior of the human being. In books on child psychology we find discussions of developmental stages, of the function of wishes and aspirations, and of the imbuing of desirable traits such as honesty and cooperativeness. How does the child acquire a general sense of values, and how can the teacher or parent awaken in him the appreciation of the religious tradition? During the past decades no discipline of thought has influenced education, in both its practical and theoretical aspects, more than psychology. I heard one of its well known representatives say that there was no longer any need for philosophy; psychology would take over the guidance of mankind.

Now we may admit that philosophy, just like religion, has done badly, which is perhaps not only its fault but due to the frailty of the human race. There was certainly need for a more experimental and observational approach to the problems of civilization and education. Only the critics who know little or nothing about the enormous range of learning problems emerging in a modern public school, will belittle the efforts and contributions of this approach. There is nothing wrong in the desperate attempt to avoid by means of experiment and statistics the vagueness connected with the interpretation and evaluation of the mental process.

Yet, the criticism and suspicion of the humanist against the so-called behavioral sciences is not totally unfounded. He misses in them the appreciation of the human being in his total "existential" situation. In order to overcome the artificial gap between the older "humanities" and the newer "sociology," we need the combination of psychology, historical anthropology, and related sciences with a philosophical anthropology which is not afraid of entering into the depth of man's existence. And whenever we do so we can hardly miss the language of symbols. This language may not always give us correct answers in the scientist's sense. But, at least, the searching questions may be asked without which man's aspect of himself becomes superficial. The larger part of human learning is not just "learning" in the usual sense of the word, but springs from the experiences of love and hatred, joy and suffering, ambition and renunciation, despair and faith, beauty and ugliness, the sacred and the devilish. The great dreams and the great religious documents of mankind are just as, and even more, revealing of man's nature than the typical modern treatise on psychology and education, for in all these great documents human life is understood as stretched between the two poles of the real and the ideal, the finite and the infinite, the achieved and the unachievable. When this insight is neglected, the scientific postulate of inclusiveness is violated, and instead of being empirical and scientific in the true sense of the word, the interpretation of human life becomes partial.

In earlier years I myself regarded it as a contradiction that John Amos Comenius, the first educator who tried to apply Baconian empiricism to the methods of teaching, began—after a brief pictorial representation of the alphabet—his *Orbis Pictus* with the symbol of the all seeing eye of God. Why begin with the most "unconcrete" lesson a textbook that is intended to relate verbal concepts to concrete objects? Yet, for the Moravian Pietist Comenius's life experience was not human unless it was conscious of the eternal vigilance of divine providence. A child could not learn to understand himself and the world without at the same time learning about the infinite and inexpressible, that which could not be pictured like a house, a workshop, or an animal, but only by means of a symbol.

Another example: one of the most prominent Italian historians, venerated by the liberals among his compatriots for his courageous fight against Mussolini and his ecclesiastical supporters, told me that the only book in the house of his poor parents happened to be an old volume of the *Divina Comedia* from which his mother sometimes read to the children. The boy did not understand Dante. The religion of the mature scholar was mixed up with a large dose of agnosticism. Yet, the greatness which he felt—and never denied—in the Florentine poet inspired him to overcome all the difficulties in the way of an indigent student and to achieve the life of a thinker and a fighter for human freedom. Somehow, he had "understood."

But profound art and thought are of symbolic value not only because they happen to use symbols. They are in themselves symbols because generations after generations have seen in them the reflected splendor of deeper dimensions of being. At the conclusion of his *Essai sur le Génie dans l'Art* Gabriel Séailles says:

> *La beauté prend une valeur symbolique. . . . Elle donne a l'esprit la jouissance anticipée de cette concorde vivante, de cette unité sans confusion, de cette concentration suprême qui acheverait la nature en réalisant Dieu.*[14]

[14]Gabriel Séailles, *Essai sur le Génie dans l'Art,* fourth edition, F. Alcan, Paris, 1911, p. 312. See also Cecil Maurice Bowra, *The Heritage of Symbolism,* Macmillan & Company, Ltd., London, 1943.

In all great human creations there lives not only what mankind knows but also what it does not know, and not only what it has achieved but what it dreams of achieving.

Here a subtle educational problem emerges, extremely evasive, yet charged with great responsibility. It says that the process of learning and teaching cannot be completely measured by its immediate success. To repeat, measurable success is of decisive importance in relation to skills. But the psychologist and teacher who, impressed by our competitive classroom situation with its demand for immediate answers, allow grades and nice answers alone to determine the content and policy of instruction, have an incomplete picture of man. With their best intentions they may do harm to exactly the finest human material. They may kill the sense of wonder.

In spite of the enormous extension of schooling we all speak of the "crisis" of our Western civilization. Certainly, this crisis is due to political and economic factors of a dimension unimagined by our ancestors. But historical factors have their weight not in themselves; they are weighed by men. With the disappearance of the sense of infinite horizons, our learning and our response to the mysteries of life have received a utilitarian, often hedonistic, direction which, rather than contributing to human happiness, has become destructive of it. The art and essence of education and culture reside in neither of the two extremes, the merely pragmatic-empirical with its contempt for the intangible, on the one hand, and, on the other hand, the romantic-idealistic with its supercilious contempt of the empirical. A healthy civilization depends on man's sense of the proper balance of the seen and the unseen, the immediate and the distant, the provisional and the final. And here lies the probably irreplaceable function of great symbols, irrespective of whether they may be of "supernatural" or "natural" origin.

The balance, when once lost in consequence of social changes beyond an individual's power, is difficult to restore. Schools and more schools, the prolongation of school age, and "better teachers" cannot be the saviors of mankind. Though it is wrong to describe a national educational system—as is the current fashion—as entirely "dependent upon the social environment" (for the life of the spirit has a certain dynamic of its own), it certainly is not independent. In concordance with our whole civilization, our public education becomes increasingly vocational and scienceminded, and this is not conducive to transcendent intuition and imagination from which spring persistent ideals and esthetically impressive symbols. More than ever mankind takes its future into its own hands and so far dormant masses become mobilized toward an increasingly rational interpretation of human life. Systematic planning—the necessity of the modern world—rarely achieves the warmth, the vigor, and the spontaneous edification which live in naturally grown relations between men and the holy, men and men, and men and their work. Thus we may ask ourselves with still more trepidation than thinking men in the period of the French revolution—when the planning began—whether the freedom of mankind from old (and certainly not always desirable) traditions will lead to true liberation, or to increasing disenchantment.

There exists an affinity between creative symbolism and creative utopias. And as all great societies live between the two poles of the real and the ideal, they are not only realistic but at the same time they project themselves forward. Yet, whereas the original utopia of a Plato, a Saint Augustine, a Morus, and a Campanella tried to give men an image of the desirable society, the modern utopia, characteristically enough, pictures him often as the victim of his own voluntary self-alienation.

In a sense, good education, too, is a utopia. It will never achieve what it intends to achieve, but it lives on the intention. The unrealizable hopes of the teacher, or parents, are the only guarantee that the realizable will not bog down in the mire of acquiescence.

VII

Conclusion

Symbols, in the sense used in this essay, are the expression of man's existential tension between the finite and the infinite, or the achievable and the unachievable. They occur whenever the transcendent and aspirational mind of man no longer regards life as self-satisfied, but creates the vision of the ought, or of ultimate value. They are, consequently, akin to the educational urge in man. Symbols are not "allegories," though the difference may sometimes be blurred. The "allegory" compares, is primarily esthetic, replaces one object by another of equal value, and puts the mind to rest. In contradistinction, the symbol discussed in this context has at the same time dynamic power (is *"maechtig"* and *"traechtig"*). It is motivational, it "points toward," it signifies the painful experience of the inadequate (*das "Un-zulaengliche"* and *"Un-zugaeng-liche"*)—that which can neither be reached nor fully possessed.

The moment the symbol loses the suggestion of human inadequateness and becomes a sign of fulfilment, it loses its uplifting strength. It may become a charm or an idol and thus degrade man instead of lifting him upward.

Symbols of the kind discussed in this context have often been considered to belong to "transcendentally" or "supernaturally" minded societies. However, there is no logical or historical reason to deny symbolic creativeness to more rationalist and naturalist groups, provided they still live in an atmosphere of aspiration and self-transcendence. (The question as to whether "transcendentalism" or "supranaturalism," on the one hand, and "rationalism" and "naturalism," on the other hand, represent more valid philosophical interpretations of life and man, has not been discussed here. The whole controversy rests, from my point of view, largely on a confusion of concepts.)

Considering the ambiguous role which symbols have played, a critical person may ask whether they are essentially desirable forms of human education. Might it not be more honest and courageous to admit man's existential suspense and uncertainty and to leave the infinite in its inexpressible grandeur? This question is theoretically justified; practically, however, man will always be the symbolmaker. The incarnation of the spiritual with all its dangers may also be man's way of spiritualizing the incarnate and thus the two, the corporeal and the spiritual, may merge in a higher unity. Furthermore, symbols not only fulfil his subjective desire for communication with the infinite, but are a part of the "objective *Geist*" (Hegel) or the "superorganic nature" (Groeber) which, created by the individual and collective mind, in turn influences the thought and behavior of persons and societies.

Though often perverted into the magical, great symbols have directed man's striving beyond the *status quo* of the already achieved toward higher levels of aspiration. Without the vision and the symbols of the transcendent and unachieved, men would gradually be satisfied with lowered standards and the education of mankind would lose one of its most effective incentives. But it must not be forgotten that even the finest aspirational symbols have the charisma not in and by themselves, but only to the degree to which man understands their transparent character and uses them for directing his thought to the superior aspects of life.

Comment by David Bidney:

I find myself very much in accord with Ulich's comprehensive paper. His position, especially as regards the existential situation of polarity, is one which I have developed with reference to cultural anthropology in my *Theoretical Anthropology* (Columbia University Press, New York, 1953). It is gratifying to note that he, too, stresses the need for a "combination of psychology, historical anthropology, and related sciences with a philosophical anthropology which is not afraid of entering into the depth of man's existence." I wish only to highlight several points suggested by his paper.

Symbols have "dynamic power" not only in the sense of being motivational and pointing toward a transcendental ideal, but also in the ethnological sense of helping to create and produce a cultural, intelligible reality which would not exist but for these symbols. Thus, symbols function not only to relieve tension but to provide the cultural forms and goals which give direction to the cultural process.

Man is indeed "the symbolmaker" and all human language is, as Edward Sapir and Ernst Cassirer have noted, a form of symbolism. What is significant of Ulich's position is that he does not reduce reality to symbolic forms, as Cassirer does, but retains the polarity of symbols and the transcendental reality which they suggest and indicate. This implies that all forms of symbolism are, as Henry Veatch has stressed, intentional in character and point to a metaphysical reality other than themselves. This point, as indicated in my work, may be generalized for culture in general.

Finally, as Ulich has observed, there is the perennial danger of confusing the "symbolic image" with the reality which it intends. In the evolution of human thought, as Tylor argued, this confusion of the subjective symbol and the objective reality is characteristic of primitive cultures and accounts in large measure for primitive magic and folklore. This identification of the ideal symbol and the actual object is not, however, limited to primitive societies, but has its counterpart in modern and contemporary societies, whenever the symbolic image and the cultural *status quo* are identified by political demagogues. The distinction between idolatry and worship of the absolute ideal in human experience, which is the hallmark of religion, corresponds to the distinction of symbolic fetishism and aspirational symbolism.

Comment by Mordecai M. Kaplan:

I venture to question the basic thesis of the paper by Robert Ulich. It is undoubtedly true that an education, which is limited to the attainable in the field of the practical pursuits is bound to foster an easy complacency. But that it is essential to impress upon the growing mind the fact that man must strive for, or aspire to, what is inherently unachievable, is open to doubt. "The unrealizable hopes," says Ulich, "are the only guarantee that the realizable will not bog down in the mire of acquiescence."

Let us test that thesis by a specific case. Suppose a person becomes convinced that personal immortality is an unrealizable hope. Would any amount of "aspirational symbolism" prevent him from "bogging down in the mire of acquiescence"? Would it not be more to the point to teach him the meaning and value of personal immortality which is achievable, so that he might use the "aspirational symbolism" as an incentive to achieve it?

Or take the case of human betterment. Would a person be more likely to strive for it if he were convinced that it is unachievable? As a matter of fact, hoping for what is "unrealizable" is nothing less than a paradox.

It seems to me that the Torah is nearer the truth, when it represents that for which man should live as attainable. Thus we read in Deuteronomy:

> For this command which I am enjoining upon you today is not beyond your power, it is not beyond your reach; it is not up in heaven, that you should say, "Who will go up for us and bring it down to us and let us hear it, that we may do it?"—nor is it over the sea,

that you should say, "Who will cross the sea for us and bring it to us and let us hear it, that we may do it?" No, the word is very near you, it is on your lips and in your mind, to be obeyed (Deuteronomy 30, 11–15, Moffat's translation).

Until modern times even the most advanced minds took it for granted that the boundaries of the knowable and the achievable were fixed, and that it was presumptuous to try to cross them. Ever since the Renaissance, man has achieved so much in the material world that he virtually stops at nothing as unachievable. He no longer has to resort to faith to move mountains. All he needs is a hydrogen bomb.

Unfortunately when it comes to self-improvement or the improvement of society, we are still content to operate with the "unachievable" and to resign ourselves to the fact that only some supernatural force which can be called into action by "aspirational symbolism" can bring about the needed transformation.

Ulich reminds us that there is as much room for "aspirational symbolism" in the domain of our natural relationships as was traditionally considered to be the case mainly in our supernatural relationships. He also warns most emphatically against converting that symbolism into magic. Would that, by the same token, he had stressed that it should be the function of "aspirational symbolism" to goad us on to advance the boundaries of the ethically and spiritually *achievable;* would that he had urged us not to be allured by that symbolism into believing that "you can't change human nature," or that "planned society must inevitably lead to totalitarianism and dictatorship," and many similar clichés, which have been the stock in trade of reactionary religion.

Professor Ulich's reply:

I agree with Mordecai M. Kaplan that nothing would be worse for the future of human society than "to resign ourselves to the fact that only some supernatural forces" . . . "can bring about the needed transformation." I had hoped to have made that point clear in my paper, but seemingly I have not succeeded.

What I call the "unachievable" or "unattainable" is not meant to say that human beings should live contentedly within their limitations and adore some supernatural forces without any attempt to reach beyond their given social and intellectual situation. But I believe that certain goals which we will never attain, but for which we nevertheless strive, help us more to go forward than that which we can seize and comprehend completely. In order to make this clear, I know of no better way than to quote a passage from an address of Judge Learned Hand to the Harvard Club at its 1952 annual dinner. (I found this passage in Harold Taylor's recent book, *On Education and Freedom,* Abelard-Schuman, New York, 1954.)

Judge Hand raises the question why some teachers had made such a deep impression on their students. He answers the question in the following words:

> And chiefly and best of all, you were in the company of those who thought that the noblest of man's works was the pursuit of truth; who valued the goal so highly that they were never quite convinced that the goal they had reached was the goal they were after. . . .

What is true of truth as an unattainable yet ever present ideal is also true of goodness, love, justice, and any other value which has raised humanity above the level of barbarism.

Comment by Joshua Whatmough:

The notion of the limit is something foreign to language. There is a paradox here. We say that a language is (or is not) "the same"; but no language is ever the "same" unless it is already dead. Its power of propresentation (or symbolism) is limitless. Hence falsehood, which is an inevitable concomitant of truth.

Ineffable, *i.e.,* "not able to be spoken." There is, of course, the negative of finite concepts here. But why seek to cover it up by the constant use of that pusillanimous negative, a vice of modern English, "rather than," when Ulich means "not"?

Language not only *is* in itself a symbolism (and a systematic one): the meaning of "meaning" is goal-directed activity, just as much as in the "feedback" of a servomechanism.

I agree that the ideal is the golden mean (balance), but not that the unromantic life is an ocean of boredom. It is the other way round. And again, if I mistake not, an educational system is not dependent upon a social environment (Ulich is right about this) but the social environment upon the educational system. A society gets the environment (in the largest sense) that it deserves, from its own system of education, which it has itself set up.

CHAPTER IX

The Symbolic Vehicles of Our Cultural Values

By THEODORE M. GREENE

Table of Contents

This paper is being written after careful study of the forty-five papers submitted to the Thirteenth Conference on Science, Philosophy and Religion. I was impressed by the keen realization of most of the writers that our cultural values are in jeopardy, and that it is imperative that we do what we can better to understand the nature and role of what R. M. MacIver has called "value-laden" symbols of expression and communication. I was also impressed by the variety of the issues raised by these papers and by the many areas of fruitful disagreement, as well as the many areas of significant agreement. The essays, in sum, demonstrated the value of, and the need for, such a conjoint enterprise. I shall conclude my paper with a concrete proposal for a further prosecution of this cooperative venture.

My effort in this paper will be a) further to clarify the nature of symbols as vehicles of value and evaluation, b) to explore some of the controversial implications of such symbols, and c) to consider how their socially beneficial use might best be promoted. It would of course take volumes to do justice to these large topics. I shall restrict myself to the systematic (rather than the historical) approach. I shall largely ignore the complex problem of scientific symbolism and the all important role of value symbols in the social sciences and in practical affairs. I shall concentrate my attention on symbols as vehicles of value, with special regard for their role in art and in religion. Some of the wider implications of this analysis will be commented on briefly in my conclusion.

1. *Sign, Normative Symbol, Art, and Sacrament*

Let us first try to delimit the basic meaning of these four terms in their relation to each other (and with due regard to some of the papers of the Thirteenth Conference and to the Notes on the Meetings of the Symbolism Seminar, The Institute for Religious and Social Studies, 1952–1953).

a) *Sign and Symbol.* I find substantial agreement that "sign" is the most inclusive of these four terms and that "sign" can be loosely defined as *anything* which points with some degree of reliability beyond itself to something else. This definition leads at once to the distinction between "natural" signs (*e.g.,* clouds indicating rain to the informed observer) and "artificial" or manmade signs with a more or less established "meaning."

I find less agreement as to the proper scope of "symbol," but I detect a tendency to label *all* "artificial" or manmade signs as symbols. So defined, "symbol" is given a very basic, inclusive, and generic meaning which permits, and invites, careful differentiation between various *types* of symbol.

b) *"Factual" and "normative" symbols.* The two chief types of symbol are easy to identify but hard to define or name. They differ in that symbols of the first type are vehicles of factual insight, whereas those of the second type are vehicles of normative or evaluative judgment. I shall label these two types "factual" and "normative," respectively.[1]

As many of the papers and Seminar discussions made clear, this rough differentiation between "factual" and "normative" symbols should not be taken to imply that they have nothing in common or that the activities they serve are radically different. Scientific inquiry has its distinctive normative components and implications. Scientific symbols are therefore not *merely* factual. Similarly, evaluations are, I believe, factual in immediate or ultimate reference, in proportion as they are responsible; they are directed to, and are intended faithfully to report on, values which, in some sense (to be determined), are themselves real or "factual." "Normative" symbols are therefore not *merely* normative.

Yet the distinction between "factual" and "normative" symbols is important. The *primary* function of the former is to convey nonevaluative factual information and comprehension of the type described by Ernest Nagel in his paper on "Symbolism and Science." Most evaluations are deliberately excluded from scientific inquiry, and the important values upon which science itself rests normally find expression in scientific symbolism only indirectly, if at all. The *primary* function of "normative" symbols, in contrast, is to serve as vehicles for many different kinds of evaluation. Such evaluations do involve, I believe, appropriate reference to "reality," if they are responsible; but such reference is, or should be, oriented to the primary task of evaluation. The symbols of evaluation are therefore *primarily* evaluative.[2]

[1] What I have called "factual" symbols are sometimes labelled "cognitive." I object, because I propose to defend the reality or "objectivity" of values *and* their knowability; and if this is the case, evaluations are cognitive, too, and "normative" symbols are *not* noncognitive. What I have called "normative" symbols are often called "evocative" or "emotive." I object to these designations not because they are incorrect—"normative" symbols *do* tend to evoke attitudes and to arouse emotions—but because, as I see it, this is not their only, or indeed their primary, function. I prefer the term "normative" because it seems freer of various negative implications.

[2] This distinction need not, at least at this stage, commit us to any specific metaphysical theory as to the ultimate ontological status of value, *i.e.,* the presence or absence of values in

c) *"Normative" symbols and the "work of art."* Analysis of normative symbols is complicated not only by their variety but also by the ways in which they subtly shade into one another. Consider, for example, this series of normative symbols: the Grand Seal of the United States of America; our flag; our national anthem; an enlistment poster; one of our political "classics," such as Lincoln's Gettysburg Address; and an explicit "work of art" whose theme is our country, such as Dos Passos's *U.S.A.* All point beyond themselves to the United States of America as a land we do, and should, cherish, *e.g.,* as possessing value for us. They do so, however, in different, though overlapping, ways.

i) *The Grand Seal* is the "coldest" of these symbols. It *suggests* the power and dignity of the state, but this suggestion is largely incidental, and it is operative only for those who are able to bring to it the requisite associations. The more I know about responsible government, the more will *any* such seal impress me by reminding me of governmental authority; the more I know about, *and respect, our* government, the more will *this* seal evoke my feelings of respect, fear, gratitude, and loyalty. Reversely, the less I respect governments in general, or our particular government, the less effective will be any governmental seal, and this seal, in arousing these emotions and attitudes in me, and the more powerfully will contrary emotions and attitudes tend to be aroused in me. In short, the Grand Seal, *per se,* is little more than a factual, nonnormative symbol. It is "value-laden" only to the extent to which *I* read positive or negative values into what it factually denotes or signifies.

ii) *The flag* is more value-laden than the Seal for reasons not hard to determine. It is colored—and colors tend to be evocative in suitable human contexts. It waves—and movement tends to catch the eye and stir the heart. It occupies a prominent place on ceremonial occasions heavily fraught with emotional overtones and patriotic fervor. We associate the flag with periods of national crisis and moments of deep personal involvement—with war and victory, with death and burial, with peacetime national activity and celebration. Had it been our custom to display and

---

what we loosely call "reality." We may eventually wish to accept a radical metaphysical disjunction between "fact" and "value," *i.e.,* a radical dualism between what "is" and what "ought to be," with due regard for resultant tensions and for the partial actualization of values in the realm of fact. Or we may, alternatively, wish to adopt a more monistic position, ascribing value in some sense to whatever is real, and interpreting science as artificially abstracting the structures and processes of spatiotemporal reality for nonevaluative scrutiny.

use the Grand Seal as, in fact, we have used the flag, it might well be nearly as valueladen for us as is the flag. But this has not been our custom; and our corporate ritualistic activities in which the flag is displayed have been so numerous, so widespread, and so consistent, that most of us have been repeatedly exposed to them and have more or less participated in them. As a result, the flag can and does tap a rich reservoir of communal sentiment and does "speak to us," as citizens, with a connotative power and urgency which the Grand Seal largely lacks.

iii) *Our national anthem* is, for most of us, more moving than the flag. Its greater normative effectiveness is due, in part, to the superior evocative power of sound over sight—a superiority which is perhaps debatable but which is supported by the apparent fact that "pure" music of a high order has a greater evocative power than "abstract" painting of a comparable high order. The anthem has, in addition, two all important characteristics which the flag lacks. First, we join in in the singing of it and thus *participate* in it, as a patriotic ritual, whereas all we can do with a flag is to watch it, raise or lower it, wave it, salute it, or march behind it. Not one of these activities can "identify" us with it, or with our fellows, or with our native land, as effectively as singing our national anthem under appropriate circumstances. Secondly, the words we sing do a good deal to remind us of what it is that we are patriotically loyal to and why such loyalty should arouse our enthusiasm. The context is historical and martial, well calculated to challenge us. The flag is described as waving "proudly"; our pride in it and what it stands for is thus explicitly invited. We join in praise of our "land of the free" and our "home of the brave," and this praise does tend to arouse our latent sentiment of bravery and whatever love of freedom we may possess. The anthem, in short, is both an evocative and a *"directive"* symbol, and its verbal directives enhance its evocative power. Unlike the flag, the anthem is thus an auditory *and* verbal vehicle which simultaneously articulates some of our basic *ideas,* invites our active *participation,* and thus more powerfully *evokes* our patriotic sentiments.

iv) It is interesting to note that typical *enlistment posters* are much less evocative than is our national anthem. This is largely because they are so explicitly propagandistic. The national anthem does, of course, have a predominantly "practical" function, *i.e.,* to arouse and express our patriotic sentiments. But, curiously enough, it is so effective chiefly because of its "artistic" character (even though it may not, in itself, be a "great" work of art), and because it largely eschews specific hortatory injunction to action. It is far more likely to impel us to want to enlist than is a poster which bluntly exhorts us to "Enlist Now!" (Even the best of enlistment posters would lack this power; we need not be distracted by the sentimental crudity of most actual posters which, in fact, eulogize not patriotism but travel, smart uniforms, pretty nurses, and, of all things, "security" and other personal benefits.) The moral, for whatever it may be worth, is plain; the *less* explicitly and boldly hortatory ("Go and do thou likewise!") a symbol is, the *more* moving (*i.e.,* effectively rhetorical) is it apt to be.

v) *The Gettysburg Address* is rhetoric of such a high order that it should undoubtedly be rated as a "great" work of art *of its kind*. I say, "of its kind," because it is patently not an instance of "pure art" (as I shall presently seek to define it). It, too, was propagandistic; it was designed to accomplish the kind of thing that our anthem is used to accomplish, *i.e.,* to sway the hearts and impress the minds of the citizens of our Republic. But it differs from the anthem in important respects. The music of the anthem is more important than the words, and even the words appeal more directly to the sentiments than to the mind; whereas the Address, however impressively it may have been delivered, derives its power primarily from *what* it says, *i.e.,* the "message" conveyed by its words—it appeals to the heart *through* the mind. The anthem, moreover, though written in a particular historical context, has become an accepted vehicle for the corporate expression of our *general* patriotism, whereas the Address remains what it was designed to be—a profoundly moving speech designed to arouse more *particularized* attitudes and to occasion a more *specific pattern of behavior* appropriate to a particular period of crisis in our history. That its "directive" and evocative power has endured, is eloquent testimony to the fact that a normative symbol can simultaneously express more particularized and more universal evaluations, *i.e.,* that its "meaning" can have both an immediate and a more enduring relevance.

vi) I have deliberately included as "unpatriotic" a novel as Dos Passos's *U.S.A.* in this series of patriotic normative symbols, in order to emphasize the crucial difference between a *"work of art"* and all the other normative symbols in the series. I shall consider in the next section some aspects of the current controversy over the nature of art. Here let me state, without supporting argument, my own functional definition of a work of art. Its primary purpose is, I believe, *to express a normative interpretation of a given subject-matter in a distinctive way*. This definition rests on the following assumptions (some of which are seriously challenged today in various quarters).

a. A work of art is *more* than its esthetically satisfying "form," pattern, or organization. Its esthetic form is, indeed, crucial, the *sine qua non* of its reality as art. But it is not *mere* form. Its form is intended to, and does, perform a function.

b. This function is not *merely* to evoke emotions, though it does evoke emotions.

c. Its function is rather to *express certain evaluative insights,* that is, an interpretation of the nature and human import of its "subject-matter," *i.e.,* whatever the artist has chosen to deal with interpretatively. The artist's motto is, as it were, "This is what I here see or apprehend, and this is my estimate of its significance for man."

d. The artist's apprehensions and evaluations are not merely "stated" in "prosaic" fashion, as in science, but are "expressed," in and through artistic form in such a way as to impel the observer to *see and feel* what the artist has seen and felt *as* he has seen and felt it. Art does not address itself merely to the intellect or merely to the emotions, but to *both* in fruitful harmony. It does not *merely* report, dispassionately, or *merely* move, emotively. It exhibits a subject-matter of human concern, and it does so in such a way as to *make evident* the artist's emotive response to this concern *and to evoke* in the observer a corresponding emotive response. It does not merely invite intellectual assent to normative propositions; it seeks to arouse in the observer a total normative response. In short, it "expresses" its meaning contagiously and passionately; it does not merely state its meaning dispassionately.

e. The primary function of art is *neither hedonistic nor practical*. Art can give intense pleasure, and it fails as art if it gives the sensitive observer no esthetic satisfaction. But its purpose is not *merely* to please. Its power to mold and move men is unequalled by any other type of normative symbol. But its explicit purpose is not to reform or to incite man to subsequent action. *Its primary purpose is normative enlightenment.* Its function is to enable men to apprehend—richly, fully, imaginatively, warmly, concernedly—the nature *and significance* of whatever is artistically exhibited and interpreted.

f. So conceived, art is the most powerful and sensitive vehicle we have for the fullbodied articulation and communication of our evaluations. We can and should explore the factual conditions of human evaluation scientifically, study their temporal manifestations historically, and discuss their validity philosophically. But only in and through art can we hope to enrich our normative insights, deepen our normative experiences, and strengthen our normative powers.

This summary account of art may suffice to differentiate it, in its purity, from the other normative symbols in our series. It is evident that they all owe something of their evocative power to their artistry. Each is, in its own way, a design which, as artistic form, is in *some* measure eloquent or expressive of the human import of its referent. Yet all are, though in different ways and to different degrees, predominantly propagandistic. Like art, they all point beyond themselves; but unlike pure art, their *primary* purpose is not to enlighten and deepen man's normative experience. If I may arbitrarily select a series of different words to make my point, the Seal might be said primarily to "signify" (governmental authority); the flag, to "signify" and "evoke" (patriotic sentiments); the anthem, to "animate" (such sentiments) by participation; the poster, to "exhort" (to patriotic action); the Address, to "guide" and "instil" a sound understanding of, and a proper attitude to (an historical challenge). Dos Passos, in contrast, "exhibits" and "evaluates" certain aspects of the American scene and "expresses" his understanding and his estimate of them in such a way as to arouse in us a similar understanding and estimate. Countless other American artists have dealt with the same scene in their respective arts, in their own distinctive idiom, and from their very different selective points of view. What they have in common is a primarily artistic approach and a primarily artistic concern, *i.e.,* the effort to express their normative insights as precisely and eloquently as possible. Their effort, in so far as it has been authentically artistic, has been, for them, self-sufficient. It has not been their purpose merely to please, or to signify, or to evoke emotion, or to incite to action. Their labor has been, first and foremost, *creative* and *contemplative,* and the response they have hoped for is a re-creative and contemplative response—no less, and no more.

My account of art will, I know, be challenged and must therefore be defended. Before I attempt this defense, however, let us briefly consider the role of art, as here defined, in religion in general and in "sacrament" in particular.

d) *Art, religion, and "sacrament."* Here I must stress the following points, all of which have already been made in one or more of the papers for the Thirteenth Conference.

i) What I have called *"normative" symbols are absolutely essential for religion.*

They are essential, first, because religious faith is basically a normative venture and is directed to a Being or beings encountered, and apprehended, as the source of value or, at the least, as essentially related to values and to human welfare. Even if religion were merely an intellectual exercise in cognition (which of course it is not), it would need appropriate, *i.e.,* normative, symbols for the articulation of man's most adequate cognitions of Deity as impregnated with, or closely related to, value. Religion involves such cognition—but it is far more than mere cognitive apprehension; it is primarily the "worship," *i.e.,* the direct, reverent response to Deity. Worship, in turn, is impossible without appropriate vehicles, and these must, by definition, be normative symbols.

Such symbols are essential to religion, secondly, because every religion is a *corporate* activity depending upon an enduring and cumulative *tradition.* No corporate activity is possible without appropriate symbols for the communication which is requisite for shared experience (*cf.* our corporate political life, our corporate participation in athletics, etc.). If people are to worship together they *must* have effective vehicles for common worship. These, in turn, can have no functional religious value unless they have a more or less established and shareable meaning, and they can have such meaning only if it has established and perpetuated itself in a living, evolving tradition. A hypothetical, newly established, *ad hoc* religion without any traditional past could not be a functionally dynamic religion. (The problem of how the religions of mankind ever got started is a very difficult problem, but the reality of this problem does not invalidate what has just been said.) No continuing living tradition is possible without suitable vehicles for the transmission of meaningful beliefs.

ii) *The arts are,* PAR EXCELLENCE, *the symbols of religious apprehension and religious worship. Why* this should be the case will, I hope, be evident after we have analyzed more carefully the nature of art and how it functions (see below, Sections 2 and 3). Here we need merely note, first, the extensive use to which all the major and minor arts have been put in various world religions, and, second, the fact that even in theology, which is man's attempt to comprehend Deity with maximum conceptual precision *within* a religious tradition, the symbols used are applicable to Deity only analogically or metaphorically and must therefore always be construed "poetically" or "mythologically," never wholly prosaically or literally. If this is true of the symbols of theology (and even, I would argue, of the philosophy of religion in so far as it really comes to grips with the God of religious worship and not merely with the "God of the philosophers"), it is true *a fortiori* of explicitly poetic and rhetorical discourse when put to religious use.

iii) *All such symbols must be distinguished from* what John E. Smith, following Paul J. Tillich, calls *"sign-events."* These are concrete historical events which are accepted as having *actually* happened and which are understood, in the context of some historically rooted faith (*e.g.,* Judaism and Christianity) as "pointing to God," as having "revelatory significance," and as being "expressive" (as actual events, not as art) of the nature and purpose of God.[3] To be understood religiously these sign-events, in turn, must be interpreted with the aid of "myth" and other forms of religious normative symbolism. In *"historical"* religions, *i.e.,* those which attach supreme importance to such sign-events (in contrast to religions which are predominantly or wholly "nonhistorical," *e.g.,* the mystical idealism of Plato, or much of Hinduism), religious symbols are, as it were, *anchored* in these accepted sign-events, *i.e.,* they are largely or wholly employed to articulate the meaning and implications of such sign-events. No comparable anchorage is operative in "nonhistorical" religions.

iv) *If religious symbolism is to function religiously it must be accepted,* to quote Amos N. Wilder, as a *"notation of reality,* however different in kind from that of science." He writes:

> Myth . . . offers . . . "news of reality." The importance of the truth represented, or the proportion of truth to error, depends upon the experience and wisdom of those who shaped the myth. The chief integrating symbols of the Bible convey real meaning and interpretative insight. They rose out of costly moral experience and were subject to the corrections of that experience. They were chiefly shaped by spokesmen and prophets whose insight is confirmed by their lives. They received negative confirmation by the sterility of opposing ideals, and positive con-

[3]John E. Smith, "The Individual, the Religious Community, and the Symbol," *Symbols and Values: An Initial Study,* Chapter X, p. 171.

firmation by the amazing fruitfulness they manifested in history. . . .
For such reasons we must assign truth-value to the picture language of
Christian faith.

Wilder then distinguishes the truths embodied in the "myths" of
"historical" religions from those expressed by "nonhistorical" religions.
He says:

> . . . we must be careful to dissociate this validation of biblical myth
> from one to which men in the Platonic tradition are often tempted. For
> them the myths represent universal ideas or ideals with little attachment
> to the historical process [*i.e.,* to "sign-events"]. We must [he is of course
> speaking from *within* the context of *Christian* faith] avoid all such ideal-
> ism here, represented recently by Santayana's striking study of the idea
> of Christ in the gospels.[4]

This insistence on the "truth-value" of all religious myth and, in
"historical religions," on the actuality and religious significance of "sign-
events," is echoed in other papers. Louis Finkelstein presumes this "truth-
value" throughout his paper on "Judaism as a System of Symbols." He
believes that "there are basic truths, regarding existence and the moral
and spiritual realms which are eternally valid"[5] (I shall return to this
claim later). Father Eugene Gallagher, S.J., agrees, though in a quite
different context.

> . . . apart from immediate religious experience of the unseen and in-
> visible spiritual realities (which, of course, is rare), I cannot know these
> religious objects through and in themselves. Moreover, as we have seen,
> they are ineffable, they cannot adequately be expressed in words: they
> must be grasped by something which enters into the field of observation.
> From these facts is born the necessity of symbolism in religion, the neces-
> sity of symbolism as an intermediary between the inadequate capacity
> of the mind and the incommunicable nature and fullness of mysteries
> and realities of religion that are too deep for words. [In support of this
> view he quotes Ralph Adams Cram, the architect: ". . . in its highest
> aspect and function art is the symbolic expression of otherwise inex-
> pressible ideas."][6]

[4]Amos N. Wilder, "Myth and Symbol in the New Testament," *Symbols and Values,*
Chapter VIII, p. 145.

[5]Louis Finkelstein, "Judaism as a System of Symbols," *Symbols and Values,* Chapter V,
p. 101.

[6]Eugene Gallagher, S.J., "The Value of Symbolism, as Suggested by St. Augustine's 'De
Magistro'," *Symbols and Values,* Chapter VI, pp. 116–117.

Ben Zion Bokser records a similar conviction in his paper on "Symbolic Knowledge and Religious Truth."

> God's essence necessarily eludes us. Classic theology . . . makes God remote and inaccessible to human life, defeating the very aim of religion which is to lead man ever closer to his Maker. We find our way out of this dilemma through the process of symbolism. . . . [These symbols] convey only a partial truth. . . . But they give our speech a pictorial and vivid quality, enabling it to meet the requirements of effective communication. . . . The cultivation of closeness to God could not be effected through verbalization alone. It is, however, pursued efficaciously through action symbols [*i.e.*, "acts" and "disciplines" of piety]. . . . Action impresses us more deeply than words . . . in affirming the religious idea. The most subtle religious ideas are thus made comprehensible. . . .[7]

I have quoted these authors (Jewish and Christian; Catholic and Protestant) at such length in order to indicate the notable agreement of Western theologians on a) the imperative religious need for normative symbols, b) the variety of such symbols—verbal (theological and "poetic"), nonverbal (in other expressive media and in "acts" of piety), c) the fact that each type of symbol has its peculiar power and limitations, d) that *all* types, to function religiously, must be judged to possess a truth-value, and e) that "sign-events" are of crucial importance for "historical" religions, though different "historical" religions anchor themselves in different sign-events and interpret them in their own distinctive ways, *e.g.*, as instances of "inspiration," as direct "revelation," or as authentic "Incarnation." The typical approach and presuppositions of the Far Eastern religions, notably Buddhism, are so distinctive (*cf.* the papers of D. T. Suzuki and A. W. Watts in *Symbols and Values*) that a different account would have to be given of their conception and use of religious symbolism. Their spokesmen would, however, agree with Western theologians in ascribing profound ontological significance to the religious experience and, therefore, appropriate truth-value to its authentic articulations.

v) *The terms "sacrament" and "sacramental"* are widely used in at least three distinguishable, though somewhat overlapping, ways. The whole universe is "sacramental," in the most inclusive sense, for those

[7] Ben Zion Bokser, "Symbolic Knowledge and Religious Truth," *Symbols and Values,* Chapter XI, pp. 173–176, *passim.*

who, with the late A. A. Bowman, find it to be impregnated through and through by Divinity.[8] The term, "sacrament," is usually used much more narrowly to signify a religious rite of special religious importance. Such a rite can, in turn, be interpreted to have a wholly or largely commemorative significance (*cf.* "Do this in *remembrance* of me"); or, alternatively, it can be interpreted (in the narrowest and strictest sense) as deriving its religious significance from the "fact" that, in and through this rite, God is in some sense (*e.g.*, via "transsubstantiation" or "consubstantiation") actually present to the worshiper and available to him as He is not at other times and even during the performance of other sacred rites.

What needs particularly to be emphasized in this connection is the profound and radical difference between a magical and a nonmagical interpretation of sacrament, particularly when a sacrament is regarded as a "real Presence" rite. Jacques Maritain and many others have rightly insisted that *both* science *and* "high" religion have evolved from a primitive magical stage to an enlightened nonmagical stage, that religion is no more essentially magical than is science, and that, at its enlightened best, it combats magic as strenuously as does enlightened science. This claim can be validated *if* we can give a meaningful definition of magic, *if* we can so define enlightenment as to distinguish it from superstition, and *if* the very possibility of enlightened religious faith is not *a priori* rejected. These are all "ticklish" ifs which we must pause to consider.

Lyman Bryson's distinction between the "primitive mind" (addicted to magic) and the scientific or "civilized" mind (free from magic) is helpful but, I believe, inadequate.

> . . . the primitive [mind] uses symbols to control nature directly, believing that they have power over events in the material world, while the civilized mind believes rather that symbols describe nature and have no power over the external world, except in so far—and this is critical —as these symbols affect the behavior of men. To oversimplify, we might say that the primitive attitude is to use symbols for the mastery of things whereas the civilized attitude, tested by scientific verifications, is to use symbols only to control or influence men. And this suggests the hypothesis that when a civilized man prays, he prays to change, not events, but the human being to whom he has greatest access, himself.[9]

[8]*Cf.* Archibald A. Bowman, *A Sacramental Universe,* Princeton University Press, Princeton, 1939.

[9]Lyman Bryson, "The Quest for Symbols," *Symbols and Values,* Chapter I, p. 4.

My comments are these: a) The primitive mind is wrong *not* in its attempt to control things (scientists, and all of us, make the same attempt) but in its *ignorance* regarding *how* things can in fact be controlled. b) Man's attempt to control or influence *men* is not automatically nonmagical (primitive man uses magic for this purpose also); it is nonmagical, once again, only in proportion as it is *enlightened*. c) An appeal to Deity in prayer is not automatically magical (unless one starts with the *a priori* dogma that there is no Deity and/or that *all* prayer is *necessarily* inefficacious). (Note Bryson's presuppositions here: "There are subtle differences between what is called magic and what is called religion but they do not affect our case.")[10]

The three crucial factors for the understanding of magic would seem to be "control," "enlightenment," and "things," "persons," and "Deity." Bryson's position, as an enlightened humanist, is clear. He approves of the enlightened (scientific) control of "things" (nature); he believes that all appeal to Deity is necessarily superstitious and magical; and he approves of man's control of other persons *provided* that it is exercised in a manner suited to the nature and value of persons, *i.e.,* is "persuasive" rather than "magical." Hence his plea, "if we are to be rational as well as effective," that, even in our dealings with our fellows, we

> distinguish between the use of power symbols as magic and their use as rational incitements to human action . . . , [and that we] trust finally to the moral values of our ideas to make their way, with the aid only of such symbols as stir men's hearts without confusing their minds.[11]

Maritain, in contrast, insists that "the sacramental sign is bound up with religion in the state of logic" (*i.e.,* is theologically defensible in the light of enlightened religious comprehension) and that it "differs essentially from the magical sign."

> None of the characteristics proper to the magical sign (physical fusion of the sign and the signified, efficient causality of the sign in itself, oscillation between distinction and identity; reference to a physicomoral environment) are to be found in the sacramental sign. The latter . . . is operative (in the sacraments of the New Law) as an instrument moved by the divine omnipotence, the principal causality of which

[10]*Ibid.,* p. 5.
[11]*Ibid.,* pp. 8, 10.

entirely and absolutely subordinates to itself such an instrument. The magical sign has as its end the exercise of a power over nature or over the powers on which nature is dependent; the sacramental sign has as its end the interior sanctity to be produced in the soul. The magical sign has as its field of action the whole extent of human life, the sacramental sign is of an order strictly religious and divine.[12]

What is evident in this passage (which loses much in being quoted out of context) is: a) the clear distinction *within* religion between "magic" and "sacrament," *i.e.,* between what is, from within a religious perceptive, judged to be an unenlightened and an enlightened conception and use of a religious rite; b) the clear implication that enlightenment is proportionate to, first, our *understanding* of whatever type of reality we are dealing with and, second, our *appropriate* response to it.

This conception of true enlightenment calls for special emphasis. Nature, man, and God can—*all three*—be both misapprehended *and* misused. Nature is gravely misapprehended by primitive man in his lack of scientific understanding, but he does at least tend to respond to nature with a kind of appropriate respect ("natural piety") which any profound "naturalism" should be impelled to honor. The modern scientist understands the structures and operations of nature far better, but he is tempted, in an exploitative culture, to lose all sense of natural piety and to plunder nature with callous insensitivity. We are slowly coming to understand some aspects of human nature more "objectively" and scientifically, but such knowledge can, we know, be put to brutal use in cruel exploitation of human beings. Primitive man tended to be both ignorant of, and exploitative toward, Diety; hence his *superstitious* resort to magic as a device for controlling and using spiritual powers for *his own benefit.* Enlightened religion is radically critical of primitive religion on *both* counts; it conceives of Deity in very different terms, and it insists on the priority of worship and on enlightened petition (prayer), not magical control, on "communion" and inner spiritual transformation rather than manipulation of Deity with the aid of manmade unspiritual hocus-pocus.

The familiar distinction between "white" and "black" magic may help us to summarize the distinctions which we have been trying to make. Any act might well be said to be magical *in proportion* as it is rooted in

[12]Jacques Maritain, "Sign and Symbol," *Ransoming the Time,* Charles Scribner's Sons, New York, 1941, Chapter IX, pp. 248–249.

ignorance, false belief, and superstition. So defined, magic is not auto-matically dispelled by a dislike of it and by the attempt to escape it. We still are subject to reliance on magic in our scientific interpretations and manipulations of nature, our dealings with each other, and our most enlightened apprehensions of, and responses to, Deity. We differ in this respect from primitive men only in degree, even though our civilized awareness of the problem may have no counterpart in the primitive worldview. We are perpetually in danger of lapsing into magic in *all* our generic activities; we escape it only *to the degree* that we achieve true understanding. Factual knowledge, in turn, is no guarantee of normative wisdom, that is, of proper valuation of, and response to, what we know. When magic is used beneficently we sometimes call it "white" magic; when knowledge is used harmfully we brand such misuse of it evil or even diabolical. "White" magic must be condemned *because* it is magical and *despite* all beneficent intent. Scientific exploitation (whether of man or nature) must be condemned for its *malevolence, however factually informed and technologically skillful it may be*. What we should all presumably work for is enlightened (nonmagical) *and* be-nevolent reflection and behavior.

The religious symbols of which we are in search, then, are the symbols which can serve us most effectively as vehicles for such benevolent *and* enlightened response to the *ultimate* in reality as a whole. It is the claim of "high" religion that certain religious symbols, properly interpreted, can and do serve this purpose and that the "sacrament," properly under-stood and used, is a distinctive type of valid and useful religious symbol. It differs (when narrowly and strictly defined) from all other religious symbols such as myths, parables, metaphors, or nonverbal symbols, in being a vehicle not only of religious *comprehension* and *communication* but also, and essentially, of Divine Power or Grace. Through them God not merely *"speaks"* to us but *"encounters"* us and, above all, affects us (operates upon us dynamically), *if* we participate in the sacramental rite in the right spirit. That they are, in fact, used superstitiously, as magical rites, by countless believers must be admitted and bitterly deplored. But this is not (*pace* Bryson) inevitable.

I have not, of course, offered any philosophical validation of enlight-ened religious faith. I have merely tried to isolate and define the essence of magic, to extend the term enlightenment to include *all* types of en-lightenment, religious as well as scientific, and to reject any dogmatic *a priori* repudiation of all religious belief as necessarily superstitious and of all religious rites as automatically magical. I can do no better here than heartily endorse, with only minor reservations, Maritain's account of man's major generic experiences of reality.

> . . . since, as I believe, religion, metaphysics, art, poetry and all the vital powers of the spirit other than the power of pure scientific thought are as well founded in truth as is science in the modern sense of the word, and since they are ever to endure, while changing their condition when the human soul passes over into the daylight regime wherein the intelligence is dominant, then, in the final analysis, the fact that they remain . . . does not imply the continuance . . . of magical or nocturnal thought. Magical thought and the magical sign are destined to be cast aside in so far as *they are magical.* . . .

I also welcome his honest confession that

> it was more necessary for religion than for any other function of human life to pass over into . . . the daylight regime of the intelligence.[13]

This concludes my initial delimitation of certain key terms and problems in the area of symbolism. The line of inquiry thus far can be schematically indicated as follows:

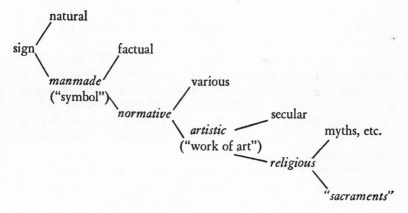

It is clear that I have focused attention upon certain terms (here underlined) at the expense of others which deserve equal attention in any well rounded study of normative symbolism. Some of these will receive

[13]*Ibid.*, pp. 249, 248.

further comment as we proceed. We must return now to the category of the artistic and consider more fully some of the current controversies regarding the nature of art. These are of crucial importance, for only if art is judged to have a certain specifiable character can it function as a powerful vehicle of secular and religious insights and of responsible cultural evaluations.

2. What Is a Work of Art?

a) *Contemporary agreements and disagreements regarding the nature of art.* There is widespread agreement among estheticians that "esthetic form," *i.e.,* the esthetically significant organization of some artistic medium, is the *sine qua non* of art. It is also generally acknowledged that esthetically satisfying form is a very mysterious thing. It is the product of creative talent or genius, not of rules; it is encounterable, recognizable, and verifiable by those who possess the requisite taste and orientation. It is *sui generis* and therefore not reducible to, or definable in terms of, anything else; it is not intellectually demonstrable by reference to any principles or laws. (One can indeed appeal to such principles as variety and unity, tension and resolution, the "organic" relationship of parts or components to one another and to the whole, contrast and harmony, etc.; but whether a given instance of formal organization does or does not satisfactorily exemplify such principles can, once again, be determined only by appeal to a cultivated taste.) In short, it is, like all irreducible ultimates in human experience, *ineffable.* It can be observed, pointed to, and enjoyed, but it cannot adequately be described discursively, or intellectually proved to exist, or scientifically assessed. If esthetic form is equated with "beauty," we can merely say, in the language of Kant and many others, that beauty is the product of genius and the "object" of taste.

Dispute arises primarily over these two questions: What is the "ontological status" of beauty? and, how self-sufficient is beauty, or esthetic form, in art? The first of these questions is, of course, a specification of the wider question relating to the "objectivity" of values in general. We shall return to this question in due course. The second question is crucial for our understanding of art.

Despite minor differences of interpretation, "formalists" are in general agreed that esthetic form *is* self-sufficient; that it is, as Clive Bell says, "significant" in and for itself. It signifies nothing beyond itself or other than itself; it is "significant" merely in being intrinsically satisfying and stimulating. When these formalists are questioned regarding the evocative, expressive, or revelatory powers of art, their answer is brief and consistent. They may admit that art does possess this power but they insist that it is extraneous to art. They distinguish between proper and improper response to art, defining the former as *exclusive* concern for, and attention to, esthetic form, and the latter as an unjustifiable concern with, and attention to, additional aspects of the work of art which, they declare, are *artistically* distracting and irrelevant. The only emotional responses which they are willing to sanction are man's *esthetic* emotions, construed as strictly correlative to "pure" esthetic form; if other emotions are in fact evoked, the purity of the esthetic experience is to that extent sullied, due either to faulty artistry, or to faulty esthetic response, or both. Here, then, we have the doctrine of "beauty for beauty's sake"—a simon-pure estheticism.

All that is positively affirmed in this doctrine regarding esthetic form and pure esthetic response must be accepted as valid, for both "pure form" and "pure esthetic response" are indeed both unique and crucial. Artistically enlightened nonformalists differ from their formalistic colleagues, not on what the latter affirm but on what they deny. Nonformalists insist that a work of art differs from an esthetically satisfying, but otherwise empty and inexpressive, decorative design, because it "says" something or "expresses" something, via its esthetic form. What is said to be thus expressed can conveniently be labelled "artistic content."

The definition of art which I would propose (as incorporating everything that is valid in esthetic formalism but going beyond it to do fuller justice to the total significance of art) is the following: *a work of art is the unique expression of authentic normative insight via the artistic organization of an artistic medium.*

I make no apology for the inclusion of the term "artistic" in this definition of art. Such inclusion is necessary because we are here dealing with a *sui generis* artifact which can be understood *only* in its *own* terms. I know no way of communicating with anyone about art who lacks all sensitivity to the uniquely esthetic factor as it appears in works of art. The definition does, however, call for elucidation.

It presupposes *three essential components* in every work of art, *i.e.,* medium, form, and content. These, too, *must* be defined in terms of one another, since they are so intimately and "organically" related. The artistic *medium* is, generically, the "language" available to the artist as his vehicle of expression. In a particular work of art it is the specific medium which he puts to specific use in his own idiom. The specific artistic *form* of a work of art is the artist's specific ordering or use of this specific medium in this particular composition. Generic artistic forms can be discovered inductively, by comparing a variety of composition in the same generic medium. Specific forms can then, if one is so minded, be thought of as unique specifications of such generic forms. The specific *content* of a work of art, finally, is precisely what is expressed *in and through* its specific form. When the contents of many works of art in the same and in different media are compared, similarities and differences will be noted. The similarities can then be described and labelled as the type or types of generic content which this or that art, and which art as such, can and does express. We can conclude, for example, that the content of art is, in intent and claim, cognitive in its own distinctive way and that the locus of "truth-value" in art is in its content or "meaning."

b) *Is artistic "content" cognitive?* The problem of how, in general, to describe what is to be meant by artistic content is one of the most difficult problems in esthetics. It is difficult, first, because the major arts, ranging from "pure" (non-programmatic) music and the "pure" dance, through architecture, painting, and sculpture, to literature (not to mention the "minor" arts, *e.g.,* ceramics, such composite art forms as the opera, and such new arts as the motion picture) differ so notably from one another and, in addition, include so many different "species," *e.g.,* nonrepresentational *vs.* representational sculpture and painting. It is difficult, secondly, because each work of art, and therefore the "content" of each work of art, is *essentially* unique and therefore not expressible in any other artistic form or medium.

It is particularly difficult, however, because the *content* of art is never adequately translatable into nonartistic, *e.g.,* scientific symbols. This fact leads the scientifically minded Nagel and many others to conclude that, whatever the content of art may be, it certainly is *not* cognitive. I quote him at some length because he has stated a widely held position very clearly and in sharp contrast to the position I have myself defended.[14]

[14]*Cf.* Theodore M. Greene, *The Arts and the Art of Criticism,* Princeton University Press, Princeton, 1940.

. . . . there seems to me a fundamental difference between knowledge codified in and communicated by scientific formulations, and what a number of writers are pleased to call the "truths" embodied in works of art. Thus lovers of the arts sometimes claim that a "significant" work of art . . . is significant because it offers an "interpretation" of some subject-matter, because it conveys a "propositional meaning," and because it expresses a truth analogous in character to the interpretations, meanings, and truths expressed by scientific statements. [Nagel cites, as "perhaps an extreme example," the claim of one of Aldous Huxley's characters that a proof of God's existence is contained in the Adagio movement of Beethoven's A minor Quartet!] On the other hand, the very writers who insist on the cognitive burden of art objects usually also insist on the unique value of works of art, and on the untranslatability of their alleged specific intellectual content into other media. This is not the place for debating the issues just outlined. I want simply to note, however, that if there is no identifiable sense in which an art object can be "translated" into other media—and I believe there is no such sense—then the "knowledge" that is supposedly communicated by works of art is generally different from scientific knowledge. Accordingly, the use of a common label for both sorts of things (whatever the sort of thing that art objects convey may be) seems to me a species of punning, and is bound to create intellectual confusions.[15]

I must challenge this statement on at least four counts.

i) Why *must* a "truth" or "insight" be completely translatable into a totally different medium? Let us suppose that "reality" does in fact have many different aspects and "dimensions" cognitively available to us, and let us suppose also that different generic types of experience mediate these different aspects to us. (Surely neither of these suppositions is *a priori* unintelligible or invalid!) Would one not then expect to find what some of us assert to be the case, namely, that mankind has, through the centuries, devised very different "languages" which are so well suited to serve as vehicles for this or that generic type of cognition that adequate translation from one generic language to another (*e.g.,* from an "artistic" to a "scientific" language) is in fact impossible?[16]

[15]Ernest Nagel, "Symbolism and Science," *Symbols and Values,* Chapter III, p. 41.
[16]I once had an argument with an eminent mathematician who insisted that I translate the "meaning" or "content" of a (nonprogrammatic) musical composition into the language of mathematical symbolism. My answer was that I would do so if he would first translate the "meaning" or "content" of one of his elegant mathematical demonstrations into music. Both efforts would, of course, be utterly futile. I could no more express the content of

ii) Why *must* a very concrete insight, well expressed in a very specific form in art, be translatable without significant loss into another specific artistic form? I am not challenging Nagel's claim that it is of the very essence of science that a scientific truth can be expressed adequately in and through more than one scientific form (though I venture, way outside my own field of competence, to wonder whether the most subtle ideas of the mathematician *can* be reexpressed in scientific prose without grave loss). But, assuming the correctness of Nagel's claim, why *must* the artistic enterprise so closely parallel the scientific enterprise?

iii) Why, as Nagel implies, *must* verification, and therefore accurate communication, *depend* upon translatability? Surely all that is required is that those who attempt to communicate with one another and to verify each other's alleged insights have at their disposal *some* adequate symbolic vehicle for accurate reflection, articulation, expression, and communication. What *a priori* reason is there for denying categorically that I, as artist, have had a real insight; that I have so felicitously expressed it in a specific work of art in a given medium that it cannot be expressed with equal, or comparable, felicity in another work of art in the same medium, or, *a fortiori,* in another medium; *and* that you, sensitive in and oriented to the "languages" of art, can accurately recapture my insight *as* I have *uniquely* expressed it in my work of art? Precisely this, I believe, is not only possible in principle but is in fact more or less successfully accomplished in artistically literate and articulate circles. (I make no claim, of course, for *perfect* expression, communication, or verification, any more than could Nagel in science. Indeed, I am prepared to admit that it is much harder to approximate such perfection in the arts than in the sciences, for a variety of reasons which I cannot here pause to explore.)

iv) Finally, why *must* scientific truth and its expression be used as the inevitable model for *all* truth and all expressions of truth—indeed as a model so sacrosanct that those of us who believe in authentic non-scientific insights are forbidden to assign "truth-value" to the nonscientific expression of such insights? When our Western culture is compared in this respect with other, notably with Far Eastern and Near Eastern, cultures; when the century old search for "wisdom" (as essentially involving insight into secular and religious values) within our

---

pure music in terms of mathematical symbols than he could whistle or orchestrate his subtle and highly complex mathematical ideas.

Western culture, from Socrates to Hegel and down to the present day, is taken into account—in these large perspectives, must not the contemporary tendency, voiced by Nagel, fall under grave suspicion of exhibiting all the hallmarks of cultural provincialism and arbitrary philosophical dogmatism?

These four comments are, of course, all negative. They are intended to challenge what I can only call dogmatic "scientism" (sharply to be distinguished from the sciences). Affirmative confirmation that art is in fact cognitive is possible only *within* the area of artistic experience, *i.e.,* of responsible artistic creation and of responsible critical response to the expressiveness of art.

The further question is sure to be raised, even by those who understand art with real sensitivity: if a work of art can indeed express genuine insights with real "truth-value," how should such insight and truth be conceived of? Insight into what? Truth about what? Irwin Edman asked me this question years ago in his excellent review of my book on art when it first appeared. He was willing to grant the claim that artists do have and do express "insights," but he objected to my defense of the notion of "artistic" truth. I, for my part, fail to see what meaning "insight" can have apart from truth in *some* meaningful sense. The real difficulty, however, lies deeper, for "insight" is surely meaningless unless it is insight *into* something, just as truth is meaningless unless it is truth *about* something. In short, my definition of art clearly implies the presence in all art of a fourth factor, over and above the medium, the form, and the content. I shall call this factor the "subject-matter" of art and define it as that part or aspect of "reality" upon which the artist chooses to focus his attention and into which he claims (at least implicitly) to have a genuine or true insight which he wishes to express in his work and, through it, to communicate to others.

c) *The nonrepresentational arts—music and architecture.* That all literature and that representational sculpture and painting have a subject-matter, so defined, is, I hope, sufficiently evident, and a corresponding claim for programmatic music and the pantomimic or dramatic dance will perhaps be allowed without serious challenge. But what about "pure" music, the "pure" dance, architecture, and nonrepresentational ("abstract" or "nonobjective") painting and sculpture? The answer to this question is not easy to give in brief compass, because it calls for a detailed analysis of each of these arts with an eye to their several distinctive expressive potentialities and limitations. All I can do here is to say a word about pure music, as exemplary of the pure dance and of nonrepresentational sculpture and painting *in this respect,* and then a word about architecture.

The generic subject-matter of pure music (and of the arts most like it on this score) is, I would suggest, the whole range of man's emotions and moods, hopes and fears, and dynamic impulses—in short, the sum-total of his "emotive-conative" states. (I link "emotive" and "conative" because these aspects of human experience are, in fact, coordinate—we never, normally, experience an emotion without some conation, or a conation without some emotion—and also because music and the arts which resemble it never seem to express one without the other.) What these arts do, I would argue, is to express, with a subtlety, precision, and range impossible in any other "languages," man's emotive-conative states *as such, i.e.,* abstracted from the behavioral, perceptual, and idea-tional contexts in which they normally occur in actual human experi-ence. (I say "normally" because they do occur in a similarly detached, unmotivated fashion in certain types of mentally sick patients, *i.e.,* pathologically. They can also be induced—as Nagel is aware—by certain drugs.) What a *particular* musical or comparable composition does is to draw on this generic subject-matter and make *specific* use of *some* of it. Hence the specificity of the musical content of specific compositions—a specificity as pronounced, and as artistically crucial, as the specificity of the composition's medium and form.

This still leaves unaccounted for, however, the role of normative in-terpretation upon which I have insisted. Does the competent composer merely *evoke* emotions, moods, and impulses in his musically enlight-ened audience, or does he somehow *express his evaluative interpretation* of them in his work? This is indeed a hard question to answer with precision and assurance. We must, I believe, approach the problem in-ductively, that is, in terms of our encounters with various types of music, and, specifically, with music which we would describe as "mature," "discerning," and "significant," on the one hand, in contrast to music which we would describe as "superficial," "trivial," and "sentimental," on the other. Both types evoke emotions and conations, the latter type no less powerfully, on occasion, than the former. But in the case of the former we are left, I believe, with the conviction that the composer has really *understood* the distinctive quality, the "stature," the heights and depths, of man's emotive-conative experience. We feel that, in his music, we have really been enabled to experience and *know* joy and sorrow, hope and despair, as we have never perhaps experienced or known them before. In the case of "sentimental music," on the other hand, we feel cheated and disgusted by the "tinsel" superficiality of the composer's "insight" into these human states. The emotions, moods, and impulses which his music evokes seem to us to be mawkish, tawdry, and devoid of depth and authenticity. Psychologically they are, of course, as *real* and far more widespread, human beings being what they are. But just as we distinguish in real life between a joy which is purified and exalted from a pleasure which is coarse and paltry, so, too, do we, I believe, distinguish between music whose content "rings true" and music whose content does not.

This analysis can be supported by another consideration of major importance, the fact, namely, that the emotions and conations which music arouses in us, *if* we submit to the guidance of the music itself and allow *it* to do the evoking (instead of using the music merely as a stimulus for some type of free association which is musically uncontrolled), are never experienced as having precisely the quality and as necessitating the kind of immediate personal involvement which characterize our actual emotions and conations in our everyday lives. It is notorious that sorrow as expressed and evoked by music is not depressing in the way in which actual sorrow is depressing. We can, in and through a musical experience, feel and know it profoundly without actually "being sad." Here, as elsewhere in disciplined esthetic response, Bullough's famous principle of "psychic distance" is, or should be, operative. It is this "distance" which enables us to know and savor the emotions and conations which music evokes, as we cannot possibly know or savor the same (or analogous) emotions during the turmoil and strain of actual living.

I conclude, then, that the composer, both in music and in the arts most like music, does find, in his creative endeavors, ample scope for "true" insight into his generic subject-matter and for suitable interpretation of the subject-matter in and through his music. *Somehow* he does, in all "good" music, succeed not only in evoking very specific emotions, moods, and conations in us; he manages to evoke them in us *in such a way* as to enable us to *know* them *and* to *appreciate* or assess them more faithfully than we commonly do when we encounter them even in our most poignant artistically unmediated experiences.[17]

We can deal with the analogous problem of architecture more briefly. What distinguishes architecture from the other arts is of course the practical use for which buildings are inevitably designed. Artists in other media do indeed often create a work of art for a specific practical purpose (*e.g.,* altarpieces, music for the Mass, "occasional" poems, etc.). They can, however, create their works with no such specific and practical use in mind, and, since the Renaissance, they have increasingly done so. An architect, in contrast, cannot possibly create an "expressive building" *as such,* that is, without regard to the use to which it might be put. Indeed, he must not only know that his job is to design *a* church, or *an* office building, or *a* private home; ideally, he needs to know the *specific* religious, or business, or domestic needs which his building is to be designed to satisfy.

This characteristic of architecture is the clue to the generic and the specific "subject-matter" of architecture. It is what architects call the "program," that is, simultaneously the generic *and* the specific use to which the building is to be put. It is, for example, to be a Protestant Christian church for a New England Congregationalist community in a certain town on a certain site (and, alas, to be built at a specified cost). Where, then, does the architect's "normative interpretation" come in? The answer involves the subtle but crucial distinction between engineering and architecture. The highly competent engineer who is *merely* an engineer will know how to satisfy the *"physical"* requirements of the "program," *i.e.,* how to achieve the requisite economy, durability, illumination, "circulation," etc. The architect must also be a master of this complex engineering craft, but he must have, in addition, two aptitudes. He must, first, be able to *grasp* the *human* implications of the "program," that is, man's "spiritual" needs in this specific type of housed activity, and he must, secondly, know how to *express* these spiritual overtones architecturally, that is, via evident and eloquent architectural structure. (This expression can be notably *enhanced* by various non-

[17] I cannot even begin to explore the conscious and subconscious processes of artistic creation for an answer to the question of *how* the artist in general, and the musical composer in particular, performs this interpretative miracle. The reader is referred to Maritain's brilliant study of this problem in his *Creative Intuition in Art and Poetry,* Pantheon Books, New York, 1953.

architectural devices borrowed from other major and minor arts, *e.g.,* by decorative motifs, fixtures, interior decoration, and landscaping; but, in first rate architecture, the *chief* expressive vehicle is the concrete "form" or organization of the building materials themselves, with full exploitation of their texture.)

This means that, in building a domestic house, the architect, if he is really competent, will understand not only domesticity in general, as it prevails in his times, his culture, and his particular locale; he will, in addition, take pains (if he is designing a "home" for a specific family and not just domestic "housing" for a real estate development) to get well acquainted with his patron and his family so that he can anticipate, so far as possible, the family's needs, both physical *and spiritual,* as specifically as possible. Only thus can he then hope to design a house for *this* family which will express as effectively as possible their particular type of domesticity at its evolving best. It is amazing what an architect can do in this regard. He can, as architect, sense the distinctive *élan* of a given family better, often, than can the family itself, and he can build them a home which will not only be "convenient" and "practical," *i.e.,* satisfy the engineering requirements of the "program," but which will "feel" and "look" right to them and to their architecturally discerning friends, and into which they can, as a family, "grow" with spiritual self-realization rather than frustration. That such a feat, difficult and rare but not impossible, requires normative interpretation, would seem obvious.

If these analyses of music and architecture are at all plausible, the much easier case for the role of normative interpretation of a subject-matter in literature and in the "representational" arts can perhaps be presumed to have been made *a fortiori.* Here, too, the expressive potentialities and limitations of each art must carefully be taken into account. Literature, because of its verbal medium, has an available subject-matter far more inclusive in scope than that of painting and sculpture. The flat surface of a painting imposes upon the painter certain limitations, and simultaneously endows him with certain generic expressive powers, which the sculptor lacks; the sculptor "in the round" has various complementary expressive assets and liabilities. The works of both, in turn, can present their chosen subject-matter, as they normatively interpret it, with a "presentational immediacy" which literature cannot rival, because the reader or hearer of a literary work must himself conjure up the meanings, conceptual and imagistic alike, of the verbal symbols and then, guided of course by the carefully planned sequence of these symbols, re-create the work itself for himself *before* he can even begin to contemplate it and assess it. These are but a few of the many complex characteristics of the several arts of which anyone who wishes responsibly to discuss the generic content of art must be aware.

d) *Can the arts express propositions?* I raise this question for brief consideration because it is often asked by those who, quite properly, want to know precisely what is meant by "artistic truth." Truth need not, perhaps, be conceived of in terms of propositions at all, but it is convenient to do so, and if truth is conceived of in this way it is fair to ask whether the claim is really being made that a work of art can actually express true or false propositions.

The answer seems to me to depend entirely upon *how* proportions are defined. If a proposition is defined (as logicians and scientifically oriented philosophers are apt to define it) as that which is asserted in a scientific statement (with or without the aid of mathematical symbolism), it follows that every proposition must itself possess as abstract character which can accurately be expressed only in abstract conceptual (scientific and/or mathematical) symbols. Those who interpret propositions in this way seem to me to be working backward *from* the symbols which they use with such precision *to* that which they attempt to express by means of this symbolism. They start with a scientific statement or assertion; they then ask, "What is here stated or asserted?" and they conclude that what is thus asserted is a proposition about reality—a proposition which is believed to be true, *i.e.,* which does justice to the "reality" in question. This "backward" movement, in turn, involves the further assumption that the "reality" in question is necessarily "structural," *i.e.,* that *kind* of reality to which abstract, *e.g.,* quantitative, propositions are able to "do justice"—the assumption, in short, that all that can *really* be known about reality *is* its quantitative structure.

If propositions are defined in this way, the claim that art can express true propositions does, it seems to me, become quite meaningless, save possibly in certain types of literature.

But suppose we conceive of reality and propositions and their felicitous judgmental expression in quite a different way. Suppose we take reality as we variously encounter it—not only in science but in our everyday experience, in moral and religious experience, and in art. In some types of encounter, notably in all normative experience, reality presents itself to us concretely, qualitatively, and as possessing value. Let us assume also that it is our desire to express, as faithfully and truthfully as we can, this concrete, qualitative, and normative character of what we thus encounter. We can do so only by i) asserting true propositions, *i.e.,* propositions which will "do justice" to *these* characteristics of what we encounter and accept as real, ii) in a *language* appropriate to such assertion. It would follow, on this approach to the problem of truth, i) that propositions should *not* be thought of as being *necessarily* abstract and quantitative, and ii) that the conceptual languages of science and mathematics should *not* be accepted dogmatically as the *only* languages of precise expression, or even as the languages best suited for the expression of *some kinds* of propositions, those, namely, related (truly or falsely) to concrete, qualitative, and normative situations or entities.

If this general approach is defensible, it makes perfectly good sense to say that a work of art can express certain propositions about certain aspects of a given subject-matter *more* nearly accurately and adequately than *any* scientific assertions could possibly express them. This would in no way impugn the precision of scientific discourse *in its own domain,* or invalidate the claim that science and mathematics can best express in their own languages *those* propositions with which they are concerned, nor would it deny that reality does have the structural characteristics which science believes it to have and which it seeks to discover and formulate with maximum quantitative accuracy and scope. What I am here urging is not a wholesale critique of science but merely a criticism of the illegitimate pretensions of "scientism" which, in its enthusiasm for scientific knowledge, insists on equating all knowledge with scientific knowledge and which dogmatically assumes that all propositions must be of the type amenable to scientific formulation and expression.

This plea is, of course, crucial for my entire analysis of knowledge and truth and, in particular, for my account of "artistic truth." I am denying the claim of the disciples of scientism (and of all other dogmatic conceptualists) to a copyright on "truth." I freely grant the important differences between "scientific" or "conceptual" truth and "artistic" truth, and hence the importance of these qualifying adjectives. But I insist that the identification of all truth with conceptual truth is invalid and intolerable. It is today the greatest *intellectual* threat to our cultural values and the most serious obstacle to the revitalization of these values in our time.

e) *The basic components of art.* I can summarize my understanding of the nature of any work of art in any medium with the help of a diagrammatic formula:

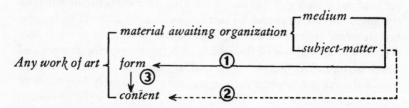

The arrows signify ①that the artist endows the work with *form* by specific manipulation of his *medium*
②that the content of the work is his interpretation of its *subject-matter,* and
③that this content is *expressed* in and through the work's *form.*

It will be obvious to anyone who understands art that the components which I have here tried carefully to distinguish are, in the work of art itself, so organically fused that they cease to function as artistic components if they are abstracted from this context, somewhat as the leaves, bark, and roots of a tree cease to function and die if they are severed from the living tree. In a painting, for example, the medium, in or of itself, is just paint; on the palette it constitutes the painter's *potential* medium only; it functions as his actual medium only *as* organized *on* the canvas. The form, in turn, is *this* specific organization of *this* specific medium; generic artistic forms are nothing but generalized abstractions (in the philosophical, not the pictorial sense) which, in themselves, have *no* artistic reality or merit. The content is precisely (no more and no less than) what *this* organization of *this* medium expresses. It loses all its artistic reality and vitality if the attempt (so common among those who do not understand art) is made to detach it from its expressive form and to "restate" it in cold conceptual prose. The work's subject-matter, finally, is introduced or exhibited by the artist entirely by means of his manipulation of his medium. In a still-life, for example, he depicts his apples and oranges via paint, and he depicts them as he does, with appropriate selection and "distortion," omission and emphasis, in order thereby to convey to the observer his normative interpretation of them. This judicious handling of his subject-matter, in turn, is so synthesized with the formal pattern of color *as such* that the *"representational"* expressiveness of the subject-matter and the *direct* expressiveness of the sheer pattern of color and line intensify one another in an endless variety of subtle ways.

What I have been describing is of course art at its ideal best—a best which only the most perfect art closely approximates. Most actual artifacts which can be labelled art because they have a modicum of artistry fall short of this ideal in various ways—in the direction of an uninterpretative realism which goes too far toward literal reproduction of the chosen subject-matter (a vice to which painting and colored sculpture are especially prone); in the direction of inexpressive and meaningless pattern, of sheer empty design (the special hazard of the abstract arts); in the direction of prosaic conceptual statement (the peculiar danger of literary prose); and, more generally, in sheer faultiness of craftsmanship and lack of significant vision.

f) *Levels of artistic appraisal.* In assessing a work of art it is helpful to discriminate between different levels or types of achievement. i) At the level of craftsmanship, a work of art can be said to be successful or to approximate to "perfection" in proportion as the artist's specific intent *in this work of art* is judged to have been realized, *i.e.,* in proportion as the artist has actually "said" what he wanted to say, however true or false, trivial or significant, the expressed content may be judged to be. ii) At the level of "truth" the work can be appraised affirmatively in proportion as the artist's expressed interpretation of his chosen subject-matter is confirmable by what we, who sit in judgment, know or can know (often with the artist's help!) about it. (This means that a critic who is relatively blind to certain truths, for whatever reason, will be an inadequate judge of the truthfulness of a work of art which seeks to embody or express these truths. We must remember that the critic is himself judged by the work of art upon which he sits in judgment, and that it may well be he who comes off second best in this judicial encounter.) iii) Finally, a truth can be either significant or trivial in varying degrees. The "greatness" of a work of art is proportionate to its total stature, the significance of its expressed insights, its profundity (its depth and breadth of vision), its inexhaustibility.

g) *The individuality, specificity, and universality of art.* My final comment is of prime importance for the analysis, in the next section, of *how* a work of art can function so powerfully as a normative vehicle. It concerns the fusion, in a work of art, of universality, specificity, and individuality. A work of art is, and remains (so long as it exists) a complex individual entity of a distinctive type. Its individuality, in turn, is the composite product of infinite specificities—of a multitude of "this-es" in multiple specific relation to each other and to the work as a whole. Everything about the work of art is entirely and irreducibly specific— the distinguishable parts of its specific medium and this medium *in toto,* the distinguishable components or aspects of its formal organization and its form as a whole, its subject-matter, in part and in aggregate, and, no less specific, its content. Not only can all these specificities, however, be conceived of as "instances" of universals (this red patch, as an instance of this hue of red, and of redness, and of color, etc.); what is so significant for our purpose is the fact that the content of the work of art, despite its complete specificity, can also be more or less universal and therefore meaningful and significant for others. This should be obvious, but it is so frequently denied that a word of explanation is in order.

Let us start with the perspective of the artist—always a unique perspective because he is a unique individual who sees what he sees with some degree of freshness and novelty in each successive work which he creates. This uniqueness of outlook and insight reflects itself inevitably in the content of his work if he has real creative and expressive power as an artist. Now, were this the whole story, his work, including its content, would be *merely* idiosyncratic and therefore, by definition, meaningless and valueless to everyone else. But, in proportion to the artist's stature, the very reverse is the case. Not by being less uniquely himself but rather by being *himself* as completely as possible, he is able to make himself intelligible to others and his work profoundly significant to others— provided, of course, that he has within himself the stuff of authentic and significant insight.

Here we have then, in all successful and notable art, the perfect fusion of uniqueness *and* wide relevance, novelty *and* pervasive human import, universality *in* specificity—in short, *significant individuality*. It is this amazing characteristic of art which, we will find, enables it to perform so notably its special function of serving as the vehicle, *par excellence,* of our cultural values.

3. *How Can a Work of Art Function as a Normative Vehicle?*

We are now in a position to relate our normative experiences, our normative judgments, and the work of art to each other, and to see, at least in sketchy outline, why the arts are, as we have claimed they are, man's normative vehicles *par excellence,* the most sensitive, accurate, and powerful symbols available to us for the articulation of our normative experiences.

a) *Values as encountered and as conceived.* Still postponing the philosophical problem of the ultimate ontological status of values, and starting, as is reasonable, with our actual value experiences, we find that the values we believe ourselves to encounter experientially are always so encountered in a *concrete context.* We come upon, and enjoy, not beauty in the abstract but specific beauties, that is, the beauty of *this* rose, *this* face, *this* work of art. The justice and love which we actually experience are not justice in general and love as such but concrete persons, acts, institutions, etc., which are more or less just and loving. The same can be said of truth as a value; we come face to face not with absolute truth but with what we judge to be specific truths expressed in some specific symbolic medium.

Nominalists seem to believe that these concrete values comprise the whole realm of value. The rest of us cannot get away from the fact that all concrete values seem to point beyond themselves to more embracing, purer, and more perfect values which they, in their concreteness, only partially and imperfectly "exemplify" and "embody." The more just a man really is, the less inclined is he to claim that he is perfectly just; it is the "saint" who is most aware of his own lack of saintliness; the greater the artist, the more conscious is he of the shortcomings of his finest creative work. Embodied values, I repeat, seem inexorably to point beyond themselves to what, for convenience (and without prejudicing the ontological issue) I shall designate as perfect Truth, Beauty, Justice, and Love. It is these "absolutes" in which, in some sense, we must believe if we are to validate man's universal sense of obligation to what *ought* to be and his feeling of tension between what ought to be and what actually is. However variously we interpret such obligation, our value experiences are permeated with it. We feel, whenever we reflect and act responsibly, that we ought to be more loving, that our laws and institutions ought to be more just, that we ought to press on for ever more truth in every area of cognitive inquiry—in short, we dare not rest content with whatever values have in fact already been concretized.

We need not, at this point, say any more about these "absolute" Values than that i) they are never themselves experientially "encounterable"; ii) that they can only be conceived of abstractly, as ideals or "universals," not yet, and perhaps never destined to be, completely actualized by and for fallible human beings; iii) that we, with our finite minds and limited range of experience, can never *fully* comprehend them *as* "absolutes," even conceptually; and iv) that we must therefore define them, most unsatisfactorily, as the largely empty but very necessary points of reference for all our normative strivings. They have a paradoxical character. We must, on the one hand, believe in them in some sense and strive to apprehend and actualize them more adequately; yet we cannot, by definition, know them for what they are in themselves. We can have fleeting and distorted glimpses of them as idealized extrapolations of the concrete values which we do know; yet only as we take them seriously can we take the finite values which we encounter in all their concreteness as genuinely valuable and as, therefore, obligating us.

The concreteness of encountered values, meanwhile, calls for further explanation because different values achieve embodiment in such different ways. The concrete context of *personal* values, or the values of persons, is the human individual—a psychophysical being with all his capacities and activities, all that he is and all that he does *as* an individual human being. The instances of *justice* which we encounter are concretely embodied either in persons and in their personal relations to each other or in the social institutions and procedures which human beings have devised to enable them to live together and to pursue common ends. The *beauties* we encounter are either natural or manmade "objects"—as concrete and specific as a flower or a landscape, a human body, a utilitarian artifact, or a work of art. Finally, the *truths* we encounter are always embodied in some specific symbolic form. We do, no doubt, speak of the truth of an insight, but I should agree with Croce that no insight is ever clear enough to be meaningful, even to the agent, until it has been articulated or expressed, at least privately, in *some* suitable language.

b) *Our encounter with concrete values.* This encounter, in proportion to its authenticity as a value experience, engages us, in turn, as *complete persons* and evokes our *total, rounded response.* Our knowledge of such values, in such encounters, is by no means merely intellectual, though it certainly involves the use of the intellect; embodied values tend to elicit from us far more than mere intellectual assent to their existence (as full bodied religious faith transcends mere deistic assent to the proposition that God exists). Our minds, our senses, our imagination, our emotions, and our will are *all* actively engaged in the transaction. This is bound to be the case for two reasons, first, because the value is encountered, as we have seen, not abstractly but always in some concrete context, and, secondly, because our awareness of it and our response to it tend to be simultaneous, not successive, experiences.

We can also *think about* an embodied value such as justice *abstractly;* that is, we can abstract it in thought from its concrete setting, and apprehend it as a generic value. We can intellectually compare different embodiments of the same generic value and assess their relative merits as successful embodiments. We can even approve of such values, both as embodied and as abstracted, and call them "good." But all such rational apprehension is but a pale intellectualized shadow of our full blooded encounter with, and involvement in, actual concrete values, for in such encounter all our "faculties" are simultaneously called into play. Our *senses* are sharply focused upon the concrete setting, our *reason* provides the requisite interpretational context, our *imagination* enables us to grasp the embodied value for what it is, an actual "object of value," our *emotions* are appropriately aroused, and our *will* generates and confirms our appropriate attitude to it and precipitates our appropriate behavior toward it. Where, in this total complex experience—so vivid, so "organic," so unified—can we validly discriminate between "apprehension" and "response"? We can, in *abstraction,* make this distinction, but in the actual experience of full fledged encounter, apprehension involves response from the very outset and is, in turn, dependent upon response. Neither is possible without the other; both are essential aspects of one and the same process. This is true even when the encounter takes time and comes to its fruition only gradually. *As* apprehension sharpens and clarifies, involvement increases; *as* we become involved, apprehension deepens.

Meanwhile, it is never merely the *value* of the object which we encounter, as in any way distinct from its embodiment, nor is it ever the embodiment, as in itself valueless, which we encounter in an authentic normative experience. What we encounter and what captivates our attention, engages our concern, and precipitates our emotive-conative response, is the *value-as-embodied,* the *total* object as an *object-of-value.* If our encounter is with a person, it is this individual as a whole, in all his endless specificity, to whom we respond in total acceptance, love, and loyalty. If it is a flower, it is this lovely flower which we contemplate with natural piety and joy. If the person, or the flower, thus encountered is threatened, we are instantly afraid and act to ward off the danger; if this effort fails, we experience more or less intense sorrow; if it succeeds and the threat diminishes we feel relief and our joy is renewed and intensified.

Thus our *total response* to the valued object in its *totality* involves, from first to last, continuing perceptual awareness, imaginative grasp, and intellectual interpretation; it also involves, from the very outset, the emotive and conative responses which, together, dynamize the complete experience.

The fact that response can and should be appropriate to the object apprehended, in no way invalidates our thesis that apprehension and response are organically interfused. The appropriate generic attitudes to nature, man, beauty, and God, respectively, can for convenience be labelled "natural piety," "loving respect," "contemplative joy," and "grateful reverence." The correspondingly appropriate behavior cannot be tagged quite so simply. We seem to be invited in each case to "commune" with the "object" apprehended in an appropriate manner, that is, to "enter into community" with nature, man, and art, no less than with Deity. But we are also impelled to *use* nature, not exploitatively but sensitively, as the true artist uses his medium; to *cooperate* with our fellows as human beings, not exploitatively but with loving concern; to *cherish* all instances of beauty, not possessively but, as Kant would say, "freely"; and to *worship and obey* God, not compulsively but in willing service and adoration. In short, our appropriate total response is indicated and controlled by the *nature* of the "object" apprehended.

Exactly the same, however, can be said of apprehension. Our apprehensions of nature and man, embodied beauty and Deity, are themselves adequate only as they "conform" or "do justice to" what is apprehended, so that mere apprehension can gradually be transformed into more and more complete comprehension. Such comprehension can be approximated, however, only in proportion as our response is, in each case, itself appropriate. If we approach nature exploitatively, in attitude and behavior, we will never be able to understand her for what she is. Without loving respect for our fellow men and the sincere effort to cooperate with them, we cannot hope to comprehend them as persons. Beauty approached with insensitive callousness and exploited in a predatory spirit cannot be enjoyed and cherished. Indifference to Deity or self-sufficient repudiation of Him condemns us to religious blindness. In short, response conditions apprehension as apprehension conditions response; they are two aspects of a single venture and develop or languish *pari passu*.

c) *Our encounter with God.* I have included the Deity and our apprehension of and response to Him in order to round out my account of man's generic normative experiences. This is fitting, not only because man's religious experience is one of his generic types of experience but because the Deity, if we believe in Him at all, must be conceived of as real, indeed, as the *most* real of all realities, with complete ontological fullness of being. The religious consciousness also reports, with great consistency, its direct "encounters" with Deity. He is, for the religiously sensitive, not an hypothesis or a mere principle of explanation (like the "God of the philosophers") but a real Being or Presence Who confronts and challenges man with existential dynamic power. He therefore differs essentially from the Values which, we have said, can never be directly encountered but only conceived of abstractly, and which, moreover, are usually conceived of as static rather than dynamic, *awaiting* discovery and *not revealing themselves* to man.

This does, of course, raise the question as to *how* we encounter God and *whether* we ever encounter Him in Himself or only in *some* concrete "embodiment." We cannot pause to explore this very difficult and controversial question. It must suffice to point out i) that the mystical tendency in all religions is to assert a mysterious but indubitable type of immediate unembodied confrontation, though even such confrontation is usually described as taking place in existentially concrete contexts, and ii) that the dominant tendency of all the great world religions has been to insist that God "reveals" Himself to man in and through the "inspiration" of prophets, in the "visions" of saints, in "marvelous" events, and, in some religions, in multiple or unique Incarnation. Even in religion, then, authentic encounter tends to be described as involving some form of concrete setting or embodiment. The heavens are said to "declare the glory of God," unusual events and "mighty works" to reveal Him; He is believed to have "spoken" to man through His chosen prophets, to have "appeared" to His saints, to be "compresent" in sacred rites participated in "with a pure heart," to be loved when "the least of these" are loved for themselves, and, in Christianity, to be uniquely Incarnate in Jesus as the Christ. These "embodiments" of Deity are *not* wholly identical with the concrete embodiments of value which confront us in our "secular" normative encounters, but they are their close religious analogues and, as such, they present us, like them, with i) something of intrinsic worth ii) which is normally experienced not as disembodied but as "clothed" in some specific revelatory vehicle.

d) *The role of emotion in normative encounter.* No problem in value theory has been more voluminously debated in recent years than the role of emotion. I cannot pause to rehearse all the conflicting theories; there is substantial agreement on only two counts, first, that emotion does play an essential role in all normative experience, and, second, that emotions have, and can have, no cognitive function. Emotive response is thus usually contrasted with cognitive awareness. Out and out "emotive" theories tend to go even farther, namely, by *reducing* evaluation to feeling (liking and disliking) and emotion and by *reducing* values to the status of *unconscious projections* of feelings and emotions into the "valued" object. So defined, values are of course not *themselves* discoverable or knowable; the term "value," when applied to anything, means merely that *our* affective and emotive responses to the thing in question are pleasant and that our attitude toward it is one of approval. (Disvalue is similarly interpreted in terms of displeasure or pain and of disapproval.)

The position I have been maintaining is, in contrast, that values as encountered *are* in some sense really "objective," that is, that they really characterize or impregnate their concrete embodiments. What I should now like to suggest, as an hypothesis worth serious consideration, is that emotions[18] *mediate* embodied values to us and make them cognitively

---

[18]More nearly accurately, the complex of closely interrelated emotive-conative-affective states. In what follows I shall, for brevity, refer to these states as "emotions."

available to us in a manner closely analogous to the way in which our senses mediate the physical world to us and enable us to know it. Note the similarity between the role of sensation in perceptual and scientific knowledge of nature and the role of emotion in evaluation.

i) Sensation is an essential component of sensory perception and indispensable for our immediate knowledge of the spatiotemporal world of nature. Similarly, "emotion" is an essential component of all normative encounters with embodied values. No such value is *really encountered* unless it evokes our emotive-conative-affective responses. This applies also to all actual encounters with Deity.

ii) Sensations *per se* prove nothing. They must always be interpreted, and they can easily be misinterpreted more or less seriously, both at the level of sense-perception (*cf.* illusion and hallucination) and at the abstract level of scientific inquiry. Similarly, "emotions" *per se* prove nothing. They, too, must be interpreted, and they, too, can be, and often are, misinterpreted more or less seriously at the level of immediate normative evaluation (*cf.* sentimental appraisal, analogous to sensory illusion, and pathological emotive states, *e.g.,* the unmotivated hopes and fears, feelings and impulses, of mental patients, analogous to sensory hallucination) and at the abstract level of normative (ethical, esthetic, theological) interpretation.

iii) We commonly refer to ideally accurate sense-perception as "veridical" and we do our best to correct all deviants therefrom. An immediate evaluation could, analogously, be called "veridical" if it were ideally adequate to the value situation in question, and it is certainly our concern to make our concrete evaluations of things, persons, human situations, works of art, and Deity as nearly "veridical" as possible.

iv) In neither case can deviations from the veridical be determined, or corrected, without reference to a wider context of relevant experience and interpretation and, in practice, without checking with other competent observers, *i.e.,* without testing our experiences against theirs and comparing their interpretations with ours for scope, depth, and clarity.

v) Sense perception is the basis of science; science starts with perception and continually refers back to it again and again, directing it to sharper and more germane focus and deriving its "empirical verification" from such accurate and controlled "observation." Similarly, value theory in any of the major areas of evaluation bases itself necessarily on relevant primary normative encounter; it starts with such encounter, purifies and directs it interpretatively, and moves toward great validity by doing it ever greater justice.

I am aware that these similarities need to be explored much more fully and that significant differences must seriously be taken into account. Our brief analysis may suffice, however, to indicate the essential but limited role of "emotion" in all evaluation. I have been assuming throughout that we cannot really be said to know or comprehend values dispassionately, without emotive-contative-affective involvement, as we cannot be said to know the world of nature in sense-perception or in science without the aid of our senses. But I am *not* claiming that "emotion" suffices for evaluation, any more than that sensation suffices for perceptual or scientific understanding. Finally, we must not think of "emotion" as isolated or detached from the total fused process of normative apprehension. It is merely an essential aspect of this process, as sensation is merely an essential aspect of sense-perception, distinguishable in abstraction but never in fact divorced from reflective interpretation. This account has at least the merit of recognizing the crucial role of "emotion" in our value experiences without reducing the latter to *mere* emotive response, and, in addition, of indicating the *cognitive* role of "emotion" in evaluation without putting upon "emotion" the entire burden of evaluative insight.

e) *The language of evaluation*. This brings us directly to the question with which we are specifically concerned in this Conference, namely, the language or languages of normative articulation and expression. What is the most adequate and most appropriate symbolic vehicle for normative judgments and normative communication? My answer is: the arts, in all their variety and gradations. That this is not an arbitrary answer can, I believe, be demonstrated.

Let us start with art at its eloquent best. Such art expresses, we have said, the artist's normative interpretation of his chosen subject-matter. It is "expressive," rather than merely "indicative" or "informative," because it is able to convey to the sensitive observer how the artist *"saw"* his subject-matter *and* how he felt about it—how he apprehended both its nature (or those aspects of its nature which were relevant to his immediate interest) *and* its significance for man. The artist's creative effort was not merely an exercise in craftsmanship; it involved his total being —his senses and his imagination, his mind, his "emotions," and his will. His work of art is the record of his total creative effort, the sensitive and dynamic product of his own complex dynamic sensitivity. It can, there-fore, mediate to us, as can no other type of symbolic artifact, the artist's total experience. Through it he is able to "express" himself and to speak to us as he cannot possibly do through any purely denotative symbolic medium. His work can also speak *for* us, often saying what we have wished to say without being able to say it; it can confirm and deepen insights of our own which, because of our linguistic deficiencies, we have been unable adequately to articulate or to clarify even to ourselves. Indeed, it might be said that in art a threefold dialogue is set in motion— first, between the artist and his work, the latter "talking back" to the artist, as it were, as it is pushed by him to completion; then, between the finished work and us, its observers, we learning from it, making it our own, and judging it, while it, in turn, "talks back" to us, deepening our insights, and, in its own way, judging us as we judge it; and, finally, between the artist and ourselves, he eloquently communicating his in-sights and evaluations to us *through* his art, and we responding, as best we can, in responsible critical comment.

The inevitable descriptive and communicative inadequacy of such critical comment, even at its best, offers further support for our thesis. The critic can dissect and point, interpret and paraphrase; but he can-not possibly restate or reexpress the *content* of the art which he is seek-ing to understand, assess, and interpret to others, and he can *really* communicate *his own* evaluations of the art he is criticizing and of the insights which it expresses only by resorting, even as critic, to language which is, in its own way, artistically eloquent, that is, to the *artistically* expressive language of "literary" utterance. Hence the repeated flights of critics into "literary" prose. When they have finished their task of historical interpretation and structural analysis and address themselves to the task of evaluation, they necessarily resort to imagistic and evoca-tive discourse.

If our analysis is valid thus far, we can extend it and apply our thesis to *all* human expression of normative encounter and *all* communication of human evaluation. The term "artistry" need not and should not be restricted to explicit "works of art." All of us are indulging in some sort of artistry all the time, however feebly and crudely, as we are evaluating all the time, and as we are, as social beings, continually impelled to com-municate our evaluations to one another. All emotionally charged excla-mations, however blunt and violent; all rhythmic and imagistic utterance, however inept or slangy; all our gestures and facial expressions; all of the emotive-conative-affective overtones of what we say and do—are not these our multiple unconscious devices for expressing our moment-to-moment evaluations of the situations in which we find ourselves and of the "objects" and persons and predicaments which we encounter? Our "popular" arts—our "funnies" and "cartoons," our jazz music and our versified jingles, our pulp magazines and our cheap movies and radio and television shows, etc., are "artistically" somewhat more articulate and expressive of the current stereotyped values of our predominantly sensate culture. Through them preeminently all our cultural tastes are formed and our popular values instilled and established. But it is only in and through our best art, in all the various media, that more authentic insights into more enduring and lifegiving values can achieve adequate expression. The tragedy of our times is that our people are, on the whole, so uneducated in the arts at their best that man's highest values and most profound normative insights, past and present, remain unavailable to them. To all but a small minority, the great art of the past and the most significant art of the present remains a closed book, an infinitely precious *potential* vehicle of communication which *might* be but *is not* communicative to the many who, in fact, either ignore it or find it incomprehensible and uncommunicative of any significant meaning.

f) *Nonesthetic uses of art.* One of the many paradoxes of our culture is our tendency, on the one hand, to value art to the point of idolizing it and worshiping it for its own sake, and, on the other hand, of profaning it by putting it to uses unworthy of its high calling. We enshrine it in museums, embalm it as a "classic" in Five Foot Shelves and lists of The Hundred Great Books, liturgize it in the elaborate social ritual of the concert hall, and solemnize it with all the unction of private "openings" and invited "showings." We thus place it in an esthetic holy of holies, insist that it be adored only for its own sake, and surround it with an opaque fog of "precious" and decadent estheticism. On the other hand, we exploit it, crudely but violently, in high pressure advertising and prostitute it by paying the artist handsomely, with money and social acclaim, to produce easy, tawdry, "popular" art in huge amounts and by selling this art at a low price in staggering quantities. We are thus overrun by little men producing trivial art to be bought and sold merely for financial profit to people craving sensuous titillation and any erotic excitation that is cheap and legal. The final irony is supplied by Watch and Ward outfits which, professing to seek to protect the public against pornographic art, succeed chiefly in making somewhat less available works of art of real merit, often of high artistic merit, such as James Joyce's *Ulysses*.

What we as a nation have hardly begun to think about trying to do is, on the one hand, to help our ablest artists in every possible way to realize their proper destiny, that is, to create as skillfully, profoundly, and honestly as possible, without regard to the market or popular taste, and, on the other hand, *really* to apply ourselves to the artistic education of the public. Our feeble efforts in both directions can be fairly assessed as mere drops in the bucket, when we compare them with the money and energy which we as a nation lavish, both governmentally and privately, on other things.

The two great institutions in our society which should be our chief spiritual bulwarks and sources of spiritual light and power, the church and the school, are also failing almost completely to apply themselves to this crucial problem and to take effective steps to remedy it.

i) What is the church doing, apart from an occasional experiment so rare as to be considered "newsworthy" by *Time,* to provide its people with religious symbols in music and architecture, sculpture and painting, literature and the liturgical "dance," which will express man's *present* religious quest and faith, and thus, as the Quakers say, "speak to our condition"? The traditional symbols are still used, almost exclusively. Some of these symbols were *once* religiously dynamic because they were created by the contemporary imagination in the contemporary artistic idiom and because they were *then* understood and used, powerfully and by the entire community, for private and public worship. But what is the church doing today to make effective use of this rich treasury of religious symbols? Is it using only the artistically best of these, as intelligently as possible, and is it carefully educating its people to understand and employ these symbols with intelligent piety? Witness the widespread use in both Catholic and Protestant churches, for example, of inferior imitative architecture (*e.g.,* bastard Gothic), of artistically revolting and religiously fatuous colored windows, of painfully "realistic" and sentimentalized representations of Jesus and biblical characters and events, of maudlin hymns, pretentious and spiritually arid anthems, sanctimonious prayers, rites rattled off with a mechanical speed reminis-

cent of a conveyor belt, moralistic sermons largely in praise of current
secular values and loyalty to the church rather than to God. Witness also
much current theology, frozen into rigid dogma, authoritarian rather
than humble, legalistic rather than persuasive, focused as often on the
multiple roads to damnation as on the highway of joyous salvation; so
often divisive, intolerant, and proud, so seldom "catholic," tolerant, and
humble.

Bryson, who seems to view all traditional religious faith and practice
with the profound skepticism of the religiously disillusioned humanist,
analyzes the alternatives open to us as follows:

> There appear to be only three ways in which our generation could do
> what a very large group of the members of this Conference say it is neces-
> sary for us to do. We could encourage the creation of new symbols of
> power and shine up the old ones believing in their magic, that is, be-
> lieving that they have direct influence on events and on our destinies.
> Is this possible to men who are wisely learned in science, philosophy,
> and religion? Or we can offer them to the people of lesser professional
> scruples who can believe in their magic, while we ourselves stand be-
> hind the scenes, making puppets dance for the good of mankind. Have
> we the stomach for this, even supposing that we could be successful?
> Or, are we proposing to ourselves a more honest task, to teach men to
> use symbols without trusting them too much, to apply their rational
> and skeptical powers to all the appeals that are made in terms of emo-
> tional loyalties?[19]

My answer to Bryson would have to be that, if these are our only
options, our cultural and spiritual future is dark indeed. The first two
procedures which he describes, *as he describes them,* are *of course* ignoble and unworthy, but the third procedure which he himself favors,
is, though commendably honest, based, I believe, upon a complete mis-
reading of religion, art, and human nature. It *assumes,* so far as I can
tell, that symbols, if they are to be taken seriously, *must* be conceived of
magically; at least he seems to imply that any symbol, to function powerfully, *must* have magical powers ascribed to it. He then offers, as our
only escape from magic, the use of symbols "without trusting them too
much"—as though a little faith could successfully combat stalwart faith,
however misguided, and as though mere creedal restraint could transform a vicious into a benevolent symbol. My entire argument has been,

[19]Bryson, *op. cit.,* pp. 9–10.

in sharp contrast, in support of i) the profound *difference* between magical and enlightened faith, *both* religious and secular, ii) the *expressive* (nonmagical) *power* of vital artistic symbols and iii) the *enlightened spiritual power* of religiously expressive (nonmagical) symbols available to religion. It is my contention that *such* symbols can and should be used in the church with *complete* honesty by the most learned and the least sophisticated alike, and that, if their true nature and function is understood, as it *can* be, *these* symbols can be believed in and used *for what they really are* with wholehearted faith and confidence. Thus men might, once again, with absolute integrity, "praise the Lord with gladness"!

This would involve *both* "the creation of new symbols" and the "shining up of the old ones"—*not,* in either case, as symbols of magical power but as artistic symbols of expressive power *and* as "sacraments," designed for, and dedicated to, *enlightened* religious worship. But if the church is really to encourage the creation of new religious symbols in and through which ancient truths can be made effectively available to the men and women of our time, it must reeducate itself artistically and achieve a far more enlightened understanding of art in general and "religious" art in particular. I venture to quote, in an Appendix, a brief description of authentic religious art which Paul J. Tillich and I were asked to prepare by the World Council of Churches for an exhibition of religious art in Chicago during the summer of 1954.

ii) The failure of formal education to grapple hard enough with the problem of how the creation and enjoyment of good art can be encouraged, is almost as notable as is the failure of the church. It is true that art has, in recent years, been introduced into our school system at the elementary level; that many colleges and universities do have some sort of art department, in a few cases a good one; that there are some ventures in the field at the public and private secondary school level; and that something is being done at the level of adult education in a few cities. It is also true that some museums and galleries are now sponsoring enlightened educational programs, and that several Foundations have, for some time, been assisting artists of talent to develop their creative ability. All this is encouraging, but it remains, in sum, no more than a pathetic beginning, if measured against the magnitude of the need and our national resources. We dare not blink our multiple failures.

Consider, for example, the present *scope* of art instruction. Only a fraction of our children get any significant art instruction at all, and the vast majority of our young people in secondary school and college get none whatever at those levels. Or consider the *quality* of the instruction actually offered. Not only is it often inferior because of incompetent teachers; it is usually very onesided in its emphasis *either* on original creation *or* on uncreative archeological and historical, *i.e.,* purely factual, instruction. Or consider the narrow vocationalism of most art schools which admit students with no more than an inferior high school education and which then limit their curriculum almost entirely to purely technical training. Small wonder that so many of our young artists have competence in their craft but empty minds and feeble insights—able to say what they will in their medium, but with nothing much to say. Our schools of architecture, music, and the dance, are, on the whole, as narrowly oriented and as vocationally minded as are our art schools. Hence the many young architects who have some training in design and some knowledge of engineering principles, but little or no cultural and spiritual stature, and therefore no understanding of true stature or spiritual "scale" in architecture. The penalties of narrow specialization in the other arts are equally obvious.

Or consider, finally, what we who teach, in that large amorphous area entitled the "humanities" are failing to accomplish, at all educational levels, with the hundreds of thousands of boys and girls entrusted to our care. How successful are we in helping an appreciable number of them to achieve *real* literacy and articulateness, let alone felicity, in their own mother tongue, not to mention one or more foreign languages; *really* to understand and love good literature; *really* to explore history with avid comprehension; *really* to see and study the crucial social and political issues of our times; *really* to study religion with sympathetic and scholarly insight; *really* to derive significance from significant philosophy past and present? This is our real job, and only as we accomplish it can our youth possibly hope to see through and resist the gross and flashy values of our economically competitive "sensate" culture.

Our corporate task, in short, is enormous on every front. We must conserve and try to revitalize the most eloquent normative symbols of the past, both secular and religious, and, through education, to make them available once again, so far as possible, in the contemporary scene. That the art of the past does in fact live for some of us and speak to us, is evidence enough that this task is not impossible. We must even more energetically promote, in *every* way, the creation, comprehension, and widespread use of new normative symbols in every walk of life and area of human concern. We must also, in the process, do what we can to help men recapture a respect for craftsmanship—for integrity and skill in the use of all the media in and through which men express themselves, and for the loving and respectful use of all these vehicles of expression and communication.

But this is only one side of the total problem, since normative symbols are of use only to those who can and will use them. A culture with a limited sense of values will always tend to neglect most of the first rate symbols at its disposal, and to invent more and more cheap vehicles for the expression and communication of the superficial values which it in fact cherishes. Great symbols are the product not only of deep need but of imaginative awareness of this need. The problem of symbolism can therefore be solved only partially by direct attack; the real solution must be sought deeper, in men's hearts and minds. True, these cannot be reached, warmed, and nourished without the aid of adequate symbols, and such symbols cannot function in a cultural and spiritual void. We are thus confronted with a vicious circle, cheap values expressing themselves in cheap symbols, cheap symbols cultivating cheap values. This circle can, however, be transformed into a beneficent upward spiral of ever better symbols and ever better values cultivating each other, *if*—but only if—our *total* cultural problem is envisaged *as a whole,* and if *all* its major aspects are studied and gradually reformed in the light of, and with the material aid of, each other. Thus, to take a single example, significant study and use of the English language cannot be divorced from the progressive comprehension and enjoyment of English literature, which, in turn, cannot be divorced from the study of, and response to, such parallel disciplines as history, philosophy, religion, and fine art, which, once again, make little sense in our age if divorced from the natural and social sciences. Only in such inclusive contexts as these can we hope to promote the cause of normative symbolism and the multiple nonesthetic uses of all the arts efficiently and wisely.

4. Some Implications of the Foregoing Analysis

I have postponed until this concluding section specific consideration of several important implications of my thesis, partly in the interest of orderly exposition, and partly in the hope that the foregoing analysis may recommend itself even to those who may be compelled to disagree with my interpretation of the highly controversial issues still to be considered. Unfortunately, or perhaps fortunately, lack of space will force me to be brief.

a) *The problem of relativism.* Here we must, I believe, make two assertions which some people regard as contradictory, but which I have found to be consistent and complementary.

i) In the light of everything we know about human finitude and the all pervasiveness of "conditioning" factors which play upon man and mold his character, ideas, languages, and behavior, the most reasonable working hypothesis seems to be that *everything* we are and think and do is not only inescapably finite but is "conditioned" in a (still largely unexplored) variety of ways. This hypothesis excludes the very possibility that man can be infallible, in part or in whole, that he can ever possess *absolute* Truth, or that *any* of *his* finite truths can ever be really "permanent" or absolutely valid. Finkelstein believes that "There are basic truths . . . which are eternally valid" and he seems at times to suggest that we mortals can apprehend them as such. Yet he himself recognizes that "the manner in which these are expressed or symbolized . . . is necessarily as relative to the life of the community as any other means of communicating ideas, including language itself."[20]

Bokser, recognizing that "as we shall always have distinctive languages to express distinctive experiences, so shall we have distinctive symbols," concludes without hesitation that "we cannot attain absolute truth in our conception of God" and quotes Erich Frank to the effect that even "the philosopher . . . can approach God or the Absolute through reason only in a negative sense, by distinguishing his object [*i.e.,* God] from his own idea of it. . . . Even the most rational idea of God retains a finite element which makes it inadequate."[21]

Such considerations as these make it clear, I believe, that *all* our insights, *however* profound and *however* expressed, are inescapably finite and relative to cultural conditioning.

[20]Finkelstein, *op. cit.,* p. 101. *Cf.* p. 102: ". . . the truly basic ideas of life or existence cannot be expressed in verbal propositions of language as it has thus far developed," in contrast to p. 103: "Perhaps the articulation of ideas, in both words and behavior, and the recognition of the relation of the two forms, is needed to identify the kind of concept which is eternally valid."

[21]Bokser, *op. cit.,* p. 5. The quotation is from Erich Frank, *Philosophical Understanding and Religious Truth,* Oxford University Press, New York, 1945, p. 99.

ii) Yet must we not simultaneously assert, with Finkelstein, our *faith* in eternal Truth and, in addition, our belief that we men are so constituted that our finite insights and truths can be made to approximate to Truth itself more and more closely? Without this dual belief—in absolute Truth as our ideal but unattainable goal, and in our ability to improve our finite insights—even our claim to partial truths and our firm belief that some of our insights are superior to, or "truer," than others, both become meaningless. And if this happens, the very nerve of all responsible intellectual inquiry is cut and serious cognitive search becomes impossible.

I welcome here the apparent support of Nagel, who is reported[22] to have said that he "was prepared to defend the notion, in some sense, of absolute truth." "What," he asked during a discussion of relativism, "is the status of the analysis which members of the Seminar are attempting to perform? Has not everyone assumed that statements made in the seminar refer to reality in a transcultural sense, that they have a truth which is not merely truth for Western culture?"

This is precisely the position which I think needs to be insisted upon if we would make sense of *any* of man's cognitive ventures. Inquiry is idle, if there is no reality with a character of its own which we can explore and know *in some fashion and to some degree,* and the very quest for *more* truth or the *"truer"* is meaningless unless we make absolute truth (I would capitalize it as Truth) our unattainable but ever approachable point of reference.

All our other normative ventures, in turn, whether in art, in morals, or in religion, seem necessarily also to imply a subject-matter or referent with a normative character of its own, whose nature would be fully embraced by absolute Truth, but which can be encountered and comprehended *by us* only partially, and expressed by us in our finite languages with only partial adequacy. To use a dangerous but useful metaphor: though all cognitive inquiry is inescapably "horizontal," *i.e.,* finitely limited and culturally conditioned, all such inquiry, if it is serious, *must* have a "vertical" reference, *i.e.,* to a "transcultural" reality and to an ideal Truth (which is *not* necessarily actual, *e.g.,* "in the mind of God") by virtue of which all our best insights *are* insights, but *only partial* insights. "Now we *see,*" but *only* "in a glass, darkly."

[22]In *Notes on the Symbolism Seminar* of March 5, 1953, The Institute for Religious and Social Studies, New York, p. 3 (mimeographed).

b) *The "objectivity" of values and the problem of responsible evaluation*. Our analysis of evaluation and its symbolic expression has implied the necessity of ascribing *some* kind of significant "objectivity" to the embodied values which we believe ourselves to encounter and, at the very least, *some* kind of authentic reality to the ideal values which we apprehend as obligating us and as calling for actualization. Is this implication valid?

Perhaps we can at least agree that if all "embodied values" are *reduced* without remainder to actual human preferences unconsciously "projected" into the "objects" which are preferred, we are condemned to a hopeless, souldestroying normative nihilism whose only motto is *"de gustibus."* If this is the whole story, any preference or evaluation is as "good" or "bad" as any other, *whatever* cultural factors may have conditioned it *to whatever degree*. The factor of "intracultural conformity" would, of course, remain operative, but *no* set of individual *or* cultural preferences could reasonably be judged to be more *defensible* or valid, *true* or *useful*, than any others. "Expertness," *i.e.*, the cultivated capacity for special normative comprehension, would also become meaningless and impossible. All argument regarding the relative merits of conflicting evaluations, whether religious or moral, social or political, would degenerate into emotive persuasion; the best factual means for realizing this or that irrational preference would remain the only subject for rational discourse in this area.

Indeed, the advocates of such nihilistic reductionism cannot *rationally* argue that it *should* be accepted by others, even if it were true, since, as William R. Dennes puts it, "truths become valuable . . . only when affection plays upon them . . . ," and nihilism provides no basis whatever for the rational defense of such "affection." Dennes is himself in this awkward predicament. Insisting as he does that "neither science nor metaphysics nor theology can yield a theoretical demonstration of moral norms or a theoretical establishment of moral ends," and that these are, therefore, "the objects and the goals, not of knowledge, but of love,"[23] he can do no more than recommend (*i.e.*, express his preference for) such love and quote Saint Paul's eulogy of love as a rhetorically persuasive device.

Dennes would, at this point, doubtless insist on distinguishing be-

[23]William R. Dennes, "Knowledge and Values," *Symbols and Values,* Appendix VII, pp. 612, 611.

tween truth as a value and the other values (moral, esthetic, religious) with which we have also been concerned, and, in company with Nagel and many others, ascribe validity to man's scientific search for "factual" truth, *i.e.,* truth regarding matters of fact, but deny any such validity to man's search for "normative" truths, *i.e.,* truths regarding objective values, whether embodied or disembodied. Yet, as Dennes himself admits, "truths become valuable, in serious senses of the term, 'valuable,' only when affection plays upon them."[24]

It would seem to follow that the value of the scientific search for truth, and the value of the acceptance of the results of such search, is itself in question and in need of independent substantiation. Why take scientific inquiry and the truths discovered in such inquiry seriously? Why value them? This is precisely the question which Dennes and Nagel cannot answer in terms of their own reasoning.

I conclude, then, that if we are compelled to accept what I have called normative nihilism as true, and if we really take the position *seriously,* we are precluded from taking seriously, *i.e.,* regarding as valuable, the very inquiries which constitute its rational support. A position which forbids us to take seriously evaluations other than those of "factual" truth and falsity, deprives us of any reasonable basis for taking even "factual" truth seriously, and therefore, *a fortiori,* the truth of the position in question. Normative nihilism, in short, is self-defeating and suicidal. It also, if taken seriously, invalidates man's alleged encounters with all esthetic and moral embodied values and all alleged encounters with Deity, and it equally invalidates all faith in absolute Values and in the Deity to Whom these encounters seem to point. It thus makes it impossible for a reflective man to take *any* of his normative ventures seriously; he can pursue them, if at all, *only* in a mood of blind irrational emotive fervor.

Some nihilistically minded sociologists and anthropologists try to escape this predicament by deliberately identifying themselves, as human beings, with the social values of their own society and culture, while admitting (if pressed) that such identification, though universal among men and necessary for self-preservation, is ultimately (*i.e.,* philosophically) indefensible. This schizophrenic device seems to me to be quite intolerable.

Other social scientists take a very useful forward step by distinguish-

[24]*Ibid.,* p. 612.

ing between man's *real* and *basic* needs (*e.g.,* for food, security, sex, etc.) and their *real* (objective) satisfaction, on the one hand, and his cultural desires and preferences which, they still claim, are *wholly* explicable in terms of cultural conditioning, on the other. But this position seems to commit them to another type of vicious dualism, whereby man's "physical" nature and needs are not only differentiated from his "spiritual" nature and needs, but are treated with a realism equally applicable to, and called for by, his "spiritual" nature.

It is only one more step to the "objectivist" position which seems to me to be so imperatively called for. This position asserts that man *as a whole* lives and moves and has his being in his *total* environment which alone, *in its totality,* can really satisfy, *not* any desire he may have, but his *real* needs so far as they are, in fact, capable of satisfaction in our universe. It follows that, if we are to live affirmatively and well, we must conduct our lives in a spirit of fruitful exploration of *all* the environmental resources, physical *and* spiritual, that are available to us. We must accept as "objective" *whatever* confronts us with an *orderly character of its own* and *whatever* can in fact satisfy our *real* needs, as *persons.* It is, on this view, our human task to search out, and to "open" ourselves to, *whatever* in our total environment, at *all* levels of experience, can sustain, strengthen, and enrich our lives.

The embodied values which we can, if we will, really encounter are "objective," then, in having a discoverable qualitative character of their own and as having, when duly encountered and responded to, this beneficent effect upon us. Absolute Values, in turn, are the necessary ultimate referents of our ongoing normative endeavors, analogous to the ultimate order of nature in which the scientist must have faith if he is to continue his inquiries. Encountered values would (pressing this analogy with science) be similar to actually encountered instances of natural order, and our responsible evaluations would be analogous to the responsible scientific judgments of the scientist. Our evaluations, like his judgments, are, of course, finite and fallible, and all our encounters, both normative and factual, are never more than partial and inconclusive; but the exploratory venture, whether scientific or normative, would be meaningful *because,* and *only* because, it was based on the faith that the venture was not futile, a search for nothing, but rather an exploration of what was real in its own right and forever both rewarded and eluded our search.

It goes without saying that this search for values, like the scientific search for factual truth, must be a cooperative enterprise and that all alleged insights must, in principle, be verifiable and confirmable by others. The sciences are at present way ahead of the normative disciplines—art and literary criticism and esthetics, individual and social ethics, theology, and the philosophy of religion—in working out an efficient methodology of inquiry with due regard for necessary criteria of normative truth, principles of normative verification, and, equally important, precise and accepted languages of critical normative discourse. Until this is done we shall continue to be bedevilled by all the ambiguities, misunderstandings, and verbal disagreements which still obfuscate discussion and block communication in these areas. Hence the urgent need for more adequate symbolism at this level of critical interpretation, as well as at the level of artistic expression.

I have not, of course, here been able to define the "objectivity" of values with anything like philosophical rigor, nor have I attempted to formulate the criteria for responsible evaluation in the generic areas of normative experience. All that I have attempted to do is to sketch, in bare outline, what seem to me to be the basic presuppositions of our value experiences, when we take them seriously, and the critical task which lies ahead. Summarized in the simplest possible terms, I have insisted that our normative experiences can and should be taken seriously; that, to do so, we must believe that in and through them we do encounter real embodied values; that these, in turn, do point beyond themselves to absolute Values, and to Deity, in which we can and must have faith; and, finally, that responsible evaluations are possible and can be progressively improved and validated with the requisite methods and the requisite artistic and critical symbols. These are, I believe, the presuppositions of most of the papers of the Thirteenth Conference, and several of these papers go far in actually showing how such responsible evaluations can be made, tested, and confirmed in ever widening critical contexts.

c) *A practical proposal.* How can the task which confronts us be most effectively undertaken? Only by *intensive cooperative* effort! The papers submitted to the Thirteenth Conference clearly demonstrate, if demonstration were needed, the great value of having experts in *all* the various relevant disciplines focus their attention upon the same problem. Our cultural predicament is much too manysided to be resolved merely by philosophers, or historians, or theologians, or art or literary critics, or scientists, or any *one* type of scholarly expert. Interdisciplinary cooperation is absolutely essential, and such cooperation must be *intensive, continuous,* and *prolonged,* if real progress is to be made. The papers of the Thirteenth Conference did much to clarify some issues and to throw light on this or that aspect of the problem, and more can reasonably be hoped for from the forthcoming and subsequent Conferences of this type. But this is not nearly enough. No progress commensurate with the complexity and urgency of our task can possibly be expected until, under governmental or Foundation or other institutional auspices, a way is found of selecting and *holding together* groups of experts from complementary fields under optimum conditions of cooperative research. Only when this was done in nuclear science was rapid progress made in that area. What is needed is a comparable venture in the area of values, motivation, and normative belief. I would therefore urge the members of the Fourteenth Conference to see whether ways and means might not be found to get such a cooperative venture financed and started in the near future.

APPENDIX

The Nature of Religious Art

By PAUL J. TILLICH
AND
THEODORE M. GREENE

WHAT IS the essence of a religiously expressive art, that is, of art that is both authentically artistic and significantly religious?

1. To be *authentically artistic* is to be artistically "alive," to possess artistic vitality. Such art is the product of the artist's creative imagination, and it exhibits to the sensitive observer the hallmarks of his fresh and untrammelled creativity. It will exemplify, on the one hand, the artist's individual style—or some phase or period of his evolving style; it

will carry, as it were, the distinctive imprint of his artistic personality, his "signature" as a creative artist. It will also, simultaneously, exemplify other more generic styles—the style of his "school," "movement" or "tradition," the inclusive style of his embracing "culture" and, above all, the style of his own historical epoch. Thus, a contemporary Picasso will be in the individual style, and more specifically in the current style, of Picasso himself. It will also be in the "expressionistic" Western European tradition; and it will be, in its own way, expressive of the midtwentieth century.

A work of art can be artistically authentic or vital without being "great" or "profound." Indeed, most authentic art of any age is not great, and much of it is relatively slight in artistic stature. But to be "real" art, whether it be profound or slight, it *must* be freshly and honestly conceived and executed. The crude art of children often has this quality, as does the art of many adult artists whose craftsmanship and whose insights are more or less inadequate.

Such art, in turn, differs radically from all "prescriptive" or "academic" art, however excellent its craftsmanship and however noble its prescribed purpose may be. For such "prescriptive" art is produced according to some formula and lacks the *sine qua non* of authentic art, that is, fresh imaginative creativity. It is "imitative"—imitative of some older style, for example, the Gothic, which was once artistically vital but which belongs to another historical epoch, or imitative of the style of some renowned artist or established "school." An artist can even imitate himself, that is, cease to be authentically creative and merely repeat his own past performances.

2. Artistically authentic art, in turn, can be *significantly religious* in two distinguishable ways, a) implicitly, and b) explicitly.

a) It is *implicitly religious* if it expresses, in whatever fashion, the artist's sensitive and honest search for ultimate meaning and significance in terms of his own contemporary culture. If religion be defined as man's "ultimate concern for Ultimate Reality," all art which reflects, however partially and distortedly, this ultimate concern is at least implicitly religious, even if it makes no use whatever of a recognizable "religious" subject-matter or any traditional "religious" symbols. Picasso's "Guernica" is profoundly religious in this implicit sense because it expresses so honestly and powerfully modern man's anguished search for ultimate meaning and his passionate revolt against cruelty and hatred.

b) Authentic art is *explicitly religious* if it expresses the artist's sensitive and honest search for ultimate meaning and significance with the aid of a recognizable "religious" subject-matter or "religious" symbols, that is, by using, in whatever way, the familiar materials of some historical religious tradition. In the Christian tradition, all biblical material and such symbols as the Cross are "religious" in this sense. The mere use of such material does not, of course, guarantee either artistic integrity or significant religious expressiveness. Indeed, much so-called religious art today is totally lacking in both artistic and religious value, despite its use of traditional "religious" subject-matter and symbolism. It lacks artistic vitality and is therefore wholly inexpressive; it is therefore necessarily devoid of significant religious content or meaning. Liturgical art which is traditionalistic and manneristic is "bad" art; the handling of "religious" material by such contemporary painters as Rouault, Rattner, Racs, and Chagall, in contrast, is authentic, explicitly expressive, religious art as here defined.

The great religious art of the past is bound to be more intelligible and acceptable to us because we are familiar with it. Contemporary religious art which is dynamic and path-finding is difficult to comprehend because it speaks to us in an unfamiliar style, and it is deeply disturbing because it is so often anguished and violent. This is, however, inevitable because each age *must* develop its own style and idiom and because our times *are* times of violence and anguish, anxiety and despair. It is not strange that our most sensitive and creative artists should so poignantly express this cultural distress in such baffling ways; nor is it surprising that they should so seldom express a triumphant faith or "the peace that passeth all understanding." We must admire their spiritual courage and their artistic integrity in an age of spiritual turmoil and anxiety. And we can be grateful to them for their notable artistic affirmations at a time when all spiritual affirmations are difficult and rare. For their art, as authentic art, *is* an affirmation of the creative imagination, and their very violence is an implicit affirmation of all the values which are being threatened and violated in these tragic times. They have at least had the courage not to retreat into an empty formalism, or a traditionalistic conventionalism, or a dishonest saccharine prettiness. This courage of theirs may well be prophetic of a new religiously oriented cultural vitality which, we can hope, is slowly and painfully coming into being in our day.

This characteristic of modern art at its courageous best has been well described by Amos Niven Wilder:

> Modern affirmation is hard won. It speaks out of intimate initiation into our cultural and spiritual crisis. . . . There is something peculiarly poignant and magnificent in the spectacle of men wringing art and celebration out of these nightmares, and saying, "Nevertheless," in the midst of the distempers that afflict the spirit today, and which afflict particularly the most gifted and sensitive.[25]

Comment by R. S. Brumbaugh:

The paper synthesizes considerations of symbolism and general theory of value in a way that brings out some of the major axiological and metaphysical implications of discussion of "symbols." It is particularly illuminating in its specific treatment of the esthetic aspect of sign-functioning. In further discussion, however, I would like to see the paper extended to take account of certain alternative positions and entities of other kinds: I will try to indicate three or four such extensions.

First, I do not see the justification of the assumption that religious experience can somehow be treated as an intensification or extension of esthetic experience. Theodore M. Greene restricts his attention, early in the paper, to "high" religions: I presume he means by this religions analogous to "high church" denominations in their stress on icon and symbol. He then proceeds to treat theological discourse as essentially poetic, and to find ritual and symbol central to religious experience. This analysis is onesided and incomplete. One aspect of religious experience is the immediate awareness that certain ideas *cannot* be symbolized, and that reliance on symbol falsifies them. This is persistent and frequent, and finds its historical expression in what one might call a "low church" point of view. To a proponent of *this* viewpoint, the injunction to invent new and viable symbols and sacraments will seem immoral, because for him "symbols" should be transcended and dispensed with, not refurbished and multiplied. Further, within the "high" tradition itself, too much seems conceded to critics in the equation of religious and esthetic discourse. I am certain that most theologians would insist that theology is propositional and literal, just as certainly as science or mathematics are: and, indeed, it is hard for me to see how one can either "believe" or "disbelieve" a creed, if that creed is a sort of poem.

Second, I do not see how one can consistently defend the objectivity of value and unity of being, as is done in section 4, yet refuse to extend the category of beauty to mathematics, science, and so on. The first three sections treat the work of art as unique, the fourth section removes any metaphysical justification for such treatment. Plato, in the *Symposium,* extends his concept of beauty from beautiful sensible objects through laws and sciences to an eternal, nonsensible form. It seems to me a false transcription of experience to deny that the same emotional feeling can accompany seeing a mathematical proof that accompanies seeing a

---

[25]Amos Niven Wilder, "Protestant Orientation in Contemporary Art," *Spiritual Problems in Contemporary Literature,* edited by Stanley Romaine Hopper, The Institute for Religious and Social Studies, New York, 1952, chap. XVII, p. 245.

painting, or to restrict "creativity" to sensuous objects—I would think an astrophysical hypothesis often shows the same sort of creation at work.

Third, the notion of a fourth, almost "anagogical," dimension of sign-functioning, which is introduced in treating "normative" signs, seems to me *either* present in all signification or in none. In the Western tradition, Augustine and Boehme occur to me as outstanding defenders of the existence of such a dimension for all signs. As in my second comment, above, I am really trying to suggest here that Greene extend his discussion of the relation of fact and value, so that the reader will be clearer as to the status of the sharp distinctions in his first three sections. As the paper now stands, it almost seems that he accepts the illicit premise of "scientism" that value and fact can be separated.

Fourth, there is a metaphysical question I would like to raise. Reality, we are told, includes both a realm of particular sensible phenomena, and one of eternal invariant structures and values. Yet the entire discussion concentrates on the texture of the sensible realm. Now, except by contrast with the realm of Platonic forms or Whiteheadian eternal objects, I do not see how one could ever come to know or to describe the nature of appearance, or sense-experience, and I would like to see these forms given more attention. To understand reality, one must feel the tension between the pure flux, with its vivid concreteness, and the pure form, with its less vivid invariability. This means that the religious man or metaphysician must be like Whitehead's God, at once sensitive poet *and* clearheaded mathematician.

Finally, I wish that more account were taken of the alternative line of practical action that is suggested by the four foregoing queries. This is a course of dispensing with symbols, as I have said; the idea of justice can still, among us, command allegiance without the picture of a large lady sitting in the middle of the astronomical system with a pack of avenging Furies held in check by leashes, though for the Ionian Greeks this sensible picture may have been essential.

Comment by Frederic B. Fitch:

I am in definite agreement with a great deal of what Theodore M. Greene has to say. His general objectives certainly have my full approval. Some aspects of his position, however, place too much emphasis on symbols and not enough emphasis on the realities back of the symbols.

I agree that art is expressive and does express various truths about reality. Some of these truths are concrete, others are abstract. Science, philosophy, and religion, in their own ways and with the help of their own symbols, also express both kinds of truths. The value aspects of reality are referred to in many of the truths expressed by art and religion. Such truths might be called "normative" or "axiological" truths. They might be called "facts about values." It is a foolish prejudice of the modern scientific movement to try to suppose that "fact" and "value" are somehow mutually exclusive and that therefore there can be no facts about values. If there were no facts about values, this itself would be a fact about values.

Science can deal with facts of all sorts. Since there are facts about values, science can also deal with such facts, and should do so to a much greater extent than it has already, using its own careful methods.

Greene seems to think that our task is primarily to "conserve and try to revitalize the most eloquent normative symbols of the past" and "energetically [to] promote, in *every* way, the creation, comprehension, and widespread use of new normative symbols in every walk of life and area of human concern." He admits this can only be done in such inclusive contexts as literature, history, philosophy, religion, fine art, natural science, and social science.

But the point is that symbols are merely tools to express, communicate, and preserve for posterity important ideas and judgments. The emphasis should not be on the symbols, but on what is symbolized. In religion the identification of symbol and symbolized is idolatry.

In philosophy it is nominalism. If we can clarify our understanding of the world (including values as part of the world), then the finding of suitable symbols to express this clarified understanding is a relatively routine and simple task. Of course the process of reaching a clearer understanding of the world is a process which itself requires correct use of symbols, so we cannot get started on this task without seriously considering symbols. But the emphasis should be on clearly analyzed concepts and the relation of these concepts to what is most directly and conclusively affirmed by experience and by other authentic sources of knowledge, if any. There is especial need for clear thinking about value concepts (in all the "inclusive contexts," of course, which Greene mentions). This is the great and important task that we must undertake if civilization, Western and Eastern, is to survive. It is not a matter of raising the banner of some new value symbol, or re-raising the banners of some old value symbols, but of first coming to an understanding of what the primary values are (and indeed what "values" are). This is to be achieved not so much by symbolists as by scientists, historians, and philosophers, working in close collaboration with students of art, religion, and literature, and using all the techniques provided by mathematics, logic, probability theory, and semantics. Here I must strongly second Greene's "practical proposal" for intensive cooperative effort.

Greene's overemphasis of the concept of symbol, however, seems to me to have led him to an undue concern with "magic" and to the view that the symbolic and socially intercommunicative aspects of religion are part of the essence of religion. Science also makes much use of symbols and much use of social intercommunication to achieve progress. But these are merely tools; and I would say that they are also merely tools for religion. No doubt religion is a practical way of life as well as a theoretical view, but the reformers have for centuries been casting away overemphasized symbols in preference to the true reality which the symbols designate; and isolated hermits have repeatedly demonstrated the possibility of religion in disassociation from the complex social ceremonies of established churches. I cannot accept the view that religion can exist only in the context of an elaborate and ancient religious tradition. The great religious geniuses have invariably *denied* a large part or all of tradition and have proclaimed a great *new truth*. The mere fact that they may have retained some traditional views, does not make religion essentially traditional. It would be unwise to reject some new religious insight, simply because we could not find a place for it in the context of religious tradition. But of course everything is traditional in the sense of having *some* relationship to tradition.

Today we need most of all a clear analysis of concepts. This can best be achieved by making full use of recent advances in logic and by collaborative research on the part of men from many different fields. But it is not just a matter of symbols, or even primarily a matter of symbols.

Comment by Howard L. Parsons:

I will limit my comments to one of the many ideas expressed by Theodore M. Greene, not only because this idea seems to me important in the symbolism of evaluation suggested by Greene, but also because the idea involves the problem of what it means "to symbolize "

The idea is this: "all concrete values seem to point beyond themselves to more embracing, purer, and more perfect values which they, in their concreteness, only partially and imperfectly 'exemplify' and 'embody.' "

My question is: What can be possibly meant by "point beyond" in this context, and what are its defensibly rational and empirical meanings, as distinctive from its meanings which cannot be so defended?

1) Is it asserted that there is a logical implication connecting concrete values and abstract values, a relation that is universally and necessarily valid? Certainly not all empiricists (or nominalists, as Greene calls them) feel compelled to treat this as a valid implication. The

necessity of deductive and inductive logic, as Hugh Miller shows, is rooted in observation of particular necessity; it is fundamentally arithmetical, and arithmetic is descriptive of the concrete, individualized events of nature, and of nothing more. Numbers begin and end in the countable events of nature. Modern science and modern logic, concerned with prediction and control of natural events, recognize no necessity of connection between the concrete and the ideal, or between nature and supernature. The particularities of nature are self-sufficient and require no entities "beyond." This question is important for the development of that for which Greene appropriately pleads, namely, a cooperative theory of value. For, ontological questions aside, the myth of realism (as Quine might call it) is by no means universal or in process of becoming universal; and presumably what is desired in theory of value is universality.

Empiricists may acknowledge that concrete values "point beyond" themselves in some sense, but few, if any, would agree that they necessarily point beyond to unencounterable and ideal absolutes. Of course, if the "abstract" is initially defined as an aspect of or derivation from the concrete, then the implication holds, for it is a tautology. But this is the exact converse of what absolutists in value-theory from Plato on have meant, namely, that the concrete is derived from the abstract.

2) Is this, then, meant: that these abstract, absolute structures of value imply or logically necessitate their concrete embodiments? This meaning is suggested by Greene's statement that "only as we take them [absolute values] seriously can we take the finite values which we encounter in all their concreteness as genuinely valuable and as, therefore, obligating us."

The claim that if and only if we acknowledge absolute values can we treat finite events as valuable, adds to the burden of the first meaning by implying that we can get to finite values and obligation only by first accepting absolute values. This is a large claim which can be justified only by begging the questions of "finite values" and "obligation," *or,* by showing that all the possible theories interpreting finite values and obligation are inadequate and that the absolutistic theory is of all theories the most adequate. Why not say that the sense of obligation arises from disharmonies between tendencies within the organism— between the tendency to detachment and the tendency to dependence, for example, or between desire and superego, or between a present good and a remembered-and-anticipated concrete good? Why not say that the sense of obligation is the sense of the organism's commitment to its concrete creative development, regardless of any specific, envisaged, ideal outcomes?

3) When Greene says that concrete values "point beyond" to "more perfect" values, does he mean that these concrete values are analogous to (or examples of) "sign-events," pointing by means of outward and visible tokens to the invisible realities of absolutes, including God? Greene seems to mean that concrete values are, taken literally, misleading, for they are as such infected with finitude and conditionality. They must rather be treated, if treated realistically, as examples, incarnations, "revelatory vehicles" of absolute values and of Deity.

If this is his meaning, then the referents of such sign-events or value-symbols are not unambiguously presented, nor are we provided with a public method by which to discriminate those referents from their misleading facsimiles. Leaving aside, as Greene prefers to do, any commitment to "the ultimate ontological status of value," and adopting Charles Morris's very general definition of "signification," as well as his definition of a denotatum (referent) as "anything that would permit the completion of the response-sequences to which an interpreter is disposed because of a sign"—we are still not informed of the character of the value-objects to which value-symbols, whether in the languages of the arts or in religious myths, point. An "object" is defined as something which confronts us with an orderly and discoverable qualitative character of its own and which can satisfy our real needs as persons. But what those objects, including Deity, might be in actual fact is not specified, and we are provided with no criteria for distinguishing true religious symbols from false ones and pathological ones from sound ones. Greene is correct in saying that "the sciences are at present way ahead of the normative disciplines . . . in working out an efficient methodology of inquiry," and we should not expect that in this comprehensive paper he should comprehend what no one today comprehends. But the tendency on his part to define absolute values initially as not "experientially encounterable," and to define Deity as something "unembodied," does not, I think, carry us any closer to the efficiency achieved by the methodology of science, for this antiempirical tendency removes values from our direct observation and public analysis and criticism. Greene may object that in his definition he is striving to formulate a general theory which can be used to describe, predict, and control concrete value-embodiments; but if so, then it is unclear where and how this theory originates in concrete observation (as I have already tried to indicate), as well as what application it may have to the prediction, control, and improved enjoyment of concrete values.

4) In what defensible sense do concrete values "point beyond" themselves? I think that Greene has indicated one important sense of the term in question in his organismic description of value. Man is immersed in a unitary context of events, and the values he experiences are a function of that protean whole. Even very slight values, faint in quality and transient in structure, are the emergents or conjunctions of processes originating in remote space and time. Concrete values "point beyond" to ever widening nexus of nature; to the many events, large and small, which converge on the present and whose line of inheritance fades into the infinite past of history and prehistory; and to the uncreated future of value and evil, of glory, and of doom, that is yet to be.

5) Thus there is a second sense, I think, in which values can be said, on rational-empirical grounds, to "point beyond" themselves. Values are generated in the natural processes of our world, and every value, as product, points beyond itself to its source, natural and discoverable, inherent in it at its formation, yet different from it. A major task for value-theory is to inquire into these generative processes: to find, in Greene's words, "whatever in our total environment, at all levels of experience, can sustain, strengthen, and enrich our lives."

Comment by Roy W. Sellars:

Valuation is Objective in Intention

I have no other comment than that of general agreement upon Theodore M. Greene's analysis of symbolism in art. I take it that he holds that subject-matter can be absorbed into the content of a work of art and yet give that content direction and significance. So far as the subject-matter remains alien to the content, it introduces a division of attention and interest, as in Victorian demands that pictures tell a story.

My querying of the admirable paper concerns his theory of values. His framework strikes me as expressing a sort of *duplication of the cognitive framework*. Just as there are things to know and gain facts about, so there is a realm of objective values to be approached valuatively.

Now I do not regard myself as a nihilist in the field of values. I am distinctly opposed to the emotive view of Stevenson and others which, I judge, has already seen its best days. I take it that valuation is an empirical job with an objective direction. We do value works of art, persons, institutions, moral rules, social ideals; and we proceed, *in empirical ways,* to determine data relevant to such valuation. Back of such employment of data is, of course, our interest, emotive and conative, in the objects to be valued. But valuation is not the mere expression of emotion. Otherwise, the best ballplayer would be the one for whom we happened to take a fancy. Surely, we have criteria for *grading* ballplayers. And such grading is an objective procedure upon which people can agree. I sometimes feel that we need a return to everyday thought and simple language if we are to make a steady advance in the theory of values. What, then, do we do in valuation of this objectively directed kind? We *commend* the object in the light of whatever we regard as relevant. In art, Greene has indicated the criteria we use and the larger setting of artistic and esthetic interest. Moral rules are reflectively judged in the light of what we regard as the inclusive goal of morality, say, general well-being. Qualifications are introduced accordingly, as, for example, in the treatment of women.

What I am driving at is the point that there are here no mysterious objects to be valued. What we value are the things, procedures, acts, institutions, around us. And our language reflects this tie-in very definitely. We are rightly asked to justify our valuations and we try to do so. But we regard this job as different from that of pure cognition. There our aim is to gain facts in a systematic way. And we regard science as having worked out the best methodology for this purpose. And here we employ the terms, true and knowledge. And I have always held what *true* here means is "acceptable as a case of knowledge." "Good" is employed in the English language in the field of values much as true is employed for cognition. We do not commend an object which we are valuing unless we are convinced that it will stand up to *relevant demands* upon it. Greene has brought out such demands in the esthetic field with admirable clarity.

In all this, it seems to me, we can be empirical. And I doubt that we can value anything which is not *also* cognizable. And I am unable to see the need for fixed absolute standards. We work out our standards progressively and improve them. That is why I object to capital letters such at Truth, Good, Beauty. Is there not a hint here of an assumption of a *realm* other than the empirical one of things, events, moral rule, and institution? And is this not the traditional burden of supernaturalism?

Like Lyman Bryson, I am a humanist. But I am not a nihilist or a skeptic. I think that valuations can be justified and that their justification pertains to the human situation. What else would be relevant to our valuations?

I have the impression that both English and American empirical thought in this field is swinging away from the absurd contrast between the cognitive and the emotive. Valuation cannot be carried on without the guidance of knowledge but the aim is not the mere gathering of facts, for now this is subordinated to the task of estimating the worth of an object of interest. The methodology of "grading" needs to be worked out with due regard to the complexity of this central human field.

[Also see comment by M. L. Rosenthal, Appendix IV, pp. 561–577, esp. 563–568.]

CHAPTER X

The Scientific and Literary Uses of Language

By ALBERT HOFSTADTER

Contents

1) *The Problem of Comparative Functional Explanation*

That there are striking differences between the uses of language in science and literature is well known. Discussions of symbolism, logic, and esthetics often refer, for instance, to the intranslatability of literary language, to the manner in which it manifests personality or exploits the characteristics of the medium or material vehicle of its meanings, in contrast with the translatability of scientific language, its impersonality and the self-effacing transparency of its medium.

291

Further, it is generally recognized that these differences are not accidental but are due to the differing functions required of language in the two contexts, of science and literary art. For the purpose of science, translatability of its propositions is necessary; a defect here would be an obstacle to the efficient conduct of the scientific enterprise. On the other hand, the purposes of literary art can be achieved only by a use of language that entails a certain resistance to complete translation into other words; so that the attempt to render the content of a piece of literature in other terms invariably results in some degree of transformation, deformation, or destruction.

What is true of translatability is also true of the other characteristic differences.

What has not, I believe, been sufficiently clarified is the manner in which the differences in language derive from the differences in purpose. One hears it often said, indeed, that there are different functions of language, that, for example, there is an informative or denotative or descriptive function fulfilled by scientific language, while there is an emotive or evocative or expressive or symbolical function fulfilled by literary language. But beyond cursory reference to these functions one does not find in the literature of the study of symbolism much extended work of an analytical character devoted to the explanation and understanding of the characteristic differences in relation to differences of function and purpose. At least the present writer has not yet met with a satisfactory treatment of this matter.

I do not pretend to offer one in this essay. I shall try only to offer a sketch in illustration of what I believe to be a proper mode of investigating the subject.

The problem is one of providing a comparative functional explanation of the differentiating characteristics of scientific and literary language. These characteristics are to be explained by showing how they are necessitated in the attempt to achieve purposes intrinsic to science or literature.

In a functional explanation everything depends on the adequacy of the end alleged to account for the characteristics of the subject under investigation. For this reason the usual statements of ends, such as have just been mentioned, cannot be taken seriously. Not all scientific language is informative or denotative or descriptive. For example, the formal logical statements used in scientific language or, again, its pure mathematical statements, are not informative, denotative, or descriptive. And it is doubtful whether many of the terms and propositions of its highly abstract theories are properly described in these terms. Similarly, such concepts as those of the emotive, expressive, symbolical, evocative, are hardly capable of covering all literary uses of language.

In general, one ought not to anticipate that a single character chosen almost at random from among a manifold should be more than a handy, occasionally diagnostic, index. One cannot expect it to be sufficient to provide theoretical insight into a subject of considerable complexity. If comprehension is what is wanted, then it is necessary to try to reach a comprehensive concept, one that makes possible reference to multiplicity and variation in function and character.

2) *Relation of Medium to Content*

a) One of the outstanding differences between scientific and literary language has to do with the relation of the linguistic medium or vehicle to the content.

In scientific language the medium or vehicle is not itself subject-matter which is organized into the content expressed by that language. A scientific statement (except in unusual circumstances, as in linguistics generally, or in particular instances, such as Goedel's proof of incompleteness or the development of semantic paradoxes) does not refer to itself or study itself in what it says. When a psychologist says that a child affected by impaired functioning of the pituitary gland tends to lack aggressiveness, he is not attempting to state a pattern of language but rather a pattern of biopsychological elements.

In a piece of literary language, on the other hand, this distinction, even separation, between vehicle and content is difficult, if at all possible, to make. The poet's words are never a mere indifferent vehicle pointing on to their meaning, and intrinsically negligible otherwise. In some cases the meanings, images, thoughts, which receive expression in a literary work are less important than the manner of expression—as though the writer were concerned centrally with esthetic values due to sound quality, rhythm, and, in general, the formal organization of the medium, and with others only incidentally. In other cases esthetic values due to the verbal medium sink to a secondary role, as in the realistic reportorial novel. There is thus a range of variation in relative dominance of esthetic value due to the verbal medium. But it is never the case that in literature of any literary merit some appreciable esthetic role is not played by the vehicle, both itself and in combination with other materials of literature, as intrinsically impressive or as contributing to a more complex effect.

In short, whereas in science language is an external means—a means of expression which is not itself an element in the expressed content— in literature language is an internal means (if "means" is the right word here)—a mode of expression which is itself an element in the expressed content.

b) Why is there this difference between scientific and literary language?

The difference occurs because of a difference between what the scientist and the literary artist are trying to do. The psychologist as scientist wants to distinguish various features of personality and behavior, including various types of aggressiveness. And he wants to discover on what such aggressiveness depends, as well as what depends on it. Thus he wants to distinguish and relate; he wants to find out what things there are, what they are, and how they depend on each other. If he supposed or had reason to believe that a child's aggressiveness depended on the language which he, the psychologist, used to refer to the aggressiveness, then he would include a reference to the language in his statement about the aggressiveness. He would say that a child affected by impaired functioning of the pituitary gland *and* by the psychologist's use of language to refer to this, tends to lack aggressiveness. He does not say this because he does not think that his use of language is an effective factor in the determination of the child's aggressiveness. Put generally, the scientist searches for *items which are involved with each other in patterns of dependence*. Ordinarily—except for the linguistic scientist—the scientist's language is not one of these items; and even where language is all or part of the subject-matter, a distinction must be drawn between the language which is studied (the language *mentioned*) and the language which refers to it (the metalanguage, which is *used*). Thus the aim of the scientist, which is to achieve a valid or credible formulation of patterns of involvement of existential items, requires that he must not allow his language to become part of the content of his assertion. He is forced to develop language which is able to distinguish itself from the content which it expresses.

It is otherwise with the aim of the literary artist. Not that the literary artist is never interested in patterns of involvement. There is nothing in the nature of literature to prevent the artist from being concerned to examine, for instance, the dependence of action upon character, or the development of character under the influence of environment, or in fact any part of the subject-matter of science. The point rather is that he is not, as literary artist, solely and exclusively concerned with the discovery and statement of such patterns.

It is much more difficult to formulate the aim of the literary artist than that of the scientist. For the present let us say that his goal is the creation of an intrinsically interesting imaginative construction, an object the experience of which is intrinsically absorbing, an intrinsically vital object of a vitalized consciousness. For this purpose, the statement of involvement patterns is merely grist for the mill, only one among the innumerable materials available. Thus, whereas the scientist seeks an order of dependence, a unity of involvement, the artist seeks an imaginative unity. And one great difference is that *the character of the imaginative object achieved by the artist depends on the character of the language he employs, whereas the language of the scientist does not operate within the involvement pattern he formulates.*

The literary artist's vehicle of expression is itself a factor involved in the constitution of the imaginative object. It functions that way for the person who experiences the object.[1]

The sound-characteristics of the words and their rhythmic movement

[1]The element of pure sound, therefore, since it suggests or reinforces underlying ideas, plays an important part in the choice of the right word. An ear sensitive to poetry cannot disregard the mere sound of the words themselves. In determining the rightful language of a poem, rhythm and accent are almost as important as alliteration and assonance. Pope shows how it may be done in a well known passage of the *Essay on Criticism* from which one couplet may serve as example:

> When Ajax strives some rock's vast weight to throw,
> The line too labours, and the words move slow.

The words in the first verse are obviously chosen to slow down the movement. Some actual striving on the reader's part is required to pronounce such combinations of consonants as *xstr, vss, ksv,* and *stw*. Each line is also made heavier and slower by the addition of two extra accented syllables where weak syllables might be expected. Pope and Keats in their characteristic thought appear meditative, deliberate, in contrast with the impetuous charioteers Dryden and Shelley. It is no accident that their verse is made up of words which cannot be read as rapidly as the careening and catapulting lines of the other two poets, for, in this choosing of words, always, and with implications far beyond the simple onomatopoeia,

> The sound must seem an echo to the sense.

D. A. Stauffer, *The Nature of Poetry,* W. W. Norton & Company, New York, 1946, p. 42.

influence and are influenced by their sense, and both sound and sense operate together in the organization of the imaginative object. It is for this reason that, while science can be understood perfectly upon silent reading, literature always loses something in the process; it is, indeed, a familiar experience that a poem which eludes comprehension in silent reading often begins to glow with significance when phrased aloud.

Thus the aim of the literary artist, which is to achieve an intrinsically arresting imaginative whole, requires that he must make his language become part of the content of his expression. This requirement is laid upon him because of the *dependence* of the character of the imaginative whole upon the language used, so that inattention to the exploitation of the characteristics of the language exacts dire penalties.

In this way, then, the difference between scientific and literary language, which consists in the relative separation between sound and sense in the one and the fusion between sound and sense in the other, can be traced to its source in a fundamental difference of aim and to the substance of what is aimed at in each case: it is because of the *nature* of what is aimed at that science is forced to separate sound from expressed content and that literature is forced to do the opposite.

3) *Scientific Organization of Subject-Matter: Involutional Order*

The difference in substance of the aims of science and literature may best be envisaged as a difference in mode of organizing their respective subject-matters into content. That is, science and literary art differ basically in their ideals of form or organization, and this difference needs to be made manifest if the characteristic differences in linguistic usage are to be explained. It would do little good to baptize these different ideals of form as, respectively, "cognitive" and "esthetic," for it is precisely the nature of the difference between a form congruent with cognitive purposes and a form congruent with esthetic purposes which requires elucidation. It is necessary to ask, rather, what kind of form *is* required for the purposes of cognition and what for the purposes of art.

I have said above that the scientist's aim is to attain to a valid formulation of patterns of involvement (or dependence) of existential items; and I want now to try to develop that notion a little further.

Science deals, as its initial and primary subject-matter, with the things of experience. This may be agreed upon independently of one's view as to the metaphysical value of scientific knowledge. One may view science in terms of an ontological realism, considering its aim to be the pure discovery of a reality whose essence is independent of any and all features of the human mind; one may thus view science as trying to assume ultimately the form of an utterly transparent window through which the outside world may be seen without distortion by medium or observer; and one may therefore tend to treat the theoretical entities of science— from sociological dispositions to subatomic particles—as literally existent entities, even though they are not things of experience or observables. On the other hand, one may take an extreme contrary view, like that of pragmatic conventionalism, which interprets science as an instrument for the prediction and control of phenomena (*i.e.,* things of experience), an instrument which is essentially an invention or creation of the human mind, bearing human characteristics in its inmost constitution; one would then view science as a tool for transforming experiential situations, a complex mode of operation applied to materials of present experience, in order to transform them into a more desirable future situation; so that the theoretical objects of science would be considered not as literally existent entities but only as useful devices.

Nevertheless, whichever of these (or any intermediate) views be taken, it must be recognized that science begins and ends with things of experience as subject-matter. The theoretical entities it introduces in between *are* introduced in between, whether they be artificial devices or literal realities behind the appearances or neither. Science starts by being puzzled by the phenomena, challenged by the multiplicity and flux of experience, and it seeks to resolve the puzzle and meet the challenge.

Now this attempt to introduce intelligibility, to understand the subject-matter to make it into cognitive content, is an attempt to bring that subject-matter into a certain kind of form, to arrange it in a certain way. The *general* character of the form of intelligibility sought to be developed in science is expressed by common phrases like "the one in the many," "analysis and synthesis," "distinction and relation." Hegel's formula is not altogether unserviceable: "The thinking activity is, in general, the apprehension and bringing together of the Manifold into unity."[2] But such phrases give only a general hint. Making a one of many is a feature of *every* meaningful variety of human behavior, from

---

[2]*Hegel Selections,* edited by J. Loewenberg, The Modern Students Library, Charles Scribner's Sons, New York, 1929, p. 99.

achieving a family life to composing a symphony. What is distinctive of the scientific scheme of intelligibility is the peculiar kind of unity-in-variety at which it aims.

This peculiarity—distinguishing scientific unity-in-variety from all other kinds—appears in connection with *inference*. It should be emphasized that the *differentia* of scientific form is something *connected* with inference, and is *not itself identical* with inference, whether actual or potential. I shall presently suggest that the term *"involvement,"* which has already been used (and which I take from Dewey's *Logic*), be reserved for this purpose.

Science seeks to unify the manifold of experience, to make the flux of experience manageable, by extending over it a network of potential inference. It counts it as an achievement when it succeeds in so formulating matters that from some set of items it becomes possible to infer in a trustworthy way to some other item. Thus science seeks a mode of unity-in-variety which will give rise to the possibility of trustworthy inference from empirical matters to other empirical matters. Let us, for brevity's sake, call such inference "empirical inference."

The distinctions which science makes, and the relations which it attempts to establish among the distinguished elements, are of sorts calculated to serve empirical inference: and the test which science imposes on its distinctions and connections, its analyses and syntheses, is the *efficiency* with which they serve empirical inference.

What is the nature of the form or organization of experiential subject-matter (and, as science progresses, of its theoretical subject-matter as well) which lies at the basis of potential empirical inference? This is not an easy question to answer. For a long time it was spoken of as "causal connection." Science, it was said, seeks to establish causal connections, to bring the whole of its subject-matter into a causal system. But the notion of causal order has proved to be so complex and so doubtful, so vague and so laden with misconception and emotional connotations, that it invites needless confusion and controversy to continue to use it. It is for this reason that I prefer to use the term which Dewey uses in the *Logic*,[3] which has not yet been overworked as a technical term, namely, "involvement."

"Inference," Dewey wrote, "is conditioned upon an existential con-

[3] He notes his debt for the term to Dr. Percy Hughes, John Dewey, *Logic*, Henry Holt & Company, New York, 1951, p. 278 n.

nection which may be called *involvement*. The problems of inference have to do with discovery of *what* conditions are involved with one another and *how* they are involved. . . . The essential consideration is that the relation is a strictly existential one, ultimately a matter of the brute structure of things."[4]

The general idea to be formulated under the term is the idea of items being dependent for their character and occurrence (what and how) upon other items. This is not a definition; the notion of "dependence" is as much in need of explication as that of "involvement." It is meant only as a suggestion of the direction of intent in using the word. Indeed, I shall not try to give here a precise definition, but am content to use it fairly vaguely. The reason is that I am not prepared to define it. A good definition must wait upon the development of a theory of scientific propositions (and concepts) adequate to handle the major sciences. Such a theory has not yet been forthcoming.

Let us then think of an involvement among certain differing items, A, B, C, . . . as a mode of interrelation of them such that the *what* and *how* of one (or more) of them depends on the *what* and *how* of the others, and such that, therefore, from some set of them an inference is possible to some other one (or ones) among them. This incidentally means that if a statement asserts an involvement, then, if that statement is true, it is possible to derive from it a true nonanalytic conditional or "if . . . then . . ." statement in which the first set of items somehow appears in the antecedent clause and the item to which inference is possible somehow appears in the consequent clause.

In accordance with this use of the term, I shall speak of the order or form in which science seeks to organize its subject-matter as *"involutional."*

[4]*Ibid.*, p. 278. For the sake of understanding of his view I add here some of his illustrations:

> A person engaged in a business undertaking is involved *with* others *in* the conditions of the situation in which the undertaking is to be carried out. In a criminal conspiracy one person is involved *with* his accomplices *in* certain activities and consequences. But the scope of involvement is not confined to personal cases. An increase in the supply of gold involves, usually, a decrease in its price and an increase in the price of other commodities. The sudden and excessive rise of the customary level of a river is involved *in* heavy rain storms and involves *with* its occurrence perils to life and property, impassable roads, etc. An outbreak of bubonic plague involves a rise *in* death-rate *with,* perhaps, a campaign to exterminate rats. There is no need to multiply instances. Every case of the causal relation rests upon some involvement of existential conditions *with* one another in a joint interaction. The entire principle of functional correlations of changes rests upon involvements, as when, in the case of many substances, increase of heat is ground for an inference to their expansion; or when the volume of gases is said to be a function of pressure and heat.

An instance[5] of involutional order is found in the content of the universal affirmative proposition when employed in the context of science, "All *A* is *B*," one of the simplest kinds of lawlike assertions. Such a proposition a) includes a *distinction* between a thing's being *A* and its being *B;* b) it also *connects* these distinct factors by a relation expressed by means of "all" and "is" (about whose meanings there is as yet no consensus among analysts of scientific language), a relation which we may here speak of as a universal compresence or association. But such a relation of universal compresence in the same subject of two distinct attributes is an order or form which makes possible inference from the presence of the first attribute in a given subject to the presence of the second attribute in the same subject. This relation is not a *logical* relation; the predicate

[5]A few other instances:

1) "A patent is everywhere, in the United States as well as in France, subject to annulment by a court before which the invention's novelty or patentability is disputed" (*Encyclopaedia of the Social Sciences,* The Macmillan Company, New York, 1937, vol. 12, p. 21). Among other things, this statement asserts an involvement between a patent's being brought before a court in the process of disputing the novelty or patentability of the invention and the patent's being subject to annulment. If true, we can then say about a given patent, *P,* that *if* the corresponding invention's novelty or patentability is disputed in court *C, then* the patent *P* is subject to annulment by *C.* And consequently, from a suit's being brought in *C* about *P* we can *infer* that *P* is subject to annulment by *C.*

2) "With Beethoven the scherzo became the most free of all the movements in the sonata group. He did not restrict it to the characteristic triple time of the minuet, but took any time that the situation required; and so far dispensed with the systematic orderliness which usually characterized works designed upon harmonic principles, that the plan of such a movement is often as difficult to unravel as that of any of Bach's merriest and lightest fugues" (C. H. H. Parry, *The Evolution of the Art of Music,* edited by H. C. Colles, D. Appleton & Company, New York, 1930, p. 336). This statement formulates a relation between a scherzo having been written by Beethoven and certain musical characteristics of that scherzo (its time, its structure) so that inference becomes possible. Thus, taken in its context, it enables us to start with a minuet by Haydn and a scherzo by Beethoven and to infer that, with some unspecified but substantial degree of probability, the first will be in triple time and will have a clearly recognizable ternary form, systematic and orderly and easy to unravel, whereas the second may or may not be in triple time, depending on the situation, and will not have a form so characterized.

3) The period of a physical (compound) pendulum with small displacement is given by

$$T = 2\pi\sqrt{\frac{I}{Mgh}}$$

where *M* is its mass, *g* the acceleration due to gravity, *h* the distance between center of suspension and center of gravity, and *I* the moment of inertia about a transverse axis at the point of suspension. By means of the relationship set up in this statement it is possible to infer, about a physical pendulum oscillating with small displacement, from any combination of three among the four characteristics *T, I, M, h* (assuming both *g* and *h* as already known) to the fourth.

does not derive analytically from the subject; it is *synthetic,* and in the context in which it is expressed it is just the sort of relation which we are to think of under the heading "involvement."

When the universal affirmative proposition is reformulated as a universal conditional proposition, "For all x, if x is A then x is B," the formal, organizational purpose it serves is even more clearly apparent. Here the variable $"x"$ ranges over the universe of discourse. Hence the subject-matter of the proposition includes *all* the individuals of the domain under consideration, not only those which possess the attribute A. To *each* of these individuals the assertion applies, that if *it* has A then *it* has B. Thus the universal conditional distributes the conditional relation between A and B (A "involving" B) over every member of the universe of discourse. It arranges the total universe of discourse into a single class, each member of which is subject to the conditional relation of A and B. At the same time, it says nothing about which, if any, of the members of that universe have A.

This, while simple as a form of arrangement, of unity-in-variety, has yet a certain power of providing for possible inferences. In point of form, there is, first, the variety of individuals, unified into a single class; second, the variety of attributes, unified into a conditional compresence; and third, the manner in which the combination of attributes is distributed over the class of individuals. And in point of inferential power, if the assertion is to be trusted, then, wherever in the wide world one turns, if one meets with something which is A, one is able to infer also that it is B. The simple lawful order in which the material is organized by this proposition makes that inference possible.

While, then, the universal affirmative (or its mate, the universal conditional) is fairly simple both in form and in inferential power, it may nevertheless be taken as a paradigm of the whole of science.[6] Science seeks to do what the universal affirmative does but on a grander scale, developing its distinctions and the complexities of its connections beyond what the simple "All . . . is . . ." itself is capable of. But the difference is not one of kind, but only of degree.

The substance of the aim of science may now be referred to as the provision of *an involutional order of the materials of experience.* In

[6]The idealist logicians, like Bradley and Bosanquet, took the simplest form of perceptual proposition as such a paradigm, and they were right in so doing. I think, however, that the universal affirmative is more effective as an illustration.

the course of its development science finds itself compelled to introduce nonobservable, theoretical entities; and if one wishes to speak of these as "existential," then our formulation of the aim of science may be broadened by saying that science seeks to provide *an involutional order of existential materials.*

4) *Organization of Scientific Language: Logical Order*

Science, we have seen, has as the substance of its aim the involutional ordering of its subject-matter, experiential or existential. I say the *substance* of its aim, because in seeking such involutional form, science seeks to achieve the possibility of empirical inference, which is a *function* based on involutional form but not identical with it (as a hammer's use in driving nails is based on its construction out of a hard material such as steel, but is not identical with it).

We have also seen that science is compelled to distinguish its language from its subject-matter. Thus science does not seek to arrange its *language* in involutional form (in so far, that is, as it is *using* rather than *mentioning* its language), but only its existential-empirical subject-matter.

Yet, in order to be able to fulfil its self-imposed task of achieving the possibility of empirical inference, science is compelled to arrange its language also; and the form of arrangement of scientific language, as distinct from the involutional order of its subject-matter, may be called *"logical."* I want in the present section to try to indicate the nature of this logical form of scientific language, and the reason why it is as it is.

Archibald MacLeish, no doubt meaning more than he should, has in his "Ars Poetica" said

> A poem should not mean
> But be.[7]

But in any event, that is just what a scientific proposition has to do— mean, I mean, not be. The separation in science between language and subject-matter goes hand in hand with the drive of scientific language

---

[7]Archibald MacLeish, "Ars Poetica," *Collected Poems, 1917–1952,* Houghton Mifflin Company, Boston, 1952, p. 40.

to be the language of "statement," a language which *refers, states, asserts, means*, without itself *being involved in* the object referred to.

The essential requirements on scientific language are twofold: 1) it is to be a language in which patterns of involvement are stateable, and 2) it is to be a language in which empirical inference is made possible. And these two requirements are closely connected with each other. For the involvement relation, as we have seen, is the sort which makes empirical inference possible.

This close connection between the two requirements is curiously and interestingly apparent in what has been called the *form* of the scientific statement. The logic textbooks conventionally distinguish between the "matter" and the "form" of a proposition by distinguishing between two categories of expressions in regard to their linguistic function. Thus, in the universal affirmative "All *A* is *B*," the expressions "all" and "is" fall into one category, "*A*" and "*B*" into another. The former are called "logical" words, the latter "nonlogical" (sometimes "descriptive," though this may be misleading, for not every nonlogical word need be used for purposes of description).

The motive for distinguishing these two categories of logical and nonlogical expressions derives from their function in *inference*. For instance, in a syllogism like "All *B* is *C*, all *A* is *B*, therefore all *A* is *C*," the derivation of the conclusion from the two premises does not depend upon the fact that the nonlogical terms "*A*," "*B*," and "*C*" appear; *any* set of three terms occurring in the proper sequence in the premises and conclusion will also give a valid derivation, as in "All *K* is *L*, all *J* is *K*, therefore all *J* is *L*." Thus the validity of inference does not depend on the *particular* subject and predicate terms of the propositions. It does depend, however, on the particular logical words; these cannot be changed at random without affecting the validity and even the meaningfulness of the linguistic construction. For instance, substitution of "no" for "all" throughout the syllogism makes it invalid; substituting "is" for "all" makes it meaningless.

If we use the variables "*X*," "*Y*," and "*Z*" in place of the constants "*A*," "*B*," and "*C*," the previous syllogism is transformed into a *schema* for syllogistic derivation, not itself an actual syllogism but a pattern for innumerable syllogisms: "All *Y* is *Z*, all *X* is *Y*, therefore all *X* is *Z*." Any particular syllogism of this form can be generated by supplying the proper constants for the variables. Such a pattern represents the *form* of a special kind of valid inference, each of the three parts representing the *form* of a proposition, and in this sense it is said that deductive inference is purely *formal* in nature, that the validity of the inference depends not upon the "matter" (represented in the nonlogical words) but upon the "form" of the syllogism and its constituents (represented in the logical words). Such a conclusion holds not only of syllogistic, but of all logical inference.

It is clear, so far, that *inference*—inference in general, including but not restricted to what we have been calling empirical inference—depends upon the characteristics of the so-called logical words (logical constants): words like "all," "some," "no," "there is," "and," "or," "if . . . then . . . ," "if and only if," "is," "is not."

The curious and interesting fact is that the statement of *involvement relations* depends upon the characteristics of exactly the same words. Thus, as we have seen above, the universal affirmative, "All A is B" is used to formulate an involvement. The kind of involvement formulated does not depend upon the particular nonlogical words, "A" and "B," but upon the logical words "All" and "is" and the sequence in which "A" and "B" are inserted. The same *kind* of involvement (though, of course, not the same identical involvement) would be stated in "All B is A." The *form* of the universal affirmative, "All X is Y," thus represents a certain kind of involvement.

There emerges the result that the element of language which conditions the possibility of inference is the very same as that which conditions the possibility of statement of involvements.[8] That is, the *logical*

[8] The matter is somewhat more complicated than appears in the above discussion. What is apparently the same statement form can be used to state what is apparently not an involvement. Thus the form "All X is Y" gives rise to "All cats are cats," and one would hardly wish to say that this latter statement expresses an involvement between being a cat and being a cat. It is only fair to say that rationalists, from the very beginning of thought about science, have tried to maintain that there is no essential distinction between the sort of relation asserted by "All cats are cats" and "All cats meow"; *i.e.,* they have tried to argue that the involvement relation (the causal relation, etc.) is essentially of the same nature as the logical relation of identity, or that all causal statements are ultimately analytic. I am not convinced; and I think that the purposes of scientific knowledge require a distinction to be made between the two. Just as logical inference is broader than inference from one empirical item to another via an involvement between them, so also statement is broader than statement of involvement relations; one can state a logical or analytical (or contradictory) matter, and one can state an accidental matter, as well as an involvement relation. *How* to distinguish statements of involvement from logical statements, on the one hand, and acci-

words of language—the words that give to language the power of formulating inference—are also the *involvement* words—the words that give to language the power of stating involvements. This does not mean that involvement relations are themselves nothing but logical relations. "All metals are conductors" does not state a logical relation between being a metal and being a conductor. But it does mean that the relation so stated is at the same time a relation of a kind which is, as it were, expressly designed for purposes of inference. Or, put otherwise, it means that the forms of meaning, the types of meaning units (statement forms) are so constructed as to be able to be linked together, extending ultimately over vast stretches of meaning; and the linkages are those of possible inference.

To the extent to which this occurs, language becomes efficient in fulfilling the requirements of the scientific purpose of formulating involvement patterns by virtue of which a network of potential inference is thrown over its subject-matter.

The logical form of scientific language is given by a) the forms of statements, b) the forms of inferences, and c) the *logical* relations obtaining among statements, relations like contradiction, contrariety, implication (such relations, like inferences, being determined by the logical words of the language). These are the "formal-logical" aspects of language; and they are registered in linguistic habits or rules of usage. Such rules include rules for combining words into sentences, for determining the meanings of complexes in terms of the meanings of their constituents, and for transforming sentences into others (rules of inference). In virtue of these rules, or of the forms and logical relations registered in them, it becomes possible for language to take on the

---

dental statements, on the other, is a problem which still vexes logicians today: the problem of defining lawlike sentences, the problem of the counterfactual conditional, and the like. For what it is worth, I venture the opinion that there is no *intrinsic* difference between an accidental and a lawlike sentence, but that the difference depends upon the context, upon the state of knowledge and the relation between the statement and other statements already accepted on scientific grounds; and the difference between logical statements and nonlogical statements is one of methodological function reflected in the rules of language: logical statements are those whose truth or falsehood is determined on linguistic grounds alone, nonlogical statements require investigation beyond linguistic grounds for the determination of their truth or falsehood. It should also be mentioned that Kant faced the same problem in the endeavor to get from the logical forms of judgments to the categories. *Cp.* Norman Kemp Smith, *A Commentary to Kant's Critique of Pure Reason*, The Macmillan Company, Ltd., London, 1918, pp. 194 ff.

logical structure of a system: to appear in the form of postulates, definitions, theorems, all arranged in due order of derivation.

The language of science assumes this form because that is the form required in order to state involvements and to link them together into the foundations of ever more extensive empirical inference.

5) *The Rhetorical Order of Literature*

Whereas science is compelled by the substance and function of its aim to distinguish between its vehicle and its subject-matter and to keep distinct the modes of organization of the two, resulting in a sharp difference between involutional form of subject-matter and logical form of vehicle, any attempt to maintain such a division in literature would be hopeless and if carried out in practice would signalize the death of the literary impulse.

It is true that a relative distinction can be made, between the esthetic possibilities of the verbal medium as such, independent of its meanings, and the esthetic possibilities of the meanings themselves. In this connection it is sometimes said that there is a quasimusical factor in literature, the esthetic employment of the verbal sounds merely as sounds for the sake of the values they have as such. That there is the possibility of such a factor is clearly the case. One has only to listen to a recitation in an unknown language to appreciate it (although probably even here there are some dim adumbrations of meaning as overtones).

But this relative distinction, between verbal and nonverbal ordering of materials, is not one of *kind of form,* like the distinction in science between logical and involutional form, but only of the *matter which is formed.* The generic kind of form which, in literature, belongs to both the sound matter and the meaning matter (images, ideas, attitudes, etc.), is the same; the difference is only one of *where* the form is, of what particular kind of thing is being formed.

Although the word is liable to a host of misunderstandings, I shall speak of the form which the literary art gives to its subject-matter as *"rhetorical,"* and I can only hope that in what follows the idea I have in mind will emerge with sufficient clearness to withstand at least the most obvious of those misunderstandings.

A beginning may be made by noting the effectiveness or impressiveness in a human being's experience of certain combinations or constructions of elements. A very simple kind of instance would be something like a *contrast*. A patch of yellow is a patch of yellow, and a patch of blue is a patch of blue, but a patch of yellow set beside a patch of blue gives a contrast, in which the patches act and react upon each other (not in a direct physical manner, independently of the experiencer, but *as* constituents within his experience), clashing with each other and yet holding tightly together, in and because of that very clash, forming a whole with a certain experienceable vital, dynamic intensity. Each of the patches gains a saliency, an intensity, and therefore an interest for the experiencer, from the peculiar relation in which it falls with the other; and the whole itself, in its own character as well as by reason of the interest of its parts, develops into something intrinsically interesting ("intrinsically," in the sense that it *itself* is interesting, not that something else is interesting to which it leads or points).

In a similar, though more complex way, a jewel is a jewel and night is night, but

> . . . a jewel hung in ghastly night,
> Makes black night beauteous and her old face new
> (Shakespeare, Sonnet XXVII).

As in the universal affirmative proposition we found a paradigm of involutional order, so here in the contrast-effect may be seen a paradigm of rhetorical (and in general of esthetic) order. A rhetorical ordering of materials is an ordering of them in such a way as to result in the building of a whole for an experience, a whole which becomes intrinsically impressive and interesting to the experiencer and in which the parts, acting and reacting upon each other, repelling and attracting each other, gain a salient relevance to each other, give to each other and the whole, and derive from each other and the whole, their own interest within that whole.

More shortly, we may define a rhetorical ordering of materials as one in which a) they produce an effect, and b) the effect is intrinsically *interesting, impressive, arresting or vital*. An effect is produced when elements in experience form a whole: for a whole is a whole in virtue of some character which it has, which only a whole can have. For instance, a contrast of yellow and blue is a whole because it is a contrast, for only a whole can be a contrast. And the character of contrast is just the effect produced by setting the yellow and blue side by side.

To be more nearly accurate, the effect produced here is not "contrast," but "yellow-blue contrast," or even better "this yellow-this blue contrast." It is important to be precise about this here because some contrasts are more interesting than others, not extrinsically but intrinsically, because of what contrasts with what.[9] It is of fairly central interest to esthetics to discover what effects are intrinsically interesting to what human beings, what combinations of what elements give rise to such effects, and why this is so. *I.e.,* there is a certain pattern of involvement here, including esthetic materials and human beings, which a scientific study would want to investigate. In this context, however, I do not wish to direct attention in that direction. Whatever be the particular combinations of particular elements which provide rhetorical order, it is the phenomenon of that order which is of concern now.

A revealing picture of an artist's search for a parallel to rhetorical order in another medium appears in Matisse's *Notes of a Painter:*

> It is necessary for me to define the character of the object or of the body that I wish to paint. In order to do this I study certain salient points very carefully: if I put a black dot on a sheet of white paper the dot will be visible no matter how far I stand away from it—it is a clear notation; but beside this dot I place another one, and then a third. Already there is confusion. In order that the first dot may maintain its value I must enlarge it as I proceed putting other marks on the paper.
>
> If upon a white canvas I jot down some sensations of blue, of green, of red—every new brushstroke diminishes the importance of the preceding ones. Suppose I set out to paint an interior: I have before me a cupboard; it gives me a sensation of bright red—and I put down a red which satisfies me; immediately a relation is established between this

---

[9] One may also think of a rhetorical ordering of materials as an *imaginative* ordering, if this latter term is conceived somewhat as Coleridge did when he spoke of the imagination as the "esemplastic power." *Cf.* Samuel Taylor Coleridge, *Biographia Literaria,* G. Bell & Sons, London, 1898, chap. XIII, and also chap. X, where he says: *"Esemplastic. The word is not in Johnson, nor have I met with it elsewhere.* Neither have I. I constructed it myself from the Greek words, εἰς ἓν πλάττειν, to shape into one; because, having to convey a new sense, I thought that a new term would both aid the recollection of my meaning, and prevent its being confounded with the usual import of the word, imagination." Only, what is lacking in the connotation as given is reference to the impressiveness, vitality, arresting character, of an intrinsic sort, belonging to the shaped one. For *every* object of human experience is a shaped one, a whole, produces an effect, has an experienced character; but not every object of human experience is *equally* interesting in-itself-to-the-experiencer. But *cf.* in chap. XIII, "(The secondary imagination) is essentially *vital,* even as all objects (*as* objects) are essentially fixed and dead."

red and the white of the canvas. If I put a green near the red, if I paint a yellow floor, there must still be between this green, this yellow and the white of the canvas a relation that will be satisfactory to me. But these several tones mutually weaken one another. It is necessary, therefore, that the various elements that I use be so balanced that they do not destroy one another. To do this I must organize my ideas; the relations between the tones must be so established that they will sustain one another. A new combination of colors will succeed the first one and will give more completely my interpretation. I am forced to transpose until finally my picture may seem completely changed when, after successive modifications, the red has succeeded the green as the dominant color. I cannot copy nature in a servile way. I must interpret nature and submit it to the spirit of the picture—when I have found the relationship of all the tones the result must be a living harmony of tones, a harmony not unlike that of a musical composition.[10]

From the field of literary esthetics and literary criticism it is possible to quote literally hundreds of reports of this same fundamental fact, the essentiality of rhetorical order to literature as the form of its materials. I cite just a few to remind the reader of the many with which he is familiar.

Marcel Proust: A picture of life brings with it multiple and varied sensations. The sight, for instance, of the cover of a book which has been read spins from the characters of its title the moonbeams of a distant summer night. The taste of our morning coffee brings us that faint hope of a fine day which formerly so often smiled at us in the unsettled dawn from a fluted bowl or porcelain which seemed like hardened milk. An hour is not merely an hour, it is a vase filled with perfumes, with sounds, with projects, with climates. What we call reality is a relation between those sensations and those memories which simultaneously encircle us—a relation which a cinematographic vision destroys because its form separates it from the truth to which it pretends to limit itself—that unique relation which the writer must discover in order that he may link two different states of being together for ever in a phrase. In describing objects one can make those which figure in a particular place succeed each other indefinitely; the truth will only begin to emerge from the moment that the writer takes two different objects, posits their relationship, the analogue in the world of

[10]The quotation is from the selection reproduced in Eliseo Vivas and Murray Krieger, *The Problems of Aesthetics,* Rinehart & Company, New York and Toronto, 1953, p. 258. See p. 255, n. 1, for information concerning the original publication.

art to the only relationship of causal law in the world of science, and encloses it within the circle of fine style. In this, as in life, he fuses a quality common to two sensations, extracts their essence and in order to withdraw them from the contingencies of time, unites them in a metaphor, thus chaining them together with the indefinable bond of a verbal alliance (*Time Regained,* Modern Library edition, translated from the French by Frederick A. Blossom).

Edgar Allan Poe: His remarks on the composition of "The Raven" are too long to quote with any degree of completeness, but, even though it may remain a question how accurate an historical description they afford of Poe's actual creative experience, some of the details will not be amiss:

I prefer commencing with the consideration of an *effect*. Keeping originality *always* in view—for he is false to himself who ventures to dispense with so obvious and so easily attainable a source of interest— I say to myself, in the first place: "Of the innumerable effects, or impressions, of which the heart, the intellect, or (more generally) the soul is susceptible, what one shall I, on the present occasion, select?" Having chosen a novel, first, and secondly a vivid effect, I consider whether it can be best wrought by incident or tone—afterwards looking about me (or rather within me) for such combinations of event, or tone, as shall best aid me in the construction of the effect. . . .

The initial consideration was that of extent. . . . What we term a long poem is, in fact, merely a succession of brief ones—that is to say, of brief poetical effects. It is needless to demonstrate that a poem is such, only inasmuch as it intensely excites, by elevating, the soul; and all intense excitements are, through a physical necessity, brief. . . . Holding in view these considerations, as well as that degree of excitement which I deemed not above the popular, while not below the critical, taste, I reached at once what I conceived the proper *length* for my intended poem, a length of about one hundred lines. It is, in fact, a hundred and eight.

My next thought concerned the choice of an impression, or effect, to be conveyed. . . . Beauty is the sole legitimate province of the poem. . . . Regarding, then, Beauty as my province, my next question referred to the *tone* of its higher manifestation—and all experience has shown that this tone is one of *sadness*. Beauty of whatever kind, in its supreme development, invariably excites the sensitive soul to tears. Melancholy is thus the most legitimate of the poetical tones.

The length, the province, and the tone, being thus determined, I betook myself to ordinary induction, with a view of obtaining some artistic piquancy which might serve me as a keynote in the construction of the poem—some pivot upon which the whole structure might turn. In carefully thinking over all the usual artistic effects—or more properly *points,* in the theatrical sense—I did not fail to perceive immediately that no one had been so universally employed as that of the *refrain*.

Poe continues by explaining how he determined where the refrain was to occur; how he chose "Nevermore"; what reasons compelled the choice of a Raven to utter the refrain; why the topic was the death of a beautiful woman lamented by her lover; how this gave rise to the opportunity of imagining the Raven answering the queries of the lover by its refrain (thus providing for "variation of application"); how this in turn made possible a progress toward a climax (growth in intensity) so that the last question, to which the answer is "Nevermore," "should involve the utmost conceivable amount of sorrow and despair"; how the *locale* was chosen to assure the effect of "insulated incident"; and other details. A few typical details: "I made the night tempestuous, first to account for the Raven's seeking admission, and secondly, for the effect of contrast with the (physical) serenity within the chamber"; "I made the bird alight on the bust of Pallas, also for the effect of contrast between the marble and the plumage—it being understood that the bust was absolutely *suggested* by the bird—the bust of *Pallas* being chosen, first, as most in keeping with the scholarship of the lover, and, secondly, for the sonorousness of the word, Pallas, itself."

Henry James: This in fact I have ever found rather terribly the point—that the figures in any picture, the agents in any drama, are interesting only in proportion as they feel their respective situations; since the consciousness, on their part, of the complication exhibited forms for us their link of connection with it. But there are degrees of feeling—the muffled, the faint, the just sufficient, the barely intelligent, as we may say; and the acute, the intense, the complete, in a word—the power to be finely aware and richly responsible. It is those moved in this latter fashion who "get most" out of all that happens to them and who in so doing enable us, as readers of their records, as participators by a fond attention, also to get most. Their being finely aware—as Hamlet and Lear, say, are finely aware—*makes* absolutely the intensity of their adventure, gives the maximum of sense to what befalls them. . . .

I recognize at the same time, and in planning *The Princess Cassamassima* felt it highly important to recognize, the danger of filling too full any supposed and above all any obviously limited vessel of consciousness. If persons either tragically or comically embroiled with life allow us the comic or tragic value of their embroilment in proportion as their struggle is a measured and directed one, it is strangely true, none the less, that beyond a certain point they are spoiled for us by this carrying of a due light. They may carry too much of it for our credence, for our compassion, for our derision. They may be shown as knowing too much and feeling too much—not certainly for their remaining remarkable, but for their remaining "natural" and typical, for their having the needful communities with our own precious liability to fall into traps and be bewildered. . . .

The picture of the exposed and entangled state is what is required, and there are certainly always plenty of grounds for keeping down the complexities of a picture. A picture it still has to be, however, and by that condition has to deal effectually with its subject, so that the simple device of more and more keeping down may well not see us quite to our end or even quite to our middle. . . . (Preface to *The Princess Cassamassima*).[11]

6) *Some Comparisons between Rhetorical Order and Involutional and Logical Order*

a) In each of these kinds of order, it is possible to distinguish between a *substantive* and a *functional* aspect. In the case of involutional order (as remarked above, pp. 301–302) there is the distinction between the involutional form (determined by the meanings of the so-called logical words) as substantive and the possibility of inference (ultimately, empirical inference) as functional. In the case of logical order, the substantive aspect consists in the formal properties of statements and inferences and in the logical relations among statements (p. 305), whereas the functional aspect lies in the possibility thereby afforded of formulating statements of involvements and of formulating inferences (ultimately empirical inferences) making use of those statements. In our definition of rhetorical order both substantive and functional aspects have been included. The substantive aspect is found in the notion of a whole-for-an-experiencer or the building of effect, whereas the functional aspect stems from the requirement that such a whole or effect be intrinsically

[11] *The Writer on His Art,* compiled and edited by Walter E. Allen, Whittlesey House, New York, 1949, pp. 134–135, 62–64, 171–173.

effective, *i.e.,* impressive, interesting, arresting, vital, that it afford an experiencer (who is willing to make the necessary effort—Tolstoi was surely wrong in requiring that literature should "infect" us without labor on our part) an opportunity to rise to a high pitch of "immanent" concern, of concern directed to the imaginative object itself.

b) In each of these kinds of order, the *relation* between the substantive and functional aspect is a means-end relation; the substantive aspect is developed in order that the functional aspect should be achieved efficiently. Science develops its involutional relations in order that empirical inference should be *performed* efficiently, and it develops its logico-mathematical forms in order that its subordinate task of *stating* involutions and *formulating* empirical inferences should be done adequately. Similarly, the writer labors, in the building of the imaginative whole of effect, to vivify and intensify, to deploy to best advantage, effects which elicit his own passionate interest and which he hopes will find kindred souls to appreciate.

c) It is the differences, however, both in substantive order and functional effect, which are of particular interest to us here. These differences lead to and become manifest in different principles and ideals of organization and method. The subject is particularly complex and subtle, and I can hope only to suggest a few directions of consideration in this place.

Rhetorical order is characterized, so far as its constitutive relations are concerned, by degrees of what has variously been called fitness, relevancy, propriety, affinity, decorum (Greek *prepon,* Latin *decorum, decentia, convenientia*).[12] This notion of fitness is fundamental to all critical interpretation of the work of art, literary or other; without it, criticism has no orientation. It can, of course, be degraded into the demand that a work of art subject itself to highly conventionalized, academic rules; but that is a degradation, both cause and effect of a deadly narrowing of taste and sensibility.

Fitness is a very broad notion, and can be used in a variety of senses and contexts. One can thus speak of a means as fit with regard to an end: the fit as the instrumental. Kant, in characterizing the beautiful as having *Zweckmaessigkeit ohne Zweck*—fitness without an end—saw

---

[12]*Cp. Dictionary of World Literature,* edited by J. T. Shipley, Philosophical Library, New York, 1953, article "Fitness" by J. C. La Drière.

beauty as grounded in a fitness of the object *to* our powers of imagination and understanding; and this, though not quite instrumentality in the ordinary sense, is yet in a way close to it.

In the context of rhetorical order, however, there are two dimensions in which fitness appears particularly decisive: i) in the construction of the imaginative whole, and ii) in the achievement of vitality or impressiveness of effect. That is, the two relevant dimensions of fitness for rhetorical order have to do with the substantive and the functional aspects of that order respectively.

i) As La Drière points out, the idea of fitness is related to the idea of unity (or unity-in-variety), but "fitness seems to be prior to unity; it is rather because its internal relations are fit that a structure presents itself as unified than because it is unified that its relations seem fit."[13]

While this is an exaggeration of one "moment" of a synthetic unity, it serves to indicate the close connection between imaginative unity and fitness of the constituent parts. One might say that the peculiar kind of unity-in-variety characteristic of the work of art is the unity of phenomenally fit, congruent, affinitive parts. This kind of fitness derives from the nature of the human consciousness in its activity of forming unitary objects (imagination). Not every existential unity need register in human consciousness as a unitary object of consciousness, and not every unitary object of consciousness need be a substantial existential unity (*e.g.,* constellations of the stars). There are laws of human consciousness, in accordance with which the mind forms objects for itself, involving the operation of factors such as attention, association, perception. In this connection, the artist is the discoverer of means and cues toward the building of such unities: a poet discovers the uses of image, metaphor, symbol, a painter discovers the uses of planes or color relations.

It is a meteorological truth that when the sun sets, it grows dark. It is a historical truth that some queens have died in the bloom of youth. Science establishes no special connection between the two facts; their relation is not one of "involvement," not, in that sense, a "rational" connection. Yet something *happens* in Thomas Nash's *Litany in Time of Plague:*

> Brightness falls from the air;
> Queens have died young and fair.

[13]*Ibid.,* pp. 240–241.

True, they are both offered as instances of the general principle that

> Beauty is but a flower
> Which wrinkles will devour:

and the even more general principle that everything in this world is doomed to death and decay. Yet that "logical" relation of coordinate instancing serves only as material for another relation, a relation of images which is felt in their congruity, their mutual enhancement, and above all in the way in which the thought of the inevitability of death and decay comes to vital realization through them. The poet achieves a single thought, playing over yet unifying a variety of thoughts, facts, images, sounds.[14]

A single act of consciousness holds its varied materials together in an act of immediacy, and is able to do so because they "fit" together to make a unified object of mind. Perceptual objects are particularly striking instances of the fitness of elements to each other in the building of wholes. A figure against a background constitutes a whole; and figure and background fit each other and fit into the whole. Dots variously distributed over a sheet fall into confusion; they fit together to make, perhaps, only the whole we call a "confused mass." Arranged in definite constellations—lines, curves, figures—they constitute a pattern, fit together to make a whole with more, and more definite, sense. One sees fitness in all objects of perception.

When we try to describe the properties of this kind of fitness—the fitness which builds imaginative unities—we find ourselves led into the theory of "form." Things fit into objects of human consciousness in so far as they exhibit formal features, such as contrast, repetition, gradation, variation, sequence, parallelism, balance, dominance, climax, type . . . ; the list enlarges itself when one begins to particularize such relations. The theory of form—so far, at least—is a theory of the peculiar kinds of relationships which items for an experiencing mind have, by

[14]"Between 'Brightness falls from the air' and 'Queens have died young and fair' there is a rational void. But a spark leaps to fill the gap, and the spark does not expire but glows on, so that the sadness of evening and the sadness of untimely death illuminate each other reciprocally, a light which is extended beyond them and reaches out some way over the human situation all round." C. Day Lewis (*The Poetic Image,* The Clark Lectures, Cambridge, 1946, Jonathan Cape, London, 1947, chap. I) overlooks the logical relation and its influence in producing the unity, but on the whole, despite the fact that his description of the unity revealed by poetic imagery is itself highly metaphorical, his way of putting it helps.

virtue of which those items are able to join together (fit) to make a whole object for that mind.

ii) But this *formal dimension* of fitness is insufficient to account for the whole nature of rhetorical order, just as the abstract formalism which, as an esthetic theory, bases itself completely on formal fitness is insufficient to account for the whole nature of esthetic value. Readers of Clive Bell will recollect that even in his theory it is *not* form alone, but *significant* form, which is the basic esthetic category. And by "significant" he does not mean *signifying* but rather *important,* capable of provoking an "esthetic emotion," capable of arousing a certain profound concern.[15]

Not every combination of line and color is capable of doing this, and hence not every combination of line and color which has form is also significant.

On this point Edmund Gurney saw very clearly:

> As regards exact rightness and definiteness of the component units . . . melodic forms stand preeminent. The rightness here spoken of is of course not of that deeper sort which implies and is implied in a *good* melody with impressiveness of a distinctly individual kind; it is a general feature of melodies good, bad, and indifferent. What is meant is that each unit falls definitely in its right place as an obviously essential part of the whole, such as it is; strike out or alter a unit here and there, and what was an organic whole is either broken into more or less incoherent fragments; or if in some exceptional instance it retains a satisfactory coherence, it is by becoming something else, recognized as another whole. . . . The whole which they make up may perhaps be weak and silly as (to use a very loose metaphor) a series of grammatical words may make a weak and silly sentence; but as in a familiar sentence words cannot be omitted or replaced (except by synonyms, and in Music there are no synonyms) without obvious destruction or alteration of the sense, so neither can single notes in a familiar tune be altered

[15]". . . when I speak of significant form, I mean a combination of lines, or of lines and colours (counting white and black as colours) that moves me aesthetically." "May we go on to say that, having seen it as pure form, having freed it from all casual and adventitious interest, from all that it may have acquired from its commerce with human beings, from all its significance as a means, he has felt its significance as an end in itself?" "But for objects seen as ends in themselves, do we not feel a profounder and a more thrilling emotion (*i.e.,* a greater significance) than ever we felt for them as means?" Clive Bell, *Art,* Chatto & Windus, London, 1949, pp. 12, 53, 52.

or replaced, except in very peculiar cases, without instantly producing this feeling of wrongness.[16]

Form in the sense of the unity-in-variety characteristic of objects as phenomena of human consciousness, is a necessary condition for the consciousness of an object at all; but it is not a sufficient condition for an *esthetically valuable* object. A fine melody has form; so also has a trivial melody; and what is true of melody is true of poem, story, play. There is an element of "significance," of "impressiveness," in the esthetic whole-of-effect by virtue of which it is arresting and vital, by virtue of which it is *intrinsically important for the experiencer of it.*

And this leads to the second dimension of "fitness" in rhetorical order. Whereas, in the first sense, components are "fit" in that they fit with each other to build *a whole-of-effect,* in this second sense components are "fit" in that they conspire rightly, cogently, effectively to build *this inherently important effect.* This is the region of taste, of sensibility, of perceptiveness. Not that one need know beforehand the effect to be achieved, but rather that one has to have the sense to feel that something important is ready to be achieved with the "right" handling of components.

This is the region, again, not merely of "words in order" but of *le mot juste,* of "the best words in the best order" (and, we may add, of the best thoughts, actions, characters, images, metaphors, symbols . . .

[16]Edmund Gurney, *The Power of Sound,* Smith, Elder & Company, London, 1880, chap. V, no. 3, pp. 92–93. See also, *e.g.,* p. 102:

and though we found the word *rightness* convenient to express the definite character and position of the component units, and perceived that this also entailed definite individuality in the resulting melodic forms, it is difficult to see that such definiteness and individuality have in themselves any necessary connection with beauty or emotion . . . (And pp. 189–190) But the perception of unity under variety, merely as such, and failing any independent ground of interest whether in the elements or in their combination, cannot make good its claim to a truly aesthetic character. There are indeed instances of which some presented themselves when we were considering the sources of architectural effect, and others might be found in polyphonic music, where the complexity and unity are both so striking that the sense of ease and power with which we grasp them becomes an important element of our enjoyment; but even here the effect would be impossible in the absence of all other elements of interest in the things combined, and such cases are quite exceptional. Unity under variety is a characteristic, or rather is the definition, of all form, not specially of beautiful form. On the above-quoted theory a prize-pig is as beautiful as a peacock, the Wellington statue as the Venus of Milo. The spectator is treated as though he were a sudden importation from another sphere, gifted with the perception of relations of fact, but without any emotional history or nature; not as the product of slow development in a certain environment, a being whose perceptions in certain directions are saturated with emotion, and whose feelings however interfused and transformed, have their primeval roots in simple experiences, and in associations whose ingredients are usually easy enough to surmise.

in the best order), of Milton's "apt Numbers, fit quantity of Syllables, and the sense variously drawn out from one Verse into another."[17]

It is the region of what the Greeks called the *Mean* (understood as a principle of perfection, not misunderstood as a principle of moderation) and of what Tolstoi called the *Wee Bit:*

> Once when correcting a pupil's study, Bryulov just touched it in a few places and the poor dead study immediately became animated. "Why you only touched it a wee bit, and it is quite another thing!" said one of the pupils. "Art begins where the wee bit begins," replied Bryulov, indicating by these words just what is most characteristic of art. . . . Musical execution is only then art, only then infects, when the sound is neither higher nor lower than it should be, that is, when exactly the infinitely small center of the required note is taken; when that note is continued exactly as long as is needed; and when the strength of the sound is neither more nor less than is required. The slightest deviation of pitch in either direction, the slightest increase or decrease in time, or the slightest strengthening or weakening of the sound beyond what is needed, destroys the perfection and consequently the infectiousness of the work. . . . It is the same in all arts. . . . Infection is only obtained when an artist finds those infinitely minute degrees of which a work of art consists, and only to the extent to which he finds them. And it is quite impossible to teach people by external means to find these minute degrees; they can only be found when a man yields to his feeling. No instruction can make a dancer catch just the time of the music, or a singer or a fiddler take exactly the infinitely minute centre of his note, or a sketcher draw of all possible lines the only right one, or a poet find the only right arrangement of the only suitable words. All this is found only by feeling.[18]

Fitness here is not simply fitting-*together,* not simply coherence within an imaginative unity, but also fitness-*for* the importance of the imagina-

---

[17]"Whatever one wishes to say, there is one noun only by which to express it, one verb only to give it life, one adjective only which will describe it. One must search until one has discovered them, this noun, this verb, this adjective, and never rest content with approximations, never resort to trickery, however happy, or to vulgarisms, in order to dodge the difficulty . . . one must discriminate, and with the utmost lucidity, all the modifications in the value of a word which are established by the position it occupies in the sentence" Guy de Maupassant, Preface to *Pierre et Jean* (Quoted in Allen, *op. cit.,* p. 229). This should be compared with the remarks of Matisse quoted earlier.

[18]Count Leo N. Tolstoi, *What is Art?,* translated by Charles Johnston, H. Altemus, Philadelphia, 1898, chap. XII, pp. 124–125. Compare the quotation from Henry James given earlier.

tive vision. It is not merely a *substantial* fitness—contributing to the building of the whole—but a *functional* fitness—contributing to the value of the whole that is built, to the vitality and impressiveness of its effect.

Such functional fitness, developing out of and perfecting substantial fitness, represents the ideal of rhetorical organization. It is the source of esthetic principles of composition and criticism. There are different modes of impressiveness, vitality, intrinsic importance: the classical beauty of balance and proportion, the romantic beauty of emotional expressiveness, the inexorable and grand sublimity of Attic tragedy, the still, brooding poignancy of the "static" drama, the echoing sadness of the pathetic lyric. Estheticians grope after a set of categories which will somehow include the unutterable, nameless multiplicity of them: Beauty, the Characteristic, the Sublime, the Expressive, the Tragic, the Comic, the Epic, the Lyric, and latterly perhaps, the Symbolic. And there are different modes of sensibility: men's minds tend, by nature and experience, toward one or the other, and social eras respond selectively, differentially to their lures. Thus taste varies, and the particular principles of rhetorical organization which formulate ideals of functional fitness will change from school to school and man to man. But wherever there is an ideal of rhetorical order, that is, wherever there is any striving after esthetic values of human experience at all, it is an ideal of functional fitness.

Functional fitness governs the choice of words and their rhythmic sequence, the selection of images and their contraposition, characters and their interrelations and interactions, ideas and their illustrations, symbols and their contexts: in a word, a sense of fitness, a feeling for the vitally impressive is the *sine qua non* of creative orientation and critical intelligence. It is at work in Keats's substitution of "Yet did I never breathe its pure serene" for "Yet did I never judge what men could mean," or in what John Livingston Lowes calls Coleridge's "imaginative transmutation of a bare hint" from the fragment of *The Romaunt of the Rose* to the 1798 version of *The Ancient Mariner*.[19]

[19]John Livingston Lowes, *The Road to Xanadu*, Houghton Mifflin Company, Boston and New York, 1927, pp. 333–334:

> There mightin men se many flockes
> Of Turtels and of *Laverockes* . . .
> Thei *song ther song,* as faire and wel
> *As angels doen espirituell* . . .
> Layis of love full wel souning
> Thei songin in their *jargoning.*

The result is that the connectedness of literary language, and its connectedness with all imagery, all represented content, with every other component of the literary medium, is a connectedness within the scope of, and constitutive of, impressive effect, of the intrinsically vitalized object of an aroused consciousness. Components of the medium are combined so as to lend force to each other in the burgeoning of the effect. Logic, grammar, common sense, the neat schemes of the understanding, the categories of science, conventional morality—all become *matter* here, to be used as is where needed as is, and to be rejected or transformed or distorted where needed.

This connectedness is most frequently spoken of as "organic"; but that is only a metaphor. The unity, and particularly the impressive and vitalized unity, of the esthetic object is one of mutual interdependence of part upon part and part and whole, but the nature of that interdependence is not the same as the nature of the interdependence of organs in a biological organism. This latter type of interdependence is due to physiological relations of involvement, or, in the higher animals, to a complex psychosomatic pattern of involvement. The parts of a poem are not organs; they do not relate physiologically or psychosomatically to other parts or to the whole. Their relations are, in a very broad sense of the term, relations of mutual "significance," of interfunctioning roles assumed in the building of the impressive whole for consciousness, relations to be studied in phenomenology and psychology; they are the counterpart to the peculiar ability of the human mind to imagine, to grow into an ardent vision; they are reducible to nothing else.

d) In science, on the other hand, the ideals of organization are two: i) the most completely universal extension of the involvement relation (so far as subject-matter is concerned) alongside a corresponding extension of the possibility of empirical inference, and ii) the most efficient

And here are Coleridge's lovely lines as they stood in 1798:

> Sometimes a dropping from the sky
> I heard the *Lavrock* sing;
> Sometimes all little birds that are
> How they seem'd to fill the sea and air
> With their sweet *jargoning*.
> And now 'twas like all instruments,
> Now like a lonely flute;
> And now it is *an angel's song*
> That makes the heavens be mute.

No imaginative transmutation of a bare hint, among all the many metamorphoses which the poem has to offer, is more wonderful than that. And "jargoning" is not so much an archaism as the one inevitable word in the world.

systematization of the linguistic formulation of involvement patterns, together with the corresponding systematization of the possibility of formulating inferences.

i) How science seeks to accomplish the universal extension of patterns of involvement; how, on the one hand, it eternally refuses to draw limits to its object, progressively widening the denotation of its symbols and deepening their connotation; how its march from the crude perceptual judgments of ordinary observation, through low level empirical generalizations, to abstract, nonobservational theory is undertaken in this interest, is a long and difficult tale, which cannot be recited in this place. There is a "fitness" here, too—if one feels compelled to use the word—but it consists in the way in which items have to be chosen to fit into the scheme of the "lawful universal," as, from among all the properties of gases, it turns out that pressure, volume, and temperature are the items to be chosen and related, if macroscopic behavior is to be accounted for.

Where literature is pushed into the discovery and employment of devices such as metaphor, metonymy, alliteration, plot-construction, in order to establish its own connectednesses, science is pushed in the direction of the mathematical, employing devices such as the relating of serial variables in terms of mathematicological functions.

This, as I have said, is a long story untellable here; but if one wished for an image of the comparison of science and literature one could do worse than to compare the Rules (Methods) of Experimental Inquiry in Mill's *Logic* with, say, Aristotle's *Poetics*. For in them we have, on the one hand, the attempt essentially to define a "causal" connection and to deduce from that definition an ideal sought for in inquiry, and, on the other hand, the attempt essentially to define a certain *genre* of dramatic effect and to deduce from that definition an ideal sought for in poetic creation.

ii) More to our purpose is the matter of the systematization of scientific language. The story here, too, is at least as long and complex as the previous one, and I can make only a few gestures at its telling. The most obvious ideal drive in scientific language is that toward assumption of the form of a hypotheticodeductive system. But it will perhaps be more useful—certainly it is simpler and more convenient—to consider some points of smaller scope here. I choose two: the *precision* of scientific language and its *translatability*.

1) There is a precision of literary language and a precision of scientific language. In literature, precision is a question of functional fitness, of *le mot juste*. In science, precision leads in the direction of logic and mathematics; as science strives toward precision it approaches more and more the form of mathematical language governed by laws of formal logic. I wish to show and explain why this is the case.

If, in ordinary English, we say that an egg is "very fragile," our meaning can be indicated approximately by a table which shows what the consequences would be in the way of deformation of subjecting the egg to different degrees of handling:

"Very fragile"

Mode of Handling	Probable Consequence
Careful, delicate	No unfortunate result
Slight pressure	No unfortunate result
Moderate pressure or slight fall	Cracking, though not disastrous
Severe pressure	Irremediable cracking and spilling
Hard drop, dashing upon floor	Thorough mess

I do not say that this is a complete account of what we have in mind in speaking of eggs as being very fragile; but, on the whole, it might be the beginning of an explication. At any rate, I believe that I have not seriously misrepresented the degree of precision embodied in the phrase "very fragile." A shipper of eggs who stamps his crates "very fragile" would be fairly satisfied if the truckmen handled them accordingly; he would not expect them to carry special instruments for aid in deciding how high to lift them before letting them fall in place.

Note that there *is* a certain degree of precision. A distinction is made, after all, between "careful" handling and "slight pressure," suggesting that being careful is subjecting the eggs to somewhat less than slight pressure; equally, a distinction is made between cracking which is not disastrous and cracking (with spilling) which is irremediable. Note also that there is a certain degree of efficiency of probable inference: if an egg is very fragile then, if it is subjected to only slight pressure, the probable result will not be unfortunate.

Science wants to know *precisely* what is connected with what and *precisely* how (for only then is it possible to have highly efficient empirical inference). From this viewpoint, the phrase "very fragile" is defective. "Careful" and "delicate" refer to the handling of eggs by persons; but are persons *involved* in the pattern that includes the cracking of eggs? Is it even a question of their being eggs? Again, is it pressure, or fall, that is to be considered essential? Or cracking, spilling, mess? How careful is careful, and how slight is slight? Such questions can be multiplied, and they all ask for further precision, precision in distinguishing out exactly which aspects of the eggs and their treatment are *relevant* and which are not, and in refining the degrees of those aspects which are to be taken into account.

When the scientist gets to work at such a problem, he emerges with concepts which will fulfil these requirements. Thus he will introduce the notions of *stress* (force per unit area) and *strain* (deformation per original unit) because experiment (and perhaps theory also) suggests a relation of involvement between these: an involvement formulatable, *e.g.,* in a numerical law such as

$$\text{Stress} = k \times \text{Strain},$$

where k (modulus of elasticity) is a characteristic of the material under investigation (*e.g.,* eggshells).

In place of "eggs are very fragile" the scientist is able to say "eggshells have a modulus of elasticity k_e." And in place of the crude table which common sense enable us to draw up, he is able to make a table in which from a particular value of the stress (accurate, say, to two decimals) he can infer to a particular value of the strain. All irrelevancies—like persons and their behavior, pressing or falling—are eliminated; thus greater precision of *distinction of relevant factors* is attained. Questions of *degree,* of stress or strain, are refined, so that greater precision of *degree or quantity within a given factor* is attained. And with proper treatment, greater precision in *specificity of inference* becomes possible, by use of standard methods of measuring probable deviations.

The movement is from a crude, qualitative method of distinguishing and connecting to a refined, quantitative method of doing the same task; the latter is more efficient as a base for empirical inference. A mathematical language (not necessarily a quantitative language), because of the rigor with which it makes its distinctions and connections, is thus the ideal form which the purpose of science requires.

More interesting, however, is the connection between precision of the scientific variety and the logical character of the language. Precision is a matter of degree of distinction, a matter of being able to cut the matter short, of being able to say, "Up to here and no further." Words such as "red" and "orange" are not precise because they do not cut colors very short; on following the spectrum we find ourselves not quite able to say that "red" applies "up to here and no further," unless we are willing to allow "here" to extend vaguely over a considerable region. Now if we cannot very well say "up to here and no further," we equally cannot very well say "not both." Thus, in the area of vagueness between definite red and definite orange, what shall we say? Red? Perhaps yes, perhaps not. Orange? Perhaps yes, perhaps not. Red but not orange? Hardly. Orange but not red? Hardly. In fact, our language begins to unravel itself, dissolve itself into unsteady mumblings at this stage.

Semanticists, Heracliteans, and dialecticians delight in such situations. They tell us that here is where Aristotelian logic, or the logic of the mere rationalistic understanding, or the logic of the concept breaks down, face to face with the immediacy and urgency of the real; here is where the mere understanding is tricked by reality into self-contradiction.

But one need not draw so hard a conclusion. One need only note that words such as "red" and "orange," "here" and "there," "now" and "then," are *vague* words, *i.e.,* relatively imprecise words, *i.e.,* words which fail to stand up in all contexts when demands are made for "either-or's" or "not-both's." That is, they are words which do not obey the logical "laws" of identity, noncontradiction, excluded middle. If one views such logical "laws" as constituting an implicit definition of verbal precision—as laws, that is, which are laws of and only of precise words—there is no great difficulty in the matter. The laws of logic are laws of language, but they are not the laws of any and all language (they are not even the laws of metaphorical language, in which a man can be a tiger); they are the laws of precise language, and precise language is language which obeys those laws.

Seen functionally, the formal-logical characteristics of language are those which language assumes in the process of the forging of precision. We do not always want our language to be precise; imprecision is sometimes a virtue; but when we want precision, we must pay its price— we must subject ourselves to the discipline of the laws of formal logic.

That is exactly what science is compelled to do. Or at least, that is the ideal limit which scientific language approaches more closely than any other form of language.

2) The scientific context of language betrays itself by the periodic occurrence of words such as "hence," "therefore," "for." It is the language of inference, and inference needs these words. They are not the same as "if . . . then . . ." taken generally. "If it snows I shall freeze my toes" does not formulate an inference but an involvement. "If it snows I shall freeze my toes; it snows, hence I shall freeze my toes" formulates a logical deduction of freezing from snowing plus the involvement of freezing with snowing. "It snows; hence I shall freeze my toes" formulates an empirical inference from snowing to freezing.

Snowing implies freezing in the sense of involvement; snowing, together with the involvement of snowing and freezing, implies freezing in the sense of *logical* implication. In a logical implication, the denial of the conclusion *contradicts* the premises; in a factual or synthetic implication, such as is used to formulate an involvement, the denial of the conclusion does not contradict the premises; this was an important point in Hume's argument.

The idea of a contradiction is the obverse to the idea of an "analytic" connection. An analytic proposition, one might say, is one whose opposite is self-contradictory, like "All squares are square" (whose opposite is, "Something is both square and not square"). Besides analytic propositions there are synthetic propositions, whose opposites are not self-contradictory, like "All dogs bark" (whose opposite, "Something is a nonbarking dog," is not self-contradictory).

If there were no such thing as self-contradiction, there would be no such thing as contradiction, and hence no such thing as logical implication, and hence no such thing as a clearcut logical deduction of a conclusion from a given, limited set of premises. Hence, if there is going to be such a thing as a clearcut logical deduction of a conclusion from a given, limited set of premises, there has to be a clearcut sort of thing that we can call "self-contradiction"; hence, also, the sort of thing that we can call an "analytic proposition" (or a logical "tautology"). And, in between the self-contradiction and the analytic proposition, there then has to be such a thing as the synthetic proposition.

A familiar kind of instance of an analytic proposition is one which predicates a synonym, such as "All brothers are male siblings," or "All equilateral triangles are triangles whose sides are all equal to each other in length." In a sense, we can think of the existence of analytic propositions as depending upon the existence of synonymy, either partial or entire. "If an object is an apple, then it is a fruit" is analytic, not because being a fruit is synonymous entirely with being an apple, but because fruit is part of the meaning of "apple."

Thus, if there can be no synonymy, there can be no analytic propositions, and hence ultimately no clearcut logical deductions of the sort mentioned above. And, conversely, if there are to be such logical deductions, there must be the possibility of synonymy in our language. Indeed, logical deduction (the carrying out of inference based on logical implication) is, one may say, just a way of explicating parts or wholes of meaning, *i.e.,* of showing verbally the entire or partial synonymies of the expressions being employed.

That is why scientific language is characterized by the possibility of *translatability*. Science must be translatable, not because it must be understood by more than one person, but because it is the language of inference, and inference is efficient only when clearcut deduction is possible. If what is meant depends on the context and varies with it, if it depends on the tone and the time and the person, so that no statement is self-sufficient as a unit of meaning but only a large contexture of language will suffice (perhaps ultimately the whole of language, as W. V. Quine has attempted to argue), then such clearcut deduction becomes impossible. You never know what you are committing yourself to in agreeing to a given statement, for you do not know the entire context.

The language of literature is not the language of inference but the language of impressive effect. For it, only the whole context determines the effect, and perhaps even, as T. S. Eliot has maintained, only the larger traditional context is sufficient to get the total effect, to get at the writer's whole meaning.[20]

20 No poet, no artist of any art, has his complete meaning alone. His significance, his appreciation is the appreciation of his relation to the dead poets and artists. You cannot value him alone; you must set him, for contrast and comparison, among the dead. I mean this as a principle of aesthetic, not merely historical, criticism. The necessity that he shall conform, that he shall cohere, is not one-sided; what happens when a new work of art is created is something that happens simultaneously to all the works of art which preceded it. The existing monuments form an ideal order among themselves, which is modified by the in-

To the extent to which translatability is possible, to that extent each statement has its own self-contained meaning, which nevertheless can be re-expressed in another statement. To the extent to which the self-contained meaning of individual statements breaks down, and with it clearcut logical deducibility and the distinction between analytic and synthetic propositions, to that extent translatability vanishes. The tendency toward translatability, the analytic-synthetic distinction, the presence of logical implication and the employment of clearcut deductions is all of one piece as characteristic of a language whose *raison d'être* is inference; the opposed tendency, toward intranslatability, toward the subjugation of the analytic-synthetic distinction, logical implication and clearcut deduction in favor of totality and impressiveness of effect, is also of one piece, and is demanded by the nature of rhetorical organization.

7) The Linguistic PERSONA

Language, because it is the utterance of a person, bears in its constitution always the marks of personality. I mean by this not the obvious fact that to a trained scientist the linguistic gestures of a person are symptomatic of the personality, nor even that to an ordinarily, or more than ordinarily, sensitive person those linguistic gestures betray the speaker's inner condition. I mean rather the, perhaps equally obvious, fact that *in* the language, in the linguistic gesture itself, there is always present, explicitly or implicitly, a speaker. Sometimes he is represented by the use of the personal pronoun, sometimes not. Always he is present in the way in which the language goes, for always the language is *his*.

The most apparent difference between the linguistic person—which I suggest we call the *persona,* the *mask* uttering the language—and the author, may be found in dramatic dialogue, or dialogue in the novel, in which the speech is that of one of the characters. Here, whether or not

---

troduction of the new (the really new) work of art among them. The existing order is complete before the new work arrives; for order to persist after the supervention of novelty, the *whole* existing order must be, if ever so slightly, altered; and so the relations, proportions, values of each work of art towards the whole are readjusted; and this is conformity between the old and the new. Whoever has approved this idea of order, of the form of European or English literature will not find it preposterous that the past should be altered by the present as much as the present is directed by the past. And the poet who is aware of this will be aware of great difficulties and responsibilities.

T. S. Eliot, *The Sacred Wood; cf.* Allen, *op. cit.,* pp. 43–44.

there are reasons for supposing that the author wished to identify himself with the character, what the author would or could say for himself is distinct from what the character says *in persona propria*. The mask from which the utterance pours is one thing, the person of the author another. Such a difference of course occurs in ordinary language; we change our masks in accordance with the occasion.

One need not know, in order to appreciate properly Milton's *On His Deceased Wife,* that his second wife, Katharine Woodcock, died in childbirth in 1658; one need not read the sonnet as a direct communication from Milton to oneself. If all knowledge of Milton's existence were destroyed, and the sonnet's author were labelled "anonymous," no really essential esthetic consequences would ensue. There is a person in the language; there is a character uttering his dream and his sentiment; this is all the person one needs.[21]

Scientific language is not without its mask. But, as science finds itself under the compulsion of separating its language from the content of its utterance, so also it is forced to separate the mask from the content. The linguistic *persona* is not part of the involvement pattern. He exhausts himself in his task of formulating the pattern and the corresponding inferences. Hence, also, being no part of the involvement pattern, *differences* in mask involve no differences in asserted content. Personal differences are ineffectual so far as the involvement pattern is concerned. *Therefore* they are irrelevant; and the introduction of them is the introduction of an irrelevancy, sometimes annoying, sometimes a hindrance, sometimes pleasing, but always an irrelevancy.

This is perhaps too strong. There are alternative possibilities in the linguistic formulation of scientific results: one can choose one's geometry, one's mathematics in general, one's favorite kind of theory,

---

[21]For the sake of having it present, I reproduce the poem:

> Methought I saw my late espoused saint
> Brought to me like Alcestis from the grave,
> Whom Jove's great son to her glad husband gave,
> Rescued from Death by force, though pale and faint.
> Mine, as whom washed from spot of childbed taint
> Purification in the old law did save,
> And such as yet once more I trust to have
> Full sight of her in Heaven without restraint,
> Came vested all in white, pure as her mind.
> Her face was veiled; yet to my fancied sight
> Love, sweetness, goodness, in her person shined
> So clear as in no face with more delight.
> But, oh! as to embrace me she inclined,
> I waked, she fled, and day brought back my night.

one's vocabulary. But, on the whole, as such choices can hardly remain merely personal (in the sense of individual) but require to be shared by the community of scientists, there is a powerful brake on variation.

The scientific *persona* thus tends to be highly impersonal and stereotyped; he does not utter his emotions because such utterance would not function for his purpose, as a judge does not utter his personal predilections because they are irrelevant to the passing of legal judgment. The scientific mask is impassive, neither stern nor mild, but direct, open, uncomplicated; it is the visage of the Truth of Fact.

On the other hand, the masks of literary language are many. They are many because they need to be many, because literature is under the compulsion of making its language part of its content. Compare, for instance, Herrick's *Upon the Loss of His Mistress* with Milton's sonnet.[22] One is confronted by two *personae* as far apart as fire and flowers: one compact of deep passion, steady devotion, sturdy faith, the other of fitful infatuation, pagan sensuousness, cleverness. The difference is audible in the rhythmic patterns, the use of classical allusions, the rhymes (how different the effects of "all-principal," "wit-it" from "shined-inclined," "delight-night"), Milton's dramatic shift to the minor key in the last two lines and Herrick's affected close on sorrow and death in the last four.

The literary mask is an inseparable part of literary content; it is an ingredient in the constitution of the whole-of-effect. There is, in literature, the constant demand, therefore, that it submit to the conditions of functional fitness. For instance, the question of the point of view in the novel (or story writing generally) represents one aspect of this comprehensive problem of the mask. Since it is possible to tell a story in different ways, from the internal viewpoint of a leading or subordinate participant in the happenings, or from an external viewpoint,

---

[22]   I have lost, and lately, these
Many dainty mistresses:
Stately Julia, prime of all;
Sapho next, a principal;
Smooth Anthea, for a skin
White and heaven-like crystalline;
Sweet Electra, and the choice
Myrha, for the lute and voice.
Next, Corinna, for her wit,
And the graceful use of it;
With Perilla: all are gone,
Only Herrick's left alone,
For to number sorrow by
Their departures hence, and die.

and since in either case the narrator will have some personality or other, with some orientation of interests, some degree of penetration, some set of moral and religious allegiances, some manner of sensibility, and will have to be made to some degree concrete, it is a question of choice of the right combination, a question no different in essence from that of choice of *le mot juste*.[23] Flaubert's remark that the artist "should be in his work, like God in creation, invisible and all powerful; he should be felt everywhere and seen nowhere," is a statement of esthetic faith and purpose, governed by the esthetic goal of justice and impartiality; it is a remark on the functional fitness of the omniscient external viewpoint. Within the same area of discussion of functional fitness of viewpoint is E. M. Forster's defense of the shifting viewpoint:

> . . . for me the "whole intricate question of method" resolves itself not into formulae but into the power of the writer to bounce the reader into accepting what he says. . . . I should put (this power) plumb in the centre. Look how Dickens bounces us in *Bleak House*. Chapter I of *Bleak House* is omniscient. Dickens takes us into the Court of Chancery and rapidly explains all the people there. In Chapter II he is partially omniscient. We still use his eyes, but for some unexplained reason they begin to grow weak: he can explain Sir Leicester Dedlock to us, part of Lady Dedlock but not all, and nothing of Mr. Tulkinghorn. In Chapter III he is even more reprehensible: he goes straight across into the dramatic method and inhabits a young lady, Esther Summersun. "I have a great deal of difficulty in beginning to write my portion of these pages, for I know I am not clever," pipes up Esther, and continues in this strain with consistency and competence, so long as she is allowed to hold the pen. At any moment the author of her being may snatch it from her, and run about taking notes himself, leaving her seated goodness knows where, and employed we do not care how. Logically, *Bleak House* is all to pieces, but Dickens bounces us, so that we do not mind the shiftings of the view point. . . .
>
> A novelist can shift his view point if it comes off, and it came off with Dickens. . . . Indeed this power to expand and contract perception (of which the shifting viewpoint is a symptom), this right to intermittent knowledge:—I find it one of the great advantages of the novel-form, and it has a parallel in our perception of life. We are

[23]There is, of course, always the possibility of adopting a shifting point of view, in which case there are a number of masks, even of masks behind masks with one mask behind all the rest.

stupider at some times than others; we can enter into people's minds occasionally but not always, because our own minds get tired; and this intermittence lends in the long run variety and colour to the experiences we receive.[24]

It would be a mistake to suppose that the viewpoint is something peculiar to prose narration; it is present in all poetry and in drama as well—in the perspective, the attitude, the mode of sympathy, reaching down into details of the manner of dialogue and monologue—in the end, in all of literature. It is so for the reason stated above, that language is utterance and that language is inseparably a part of the content of literature.

This functional omnipresence of the *persona* in literary language leads to an important aspect of literary communication. All language is communicative. Scientific language is communicative, as well as literary language. But there is a significant difference.

In communication we are brought to a consciousness of an object from a point of view. What is communicated is not an object that can be separated from a perspective upon it, but only a compound of object and viewpoint. (One may, of course, if one wishes, include the viewpoint in the total esthetic object; and one would then distinguish in the total object between the objective and subjective aspects of the object. This is merely a matter of words.)

It follows that the *total* "effect" in literature (inclusive of all partial effects) is always of the nature of a "vision." However distant and detached, however merely contemplative our attitude be in reading literature, there must always be some degree of empathy, of *"verstehen,"* of living oneself into the point of view, of having the vision. Without it communication fails and literature disappears.

There is such an element in scientific communication, but it is reduced, in accordance with the demands of efficiency, to the vision of implications and significances (empirical inferences and involvements). Every other factor in vision is played down in science, on purpose. (There is nothing wrong about this. It is necessary.)

This is the reason why scientific language is impersonal and literary language is personal. To be personal, literary language does not have to be impassioned, highly emotional, fervid, or hysterical. The language

[24]E. M. Forster, *Aspects of the Novel,* Harcourt, Brace & Company, New York, 1927, pp. 118–123.

of wit may be perfectly moderated and controlled; and a restrained simplicity may be more powerful than the wildest flourish:

> So here I am, in the middle way, having had twenty
>   years—
> Twenty years largely wasted, the years of *l'entre deux*
>   *guerres*—
> Trying to learn to use words, and every attempt
> Is a wholly new start, and a different kind of failure
> Because one has only learnt to get the better of words
> For the thing one no longer has to say, or the way in
>   which
> One is no longer disposed to say it. And so each venture
> Is a new beginning, a raid on the inarticulate
> With shabby equipment always deteriorating
> In the general mess of imprecision of feeling,
> Undisciplined squads of emotion.[25]

The consequences of this difference in communicativeness of scientific and literary language for their respective functions in life cannot be overstated.

Science is an extension, through the use of the powers of the intellect, of animal readiness to act upon the significances of things. Its dominant function is the development for the human mind of schemes by which the mind can estimate the probable consequences of given conditions. There is, as I have said, an element of vision in it; and persons who devote themselves to science as a career find in this vision a certain interest of a sort continuous with the interest all find in esthetic vision. But that, while an important function for the scientific thinker, is a function of secondary importance in the life of men, as whole men and taken together.

Science does not make men respond to the significances of things in one way or another; it gives them those significances and they respond in accordance with their interests and bents.

Literature, while it also makes use of scientific significances (to a limited extent, the limitation varying with its esthetic purpose), communicates things that are in some way important: it communicates things in their impressiveness, their qualities in experience, their values, together with modes of realizing such qualities and values. In this re-

[25]T. S. Eliot, "East Coker," V, from *Four Quartets,* Harcourt, Brace & Company, New York, 1943, pp. 16–17; but there is a bit of posing in this that robs it of pureness.

spect, the scientific communication of intellectual vision falls under the general heading of literary communication, and is one part of it. But literature ranges far and wide in communicating different modes of vision and value.

Literature does not make men respond to the qualities and values of things in one way or another; it gives them those qualities and values, and they respond in accordance with their interests and bents.

But the difference between science and literature on this score remains substantial. For literary communication, by leading to the cultivation of different viewpoints as well as different subjects, by leading us from *persona* to *persona,* is a great laboratory of the human spirit. Where science narrows down its *persona* to the one impassive type, literature opens up the possibility of "understanding" (in the sense of Dilthey's *"verstehen"*) the multifarious forms of the spirit. It thereby offers the possibility of that refinement of sensibility which is one, though not all, of the necessary conditions for attaining the status of authentic humanness.

8) *Retrospect and Prospect*

In the foregoing remarks I have attempted to sketch briefly the outlines of a comparative functional treatment of some of the differences between the languages of science and of literature: in particular, differences in i) the relation of medium to content and ii) the organization of subject-matter and medium, specifically the differences of involutional-logical and rhetorical organization, leading to iii) differences in regard to precision, translatability, and personality of language.

These are plainly only a few of the many facets of both languages which can be studied in a functional manner, and there is much more to be said about them than the short, crude remarks here made. It is my belief that research directed along these lines, however, can be of aid in our understanding of the nature of the languages of science and literature—and of other areas of experience as well, law, morality, and religion, for instance.

There is an underlying and pervasive question of method which arises in the context of functional explanation and which must become a matter of constant preoccupation. It is a question of the relation between the conception of the end and the conception of the characteristics of the subject-matter to be explained by their role in the attainment or constitution of the end. The temptation is to fix upon some conception of the end beforehand, *a priori,* and then—without consideration of any change in that conception due to the investigation—to proceed to relate the characteristics to it.

The danger is that the facts of the case may be sacrificed or distorted in the interest of maintaining an initial conception of the end. To be sure, the end initially entertained may be the result of induction: it is said that Aristotle's conception of the substantive content and psychological effect of tragedy was an induction from the experience of the Greek audience with its great tragedies. The actual text of the *Poetics,* however, does not make manifest any serious inductive investigation undertaken by Aristotle; and it remains a question whether, for instance, the arousal of pity and fear (and their purgation through this means) was in actual fact either the intention of the Greeks or their actual dramatic experience.

Moreover, ends and means in language (as in all human behavior and experience) are not easily separated. Perhaps the best way to reach a conception of the end is by examination of the means so as to see what is and can be accomplished by them. Take, for instance, our initial formulation of the end in literature (pp. 294–295) as "the creation of an intrinsically interesting imaginative construction," or the later formulation of it in the garb of a definition of rhetorical order (p. 307) as an ordering of materials "in such a way as to result in the building of a whole for an experiencer, a whole which becomes intrinsically impressive and interesting to the experiencer and in which the parts . . . give to each other and the whole, and derive from each other and the whole, their own interest within that whole," or the briefer version of rhetorical order (p. 307) as an ordering in which an effect is produced which is intrinsically impressive, interesting, arresting, vital.

I would not boast about the theoretical pregnancy of these formulations. They suffer from what Hegel would have called "abstractness": they do not in themselves suggest the detailed constituents or the detailed ordering of the whole which they try to denote. The problem is, how to achieve a comprehensive formulation of the end which would so relate it to the means that it would be "concrete" rather than "abstract," that it would make fruitful reference to the inner articulation of the denoted whole.

If now we look at one of the characteristics to be accounted for, say the nature, place, and function of the *persona* in language, we see that the extent to which that phenomenon is studied determines the extent to which the effects achievable by language can be, on that side, concretely understood. If, as I have noted, *no* element of literary language is immune from exploitation as material for the total effect, then the *persona* also is not immune. It follows that the way or ways in which the *persona* does or can operate *must* constitute one aspect of the end of the literary use of language. Hence a more concrete account of the end of literature than any of those I have formulated would include a reference to this factor. It would take up and give serious weight to a point which I have only mentioned (p. 331), namely, that "the *total* 'effect' in literature (inclusive of all partial effects) is always of the nature of a 'vision.'" It would have to spell out what "vision" is, and how other effects fall within the compass of "vision." In this way, research into the details of means and characteristics—undertaken perhaps under the guidance of an initially inadequate conception of the end—would react to throw light upon the end and lead to a better formulation of it. Thus while in one sense the fact that poetry uses metaphor or personification or rhythm is explained by reference to a poetic end, in another sense the nature of the poetic end can be discovered only by examination of what metaphor, personification, rhythm are and can do.

These remarks hold not only of the language of literature, but of that of science and of every other field of human experience, and, more generally, of the whole attempt to deal with expressive human experience, *i.e.,* experience in which human beings make a content in and for experience by the use of materials as a medium.

Comment by Stanley Edgar Hyman:
   Albert Hofstadter's definition of art as "an intrinsically interesting imaginative construction" seems to smuggle in the idea, in that word "intrinsically," that this interest inheres in the work independent of audience or observer. Hofstadter specifically disclaims this when he introduces the "experiencer," and defines "intrinsically" to mean "that it *itself* is interesting, not that something else is interesting to which it leads or points." At this point I would be tempted to give up my resistance to the word as an insignificant terminological quibble, did he not shortly after quote without protest Poe's account of the creation of "The Raven," which argues precisely those stylistic absolutes, independent of the experiencer, to which I feel his "intrinsically" opens the door. With the tentativeness befitting a literary man arguing matters of vocabulary with a professor of philosophy, I would suggest that Hofstadter might avoid starting some of these hares by substituting some less misleading word or phrase for that "intrinsically," perhaps *"per se."*

[Also see comment by M. L. Rosenthal, Appendix IV, pp. 561–577, esp. pp. 563–572.]

CHAPTER XI

The Literary Symbol

By WILLIAM Y. TINDALL

THAT SYMBOLS offer ways of presenting thought and feeling and of celebrating or constructing suitable worlds, though plain to Moses and other authors before the time of Blake, has been plainer since then. Melville, Baudelaire, and Ibsen come readily to mind, but the twentieth century, which is my principal interest, brought with it an even thicker crowd of romantic symbolists, including the greatest writers of our period. Not only Yeats and Joyce, Valéry and Proust, Wallace Stevens and Faulkner, Mann, Kafka, and Conrad—all writers of the first order —but even more popular, though no less important, writers such as F. Scott Fitzgerald and T. S. Eliot, making symbolic worlds of symbolic elements, have shaped our vision of reality.

Consider Dr. T. J. Eckleburg's eyes in *The Great Gatsby:*

> About half way between West Egg and New York the motor road hastily joins the railroad and runs beside it for a quarter of a mile, so as to shrink away from a certain desolate area of land. This is a valley of ashes—a fantastic farm where ashes grow like wheat into ridges and hills and grotesque gardens; where ashes take the forms of houses. . . . But above the gray land and the spasms of bleak dust which drift endlessly over it, you perceive, after a moment, the eyes of Doctor T. J. Eckleburg. The eyes of Doctor T. J. Eckleburg are blue and gigantic— their retinas are one yard high. They look out of no face, but, instead, from a pair of enormous yellow spectacles which pass over a nonexistent nose. Evidently some wild wag of an oculist set them there to fatten his practice in the borough of Queens, and then sank down himself into eternal blindness, or forgot them and moved away. But his eyes, dimmed a little by many paintless days, under sun and rain, brood on over the solemn dumping ground.[1]

We may not know precisely what symbols are or what they "mean," but Fitzgerald's desolating image, which recurs throughout the novel,

[1]F. Scott Fitzgerald, *The Great Gatsby,* Charles Scribner's Sons, New York, 1925, p. 27.

is what most would call a symbol. If this vision of eyes is a functioning part of a larger structure, as the single eye on a signboard in the last part of Faulkner's *The Sound and the Fury* or the eyes of Beatrice in Eliot's *The Hollow Men* are obscurely portentous but essential constituents of that novel and this poem, it becomes apparent that symbols may serve as elements of a work. That the work itself may be as symbolic as its elements is not unlikely.

The Cocktail Party seems a symbol composed of symbols, not there to be explained but to play their part in a conspiracy. Peripheral suggestions of gin and water, of making dishes out of nothing, and of single eyes may limit or deepen the total effect and excite the critic, but the audience, taking them as they come, enjoys the experience to which they contribute. As if referring to members of this audience, Eliot's Thomas Becket says: "They know and do not know."

The masters of those who know tell us that symbolmaking is our natural activity and our condition. Catching up with artists or trying to account for them, recent philosophers provide an assurance that the value we place on symbols is not misplaced. Whitehead regards symbolism, if I understand him correctly, as a mode of perception and a cause of error, but, although he talks about literature at times, he is too general and indifferent to help us with the literary symbol. Ernst Cassirer, who seems more to the point, says man is a symbolic animal whose languages, myths, religions, sciences, and arts are symbolic forms by which he projects his reality and comes to know it: "What reality is apart from these forms is irrelevant."

As these philosophers assure us, all perception, all our fanatical pursuits, and all our arts may be symbolic in some fundamental sense at all times, but at certain times symbolism has become conscious and deliberate. It is with one of these periods that I am concerned and with one of the arts. Before trying to define the literary symbol as it is used in our time, I must try to explain symbol and tell the difference between symbol and sign or at least fix their usage. Webster says that a symbol is "That which stands for or suggests something else by reason of relationship, association, convention or accidental but not intentional resemblance; especially, a visible sign of something invisible, as an idea, a quality or a totality such as a state or a church." Something that stands for or suggests something else is a good definition of the word as we use it in the marketplace but too general and maybe too clear for the closet. I prefer "a visible sign of something invisible," although this would seem to exclude unwritten music or music as we hear it. Webster's echo of the catechism or the prayerbook might be intensified and the definition made more inclusive by saying that a symbol is the outward sign of an inward state. By inward state I refer to feeling or thought or a combination of the two. However, this gets us, as it got Webster, into trouble with the word sign.

The words symbol and sign are commonly interchangeable yet at times some of us mean one thing by sign and another by symbol. That is a cause of trouble and this is another: sign, taken to mean an exact reference, may include symbol, and symbol, taken to mean a suggestive device, may include sign. Since Dr. T. J. Eckleburg's eyes occupy a signboard, they are plainly a sign, yet we agree or, I think, should agree that they are as plainly a symbol, which, in this case, must consist of a sign. If we define sign as an exact reference, it must include symbol because a symbol is an exact reference, too. The difference is that a sign is an exact reference to something definite and a symbol is an exact reference to something indefinite. Less of a paradox than they seem, exact and indefinite will get along more comfortably together if we consider the senses of exact, one of which is suitable. Dr. Eckleburg's eyes are a sign referring to Dr. Eckleburg and his business. As a symbol they suggest, to use Webster's word, more thoughts and feelings than we could state; for if we stated as many as we could—the wasteland, the suburb, the modern world, futility, or moral censure—some would be left over and some would remain unstatable.

As I shall use it, the word sign means a one-to-one correspondence. Example: the American flag is a sign of the United States, used to identify post offices, income tax bureaus, and ships. The flag may also suggest Iwo Jima, General Grant's cigar, and graduation day—as the sign "Times Square" on that corner suggests as much as it indicates. The sign may have symbolic values, but ignoring connotations, overtones, and suggestions, I shall regard the sign as a pointer. Indifferent to the sign as symbol or as the container of a symbol, I prefer to look at the symbol as a container of a sign, upon the flag, for example, as a symbol which happens by proximity to indicate a post office. Those eyes as suggesters of many things, some of them nameless, seem more entertaining than as references to an oculist.

If we receive sign as pointer and my variation upon Webster's second try as an approximate account of symbol, we may accost art as symbol and symbol in the arts. According to Cassirer's *Essay on Man,* as we have seen, art is a symbolic form, parallel in respect of this to religion or science. Each of these forms builds up a universe that enables man to interpret and organize his experience; and each is a discovery, because a creation, of reality. Although similar in function, the forms differ in the kind of reality built. Whereas science builds it of facts, art builds it of feelings, intuitions of quality, and the other distractions of our inner life—and in their degrees so do myth and religion. What art, myth, and religion are, Cassirer confesses, cannot be expressed by a logical definition.

Nevertheless, let us see what Clive Bell says about art. He calls it "significant form," but what that is he is unable to say. Having no quarrel with art as form, we may, however, question its significance. By significant he cannot mean important in the sense of having import, nor can he mean having the function of a sign; for to him art, lacking reference to nature, is insignificant. Since, however, he tells us that a work of art "expresses" the emotion of its creator and "provokes" an emotion in its contemplator, he seems to imply that his significant means expressive and provocative. The emotion expressed and provoked is an "esthetic emotion," contemplative, detached from all concerns of utility and from all reference.

Attempting to explain Bell's significant form, Roger Fry, equally devoted to Whistler and art for art's sake, says that Flaubert's "expression of the idea" is as near as he can get to it, but neither Flaubert nor Fry tells us what is meant by idea. To "evoke" it, however, the artist creates an "expressive design" or "symbolic form," by which the spirit "communicates its most secret and indefinable impulses."

Susanne K. Langer, who occupies a place somewhere between Fry and Cassirer, though nearer the latter, once said in a seminar that a work of art is an "unassigned syntactical symbol." Since this definition does not appear in her latest book, she may have rejected it, but it seems more nearly precise than Fry's attempt. By "unassigned" she probably intends insignificant in the sense of lacking sign-value or fixed reference; "syntactical" implies a form composed of parts in relationship to one another; and a symbol, according to *Feeling and Form,* is "any device whereby we are enabled to make an abstraction." Too austere for my taste, this account of symbol seems to need elaboration, which, to be sure, her book provides. For the present, however, taking symbol to mean an outward device for presenting an inward state, and taking unassigned and syntactical as I think she uses them, let us tentatively admire her definition of the work of art.

Parallel symbolic forms, says Mrs. Langer, the arts differ from one another in materials and in what is symbolized. As music uses sounds, painting colors, and sculpture stuff, so literature uses words to create an image of time, space, or dynamic patterns of feeling. Music attends to virtual time, painting to the semblance of space, and literature to vital patterns. However referential or discursive the materials and elements or constituent parts of painting or literature, these arts are as irrelevant and nondiscursive as music.

Words, which she finds trivial in themselves, seem more than materials of literature. Its elements may be character, action, and image; but words, more than the matter from which these elements that compose the form are made, also serve as elements in their own right as her metaphor of syntax should imply. Poetry is made of words, as Mallarmé once observed, not of ideas; and according to Conrad, words are "symbols of life," having power in "their sound or their aspect to present the very thing." Since things as they are exist in words and by them, he continues, words must be treated with reverence lest "the image of truth abiding in facts" be injured. The potency of the real thing, Cassirer agrees in *Language and Myth,* is contained in the word that creates it. If language, as he says elsewhere, is a symbolic form, literature uses elements of one symbolic form as those of another. Words are symbols, but like most symbols they are not without significance or sign-value, as the grammarian's connotation and denotation imply. If words are elements as well as materials of literature, a poem, differing in this respect from a sonata or a plastic abstraction, is a symbolic whole composed in part of references. At once assigned and unassigned, literature troubles esthetic philosophers and moralists alike.

My interest in literature is not that of the philosopher, still less that of the moralist. Cassirer talks about art in general as symbolic form, and Mrs. Langer about poems as symbols, whereas I have in mind not only that but the symbolic elements that compose the poem. My examination of the literary symbol proceeds from constituent images to whole works. Since the image is an approximate epitome of the whole, we may acquire understanding of the literary symbol from a return to Dr. Eckleburg's eyes.

Taking that signboard as the image, we recognize it as a definite object or at least as the semblance of an object, to which, nothing much in itself, experience and memory have given import. We know that eyes, even virtual eyes, are for looking, watching, rebuking; and with them we associate many other activities and attitudes, which we can feel more easily than explain. If the signboard were alone in a kind of nothing, we might not know which of these implications to pick from memory or feeling and which to reject. Situated as it is, however, near a commuter's railroad between Wall Street and a suburb, near a highway for homing brokers, and in the middle of a waste of ashes and shacks, which is presented by charged, desolating words, that signboard or rather its meaning is at once enriched and limited by context. I agree that this would be no less true if the signboard found itself in a kind of nothing, for nothing as context becomes something. No constituent image is without context and every image owes context part of what it bears. Since context owes as much to image, the roads and ashes and all the implied commuters acquire import from those eyes. By reciprocal limitation and expansion, image and context, two interacting components of what they create, carry feelings and thoughts at once definite and indefinite. The composite of image and context constitutes a symbol.

This image in context is an element of *The Great Gatsby,* but if it is an epitome of the symbolic whole in which it functions, it is no more than approximate; for although work and image alike are made up of elements which, working together, present a feeling and maybe an idea, the constituent image has immediate literary context and the work has not. Of course we may take the state of society, the literary tradition, what we know of the hand that wrote the book and what we feel of the hand that holds it, time, place, and the weather as a kind of context with which the work may interact; but such circumstance, of the sort that surrounds all our affairs, is too general and remote to serve as more than a parallel to the surroundings of Dr. Eckleburg's signboard. The work as symbol, therefore, differs from the image as symbol in lacking the limitation and enlargement provided by immediate context. Work and image may have similar syntactical structure and function, but without immediate context, the work, less narrowly directed, is harder to apprehend. This lack is more or less supplied by the greater richness and complexity of the internal relationships that, providing control and enhancement, compose the whole.

The literary symbol, whether a work or one of its parts, is clearly an embodiment. As the spirit or vital principle occupies our bodies and shines out, so thought and feeling occupy the form, shape, or body that we call symbol. With the symbol or something like it in mind, Shakespeare's Theseus in *A Midsummer-Night's Dream,* considering madmen and poets, speaks of "shaping fantasies, that apprehend more than cool reason ever comprehends."

> And, as imagination bodies forth
> The forms of things unknown, the poet's pen
> Turns them to shapes, and gives to airy nothing
> A local habitation and a name.

If we may take these verses as references to the literary symbol, it is a thing made by the shaping imagination to body forth an unknown airy nothing. Although made by the poet's pen and composed of words, these words, no longer in the service of cool or discursive reason, serve nondiscursive purposes; neither practical nor logical, the poet's speech is the builder of symbolic forms. Shakespeare again has the words for this kind of speech, no longer speech but shape, in *The Tempest,* where, speaking of shapes, gesture, and sound, one of his people calls this nondiscursive though expressive form "A kind of excellent dumb discourse."

Unlike the sign, which interests us less for what it is than what it points to, this dumb discourse is interesting in itself. Unlike the sign, it cannot be separated from what it stands for; for it is what it stands for or else part of it by a kind of synecdoche. Not entirely translatable and without substitute, it resists what Wilbur Marshall Urban in *Language and Reality* calls "expansion." That transcendental philosopher, who believes that a symbol is a "condensation of meaning, of unexpressed reference," holds that it may be "expanded into expressed reference" or discourse. If that were so, there would be no need to employ symbols; for as the dancer said, "If I (could say what) it meant, I would not have to dance it." Justly rebuked for those notions, Urban has retired to the arms of New Critics. But the symbol remains, calling for explanation and resisting it. Though definite in itself and generally containing a sign which may be identified, the symbol carries something indeterminate and, however we try, there is a residual mystery that escapes our intellects. As Carlyle said, and what he said is true to our impression, the symbol at once reveals and conceals.

The symbol conceals what it carries and resists total explanation because it is founded upon analogy, which, philosophers say, is primitive, childish, and irrational. Cassirer has told how primitive man confused analogy with fact, and Whitehead, seeking things as they are, has found in analogy a cause of modern error; but men of letters, recovering an ancient illusion, have made of it a device for presenting apprehensions, counteracting the world of fact, and creating something more suitable. If symbol is analogy, it is related to metaphor, but the account of that relationship can wait for a while. For the present it is enough to say that the symbol seems a metaphor one half of which remains unstated and indefinite. As in metaphor, the halves of the equation may be related by partial similarity, which is qualitative at times and structural or functional at others, but hardly ever imitative or representative. Dr. Eckleburg's eyes and their environment are an analogy for an unexpressed feeling and thought about our condition, not an imitation of it.

The creator of such a symbol is not unlike Henry James's antique dealer, who, taking the golden bowl from its box, "left the important object—for as 'important' it did somehow present itself—to produce its certain effect." Since the writer displays his important object to a reader for enjoyment or interpretation, the relations of writer and reader to symbol and to each other must be examined. Does the writer use a symbol to express what he cannot say discursively or does he create it to find in the process of embodiment what he wants to say? *Express* is a common term and not altogether inaccurate; but I doubt that a writer, unless writing discourse or allegory, tries first of all to express himself. He tries to create something to embody and discover his concerns, and he is often astonished at the expressive adequacy of what he has made. Now independent of him, his creation and maybe his expression, the symbol he has made offers something, and not necessarily what he puts or finds in it, to the reader. Does the symbol *evoke* something from the reader, *suggest* something to him, or *create* something in him? Does it *present* or *represent* something to him? These verbs, which are tricky, have been generally used to define the relationship of symbol and reader. Although the symbol may represent something to him in the sense of stand for or exhibit, plainly it does not re-present it but presents it for the first time unless the symbol is traditional and commonplace. Moreover the word *represent* has unfortunate associations with "representative art." *Evoke,* used by Mallarmé, Yeats, and Eliot, is a metaphor taken from magic to fix our impression of something called from us by symbol, but this word puts more emphasis upon our reaction than upon the symbol, which, more than a stimulus, is, after all, the important thing. There before us like a fact, it is indeed a fact in the sense of something made or a fiction, though our reaction to it may be eccentric or irrelevant. Many have called the symbol a device for suggesting more than it says. *Suggest* is a better word than evoke; for by its root it means to carry, and the symbol not only presents something to us but carries it. *Create* may also refer to symbol and reader; as the artist creates it, so it may create something that we have never encountered before. Letting poets use *evoke* and critics use *represent,* I shall try to confine myself to *create, present,* and *suggest,* and if I use *express* or *mean* and the like, it will be loosely, to avoid monotony, and in spite of Ogden and Richards.

Once I thought of beginning my essay in this fashion: the literary symbol is indefinite, and, logicians tell me, the indefinite cannot be defined. That would have exempted me from attempting a definition, which, if we may judge by previous attempts, is difficult and unsatisfactory. Second thought, however, made it clear that the symbol, though offering the indefinite, is definite enough in itself to demand definition. Here is a provisional one, which must be restricted in places and expanded in others by my essay as a whole:

The literary symbol, an analogy for something unstated, consists of an articulation of verbal elements that, going beyond reference and the limits of discourse, embodies and offers a complex of feeling and thought. Not necessarily an image, this analogical embodiment may also be a rhythm, a juxtaposition, an action, a proposition, a structure, or a poem. One half of this peculiar analogy embodies the other, and the symbol is what it symbolizes.

I am afraid that my definition, hopelessly general, might fit all literature at all times; for, according to it, "Jack and Jill went up the hill" is plainly symbolic, and since words are symbolic, other literature is symbolic, too. But there are differences in degree between *Tom Jones,* let us say, and *Moby Dick.* What I have in mind is less literature in general than *symbolist* literature, my term for writing deliberately symbolic and for writing in symbolist periods which, though not necessarily deliberate, takes its method from current practice. Most of the writers I shall consider are conscious symbolists—not that it matters whether they are or not; for what matters is the kind of thing they made. I think we can recognize the difference in degree that separates their work, if it is symbolist, from *Tom Jones,* which may be symbolic. The mark of distinction is embodied or immanent analogy.

Returning to the conscious or unconscious use of analogy, let us consider the statements of four symbolists. In a letter to Mrs. Hawthorne about *Moby Dick,* Melville said:

> Your allusion for example to the "Spirit Spout" first showed to me that there was a subtle significance in that thing—but I did not, in that case, *mean* it. I had some vague idea while writing it, that the whole book was susceptible of an allegoric construction, & also that *parts* of it were—but the speciality of many of the particular subordinate allegories, were first revealed to me, after reading Mr. Hawthorne's letter, which, without citing any particular examples, yet intimated the part-&-parcel allegoricalness of the whole.

By allegory he meant, I think, what we mean by symbol. Happy to discover what he had made and tolerantly aware that what his creation carries is an affair between the reader and a book, no longer the creator's but an object for creating feelings and ideas in others, Meville appears to have been no more than partly conscious of what he was creating. In his Preface to *Paludes,* an early work, André Gide says:

> Before explaining my book to others, I wait for them to explain it to me. To explain it first is to limit its sense; for if we know what we wished to say, we do not know if we have said only that.—One always says more than that.—And my interest is what I have put into the work without knowing it,—the unconscious part that I like to call God's.—A book is always a collaboration, and the greater its value, the smaller the part of the scribe. As we expect all things in nature to reveal themselves, so let us expect our books to be revealed by readers.[2]

Speaking in a letter of the symbolic character of all art and of unconscious and conscious symbolism, D. H. Lawrence said that while much of his own symbolism was intentional, some of it escaped his notice until later. In an interview William Faulkner, speaking of how critics take his images, said: "I'm just a writer. Not a literary man. . . . Maybe all sorts of symbols and images get in. I don't know. When a good car-

2André Gide, *Paludes,* Gallimard, Paris, 1941.

penter builds something, he puts the nails where they belong. Maybe they make a fancy pattern when he's through, but that's not why he put them in that way." Although Faulkner's statements to his public not uncommonly reveal tongue in cheek, maybe those nails are an analogy for analogies.

Whether consciously, unconsciously, or with a profession of this or that, authors make symbols and readers receive them. We must discover, if we can, the function of symbols and for whom they are designed. As for the second of these, a symbol in a novel may serve a character, the author, the reader, or the critic.

Some symbols, plainly for a character in the book, are there to carry something to him and by his reaction to enlighten us about him. If like the elderly gentleman in Joyce's "An Encounter," the character responds to hair and whips, we understand his nature a little better. To find how the symbol serves the author we must consult psychology and history (which I do not propose to do here); for time and fixation may determine usage. Beyond these he may use symbols to embody what he cannot think, to discover what he feels or to express it, or, if he is an artist like Faulkner, to function as elements in a design. Convinced of the inadequacy of discourse for all that lies outside the rational and the prosaic or persuaded that things as they are are not entirely explicable, he may resort to analogical embodiment, which is useful, too, for supplementing a discursive meaning with overtones, qualities, and implications beyond logical handling. "Where there is an obscurity too deep for our Reason," says Sir Thomas Browne, " 'tis good to sit down with (an) . . . adumbration." Dissatisfied with what is, the author may use the symbol to create something better. For the philosopher, the psychologist, or the historian it is all right to inquire into the relation of author to symbol, but not for the critic, lest he commit the "intentional fallacy."

To a point the reader may share the author's concerns and find in the symbol a reminder of his own; but for him the principal function of symbol is organizing his experience and enlarging it. This supposes apprehension of the symbol, but even if careless of it, the reader may respond beneath the level of awareness and find himself surprised by an enrichment he cannot account for. Perhaps this is the commonest and best way to take symbolist writing. For critics, however, unawareness is a fault. Their response to symbolism, far keener than that of most authors and readers, is of two kinds: exercising ingenuity as over a puzzle, they may explain meaning and reduce embodiment to discourse; or, if esthetic, they may try to fix the function of parts in the whole.

For author and reader the symbol is unitive. By its roots, as the dictionary tells us, the word symbol means throwing or putting together. Taken from one realm of experience, vegetable nature, for example, to serve in another, let us say the moral, the symbol joins those realms. By uniting the separate it can organize experience into a kind of order and, revealing the complex relationships among seemingly divided things, confer peace. Men of God praise the symbol's mediatory power. Whether verbal or iconographic, the religious symbol, and the political, too, can unite man with man and man with something greater than he, society or God. Jung, speaking of the symbol as reconciler, finds it uniting the unconscious with the conscious, and Whitehead finds it connecting modes of experience. In a world as scattered as our own this ability is not without value. More important or at least more immediate for us is the power of the symbol to put parts of a literary work together in the service of the whole.

The symbol may put things together, but we must find if it puts author and reader together by establishing communication between them. This problem, approached when we noticed the verbs used to express the relationship of author, symbol, and reader, must be faced. The trouble with the symbol as a communicator is that, although definite in being the semblance of an articulated object, it is indefinite in what it presents. In the first place the symbol is an analogy for something undefined and in the second our apprehension of the analogy is commonly incomplete. Moreover, the terms of the analogy are confused. Since one is embodied in the other, our search for a meaning apart from the embodiment must return to it and we are left with a form, at once definite and indefinite, and significant perhaps only by seeming important.

For communication there must be reference to actuality or to something accepted. The symbol may communicate by incorporating a sign or a traditional association. In so far as it has significance in the sense of containing a sign, it may unite author, reader, and fact, but significance is the symbol's lesser part. The greater part, remaining mysterious, carries no guarantee of communicating. As we have seen, the author's community with his symbol is often incomplete; therefore what passes between him and the reader through intermediary embodiment must be less nearly complete. When we pass beyond significance, communication is uncertain or partial at best. What the reader gets from a symbol depends not only upon what the author has put into it but upon the reader's sensibility and his consequent apprehension of what is there. The feeling of profundity that accompanies it comes from a gradual but never final penetration of the form. T. S. Eliot's remarks about the poem seem relevant here: an independent object, the poem (or symbol) stands between author and reader, related in some fashion to each, but the relationship between author and object is not necessarily similar to that between object and reader. It may express the author and suggest to the reader, but expression and suggestion need not coincide. I. A. Richards, Eliot's opposite, who finds poetry the highest form of communication, finds it so by reducing symbol to sign. If the symbol, apart from incorporated sign, has little value as communicator between author and reader, its value may lie in communication between itself and the reader. What it submits to him and what he receives, however, may be different things. Nevertheless the value of the symbol to readers must be sought in this imperfect relationship.

Maybe the symbol has value as a way of knowing; but the meaning of knowing depends upon one's school. If one belongs to the scientific school, knowledge means acquaintance with fact, the sign becomes the instrument of knowing, and, as Ernest Nagel has pointed out, the symbol of science, a fiction ancillary to sign, is only a means of arriving at it. In the sense of direct reference to fact, the literary symbol, like that of science but worse, is so far from cognitive that even the sign it incorporates seems useless or vague. If we take knowledge to mean acquaintance with truth, the literary symbol, equally uncertain, may seem a more suitable instrument. However, Yeats, an old man at the time, said: "Man can embody truth but he cannot know it." By "know" in this place he seems, like a rationalist, to mean apprehend by discursive reason, though we should expect a romantic poet to find the symbol a way to another kind of knowledge: intuitive (immediate apprehension without logical interference) or else emotional. For him, the symbol, embodying intuitive truth and feeling, might present something which, although imperfectly received, feels like knowledge. As a character puts it in a novel by Charles Williams: "I sometimes think the nearest we can get to meaning is to feel as if there was meaning." Virtual knowledge, addressed to our feelings, might be what the symbol carries. But "virtual" implies that true knowledge is scientific and so does the quotation from Yeats.

Before we accept that meaning of knowledge we should consult Cassirer, an enemy of "naive realism," to whom scientific knowledge is one of many kinds, each from a symbolic form for showing what reality is like. The literary symbol, which presents knowledge of its own reality, may not communicate this knowledge, but by its form, which corresponds in quality to a nature of things, creates it. In so far as we apprehend the form we, too, are informed. The value of the symbol, if we accept this account of it, lies therefore in creating a vision of reality and submitting it to our apprehension. Not only creative but heuristic, it serves to discover the reality it shapes. Perhaps in view of the narrow sense of "knowledge" it would be better to speak of the literary symbol not as a way of knowing but of extending awareness or of conceiving in the sense of becoming filled with or pregnant.

If feeling is part of conceiving, we must consider feeling, which may be of several kinds. Aside from that experienced and embodied by the author, feeling may be our reaction to the stimulus afforded by the embodiment, a sign for us, if we are sensitive and experienced, that something of value is there. But those who find fallacies congenial tell us that this is subjective and, except for indication of possible value, unreliable. In the second place, the feeling may be that embodied in the symbol and offered to us. This, as T. S. Eliot says in "Tradition and the Individual Talent," is objective, impersonal, and "significant." In the third place, the feeling may be what the embodiment creates. Equivalent to an apprehension of the feeling in the symbol, this is not so much a feeling of our own as an awareness, at once distant and sympathetic, of immanence— by a kind of empathy. If that is the case, contemplation of feeling rather than feeling itself marks our happiest encounter with these fictions.

As the feeling in the symbol is more important than our emotional response, so the symbol is more important than what, by virtual analogy, it suggests. Lacking embodiment and the semblance of actuality, what it suggests turns back to its source to recapture a body and enlarge it. The symbol is not there like a sign to point to something else, to take the place of something else, or even to stand for it, but to display itself with all it has created and welcomed home. The trouble with Whitehead in this connection is that he thinks a symbol may be exchanged with what it symbolizes, as if the halves of the peculiar equation were of equal importance. This may be true of certain signs or of symbols that only convenience recommends, but it is far from true of literary symbols. Our concern, less with disembodied souls than with embodied ones, keeps our metaphysics warm—or, to call upon a more classical poem, the symbol haunts us with its body on.

To find how to approach a haunting body let us consider critics of Moby Dick, that great yet exemplary symbol. In *The Enchafed Flood,*[3] an investigation of "romantic iconography," W. H. Auden says: "A symbol is felt to be such before any possible meaning is consciously recognized; *i.e.,* an object or event which is felt to be more important than the reason can immediately explain." This seems almost unobjectionable, but he continues: "A symbolic correspondence is never one to one but always multiple, and different persons perceive different meanings." He proceeds to illustrate this point by stating what Moby Dick means to Starbuck, Ishmael, Ahab, and the captains of other ships. Since each interpretation differs from the others and each is thoroughly explicit, we must conclude that the meaning of the whale is both multiple and definite. This seems Auden's own position; for although he allows multiplicity of meaning, he inclines to allegory and sign, and we are left with a series of clear equations. Not multiplicity of definite meanings, however, but indefiniteness is the mark of the symbol, a conclusion too obscurantist perhaps for Auden's brilliant mind. This reasoning engine, reducing symbols to signs, provides a fitting introduction to some of the other commentators who, like Auden's mariners, are devoted to significance.

During the course of *Studies in Classic American Literature,*[4] D. H. Lawrence comes to Moby Dick: "Of course he is a symbol. Of what? I doubt if even Melville knew exactly. That's the best of it." Later on, however, reproving Melville for a transcendentalism unlike his own, Lawrence refuses to accept the story as "a voyage of the soul." He prefers to take it literally as a "sea yarn." That is a good beginning: the whale is a whale. But he also seems more than whale, and Lawrence, unable to resist, leaves the literal story he has been enjoying for a definite interpretation in the light of his philosophy: "What then is Moby Dick?—he is the deepest blood-being of the white race. . . . And he is hunted . . . by the maniacal fanaticism of our white mental consciousness." If we contemplate the image of the whale, we must admit that it embodies sex-

[3] W. H. Auden, *The Enchafed Flood,* Random House, New York, 1950, p. 65.
[4] D. H. Lawrence, *Studies in Classic American Literature,* T. Seltzer, New York, 1923, pp. 214, 238.

ual suggestions. That it presents the phallic being endangered by the mind is possible, but it seems illiberal to exclude possibilities which are as plainly embodied. Each of us, carrying his own baggage to the symbol, admires what he has brought without care for what the pile obscures. The symbol seems to invite this undertaking; but our excuse must be that we find it hard to endure the indefinite.

The medieval bestiary includes the whale. In the first part of the verses devoted to that fish, he is described, and in the second his significance is defined. This emblematic habit of mind, persisting to our day, limits or disembodies Moby Dick, who, becoming a mirror for critics, "represents" or "signifies" their anthropological, political, sociological, or psychological concerns. Almost as if he had such critics in mind, Melville includes the following quotation in his prefatory "extracts": " 'My God! Mr. Chace, what is the matter?' I answered, 'We have been stove by a whale.' "

Although William Ellery Sedgwick calls the whale an "emblem" of the mystery of creation, he refuses to make definite equations of symbols: "No statement as to their meaning can convey how vital, how meaningful these symbols are. Separately and in relation to each other [the whale, Ahab, and the sea] will not be held to any final definition or any fixed subject-object relationship." Interrelated yet unlimited, he continues, they baffle the intellect. Charles Feidelson, who agrees that the symbol is supralogical, finds *Moby Dick* a philosophical quest. Seeking vision through images of whale and sea, the voyaging mind approaches Emersonian knowledge of reality. Newton Arvin, who confuses Melville with himself at times, parodies Dante at others. The literal, Freudian, moral, and mythical meanings of his whale fail, as he says, to exhaust it. For other men other whales.

Not entirely aware, perhaps, of what he was composing, Melville was conscious enough to include passages which serve not only as elements of his book but apparently as clues to how we are to take it and how not. At the Spouter Inn, for example, Ishmael confronts a painting "so thoroughly besmoked, and every way defaced, that in the unequal crosslights by which you viewed it, it was only by diligent study and a series of systematic visits to it, and careful inquiry of the neighbors, that you could any way arrive at an understanding" of "such unacountable masses of shades and shadows." Contemplating this obscure and marvellous object, he is puzzled yet compelled by its "indefinite sublimity" to try to find what it is. "Ever and anon a bright, but, alas, deceptive idea would dart you through. —It's the Black Sea in a midnight gale. —It's the unnatural combat of the four primal elements. —It's a blasted heath. —It's a Hyperborean winter scene. —It's the breaking-up of the ice-bound stream of time. But at last all these fancies yielded to that one portentous something in the picture's midst." His "theory," tentative and based in part upon the opinions of many aged persons, is that the portentous something in the middle is a whale. This painting is plainly an analogy for the whole book. Ishmael's compulsive attempt at explanation corresponds to the predicament and endeavor of reader, critic, and maybe the author. It is worth noting that Ishmael, content at last with discovering the image, stops short of its significance—though his preliminary speculations about it are better than those of most critics.

A little later Father Mapple finds a definite lesson in the story of Jonah and the whale. That this, however, is not how to take the story of Ahab and the whale is suggested by the Ecuadorian doubloon, nailed by Ahab to the mast as an incentive to the discovery of Moby Dick. This golden coin from the center of the earth, richly stamped with a design of three mountains, a tower, a flame, a cock, and half the zodiac, revered by the mariners as the White Whale's talisman, invites interpretation. In "some monomaniac way" Ahab finds these strange figures significant; for as they say in Emersonian Concord, "some certain significance lurks in all things, else all things are little worth, and the round world itself but an empty cipher, except to sell by the cartload, as they do hills about Boston, to fill up some morass in the Milky Way." Not only monomaniac but egocentric, Ahab sees the coin as an image of himself and the world, which "to each and every man in turn but mirrors back his own mysterious self." Healthier but allegorical, Starbuck sees the sun as God, the valleys as our life, and the three mountains, "in some faint earthly symbol," as the Trinity. Stubb, fixing upon the zodiac, thinks of Bowditch and the cycle of life. Flask sees the coin as money for cigars. "There's another rendering now; but still one text." Only feebleminded Pip, a critic of critics, makes an admirable comment: "I look, you look, he looks; we look, ye look, they look." We are left with the object and lookers at it. Whether monomaniac, eccentric, or practical, these lookers are mistaken. Far from being a clue to the interpretation of the book, as some critics have taken it, this episode of the doubloon shows how not to interpret *Moby Dick* or any other symbolic form.

The chapter on the whiteness of the whale seems more exemplary. "What the White Whale was to Ahab, has been hinted," says Ishmael. "What, at times, he was to me, as yet remains unsaid." Taking a quality for the whole, he finds whiteness ambivalent, full of warring contraries, and universal. A "vague, nameless horror," on the one hand, it serves, on the other, to "symbolize whatever grand or gracious thing." Few are "entirely conscious" of the effect of whiteness in either of its aspects. Even Ishmael, who is conscious enough, finds the meaning of whiteness so "well nigh ineffable" that he almost despairs of putting it into "a comprehensible form"; and "to analyze it would seem impossible." By analogy and example, calling upon white towers, white mountains, and white seas, he suggests "the nameless things of which the mystic sign gives forth such hints." Is it "a dumb blankness, full of meaning?" he asks. "Is it that by its indefiniteness it shadows forth the heartless voids and immensities of the universe?" After such questions, analogies, examples, and contradictions, which build up the feeling and idea of indefiniteness, he concludes: "And of all these things the Albino Whale was the symbol."

Let us see how that symbol is composed. By description Melville presents the whale's indifference, its ferocity, and its "uncommon bulk." By the action and the nature of the sea, the ship, and the quest he improves the whale's solidity and complicates his import. "The overwhelming idea of the great whale himself" is further qualified by the thoughts of those in quest of him: Ahab's idea of him as the "incarnation" of all evil and Ishmael's idea of him as a thing of the "wonder-world," a "grand hooded phantom" which, midmost in the "endless processions of the whale" that floated through his soul, seemed "a snow hill in the air." From discursive chapters on the whale's anatomy, the history of whaling, the process of trying whales out, and the like, the image acquires greater body and depth—as Somerset Maugham, omitting these elements from his edition, failed to see. "Taken with context," however, as Father Mapple observes, "this is full of meaning." His observation, which refers to an incident of Jonah's life, may be taken as a reference to Melville's whale; for the monster is made by an interaction of image and context.

Melville shaped them to embody his vision of reality. His success is shown by the variety of critical interpretation. Working within the limits of his fixation or his gift, each critic takes an aspect or two of Melville's vision as the whole, and each critic is more or less justified by parts of image or context. Those who are fitted to find sociological or political significance are encouraged by the emblematic ending of the book. Those who are devoted to Freud find evidence in Ahab's missing leg. Those who prefer the metaphysical find ample corroboration everywhere. But that whale in context is more than a thing to a man. All things in heaven and earth, unassigned and indefinite, he embodies our feeling when face-to-face with ourselves and with what surrounds us.

To every dog his patch; but what of the undogmatic critic? If, preferring the whale to the part, he finds the image a general vision of reality, inexpressible save by itself, he incurs the danger of monotony; for the same thing might be said of *Ulysses, The Trial,* or *Bateau Ivre.* But however general, each symbol is particular in feeling and quality, and the critic, without trying to define the indefinable, may suggest its singularity. By analysis of image and context he may reveal the shape of the image, the relation of part to part and to the whole, and the function of each part. For aid he may consult the author's intention, if he can, and the circumstances of time and place. Anything goes as long as we remember that the text is the thing and that the symbol, an apparent object, is the object. Contemplating that appearance, we may find it becoming what Wallace Stevens calls a "transparence," but if, like Ahab and his critics, we find it becoming a mirror, we must look again.

Since the critic's region is on the other side of logic, he has no rational way of proceeding from analysis of part, function, and whole to a judgment of value. For that reason most analysts never mention value. If, however, the critic feels that art has value which analysis fails to guarantee, he must call upon intuition and feeling for help, not only the sudden intuition and feeling that accompany discovery of the object but the feeling that accompanies the apprehension of feeling in it. Analysis, justified by these feelings, may help to account for them. "I no sooner felt," says Coleridge in *Biographia Literaria,* "than I sought to understand." However coldblooded and objective the "exegetical inquirer" may pretend to be, he is a feeler; for we feel more than we think. If he is sensitive, feeling must attend and direct his analysis and assist his apprehension of feeling in the object. Maybe such feeling is another word for taste or for what Mr. Eliot calls sensibility. If, ignoring his commendation, we fear subjectivity, we must try to endure our condition. If in this doubtful region, fearing the danger of obscurantism, we long for

Euclid, we must recall that the symbol, occupying another region, does what discourse cannot do. The best equipment for a critic of symbolist literature is what Keats called Negative Capability: "being in uncertainties, mysteries, doubts, without any irritable reaching after fact and reason," and "remaining content with half-knowledge."

II

The literary symbol, I repeat, may be the work or one of its parts. Of these the image is the principal kind. Before we approach it, however, or, passing from the simple to the complex, proceed beyond image to other parts and to the whole, we must reconsider the meaning of image. Earlier I called the participating image an epitome of the whole or all but its epitome. It is fitting, before we receive that, to consult authority and establish our usage; for nothing is slipperier than a word. The imagist school, founded by T. E. Hulme, promoted by Ezra Pound, and adorned by T. S. Eliot, may offer help.

In "Notes on Language and Style," a posthumous paper published by Eliot in his *Criterion* (July, 1925), T. E. Hulme defines the image as an analogy, offered to the senses, expressing a vision. This analogy, composed of definite words, is a solid thing which may take the form of a metaphor or an unattached concretion. A follower of Bergson, Hulme prefers analogy to logic as a way of expressing and knowing. His image not only makes the poet's thought and feeling apparent to himself and the reader but, preceding thought and feeling, creates them. As defined by Hulme, therefore, an image is not unlike a symbol. Both are solid analogies, but whereas our symbol, presenting itself, suggests something indefinite, his image, suggesting something almost as definite as itself, seems limited, if not altogether assigned. These notes, though fragmentary, may approximate what Hulme said in his seminar on imagism.

Ezra Pound attended it. In *Gaudier-Brzeska,*[5] a Vorticist manifesto, he distinguishes image from symbol. For him the symbol has a fixed, traditional meaning. However definite, symbols such as cross or crown are associated with a "mushy" technique. The image, on the other hand, has "variable significance." Particular, precise, and impersonal, it is "that

[5]Ezra Pound, *Gaudier-Brzeska,* John Lane & Company, New York and London, 1916, pp. 102–103.

which presents an intellectual and emotional complex." The spheres in Dante's *Paradiso*, he says, are an image which, although known directly, we may explore. The trouble here is definition: his symbol seems our sign and his image our symbol.

Feeling his definition inadequate, however, he turns to autobiography and further example. One day in the *Metro* he saw beautiful faces of straphangers as a nonrepresentative color-pattern. No painter, he went home to find expression in the image, the poet's pigment. There, after an attempt which proved of "secondary intensity," he composed the following *hokku*:

> The apparition of these faces in the crowd:
> Petals, on a wet, black bough.

This *hokku*, he continues, records the precise moment when a thing outward and objective transforms itself into a thing inward and subjective. The image is a "radiant node or cluster or vortex from which and into which ideas constantly rush. . . . In decency one can only call it a vortex." A radiant thing and a vortex are opposites, one going out and the other in. But since his vortex, which receives and confuses the reader's ideas, remains alone at the end of the definition, we might assume that Pound's image is like those ink blots where neurotics find what they think is there—or like Moby Dick among critics. Pound's *hokku*, plainer than his definition, suggests, however, that his image is an analogy, a metaphor in this case, that embodies feeling if not idea.

T. S. Eliot, a disciple of Pound and Hulme, commended the metaphysical metaphor for combining idea and feeling. His objective correlative, amounting to a definition of image, is a verbal formula outside poet and reader for presenting something inside them but to neither alike.

In his lectures on the poetic image, Cecil Day Lewis is closer to Pound but somewhat less precise. The symbol, standing for one thing alone, says Lewis, is denotative, whereas the image is "infinitely resonant." After fumbling that point a while, he concludes—if so definite a word may be used for what he does—that "images are elusive things." Inclining somewhat to the other side—if one can speak of sides in a matter like this—Caroline Spurgeon, famous for studying Shakespeare's imagery, freely exchanges the words, "image," "metaphor," and "symbol." For her the image is a word picture used by a poet to "illustrate, illuminate and embellish his thought." Removing Shakespeare's images from context, she classifies them by subject and makes charts. Both this venture and that definition are a little dubious.

Applauding the insights of Hulme and Eliot and the example of Pound, we are now in a position to reconsider the image. My definition, though based upon example, welcomes authority. The image, like the symbol of which it is a principal kind, appears to be a verbal embodiment of thought and feeling. An analogy ranging in scale from the relative assignment of metaphor to the unassigned, the image presents what it carries. The word "image" may refer to the symbolic whole or to an element depending for part of its burden upon context. It is to image in its capacity of functioning part, however, that I shall confine myself here. My image, less than the whole, is a constituent symbol.

Take, for example, this image from Eliot's "Prufrock": "men in shirt-sleeves, leaning out of windows." One of many parallel concretions, this one acts with them and with elements of other kinds to create by interrelationship the figure of the hero and the vision he embodies. By itself this image suggests loneliness, frustration, despair, and maybe, since a window is for looking out of, longing. Shirt-sleeves and window-leaning, implying class and deportment beneath those of Prufrock or Eliot, show the hero's extremity. Relationship with other images enriches the figure at the window in whom for the moment Prufrock sees himself. There is contrast between those covered arms and the arms, elegantly braceleted and "downed with light brown hair," that Prufrock has just imagined. He sees the shirt-sleeved man at dusk. This time of day connects him with the opening conceits of evening, the patient etherized upon his table, and the catlike fog. The following image of the lonely "pair of ragged claws" at the bottom of some sea and that of rolled trousers, suitable for wading but not for deeper excursion into the waters of life, enlarge the man at the window as he enlarges them. These images and others, together with tone, rhythm, questions, statements, and periodic deflations, work upon each other and upon the whole until something emerges, at once the sum of the parts and, beyond that, the result of their interaction. We are moved, as Eliot observes at the end of "Preludes," another sequence of "sordid images," by "fancies that are curled around these images." What they compose is an embodiment of our condition. Qualified by the nature of the elements, this vision includes the sexual, social, and spiritual plight of the individual and, what is more, the state of the times. "The Love Song of J. Alfred Prufrock" has proved popular because through it we conceive more about ourselves and our reality than we can through the most discursive of daily papers or the biggest of little magazines. Prufrock's man at window is an element of this large vision and its epitome.

Baudelaire's giantess is a larger example. Like Prufrock himself, a body expanded by elements that surround it, she is central in the composition she informs:

La Géante

Du temps que la Nature en sa verve puissante
Concevait chaque jour des enfants monstrueux,
J'eusse aimé vivre auprès d'une jeune géante,
Comme aux pieds d'une reine un chat voluptueux.

J'eusse aimé voir son corps fleurir avec son âme
Et grandir librement dans ses terribles jeux;
Deviner si son coeur couve une sombre flamme
Aux humides brouillards qui nagent dans ses yeux;

Parcourir à loisir ses magnifiques formes;
Ramper sur le versant de ses genoux énormes,
Et parfois en été, quand les soleils malsains,

Lasse, la font s'étendre à travers la campagne,
Dormir nonchalamment à l'ombre de ses seins,
Comme un hameau paisible au pied d'une montagne.

By a pun which involves *gea* or goddess of earth, Baudelaire's *géante,* who plainly becomes the landscape by uniting with *campagne* and *montagne,* enters regions of myth and fruitfulness and takes her place with Mrs. Bloom, the "gea-tellus" of *Ulysses.* The relationship of hero and giantess serves to expand them both. Two similes, those of the voluptuous cat at the feet of a queen and of a hamlet at the foot of a mountain, and two actions, crawling over her enormous knees and sleeping in the shade of her breasts, fix their strange encounter. In it we may see mother, son, and all the troubles of Oedipus, the masochist and his lady, and the relationship of man to whatever else woman can embody, the metropolis, perhaps, or things as they are. Not only the relationship but the attitude of the hero serves to solidify our giantess. His tone, as remote from her as he himself is close, contributes to the ambivalence that determines our view. Classical and distant in rhythm and diction, the poem is decadent in theme. This quarrel of grand manner with outrageous substance serves to present adoration and Swiftian disgust, gratification and horror, abandonment and reservation. Attitudes, tone, and relationship alike help to create the atmosphere of dream that clothes enormity and makes it more portentous.

Opening another aspect, *verve* in the first line, from Latin *verbum,* means poetic power or imagination. Nature the imagemaker creates the giantess as the poet the poem, which, becoming one with monster, reveals the monstrousness of all creation whether biological or literary. The poet-hero's attitudes toward these creations, however mixed, unite at last in acceptance. "I accept the universe," said someone whose name escapes me. The feeling and idea of more than such acceptance are embodied in this poem. Though *"La Géante"* and "Prufrock" are alike in being visions of reality, Eliot rejects the reality he apprehends, while Baudelaire, with greater understanding and humanity, accepts it. His image is the symbol of that complex acceptance. By itself neither acceptance nor rejection constitutes merit; but the depth, quality, and scope of what an image incorporates or forms are among its values. Nothing but these forms could acquaint us with the realities and attitudes they present.

The central image, surrounded, supported, and enlarged by other elements, is no less conspicuous in Kafka's *Castle* than in *"La Géante."* But this enlargement of the image, however notable, is no more important than its thematic elaboration. The recurrent image, made known by Wagner's motifs, has become increasingly evident until it seems almost a mark of better fiction in our time—though by no means peculiar to it. The device has become so apparent that Wellek and Warren find the symbol dependent upon repetition. *Rhythm in the Novel* by E. K. Brown is a more elaborate study of the recurrent or "expanding" symbol, which "accretes meaning from a succession of contexts," and, as he might have added, gives it back to them. His analysis of "hay" in E. M. Forster's *Howards End* is excellent. This image, which occurs on the first page and the last and here and there between, acquires more and more from recurrence until it embodies the meaning of the novel and imposes a kind of order. Proust's little phrase from Vinteuil is a more illustrious example of the same device. Inspired perhaps by Wagner's motifs, such images differ from his in expanding as they recur.

Take, for example, the image of snow in "The Dead," the last and best story of Joyce's *Dubliners*. The book, which concerns the paralysis and death of his country and moments of self-realization on the part of his moribund heroes, finds its climax in the party given by Aunts Kate and Jane Morkan in this story. As we soon discover, their party is an embodiment of death and all the people there are living dead, though each has some connection with life and at least the possibility of living, if not much opportunity for it. The image of snow in connection with this party and those guests gradually accumulates and embodies the principal meanings. As it acquires them it gives them back to context.

The time is Christmas, season of birth and of the year's death. As Gabriel Conroy, the principal figure, enters the house, his aunts observe that he must be "perished alive" from cold. "A light fringe of snow lay like a cape on the shoulders of his overcoat and like toecaps on the toes of his goloshes." Outside the air is cold yet fragrant in contrast to the deathly festivities within, as Mary Jane plays her academy piece on the piano and aunts "toddle" about. Later, after his encounter with Miss Ivors, who leaves the party, almost successfully repudiating death, Gabriel thinks: "How pleasant it would be to walk out alone, first along by the river and then through the park. The snow would be lying on the branches of the trees and forming a bright cap on the top of the Wellington Monument. How much more pleasant it would be there than at the supper-table." About to commence a speech commending the past, Gabriel thinks again of the snow and the pure air out there in the park: "The Wellington Monument wore a gleaming cap of snow that flashed westward." The recurrence of snow and of the Wellington Monument begins to claim our attention. As the guests leave with more good-nights than realism would require, Mary Jane observes that snow is "general all over Ireland." Even the statue of Dan O'Connell, the liberator, has patches of snow on it. Safe at last in the Gresham Hotel, Gabriel and Gretta, his wife, go to bed, but wakeful and shattered by a sudden awareness of himself, he sees and hears the falling snow: "His soul swooned as he heard the snow falling faintly through the universe and faintly falling, like the descent of their last end, upon all the living and the dead."

This recurrent image, taking what it carries from context and tradition, sometimes supports the meaning of the party and sometimes all that seems its opposite. Since snow is a form of water, a traditional image of life, it holds the possibility of thawing. Ambivalent, therefore, it may hold suggestions of life as well as the death to which its coldness and whiteness appear to confine it. Of the peripheral images which help to determine these relationships, Gabriel's goloshes are important. Designed for keeping out water and snow, these articles point to his character. He even insists that his wife wear goloshes although she prefers to walk unprotected in the slush: "The next thing he'll buy me," she says, "will be a diving suit." Like the macintosh carried by Lenehan in "Two Gallants," an earlier story, or the brown macintosh that becomes a motif of *Ulysses,* Gabriel's goloshes, fixing his hostility to water and snow, prove snow's connection with life, which, as we have seen, attracts him now and again. Another of these peripheral images is the cold in the head: "Everybody has colds," says Aunt Kate. Going home in the snow, Gretta caught one the year before; and this year Bartell D'Arcy, the tenor, is too hoarse to sing. "Mr. D'Arcy doesn't like the snow," says Aunt Kate; but since he is one of the least deathly people at that party, his dislike, emphasizing the deathliness of snow, strengthens that aspect of the ambivalent image.

By its whiteness snow is connected with Lily, the caretaker's daughter, whose name is the first word in the story. That this is not accidental is shown by the flower's traditional connections. Not only for funerals, the lily is for Easter as well. When Lily brings Gabriel three potatoes (roots, seeds, and images of Ireland), she offers life to his deadness. By its whiteness snow offers contrast to Mr. Browne, who, as he says, is "all brown," and who, as Aunt Kate observes, seems "everywhere." Since Joyce has associated brown with decay and death throughout the book, Mr. Browne, issuing out into the cold to fetch a cab, lends snow a kind of vitality. As it lies fresh, white, and cold in Phoenix Park and by the river, obvious signs of resurrection and life, Gabriel carves a "fat brown goose" indoors. That this object, which collects and carries all the meanings of the party, is opposite to the "wild geese" who fled Ireland for foreign parts is suggested by the lady who, when offered a wing by carving Gabriel, refuses it.

In spite of all those goloshes and colds in the head, therefore, snow takes on the color of life and reflects it upon the ambiguous narrative. Gretta's lover, fearless of rain, may have caught his death of cold from melted snow in that garden long ago; but although dead, he is more nearly alive at the end of the story than Gabriel, confronting his own inadequacy. His tremendous final vision of the falling snow, which seems at first glance his union with all the dead, seems to prove on closer inspection an acceptance of death as part of life. Like Thomas Mann's Hans Castorp, who also has his vision in the snow, Gabriel, losing his old identity, may emerge mature from his shattering experience. Leaving goloshes behind, he may go for a walk next morning in Phoenix Park where the Wellington Monument, at once phallic and funereal, may remind him of the nature of things as he passes by. The image of snow carries these meanings to us as well. The last of a recurrent series, which has gradually gathered contradictory meanings, the final image, having received and united them, offers them to our sensibilities for penetration. In traditional fiction, narrative and characters assume the weight of meaning, and images, if there at all, are there to embellish it. But in Joyce's symbolist story, images by a grand "consult" among themselves and with action and character carry the heavier burden. If, attending to action and character alone, we ignore these images, we miss the vision entirely—as those did who used to think Joyce a naturalist.

It is plain that structure, which is partly determined by narrative line and the development of character, is served no less by thematic elaboration of images, which by bringing part together with part and by uniting them at last helps bring them into such harmony that the whole, as Joyce would say, has radiance. Not all particulars of "The Dead" are centered by the snow. Some of them, like the story of the hospitable monks in their coffins, agree with the general idea of death rather than with death's ambivalent image. But sometimes even such unlikely materials as Gabriel's story of his grandfather's horse, who, fascinated by King Billy's statue, walks round and round it, are brought under the command of the recurrent image. This story, which suggests Ireland's political condition, takes its place in the expanding system by relationship with Miss Ivors, the statue of Dan O'Connell, the Wellington Monument, and, by indirection, the snow. Acting his story out, Gabriel "paced in a circle round the hall in his goloshes."

As symbol can serve structure, so structure can serve as symbol. There is no necessary connection between the structure of a symbol and that of what it symbolizes, but structures as well as images can embody thought and feeling. Yeats's "Who Goes with Fergus?"[6] is a good example:

> Who will go drive with Fergus now,
> And pierce the deep wood's woven shade,
> And dance upon the level shore?
> Young man, lift up your russet brow,
> And lift your tender eyelids, maid,
> And brood on hopes and fears no more.
>
> And no more turn aside and brood
> Upon love's bitter mystery;
> For Fergus rules the brazen cars,
> And rules the shadows of the wood,
> And the white breast of the dim sea
> And all dishevelled wandering stars.

This great poem, one of Yeats's best, teases our curiosity as it quiets our anxieties by finality of shape in strange union with indeterminateness of sense. But the mystery is not so deep as William Empson in *Seven Types of Ambiguity* thinks. If we take the poem in the large context of what Yeats was obsessed with at this period, it becomes apparent that the opening question, which may seem invitation or warning, is invitation with implicit reservation perhaps. Longing for refuge from the world in some island, Yeats wrote poem after poem on the theme: "The Wanderings of Oisin," "To an Isle in the Water," "The Indian to his Love," and, of course, "The Lake Isle of Innisfree." In a letter to Katharine Tynan, written a year or two before "Fergus," he says that while correcting his poems he has noticed that most of them concern flight into fairyland or a summons to it. In other letters to her he calls Howth (an almost island) a "region into which one should wander from the cares of Life," and speaks of retreating to a complete island as "an old day-dream of my own." The poem before us seems a dream of exchanging the troubles of reality for insulation, and the trouble that invites retreat is love with all its hopes, fears, and moody brooding; for Yeats had known Maud Gonne a year or two by this time. In the peace of this island, the Land of Youth no doubt, adult responsibilities such as Fergus shirked will be replaced by dancing, games of war, poetry, and magic. The "brazen cars," a possible reference to solar myth,

---

[6]William Butler Yeats, *Who Goes with Fergus,* The Macmillan Company, New York, 1935, p. 49.

seems paternal, but the atmosphere, clearly maternal, suggests regression.

Our immediate concern, however, is structure. The poem begins with a question, the more effective for its uncertainty. A question is the embodiment of a feeling and attitude. This question is followed by a double chiasmus or crossing of separated elements, prepared for by the adjective, "woven." The third line of the second stanza is hard and triumphant. After that by sound, rhythm, and sense the poem declines softly into peace. "White breast" and "dim sea," spondees, interrupt that soft relapse only to call attention to the comforts of mother. We have, then, the following structure: a question, a chiasmus, a triumph, a decline, and peace, all passions put aside. Because we have known this pattern or find it possible, we respond. While our minds are occupied by the particulars of Yeats's problem, our feelings, more sensitive to such things than our minds, accept the structure these particulars compose. What the structure offers is the shape and quality of an experience. Since, conditioned by what it gets from sense, tone, and rhythm, this shape alone corresponds to that experience, there is no other way of expressing or creating it, and those who try by discourse are shape-changers.

A conscious symbolist, to be sure, Yeats may not have been altogether aware of what he was creating. Faulkner, who professes himself indifferent, may have been more nearly conscious of what he was about in *Absalom, Absalom!,* his greatest novel and my example of work as symbol. No writer knows entirely what he has made as no reader what he has before him.

Form or the work as a whole differs from structure as any whole from one of its parts. So far we have examined the image, its thematic elaboration, and structure as elements of a thing in which they function. Since that thing, the expressive or symbolic form, is greater than the sum of its parts or different from them in quality, the analysis of parts, stopping this side of what we are after, must be replaced by contemplation of the whole. Maybe the apprehension of the *gestalt* is immediate, but, incurring the dangers of impressionism, it is not always accurate. Analysis of parts, helping to keep our eyes upon the work rather than upon ourselves, may lead to a second and more objective apprehension or a third. The series seems endless. Though each apprehension may be richer than the last and more nearly accurate, a work like *Absalom, Absalom!* is too large and too complex to be mastered entirely. The relations of part to part and of part to whole escape analysis because they work below awareness. Moreover, in spite of our illusion of "spatial form," we follow the novel in time as we turn the pages and neither our memories nor our notes are adequate. The novel as a whole is never before us. Trying to keep our eye upon it, despairing of finality, reporting our most recent apprehension, we must do what we can. Maybe we are little better than impressionists, however much we may detest the thought of it. But this must be our comfort: our impression, though discarded tomorrow for a better one, may help the more casual reader.

Absalom, Absalom! is the story of Quentin's effort to understand the career of Sutpen, the nature of the South, and, beyond these, to realize himself. In his cold room at Cambridge, Quentin tells Shreve what others have told him and he recalls; and those roommates, calling upon imagination, create what must have been. Sutpen, seeming at first the center of the story, finally seems the material for these fictions. What Marlow is to Kurtz in *Heart of Darkness,* Quentin is to Sutpen. Like Marlow, Quentin is the center, and his mind is both our theater and our factory. More than materials, Sutpen and the South are Quentin or his greater part.

The elements of which Quentin composes his fiction are familiar. The central image is Sutpen's house, intended to surpass the mansion in Virginia where he suffered his trauma. Designed to shelter a great family, constructed in fury, almost attaining magnificence, the great house falls into decay at last and final destruction. To Sutpen the house is the symbol of his dream and to Quentin a symbol of the South. To us, bringing parts together and centering feelings, it presents the troubles of Quentin. Of the other images, no less recurrent, we need consider only one. Memories of wistaria, serving to connect Rosa, Quentin's father, and the South's brief summer, carry much of the burden of Quentin's nostalgia and despair. Shreve, in his overcoat, looking out at northern snow, may be cynical about wistaria, but to Rosa, Quentin, and the reader the flower becomes what Rosa calls a "globed concentrate."

Rosa's metaphorical extravagance, recurring metaphors of fever and swamp, ponderous sentences without definite shape, actions in slow motion—all these are expressive devices that help create the feeling of nightmare. That thick atmosphere, giving the vision its quality, is one of the principal elements of the form. It may be that dream, logically considered, is a way of showing that Sutpen, Rosa, and the South lived in a dream that Quentin is redreaming, that "too much, too long remembering" is nightmare. We can be certain that Rosa's incubus oppresses us as it obsesses Quentin and that reading the book is our nightmare. As in the worst of fever dreams, we are compelled to endure a thing again and again.

The structure is circular. Around Quentin as center, Rosa's story of Sutpen describes the inner circle. Next, describing a larger circle around that center, comes the version of Quentin's grandfather and beyond it that of his father. Then comes Shreve's hypothetical construction and finally that of Quentin himself. These concentric circles, however, are less circles than segments; for none is complete and each at another radius repeats segments of the others. "Maybe nothing ever happens once and is finished," says Quentin. "Maybe happen is never once but like ripples maybe on water after the pebble sinks, the ripples moving on, spreading . . . across its surface . . . to the old ineradicable rhythm." This two dimensional image, which suggests the structure and its effect, is less exact perhaps than Rosa's three dimensional "globy and complete instant" that "repeats (repeats? creates, reduces to a fragile evanescent iridescent sphere) all of space and time and massy earth." Concentric spheres correspond more closely to the final vision than any of their elements. With all it carries of character, image, feeling, attitude, and tone, this globy structure approximates the form or the synthetic whole.

Being from Vermont or some other place, we may have little concern with the South or with the troubles of a Southerner; but raised by form to generality, these local matters, far from being the point of the book, become all memory and guilt and all obsession. Like *Finnegans Wake,* another nightmare of history where all things go round and round, this fictive thing presents a vision of times, place, and their burdens.

Comment by Stanley Edgar Hyman:
  As almost the only paper in the fine arts group that goes into any detail about specific symbols, as opposed to the general discussions of the nature of esthetic symbolism by Albert Hofstadter and Theodore M. Greene, William Y. Tindall's essay is invaluable, and suggests that we might profit by much greater concreteness, as the political section does in such topics as "The Queen as Political Symbol" and the religious section in such topics as "The Hebrew Text of the Bible." It seems to me therefore particularly a shame that Tindall quotes uncritically William Faulkner's statement that his symbols and images are not the work of conscious craft and intention, but just "get in." Tindall later somewhat modifies this effect by suggesting that in *Absalom, Absalom!* Faulkner "may have been more

nearly conscious of what he was about." Faulkner's statement is patently absurd, the sort of primitivist posturing he indulges himself in when he tells newspapermen he is just a simple farmer, as any reader of *A Fable,* with its elaborately workedout parallel with events of the Passion, can hardly avoid knowing. The matter of intention is not always important and is frequently unknowable, but no profitable discussion of literary symbolism can begin from the idea that these effects and organizations are accidental or fortuitous. The best place to study literary symbolism for our purposes, in fact, is in the work of the most highly conscious artists. Tindall knows all of this, as his studies of Joyce have certainly shown, and it is regrettable that in printing Faulkner's remarks without discounting them, he somewhat cancels out the effect his paper otherwise gives of looking at specific symbols in literature to see what the writer was doing and how he set about doing it, surely the best starting point for our discussions.

Comment by Howard L. Parsons:

William Y. Tindall rightly reproves those critics who, like the interpreters of Rorschach blots, read in the symbol only their own feelings and mistake these for the objective significance of the symbol. The literary symbol is unique and incommensurable; its meanings cannot be marked out and measured; it is an analogy and epitome of being, borrowing from that being its complexities and mysteries and lending to them the intensities and subtleties and orders of the imagination. We cannot pass beyond it. "The symbol, an apparent object, is the object." It is no mirror held up to nature or man; it is nature and man transmuted and spiritualized. It is transparent.

My question has to do with another dimension of art—a dimension which underlies or embraces the objective and the subjective. It is a metaphysical, or, if you will, a moral one: in addition to being a delightful dumb discourse, a life beyond life and a habitation of spiritual and invisible creatures who haunt us with their body on—do not symbols, by a kind of indirection and adumbration, signify a life and a movement, a richness and complexity of feeling and thought yet to be, a fountainhead of new feeling and form which lies outside the explicit work of art, remoter and deeper than its qualities, suggested and unassigned? Ought not the symbol direct us back and down to that life-source itself, its generative and forming and transforming power, from which the symbol gathers into its lofty forms harvests not altogether its own?

Searching Tindall's essay for an answer, I find myself caught in a curious ambiguity, swayed to and fro in the uncertainty of pleasure and then pain. Perhaps that is the intent of his somewhat symbolic account, to leave the question as Keats would leave it, "remaining content with half-knowledge," since the symbol is something "calling for explanation and resisting it," and since art, like the inspirational symbols of Ulich, is ambiguous; in which case my Reason is as presumptuous as the critics of *Moby Dick* and rushes into those depths of living waters where angels of Feeling most delicately tread.

On the one hand, following the tradition of the symbolists, the symbol, we are told, exists "to display itself with all it has created and welcomed home." The symbol and the life it presents, creates, and celebrates, are sufficient unto the form they use and the immediate qualities they evoke. On the other hand, the symbol creates and discovers an experience and a world too obscure for science and too deep for philosophical definition. The symbol embodies, reflects, and enlarges the infinite variety of the feelings it intuitively suggests. It refers in exact ways tö the domain of the unnumbered and indeterminate. It adumbrates. It is an iconic sign, epitomizing and condensing the immensities, nuances, and mysteries of existence.

If Tindall answers that all these indefinite overtones and adumbrations are by definition part of the symbol or the image or the art work, then I ask: "Does not the art work spring from a source beyond itself?" And if he replies, "Yes, from the creative or conceiving power of the artist," then I ask: "Does not ordinary no less than expert experience reveal that the artist in creating submits to or undergoes an unconscious transformation of feelings and thoughts?" Is there not a "collaboration," a revelation of which the writer is, as Gide is quoted to say, the mere scribe? And is he mistaken in calling this "unconscious part . . . God's"? Leaving aside particular theologies and the origin and locus of this creative power, do we not have evidence (as that gathered by Eliot Dole Hutchinson on creative endeavor) that such a power, especially in great art, does in part impel and produce the creations of men, innovating intuitions of quality and of form?

Does not this also mean that art, so far as it is great, would refer men back to this source of all greatness—as great art has unconsciously done? Ought not some art, at least, as an outward and visible symbol of an inward and invisible state of creation, bear witness to the life and inexhaustible goodness of that movement of creation? Perhaps art is transparent. But seeing through it and beyond it, is not our attention directed to that of which it is the expression and emblem, its little creation and form being but a miniature of what science and philosophy and all the other symbolic worlds are, including the great Universe itself? Art is transparent; it should lead us across to the matrix and parent of all created goods. Art should be a lens of intensification, polar in its reference: a window revealing unto us the unspeakable and expressive Light of all creation. Always "there is a residual mystery that escapes our intellects." But how deeply may our intellects penetrate? Do we not now see in part through the glass of art an elusive working that commands allegiance by virtue of its worth, that evokes reverence by virtue of its redemptive power?

The mediocre, proud, or egoistic artist fashions a graven image, and falling down in his demonic rite impoverishes his life and the life of his fellow man by the worship of such richness. An artist, says Valéry, never finishes a work, he abandons it. For the great artist his symbols are insubstantial pageants, nothing but smoke and dust, embodied souls but transient, testifying in glorious passage to the power of creation, creating and presenting to us "a vision of reality and submitting it to our apprehension." Art persuades us to a love and devotion for the sovereign force of creation by the sheer unexhortative power of beauty, soothing or terrible; it mediates to us its vital source by stirring in us the life that was first conceived and nurtured in it.

[Also see comment by M. L. Rosenthal, Appendix IV, pp. 561–577, esp. 570, 575–576.]

CHAPTER XII

Symbolism in Architecture—
The Decline of the Monumental

By JOHN ELY BURCHARD

I. *Buildings and Symbols in History*

THERE HAS never been a time before now when men's buildings, and particularly their religious and political buildings did not play a symbolic role. Often, indeed, this role was a dominant one. From the time of Egypt at least through the late Middle Ages, the symbolism of the architecture was among the most important symbolisms. Commencing with the Renaissance, perhaps, and certainly by the time of Napoleon Bonaparte the symbols of architecture commenced to be devalued, and there can be little doubt that as Giedion says, "We—in our period—are deep down on the ladder of non-materialistic meaning."[1]

This symbolism was expressed at all levels. On the broadest scale architecture has often remained as the largest symbol of a whole culture. It is only natural that architects should evoke reminiscences of other eras through their recollections of buildings, just as poets might identify the same periods by works of poetry, or philosophers by theories of the times, or, less frequently, scientists by scientific achievements. And there is really no period which cannot provide more than one kind of quick association. It is instructive, however, to play a sort of child's game of response. Select a large historical period at random and ask a considerable group of generally well educated adults what work of man first comes to mind in association with the period. For many early periods the work is likely to be a piece of architecture or at least of construction.

Is the architectural symbol for Egypt not the Great Pyramid, rather than the cave temples? And is there any association that will be generally made with Egypt more frequently than the association of the pyramids? Athens is full of recollections. Would the Parthenon or the Erectheum of the Acropolis in general not spring to mind more frequently than

[1]Sigfried Giedion, private communication, June 10, 1954.

371

the tragedies, or the teaching, or even the concepts of the *polis* of *arete* and *hubris?* Is the symbol for Rome the circus, the bath, the aqueduct, the forum? Or is it the *fasces,* the courts of law, the marching legion, the pantheon of gods? Is not the quick response to the Middle Ages a picture of the cathedral or the castle, rather than the iconography, the manuscript, the abbatial organization, even the crusades? But is the answer for the Renaissance nearly so explicit? Do the houses of the *condottieri,* even the tower of Giotto or the Palace of the Doges, or the Duomo of Florence, or its Baptistery—do these represent our first association with this time? And how much less may we say for the urban squares of Georgian England, refined and valuable as they were; or the meeting house and the village green of Colonial America? Are not these associations much less specific? Has the importance of architecture as a symbol for the totality of the times not shown a fairly continuous regression, with perhaps a momentary upsurge in the Middle Ages?

There is one risk in such a conclusion. Architecture of earlier periods has been among the most durable of man's artifacts. The high degree of association with architecture characteristic of the earlier times *could* be due to a paucity of other relics to provide association. This warning is worth posting but is probably not serious. There are other relics and there is also the evidence of our own times.

The situation of architecture in our times simply reflects the situation of painting. Indeed, as will be shown later, many critics are of the opinion, not only that painting has had an enormous effect upon contemporary architecture, but that it is still in painting that future architectural trends are to be detected.[2]

If this be so, we can learn something from observations about painting. A particularly relevant one was made by W. G. Constable in his paper at the Thirteenth Conference on Science, Philosophy and Religion.

---

[2]The outstanding example is of course the relationship between the nonobjective painting of Piet Mondrian and the buildings by Ludwig Mies Van Der Rohe, and those derived from them, such as the Equitable Building in Portland by Belluschi, Lever House, and countless other examples by Skidmore, Owings and Merrill, the Biology Building at Massachusetts Institute of Technology by Anderson and Beckwith, and indeed a whole array of similar structures all around the world. To relate this only to the work of Mondrian and of Mies Van Der Rohe is of course a majestic oversimplification which could not be tolerated in an architectural discussion, but which is perhaps justified in this context.

Or, to take a third example, when the idea develops of a work of art being primarily a means of expression for its maker, and only secondarily a means of communication to other people, the use of symbols becomes less necessary. Since the early nineteenth century, this idea of a work of art . . . has taken increasingly firm root.[3]

The same statement may be made, *mutatis mutandis,* about architecture. It will be a principal thesis of this paper that there has been a steady devaluation of the symbolic purposes of architecture, beginning certainly not later than the opening years of the nineteenth century, coincidental indeed with the attitudes of painters described by Constable. It can hardly be coincidence that the phenomena should have run in parallel lines. But before enlarging on that thesis it may be well to set forth a little more evidence that buildings of earlier ages were in fact symbolic.

S. I. Hayakawa[4] has established a structure involving stages in the communication among people and the creation of societies. The first stage he calls "Organization around a Physical Symbol," the second "Organization around Verbal Symbols," the third "Organization around Shared Perceptions." The first stage is characterized most frequently by buildings or their prototypes, simple space organizations.[5] In the second

[3]W. G. Constable, "Symbolic Aspects of the Visual Arts," *Symbols and Values: An Initial Study,* Chapter XIV, p. 213.

[4]S. I. Hayakawa, *Adult Education as a Time-Binding Process,* Center for The Study of Liberal Education for Adults, Chicago, 1954.

[5]In the planning of his paper Hayakawa (*ibid.*) has relied heavily on the writing of the English anatomist, J. Z. Young, and his book, *Doubt and Certainty in Science.* (Clarendon Press, Oxford, 1951, pp. 95–98.) What Young says on this point and what Hayakawa adds are worth quoting in full:

"Some of the earliest of these (human) assemblies occurred at prominent hills of suitable shape, on and around which large numbers of people came together. One of the clearest pieces of evidence that we have about early social man is that he soon began to build large *artificial* hills. Objects nearly as big as anything we build now were the product of some of the early agricultural communities, nearly 10,000 years ago. Such huge objects are found all over the world—an English example is Silbury Hill in Wiltshire. I suggest that the value of building these objects was that they and their names were the signs by which men were trained to react to each other in such a way as to make society possible. At first, this must have been learned by all coming together at one place. Ritual feasting (and other ceremonies) are occasions of training of the brains of the members of the community, so that they shall continue to react correctly, and hence get a living by cooperation and communication. Mankind has gone on assembling and building assembly places ever since. It is assuredly one of the features that the biologist should notice about him.

"The hill is a very convenient symbol because it is easy to ensure that the association is quickly formed. Everyone can stand or sit on the symbol while the ceremonies are performed. . . . But there are obvious disadvantages about large symbols too. If they are

stage the building has not disappeared as a symbol but a verbal symbol has had to be added to make sense out of the building symbol which otherwise cannot have a universal meaning, as it is well known that its counterpart exists in another place, indeed that there are often many counterparts.

Next in the history of human cooperation and communication (writes Hayakawa) came Stage II, which I shall call the Stage of Organization around Verbal Symbols. Let me quote again from Professor Young:

". . . each temple has its own spirit. How then can all temples serve as a means of association for a large group? At some stage arose the habit of speaking of a single god, resident not in one but in many temples. This was a discovery of very great power. The peoples who first learned it produced one of the greatest of human advances."

Indeed it was a great advance to go from the physical to the verbal symbol, for the separate temples at Miletus and Rome and Carthage and Athens could then be defined as the dwelling places of one God, whose spirit is everywhere. In short, progress from the physical to the verbal symbols enabled social organization among people who lived much too far apart ever to meet in one place for an annual ceremony memorializing their solidarity. Everyone who acknowledged the name of the one God and the appropriate beliefs and dogmas that went with that acknowledgment could be recognized as belonging to the same community.

But this transition was not an easy one to make

As Professor Young says; "It seems at first quite illogical. . . . How could one person live in many places? An example of this was the dilemma of David when driven out of Israel to live among the Philistines. His god was associated with the particular soil from which he had been expelled, so he felt separated from his god and actually—and this is the point—he felt unable to worship him. Naaman overcame a similar difficulty by carrying two sacks of hallowed soil with him on a mule. But the real solution of the problem came by emphasis on the

---

to act as signs for the whole of a big population it soon becomes hardly possible to get everyone on or in. You can, however, have a lot of rather smaller objects or temples, in place of the original natural holy mountain. Their construction may be reckoned as the first act of making tools of communication, the direct ancestor of television engineering we might say. . . ."

As we read these lines from Professor Young, the hearer has no doubt been reminded, as I have of other instances of the Stage I type of organization around physical symbols; the Indian burial mound; shrines, churches and temples; the Ark of the Covenant of the Old Testament.

name of the god. . . . The worship of the name of one god, not associated with any one place, was surely the symbol that provided the cement for the next stage of human evolution, in which we still partly are."

Hayakawa points out that there remains a residual affection for the central meeting place, that Mohammedans turn toward Mecca to pray and try to visit it at least once before they die, that the Roman Catholic pilgrimage to Rome is an aspiration of their devout.

> But Christians, taking full advantage of the abstractive capacity of the verbal symbol, have also long known how to consecrate a holy place in the wilderness by putting up a cross out of the trees they find there, as is often told of Catholic missionaries in early pilgrimages.[6]

Still it is true of most places of pilgrimage, whether the purpose be religious, or political, or simply in reverence for a great past achievement, that they are not barren sites. Mecca, Jerusalem, Athens, Rome are sites, but they also have buildings, and we have come so far from primitivism that we could scarcely identify them without their principal buildings. The aborigine of Australia can still find a holy place in the bush which has no construction on it, no perceptible path to it, no tree or rock which would identify it to the Western eye. But the aboriginal knows where the place is and can travel to it over long distances. These perceptions left us long ago, and the building we know to be an essential part of the holy or the governmental place, not only for the practical purposes it serves, but for the symbolism it provides.

This second stage of organization around a Verbal Master Symbol reached its high point, according to Young, in the Western world in the Middle Ages, but other times added by Hayakawa would include the Mohammedan world of the eighth century, the Ottoman Empire of the sixteenth century, the T'ang Empire of the seventh century, and the Byzantine Empire at its climax in the tenth century. In this second stage the building still played an essential role in the process of symbolization.

Stage III is something different. Hayakawa regards this stage, the Stage of Organization around Shared Perceptions, as perhaps the greatest advance of all in the history of human communications. His stages overlap to a great extent, and so it is not surprising that he finds his first example in a communication from Strato while he was head of the

[6]*Ibid.,* pp. 2, 3.

Lyceum at Athens in the third century B.C.[7] The importance of the statement according to Hayakawa is "that, instead of saying, 'Listen friend, since I acknowledge the same god as you, you know that you can believe me when I say that air is a material substance,' he says, 'You don't have to take my word for it; you can see for yourself.'" Hayakawa believes that we are at present in transition from Stage II to Stage III concepts of morality. The latter he asserts is even more general and all embracing than the former which is no longer adequate. "The emergence of the new morality is slow, because all of us are struggling under the weight of sackloads of the holy soil of Israel, unable, like Naaman, to understand that it is possible to love and pray without them."

I have spent so long on this thesis because it affords the wall against which we may choose to test later the theories of many present critics of art and architecture that a new symbolism is possible in an architecture which has admittedly lost it, and to test also their ideas of what that symbolism is to be. I myself am unable to reconcile their notions with those of Hayakawa.

Let us return briefly to a few more examples of symbolism in architecture. The dome may offer a primary example. It was more than a method of construction. Indeed its structural importance may often have been minor. The terms for it in ancient times were various and suggestive, "*tholos,* beehive, onion, melon, bulbous, *omphalos,* pine cone, helmet, parasol, cosmic egg, heavenly bowl."[8] Many of these are of course simply physical descriptions but a few are symbolic. "In the naive eye of men uninterested in construction, the dome, it must be realized was *first of all a shape* and *then, an idea.*"[9] The effect of the dome as idea will be recognized by anyone who has stood beneath the canopies of Hagia Sofia.

[7]The quotation runs:

> We must first correct a popular illusion. It must be clearly grasped that vessels which are generally believed to be empty are not really empty but are full of air. Now air, in the opinion of the natural philosophers, consists of minute particles of matter for the most part invisible to us. . . . To prove this make the follwing experiment. Take a seemingly empty vessel. Turn it upside down, taking care to keep it vertical, and plunge it into a dish of water. Even if you do depress it until it is completely covered no water will enter. This proves that air is a material thing which prevents the water entering the vessel because it has previously occupied all the available space. . . . If . . . you lift the vessel vertically out of the water and turn it up and examine it you will see that the interior of the vessel has remained perfectly dry. This constitutes the demonstration that air is a bodily substance.

The quotation is from Benjamin Farrington, *Greek Science,* Penguin Books, Harmondsworth, England, 1949, II, p. 32.

[8]Baldwin Smith, *The Dome,* Princeton University Press, Princeton, 1950, p. 5.

[9]*Ibid.,* p. 5.

It is hard to recall any early period where the community buildings and those destined to religion did not include symbolism. In Egypt, for example, there is no line, no gesture in the reliefs, which has not a symbolic meaning, even down to the triangle of the pyramid.

And the symbol is powerfully related to the attitude of the community. The Egyptian monuments tell us clearly enough and reminded the Egyptians, too, that the preservation of the body was essential to the immortality of the soul; the temples insist that the religion is exclusive, not for the people, but carried on in the sanctuary by the king and the priest.

In contrast, the democratic Greek temple proclaimed the Greek democracy by its lack of privacy. Here only a small *naos* was reserved for the god. The emphasis was on the open colonnades, available to all the people. "Egyptian temples were a royal prerogative, Greek temples were the people's patrimony."[10]

And so it was everywhere else. The Assyrians and Persians, warriors and hunters more concerned with material than spiritual matters, reminded themselves of this, as well as they remind us, by the ubiquity of the hunting scene and the animal of prey and the inconsequential nature of the temple.

We need to be cautious here of course. A building may simply be an expression of its time, or an expression of its purpose. It becomes a symbol, only if, in addition to expressing its purpose for the benefit of history, it reminds the people of its time of its purpose, and if that purpose is enhanced by the symbol. The United Nations complex might have been a symbol as well as a lot of rentable property, the building for Lever Brothers on Park Avenue may express its purposes admirably but may not become a symbol.

We need not wear out the examples to the end. The building as symbol reaches its apogee when it is combined with sculpture and painting in an inextricable whole, when iconography dwells on and in architecture. Such demonstrations can be found in many times, notably of course in Buddhist temples and in the Romanesque and Gothic churches of France. It is the measure of their greatness and the real distinction which sets them off from the lesser Gothic of England, that they did so intertwine the symbolic of the building with the symbolic of the art.

Symbolism was to be found of course in every part of the cathedral.

[10]Sir Banister Fletcher, *A History of Architecture*, 16th edition, Charles Scribner's Sons, New York, 1954, p. 6.

The transept may well have been introduced first as a space gainer, but what was outlasted as a convenience remained as a symbol. The Greek cross plan, on the other hand, was manifestly symbolic from the outset.

This is not the place to develop *in extenso* the enormous impact of the architecture of this time, the iconographic part of which has been so fully discussed by such men as Emile Male.[11] It is often hard for us to understand the full impact of this symbolism of another time. Just as business men and economists in general may distrust the notion that the Trobriand Islanders indulge in their interchange more for ceremonial than for economic reasons, so it is hard for us of the twentieth century to feel fully that Malraux is right when he says of the people of the Middle Ages and their attitude toward "art":

> The notion of art as such must first come into being, if the past is to acquire an artistic value; thus for a Christian to see a classical statue as a statue, and not as a heathen idol or a mere puppet, he would have had to begin by seeing in a "Virgin" a statue, before seeing it as the Virgin.[12]

But Malraux is almost certainly right. The fate of the personages on the tympanum at Bourges, meeting Saint Michael and going either to Abraham's Bosom or to the Jaws of Leviathan, was a fate which could be universally anticipated by every passerby. How different these circumstances from those of another day, when as Malraux again reminds us, "As motifs of the age during which the machine and Europe conquered the world we are given—the dish of apples and the Harlequin."[13]

So in the architecture of the Middle Ages we have the Mirrors of Vincent of Beauvais, the Mirror of Nature, the Mirror of Knowledge, the Mirror of Morals, the Mirror of History. Each is full of its symbols, the beasts, the evangelists as animals, the trivium and quadrivium, the wheel of fortune, human destiny, the virtues and the vices, the active and the contemplative lives, the tree of Jesse, the patriarchs and the kings, the processions of the prophets, the evangelists, the characters of the apochrypha, the passion, the miracles, the saints and the golden

[11] Emile Male, *L'Art Religieux du XII Siècle en France,* Librairie Armand Colin, Paris, 1924; *L'Art Religieux du XIII Siècle en France,* Librairie Armand Colin, Paris, 1925; *L'Art Religieux de la Fin du Moyen Age en France,* Librairie Armand Colin, Paris, 1925.

[12] André Malraux, *The Voices of Silence,* translated by Stuart Gilbert, Doubleday & Company, Inc., Garden City, New York, 1953, p. 53.

[13] *Ibid.,* p. 414.

legend, the apocalypse, the Last Judgment—all this and more, attesting to the truth of the remark of Suger:

> *Notre pauvre esprit est si faible que ce n'est qu'à travers les réalités sensibles qu'il s'élève jusqu'au vrai.*

And in the architecture of the middle twentieth century we have as symbol, the column and the beam!

The extremity to which this has gone may be reserved for later discussion. Here let us only note a paper produced at the 1952 Conference by the late Erich Mendelsohn,[14] one of the great contemporary architects, and one of more poetry and sensuous attachment than most. Yet in this paper he was so preoccupied with structure as the essence of contemporary architecture as to be almost blind to true symbols. He implied that structures were fundamental to man, when of course all the evidence of anthropology would deny this, as it is also denied by matter earlier cited here concerning the Australian aborigines and in the citations from Young.

But the dimension of the sterility of the symbolic aspirations of the best current architects is revealed in a more startling way by the fact that Mendelsohn in this same paper could lavish enormous praise upon Gothic architecture based entirely on its structure, and ignore the iconography as though it were not an essential element of this architecture.

This is of course an element which modern architects have almost completely ignored, and have zealously effaced from their buildings. The structure has become for many of them a private symbol. They do not have the advantage of the lexicons of symbolism which were current in the times when the symbols of painting and of architecture were not private.[15]

---

[14] Erich Mendelsohn, "The Three Dimensions of Architecture—Their Symbolic Significance," *Symbols and Values: An Initial Study,* Chapter XVII, pp. 235–255.

[15] See Constable, *op. cit.,* pp. 210–211.

Single figures with symbolic identifications were not limited to religious purposes. In the Christian era, for example, they appear as Virtues and Vices, a famous example being those by Giotto in the Arena Chapel at Padua; while throughout the Middle Ages, symbolic representation of the seasons, and of the months, were used. Likewise, the representations of animals in the bestiaries of the Middle Ages were often meant to convey a moral idea. In this connection, a vast mass of learning was accumulated in the encyclopedias of the Middle Ages, such as that of Vincent de Beauvais and later compilations such as those of Vincenzo Cartari . . . or Cesare Ripi. . . . From these can be seen not only the wide range of the symbolic apparatus put at the service of artists, but some idea gained of the continuity of that apparatus, and how a symbol connected with one figure could be transferred to another, or some particular figure be given another's symbol, to reflect ideas of different communities and different periods.

These comments on Mendelsohn's statement must not be taken as a criticism of him. If they are a criticism of anything, they are a criticism of the times. It would have been dishonest of Mendelsohn and of any other contemporary architect to seek a symbolism that was not there, to rely as their predecessors did on vanished stimuli. The significance of the attitude of Mendelsohn (or of Mies Van Der Rohe, or Gropius, or le Corbusier) is that they *are* men of their time, men of the Stage III of Hayakawa.

Yet the general human desire for something more convincing than the logical Stage III is evident all around us. And the residual power of the symbols is enormous.

The Indian temples of Trinidad are scattered all over the island and are the focal points of those large agglomerations of Indians—"coolies" as they are called by the negro majority—that form nearly a third of the island's population. Mosques, whose crescent-topped minarets fly the flag of Pakistan, bear witness in the towns to the presence of transplanted enclaves of Islam but the rural Indian population is predominantly Hindu. Occasional cemeteries with their little forests of turbaned monoliths mark the resting place of country Moslems.

This temple (*i.e.,* at Pinal) lies at the south between the chapel of the famous Black Virgin and the nightmarish reeking acres of the Pitch Lake where Raleigh careened and caulked his galleons. Throughout this region, the black features of the Africans are replaced by the finer bone structure of the Hindus, and the battered plaited sombreros of the black labourers in the plantations by pugarees of many colours, and by flowing saris. These Indians are the descendants of indentured labourers that came from India to the Caribbean in hundreds of thousands after the emancipation of the slaves, to work in the canefields and reinforce the waning labour market that the abolition of slavery had, from the planters' point of view, so drastically depleted. Few of them ever returned to India, and all the Antilles now have an Indian minority which has been rooted in the soil for four or five generations. Many of them are losing their language and their religion and are imperceptibly melting into the heteroclite cosmopolis of the West Indies. Trinidad will be the last stronghold to resist this absorption, for here the priests still maintain their sway, and jealously cling to a language, a religion, a music, and a way of life that elsewhere is vanishing fast.

Among the rambling villages of trash-roofed huts in a forest of bamboo, palm, bread-fruit and paw-paw trees, the white temples rear their phenomenal towers and domes and pinnacles. An image of Hanuman, the monkey-god of the Ramayana, stands on the triple arched façade, one stone leg advancing in the first step of a grave religious saraband. Passing beneath the scalloped indentations of the doorway into the glaucous penumbra of the temple, the visitor is surrounded by frescoes of the gods of the Hindu Olympus. Cobras and eagles writhe and fly across the flaking white plaster in a turmoil of primary colours. Mahadeo brandishes a scimitar, Ganesh, the elephant-headed, sits cross-legged, his trunk twirling like an inverted question mark among a multiplicity of arms, and Krishna applies his lips to the mouthpiece of a long flute. Red-green, ochre, and blue figures, whose names and functions even the priests have forgotten, are painted in innumerable hieratic postures with a sort of uncouth, conventional, virtuosity. Every decade the name of one of these shadowy numina vanishes from men's minds. Eventually nothing will remain but these multi-coloured, ambiguous, two-dimensional symbols, portentously enjoining, threatening, admonishing or lamenting, for reasons that nobody can remember.[16]

Would this have been the fate of the Gothic iconography, too, had it not been for Western scholarship? Was it scholarship rather than faith that has kept alive what remains of these symbols? Is this suggested by the sterility of the symbolism of a contemporary church, no better in a Roman Catholic edifice where symbolism is consequential than in a Unitarian one where the symbol is effectively excluded?[17] Is this because Stage III of Hayakawa has advanced far enough so that this faith is really also being "assimilated"? Or is it perhaps because the faith no longer needs this kind of symbol or even visual aids of any importance? These are matters which will bear further investigation.

II. *Monumentality and Symbol*

The subtitle of this paper is "The Decline of the Monumental." This was adopted with full recognition that *monumental* as defined in English and American dictionaries is in no sense equatable exactly to

[16]Patrick Leigh-Fermor, "West Indian Hindu," *The Architectural Review*, vol. 104, no. 620, August, 1948, pp. 93–94.

[17]Some of the most interesting efforts to build churches in the contemporary manner have been made by the Roman Catholic Church of course, and there are notable examples of freshness of view both in the buildings and also in the essays of Father Thomas Merton, praising the barns but not the gate house at Gethsemane. Still the recent American church which most conveys the feeling of reverence and which is *in toto* a symbol, is the Lutheran church in Minneapolis designed by the late Eliel Saarinen.

symbolic. The reason was to emphasize the historical significance of a discussion which began in 1944 and which has not yet died away, a discussion between makers and critics of contemporary architecture.

In 1944, the Swiss historian-critic, Sigfried Giedion, gave an address before the Royal Institute of British Architects on the subject, "The Need for a New Monumentality." This address was first published in a symposium edited by Paul Zucker.[18] As a result of the publication, *The Architectural Review* of London organized a symposium on the subject proposed by Giedion and published it in 1948.[19] This symposium was well designed and elicited serious comment from a group of distinguished contributors, including, Gregor Paulsson, Henry-Russell Hitchcock, William Holford, Walter Gropius, Lucio Costa, Alfred Roth, and Giedion himself. This symposium still remains the most significant current contribution to the subject, far outshadowing something along the same lines developed in February, 1948, at The Museum of Modern Art in New York.[20] At a later date Mumford made an important contribution to the original *Architectural Review* symposium in the form of a separate comment.[21]

[18]Paul Zucker, *New Architecture and City Planning,* Philosophical Library, New York, 1944. Giedion's statement is on pp. 549 ff. and is in startling contrast to the pedestrian nature of most of the contributions to this book.

[19]"In Search of a New Monumentality," *The Architectural Review,* London, vol. 104, no. 621, September, 1948, pp. 117 ff.

[20]"What is Happening to Modern Architecture?", *The Museum of Modern Art Bulletin,* vol. XV, no. 3, Spring, 1948. This symposium touched on our question only from time to time, although there were many references to Giedion's thesis. It was based on a statement by Lewis Mumford in the *New Yorker* for October 11, 1947, and massed a great many, perhaps too many, men of reputation, including *Alfred H. Barr, Jr., Peter Blake, Marcel Breuer, Walter Gropius, Frederick Gutheim, Henry-Russell Hitchcock,* Philip C. Johnson, Edgar J. Kaufmann, Jr., Albert Mangones, John McAndrew, Walter McQuade, *George H. Nelson,* Matthew Nowicki, Eliel Saarinen, Vincent Scully, Edward D. Stone, *Christopher Tunnard,* Mario H. G. Torres, *Ralph T. Walker.* Those in italics made speeches. Speeches were also made by *Gerhard Kallmann, Talbot F. Hamlin,* and *Lewis Mumford.* Unfortunately for the light which might have been shed on our problem by sober consideration from any three or four of the panelists, the whole question was loaded and the discussion degenerated largely into a trivial ideological contrast between the *"International"* and the *"Bay Region"* styles.

[21]Lewis Mumford, "Monumentalism, Symbolism and Style," *The Architectural Review,* London, vol. 105, no. 628, April, 1949, pp. 173 ff.

The discussion has subsequently spread to South America, *cf.* several issues of *Revista de Occidente Argentina,* Buenos Aires, but the important pieces remain the original Giedion paper, *The Architectural Review* symposium of 1948, and Mumford's *addendum* in the same journal in 1949.

Those with great interest may also wish to consult some of the issues of *Progressive Ar-*

Giedion's proposal was a simple one. He set forth his own definition of monumentality. He then suggested that symbols had decayed in architecture ever since the time of Napoleon I, and that pseudomonumentality had finally become the order of the day. He argued that reforming architects had had to sweep away many things in order to rid architecture of such defects as pseudomonumentality. During that time it was necessary to be severe. Now the time had come for the architects to look again for a way to provide symbols in buildings. It was essential to his argument that the architects could *create* symbols whether or not there was demand for them and of the collaborators only Gropius seemed to disagree with this point. As to the nature of the symbols the various discussants disagreed, although there was some consensus that they might be found in social building. One or two thought there was no longer any need for "monumentality." Giedion himself now takes the position that the symbols will be "anonymous," which at once includes the concept of the civic social symbol and something more subtle.

I believe that we are on the threshold, at the beginning of a new period of symbolism. There are ample signs for it from pure science . . . and there is a whole development in painting and sculpture which announces from the side of our psychical background that we are striving and in a very different way to reconquer a symbolic expression. . . . In the Massachusetts Institute of Technology lectures I tried to define what will distinguish our symbols from those of bygone periods by quoting the research of the Warburg school of psychology and Sarton's definition that today "symbols have to spring directly to the senses." I cited at this occasion the forms of Arp, Leger, and others all showing that for reasons we cannot explain or cannot explain at the moment, certain similar forms in the individual work of each of them leave a psychic impression on us. . . .

The symbols which our period is forming I call "anonymous symbols" as they are attached to no religious faith or political system but they are direct projections for what is going on in the human soul.

The myths which—in their origin—belong always to a later period (most of them show by certain of their features that they are moulded only at the beginning of the historical period), the myths will in our period be much more attached to the inner happenings of the human soul, just as the symbols are today.

chitecture for early 1949. An editorial by the editor of this journal, Thomas Creighton, touched off correspondence by Mumford, Hamlin, and others.

This does not exclude at all that by some—*badly needed*—event of an *inner* change all these anonymous symbols and mythical fragments will get more than a personal significance, will become a reinforced meaning, just as the hieroglyph for life or the hieroglyph for perseverance became amulets through the whole Egyptian development.[22]

It is to a discussion of the premises and implications of this position that most of this paper is devoted.

The consideration of Giedion's thesis requires, in the first instance, an understanding of his concept of the meaning of *monumentality,* and an acceptance of that meaning at least for the purposes of the discussion.

In his first statement Giedion defined *monumentality* by saying that it "derives from the eternal need of the people to own symbols which reveal their inner life, their actions and their social conceptions."[23]

This is a definition which of course is more comprehensive than the customary one in American dictionaries at any rate. The panelists for *The Architectural Review* necessarily took some time in discussing it. Here let us dismiss that kind of discussion with but a brief look at its highlights, in order that, accepting the definition for the purposes of the paper, we can move to more important things.

Hitchcock, for example, outlined a series of qualities which we have come, at least in architecture, to associate with the monumental. Though these are not found in the dictionary definition, they are germane. These qualities were durability, solidity, dignity, serenity, concentrated unity, large size or at least large scale, a testimonial consciously or unconsciously for the future, with the suggestion that the monument is nearly always unconscious in its time. Finally, he suggested that the monument should have a fundamental emotional impact.

The panel on the whole agreed with these limitations, though they pointed out that durability might not be a fundamental quality, solidity might be a residue from a different age and kind of construction. The matter of scale was questioned, and of course if it is maintained, the term *monumental* will not be as comprehensive as the term *symbolic,* al-

[22]Sigfried Giedion, private communication, June 10, 1954.
[23]Zucker, *op. cit.,* pp. 552–553.

In the private communication of June 10, 1954, Sigfried Giedion revises this slightly to read, "Monumentality consists in the eternal need of the people to create symbols revealing their inner life, their religious and political aspiration." This may have been written from memory and the distinction between *own* and *create,* or between *actions and social conceptions* and *religious and political aspirations* may not be significant.

though most architectural *symbols* have in fact been large in scale. The notion that the monument should have a fundamental emotional impact is of course intrinsic also to the notion of *symbol*.

The most difficult of these assertions, though it was not much challenged at the time, was that the genuine monument is unconsciously provided for the future and that the monument which is consciously provided is probably already pseudomonumental and therefore made up of decayed symbols. My difficulty with this comes in reconciling it with the Gothic cathedral, for example, which was certainly aware of what it was doing, and which was built not only for eternity but with an eye to the current flock. If by accepting the Hitchcock definition I had to admit that the Gothic cathedral was *pseudo,* then I would have to give up the definition. But this quality is important in understanding some of the argument that was to follow, and it was generally accepted, save with reservations of the kind entered by Gropius who said that though this may have been characteristic of the monumentality of the past he believed that in the future its "equivalent is a new physical pattern for a higher form of civic life, characterized by flexibility for continuous growth and change." A similar reservation was entered by Holford.[24] Paulsson, of all the panel, produced quite different definitions which may be left out of this discussion although they were sharp and technically accurate.[25]

[24]"In Search of a New Monumentality," *op. cit.,* pp. 117–128. Individual page references for the quotations will not be supplied here, in view of the brevity and importance of the entire document.

[25]*E.g.,* from Paulsson:

Other writers have formulated the problems of architecture in our times as follows: The modern architect has had to create a *tabula rasa* in order to free architecture from traditional conventions devoid of all vital force. He has rationally solved the problem of the "single cell." Similarly he has attacked the urban problem in its functional aspect. These endeavors however are not sufficient: we must reconquer the "monumental expression." [This is a paraphrase of Giedion's statement.]

The term used is not synonymous with "the expression of emotions" or any general aesthetic qualities. It is a distinct and innate quality with a special social function, and should be used only in connection with buildings of a particular character—*e.g.,* "In ancient Greece monumentality was used rarely, and then only to serve the Gods and, to a certain extent, the life of the community." Europe, since the time of Napoleon, has been unable to express this monumental quality in its architecture; it has only succeeded in being pseudomonumental.

This picture of the problem contains a dualistic concept of architecture, since it postulates two categories of buildings; the purely functional and the monumental. For the moment I present this question without attempting to give an answer. The problem is: *Does not the demand for monumentality as an inherent aesthetic quality in iself lead to some form of architectural idealism?* The assumption that certain buildings are to have an expression of monumentality may be correct or incorrect. If correct, what is meant by monumental?

We may as well start out by pointing out that the modern meaning of the word is the result of a change in its significance. In Latin the word monumentality is never con-

The Architectural Review accepted for its discussion, as we should for ours, the term *monumental* as the focus of discussion of the need for broadening the modern architectural idiom, but it felt, as we may, that its aptness was debatable.

Still it is likely that as a result of these discussions which began seven years ago and the continuing use of the term in them we may see some modification of the old meaning of *monumental* in the direction of Giedion's usage. This is suggested, for example, by a letter from Talbot F. Hamlin to *Progressive Architecture*:

> I am all for structural research in its own place but I believe that society and the individual both demand first of all an ordered environment which they can come to love because it is beautiful and an environment which will be emotionally expressive of their deepest feelings. I feel somewhat the same about monumentality. Man always wishes somehow to transcend the limitations of his individual life. Any building or group of buildings which comprises elements of more than individual significance may rightly search to express something of this super-personal feeling. One thinks at once of community buildings, town squares, government buildings, churches, synagogues, as places in which this quality is or might be dominant. One thinks, too, of industrial buildings, or dams, and powerhouses where men work together in a

---

nected with aspects of a building, but only with a land survey, *e.g., cippus monumentalis,* a border post serving at the same time as a memorial.

The word therefore has no aesthetic distinction. Classic Rome used to characterize its buildings with adjectives like *magnificus, splendidus, decorus,* and nouns like *maiestas* and *dignitas.* Of these *dignitas* became the term used most frequently as a means of particular characterization. Vitruvius, for instance, describes a building without columns as purely functional, but with columns it is designated as *dignitas.* The columns therefore had for Vitruvius, an aesthetic-psychological as well as an aesthetic-sociological function. This concept of *dignitas* as a distinct architectural quality goes back as far as Cicero. He discusses in *De Oratore,* the dignity of columns for temples and porticoes as distinct from their practical value (*tamen habent non plus utilitatis quam dignitas*). In analyzing the temple of Jupiter on the Capitol this quality surprisingly emerges as a specifically individual property. Cicero describes the pediment of this temple as having arisen out of an original need for conveying rainwater, but that at the same time the form showed dignity (*utilitatem templi fastigi dignitas constructa est*) and this property was of such importance that *were the temple to be erected in Heaven where it could never rain,* it would still need the pediment for its dignity (*nullam sine fastigio dignitatem habiturum fuisse videatur*).

It is here for the first time we meet with an aesthetic concept as an isolated factor which can be taken from or added to an object. A clear objective and idealistic quality. There is an aesthetic criterion which lends the abstraction of beauty to all objects of art.

We should certainly call the temple of Jupiter on the Capitol monumental today. But in so doing we should not only acknowledge it as beautiful but magnificent as well in dimensions and outlay, imposing, vast and noble. For this particular purpose the beautiful becomes synonymous with the magnificent . . . the monumental . . . may not be identified solely with the beautiful. It is only a kind of beauty and occurs—if we adhere to the real meaning of the word—*only under certain psychological and sociological conditions.*

communal spirit to produce goods or power for communal use. Buildings built merely for private profit are individual and should not, under this definition, strive for monumental quality. It is perfectly true that men yearn for an order in their surroundings of more than personal scope and that this desire is frequently starved and thwarted in much modern building. True monumentality for our age will arise inevitably when we succeed in developing really expressive solutions to many different social building programs.[26]

Mumford's comment on these definitions may suffice to close this part of the consideration:

The qualities that Dr. Giedion would like to reinstate are, if I understand him rightly, manifold; they might be treated under the heads of symbolism, of visible hierarchic order, of aesthetic expressiveness, of civic dignity. Unfortunately these terms are almost as full of insidious meanings as monumentalism, and are as capable of being misunderstood. Perhaps the best way to restate Giedion's thesis would be to say that it is not enough for a modern building to be something and do something; it must also say something. . . . This new interest in the expressive element seems to me healthy; it means, or it should mean, that modern architects have mastered their grammar and their vocabulary and are ready for speech.[27]

The question remains whether in the sense used here they have anything to say.

The only other question debated on the definition of monumentality which might momentarily deter us was whether it was appropriate in these days to set certain buildings apart for monumental consideration and deprive others of that privilege. This was raised though not answered by Paulsson.[28] Hamlin approved in his letter just quoted and took it for granted that it would be so. The same position was taken by Horatio Greenough 100 years ago[29] and it seems to accord with all his-

[26]*Progressive Architecture,* vol. 30, February, 1949, pp. 9–10.
[27]Mumford, *op. cit.,* p. 173.
[28]*Cf.* note 25.
[29]In *American Architecture 1843,* reprinted in 1947 as part of *Form and Function, Remarks on Art,* by Horatio Greenough, edited by H. A. Small, University of California Press, Berkeley, 1947, pp. 64–65, the relevant passage goes:

The edifices in whose construction the principles of the architect are developed may be classed as organic, formed to meet the wants of their occupants, or monumental addressed to the sympathies, the faith, or the taste of a people. These two great classes of buildings, embracing almost every variety of structure, though occasionally joined and mixed in the

toric positions. It would require an abnormally romantic view of the "century of the common man" to expect that there should be no distinction between its buildings, that some ought to be monumental and some ought not to be. The easy conclusion that commercial and industrial buildings should manifestly not be, while governmental buildings, churches, and perhaps communal establishments should, seems to me to have been too readily drawn by most of the collaborators. Which buildings are to be important, which monumental, which symbolic, remains for the times to determine; and it will be the times and not the architects which will in the long run prevail.

May we then accept the original Giedion definition and go on? "Monumentality consists in the eternal need for the people to create symbols revealing their inner life, their religious and political aspiration," or "Monumentality derives from the eternal need of the people to own symbols which reveal their inner life, their actions and their social conceptions."[30]

What are the remaining points of the proposal?

1) That the symbols have decayed since the time of Napoleon I
2) That modern architects in making their revolution had to do it the hard way; first to extirpate everything, then to start afresh on a three step program of which the first two have successfully been taken
   a) Creation of the single cell, the house
   b) Solution of the problem of urbanism
   c) Reconstitution of monumentality. This is the hardest and most dangerous.
3) That *c* is essential, because there is a need for monumentality as here defined
4) That symbols *can* be invented or composed.

Beyond that others have suggested directions which the new symbolism may take.

---

same edifice, have their separate rules, as they have a distinct abstract nature. In the former class, the laws of structure and apportionment, depending upon definite wants, obey a demonstrable rule. They may be called machines, each individual of which must be formed with reference to the abstract type of its species. The individuals of the latter class, bound by no other laws than those of the sentiment which inspires them and the sympathies to which they are addressed, occupy the positions and assume the forms best calculated to render their parent feeling. No limits can be put to their variety; their size and richness have always been proportioned to the means of the people who have erected them.

[30]See p. 384 and note 23.

III. *The Decay of the Symbol*

The historical evidence that the symbols have decayed is as plentiful as the evidence that buildings once were important symbols. Just as I did not try to mount an imposing case for the latter assertion, so I shall not for the former. The evidence is all around us in the tired Tudor of the Princeton Graduate College, in the lovers' knots of Saint Thomas, in the romantic restoration of unromantic Williamsburg. But we need seek deeper.

Giedion has been oppressed with the decay of symbols for a long time and gives a good deal of attention to it in the second book of his planned great trilogy.[31] Although the decay of the symbol may have begun with the Renaissance, it was in full force by the early nineteenth century, long before the Industrial Revolution gave it the *coup de grace*. Of Napoleon, Giedion says that his tragedy was that he did not cast a new and vital form from the favorable opportunities opened by the revolution. It was not only his fate but that of the whole nineteenth century. Instead of forging new and lasting forms he did an about face. He tried to imitate the old dynasties of Europe.

> He lost the eighteenth century feeling for totality. He became unsure of himself. He needed something to lean on, for the problems of life could not be brought into meaningful shape. His immense appetite for power and craving for conquest found no social channel that it might have constructively filled.
>
> So he lost himself in the social sphere like the self-made man of the later industrial era whose taste failed him when he leaned on it to scale social heights. He willed a style worthy of the Caesars and of himself and did not deal in half-measures in making this setting his own.
>
> Behind all this is the reminiscence of imperial Rome. From the Renaissance on, the Classical panoply had served time and again; arabesques, trophies, torches, the horn of plenty, palms as used by Robert Adam, the Roman eagle with thunderbolts, the swan, the genii, the winged griffon, sphinxes, Hermes, lion heads, helmed warrior heads or Olympian scenes, symbols of power and fame. Singly or in groups this treasury of emblems is spread upon the walls, or in miniature form, nailed to furniture.
>
> The variety of emblems on the power and fame motif is almost im-

[31]Sigfried Giedion, *Mechanization Takes Command,* Oxford University Press, New York, 1948.

possible to digest. . . . The ornament is chosen and assembled from various conventional motifs. Its elegance of line cannot be denied but it no longer flows freely from the springs of invention. . . .

The motifs multiply. But do they ever reach the threshold of feeling? Are they not rather like advertisements that one carelessly passes by, having seen them too many times? Do not the eagles, lion heads, torches, and griffons too insistently stress the envied Roman ancestry? And the trophies, the genii with palms, the spears and swords, encrusted on furniture and walls, do they not speak too often of victories?

What takes place in the Empire style is nothing other than a devaluation of symbols. As Napoleon devaluated nobility, so he devaluated ornament.

This devaluation of symbols is seen time after time in the Empire style. The laurel wreath, which the Romans used sparingly because of its significance, forms almost the trademark of the Empire style. Beginning in the Directoire, it appears singly, but now it spreads like ivy over entire pilasters, or is stamped upon the walls of the Tuilleries throne room. . . . And is it not telling that one felt no incongruity in using friezes of crowning victories with palms even on teapots? Or that the thrysos staff, carried in Antiquity by the worshippers of Dionysus only at the most solemn festivals, now serves as a curtain rod?[32]

Mechanization, in Giedion's view merely enlarged these symptoms to undreamed of proportions. The elements of decay lay ready in the man of 1800. It was not mechanization *per se* which devalued the symbols, but the way in which mechanization was employed.[33]

The pathos of a decadent society that has made its home in an operatic setting is not to be taken in earnest, but what the Surrealists mockingly portray is at bottom the same phenomenon that Henrik Ibsen, living within the period, attacked in deadly earnest and incarnated in his personages, the ceaseless roaming in search of one's soul. . . . There, as here, it is the nineteenth century, never finding the way to its true self, devaluating symbols, without shaping new ones.[34]

[32]*Ibid.*, pp. 338–341. He might have cited as a relic of this into the twentieth century the enormous German compendia of ornament which helped the architectural draftsman of my youth. Here were all the symbols of the Empire and many others, all commonly degraded and lacking by this time even the elegance of line which was usually produced by Napoleon's designers, Percier and Fontaine.

[33]*Ibid.*, p. 345.

[34]*Ibid.*, p. 388.

And of course the difficulties persisted into the twentieth century even augmenting themselves. The men of the twentieth century did learn not to observe many of the desecrations. How many readers would be surprised as I was to come on the following clipping in a newspaper a few weeks ago? "When your eye follows over the white dome of our Capitol it is caught by a delicate figure poised on the very top. Actually this bronze figure weighs almost 15,000 pounds." "The figure represents Freedom and was moulded in clay by Thomas Crawford in Rome. The clay model was shipped to America and here cast in bronze and hoisted to its present position in December, 1863."

How many Americans are aware that a gigantic symbol of Freedom rests at the peak of the national Capitol, or would be aware of the meaning of the "delicate figure" if not suitably instructed?

Other problems besides those of taste have come in to beset us. There is, for example, the problem of scale. It is not, on the whole, the church or even the democratic state which now controls the power of scale. Saint Patrick's might not be diminished by Rockefeller Center, if it were good enough, but is Saint Patrick's good enough?

It was to deal with problems such as these that the iconoclasm of the modern architectural schools was adopted. It is easy to make fun of it as E. H. Gombrich did in his paper of three years ago: "If the Victorians took their visual metaphors from the museum, we take ours from the operation theater and the factory,"[35] but this is neither accurate nor fair. It is hard to overestimate the satisfaction we felt as we saw the worn out symbols toppling from the buildings and there are none who would wish them back on present work.

Yet the difficulty continues. The surgery has not made ready for the cure. On the one hand, there are countries where the surgery was not practised. And Mumford has said that when the Russians returned to the ponderous forms of classicism, "the typical architecture of autocracy and bureaucracy," she was not merely exposing a reactionary esthetic but was denying the "common world which men of goodwill seek in all countries to build; and its official adoption in the thirties warned all sensitive observers in advance, of the turn towards isolationism and imperialism that Russian policy was taking."[36]

[35]E. H. Gombrich, "Visual Metaphors of Value in Art," *Symbols and Values: An Initial Study,* Chapter XVIII, p. 266.
[36]*The Architectural Review,* vol. 105, no. 628, April, 1949, p. 174.

This is strong gospel, for if one believes Mumford's last conclusion and then examines the buildings the United States Government was producing officially at the same time, he will be unhappy at the logical *sequitur.*

But the troubles are not only in Russia and not only in eclectic buildings. Most of the modern architects agree that they have been unable to find the symbols, yet. And surely the evidence is all around us. What more dramatic example could be found than the United Nations buildings on the East River, which ought by their purpose to have had such a strong and noble symbol, and which as buildings say so little? By size and scale they are monumental, but everyone senses that they fail to proclaim a new world. Was this because the new world was not to come, and so the architect could not be given the inspiration? This is perhaps too mystical to swallow. Was it because the architects were instructed not to commit too much, to produce a building which in the words of George Nelson showed "an attractive arrangement of rentable space, but no monument to a great ideal?" "The ideal exists but the politicians are no longer its carriers."[37]

Or was it because as Hitchcock suggested while the buildings were building, that under the circumstances, amounting to a sort of committee design, it was improbable that they would present a strong symbolic expression of their significance? No doubt this was true, but what an ironic commentary that an international committee could not provide a symbolic statement for buildings which were in themselves essentially for the use of international committees! In any event the failure was manifest.

Still international committees may be left out and the trouble persists. Consider, for example, the colossal statue by Bruno Giorgi, called *Il Iuventude Brazileira,* and intended to symbolize the youth of Brazil. Or consider rather what was said about it in the October issue of the very same *The Architectural Review* which only one month earlier had published the vital symposium on monumentality, a magazine which covering all sides, is known to favor the contemporary. Said *The Architectural Review:*

These photographs have been taken less with a view to showing its intrinsic merits as a piece of sculpture than to demonstrate its value as

[37]*What is Happening to Modern Architecture?* op. cit.

a feature in the townscape. And whether it is seen as a linking element between architecture of the twentieth and eighteenth centuries, as a dramatic incident in an already dramatic skyline, as an organic foil to the mathematical regularity of modern architecture, or as a motif giving directional emphasis to the serpentine curves of Burle Marx's layout, what it chiefly symbolizes is the march of sculpture from the museums back to the streets and gardens where it rightfully belongs."[38]

Shades of the Virgin of Chartres who would never have been spoken of thus in her heyday! What became of the symbolization of the youth of Brazil?

But perhaps the grimmest evidence of all can be found in the work of one of the greatest of contemporary architects, Ludwig Mies Van Der Rohe, when he designed the chapel for the Illinois Institute of Technology. Here the architect's worship of the column, the beam, the pane of glass, and the filler wall of brick, ran headlong into the worship of God which presumably was desired by those who caused the building to be built at all. If any symbol won out it was the symbol of the steel section. It is hopeless for a man, no matter how talented, to build a building which is supposed to present a symbol in which he has lost faith. And this is the true dilemma of most of the architects of this day—and most of the rest of us, too, for that matter.

Although Giedion is on the whole optimistic and thinks that the devaluation of symbols may not yet be dangerous, I do not have the same optimism. Giedion suggests that the palaces of Babylon and Nineveh, "all by the way, short lived edifices," also presented decaying symbols. But I do not find the analogy reassuring.

Lewis Mumford has made an eloquent exposition of the problem of the decayed symbol and the absent monumentality in his *The Architectural Review* article.

> Architecture grows to self-consciousness and mature expression out of the elemental processes of building, mainly by concern over symbolism. However constant the mechanical functions of a building may remain— so that the form of a court of justice could be taken over by the Christian Church, because both buildings were designed to hold a crowd—the needs of language differ from generation to generation, as each fresh experience of life gives us something new to communicate, or as new evaluations change the relationship of one social institution to another.

[38]*The Architectural Review*, vol. 104, no. 622, October, 1948, p. 197.

There are many points of difference between verbal expression and plastic expression; but the need to assimilate and record new experience is common to both. All this is plain in the transformation of historic forms: no internal technical development in building will explain the abandonment of the audacious verticality and sculptural exuberance of medieval building for the more elementary technical forms of Renaissance building, with their horizontal lines, their repeating patterns, their standardized ornament; nor will any purely aesthetic reaction explain the positive hatred with which, by the end of the eighteenth century, especially in France, all Gothic building was viewed by "progressive" minds. What is superficially a change of form turns out to be something far deeper; a change of meaning. Ornament and decoration sometimes record changes of feeling, sentiments, and attitudes faster than construction. But construction itself is the main language of expression, and is at the service of many different human purposes, other than those satisfied by the building proper. The height of a spire meant religious aspiration in the thirteenth century; in the form of a skyscraper, it means publicity and self-advertisement in the twentieth century; yet in more than one medieval church, from Luebeck to Florence, the height and scale of the Church also represented the conscious self-assertion of the bourgeoisie over the clergy; so there is a significant connecting link between the two.

Now we live in an age that has not merely abandoned a great many historic symbols but has likewise made an effort to deflate the symbol itself, by denying the values which it represents. Or rather, our age has deflated every form of symbolism except that which it employs so constantly and so unconsciously that it fails to recognize it as symbolism and treats it as reality itself. Because we have dethroned symbolism we are now left, momentarily, with but a single symbol of almost universal validity; that of the machine. We should understand certain aspects of modern architecture during the last generation a little better if we realized that many modern architects were trying to pour into this restricted mode of symbolism all the feelings and sentiments that had hitherto flowed freely into love and religion and politics. Much of what was masked as functionalism was in fact fetishism; an attempt, if I may use Henry Adams' well-worn figure, to make the Dynamo serve for the Virgin. . . .

. . . In essence the monument is a declaration of love and admiration attached to the higher purposes men hold in common. An age that has deflated its values and lost sight of its purposes will not, accordingly, produce convincing monuments. Dignity, wealth, power, freedom, go with the conception of monumentality; and its opposites are meanness, poverty, impotence, standardization. Pride and luxury, it is true, often produce bad monuments; but poverty and humility, if left to themselves, would never produce any monuments at all. Most ages, to make the monument possible, have (in Ruskin's terms) lighted the lamp of sacrifice, giving to the temple or the buildings of state, not their surplus, but their very life-blood, that which should have gone into the bare decencies of life for the common man. This fact is responsible for democracy's distrustfulness, its grudging attitude, toward the monument. But though often painful in the giving, these sacrifices were not without their reward even to the giver, whether that gift was voluntary, as often in the building of the Cathedrals, or exacted by physical force, as in the taxes that made possible the pomp and grandeur of great courts. Denying the claims of the flesh and the prosperity of the household, buildings of permanent value, enriching the eye, sustaining the spirit, not for a few passing days, but for generations and centuries actually came forth.

To remind oneself of these conditions is almost to explain why we have lost, to such a large degree, the capacity to produce monuments in our time. If surplus wealth were sufficient to produce monuments, we might produce them today as easily as we produce much more costly things like cyclotrons and atomic piles. Never before, surely, has so much physical power and physical wealth been available. But for all this, we spend money for monuments with a bad conscience, when we spend it at all. This bad conscience is the product of middle-class convictions and middle-class standards of course; the poor, precisely because their lot is so constrained, have never lost the sense of life which produces the monument; consider how they will spend on a wedding, and even more on a funeral, the money that might have been "better" spent—but who shall define and justify this better?—for their children's food or clothes or education. To raise all living standards to a decent level, at least to the minimum of existence, is the aim of modern man; not to elevate and sanctify one side of life at the expense of every other aspect. Plainly there is reason for this choice; too easily did the upper classes in other periods justify the poverty of the poor and the deprivations of the needy, in order to make possible the grand, the superfluous, the beautiful. But as we approach a high general level of comfort today, the danger is just the opposite; that we forget the function of sacrifice; which means ultimately the arrangement of the good of life, not in the order that produces merely physical survival, but in the order that conduces to continued spiritual development. If we were better prepared to accept sacrifice, there might be less danger to mankind from the cyclotrons and atomic piles, to whose existence we dedicate every available penny. We spend lavishly on mechanical means; we scrimp on the ultimate human ends. That is why modern monuments are far to seek.[39]

IV. *The Modern Revolution*

Giedion's thesis seems to me at this point to need some criticism. He stated, it will be recalled, that the modern architects had to make their revolution the hard way, they had first to extirpate, then to reconstruct on three stages, first, at the level of the single cell, the dwelling house, second, at the level of urbanism, and, finally, at the third level, the most difficult, that of the recapture of monumentality. As to the first contention we may fairly take it as granted. Nothing short of a violent purge could have done in the 1920's or even at the turn of the century. We may also admit that the modern architects have effectively changed the single cell, the house. Whether all the change is for the better remains to be seen; there is little recognition, for example, in most of the designs that individuals often want privacy, a small dark place to which they may retire alone.

But to say that they have managed the problem of urbanism goes much too far. They have in fact been able to affect but a few cities directly and not many more indirectly. Statistically the number of dwelling houses of modern design is probably small; statistically the number of successful urban plans is minuscule. Theoretical plans do not mean much, and though the modern architects talk much of urbanism, we have principally only their own assertions to go on that they have passed this barrier.

But the notion that they have deferred the attack on the monumental will not stand any inspection at all. The plain fact is that the society has not asked for the monumental or the symbolic, either from reactionary or from contemporary architects. There is no evidence to support the notion that the society has refrained in revulsion from the things the reactionary people used to do; no evidence that the modern architects have not tried as hard as they could to obtain monumental tasks; no evidence that they are any too well qualified for the tasks either, if the

[39]Mumford, *op. cit.*, pp. 177–179.

overwhelming scale of most of the present great American urban proposals from Boston and Chicago to Los Angeles is any evidence. There is little to suggest, for example, that Boston will in any way be a more human place to live, if the great complex over the Boston and Albany railroad tracks should come to fruition; while the Chicago proposals separate the buildings by such magnificent distances that people with the slightest infirmity will need moving sidewalks to keep them from freezing in the winter and cooking in the summer as they pass from towering mass to towering mass. Yet this is societal architecture for a society in which the old and partially infirm are steadily increasing proportional to the entire society.

But these cavils are not of the greatest importance, for Giedion is clearly right when he says that the hardest of the three tasks is to recapture a monumentality which is gone and which now no longer seems to be desired.

V. *The Need for the Monumental*

It is then necessary to ask whether there is any need to recapture the monumental and the symbolic in buildings. There are architects and planners who think not. George Nelson says that several negative positions might be taken. The first is that we have actually created monuments unconsciously, and with them symbols, as we have built our industrial society, our dams, bridges, and factories. The problem thus solved itself before it was discovered. He reminds us that monuments often turn out to be different than expected by their builders, and conjectures that the Romans may have expected to be remembered for their temples and law courts, and not the baths, roads, and aqueducts by which we actually remember them. Perhaps then someday tourists will visit the ruins of Radio City, as we now visit the Coliseum.

A second reaction he says is that we do not need monuments in our time, because they are clearly out of place, both by nature of their structure and because we need other things more. This utilitarian view embraces the middle class notion of extravagance and waste, in the face of need, which Mumford described earlier. On either of these counts however the need for monumentality might be denied.[40]

40George H. Nelson, *"Stylistic Trends in Contemporary Architecture,"* Zucker, *op. cit.,* pp. 573–575.

Gregor Paulsson opposed the need for monumentality most violently and essentially on the ground that it is antidemocratic. He was obviously using his own definition of the monumental, but if we concede any extra cost of human effort for the symbolic or the monumental, then he would still make his point. He quoted Burckhardt to the effect that the chief motive power behind the Renaissance was the desire for self-glorification which monumentality served so effectively. He argued that monumentality was almost always sought in antidemocratic times and that it was not democratic but Hellenistic Greece that aimed for the magnificent in dimensions or outlay. The whole idea of monumentality he asserted to be associated with dictatorship, and said that the word monumental should be removed from the lexicons of democracy.

Modern architecture could in his opinion be shaped to express pomp, dominance, and mass appeal, but it would be wrong in a democracy because it would divert our attention from the chief problem of architecture, namely, to provide people with the best possible physical environment. The totalitarian states had used monumentality as one of the ways to drug people, so there would be danger in democratic states if they indulged in it. He ignored or did not regard conspicuous landmarks, *i.e.*, monuments, as an element in the total environment even of a poor and democratic people. Finally, he denied with vehemence the idea that some buildings might be monumental and others, because of their purposes, denied that right.

> The very demand for monumentality insures that the public buildings will be qualitatively different from the secular buildings, and on the basis of this difference in kind a special form language will arise. And this will almost certainly be classic in nature. The risk of this leading to academic escapism is greater than ever. The modern architect has derived all his creative force, all his revolutionary ability, through the very fact of his *denial* of this aesthetic difference in categories and his most decided defence of the thesis that the artistic value is principally the same—naturally not actually so—in the design of cutlery, a workers' home, an underground station, a town hall.[41]

Alfred Roth took much the same position, and in combination with what Paulsson said summed up the objections of those modernists who oppose the recall of monumentality. Roth mentioned the same bad associations of the monumental with the totalitarian, added that monu-

[41]Gregor Paulsson, "In Search of a New Monumentality," *op. cit.*

mentality exists in all genuine works of architecture anyway and cannot be turned off and on like a water tap. But in particular he reemphasized Paulsson's contention that it was anathema to the modern architect to accept any attempt to divide buildings into nonmonumental and monumental according to their functions, that is, everyday and symbolic. This is the essence of the negative position.[42]

But George H. Nelson in The Museum of Modern Art discussion said something outright which may have been in the minds of the others as well, although they were not explicit about it. Nelson remarked:

> Most of what happens to architecture is out of the hands of the architects. No architect alive has produced a church or government building that evokes a deep emotional response from the beholder. *Faith in the institutions no longer exists and even genius is powerless in face of this fact.*[43]

This is not my position.

The arguments stressing the need for monumentality were less detailed but quite as dogmatic. There was Giedion's original statement. Gropius seemed to join himself to this general point of view, hoping however that size would not be a criterion, that the new monuments would be fitting for the modern man who has discovered that there is no such thing as finality nor eternal truth. The old monumentality, suited for a static society, would no longer serve he thought, so he tended to identify monumentality with flexibility for continuous growth and change, a desideratum no doubt, but perhaps not one which is aided by calling it monumental. But Gropius also uttered a warning somewhat in the vein of Mumford's:

> But higher spiritual aspirations of a period, which will reach beyond utilitarian aspects worth being expressed in its physical surroundings can develop only slowly, subconsciously. We cannot force the issue, for emotions cannot be trained. All we can do actively—through education, is to free our intuitive qualities from frustration by giving the same emphasis on learning by doing as on intellectual fact knowledge. Not until creative art is reinstated in everybody's mind as being of equal rank with scientific invention can spiritual aims of humans be visibly expressed and be understood. When the prevailing philosophy of "time is money" will have yielded to a humanly higher civilization, will the

42Alfred Roth, *ibid.*
43George H. Nelson, *What is Happening to Modern Architecture, op. cit.*, p. 12.

"reconquest of the monumental expression" lie at hand? But it will not come back as the "frozen music" of static symbols, but as a dignified inherent quality of our physical environment as a whole, a *quality* in process of continuous transformation.[44]

It is perhaps not surprising that in a group dedicated to belief in the visual arts no one raised the fundamental question as to whether the visual symbol was any longer necessary at all for major stimuli in a verbal world, and a world in which the visual symbol had been put to work all day long in the service of sales.

VI. *What Sort of Symbols or Monumentality in Building?*

We have come now to this point: most of history seems to have shown us buildings of great importance which had large symbolic overtones and often direct symbolic appeals. We realize we must proceed with caution even here, for we know that a symbol does not always mean the same thing to everyone. In the Thirteenth Conference, Constable gave us the example of the housewife who could use a Persian carpet but remain indifferent to its symbolism, and Gombrich the example of upright poles which anthropologists and presumably also the erectors of the poles would interpret differently than you and I. But these are examples in reverse, for they presume that the symbols were more viable in their time than they are now. It is also possible that we may overestimate, from our present knowledge, the power of a symbol in an earlier day. Still, on the whole, we conclude that there was powerful symbolism associated with buildings directly and through iconography, with wavering intensity but generally with considerable force from the beginning of recorded history down at least to the Renaissance, and that this was a world and not a Western phenomenon. The symbols were most usually, moreover, attached to buildings of Church or of State.

Since anyway the beginning of the nineteenth century, we think we can see a more or less steady devaluation of visual symbols, in painting, too, but particularly in those associated with architecture. For many of those which remained the associations have become bad. Thus symbols of the Roman Republic now recall Fascism and not the Senate and the Roman people. This devaluation has been ascribed to Napoleonic ambition, followed by mechanization, but other forces may have been at

[44]Walter Gropius, *ibid.*

work; for example, the world may have needed fewer symbols after Galileo. This has not been developed in the argument, but it is surely a possibility.

In any event the modern architects assert that when they came on the scene things were in such a mess that only an iconoclastic action would suffice. There were symbols everywhere, in profusion, but they had lost their meaning, monumentality had been corrupted into pseudorepresentations. The public, too, was weary of this, even if it did not know it.

In the housecleaning which followed there seems reason to doubt that the public did know it, for it scarcely welcomed with open arms the innovators, the extirpators. But as time has gone on the public has come to understand, or to tolerate, or even to enjoy the results of the housecleaning.

During the cleaning all the symbols had to go, and at first the architects could tackle only simple problems such as the dwelling house, then having solved that problem, the slightly more complex one of urbanism. And now, they seem to be saying, they are readying for the most difficult and dangerous task of all. But they are not quite so agreed about the nature of the big task or the need for undertaking it, as they were about the need for cleaning house a half-century ago. This big and dangerous task is "the reconquest of the monumental expression."

On the whole, they do agree that the society has long been starved for symbols in its building. They cannot agree on what monumentality is exactly, or on whether it is appropriate for modern democracies. Some fear it for its associations, some object to setting any classes of buildings off for symbolic or monumental treatment unless all are so symbolized. Some object to any wasted effort on spiritual food in the shape of symbols, so long as anyone anywhere is starving for physical food. They recognize that other times have accepted such a way but think it beneath us. Even if some buildings are to be set off for symbolic treatment, they do not agree as to which ones; many say only social buildings, others would retain or restore the ancient virtues of church and state; but at least one says that nobody believes in either any more.

Perhaps I might state my own position here. The position of those who oppose monumentality and symbolism in a democracy seems to me to be hopeless, sentimental, and nonsensical. There is no reason why democracies may not now, as they have in the past, build monuments to their faith in their form of government—no reason why we as individuals should not be impressed by symbols of our collective strength. The dignity and simplicity of England's coronation ritual put to shame the overdrawn march of the sweating legions in the Red Square, and incidentally the oversimplicity of our own inaugural ceremonies. The coronation ritual is not only an example of monumental symbolism appropriate for a democracy. Unlike the less satisfactory rites in the United States or the U.S.S.R., it is neither invented or composed, but is rather an inheritance from the ancient magical rites of divine kingship.

The denial of monumental architectural symbols to a democracy is in essence a denial of faith in government, religion, or anything else. It is a confession of the abject failure of humanism. It is sentimental when it insists on attaching all the symbols to a properly detested totalitarianism, and nonsensical, too, as it presupposes that most of the people have made the same transfers of symbol which have occurred to Nelson, Paulsson, and Roth. This is simply not true. And the position is sentimental also when it proposes that either all buildings shall be symbols or none—not only sentimental but something worse, for this is not as the contenders fancy a democratic position but an egalitarian one. By their standard everything Washington, Jefferson, Adams, and Madison stood for was undemocratic.

In short, their position seems to me to lead to disaster. In the words of Whitehead:

> The art of free society consists first in the maintenance of the symbolic code; and secondly in fearlessness of revision, to secure that the code serves those purposes which satisfy an enlightened reason. Those societies which cannot combine reverence to their symbols with freedom of revision, must ultimately decay either from anarchy, or from the slow atrophy of a life stifled by useless shadows.[45]

Most of them seem to have tacitly accepted the assumption that symbols can be created by intellectual will and that the contemporary architects are the ones to interpret and design the symbols for the public. Mumford is happy that the contemporary architects are now ready to talk; he does not add whether he thinks they have anything to say. Gropius alone enters the strong *caveat* that only evolution and time will reveal the need for the symbol and the nature of the symbol needed.

[45]Alfred North Whitehead, *Symbolism, Its Meaning and Effect,* The Macmillan Company, New York, 1927, p. 88.

The evidence of their own creations would not seem to many of us to support the notion that contemporary architects have a highly developed symbolic sensitivity; or that where they seem to have some it is anything but intellectual. They may well suffer from the same problem as the modern painter who has fled to personal symbols and who, in effect, says to the world: "when I mean what I mean I mean it, whether you or anyone else knows what I mean or cares; or whether I will or will not choose to mean tomorrow the same thing I mean today." A symbol must be understandable without footnotes or scholarly exegesis by some minimum number of people before it can properly be called a symbol, and we might suppose that minimum number to be greater than one. In fact, we can hardly sensibly expect that the number who comprehend a symbol in common can really be a small number at all, in a modern world which reserves so few privileges for its priesthoods. The powerful symbols of which we spoke at the beginning were certainly well comprehended by a majority of the society.

Stanley Edgar Hyman[46] has pointed out that symbols like those of the coronation, deriving from historically remote rituals, which he calls "mythic," are of ancient anonymous collective origin. The architect or the poet who does not inherit them in a viable state may bewail their absence, but must do without them. Hyman then considers the private symbols that architects or other creators may invent or compose. These he calls "esthetic." Their power and meaning may be equally great but must tend to be less universal. The extent of the power may depend primarily on their creator's art. The extent of their meaning may rest on other grounds. It is a safe conjecture that the grizzly bear who warns us against forest fire is more widely understood and more effective upon action than any number of esthetically superior drawings, not even excluding the Christmas cards of Grandma Moses.

There is little doubt that the Lincoln Memorial in Washington is more powerful as a symbol than either the Washington obelisk or the Jefferson Rotunda. The Lincoln Memorial has doubtless an absolute esthetic superiority over the other two memorials but not over the White House or the Capitol. Does the Lincoln Memorial owe its power to the architectural skill, or to the famous inscriptions on its walls, or simply to the legends after Lincoln which have never clustered so readily

[46]Comment on this paper, prepared for the Fourteenth Conference on Science, Philosophy and Religion.

around the aloof Washington and the intellectual Jefferson? Is the Lincoln Memorial, monumental certainly, undemocratic? Does any of its power derive from its use of an architectural style associated with the great Athenian democracy? One would guess not, on the ground that most people who stand reverently in this temple are quite unaware of what Athens was like in the fifth century before Christ, and considerably more aware of the covered wagon and the Sangamon River, neither one of which appear at all. Would a Lincoln memorial built today in the private language of Mies Van Der Rohe have the same evocative power?

The way one answers the last question will intimate how he might answer larger questions. My own view of these questions can be briefly summarized as follows:

The dilemma of the architect but mirrors that of the painter or the writer. He has forgotten or chooses to ignore the myths and the legends. He has done this deliberately. It is not certain that the people have so readily cast away the influence of the past. But, having rightly or wrongly cast them away, he has to grope for generalized symbols in a dark and overpersonalized world.

This is a world in which the individual man is marked as unique and self-sufficient, independent of faith, independent of respect for government, independent of an aspiration common to and well understood by a large group of fellow humans. That this is quite silly and cannot last, I take as self-evident. But, as long as men are convinced that it is so, there will be no occasion for men to call for symbols or to welcome them when they are proffered. Far from being "anonymous," which is what great symbols based on myth or legend are bound to be, the symbol of a Motherwell or a Kooning is highly individual. Whatever it says to its maker, it says nothing to the rest of the world; or rather it says everything, so that the viewer is like cloudwatching Polonius waiting for a Hamlet. If we are to call such symbols "anonymous," then we may also have to say that anonymous symbols, so defined, may well be no symbols at all. "I asked for bread and ye gave me a stone."

Comment by Howard L. Parsons:

To understand the decline of the monumental, I think we must understand the role played by monumental symbols in lives of peoples up until recent times, and the factors leading to the rejection of these symbols, and hence monuments, in modern times.

In their aboriginal and most fertile function, symbols arise and are perpetuated as ways of facilitating human fulfilment and group survival. Meanings are *means* to life as men hold and cherish it in common. Symbols are created in communities and are used in communities; communication is the soul of community. Symbols evoke common emotions like fears and aspirations; they incite common actions, propelling or arresting or holding back men; they direct attention to a common world, commonly felt, known, appraised, acted on, enjoyed, or shunned.

Historical analysis of human cultures reveals the simple fact that, while the basic symbolic processes of a given culture are common to all subgroups within that culture, the dominant control exercised over the making and remaking of symbols lies in the hands of relatively few men who in like proportion exercise a dominant control over the economy. Ordinarily the task of fashioning, propagating, and rendering efficacious the symbols of the culture is given over to some group of specialists, such as scribes, priests, chroniclers, publicists, ministers of state, and the like. Accordingly, the coherence, common loyalties, and guiding aims of the society are secured, through the evocation of common emotions, actions, ideas, and values.

Thus Gregor Paulsson is correct in asserting the antidemocratic nature of monumental symbols, not to mention all symbols. In so far as the symbolic life of a culture has been shaped preeminently by a few men—and surely this has been the case with large scale architectural monuments necessitating mass labor and oligarchic planning—then the motives and effects of that symbolic life must be at best benevolently nondemocratic. The most sensitive and enlightened elite benevolence cannot faithfully and exhaustively express or take account of the feelings of a whole people. And while it is true that the millions of Egyptian slaves who labored and died to build the pyramids may have, if they chanced to survive the labor, felt the monumental sense in the face of those massive tombs designed for their masters—still the effect accompanying those feelings was certainly not a liberation from the conditions of their physical and psychic slavery. Indeed, as party to the process of totalitarian symbolbuilding, those slaves had forged their own intangible chains and reared their own invisible prisons and collective mausoleums. So it has been throughout much of human history. And so it must be so long as economies and symbols are the workings of a few puppeteers.

But symbols, as Robert Ulich points out,[47] always possess the peculiar character of expressing both the infinite and the finite; while they reveal man's "self-glorification" they also confer quality and order upon his living; they are a strange mixture of power over and liberation from, of despotism and democracy, of pride and humble service. Overtly, they bind men under the yoke of an empire or some other institution; indirectly, often, they level king and commoner alike by bringing all men into the presence of powers which command or threaten or lure or persuade, simply by reason of their transcendent character which stands over against and above all men. It is not curious that artists and artisans in the service of rulers should have discovered this secret power of incantation in symbols and particularly in monumental symbols, and should have employed them to their own advantage; for all men want the dramatic, the symbolic, the monumental.

What did the medieval churches mean to men? Extravagant pomp and papal power—and obedient meekness and selfless love. What did the art of the Renaissance import? Indulgent passion, arrogance, and unbridled potency—and exuberance of healthy vitality. Monuments bind men together by eliciting common loyalties, even in the midst of internal conflicts among the members of the community. They do so because they point men beyond the differences of the immediate and ephemeral to what lies beyond the local perplexities and antagonisms. And so long as the symbolic life joins together what the economic life has put asunder, the community will persist. Eventually, however, because of the tensions generated between the rulers and other elements in the society, the cohesive cement and façades of symbolic meanings, being strained and stretched from within, can no longer hold, and the house divided against itself must fall into decay.

Humanism is a protest against the tyrannical and enslaving causes and effects of symbols.

[47]Robert Ulich "Symbolism and the Education of Man," Chapter VIII.

Humanists center their critical fire on monuments; these are large targets easily pene-trated—decay has, in such instances, already set in, and the demolition proceeds with logical finality. Humanism properly protests against the folly and fatuous devotion en-gendered by the symbols of old. But because they repudiate the rich, warm; pulsating, adumbrative spell and mystery of the monumental—what may humanists offer in its place? Nothing but arid bones and, in our own time, mechanization, sterile design, and legends of extraterrestrial robots. When you destroy the organic impulse and rhythm and movement of life, with its sense of an all embracing Source or Aim or Whole, the best possible substitute is a mechanical imitation.

The failure of humanism was not that it put man on too high a pedestal but that it did not put him on a high enough pedestal. In exorcising the devils of superstition, humanism also cleansed the dikes of guardian angels, of good geniuses, and of Jacob's ladders of imagination. Being master of himself, man has no monsters of hell and surely no gods to struggle with; being a monument himself to his own meaning and destiny, man cannot lose himself in the experience of some supreme Monument, taking into his own small life the character of the Great Stone Face. So the decline of the monumental sense is a decline of the sense of man's majesty and dignity. That sense does not signify the diminution or deg-radation of man before the exaltation of some overreaching and overwhelming power. Rather, it means that man feels caught up and transmuted in some "sense sublime" of a transcendent presence or purpose from which he borrows a sublimity and beauty that en-hances his own importance. What is of great moment must render man's own moment rich and complete, until he is touched by what is eternal amid passage; what is magnificent, seizing him with awe or soothing him with understanding and peace, must magnify man the perceiver; it must lift up, but at the same time chasten and cleanse.

Yet humanism teaches us, in its faltering and indirect way, the dignity of man. It de-clares eternal war against all forms of tyranny over the minds and bodies of men. It cries out against the carnage of human resources and the tragedy of frustrated human potenti-alities, as these are caused and compounded by the symbols of the past. And so, as Mum-ford points out, modern man, still dimly remembering the poverties and indignities suffered by his recent ancestors under foreign monarchies, looks with suspicion upon the diversion of life's energies into the building of the monumental. Man asks for bread, but he is given sticks and stones, glass and steel; he seeks God, and receives a temple; he yearns for the altar of a sacrificial faith and the common rules of righteousness and is purveyed a golden and presumptuous idol. Mumford blames the timidity and possessiveness of common men for this tragedy; but does not an equal amount of responsibility and blame lie with those whose decisions determine the goods and rewards of art and the common life? The tragedy is that all of man's dynamic hungers and deepest tendencies are diverted and vaporized in the overruling symbols of his culture, and the monumental in particular, mixed as it is with pretension and a certain element of the *mysterium tremendum,* becomes an easy substitute for what is truly grand and magnificent in man's life. Man wants the third stage of Shared Perceptions wherein he day by day builds and celebrates, in the bodies of his own actions, the living monument of growing knowledge, love, and mutual aid; and the fourth stage, wherein men surrender themselves freely to the master demands of a creative power that has built and still builds through time the great chain of being and the ever evolving monu-ment of material and living forms.

What is the ultimate meaning of the monumental? We find it difficult to name with pre-cision. For what we hold to be dear and durable about the monumental experience is that it contains what can never be exhausted in symbols or confined by this physical vehicle. The monumental impresses on us, momentarily, a vision of what is everlasting; it deposits in us a passing image of what does not pass, yet what is forever transforming our own perspec-tives and remaking our own monuments. The monumental puts us in touch with unfathomable depths, almighty destinies, unfading and ever brightening glories, and irrevocable dooms. It makes what is weak in us strong, and by absorbing our little day it stretches out our time beyond itself into what abides and prospers through all times. By redeeming us from the fears and doubts of our creatureliness, the monumental finally gives us peace, for it becomes testimony to a richness that cannot be counted and a power that cannot be overcome.

What, then, of the restoration of the monumental in our own time? Burchard suggested that great monuments are the products of ages of faith; the purer the faith, the more perfect the monument, the more transparent its revelation of the fountains of living waters from which its own crystalline symmetry springs. Faith is endogenous and creative; Jesus likened it unto a wild flower, which toils not but grows and spins spontaneously its own walls and roof and crowning penthouse. Still, the conditions of faith lie partly in man's control: his economies, technologies, artistic techniques, families—all the material and psychic powers which sustain him—must be reconceived and remade so that, the roots of creative love being watered, the symbols of celebration may unfold to shield and beautify and bless the hearths and pathways, the yards and woods, of our common life.

For what is the right function of symbols? It is to release the spiral and mainspring deep within creative man; to embody the grandeur and power and beauty of life in some body which, like the bodies of our children or our students, perpetuates the heritage and secret of man's quest; to liberate life, as symbols themselves are liberations, to the creative power bound up in life and in all its symbolic functions; to let the slumbering angel of Michelangelo out of the marble, not as an immobile marble, a dumb idol, mute and passive in the dark corner of a museum, but as a vital and moving expression which is a joy forever and is always calling forth the spirit of creation, of resurrection, and redemption in others. Not only should symbols, as Giedion is quoted to say, satisfy "the eternal need of the people to create symbols revealing their life, their religious and political aspiration"; but in showing what is mighty and enduring and in evoking reverence toward what may be strong or striking or tragic or triumphant in his world, symbols should carry men out of themselves and cause them to shed their shoes, knowing they stand on holy ground. "Man always wishes to transcend the limitations of his individual life"; and symbols are the stepping-stones, the springboards, the ladders which lead him into an experience beyond symbols but served by them.

So a monument, or even the monumental experience which it generates, is not an end in itself. The long Hindu and Chinese traditions teach that, in its ultimate uses, the symbol dissolves into an all pervasive reality or experience which cannot be named but which can only be contemplated, enjoyed, and served. Monuments, like all symbols, are only outward and visible meanings for inward and invisible values. Because these meanings are ordinarily incarnate in some relatively permanent medium, the decay of symbolic meaning and value is more easily detectable in monuments than in the more changeable and insubstantial art forms such as poetry or music. A monument, as Mumford says, "is a declaration of love and admiration attached to the higher purposes men hold in common." It is a crystalline deposit purified out of the stream of the common life; it is the power of history made articulate, the network of material and common meanings lifted and sublimated into a life of its own. And a great monument declares in a great way a great event, as the heavens declare the glory of God. A monument exists to vivify and celebrate those purposes of which Mumford speaks, and to hold them up above the flux of time and the vicissitudes of history and cultures. Yet, let those purposes die or change, and the monument becomes a mockery, a deserted village or a vacated shrine, fit only for some archeological analysis or romantic lament: "My name is Ozymandias, king of kings." The best monument men could hope to build would be a monument that in all its strength and commanding beauty would say of itself, in resignation and in humor, and in the spirit of sacrifice proposed by

Mumford: "This, too, shall pass away." It would be the kind of art which, like the words of Jesus, would be so close to the facts of life and death themselves that its symbols would become household words indistinguishable from those abiding realities, and its speaker would lose his identity in the power to which he addressed himself and commended men. Or as Jonson says of Shakespeare, who still lives like an anonymous impersonal power in his plays,

> Thou art a monument without a tomb.

The monument is a living sacrifice to life itself, its child and devoted servant. As such, it would point beyond itself to its source and ground, to the creative and rounding force in history which never decays but forever outlives its own creations and, in the very center of decay and tragedy and death, gathers its resources unto iteslf and passes on,

> Tomorrow to fresh woods and pastures new.

[Also see comment by M. L. Rosenthal, Appendix IV, pp. 561–577, esp. 572–575.]

CHAPTER XIII

The Hebrew Text of the Bible:
A Study of Its Cadence Symbols

By LOUIS FINKELSTEIN

URING THE past five years, I have spent much time studying and
discussing with others the problems of communication through
symbols. Naturally, my mind has continually reverted to the use of symbols in the religious tradition in which I was reared and especially in the
literature with which I deal most frequently, namely, the Hebrew Scriptures and the writings based upon them.

For me, the Hebrew text not only expresses ideas, but also elicits attitudes. I do not know whether the description of its effect upon me
corresponds to that upon others, whether in limited or large groups.
That study I leave for scholars in specific fields. Here I can only record
my experience, and offer examples of one type of distinctive symbolism
in the Hebrew text which seem to me particularly fascinating.

Before describing this particular type of symbol, let me clarify what I
believe to be its purpose. As I read the Scriptures, they have among their
many goals the mission to acquaint the reader with the concept of the
One God, Creator of all things, Father of all mankind, eternal, beyond
human vision or real comprehension, timeless, infinitely wise, infinitely
powerful, a King whose empire is the All. In the endeavor to win men
to the understanding of this Deity, Who is beyond classification, and in
its vigorous attack on idol-worship, Scripture necessarily struggles to
elicit in the reader a sense of the nearness of God, and the possibility of
approach to the Deity with an intimacy closer than would be possible in
any other human relationship.

The effort to understand the greatness and power of God requires an
appeal to reason. The effort to convey His nearness, His affection, and
the sense of His intimacy, and to evoke our love for Him, is necessarily
an appeal to the emotions.

The first part of this effort is thus generally directed toward our intellect: the Scriptures desire us to know the greatness and transcendence of God. The second part is directed to our emotions: the nearness of God needs to be felt, rather than understood. Indeed, perhaps it cannot be understood, and may, in large measure, only be felt.

A Galilean Jewish sage of the third century, Rabbi Johanan ben Napaha, remarked on this double purpose of Scripture and asserted that whenever Scripture has occasion to stress God's greatness it takes care immediately also to assert His humility and gentleness. He offers several examples from the Five Books of Moses, the Prophets, and the Hagiographa. But, actually, one of the best examples is offered by the first chapters of Genesis. The two accounts of creation are intended to supplement one another. The first asserts God's endless power and His transcendence; the second, His dependence on man for the fulfilment of His purposes on earth and His close association with man (described in anthropomorphic terms to clarify beyond question the intimacy of the relationship).

Quite apart from the conviction of the Sacred Writers that God both transcends the world, and is in intimate association with it, and particularly with man, they were under the most urgent pressure to stress His nearness to man, because the sense of intimacy with pagan deities was one of the foremost attractions idolatry could offer. The Baal, Zeus, and Jupiter were so human that the simplest peasant could understand and love them. Their moral weaknesses and their intellectual and other limitations tended to endear them. The Baal was dependent on his worshipers for their gifts, for the very food he consumed, for the pleasure they gave him through the dance, through music, and through sacrifice. The human tendency to love those dependent on us, far more than those who help us, increased the propensity to Baal worship in biblical times.

While the Prophets, true to their calling and conviction, had to declare day in, day out, the absurdity of a theology which made gods dependent on men, and in which men created deities instead of *vice versa,* they also tried their utmost to satisfy what we would call men's psychological need to sense intimacy with the Deity and to be in the position of helping Him.

One of the ways they apparently sought to achieve this purpose is through the cadence and lilt of the words that express their ideas. Even the most solemn and majestic scenes of God's manifestation are described in words and phrases whose very melody suggests a Being Who beseeches, rather than commands. God can have His way, Scripture indicates in its peculiar word structure, all the time; but securing obedience through power is frustration for Him. He wants us to serve Him, out of love and reverence, and not for lack of choice. This theological paradox is not altogether omitted from the discursive and assertive phases of biblical literature; but becomes manifest with the greatest clarity in the examination of one's emotional reaction to the sound of the words, rather than merely to their meaning.

Naturally, this lilt and cadence of the original Hebrew is almost always necessarily lost in translation. Hence it comes about that in all versions of the Hebrew Scriptures, save the original itself, God appears austere and remote, to a degree which shocks the reader accustomed to the Hebrew text. I was well out of my childhood when I first came across theological works based on translations from the Hebrew, and realized that many people regarded the God of the Hebrew Prophets as austere, remote, unloving, and far away from need for man's affection. So completely had the sound of the Hebrew verses and the chant accompanying them, as well as the insights based on them, permeated my heart and mind, that for years I did not understand the meaning of some of the discussions based on translations.

Perhaps the reader not acquainted with the Hebrew text will be able to follow the different types of suggestion which emanate from the Sacred Word, if I give here some examples of the manner in which cadence and lilt are used to convey moods and even ideas. The following study may thus be of some value to theological students, and may also serve other scholars as an example of the different ways in which language operates.

It may be best to begin our examination with a scene where the sound effects can scarcely be mistaken, though its theological significance may not be evident.

In the encounter of King David and the Prophet Nathan, after the incident of Bathsheba, the Prophet, rebuking the King for his transgression, resorts to a telling parable which describes a rich man with numerous herds who steals his neighbor's one lamb. Having stirred the King to fury against the selfishness of the thief, so that he declares that the scoundrel deserves death, the Prophet, according to the King James Version, proceeds, "Thou *art* the man" (II Samuel 12.7). The authors of the King James Version doubtless intended to suggest that the Prophet uttered these emphatic monosyllables in sounds of thunder. It is unnatural to pronounce them except with great emphasis.

In the *New Yorker* (November 14, 1953) Dwight Macdonald reminds us of the nonassertive symbolism of these and similar expressions in the King James Version; and complains that the new Revised Standard Version reproduces the Hebrew, simply as "You are the man." Accustomed to this colloquial expression, we are likely to read it, "You're the man," which has mere denotative and little connotative power.

However, the Prophet Nathan did not address the King in either Elizabethan or modern English, but in the Hebrew of the tenth century B.C.E. He brought his story to a climax in a brief iambic verse in which the consonants are particularly *un*emphatic. He actually said to the King, when the latter had reached the height of his indignation, " *'attah ha-'ish.*"[1]

These words do not suggest awesome thunder or even anger. Obviously the Prophet, rebuking the King, did not forget that he was addressing royalty. The Prophet did not raise his voice. Having persuaded the King of the infamy of the deed, the Prophet could afford to be moderate and subdued in his condemnation. We can almost see him bend down toward the King, as the latter sits on his throne, and, lest they be overheard, whisper the dread words, " *'attah ha-'ish.*" Having uttered these softspoken words, the Prophet continued, unable entirely to control his indignation. He opened his explanation of the brief remark with apparent calm, describing how God had lifted David from obscurity to the throne, and had given him his master's house and harem. God was ready to give him even more. And now, as the Prophet came to reflect on David's action, he found himself almost audibly gritting his teeth, saying, according to the Hebrew text, *"maddua' bazita 'et debar*

[1]For the convenience of the reader, I use a transliteration which most nearly suggests the corresponding Hebrew sounds, though that necessarily departs from technical, scientific transliteration, which serves other purposes. The apostrophe indicates the soundless *'aleph* of the Hebrew alphabet; the inverted apostrophe the *'ayyin* which in most modern Hebrew dialects is also soundless, but doubtless was pronounced by many in ancient times, and is still discernible in some Hebrew dialects today. A diacritical point under *h* indicates that the original is an *ḥeth*, which has more sound than the simple *heh* (virtually, the English *h*); that under the *s* indicates a *ṣadi* which was and is pronounced in a variety of ways, today generally as *ts*, but in ancient times doubtless more like its present Arabic counterpart, a throaty sibilant; the *shin*, corresponding to the English *sh* is transliterated *sh*. My religion forbids me to pronounce or to write a transliteration of the tetragrammaton, which is the especial and ineffable name of God, and it is therefore indicated by the form YHWH, suggesting the consonants of the word.

YHWH." The discursive force of the words is sufficiently rendered by the King James Version "Wherefore hast thou despised the commandment of the Lord?" but there is nothing in the translation to reproduce the emotional force of the Hebrew original. The compactness of the Hebrew phrase which contains only eight syllables, contrasts with the prolixity of thirteen used for the same idea in English. Moreover, the repeated explosive sounds, especially the dentals, the harshness of the *zayyin,* make one feel the deep emotion of the Prophet as he tried to control his temper, and to speak to his royal master with deference.

The same contrast between the force of the Hebrew original and the translation is evident in the Ten Commandments. The sixth commandment, "Thou shalt not kill," has awesome power in the King James Version, like that of the quadrisyllabic sentence used (in that Version) by the Prophet in addressing King David. The translators could not find a similar expression for the seventh commandment and wrote simply, "Thou shalt not commit adultery." But in the eighth commandment, the translators return to the four syllable sentence, "Thou shalt not steal." The ninth though longer, still retains the power of the sixth and eighth commandments, "Thou shalt not bear false witness against thy neighbour." And so does the tenth, "Thou shalt not covet thy neighbour's house, thou shalt not covet thy neighbour's wife, nor his man-servant, nor his maid-servant, nor his ox, nor his ass, nor anything that *is* thy neighbour's" (Exodus 20.13 ff.).

However, none of this emphasis is discernible in the Hebrew original. The sixth commandment reads simply *l'o tirṣah;* the seventh, *l'o tinaf;* the eighth, *l'o tignob;* the ninth and tenth in longer sentences are equally unemphatic. This is not because the Ten Commandments are without special stress in the Hebrew Scriptures, the whole story of the Redemption from Egypt, and even from the Creation of the world leads up to them. But as the *midrash,* responding to unasserted symbols of the Commandments, remarks, God appeared on Mount Sinai like an old man, full of mercy.[2] He did not shout at His children. As in the incident of God's appearance to Elijah,[3] the Divine Vision was surrounded by awesome spectacles and fearful sounds; but God Himself spoke in a low voice—with the sound of Moses himself, according to the *midrash.*[4]

[2]*Mekilta, Behodesh,* chap. 5, edition Horowitz, p. 219.
[3]I Kings, 19.
[4]*Midrash Tehillim,* chap. 18.29, edition Buber 78b. The same idea is expressed in other *midrashim,* some of which assert that the Divine Voice adjusted itself to the capacities of

Like a grandfather trying to win his grandchild to observance of the moral law, God reminded the Israelites that He had redeemed them, and then proceeded to warn them against the evil temptations lurking about them. He mentioned the penalties which were sure to follow violations of the Commandments, not as threats, but as inevitable consequences of evildoing, and good reasons for avoiding it.

The commandment to keep the Sabbath is put into the words, *"zakor 'et yom ha-shabbat leqaddesho."*[5] And apparently because the first word begins with a somewhat harsh dental sound, it is replaced in the Deuteronomic text with the softer sounding *"shamor."*[6] The Rabbinic Sages, of course, noticed the difference in text, and maintain that the Divine Voice spoke both words simultaneously.[7] Lest what has been said suggest that the Hebrew language itself or the Prophetic dialect is incapable of harshness and emphasis, it will be well to consider some examples, in which fierce denunciation is expressed in the very sound of the words. Thus when King Ahab unjustly seized the vineyard of Nabot, Elijah was commanded to meet the King and denounce him with the words, *"ha-raṣaḥtah ve-gam yarashta"* ("Hast thou killed, and also taken possession?" according to the King James Version, I Kings, 21.19). The English version cannot reproduce the fierceness of the Hebrew with its emphatic dentals, and particularly the sound of the *ṣaddi* (almost *ts*), as well as the deep sound of the repeated guttural *resh,* and the harsh explosive *g*. The Prophet continues, *"bi-meqom asher laqqaqu ha-kelabim 'et dam nabot yaloqu ha-kelabim 'et dameka gam 'attah"* ("In the place where dogs licked the blood of Naboth shall dogs lick thy blood, even thine," King James Version). Again the Prophet uses the hard *g* for his furious anger; again he resorts to the guttural explosive *q* (whose sound has been softened to a mere *k* in modern Hebrew, but in the ancient pronunciation was doubtless much harsher); the whole verse is punctuated with the explosive dental, *dalet.*

each hearer, the older people heard it according to their strength, the younger ones according to theirs (*Midrash Tanhumah,* Exodus 25). There is no real contradiction between these views and that which holds that God gave Moses power to speak with the sound of the Divine Voice itself, for God spoke only to Moses, and the voice of Moses had to be heard by all Israel, encamped at the foot of the mountain (*Mekilta, Bahodesh,* chap. 4, edition Horowitz, p. 216).

[5]Exodus 20.8: "Remember the sabbath day, to keep it holy."

[6]Deuteronomy 5.12: ("Keep the sabbath day to sanctify it." King James Version).

[7]*Mekilta, Bahodesh,* chap. 7, edition Horowitz, p. 229.

When Adam is sentenced by God for having eaten the forbidden fruit, there is a similar grouping of dentals, the *qof* and the *resh*. *"ve-qoṣ ve-dardar taṣmiaḥ laḵ, . . . bezeat 'appeḵa toḵa'l leḥem . . . ḵi 'apar 'attah ve-'el 'apar tashub"* ("Thorns also and thistles shall it bring forth. . . . In the sweat of thy face shalt thou eat bread . . . for dust thou *art,* and unto dust shalt thou return." Genesis 3.18–19). Almost as harsh sounding is the sentence of the serpent. *"ḵi 'asita zot 'arur 'attah miḵol ha-behemah u-miḵol ḥayyat ha-sadeh 'al geḥonehah teleḵ ve-'apar toḵa'l ḵol yemé ḥayyeḵa ve-'ebah 'ashit beneḵa u-ben ha-'ishah uben zar'aḵa uben zar'ah hu yeshupeḵah rosh ve-'attah teshupenu 'aqeb"* ("Because thou hast done this, thou *art* cursed above all cattle, and above every beast of the field; upon thy belly shalt thou go, and dust shalt thou eat all the days of thy life; and I will put enmity between thee and the woman, and between thy seed and her seed; it shall bruise thy head, and thou shalt bruise his heel." Genesis 3.14–15).

On the other hand, the Judge of the whole world cannot bring Himself to be harsh in sentencing Eve. The words He addresses to her are brief, and the penalty far lighter than those imposed on her fellow sinners, Adam and the Serpent. Similarly, the very melody of the words is less severe. *"harbeh 'arbeh 'iṣboneḵ ve-heroneḵ be-'eṣeb teledi banim ve-'el 'isheḵ teshuḵateḵ vehu yimshal baḵ"* ("I will greatly multiply thy sorrow and thy conception; in sorrow thou shalt bring forth children; and thy desire *shall be* to thy husband, and he shall rule over thee").

The Divine sentence against Cain after the murder of Abel is even more emphatic than that against Adam, for his sin. The Hebrew reads, *"'arur 'attah min ha-'adamah 'asher paṣeta 'et pihah laqahat 'et demé ahika miyadeḵa"* ("And now *art* thou cursed from the earth, which hath opened her mouth to receive thy brother's blood from thy hand," Genesis 4.11).

When the Israelites in the Wilderness worship the Golden Calf, God Who has brought Moses into the heavens to receive the Commandments, abruptly commands him, *"leḵ red ḵi shiḥet 'ammeḵa"* ("Go, get thee down; for thy people . . . have corrupted *themselves,"* King James Version, Exodus 32.7). The remainder of the verse is necessarily less powerful; the force of the command is virtually exhausted in the opening spondee.

The very same words occur also in another connection, where their use together suggests impatience with Moses on the part of the Master. Just before the revelation on Mount Sinai, when the Divine Glory has descended on the mountain, God suggested that Moses descend to the people to warn them once more not to try to penetrate to it, to see the Divine manifestation more clearly. Moses replies that the people have been sufficiently warned. To this God replies, *"lek red"* (King James Version, this time, with apparently correct emphasis; "Away, get.thee down," Exodus 19.24). But the force derives more from the sound of the words, than from their literal meaning.

On the other hand the combination *"lek leka,"* used by God in calling on Abraham to leave his father's house and settle in Canaan, and again in asking him for the sacrifice of Isaac, is singularly sweet and tender. The repeated *lamed,* the combination of the two words into virtually a single one of two syllables, with the accent on the second, has a totally different effect from the spondee *lek red.*

These examples indicate how the melody and cadence of the Hebrew are utilized by the authors of Scripture to convey ideas which stir emotions far more deeply than could mere prose. It is obvious that words are chosen not only for the meaning they convey, but also for the overtones inherent in their sound effect. The Prophets did not speak or orate, they chanted their messages. And while the stories of the Torah were written, they were also intended for reading aloud, either at synagogue services or to children; and so the sound effect of the words and groups of words is utilized to reinforce the lexicographical meaning.

A study of the way in which the Prophets communicated these emotional overtones is still to be made. Perhaps it need not be left entirely to subjective interpretation, for it soon becomes clear that certain sounds and combinations of sounds were considered severe and harsh, while others were considered (and doubtless were) soft and tender. On the whole, it may be said that short words, with explosive dentals and guttural sounds suggest rigor, determination, resentment, indignation, and anger. The *r* sound used in connection with the gutturals apparently partakes of their harshness. On the other hand, the *m* and *n* sounds are intended to suggest tenderness, softness, forgiveness, and kindness; the *r* sound in association with them likewise suggests kindness; and so does the sound of *shin,* with its hushing quality. Hence the priestly blessing has a quality of great mercy and kindness implicit in its very sound:

> "*yebarekeka YHWH ve-yishmereka*
> *ya-'er YHWH panav 'eleka vihuneka*
> *yisa' YHWH panav 'eleka veysasem leka shalom*."
> ("The Lord bless thee, and keep thee:
> The Lord make His face shine upon thee, and be
> gracious unto thee:
> The Lord lift up His countenance upon thee, and
> give thee peace" Numbers 6.24–26).

Perhaps the most effective musical overtones in all Scriptures are those found at the beginning of the consolatory prophecies in Isaiah, chapter 40. The Hebrew reads: "*nahamu nahamu 'ammi y'omar 'elohekem*." The very sound of the letters suggests the mother comforting her children, and the meaning, "Comfort ye, comfort ye my people, saith your God."[8] The Prophet continues, "*dabberu 'al leb yerushalayim ve-qir'u 'eleha ki mal'ah seba'ah ki nirsah avonah, ki laqehah miyyad YHWH kiflaim kekol hat'oteha*" ("Speak ye comfortably to Jerusalem, and cry unto her, that her warfare is accomplished, that her iniquity is pardoned: for she hath received of the Lord's hand double for all her sins").

The first verse of this prophecy contains not a single dental, and there are relatively few in succeeding verses. The Aaronic blessing contains not one.

A similar soothing effect is produced on the ear by the verses of the *Shema,* selected as the portion to be recited each day, morning and night, as a declaration of loyalty to God and His Torah. The English of the first verse of the *Shema* reads (according to the King James Version), "Hear, O Israel: the Lord our God *is* one Lord" (Deuteronomy 6.4). The passage continues, "And thou shalt love the Lord thy God with all thine heart, and with all thy soul, and with all thy might. And these words, which I command thee this day, shall be in thine heart: And thou shalt teach them diligently unto thy children, and shalt talk of them when thou sittest in thine house, and when thou walkest by the way, and when thou liest down, and when thou risest up." While the words speak of love, there is little tenderness in their sound. However, it is quite otherwise in the Hebrew. The first verse of the Hebrew reads: "*shema' yisrael YHWH 'elohenu YHWH 'ehad*." The cadence suggests beseeching,

---

[8]My attention to the sound effect of these words was first aroused some forty years ago, in class lectures by the late Professor Israel Friedlaender.

rather than commanding. So do the following verses: *"ve-'ahabta 'et YHWH 'eloḳeha be-ḳol lebabeḳa u-be-ḳol nafsheḳa u-be-ḳol me'odeḳa, vehayu ha-debarim ha-'eleh 'asher 'anoḳi mesaveḳa ha-yom 'al lebabeḳa, ve-shinantam le-baneḳa, ve-dibarta bam be-shibteḳa be-beteḳa u-beleḳteḳa ba-dereḳ u-beshoḳbeḳa u-beḳumeḳa."* The repeated *lamed* with its lilt suggestive of softness and love, the hushing effect of the *shin,* the consolatary *mem,* make the recitation of the passage not the repetition of a commandment, but an assertion of God's love, and of His desire that man love Him.

A similar effect, both tender and soothing, is produced in the famous passage detailing the Divine attributes (Exodus, 34.6 f.) : *"YHWH YHWH 'el raḥum ve-ḥannun 'ereḳ 'appayim ve-rab heṣed ve-'emet noṣer ḥesed la-'alapim nose 'avon va-pesha' ve-ḥatta'ah"* ("The Lord God, merciful and gracious, longsuffering and abundant in goodness and truth, Keeping mercy for thousands, forgiving iniquity and transgression and sin." King James Version). However, the verse continues with quite different sounds to stress also the severity of the Divine penalties: *"ve-naqqe' l'o yenaqqe' poqed 'avon 'abot 'al banim ve-'al bené banim 'al shileshim ve-'al ribbe'im"* ("and that will by no means clear *the guilty;* visiting the iniquity of the fathers upon the children, and the children's children, unto the third and to the fourth *generation"*). We have already observed the force of the ancient *qof,* repeated in this brief passage thrice, twice in the emphatic *piel,* where its force is doubled; and we observe further the explosive *b* sound in the second half of the verse. It is clear that beautiful verse is meant to suggest by its very melody both the mercies and the severities of the Divine Moral Law.

The sound of the Hebrew words can produce effects other than those of either severity or tenderness. The Book of Genesis opens with verses which suggest the murmurings of the primeval waters and their hushed sounds. *"bereshit bara' 'elohim 'et hashamayim ve-'et ha-'areṣ ve-ha-'areṣ hayeta tohu va-bohu ve-ḥoshek 'al pene tehom ve-ruaḥ 'elohim meraḥefet 'al pene ha-mayim."* The repeated *m, r,* and *sh* sounds suggest a forest or a body of water, with the waves lapping the surface in the darkness. All this is of course quite lacking in the more prosaic, though beautiful translation of the King James Version, "In the beginning God created the heaven and the earth. And the earth was without form and void; and darkness *was* upon the face of the deep. And the spirit of God moved upon the face of the waters." The combination *"ruaḥ . . . meraḥefet"* is doubtless deliberate, so to speak; it gives a deep sense of the brooding of the Divine Spirit amidst the eternal silence of the beginning of things. The story continues, in Hebrew, *"vay'omer 'elohim"* ("and God said") *"yehi 'or"* ("Let there be light"). The suddenness with which the brief sounds *"yehi 'or"* burst upon us after the long introduction is clearly intended to suggest the suddenness with which the Voice of God broke upon the primeval stillness.

The English, "Let there be light," seems to reverberate through the empty spaces, like the loud voice of a master, walking into a dark room, shocked by the darkness. The Hebrew words may be said either loudly or quietly; in either case their force derives from their economy of sound. The Master is not interested in commanding or in being obeyed; He is concerned with the light, and wants it produced with the least possible effort on His part. He claps His hands, as it were, and His will is done.

When God discovers that man is unworthy of the faith He placed in him, He is sore at heart. The Divine sadness is expressed in moving tones: *" 'emḥeh 'et ha-'adam 'asher bara'ti me'al pene ha-'adamah me-'adam 'ad behemah 'ad remes ve-'ad 'of ha-shamayim ki niḥamti ki 'asitim"* ("I will destroy man whom I have created from the face of the earth; both man, and beast, and the creeping thing, and the fowls of the air; for it repenteth me[9] that I have made them." King James Version, Genesis 6.7). (A similar phrase occurs in an elegiac passage in Jeremiah 9.9, King James Version, 9.10): *"me-'of ha-shamayim ve-'ad behemah nadedu halaḳu"* ("both the fowl of the heavens and the beast are fled; they are gone"). The repeated *m* sound, together with the *shin,* has in these passages a sound of mourning and utter sadness. The same configuration of sounds appears in David's lament over Saul and Jonathan, especially in its final, heartrending verses (II Samuel, 1.23 ff.); in the lament over Abner the alliterative *lamed* is stressed with a similar effect (II Samuel, 3.34).

A few verses later, God tells Noah of His decision to destroy man. He articulates His sentence as usual in harsh dental sounds, *"qeṣ kol basar ba' lefanai"* ("The end of all flesh has come before me," King James Version, Genesis, 6.13). Having uttered these decisive and harsh words, He proceeds gently and comfortingly to explain His sentence to Noah, and advise him to find safety in the ark; *"ki male'ah ha-'areṣ ḥamas*

---

[9]The authors of the King James Version render the Hebrew with the impersonal, "it repenteth me," to avoid anthropomorphism; the word means, literally, "I am sorry."

mi-penehem ve-hineni mashḥitam 'et ha-'areṣ" ("for the earth is filled with violence through them; and behold, I will destroy them with the earth." King James Version).

In a remarkable passage, Deuteronomy 28.3 ff., we are enabled to observe the way the substitution of a single word in repeated verses, will create a totally different sound effect for the whole passage. These verses contain first the blessings promised Israel, if it would observe the Commandments, and then the penalties to which it would be exposed for transgression. The blessings read: *"baruk 'attah ba-'ir u-baruk 'attah ba-sadeh. baruk peri bitneka u-peri 'admateka u-peri behemteka shegar 'alapeka ve-'ashterot so'neka baruk tan'aka u-mish'arteka baruk 'attah be-bo'eka baruk 'attah beṣe'teka."*

When the curse is to be pronounced, the word *" 'arur"* is substituted for *"baruk"* in each verse. The difference in effect is vast. The repeated *"baruk"* gives the whole passage a loving tenderness, which becomes almost harsh when the hard sounding *" 'arur"* replaces it. (The King James Version reads for the first passage, "Blessed *shalt* thou *be* in the city, and blessed *shalt* thou *be* in the field. Blessed *shall* be the fruit of thy body, and the fruit of thy ground, and the fruit of thy cattle, the increase of thy kine, and the flocks of thy sheep. Blessed *shall* be thy basket and thy store. Blessed *shalt* thou *be* when thou comest in, and blessed *shalt* thou *be* when thou goest out." In Deuteronomy 28.16 ff., the passage is repeated *verbatim,* except for the substitution of "cursed" for "blessed," and a change in the order of the verses.)

For one reared in the Synagogue, the sound effect of many passages, particularly of the Pentateuch, is further enhanced by the chant. Thus, on fast days, when the passage including the attributes of God, mentioned above, is read publicly, a particularly moving chant is used in some rites, giving great emphasis to the tenderness of the passage. Similarly the melodies used for the Pentateuch readings of the High Holy Days (*Rosh ha-Shanah* and *Yom Kippur*) cause a special love and tenderness to attach to those portions, even when they happen to deal with ritualistic laws, otherwise quite prosaic. But the stirring power of the melody becomes far greater when it happens to coincide with the denotative theme of the passage.

Thus, when Isaac innocently asks Abraham, why he had brought the fire and the wood for the sacrifice but no lamb, Abraham replies, with heartbreaking sounds, in which we can almost hear his tears: *" 'elohim*

yir'eh l'o haseh le'olah beni" ("My son, God will provide himself a lamb
for a burnt offering." King James Version, Genesis 22.8). The repeated
lamed together with *resh,* in a few brief words, has the usual effect of
arousing pity. But when chanted in the Synagogue with the particular
melody assigned to the passage for the festival of *Rosh ha-Shanah,* its
force is multiplied many times.

Some writers had apparently an especial feeling for particular sounds,
or at least utilized particular sounds to produce the effects they desired.
One of them was the author of the Book of Ruth, who seems to use certain sound expressions to portray the character of his main figures. Thus
when Ruth says to her mother-in-law, "Intreat me not to leave thee: *or to*
return from following after thee; for whither thou goest, I will go; and
where thou lodgest, I will lodge: thy people *shall be* my people, and thy
God, my God. Where thou diest, will I die, and there will I be buried: the
Lord do so to me, and more also, *if ought* but death part thee and me."
(1.16–17), the very lilt of her words, even in English, carries an emphasis
which is deeply moving. In the Hebrew original, Ruth spoke not with
emphasis, in a confession of faith and loyalty, but with deep personal
love for her deceased husband's mother. In the English Ruth is attracted
to the faith of Israel. Her words in Hebrew are: "*'al tipgei bi le-'azek
lashub me-'aharayik ki 'el 'asher teleki 'elek, u-ba'asher talini 'alin,
'ammek 'ammi, ve-'elohayik 'elohay. ba-'asher tamuti 'amut, ve-sham
'eqaber, ko ya'aseh YHWH li ve-ko yosif ki ha-mavet yafrid beni
u-benek.*" Even in transliteration, the particular emphasis on the *lamed*
sound, as well as the tender *m,* cannot be overlooked.

The author repeatedly makes use of this configuration of sound effects, because apparently he regards it as most effective, and perhaps because it was powerful in his particular dialect. When Boaz awakens to
find Ruth sleeping at his feet, he praises her, and ends his remark with
the words: *"lini ha-laylah vehayah baboqer 'im yige'alek tob yig'al, ve-'im
l'o yahpoṣ le-go'olek u-ge'altik 'anoki. hai YHWH shikbi 'ad ha-boqer"*
("Tarry this night, and it shall be in the morning, *that* if he will perform unto thee the right of a kinsman, well; let him do the kinsman's
part: but if he will not do the part of a kinsman to thee, then will I do
the part of a kinsman to thee, *as* the Lord liveth: lie down until the
morning." King James Version, Ruth 3.13).

It seems scarcely probable that this conjunction of sound in different
parts of the book (and also in other passages) can be mere coincidence.

The reader will see that I am trying to translate into discursive signs the emotional impact made upon me by the different cadences of Scriptural verses. Undoubtedly, this emotional impact is related to the circumstances under which I first heard or read these verses, the cantillation provided for them, and the synagogue setting in which they are uttered. Nevertheless, it seems possible that there is some force inherent in the sounds themselves.

If this is correct, the divergence of the authors of the King James Version from the cadence of the Hebrew may itself reflect a special theological concept. Those masters of the English language could have preserved the softness and tenderness I find in so many passages, had they recognized it in the original. But they doubtless felt, as have so many interpreters of prophetic religion outside the Jewish tradition, that the God of the Prophets was remote and austere, a King, rather than a Father; and that this conception of Him was the only one possible in the age of the Prophets.

At any rate, the King James Version not only fails, like other versions, to suggest the tenderness and sweetness the Hebrew cadences ascribe to God. It goes much further. It deliberately utilizes a cadence which tends to make Him remote and unapproachable. This cadence, the fruit of so much earlier philosophical and theological exegesis, has helped put its stamp on later thought.

So prevalent is the usual conception of the Prophetic God as austere and distant, that the thesis here maintained may seem to some readers impossible of acceptance. Yet the current view seems equally unrealistic and utterly out of accord, to one reared on the Rabbinic interpretations of Scripture and on the Hebrew text.

Accepting the abstract intellectualism of Maimonides and his followers in their approach to the Deity, the student of Scripture in Judaism feels he can attain a depth of communion with God in prayer and in the performance of the Commandments, which is the profoundest experience in all his life. Indeed, the dogmas of Maimonides himself have, as is well known, been formulated as a hymn, whose words contain philosophical-theological abstractions, but whose sound is deeply stirring and —put to the music of the traditional melodies—capable of reducing one to tears, particularly during the High Holy Days.

Perhaps in some future studies I may be able to indicate how these effects are achieved through the very text of the prayers, and how different schools of Jewish theology sometimes expressed their opposing concepts of God through differences in poetic cadence, as well as in diction.

Comment by Swami Akhilananda:

It is no wonder that Louis Finkelstein and other such scholars are often amazed by the misinterpretation of the Hebrew text. The same can be said about the misinterpretation and erroneous understanding of the Hindu conception of God by Western thinkers, when they used to say that Hinduism is polytheism, and when they now say that it is a metaphysical concept.

How interesting it is to note that the various sounds, as uttered by the Hebrew prophets and quoted by Finkelstein, express different qualities of the divine Being. Cadence and rhythmic notes symbolically express different phases of that ultimate Reality. Every religion has its symbolic expressions for the various aspects of God. It is but right that this is so. We human beings with our finite minds cannot wholly comprehend the Absolute—God. Yet we have our own individual ways of approaching that Reality. So the Hindus say:

> Truth is one; men call it by various names (Veda). There is but one God and endless are His names and aspects in which He may be regarded. Call Him by any name and worship Him in any aspect that pleases you. You are sure to realize Him (Sri Ramakrishna).

So the differences will remain in religious approach to God.

We can support Finkelstein's thesis, from Hindu tradition, that sounds and cadence give different meaning from what is assumed by man of the Western thinkers. The word *Brahman* means God. If we add *Nirgun* to *Brahman* it means Absolute, without name form, and qualities. If we add *Sagun* to *Brahman* (instead of *Nirgun*), it means personified Absolute with qualities and attributes. When the word *Brahmâ* is uttered, it means the creative power of *Sagun-Brahman*. This shows that a little intonation or addition of a prefix or a suffix can change the meaning. Cadence also changes the feeling of an individual toward the Absolute.

We make an erroneous judgment if we regard Philo and Maimonides as mere conceptual philosophers. It is true that they approach God through the intellectual method, which the Hindus call *Jnana Yoga,* yet they have emotional satisfaction. We can cite as examples of this Saint Dionysius and Meister Eckhart in the Christian tradition, Plato and Plotinus in the Greek tradition, and Sankara, Swami Vivekananda, and others in the Hindu tradition.

We understand from the Hebrew writings that God is not merely transcendent but He is also immanent, as indicated in the Psalms and other writings. Our understanding of this is that the Reality is both immanent and transcendent. The world and man, as we perceive them at present, are not the Absolute. In that sense God is transcendent, but the world and man as they really exist are based on that immanent Being. So the Psalms declare that one can feel the presence of God everywhere. The transcendence and immanence of God are perceived by different individuals in any of these religious groups according to their spiritual evolution. The symbols and cadence that are used only indicate both the immanence and transcendence of God. The use of symbols and cadence is absolutely necessary for our comprehension of God by this finite mind.

Comment by David Norimoto Iino:

Louis Finkelstein is enlightening in making me see that the force of the Hebrew original derives more from the cadence and lilt of the words than from their literal meaning and that English translations err in making the God of the Hebrew prophets stern and remote. In reading English translations of classical Japanese literature I, too, have felt that the meaning of the original is distorted in the translation. The reason is due to the inability of the translation to convey the sweetness and pathos of the original. Japanese is symbolic in the sense of being suggestive and poetic. When a master of Japanese uses it, it can engender in the reader an appreciation hard to explain through anything but Japanese. Writers of the shorter forms of poetry can let the briefest form express the deepest thought. What Finkelstein says about the Hebrew economy of sound is the ideal of Japanese poetry, too.

His insight into the tender mercy of God is more in line with what the facts of experience seem to bespeak as to the nature of God. The God of human experience is not a hidden and austere God. Such an idea is a product of the emotions frustrated by the observation of the darker side of life which a God Who is not strictly almighty could not eliminate wholesale. A view such as Harold DeWolf's that the Greek New Testament gives the attribute of God almighty παντοκράτωρ due to mistranslation of the Hebrew word *Shaddai,* supports Finkelstein's position.

I agree with him as he attributes the effectiveness of Hebrew symbolism to its appeal to both our intellect and the emotions. Symbolism is not fruitful without these two appeals. I disagree with those who regard faith as the only vehicle of revelation. Faith, in the last analysis, is something symbolic and emotional. But we cannot have faith in what is not convincing unless we deceive ourselves or stop thinking. Comprehension through our total experience is what can best engender the emotional reaction called faith. In fact these two appeals coalesce. What is incomprehensible is not apt to be the object of a genuine emotional appreciation. And such an object is likely to be studied painstakingly that its meaning may be grasped by our intellect also. For example, scientific study of the Universe has been given an added impetus because of the religious faith in the divine creation of the world. The latter has been more firmly validated by the metaphysical scrutiny of the whole. A philosopher of religion who would like to see more evidence is deeply appreciative of information on the Hebrew religion at its truest revealed by Finkelstein's research and experience. Narrowness is the enemy of the love of truth. The closed mind too proud to learn from another means death to religion. One's intellect and emotions must be enlightened by new fact and value.

Finkelstein implies the coalescence of religions. The God of the Hebrew religion is closer to the God of Jesus than English translations of the Old Testament depict Him to be. The graciousness of the same God is revealed in Buddhism which regards the cosmic radiation of Buddha's spirit as something like the mercy of the full moon adorning not only the lake but the smallest of the dew drops on the windblown leaf. *Jodoshinshu* has it that a man who has reached the shore of salvation is so grateful as to feel constrained to return to this world again so as to be a Buddha to his neighbors that they, too, may join him in attaining salvation. Whenever there is an ideal value we should see the revelation of the same Father of Mankind. The uniqueness of each religion should be studied carefully but that should not deny the coalescence of all religions.

The basis of all experience is emotional. In the process of knowing any object, our interpretation of its nature is always colored by the emotional reaction of the knower to a much greater extent than most thinkers assume. This is what Finkelstein stresses as he refers to his cultural background and home training, influencing his own appreciation of the cadence and lilt of the original text of the Hebrew Scripture. This has a wider application than that which he envisages. The discernment of the nature of anything, whether it be a stone, a country, Scripture, is symbolically emotional. Especially about the knowledge of God we must say that there is more room for the emotions to do their work of distorting, denying, or exaggerating, for He is the vastest object there is. The limitations of language as a symbol of communication are aptly stressed by A. N. Whitehead. Between God and man there is no language except our symbolic interpretation of the signs of the times, nature, history, Scripture, our own inner lives. As we think about the meaning of symbolism in the realm of religion, we see that its use must be carefully supplemented by coherent thought. Without coherence symbolism is like a boat without the rudder.

Symbols must be easy to understand if they are to appeal to the masses of people. From this point of view the Fatherhood of God is a good symbol. It is found in Plato (the πᾱτήε of *Timaeus*, 28C), in the Hebraic religion, and the religion of Jesus. Since this is a most important symbol, we must interpret its true meaning in the light of our total experience. To God the problem of communication through symbols must be a matter of the deepest concern for He, throughout the ages, has done His best in communicating His message of peace and love, not through language but through symbols scattered everywhere in the universe. The whole cosmos is a system of divine symbols of the Fatherhood of the God of mankind.

Comment by Hajime Nakamura:
In the East also we find phenomena somewhat similar to the facts pointed out in this paper.

Poems of Zen Buddhism were originally composed in medieval Chinese, and their vocabulary was highly colloquial in comparison with that of the Chinese Buddhist Scriptures composed before. A lot of Zen terms were adopted from daily life conversation. The style was familiar to the Chinese of those days, and the sentences are very easy to understand. Their cadence or lilt was congenial to them. But Japanese traditional scholars translated them into literary, archaic Japanese with most Chinese words intact, *viz.*, most of the important words in them have been preserved intact (not translated) in traditional Japanese translations, although the cadence or lilt of the original Zen poems was completely lost in Japanese translations. The traditional Japanese translations of Zen poems sound very difficult and abstruse for Japanese common people, for those colloquial or vernacular Chinese terms look very strange and awkward to them, especially to younger people nowadays. Americans read the poems in the translations of Daisetz T. Suzuki and others, which can be read easily or congenially, whereas traditional Japanese translations of Zen poems give the impression of being highly abstruse or awkward. That is why Zen poems are becoming more and more unpopular among younger Japanese.

This holds true with Chinese versions of philosophical Sanskrit poems. For example, the Madhyamaka-Śāstra of Nāgārjuna, the Buddhist philosopher (second to third century A.D.), was composed in *slokas,* the most popular form of Indian poetry. Every Indian intellectual of those days could understand the purport, and enjoy the rhythm, of the work. However, the Chinese version was set forth in an abridged form, which, together with its foreign provenance, went the length of giving the impression of extreme abstruseness even to Chinese intellectuals of the past.

By accumulating phenomena of this sort throughout East and West we might expect finally to acquire some general conclusions in the long run.

Comment by Joshua Whatmough:
If the argument is that in a given language certain phonemes or groups of phonemes (other than merely onomatopoetic) have inherent meaning, this is not acceptable to Linguistics. What is true, is that such a specialized meaning as appreciative or esthetic may come to be acquired from a few words—one or two will do—as it were by abstraction, and then be extended to other words. Historical considerations regularly show that a certain sound-group, *e.g.,* initial *sl*—in English (said to be depreciatory: *slip, slop, slump, slave*) is etymologically of quite diverse origin. In what sense do we react to the "sound of the words, rather than merely [!] to their meaning"? Is not the sound, even of a word of unique occurrence, *part of* the meaning? The meaning, however, is properly given by phonemes and the patterned sequence of phonemes. It is not through *phonetic*, but through *phonematic*, values that "language operates" chiefly, a distinction hardly realized by those who are not linguists.

I agree entirely about the inadequacy of translation, which always distorts the message, except in such expressions as "two and two are four," in which the terms are entirely arbitrary.

But form (*i.e.,* structure) plays a far greater role than acoustic features. The same sequence of sounds may differ totally in meaning not only when reversed (God; dog), but even in words differing only by one phoneme. Is *ame* (*aim*) filled with a content of meaning because of a supposed "pleasing" sound? Rhyme would be impossible if this were true. We all remember *South Pacific:* "There's nothing like a *dame . . . same . . . name . . . frame.*"

CHAPTER XIV

The Evocative Symbol

By WILLIAM F. LYNCH, S.J.

I SHOULD LIKE to focus my small part in this discussion on symbolism immediately. I shall be interested, not in any kind of total exploration of the nature and values of the symbol, but in one delimited but major drive in the habits of symbolism as we know it in our generation. That major drive can be summarized at once in the following way: the symbol is evocative, it looks to the creation and nurturing of energies, life, and aspirations at the interior of the human person. Its eye has become largely turned inward and not outward. It is in danger of taking a new and almost exclusively psychologistic path. Much of this major drive is fundamentally uninterested in "actuality." It is in danger of letting the ideas of actuality, truth, event, disappear out of the symbol situation.

This is a rough and tentative statement for exploration. Once again, it is not meant as an accurate and total summary of where we stand at the present moment in our civilization over against the symbol and symbolism. But the purpose of this Conference may be well served if tentative positions are sharply taken and highlighted as a preliminary to our common debate.

My own discussion will take the following simple form: a running documentary and analytical summary of those evocative and nonactual drives in the contemporary concern about the symbol which I have already suggested as surely a problem and possibly a disease. It will receive its sharpest focus in a discussion of the tendency of the modern symbol to move into the areas of magic and manipulation.

I

It will help very much to begin with a simple, almost diagrammatic outline of the potentially double orientation of every symbol as this double orientation, evocative and transcendental, psychological and "actual," is proposed by Jacques Maritain:

In the work of art . . . we meet with what can be called the *direct* sign (indicating an object) and the *reverse* sign (making manifest the subject). . . . The letter *A* signifies the sound A, mourning signifies death. But the sign can also act in a reverse sense: while making manifest an object, it can—by an inverse or retroverse signification—denote the very subject who makes use of this sign: his condition, his dispositions, his secrets which he does not even admit to himself—the subject being then taken as object by some observer.[1]

Note well that though we can reduce this pattern to a diagram,

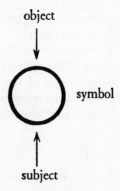

we cannot reduce it to a simplicity, for the processes by which the discovered or created symbol flows out into actuality and back into the subject are extremely complicated. The objectivist with a passion for the referential value of the symbol would be overdoing his case were he to minimize its evocative qualities, or if he were to try to establish some kind of awkward priority and posteriority in these outward and inward processes. Actually symbolic propositions and facts in art and religion either are capable of creating enormous echoes in the psyche or they are without *human* meaning; actually, too, it seems highly probable that the outward and the inward flow of the symbol, the cognitive and evocative, occur psychologically *in the one act* and need not be defended against any awkward descriptions of time sequences.

Now two things may occur to disturb the complex balance of this single psychic act of cognition and evocation. Symbols may (though we will not for the moment go into the etiology of this situation) lose their

[1] Jacques Maritain, *Ransoming the Time,* Charles Scribner's Sons, New York, 1941, p. 253.

human and evocative quality, and only retain an increasingly meaning-less and nominalistic quality of reference to an object, of whatever kind of world it be. The symbol then becomes a dead formula, incapable of raising any repercussions in the human person. No sane man would praise this kind of symbol situation. Nevertheless, it is the larger point of this paper that it is an even more unfortunate situation when the flow of symbolic energy out into the actual and the objective comes to the dying point and we deal with symbols from the exclusive point of view of creating inward states in man, of providing spiritual and political energies and harmonies within him. Whether this latter is not indeed a great contemporary phenomenon and whether it can accomplish its goal are the questions cordially raised in these pages.

A

The literary imagination was hardly the first to disturb our delicate, diagrammatic balance in favor of psychologism (we cannot take the time here to review the history of ideas metaphysical and theological that led to the collapse in the West of the metaphysical and theological object). But the men who trade in the making of the life of the imag-ination are the final formers of our most habitual symbols and images—so that it is right to pick and choose first from their psychologistic habits.

One thinks quickly of Proust and his cup of tea[2] and of Proust and his bar of music:[3] the attempt in each case to win back, through fortu-

---

2 I drink a second mouthful, in which I find nothing more than in the first, a third, which gives me rather less than the second. It is time to stop; the potion is losing its magic. It is plain that the object of my quest, the truth, lies not in the cup but in myself. The tea has called up in me, but does not itself understand, and can only repeat indefinitely, with a gradual loss of strength, the same testimony; which I, too, cannot interpret, though I hope at least to be able to call upon the tea for it again and to find it there presently, intact and at my disposal, for my final enlightenment.

Marcel Proust, *Swann's Way,* Modern Library, New York, 1928, p. 55. Reprinted by permission of Random House, Inc.

3 The little phrase was associated still, in Swann's mind, with his love for Odette. He felt clearly that this love was something to which there was no corresponding external signs, whose meaning could not be proved by any but himself; he realised, too, that Odette's qualities were not such as to justify his setting so high a value on the hours he spent in her company. And often, when the cold government of reason stood unchallenged, he would readily have ceased to sacrifice so many of his intellectual and social interests to this imaginary pleasure. But the little phrase, as soon as it struck his ear, had the power to liberate in him the room that was needed to contain it; the proportions of Swann's soul were altered; a margin was left for a form of enjoyment which corresponded no more than his love for Odette to any external object, and yet was not, like his enjoyment of that love, purely individual, but assumed for him an objective reality superior to that of other concrete things. This thirst for an untasted charm, the little phrase would stimulate it anew in him, but without bringing him any definite gratification to assuage it. With

nate sensation, to a memory or to a heaven-charged depth in the self; the return again and again to the symbol image, to this powerful, this evocative cup of tea; but my complaint is that there is no real interest in the tea, nor in the music; there is no real oscillation between these finite, human things and the dream of the past, so that the more the one would be plumbed, the more would the other, too. Indeed, there is the feeling that the *actuality* of these contemporary sensations is an obstacle to the invocation, the daylight of it is a too clear consciousness that must be overcome. These are secret, tenuous notes in the real world which help us to overcome reality, only open to an elite perceptiveness. There

the result that those parts of Swann's soul in which the little phrase had obliterated all care for material interests, those human considerations which affect all men alike, were left bare by it, blank pages on which he was at liberty to inscribe the name of Odette. Moreover, where Odette's affection might seem ever so little abrupt and disappointing, the little phrase would come to supplement it, to amalgamate with it its own mysterious essence. Watching Swann's face while he listened to the phrase, one would have said that he was inhaling an anaesthetic which allowed him to breathe more deeply. And the pleasure which the music gave him, which was shortly to create in him a real longing, was in fact closely akin, at such moments, to the pleasure which he would have derived from experimenting with perfumes, from entering into contact with a world for which we men were not created, which appears to lack form because our eyes cannot perceive it, to lack significance because it escapes our intelligence, to which we may attain by way of one sense only.

Ibid., pp. 306–307.

ªComment by James Collins:

The classical philosophical counterpart to these texts from Proust is found in Kierkegaard's *Repetition*. Here we are given the fable about the poetic individual who returns to the same theater in the hope of recapturing a lost moment of pleasure and feeling of ecstasy. Although he fails in this particular quest, he continues to grasp at external events as a means of returning to some purely private heaven within his own experience. The mind which allows imagination to dominate and to dictate the fundamental relations to the world, finally ends by becoming a pitiful and slightly foolish slave of passing moods and fancies. The purely evocative personality has illusions of omnipotence, turning the actual world totally in an inward direction, until some slight excess of unyielding actuality dispels the feeling. "In me all was ominous, and everything was enigmatically transfigured in my microcosmic bliss, which was able to transform into its own likeness all things, even the observations which were most disagreeable and tiresome, even disgusting sights and the most fatal collisions. When precisely at one o'clock I was at the highest peak, where I surmised the ultimate attainment, something suddenly began to chafe one of my eyes, whether it was an eye-lash, a mote, a bit of dust, I do not know; but this I know, that in that selfsame instant I toppled down almost into the abyss of despair (Soren Kierkegaard, *Repetition,* translated by Walter Lowrie, Princeton University Press, Princeton, 1941, p. 76)." The double price paid for overstressing the subjective direction of symbols is, first, that the meaning itself loses its determinate boundaries and relations and thus dissolves into mere euphoria, and next, that the dreamer loses the capacity to see the human significance of the familiar things of our world. Thus Kierkegaard's playgoer returns to his room and is overcome with nausea at the sight of the furniture and homely surroundings. Sartre has universalized this disgust on the part of the thinker who finds no meanings and references but must pretend to be their creator in every respect.

is here no high and muddy entrance into the actual, no theory of a deeper entrance into the actual, into the daylight world, in order to tie down a surer dream. If there is any digging here, it is a digging into the past and the self, never into the tea (we have said there is no true oscillating movement)—in the sense that Blackmur has put so well.[4] This is the kind of fundamental fear of the resources of the thick and nonvague world of consciousness which finally made Jacques Rivière turn his back on the Symbolistes because of his own needs:

> The first of these needs, directly implied by all his criticism thus far (of Symbolism) is for the palpable . . . the work of art itself, just as its source in the material world, must even typographically be thick, long, "a cake of earth and stones," no longer haunted by "blank pages," nor built on "absence," or even "silence"; for these are not the things of man.[5]

Wagner has taught us in an extensive way the uses of the symbol to evoke the dream, the uses of a tenuous real that must evade the note of the actual:

> . . . the ship which carries Isolde is not a ship in its own right, but only those aqueous and unfixed qualities which it shares with the lost beginnings of passion. As for the wind, it would ruin everything to know its velocity in knots.[6]

And I think of Yeats in his pleading hymn to the magicians of the imagination to overcome the actuality of old age by building a new inward city in "Sailing to Byzantium":

> O sages standing in God's holy fire
> As in the gold mosaic of a wall,
> Come from the holy fire, perne in a gyre,
> And be the singing-masters of my soul.
> Consume my heart away; sick with desire
> And fastened to a dying animal

[4]R. P. Blackmur, "Unappeasable and Peregrine: Behavior and the Four Quartets," *Thought,* vol. XXVI, no. 100, Spring, 1951, p. 63:

> . . . his poem would seem to tell us, with examples, that man's ideals ought to be nourished by the cumulus of manifestations of the real into the actual (and of the actual into the real; for it is a reversible relation).

[5]Bradford Cook, "Jacques Rivière and Symbolism," in *Yale French Studies (Symbol and Symbolism)*, no. 9, p. 109.

[6]Francis Fergusson, *The Idea of a Theatre*, Doubleday Anchor Books, New York, 1953, p. 93.

It knows not what it is; and gather me
Into the artifice of eternity.

Once out of nature I shall never take
My bodily form from any natural thing,
But such a form as Grecian goldsmiths make
Of hammered gold and gold enamelling
To keep a drowsy Emperor awake;
Or set upon a golden bough to sing
To lords and ladies of Byzantium
Of what is past, or passing, or to come.[7]

Indeed, there was through so many of the Symboliste theorists the note of a resort only to certain well selected regions of the actual which could function (God knows why) magically. Magic, mysticism, esotericism, the occult, a new theosophy, were in the air.[8] The finite and the human reality was no longer being lived through or in; it was being manipulated, used, exploited. Let us call it the new scientific (almost mathematical) instrumentalization of the actual in the interest of the restoration of what André Gide[9] himself called the Lost Paradise. The new poets had turned their backs on the old allegorical and conceptual poetry

---

[7] W. B. Yeats, "Sailing to Byzantium," *Collected Poems,* The Macmillan Company, New York, 1951, p. 192.

[8] Ces aperçus suffisent à démontrer que la science et l'esprit moderne se préparent sans le savior et sans le vouloir à une reconstitution de l'antique théosophie avec des instruments plus précis et sur une base plus solide. . . . Alors se confirmeront les paroles d'un écrit hermétique contemporain, et elles ne sembleront pas trop audacieuses à ceux qui ont pénétré assez profondement dans les traditions occultes pour soupçonner leur merveilleuse unité: "La doctrine esotérique n'est pas seulement une science, une philosophie, une morale, une religion. Elle est *la* science, *la* philosophie, *la* morale, *la* religion dont toutes les autres ne sont que des préparations ou des dégénérescences, des expressions partielles ou faussées, selon qu'elles y acheminent ou en devient."

Schuré, *préface des Grands Initiés,* 1889.

Il doit y avoir quelque chose d'occulte au fond de tous. Mallarmé, *Les Mystères dans les Lettres,* 1896.

Toute chose sacrée et qui veut demeurer sacrée s'enveloppe de mystère. Mallarmé, *L'Art pour tous,* 1862.

For other similar texts *cf.* Guy Michaud, *La Doctrine Symboliste* (Documents), Paris, 1947.

[9] Triste race qui te disperseras sur cette terre de crépuscule et de prières! Le souvenir du Paradis perdu viendra désoler tes extases, du Paradis que tu rechercheras partout—dont viendront te reparler des prophètes—et des poètes, que voici, qui recueilleront pieusement déchirés du Livre immemorial ou se lisait la vérité qu'il faut connaître. . . . Le Poète est celui qui regarde. Et que voit-il?—Le Paradis. . . . Car le Paradis est partout; n'en croyons pas les apparences. Les apparences sont imparfaites: elles balbutient les vérités qu'elles recélent; le Poète, a demimot, doit comprendre,—puis redire ces vérités.

Michaud, *ibid.*

—no need to say that. But had not many of them, as Allen Tate[10] saw it, come back ironically to the same pitfall, the instrumentalizing of the real in the interest of the useful, of some form of power? What is the organized shape and meaning of the human?—it did not matter. It was more important that symbol and human sensation should function in the interest of an inward peace and paradise. And this is precisely the issue I many times raise: the noncognitive exploitation of symbols. If we insist that they be rooted in cognition and the restoration of the balance with whose description this paper began, it is not because we minimize the status and power of symbols; we very well recognize and acclaim their extraordinary power for creation and destruction in human life.

B

There are many kinds of play for the imagination—and this is good, as long as it quite knows it is playing.[11] And who would not admit that

10 There is therefore a distinction to be drawn between a kind of writing in which allegorical meanings are fused with the material, and pure and explicit allegory. It is the difference between works of the creative imagination and the inferior works of the practical will. The reader will recall my first proposition: the power of creating the inner meaning of experience is a quality of the imagination. It is not a construction of the will, that perpetual modernism through which, however vast may be the physical extent of the poet's range, the poet ignores the whole of experience for some special interest. This modern literature of Platonism—a descriptive term used to set apart a kind of work in which the meanings are forced—carries with it its own critical apparatus. It is known at present as the revolutionary or social point of view. Since the rise of science it has been also the "capitalist" point of view. For our whole culture seems to be obsessed by a kind of literature that is derivative of the allegorical mentality.

Allen Tate, *On the Limits of Poetry*, Swallow Press, New York, 1948, pp. 98–99. Reprinted by permission of the publisher, Alan Swallow. Copyright 1948 by Allen Tate.

Mr. Richards' theory of the relation between poetry and our beliefs about the world appears novel to some critics. It is the latest version of the allegorical, puritan and utilitarian theory of the arts—a theory that is rendered, by Mr. Richards, the more plausible because it seems to give to the arts a very serious attention. The British utilitarians, a century ago, frankly condemned them. So, with less candor, does Mr. Richards: his desperate efforts to make poetry, after all, useful, consist in justly reducing its "explanations" to nonsense, and salvaging from the wreck a mysterious agency for ordering our minds.

Ibid., pp. 107–108.

11 Imagination is beyond good *and* evil, but it is only with the help of imagination that I can become good *or* evil. Without imagination I remain an innocent animal, unable to become anything but what I really am. In order to become what I should become, therefore, I have to put my imagination to work, to limit its playful activities, to imagining those possibilities which, for me, are both permissible and real; if I allow it to be the master and play exactly as it likes, then I shall remain in a dream-like state of imagining everything I might become, without getting around to ever becoming anything. But once imagination has done its work for me to the degree that, with its help, I have become what I should become, imagination has a right to demand its freedom to play without any limitations, for there is no longer any danger that I shall take its play seriously.

W. H. Auden, "Balaam and the Ass: The Master-Servant Relationship in Literature," *Thought*, vol. XXIX, no. 113, Summer, 1954, p. 260.

the creation of inward energy, of an inward heaven and harmony, is also a blessed thing? But there are dangers in real illusions and escapes, when the play becomes increasingly serious. This occurs on a larger and larger scale as our culture goes in more and more for evocation and less and less for the cognitive. Let me illustrate this again, from what is surely a central passion in literature, the writing of tragedy.[12]

About tragedy, might we dare go along with the simple thesis that, wherever it has come off well and best, wherever, therefore, there is no discussion about the achievement (as with the Greeks), this achievement has been cognitive and actual. The dramatist, let us say in the *Oedipus,* has really faced into the finitude of man, to the finest point of helplessness, the collapse of human energy, death. It is by this facing, without distraction, into the exceedingly concrete innards of what we may (for want of a better word!) call the finite structure of the finite and limited human situation, that the extraordinary exaltations which belong to tragedy are evoked. Now exaltation can, indeed, come only from some form of the sublime, but here the facts of the true tragic text indicate that the sublimity is not in the greatness of man (his heroicity, his nobility in pain, etc.) but in the extraordinary depth of his finitude when it is, without distraction, really confronted.

Put the shoe on the other foot and what happens? I would say, very bad tragedy. If you begin with the concept of exalted man, if you begin with the desire to produce exaltation in an audience through tragic symbols, most of the evidence of contemporary American attempts at tragedy indicate that there will be two results: 1) The sublimity of the true (and awesome) depths of the finite is turned into a flat and contemptible, a small and Manichaean reality that must be rebelled against by the human spirit, if indeed man is emotionally to secure *any kind of* salvation. 2) This human spirit must find greatness and exaltation in its own size and capacity for resentment. In the concrete texts this leads to an exaltation of human energy, to protagonists who, far from cognitively discovering the finite, are chockfull of all those inauthentic energies that are found in the last acts of so much American tragedy.

The modern tragic hero does very well with his confrontation of

---

[12]The material on tragedy from a previous article ("Confusion in Our Theater," *Thought,* vol. XXVI, no. 102, Autumn, 1951, pp. 342 ff.) is here restated in the light of the question of the cognitive *versus* the purely evocative and because of the later necessity I meet in this paper of correlating the problem of tragedy with that of the freedom of the imagination.

finitude, very well up to the last and finest point of finitude. But because fundamentally he cannot trust actuality and the conscious sense of limit to lead him anywhere, he must turn away from this finest and last point to indulge in all the fierce and powerful gestures of the romantic hero.[13]

[13]The amount of energy still left at the conclusion of contemporary tragedy is really extraordinary:

A) Examples from the dramatists: 1) Henrik Ibsen, *Enemy of the People:* "The Strongest man in the world is he who stands most alone." 2) Maxwell Anderson, *Winterset:* "And Mio—Mio, my son—know this where you lie./ This is the glory of Earth-born men and women./ Not to cringe, never to yield, but standing/ Take defeat implacable and defiant/ Die unsubmitting." 3) Clifford Odets, *Till the Day I Die:* "Let him die/ Let him live." 4) Odets, *Awake and Sing:* Ralph. "Right here in the house! My days won't be for nothing. Let Mom have the dough. I'm twenty-two and kickin'! I'll get along. Did Jake die for us to fight about nickels? No! The night he died I saw it like a thunderbolt! I saw he was dead and I was born! I swear to God I'm one week old!" 5) Paul Green, *The Field God:* "We are God—Man is God. That's the light, that's the truth. It will set them free. And love shall abide among us to the end."

B) And I extract from the theoretical essays and books on the subject of tragedy the following romantic pearls. They are really incomparable:

   1) The theater in general is nothing but the place for the development of the human will. . . . What I do not see is a dramatic renaissance whose dawn has not been announced, as it were by some progress or some arousing of the will.

   2) . . . in tragedy is embodied the eternal contradiction between man's weakness and his courage, his stupidity and his magnificence, his frailty and his strength. . . . Christianity trains men to endure evils, not to perform great actions.

   3) . . . suffering borne with dignity, with the indestructible strength of man's spirit. . . . The truly tragic hero "will weep no more," he "will endure." The ecstasy is not to be shunned. At this height he is alone, unique and sufficient. This is tragic dignity. . . . The spiritual elevation that can come only when a hero has learned to find his strength within himself is the keystone of the structure of tragedy. . . . Eliot has written a dramatic poem, a metrical drama, but not a dramatic tragedy. His philosophical pattern is in relation to tragedy "ignoble"; like Samson, Thomas à Becket finds his strength not in himself but in God. . . . Such plays have a religious rather than a tragic ending. They offer consolation in a dogma, not, primarily, in the strength of man.

   4) . . . it somehow or other follows from the belief that man has a certain dignity, and even grandeur, that the sight of a man collapsing in evil circumstances is the most marvelous spectacle in the world.

   5) . . . though life might be difficult and fate unintelligible, man had moral and emotional and intellectual qualities which could triumph over his fate or at least make him superior to it . . . though vanquished he need never be ignoble.

[b]Comment by James Collins:

Facing the concrete innards of the finite is surely a condition for a return of sanity in the world of fact and symbol, but is not adequate by itself to achieve the new wholeness. From Feuerbach and Nietzsche to Gide and Heidegger, the call has been for men to make a lucid and unblinking appraisal of their finitude. There is actually a grand debate over what does constitute an honest and accurate account of limited human nature and its situation in the cosmos. This quarrel cannot be settled solely in terms

I therefore take him as a kind of ultimate symbol of the dealings of so much of the modern imagination with the limited and actual image or symbol. We cannot quite trust that the exploration of its full, finite concreteness will really lead us anywhere. We have, too often, to exploit its tenuous, noncognitive, vague, suggestive power for the evoking of quick infinities in our souls.

C

A typical and more immediately relevant example of the central problem of the modern symbol is, of course, that of the symbol and belief, myth and belief, poetry and belief. There is no intention here of critically examining the final epistemology of this question or of proposing helpful and didactic solutions. Once again all that needs emphasis is the structure of the new symbolic situation into which we have been forced, the total pressure toward the inward evocation.

At any rate, our belief in the referability of a good many symbols to an order of fact and truth collapsed somewhere. But because it is entirely clear to us that neither the soul nor civilization can endure without symbols or "myths," we have insisted on keeping them, though they are now expected to operate on an exclusively psychological level. We have executed a good deal of sleight-of-hand and created a good number of intricate dichotomies in order to make this possible. The world of values, for example, has been neatly divorced from the world of fact and we need not, therefore, labor any more to keep the two laboriously related.

---

of attitudes and appropriate symbols. It calls for philosophical analysis of the nature and implications of our human condition. Thus the various playwrights cited here could appeal to Simone de Beauvoir's maxim that authentic existence "must assert itself as an absolute in its very finiteness; man fulfills himself within the transitory or not at all. He must regard his undertakings as finite and will them absolutely. . . . Man must, in any event, assume his finiteness: not by treating his existence as transitory or relative but by reflecting the infinite within it, that is, by treating it as absolute" (Simone de Beauvoir, *The Ethics of Ambiguity,* translated by Bernard Frechtman, Philosophical Library, New York, 1948, pp. 127, 130). This is a typical philosophical expression of heroic or tragic finitism. It is the closed way of viewing the finite, as though to open it up to another perspective of transcendent reality would be to lose freedom and dignity. Whether there would be this loss upon an admission of the dependence of finite man on the infinite God cannot simply be assumed: it is the very point at issue. Man must certainly fulfil himself within time and history, but it does not follow that his historical existence must be treated as if it were self-sufficient and sealed off from all reference to the eternal. This "as if" is just as much a matter of bad faith and dangerous pretense as are the dodges of those who try to evade all responsibility by appealing to impersonal codes or conventions.

Santayana has written several sentimental books to prove to us that this can and must be done, and certainly no one more than Santayana has been able to make the New Platonism sound more beautiful or more empty. But he had, of course, been long preceded by the eminent theologians of the nineteenth century, men like Auguste Sabatier,[14] and Alfred Firmin Loisy,[15] who had devoted all their great talents to placing the creedal symbols of Christianity within an invulnerable world of value and invocation where they would not be open to the attacks of history and science, or open to the need of referability to the actual.

In the realm of poetry, I. A. Richards has, of course, given us one of the classical documents that help to salvage the poets from being intricated too deeply in the question of belief.[16] He has very neatly provided us with a system of "objectless beliefs." Edmund Wilson has provided us with similar materials (though I must say, according to a previous vein of reflection, that his theory of tragedy always struck me as non-cognitive, indeed: the picture of the *Oedipus* establishing a harmony in the conflict of human drives, as poor Oedipus himself collapses all over the place, always seems quite funny and a possible subject for a good comedy).

I prefer to conceive that any literary organism, far from even being merely an evocative object, is something far more than an object, and that it is difficult to satisfy oneself with the traditional esthetic of so many thinkers who continue to think entirely in such terms as those of "object," "creation," "making," and beauty. Must we not come back finally

---

[14]*Cf.* Auguste Sabatier, *Outlines of a Philosophy of Religion Based on Psychology and History,* Hodder, London, 1897; and *Religions of Authority and the Religion of the Spirit,* Williams & Norgate, London, 1910.

[15]*Cf.* Alfred Firmin Loisy, *Religion et humanité,* Nourry, Paris, 1926.

[16]This is the way in which Richards justifies the "pseudo-statements" of poetry: "A pseudo-statement is a form of words which is justified entirely by its effect in releasing or organising our impulses and attitudes (due regard being had for the better or worse organisations of these *inter se*)"; and for the collapse of belief, his remedy is "to cut our pseudo-statements free from belief, and yet retain them, in this released state, as the main instruments by which we order our attitudes to one another and to the world. Not so desperate a remedy as may appear, for poetry conclusively shows that even the most important among our attitudes can be aroused and maintained without any belief entering it at all. Those of Tragedy, for example. We need no beliefs, and indeed we must have none, if we are to read *King Lear*. Pseudo-statements to which we attach no belief and statements proper such as science provides cannot conflict. It is only when we introduce illicit beliefs into poetry that danger arises. To do so is from this point of view a profanation of poetry." I. A. Richards, "Poetry and Beliefs," from *Critiques and Essays in Criticism, 1920–1948,* selected by R. W. Stallman, Ronald Press Company, New York, 1949, pp. 330–331.

to the fact, complicated to be sure and stated here in an oversimple form, that the poem is also a word, albeit a highly organic one? And if it be also a human word we are immediately thrust back into another facet of the perpetually important problem of the double reference and direction of the symbol. We are indeed headed inevitably for some discussion of the question of poetry and belief, but this latter issue can be first viewed as only a phase of the even broader issue of poetry and meaning, poetry simply as a word that says something.

Surely it is the desire of man that all meaning be packed into an object, and that the object overcome the abstractions and inadequacies of discursive thought, becoming an object of direct vision capable of arousing marvelous echoes and rest in the human soul. Thus it is inevitable that poetry should strain after a pure "logic of feeling," or a pure "logic of the imagination"—which was certainly what a man like Mallarmé was straining after. But the great question is whether, as we try to do this, we are not trying to do something inhuman, or, better, nonhuman, and whether, in so doing, we are not restricting ourselves to one order of thinking, and that the order of pure sensibility, thus abandoning all those other proportional human expressions of actuality that might come to the enormous aid of sensibility. Perhaps this is what Eliot means when he says that Dante is the artist for the study of the modern poet, and this in a sense is the total burden of what is said by Francis Fergusson in his two splendid books, *The Idea of a Theatre* and *Dante's Drama of the Mind.*

We begin by saying, then, that there is no such thing as a pure literary *object*; it is also a word, that is the simplest thing we can say of it, and all the current interest in the medieval science of meanings, fourfold meanings, and levels of meaning, is only a refined expression of the possible worlds in which a word can function as such. Eliot puts the matter in a reasonable way when he says:

> The process of increasing self-consciousness—or, we may say, of increasing consciousness of language—has as its theoretical goal what we may call *la poésie pure*. I believe it to be a goal that cannot be reached. I believe that poetry is only poetry as long as it preserves some "impurity" in this sense: that is to say, as long as the subject matter is valued for its own sake.[17]

[17]T. S. Eliot, "From Poe to Valéry," *Hudson Review*, vol. I, no. 3, Autumn, 1949, pp. 327–342; see especially pp. 337–339.

And I add another effective summary from Denis de Rougement:

> . . . the work of art is an object of which the raison d'être necessary and sufficient is to *signify,* organically, and by means of its own structure. Whether it consists in a structure of meanings, or forms, or sounds, or ideas, the work of art has for its specific function the bribing of the attention, the magnetizing of the sensibility, the ensnaring—and at the same time it must orient existence toward something which transcends sounds and forms, or the words so assembled. It is a trap, but an orientated trap.[18]

Once again let us admit that we all have a proper hankering to deal with objects, pure, self-enclosed objects that are the forms of pure vision and help us to explore ourselves. And as there must be meanings we cannot help but hanker that the meanings really get into the words and not "transcend" them. This is only another way of saying an even more important thing, that we long for the union of our total human and terrestrial actuality with a world of meanings. We would like our world to signify without becoming less actual for doing so, without being reduced to a sign or a meaning.

If we have not yet become sensitive enough to the reductionism of the actual that we have got used to calling psychologism, if we have not yet quite seen that there is such a thing as scraping the bottom of the barrel in that direction, at least we had long ago developed a profound distaste for that other and reverse form of reductionism which consists in reducing the real and terrestrial to pure meaning.

We have a perfectly understandable horror of being reduced, either ourselves or our world, to a set of symbols or illustrations or meanings. The issue then is not only to recover, if we can, the outward directions, the true meaning, the real commitment of a set of symbols that may again actuate spiritual and political life. The real and final issue is to discover such symbols as can do all this and yet keep the tang and the density of actuality. It is necessary that, if Beatrice again become a symbol, she should not become a romanticized shadow full of cheaper and quicker magics, but should retain all the human actuality of the woman of Florence. It is only by recovering a profound identity of the actual and the symbol that we will overcome our current temptations to magic

[18]"Religion and the Mission of the Artist," in *Spiritual Problems in Contemporary Literature,* edited by Stanley Romaine Hopper, The Institute for Religious and Social Studies, New York, 1952, p. 176.

and psychologism. And when we say "magic" we need no longer think in terms only of the sophisticated work of an elite poetic sensibility; as these things always do, this superior magic has penetrated, in a more vulgar form, to the level of popular culture where the people themselves are being daily inoculated with enormous doses of charms, tricks, and potions—of such a kind as hide the true face of the finite from them and induct them quickly into false heavens and cheap infinities. But we shall return to this critical point a little later; it is only inserted here that the sense of our argument may be felt thus early in its widest implications.

The correlations, identities, separations, enforced dichotomies between actuality and symbolism have always presented our civilization with a series of crises; we are not the first to confront such a crisis (though its range and depth may very well be in our case unprecedented). If we here cite some examples from the history of scriptural exegesis, it is, first of all, by way of illustrating our problem, but it is, secondly, good to remember that this was the first large ground on which our own current crisis was worked out for the human imagination.

The exegesis of the Bible had met its own crisis. It had passed through periods of the temptation to reduce the literal meaning, the "letter," the actual historical event, the *gesta,* to a shadow or to a meaninglessness that could provoke meaning (if only the disturbing actualities were eliminated!). Beryl Smalley[19] compares this period's attitude to the literal historical text as an affair of "stepping through the looking glass," like Alice herself, of looking through the text and not into it.

But by the time of the thirteenth century, the tide had swung full and permanently around to the centrality of the literal text and history as a source and foundation for all allegorical, tropological, and anagogical meanings. Thomas Docking speaks in his lectures at Oxford of the "subtle, noble literal sense." In an earlier day Saint Gregory had decided that the measurements of the Temple made no precise sense (they would make the door bigger than the walls!), and rightly made no sense, the argument seemed to be, because it would only be by a proper vagueness, that this house could function to represent, on higher levels, a tabernacle, a sanctuary, a city. But Hugh of Saint Victor, a better textualist, cor-

[19]Beryl Smalley, *The Study of the Bible in the Middle Ages,* Clarendon Press, Oxford, 1941.

rected the measurements to make physical sense, so that it was, after all, out of the dense and precise reality of an actual human house that the original writer did indeed draw his splendid meanings. Nor did the commentators hesitate to identify the symbolized passion of Christ with all the crude reality of Noah being seen naked and derided by his son. With Christ Himself they had, of course, a preeminent theological warrant for not leaping too quickly (and magically!) out of the facts of His life and personality to grasp some vague Godhead. No one had ever cared much about the precise details of the life of Apollo (who was indeed entirely symbol) but Christian spirituality doted on every detail, in all its density, of the life and passion of Christ, where the actuality and the thing signified were so completely one.

To get the real into the actual is, again according to the phrasing of Blackmur, the whole burden of our plaint. First of all, this entails a new respect for the real and a growing contempt for pure psychologism; and then a new contempt for magic and tenuosity over against a respect for the actual and for density—for in what other world must we live?

But one more word on this legitimate passion of ours that the signs of meaning be located in immediate objects of vision, so that there be no need of leaving the latter to get to the former. Kierkegaard has given us his warning that there are two forms of the immediate, with a great abyss between them. The first is the immediate of the esthetic man, the man of sheer sensibility, who by luck, by chance, by genius, by non-decision, by making all things the Platonic occasion for the creation or the evoking of beauty, releases us from the Ixion wheel of struggle. To begin there is understandable for man; it is a kind of natural childhood for the artist. But if one is to rise to a new and final form of immediacy, that of Faith, where again but on a higher level and for different reasons, the strains of the will and the discursive reason may again be abandoned, it will only be through a mediating stage of the ethical—where evocative beauty is no longer the absolute, but beauty is chosen over beauty in the name of good, where decision and the finite terms of my existence press down in quarreling forms upon the soul.

I mean this in part as an analogy. Many men have been critical of the insertion of real meaning or belief into our symbols. Now this insertion really involves a twofold discussion: 1) It involves the descent of the historical forms of Christian belief into natural symbolism in such a way that some organic union really emerges from the descent. Here we have to do with the question really of the relation between historical and natural symbolism, and we shall have something to say about that in our next section. 2) But what of the men and symbolmakers who do not believe and who are obligated to make the ascent but are still closed in the self-enclosed, evocative symbol? Are there now, in this roughest of moments of human history, certain things we can now at last, without hesitation, say to them?

a) We are, I think, now entitled to say first to them that they no longer have the right to remain in this initial and easy immediacy of pure sensibility. We can no longer go any further in this direction, or in the direction of the bottom of the barrel of the psyche. Or better: even if we could, it would make no difference; we begin to be alive to a new awareness that there lie so many dead ends. We are all, I should say, dedicated to the idea of the freedom of the imagination. But freedom of sensibility is not a mature freedom for the imagination and requires moving on.

b) If this new adventure in order is to be successful, it must pay the price of passing through many painful mediating stages. The new symbolmakers must consent to using all the intellectual resources that belong to man, all the possible levels of human discourse (in order that their symbols may reach a level of conviction, and not of manipulation of souls, a level of meaning which the medievalists contained under *quid credas*). They must also make many moral decisions and commitments; I do not mean they must become propagandists (but they must pass beyond first immediacies of "beauty"—a word we could often do without —and pass through the world of good and evil, through the world of "tropological" meaning, through the actual human world which always requires decision and rejection, the order which the medievalists called *quid agas*). Here the imagination, since it deals more than anywhere else with the concrete materials of the actual, will feel that, by entering into such an order as this, it is losing its freedom. And this indeed, this fear of the loss of freedom in the face of the finite actual, is perhaps the great crisis for the modern imagination.

There will be many feinting before this crisis gets solved. Sometimes there is the feinting in the direction of the dialectic, the yes and no of André Gide, the desire to taste everything in its own pure taste, unpolluted by any other taste. It is the uncommitted freedom that speaks ironically in terms of the detachment of the poor man of the Gospel.

Another feint away from the problem is that of Scobie in Graham Greene's *The Heart of the Matter,* where the evasion of the imagination lies in a description of its own tragic helplessness to commit itself. Scobie pities his wife and he pities the other woman and he pities God and, standing thus completely outside of himself, he offers his damnation to God, proposing to choose without choice. In the one case it is the dialectic, in another it is pity, that keeps the imagination in the initial immediate of freedom, within one of the manifold ruses of the esthetic man of Kierkegaard.

Let it be said again that one of the great fears of the modern imagination is that it will lose its freedom if it inserts itself with decision into the limited actual world. Allow me to take a minor risk. I would propose that the great debate we must work out is whether the imagination wins its freedom by seeking quick infinities through the rapid and clever manipulation of the finite—or does it win it by passing through all the rigors, densities, limitations, and decisions of the actual. And this debate has application to both our intellectual and our vulgar cultures, for, though these were never divided by so terrible an abyss of misunderstanding, yet they are tied together by different levels of this common problem of the path to freedom and joy. Between Hollywood and some of the secret desires of the more sophisticated symbolmakers (in both culture and politics) there is a secret but real kinship.

These present pages are meant to be a brief sketch of possible modern applications of the ways in which *for us* the medieval theory of fourfold levels of meaning for images and symbols will make some sense—and will give some kind of depth and conviction to our symbols and myths. So many lines have been given to the analogy from Kierkegaard and the idea of the penetration into the finite actual because I conceive it to be the modern counterpart of the problem raised by the tropological level of the medieval image. To use the language of the "freedom of the imagination" and "confident penetration of the limited finite" avoids, and properly avoids, the pejorative connotations of the phrase, *"sensus moralis"* or *"quid agas."* The poetic or symbolic imagination is not didactic or moralistic but it is completely moral in the sense of human when it chooses the actual, and, within the actual, the actual over the actual.

What of the level of belief (*quid credas*) in the symbol? Let me put one suggestion here succinctly. The words, "actual" and "actuality" and "limited finite," have been recurring like a litany through this paper. But with malice aforethought. For the temptation for our imaginations these days is the temptation to Manichaeism, to a contemning of the actual, a fear of the finite, a distrust of the potency of the limited thing or moment or image—correspondingly, there is the temptation to escape, to cover the face of the finite with a superficial charm, and to create quick compensating heavens. Now the order of belief called Christology (if I may give a limited definition for the purposes of this paper) is a belief in the capacity of the human actual, if we imagine and live through it, to lead somewhere. The essential meaning of Christ is that He rejected the way of tricks and magic and power and quick infinities as redeeming ways, and chose instead to walk through the mysteries of man (thus I refer to the actualities of man and all the stages of human life) as a way into God. Thus all Christians talk about the "mysteries of Christ" but they do not talk enough about the mysteries, I mean the realities, of man—through which He, Christ, walked and imagined as a path to freedom and the infinite. It is easy enough to believe in the virtue of infinities, but it is harder to trust in the finite and the actual as a way to them. A properly understood Christology should provide the theological energy required for that penetration for which we no longer seem to have the heart or the energy. I do not say that Christology must get into the poem or the symbol, but what we may call the Christic act, the act of athletic and confident penetration of limit, of the actual, and the human, can again become the model and energizer for the poetic imagination and for the total act and attitude of any human culture. What other firmer *quid credas* could there be for the poet or for popular culture?

Let us be very frank to acknowledge that such words as "belief" and "faith" have come to have the connotation of the irrelevant and the extrinsic so far as the life of the poetic and symbolic imagination is concerned. And they are so often taken themselves as rather magical and compensatory attitudes that might somehow make up for the flatness or the horror of the finite. Well, I am simply not talking about such belief and such faith. Rather I am thinking of the true Christian action which is the dynamic story of the penetration of the finite *usque ad mortem,* and the redemption of the actual; it is not a story of redemption from the actual. The greatest task before us is the restoration of confidence in the human and in the concretions of *our* limited world, a confidence in the power even of our weakness and our death, with the

mud that goes with the one and the blood that goes with the other. All
we are ultimately saying, therefore, is that we are indeed living in a
Manichaean period of alienation, and that we must not now, in our
anxiety, choose symbols, in the name whether of beauty, or evocation, or
successful politics, which will only exacerbate our present situation.

D

There was a promise in our last section to examine the burden that
rests upon the men of belief, those in our civilization who think they
possess points of referability and commitment for our symbols, to make
a descent and to contact the natural images of the human imagination.
It would be a pitiful affair, indeed, not to say pitiless, if they satisfied
themselves pretentiously with some easy and satiric appraisal of evocation. For, after all, evocation, we can agree, is the only thing that really
matters, whether for the poet or the Christian. Our only possible quarrel
is with those fine spirits among the Symbolistes or those vulgar spirits in
Hollywood who have, in sophisticated or vulgar mode—at any rate, by
noncognitive modes—corrupted the idea of evocation. All that I wish to
say at this present stage of our discussion is that this idea remains corrupted as long as it is not an evocation by and toward the actual and the
historical. In brief, then, I should like now to look at the differences and
the relations between historical and natural symbolism. And we may
briefly define the men of belief as those who, with every concomitant
obligation, believe in and possess *historical* symbols.

If it is permitted for a moment to talk on the level of the vocabulary
of Jung, let us look at the symbolforming archetypes in the soul. These
centers of energy and of images push out an incredible history of myths
and symbols. These are all, in a measure, distinct but finally they are all
indistinct. There is no longer a Hero, but a Hero of a Thousand Faces,
serving their purpose all, but who cares who was the second cousin of
any of them; or who cares too much whether the actual hair of the
Prince or Princess was henna or black. As Mr. Auden says, it is important that Tristan should not be an actual man, or Iseult an actual
woman; they must have picked each others' numbers out of a hat.

A purely natural symbol is best left anonymous. There is Kierkegaard's distinction between the Socratic *occasion* and the Christian moment. In the spirituality of the occasion, the eternal may be contacted

everywhere, through everything; in the spirituality of the moment, it is only in this moment, this thing, this person. If Apollo and Christ are occasions, they are identical. But actually nobody is ever asked to love Apollo, and nobody has the slightest interest in his cousins—or in any other part of his "actuality." Here the scholar must examine Christian spirituality: it pours endlessly over the concretions of Palestine, every step, every word, every limited movement of the Hero. The love of love is over with. The question Christ asks Peter is "Lovest thou *me?*"

It has been suggested earlier that the surrender of an initial freedom for the entrance of the imagination into the exploration of the limited is the necessary condition of a higher freedom. Something similar is now true of the surrender of the imagination to historical symbolism. On the surface this surrender is an abandonment of freedom. It is a temporary rejection of the universality of the Eternal Idea (found everywhere, with occasion everywhere, and commitments nowhere) and the bewildering efflorescence of the archetypal inward form—and an acceptance of the precise, limited, singular, and absolutely unique event (with all that that means for scandal to the mathematical intelligence and the universal faculty of fantasy). But I think it is a plausible proposition that the natural symbolic powers of the religious imagination began to wither and collapse with the collapse of the historical and dogmatic symbol in the seventeenth century.[20] And the reverse is also true, according to the brilliant analysis of Jean Daniélou in his "The Problem of Symbolism":[21] for the historical symbol, finally, does not at all cancel out the glories of the natural symbol, but rather assumes it all up to its own level of actuality, devotion, and commitment. Level after level that was once repetitive and anonymous, or vague and searching for form and reality, now shares in the uniqueness and historicity of true events. a) The types or figures, the half-history, of the Old Testament became completely history: for Christ is its lamb, its brazen serpent, arc, ram which Isaac saw, cloud by day, pillar of flame by night, promised land, tree of life, cluster of grapes, manna, and many things besides; b) and the force which could have evaporated out of natural symbols—it threatens again to do so with us despite our frantic concern—is vitalized as these symbols

[20]*Cf.* Malcolm Ross, "Fixed Stars and Living Motion in Poetry," *Thought*, vol. XXVII, no. 106, Autumn, 1952, pp. 381–399; and his "History and Poetry," *Thought*, vol. XXVI, no. 102, Autumn, 1951, pp. 426–442.

[21]Jean Daniélou, "The Problem of Symbolism," *Thought*, vol. XXV, no. 98, September, 1950, pp. 423–440.

are raised to levels of historical commitment they could never have aroused: for Christ is water, gold, butter, food, a harp, a dove, the day, a house, horseman, merchant, fig, gate, stone, book, wood, light, medicine, oil, bread, arrow, salt, turtle, risen sun, way, and many things besides.[22]

Surely, all purely human history is made by men, but there is a sense in which the archetypal and imageforming forms of the soul can never make history or by themselves climb up to its level of actuality and uniqueness. Is there not a sense in which the imagination of the sleeping Earwicker of Joyce courses through universal history and finds in it, or makes in it, the expressions, on every level, of all its own great forms? —and yet there is no history in it. Do not these interior forms and desires always threaten to destroy history by reducing it to their own structures —as perhaps Thomas Mann does in his story of Joseph?[23] I hesitate to give a cruder example of this particular form of reductionism, lest again we do injustice to the finer spirits. But it will not be misunderstood. One day I saw a movie which contained perhaps the ultimate example of how the imagination can throw all the orders of reality together into a common pot and exploit them for its own manipulating, emotional purposes. The name of the circus movie was "The Greatest Show on Earth." In the scene that sticks in the memory, a circus crescendo had arrived; the elephants pranced in glory; on their backs were sets of American beauties, clad in very little; and the band was blaring. It was blaring "O Come Let Us Adore Him."

Perhaps, though, we really get at some of the more crucial pinpoints of this discussion by making two observations:

1) We have just passed through a whole long era of history during which the historical had come to take on the connotation of the *primitive*. The historical and actual symbols of Christianity had come to be

[22]Chosen from the endless Christic symbolism one might rapidly review by scanning indexes XLVI–XLIX of Migne's *Patrology*.

[23]Jean Daniélou (*loc. cit.,* pp. 438–439) points out the corresponding danger in the tendency of the allegorical imagination to reduce everything to an illustration of Idea:

> Philo of Alexandria looked at the realities of the Old Testament and, instead of seeing in them the figure of eschatological events, came to view them as the image of cosmic realities. With him the history of Moses turns into a myth, into an image of the life of the universe or the ideal model of the soul, and down to the very last degree the historical signification of the book has disappeared. . . . The Relation between myth and revelation, therefore, involves a perpetual tension. Revelation needs cosmic symbolism if it is to take hold of the vitality of reality with a new grip, but it must always be on its guard against allowing itself to be assimilated by this symbolism.

looked on as vulgarizations of the work of what we have earlier been calling the mathematical intelligence and the psychologistic, indeed the divine and autonomous, imagination. But it should be a lesson for us to remember the curious twists and reversals in the scholarship of what is "primitive" and what "sophisticated." Certainly Philo thought his "rational" version of scriptural exegesis a more sophisticated one than that of his earlier, actualizing Jewish brethren. But just as certainly, later Christian exegetes, with their emphasis upon the creative *littera* and history of the text, thought they were moving away from the primitivism of many philosophers and Alice-in-the-looking-glass commentators. I have the feeling that we are again on the rebound toward the actualities of history and shall soon conceive ourselves as having overcome another— and this time Cartesian—period of the primitive. At any rate, we should be a little more on our guard against the superficial fascinations of words —and the moods that go with them—like the primitive and the sophisticated.

We shall probably come quickly to suspect a little less the *precise* decisions of God that are represented by the historical symbolism of Christianity. And be scandalized a little less. For the actions of God have, indeed, always been scandalously precise, picking things, and shapes, times, places, and people. Perhaps the most disconcerting example is the way in which He chooses that His ultimate place of worship be made in the early pages of the Old Testament (Exodus 25, 9 ff.) :

> According to all the likeness of the tabernacle which I will shew thee, and of all the vessels for the service thereof: and thus you shall make it:
> Frame an ark of setim wood, the length whereof shall be of two cubits and a half: the breadth, a cubit and a half: the height, likewise, a cubit and a half.
> And thou shalt overlay it with the purest gold within and without: and over it thou shalt make a golden crown round about:
> And four golden rings, which thou shalt put at the four corners of the ark: let two rings be on the one side, and two on the other.
> Thou shalt make bars also of setim wood, and shalt overlay them with gold.
> And thou shalt put them in through the rings that are in the sides of the ark, that it may be carried on them.
> And they shall be always in the rings, neither shall they at any time be drawn out of them.
> And thou shalt put in the ark the testimony which I will give you.

Thou shalt make also a propitiatory of the purest gold: the length thereof shall be two cubits and a half, and the breadth a cubit and a half.

Thou shalt make also two cherubims of beaten gold, on the two sides of the oracle.

Etc., etc.

This is surely a long call from the death of actuality in the imagination of Wagner (who, you recall, would have had scant respect for ship measurements and precise knottage) or in the imagination of Poe (about whom Allen Tate goes so far as to say: "No other writer in England or the United States, or, so far as I know in France, went so far as Poe in his vision of dehumanized man"). It is also very far from the complete romanticization of love in the cinema, where an actual woman would not stand a chance. And as for the precise modes of death among us, how these are concealed in the fog of a too quick beauty, we can reread the too pitiless satire of Evelyn Waugh, *The Loved One*.

2) So much in general for the debate that goes on among us, at least subconsciously, on the equation between history and primitivism in the making of myths and symbols. The second crucial pinpoint which disturbs us is that of the freedom of the imagination, which we subtly conceive to be impossible if, abandoning for a time the high path of the priestly, magical, and "creative" imagination, we take instead the low path of the historical and the actual. I have said this before, but should like to close with a few further repetitive notes on this critical question.

How shall we be free? We put this discussion on the right level by agreeing all of us—as we surely do—that freedom is the only thing that matters. And perhaps its highest form is *the freedom of the imagination*. The worrisome people might think here of nothing but the sexual imagination, and might drag us down to discussing this issue on the least important level of freedom. For on this level there is no problem in liberating the imagination; at least, no effort is involved. No, when I speak of the freedom of the imagination, I speak of it as the prime vocation of the human race, as the occupation of the poet and the saint; just as we can conceive the rigidities and fixities of the imagination to be one of the great sources of all our sicknesses, and of our idolatries.

In a word, my attitude toward the "liberation of the imagination" is, to put it mildly, that I am heartily, passionately, and theologically for it, in the same sense that—and because—I am in theology a Christian. The only thing at issue, therefore, is the incredibly difficult one of how we shall get to that point of liberation. Certainly it is no game for a child. It requires more than the resources of a Jungian psychologism and magic; it requires, in addition, all the resources of the actualities of nature and the historicity of grace. To conceive, in fact, that Christian theology (*quid credas*) has any other goal but this freedom of which we speak is to talk of it as something other than it is.

Northrop Frye seems always intent on telling us that poetry (I think he also means the free creative spirit of the poetic imagination) has "an authority which cannot be overruled by any other aspect of human activity." If I do him no injustice, he cannot help but regard theology as another special, isolated, and narrower field of human activity. This writer must confess that he simply cannot think according to this departmentalized mode. He has no objection, again to put it mildly, to the full exercise of fantasy, and to the free creative exercise of the poets' "Let this be," or to the full exploration of the forms of the psyche. All that I wish to add in this paper to such a "no objection" is that I wish to equate the problem of freedom with the problem of tragedy. Neither problem is solved, neither freedom nor tragedy achieved finally, without the imagination consenting to enter into the dread gate of the actual, finite, limited human situation. (Here we are speaking not only of the poet but of the people who, in their total cultural act, are pretty badly off right now.) To ask the creative imagination so to enter, sounds indeed like the end of freedom. I do not conceive that it is, but I do believe it cannot be done without courage and belief. That belief is what I call Christology; for being God, and creative indeed, He did not think it robbery that He should take on the form of a servant.

Comment by Swami Akhilananda:

William F. Lynch, S.J., is right that a symbol must have both objective and subjective elements in order to be of real value in any field of discipline. Unfortunately, symbols are often used not merely from the evocative standpoint but also for pragmatic purposes. On the other hand, if the symbols are used to signify an ideal for itself and to evoke the highest signifying elements from the subjective, as well as the objective point of view, then they are constructive, creative, and elevating. The swastika was used by the Buddhists and it evoked the highest and most glorious qualities of human nature, while the symbol itself became a blessing not only to individuals but also to mankind. Then the symbol was used much later by the Nazis (in reverse appearance) and it evoked narrow nationalistic and racial feelings. It apparently gave the idea of sacrifice and love, yet it produced a result opposite from that attained by the Buddhists in their use of the swastika. This shows that the same symbol can evoke different feelings when it is used for different purposes. Both subjective and objective effects are diametrically opposite, as we observe in these two instances.

Hence, one should be very careful in interpreting a symbol. Certain ethical and spiritual values should be thoroughly emphasized in the use of religious symbols. The Cross is indeed a glorious evocative symbol, as Father Lynch explained it, and we all agree with him. But it is also known that the Cross was employed not only for the evocation of glorious qualities of Jesus but also for narrow, sectarian feelings and destructive uses.

Symbols are used extensively by all religions. It will not be right to say, as Father Lynch implied, that Christology is the final evocative symbol of transformation or "redemption" of man, as different religions use different symbols to reach the same goal, each according to its historical background. It is true, generally speaking, that the Jews and Mohammedans in a sense do not use external symbols in the same manner as the Christians, Buddhists, and Hindus. It is quite possible that symbols are sparingly used by the former, because they contacted many primitive groups in the earlier days of their development who personified nature and thereby used many aspects of nature for their religious life. Many primitive symbols signified magic, incantation, and cure, not the glorious purposes of spiritual evolution. It seems to us that the most important reason for the lack of symbolism in Judaism and Mohammedanism is that they felt the Infinite to be unapproachable by the finite mind and therefore they should not symbolize. They do use certain types of symbols to evoke the same noble sentiments found in Christianity and other religions.

Symbols represent the inevitable search for the Infinite or God. The Infinite as such cannot be the object of thought so long as the mind operates on the finite plane. After all, this finite mind is limited to time, space, name, and form. The moment we try to comprehend the Infinite we cannot help resorting to symbols. They may be of different types, visual or auditory. The use of any type of symbol is meant for the evocation of the nobler qualities of the human being and for the training of the finite mind to comprehend the Infinite. That is the very reason the mystics of various schools of thought in all religious traditions have used one or another of the symbols signifying God.

We agree with Father Lynch in his reply to the critics regarding the loss of freedom in the use of certain symbols or in the submission of the individual to the historical Jesus. In studying the lives of persons who transcend the limitations of the immediate objective world and rise to the transcendental through immediate and direct perception of the Reality, it is found that they have to give up their so-called freedom, in the limited sense, of self-expression and self-assertion. So, the real requirement for the understanding of the Reality is self-imposed self-discipline, self-control, and self-transformation. In order properly to use a symbol that leads us to the realization of the All-Loving Being, or the Absolute, this sacrifice is needed. To be exact, this is not real sacrifice, it is only expansion of inner consciousness. A child uses toys; but as it grows it gives up toys and enjoys living companions. So when a man becomes mature he gives up the limited sense of freedom in order to achieve the supreme type of freedom, namely, experience of God. This alone gives real freedom which negates all limitations.

Father Lynch is correct when he says that the historical Jesus, "mysteries of Christ," provided opportunities to man to go beyond himself, enter the presence of God, and be united with Him. But we must also recognize the use of other such symbols, historical and other, which lifted and are still lifting people of various religious traditions to the same goal advocated by Father Lynch. Great Jewish, Hindu, and Buddhistic mystics, and Sufi Mohammedans reached the same goal using their own historical symbols, as did the Christian mystics by following and using Christology. We admit that the symbol of Christ and the Cross means something positive and dynamic, more than Apollo. The personality of Christ evokes love, sacrifice, and forgiveness in His followers. Similar qualities have also been evoked by other personalities and other symbols in various religious groups.

We have to admit that different individuals function on different levels of mental development. Some need remembrance, the passion of Jesus, the life of Buddha or Krishna, as the evocative element for the highest understanding of God. Others can reach the same goal by using subtle symbols. Then again there are others who need tangible symbols with name and form to evoke the higher spiritual aspirations and to lead them to the highest spiritual realization. There are still others who need grosser forms or symbols for the same achievement. They need elaborate ritualism to evoke the same sentiments. It will be a mistake for anyone to think that one ritualism is idolatry and the other ritualism is real religion. The use of ritual remains the real instrument of spiritual development and the symbol is the doorway to spiritual evolution when it is used properly. Otherwise rituals become actually "magic." So it is the duty of real spiritual personalities to guide and help the average man and woman to grow gradually from the grosser use of symbols to higher use, until they reach a state in which God or the Infinite is realized and man is transformed and redeemed.

Comment of Martin C. D'Arcy, S.J.:

I read the paper by William F. Lynch, S.J., with great interest and regard it as quite remarkable. It develops a new way of approach, which seems to me to open out new possibilities of understanding between literary criticism, philosophy, and religion.

Comment of Francis Fergusson:

I found Father Lynch's paper very stimulating and suggestive. It is in effect a criticism of that very important part of modern literature which stems from the *symboliste* movement of the past century, and an effort to distinguish this modern, subjective symbolism from the more objective and traditional symbolism of the classic Christian tradition. Father Lynch has thought deeply and read widely about these matters, and what he has to say here should be of interest to anyone who is concerned with contemporary attempts (especially in literature) to find a significant and viable symbolic technique.

Those who are not Catholic (I am not a Catholic myself) will of course be unable to go all the way with Father Lynch. But I understand that his paper is designed as a contribution to a discussion by a number of authors with various philosophies. As such it is very valuable and very instructive.

CHAPTER XV

Being and Value

By WHITNEY J. OATES

IN THIS CONFERENCE on "Symbols and Society," it goes without question that much attention must be paid to the various ways in which symbols function as spurs to human action. Quite obviously symbols would not have this evocative power, were it not that value or values are in some way deeply embedded in the complex of symbols and things symbolized, whether the symbol be verbal, a gesture, or in any other medium. To some it may have become a kind of end in itself. As my friend, Father William F. Lynch, S.J., has observed, "The evocative power of the symbol, *i.e.,* its ability to produce extraordinary repercussions in the human soul, has been divorced from any attachment to or penetration into actuality and finite reality and what we call truth." In other words, symbols in their capacity of giving expression to values, have been kept in a psychological order, and have been more or less radically separated from the order of fact, or reality, or existence, or actuality—whatever designation you may choose to employ.

This problem, *i.e.,* the relation of Being and Value, seems to underlie or to be fundamentally germane to any discussion of symbols. It is therefore my intention to examine it briefly in the metaphysical positions of Plato and Aristotle, after considering how the problem is handled by A. J. Ayer, Nicolai Hartmann, and Saint Augustine, and I trust that the reason for selecting this particular trio may become apparent in due course.

The problem itself has been noticed on several occasions in the previous deliberations of the Conference on Science, Philosophy, and Religion, and those of The Institute for Religious and Social Studies. For example, in the record of a seminar held March 5, 1953, Lyman Bryson held that the "reals" recognized by a given culture are functions of its valuational processes. This observation apparently precipitated a debate on the concept of reality in terms of the following question, "Is 'reality' a postulate of cultural valuation, or is there a 'reality' prior to and independent of all cultural processes?"

Howard Lee Nostrand, in his paper contributed to the Thirteenth Conference, remarked:

> At least three ultimate explanations of values appear to be mutually exclusive and irreconcilable. As Edgar S. Brightman has listed the three views in his article "Axiology" (Runes's *Dictionary of Philosophy*) they hold respectively that ultimate values are purely subjective imaginings; or metaphysical realities; or logical essences which subsist independently of being known, yet without existential status.

Dean William R. Dennes of the University of California, in his paper for the same Conference, entitled "Knowledge and Values," was categorical in his insistence that Being and Value should be kept separate. In arguing against "metaphysics" as a ground for value judgments, he says we cannot logically "determine from what really is what really ought to be: to derive from judgments of fact, judgments of value. It could only be by taking the symbols, 'good,' to mean precisely what is meant by 'real,' and nothing more than is meant by 'real,' that we could say that metaphysics, as a theoretic discipline, determines or demonstrates the nature of value. But then our statement, 'what is metaphysically real, and only that, is good,' would mean precisely what is meant by either one or other of the empty truisms: 'Whatever is metaphysically real, and only that, is metaphysically real,' or 'Whatever is good, and only that, is good.'" Or again, later in his paper, he asserts, "We must distinguish clearly between facts and *values;* for no theoretical mistakes can be more destructive than those that neglect either facts or values, or pretend to reduce one to the other, or confuse the two and thereby fail to recognize the relevance each has for the other by virtue of their very differences."

Another paper of the Thirteenth Conference by Mordecai M. Kaplan contains a paragraph which reflects in general the point of view to be set forth in the following pages:

> Reality is for a long time conceived as whatever has to do with man's purposes, of which he becomes progressively aware from day to day. Nothing is experienced or known apart from what it means for some human interest. Nothing is a mere fact. Everything is either a good or an evil, or, in modern terminology a value or a disvalue.

These are merely brief indications of the relevance of the problem of Being and Value to the theme of the present Conference. It is hoped that hereby a proper context has been set for the discussion which follows.[1]

The incorrigible Lucian, whose eye for the weaknesses in others as well as in himself was unsurpassed, spared none of the great in the Greek philosophical tradition. In one of his well known dialogues, he singled out Aristotle for attack, and caught in the focus of his satire that aspect of the great philosopher's ethical position which has been characterized often as "practical," prudential, and this-worldly. In the dialogue, which is set in Hades, Diogenes is chiding Alexander, but lately dead, for lamenting his recent loss of his power, his imperial trappings and all the other tokens of his earthly splendor. Diogenes asks, "What, crying? Silly fellow! Did not your wise Aristotle include in his instructions any hint of the insecurity of fortune's favors?" Alexander retorts, "Wise? Call him the craftiest of all flatterers. Allow me to know a little more than other people about Aristotle; his requests and his letters came to *my* address; I know how he profited by my passion for culture; how he would toady and compliment me, to be sure! Now it was my beauty —that too is included under the Good; now it was my deeds and my money; for money too he called a good—he meant that he was not going to be ashamed of taking it. Ah, Diogenes, an imposter; and a past master at it too. For me the result of his wisdom is that I am distressed for the things you catalogued just now, as if I had lost in them the chief goods."[2]

The so-called "realistic" or practical attitude of Aristotle's thought, so skillfully delineated by Lucian, has attracted many of a more pragmatic temper of mind, while to others the Aristotelian position has seemed unelevated and in certain respects distasteful or inadequate. What actually Lucian's critique suggests is the widely divergent reactions to the Aristotelian point of view which have emerged in the course of the history of Western thought. It is true that the more Platonic is one's view, the more inadequate does the Aristotelian approach appear to be. This, in turn, suggests the profundity of Coleridge's familiar dictum that all men are born either Platonists or Aristotelians. That this rather ambitious dichotomy of the human race is in a real sense valid, is vividly

---

[1]The balance of the text of this paper is adapted from the manuscript of the first chapter of a projected book on Plato, Aristotle, and the problem of value.
[2]Lucian, *Dialogues of the Dead*, xiii.

prefigured in the genuine opposition, primarily on metaphysical grounds, which existed historically between the master, Plato, and the brilliant pupil, Aristotle. Though the ground of the conflict lay in metaphysics ultimately, to the individual whose technical knowledge of the more abstruse philosophical problems is somewhat slight, the difference appears most clearly in the area of value. While, on the one hand, the casual reader of Plato can readily observe in the Theory of Ideas, and in the supreme Idea of the Good, a coherent theory of value that is essentially other-worldly in character, on the other, a like reader of Aristotle can see a commonsense mind, aware of things "as they are," and reacting in value judgments, particularly in ethics and literary criticism, as any "sensible" man would. On closer reading, however, the value theory of Aristotle, appealing though it may be in its "realism," appears in the main to lack the coherence found so clearly in Plato.

The thesis, briefly stated, which the present paper will attempt to suggest is simply this: when Aristotle rejected the basic metaphysical theory of his master Plato, *viz.,* the Theory of Ideas, he developed an empiricist metaphysics which permitted him to build upon the logical aspect of Plato's Ideas, and at the same time to make startling advances in ontology and epistemology, but which prevented him from coming to grips adequately with the problem of value and its relation to being. In other words, I am inviting a comparative study of Plato and Aristotle concerning the relation of being and value.

There will be two serious difficulties to overcome in the presentation of this thesis. The first lies in the fact that the isolation of and speculation about the problem of value as such is a relatively recent phenomenon in the history of philosophy. Consequently a modern interpreter who approaches the thought of Plato and Aristotle with particular reference to its implications for the problem of value, stands in grave danger of projecting back modern modes of thought and speculative climate which had not recognized value as such as one of the persistent and analytically isolable problems of philosophy. However, the difficulty can with proper precaution be overcome. Though indeed neither Plato nor Aristotle, we can suppose, ever explicitly asked himself the question, "What is value?", yet throughout their writings, as everyone knows, they are both implicitly and explicitly concerned with all the varied phenomena of evaluation. Consequently what the modern philosopher would call "value theory" is to be found imbedded in the texture of the writings of these two monumental ancient thinkers, save in those areas which are either logical or descriptive or "scientific." Obvious cases in point would be the puzzling second half of Plato's *Parmenides* or the mathematical or physiological sections of the *Timaeus*. In Aristotle, the strictly logical *Organon* or the biologically descriptive *Historia Animalium* should suffice as illustrations.

For evidence wherewith to reconstruct the "value theory" of either Plato or Aristotle, the interpreter will be obliged to scrutinize almost completely the body of their extant writings. He can legitimately use any passages which involve value judgments expressly, as well as those which by implication readily suggest presupposed value criteria. He must only be on his guard not to lose sight of the context from which the passages are drawn, for most often their meanings will not be confined to that which has a bearing upon value alone. The ancient thinker, even when dealing with the nature of "goodness," was not accustomed to limit his meaning philosophically to "pure value," but rather to have within his speculative range other closely related philosophical areas.

The other difficulty will arise as the negative character of the thesis concerning Aristotle's value theory begins to appear. In fact, the analysis will attempt to indicate a lack of coherence, and perhaps even confusion, in questions of evaluation, which tend to vitiate the whole effectiveness of Aristotelianism. There may even be adequate ground to contend that the major reason why Aristotle is so frequently obscure and difficult to understand lies in the absence of any comprehensive metaphysical ground for his value judgments. Or, to put it in another way, Aristotle never seems to have consistently felt the obligation to relate explicitly his evaluational speculation with those other aspects of his thought in which he achieved such outstanding success. But, as can readily be seen, merely to affirm that Aristotle was confused in his value thinking is not enough. Such an assertion, in its stark negativity, presupposes that there is a value theory, consistent and coherent, by means of which the weaknesses of this aspect of Aristotle's thought may, by comparison, be brought to light. That this difficulty involved in the negative thesis must be fully met, goes without question.

An obvious, though inadequate, method of solving the problem would be merely to set up Plato and his Theory of Ideas as the norm, for whatever may be said on metaphysical grounds against the Platonic position, it must be admitted that from the value point of view it is thoroughly coherent. Such a solution must be rejected, for it seems to imply that there is a "value theory" which in its human formulation has attained to the inexpugnable level of an absolute. Absolutes of this order are suspect, not only because they fly in the face of the brute datum of human finitude, but also because they in fact deny the fundamental character of philosophical speculation as quest. Philosophy basically is process. Once it becomes reduced to a series of absolute formulas it is defunct. Rather a solution to the present difficulty seems to lie in seeing the value problem never in isolation but always as it is functionally related to all the other aspects of philosophy. Or, to put it in its most summary form, it appears to be impossible to consider being and value apart from each other. Evidence for this conclusion seems to lie in the historical phenomenon that, for example, a philosophical system which seeks to confine itself solely to an analysis of being seems automatically by implication to construct or to adopt for itself a more or less inchoate accompanying value theory.

Aristotle, to a degree, in his reaction against Plato has done just this, as it is hoped that the present argument will suggest. In a sense he gives himself away in the phrase which G. R. G. Mure has chosen as the epigraph for his excellent discussion of Aristotle,[3] τὸ πάλαι τε καὶ νῦν καὶ ἀεὶ ζητούμενον καὶ ἀπορούμενον, τί τὸ ὄν, "The eternal question: What is Being?"[4] The history of philosophy, and indeed, some of its more recent developments in the field of value theory indicate that the eternal question should be, "What is Being—and—Value?"

The history of Western philosophy has produced myriads of views of Reality, of human life and the world, of values, of God, and of the supernatural. Though these views are almost infinitely various in their several details, they can in general be classified into three main groups which may be called somewhat arbitrarily Naturalism, Humanism, and Theism. It is most instructive to observe in each of these classes the characteristic attitude of the view in question concerning nature, the nature of man, reality, and that which is valuable. Naturalism, according to this classification, comprises all those philosophies which are basically materialistic or mechanistic, and above all in the biological sphere adhere to the principle of continuity. The Naturalist is impressed by the haziness of the line which marks off the animate from the inanimate, and

[3]G. R. G. Mure. *Aristotle,* Oxford University Press, New York, 1932.
[4]*Met.* 1028 b 2–4.

in the animate category sees an unbroken continuum, ranging from the most minute unicellular organism which possesses "life" on up to man, traditionally regarded as the most complex of living beings. No difference in kind, *i.e.,* no qualitative difference, is recognized normally in the series, but only a difference in degree, which is at bottom quantitative. Man and the amoeba, in other words, are in the same qualitative category, and are separated from each other by degrees of complexity which can be quantitatively measured. If Reality (that is, Reality with a capital *r,* or as Sir Arthur Eddington is alleged to have designated it, "Reality, loud cheers") be defined as comprising *everything* that has existence, the Naturalist makes it coextensive with the universe of space and time, and hence would deny the existence of God or of any transcendental element in things. Man's consciousness tends to be regarded as a bundle of conditioned reflexes, or an epiphenomenon. As an inevitable concomitant of the materialistic hypothesis, the validity of the concept of free will is usually denied, and man is conceived as a being determined completely by his hereditary physiological makeup and by his physical and social environment.[5] In the sphere of values, both esthetic and ethical, the Naturalist usually propounds a subjective and relativistic position. Ultimately values are determined by a hedonistic calculus and sanctioned by pleasure and pain reactions. What is pleasurable is good; what is painful, evil.

Perhaps the best illustration of Naturalism, because it is relatively simple, is to be found in ancient Epicureanism. In it, as we may gather from its leading exponents, Epicurus and Lucretius, we have most of the features described above. Certainly, reality is equivalent to the space-time universe, even though the orthodox Epicurean held that the universe is infinitely extended. All things are compounded of atoms and void, and all natural, as well as psychological phenomena, are explained

[5]This, and the subsequent descriptions of Humanism and Theism are drawn, it is fully acknowledged, in the most general terms, and are expressed in this way in order to designate the basic tendencies of the three different views. Not every philosophical system fits precisely into one of the three categories. For example, the position of John Dewey, in all its facets, may be regarded as Naturalistic in so far as it places supreme confidence in science and the so-called scientific method, while it is Humanistic in so far as it is a doctrine proclaiming, in the liberal tradition, the rights of individual men, human freedom, and the values inherent in political democracy. An unfriendly critic, however, might protest by pointing out that Dewey ultimately is a Naturalist, and that there is no sound basis in Naturalism wherewith to sanction his humanistic liberalism. It may be that Dewey is attempting to have his metaphysical cake and eat it, too.

in terms of this hypothesis. Pleasure is the highest good, and all value judgments are ultimately referred to this absolute norm. To be sure, the Epicurean hedonism is enlightened. The creed is far different from that of the crude voluptuary, and characteristically the pleasures which accrue from elevated intellectual pursuits or from friendship and similar human activities are given the highest place, but they are finally determined by the subjective reaction of the individual. In only one respect does Epicureanism depart from the standard features of Naturalism, since it does maintain the freedom of the human will. Through the well known attribution of the capacity to "swerve" to the individual atom, the Epicurean could account for the power of human beings to initiate action. It is thus that Epicureanism avoids the trap of a complete determinism, but still the criterion which controls moral action remains the carefully calculated long term pleasure reaction of the moral agent.

The second great class among *Weltanschauungen* may be called Humanism, even at the risk of some confusion because of the wide variety of meanings which have from time to time been given to the term. Humanism here intends to designate that view of man and Reality which, like Naturalism, sees man as part of biological nature, but at the same time believes that there is a dimension in man, not possessed by the other beings in the biological order, yet sufficient to differentiate him qualitatively from the rest. In short, Humanism denies at bottom the principle of continuity. The major ground for thus assigning a special position for man lies in his capacity to have both ethical and esthetic responses, as well as in his possession of the faculty of reason. Humanism would not limit Reality necessarily to the physical and temporal extension of the universe (specific examples of Humanisms differ on this point) but, at any rate, the view would hold that intrinsic in Reality are certain absolute norms or standards of value. These principles are absolute, are deep in the heart of things and are external to and unconditioned by any human subject. Yet Humanism would insist that it is possible for man to grasp and know these principles, and govern his life accordingly. Though he does adhere to his belief in the existence of these absolute standards, the Humanist shares with the Naturalist the conviction that no Divine Being lies behind the universe. Man in his view, because he possesses reason and is capable of ethical insight, is in complete control of his own destiny, and will, at some future time be able, by virtue of his own powers, to solve the problems presented to him in the human predicament.

In ancient philosophy, despite the fact that both Renaissance and modern Humanisms stem from it, it is difficult to find a system which in every point coincides with Humanism as it has been delineated. Both Platonism and Aristotelianism fall in part within the category. Plato and Aristotle both would deny the principle of continuity in nature, and would assign a special position to man because he possesses the faculty of reason. Plato's Ideas certainly are absolute norms, but Plato would not assert that man could apprehend them completely or could totally exhaust their meaning. Yet Plato would contend that man possesses the power to orient himself properly toward these Ideas, as the ultimate principles in Reality. But, as distinct from the normal Humanism, Plato does postulate the existence of God, Who has functioned as the great Artificer of the universe and Who does control in some measure the things and events therein. Aristotle, on the other hand, would insist that man through reason is capable, in an absolute sense, of solving his problems, though Aristotle by no means can postulate the separate existence of absolute norms or values. Also, for Aristotle, God occupies a supreme position in his metaphysical scheme, a fact which further would differentiate his system from "normal Humanism." Historically, it may be observed that Humanism has emerged by a kind of amalgamation of Plato and Aristotle into a view which tends to elevate man and his reason into the supreme position in Reality.

Theism, or the religious view of Reality, shares certain beliefs with both Naturalism and Humanism, and to this extent absorbs them within itself. With Naturalism it recognizes the biological aspect of man's nature, and with Humanism it denies the principle of continuity in nature. With Humanism it postulates the existence of absolute norms or standards of value, but unlike Humanism, it postulates the existence of God, Who as Creator is the supreme source of these values. Though Theism recognizes the superior status of man among spatiotemporal things, it insists that Reality has within itself a supernatural dimension over and above the natural order, from which man derives his especial worth and without which he is incapable of working out his own destiny. To a greater or a lesser degree all the great religions of the world maintain this view of man and Reality, and, of course, Christianity gives it its most explicit formulation.

Even in these brief analyses it should be clear that there is an inevitable functional relation between theories of value and of being. If this be so, then any philosophy which addresses itself specifically and exclusively to the one or to the other would appear to run the risk of having its system vitiated by the failure properly to attend to the excluded problem and the relation of it to the sphere selected for analysis. Thus, if a system attempts to be exclusively a philosophy of being, the problem of value will receive short shrift. On the other hand, a philosophy which singles out value for its sole sphere of investigation will suffer for want of an adequate ontology. In fact, this phenomenon, to be found so often among philosophers, *viz.,* to abstract one area from the total philosophical context, and to analyze it to the exclusion of all else, has constituted perhaps the gravest of all philosophy's liabilities. Of course, it cannot be denied that these investigations have produced significant results, but in all but the rarest of cases, these positive results have failed of complete fruition, because they have not been produced by a method which analyzes always in full context. Speculation in isolation seems always to tend to be more and more rationalistic. This is virtually inevitable, for the further a thinker departs from the full context of philosophy, *i.e.,* the complete range of philosophical data of all orders, the greater must be his reliance upon the rationalistic criterion of inner coherence or consistency. Naturally the further he goes in this direction, the less recognition will he give to the criterion of correspondence.

An interesting illustration of this philosophical "isolationism," *i.e.,* of the tendency to explore one philosophical sphere to the exclusion of all others, can be seen in recent times in the development of logical positivism. The position as it is expressed in A. J. Ayer's *Language, Truth, and Logic* is most instructive.[6]

Whatever one's reaction to logical positivism, and to Ayer's version, may be, there can be no doubt about its service as a wholesome corrective to the airy metaphysics of nineteenth century German idealism or its British counterpart. In England, at least, it has amounted to a strong reassertion of the characteristic tradition of British empiricism. For example, in 1910 Hume is reported to have been largely out of favor among English thinkers, but now the mode, largely under the impulse of logical positivism, has reinstated him as one of the great figures with whom to conjure in the history of philosophy.

[6]A. J. Ayer, *Language, Truth, and Logic,* 2nd edition, Victor Gollancz, London, 1946.

Now Ayer is consumed with the most laudable desire to say only that which makes sense, and that which is true. His test of "sense," shared, one can suppose, fundamentally with all other logical positivists, amounts to a scrutiny of each statement or proposition to see whether or not it may be empirically verified. Obviously, scientific propositions, which can be verified by the scientific or laboratory method, are true, *i.e.*, "make sense," though they are not absolute truths but only probable truths. According to Ayer, when he comes to deal with mathematical propositions, which by their nature cannot be empirically verified, such propositions are "true" because under analysis they are revealed to be ultimately tautologies. They are *a priori,* and, as tautologies, are logically certain. Other propositions which involve the data of ordinary sense experience may be regarded to all intents and purposes as "true," though their truth or the "sense they make" may, like scientific propositions, only attain a reasonably high degree of probability. Probable truth rather than absolute truth seems to be introduced in Ayer's thinking, because experiential data are rather cantankerously intractable, and no "scientific" method of verification can be devised to produce absolutely certain results.

Ayer's position, as thus far expounded, has much to commend it. Certainly "scientific truth" is worthy of the highest regard, because it has been tested again and again by independent experimenters. Also, the acceptance as probably true of the propositions which at a fairly elementary level are verified in human experience could hardly find an opponent in anyone who somehow or other believes that there is such a thing as common sense. As for Ayer's conviction that mathematical propositions are tautologies, it seems difficult to believe that a philosophical mathematician would accept this view. Perhaps Ayer quotes Poincaré inadvisably on the point (for it seems so damaging to Ayer's own position) who remarks, "If all the assertions which mathematics puts forward can be derived from one another by formal logic, mathematics cannot amount to anything more than an immense tautology. Logical inference can teach us nothing essentially new, and if everything is to proceed from the principle of identity, everything must be reducible to it. But can we really allow that these theorems which fill so many books serve no other purpose than to say in a round-about fashion 'A = A'?"[7]

---

[7]Jules Henri Poincaré, *La Science et l'Hypothèse,* part I, chap. 1, quoted by Ayer, *op. cit.,* p. 85.

Fortunately in the present context it is not necessary to investigate further the difficult question concerning the philosophical status of mathematical entities, but Ayer's views concerning the propositions of metaphysics, morality, and religion are definitely in point. To his own satisfaction, at least, Ayer believes that he has eliminated metaphysics. He does so with an astonishing bravura and with great simplicity. Since metaphysical propositions involve heavily *a priori* conceptions and hence are not susceptible to empirical verification, they are quite literally nonsense. For any who, hitherto denied the light of logical positivism, have been foolish enough to suppose that the great monumental figures in philosophy are metaphysicians, Ayer has a word of comfort. He asserts quite categorically that the majority of the "great philosophers" were not essentially metaphysicians in his sense, and thus reassures "those who would otherwise be prevented from adopting our criterion by considerations of piety."[8]

Ayer disposes of the possibility of religious knowledge and the question of the existence of God (which he spells uniformly with a lower case *g*) with equal celerity.[9] Religious knowledge is impossible because it cannot be verified empirically. As for the existence of God, Ayer insists, and quite correctly, that it cannot be demonstratively proved, but his argument for the point is interesting. To prove anything demonstratively, its terms must be *a priori,* for only *a priori* propositions are logically certain, and they are logically certain only because they are tautologies. That God exists cannot be deduced from an *a priori* proposition, because from such a proposition only a further tautology can be derived. Therefore, there is no demonstrative proof for the existence of God. But Ayer goes further to insist that there is no way to prove that the existence of God is even probable. He argues that if God's existence were probable, "then the proposition that he existed would be an empirical hypothesis."[10] But this cannot be shown, and upon further analysis the term, God, is revealed to be a metaphysical term. Hence the proposition, "God exists" is shown to be a metaphysical proposition, and therefore is nonsense. It should be added that Ayer goes on to show how the views of the atheist or agnostic are equally nonsense for the same reason. The agnostic holds that the existence of God is a possibility

[8]*Ibid.,* p. 41.
[9]*Ibid.,* pp. 114 ff.
[10]*Ibid.,* p. 115.

which has no compelling ground for acceptance or rejection. The atheist believes that the nonexistence of God is probable. Both views, according to Ayer, are nonsense, because all propositions which involve in them the metaphysical term, God, are automatically nonsense.

To complete his demolition of religion, Ayer proceeds to deal with the content of the religious experience of the mystic. The mystic avers that God is a mystery Which transcends human understanding, "the object of a purely mystical intuition, and cannot therefore be defined in terms which are intelligible to the reason." Ayer takes the impossibility of being able to define God in intelligible terms to be the equivalent of the admission "that it is impossible for a sentence both to be significant and be about God." He goes on, "If a mystic admits that the object of his vision is something which cannot be described, then he must also admit that he is bound to talk nonsense when he describes it."[11] Ayer cannot say *a priori* that the mystic's intuitive method is invalid. He rather waits to see the propositions which the mystic formulates about his intuitions in order to subject them "to the test of actual experience," or "in order to see whether they are verified or confuted by our empirical observations. But the mystic, so far from producing propositions which are empirically verified, is unable to produce any intelligible propositions at all." . . . "The fact that [the mystic] cannot reveal what he 'knows,' or even himself devise an empirical test to validate his 'knowledge,' shows that his state of mystical intuition is not a genuinely cognitive state. So that in describing his vision the mystic does not give us any information about the external world;[12] he merely gives us indirect information about the condition of his own mind."[13]

After having followed the analysis of Ayer's position thus far, it should take little imagination to anticipate the nature of his ethical views. In ethics Ayer descries four classes of propositions. First, there are those which define ethical terms, or "judgments about the legitimacy or possibility of certain definitions. Secondly, there are propositions describing the phenomena of moral experience, and their causes. Thirdly, there are exhortations to moral virtue. And, lastly, there are actual eth-

---

[11]*Ibid.,* p. 118.

[12]Ayer's own "metaphysics" can virtually be reconstructed on the basis of this one sentence. A cardinal feature would be that Reality and the external world are equivalent. Also only in the most incidental sense would the mystic be interested in giving us any information about the "external world."

[13]*Ibid.,* p. 119.

ical judgments."[14] Ayer limits ethical philosophy to the first class. Class Two is the proper subject-matter of psychology or sociology. Class Three comprises commands to act, and as such "do not belong to any branch of philosophy or science." The nature of the propositions of Class Four Ayer is unwilling to categorize with undue precipitation. He first addresses himself to the question "whether statements of ethical value can be translated into statements of empirical fact."[15] After rejecting both subjectivist and utilitarian analyses of ethical terms, Ayer asserts first "that, in our language, sentences which contain normative ethical symbols are not equivalent to sentences which express psychological propositions, or indeed empirical propositions of any kind."[16] Descriptive ethical symbols, on the other hand, are not in Ayer's view indefinable in factual terms. Only the normative apparently is suspect. In other words, if one says that such and such an act is wrong, if this constitutes a moral judgment, "wrong" is a normative symbol. But if by the statement that the act is wrong, we mean that a specific society disapproves of it, "wrong" is a descriptive symbol, and the proposition, now become legitimate, respectable, and factual, is one of the ordinary sociological sort.

Naturally Ayer in turn rejects the "absolutist" view of ethics, which rests ultimately upon what to him is anathema, *viz.,* a mysterious intellectual intuition. Having rejected all the standard ethical solutions, Ayer is really in an unhappy plight. Hence he is reduced to asserting that statements involving moral judgments are merely the expression of moral sentiments. Any man who disagrees is likewise expressing his moral sentiments. There is no point in asking which one is right, for neither "is asserting a genuine proposition."[17] The normative ethical term is purely "emotive." Thus ethical judgments can in no sense have any objective validity whatsoever. Arguments on moral or value questions merely reduce themselves, if we are to believe Ayer, to pitting one set of feelings over against another. We resort to argument, so he says, "in order to win our opponent over to our way of thinking."[18] But such arguments really resolve themselves into a consideration of the facts of the case. If agreement on the facts is achieved and there still is a dis-

[14]*Ibid.,* p. 103.
[15]*Ibid.,* p. 104.
[16]*Ibid.,* p. 105.
[17]*Ibid.,* p. 108.
[18]*Ibid.,* p. 110.

agreement concerning the value in question, there is nothing to be done between the disputants except to abuse each other. In the ethic of Ayer, there can be no argument about the validity of moral principles; there can be only agreement or conflict of feelings.

So confident is he of the soundness of his position, that he is able to engage in the following self-appraisal: "If anyone doubts the accuracy of this account of moral disputes, let him try to construct even an imaginary argument on a question of value which does not reduce itself to an argument about a question of logic or about an empirical matter of fact. I am confident that he will not succeed in producing a single example."[19] In the first place, this remark is a trifle odd, since on the preceding page he has described a dispute between individuals with different moral "conditionings" who agree on the facts in a given case but still disagree on the moral value under discussion. Perhaps Ayer would evade the issue by insisting that what would ensue under these conditions could not accurately be designated an argument. And, secondly, it is difficult to refrain from wondering about the kind of philosophical *milieu* in which Ayer has discussed or "argued" about questions of moral value.[20]

No doubt the foregoing account of Ayer's position has resulted in some distortion because of its foreshortened character, but at the same time it seems certain that its skeletal structure, apart from refinements in detail, cannot be understood in any fundamentally different terms. In any event, the discussion should have revealed the philosophical consequences of starting an inquiry of a strictly ontological and epistemological character, constructing a series of absolute principles, and then after having become tightly hedged about by the principles to turn to questions of moral and religious value. Ayer asks, "What is being and how do we know it?" Roughly, the answer is that being is the external world (here let us not forget that mathematical and logical propositions are tautologies which we spin out in a simon pure, *a priori,* mental realm of ultimately undifferentiated identity) and that we know it by experience, and that we know we know it if we can express what we know via verbal language or symbols in propositions which can be empirically verified. If this theory of being and knowledge is accepted, then value and, of course, religion are nonsense. At bottom, it comes to something

[19]*Ibid.,* p. 112.
[20]Perhaps Ayer would regard this last remark as abusive.

like this: if one admits the ultimacy of Ayer's principle of verification, the rest follows with an overpowering inevitability. And no one, to give Ayer his full due, can say that he did not see the argument through to its appallingly nihilistic conclusion in the realm of value.

Suppose one should ask for a sanction for the principle of verification. Search his volume thoroughly and the best that emerges is that the principle somehow or other has a "scientific" aura about it which should make it automatically acceptable to any rightminded man. But upon inspection, though we are supposed to believe that it is a scientific principle, actually it is found to be a philosophical principle or, *pace* Ayer, even a metaphysical principle, and, as such, really functions as a value principle.[21] As a metaphysical principle it must be reached via philosophical or metaphysical methods, and must be defended and supported by the same methods. Metaphysics has only one proper meaning and that is the philosophical inquiry into first principles. Ayer is by no means the first man to assail metaphysics when it has lost touch with the manifold of philosophical data. But to "eliminate" metaphysics is merely to lock the front door while permitting what can only meaningfully be called metaphysical first principles, to enter through the rear window, unexamined and untested. It seems difficult to see in the principle of verification anything other than a fiercely tyrannical metaphysical absolute. Like many another principle it has its spheres where its value and appropriateness are unquestioned. In this case these are obviously science and certain domains of human experience. But why should it be that thinkers who have grasped a principle which operates beautifully within its appropriate sphere can never resist the temptation to universalize it, and thus work havoc or produce nonsense in areas to which the principle is palpably alien?

It may be possible that Reality is constituted as Ayer supposes, but if it is so we must conclude that the vast majority of men, from the humblest to the great masters of thought and art, have been most monstrously humbugged. However appealing the logical positivist theory of value (or, had we better not say, theory of no-value?) may be to some, it is a matter of historical fact that men simply have not lived that way, nor is there any conceivable reason to suppose that they will. The broad experience of men (not Ayer's combination of experience and verifiable

[21]The principle of verification reveals truth. Would any one be prepared to deny that truth is a value?

propositions) indicates that the philosophical attempts to resolve the problem of value must take a different course. The reduction of value to nonsense is clearly no solution. Ayer's peculiar analysis of the problem of being, and its consequences for the problem of value, should suggest that the attack must somehow be simultaneous on both. Being and value, though analytically distinguishable, are, it seems, in reality deeply interconnected.

In sharp contrast to the philosophy of logical positivism, Nicolai Hartmann has elaborated a fully wrought theory of value.[22] In his thought there is a concentration upon value as such, and there is relatively little attention paid to the question of being. As a result, it is not surprising to see that an opposite weakness to that of Ayer tends to appear. Hartmann definitely is in the tradition of postKantian German Idealism, and in his ethical thinking, he professes a great obligation to Aristotle, whom he calls "the ancient master of ethical research."[23] Though large sections of Hartmann's work give the reader a sense of dizzying complexity, still he has taken pains to specify the first principles in terms of which he works out his theory. His goal is to present a concrete ethic of values, and he takes his start from two fundamental concepts which had been developed by two of his German predecessors in sharply contrasted fields.[24] One principle comes from Kant who had "in the apriority of the moral law a well considered and a unified knowledge of the absoluteness of genuine ethical standards." But Hartmann believes that Kant did not have "the concrete perception and the breadth of sympathy which would have given this knowledge full recognition." The other concept is that of "the manifoldness of values which Nietzsche—though only from a distance—had discerned." Hartmann adds, "Nietzsche was the first to see the rich plenitude of the ethical cosmos, but with him it melted away in historical relativism."[25]

---

[22]Nicolai Hartmann, *Ethik,* Walter de Gruyter, Berlin, 1926. The quotations in this chapter are from the English translation by Stanton Coit in three volumes, originally published by George Allen & Unwin, Ltd., London, 1932. The extracts are used with the permission of the original publishers as well as the Macmillan Company, the American publishers.

[23]*Ethics,* vol. I, p. 16. All references to Hartmann will be given in the English translation.

[24]*Ibid.*

[25]These quotations all can be found in *Ethics,* vol. I, p. 16. One perhaps may doubt the rather extravagant claim that Nietzsche was "the first to see the rich plenitude of the ethical cosmos."

For our present purpose, in considering Hartmann's self-styled amalgam of Kant, Nietzsche, and Aristotle, by all odds the most important element is the Kantian aprioristic principle. Hartmann takes as his starting point that the *a priori* awareness of values on the part of human beings, or what he calls alternatively "the valuational consciousness," constitutes absolute proof of the absolute and objective existence of values. One remark which he makes when he is discussing the bearing of the distinction between form and matter upon an autonomous ethical principle discloses without ambiguity the orientation of his thought:

> Values may be as formal or material as they please, only they must be something self-dependent, they must be independent of all extraneous principles, and the valuational consciousness in regard to them must be aprioristic. If by the aprioristic we do not understand a function, but only the specific way of knowing something objective which, as such, can be as well understood as mistaken, there is no difficulty in regard to the material content of values.[26]

Hartmann is obviously trying to get away from what he regards to be the undue formalism of Kant, *i.e.,* he is trying to inject into ethics some of the concrete material of Nietzsche's "rich plenitude." This purpose leads him to insist: "Valuational structures are ideal objects, beyond all real Being and Not-Being, also beyond the really existing feeling of value, which alone grasps them.—But that they are something which as regards content are material and not empty, abstract forms, makes them capable by their nature of being actualized—in so far as they are not actualized. Consequently, on account of their concrete nature they are capable of determining the content of laws which have a bearing upon positive moral life. For only positive contents are capable of being commanded and actualized, but empty forms and abstractions never.— This is why ethics—precisely as a consequence of Kantian apriorism— must be a material ethics of values."[27]

What then is Hartmann's philosophy of Being? What is his ontology? The answer to this question is by no means easy. Implicitly, in the light of his use of the terms "real" and "actual," we get a sense that Being is pretty much the world as we find it, *i.e.,* the objective universe of space and time. The world is filled with persons who possess a "feeling of

[26]*Ethics*, vol. I, p. 170.
[27]*Ethics*, vol. I, p. 180.

value" and participate in a complex of events. Thus much is certainly implicit in Hartmann's phrase which asserts that "valuational structures are ideal objects beyond all real Being and Not-Being." So the sum-total of things is presented as consisting, on the one hand, of a realm of "real Being and Not-Being," and, on the other, of a realm of values, self-subsistent and self-substantiating.[28] These "valuational structures" somehow or other have the capacity to get themselves "realized" or "actualized" in the realm of "Being and Not-Being." This actualization is brought about by human persons who can be regarded as genuine moral agents, for they first become aware of valuational structures because they possess the *a priori* valuational consciousness. And next, because their awareness is so vivid, the phenomenon of moral conscience takes place, and they feel themselves under obligation to bring into "actuality" the values which they have apprehended *a priori*.

Having postulated such a theory of total Reality, Hartmann devotes

[28]Hartmann reveals explicitly in one passage that he sees these two realms as I am attempting to present them. He is discussing Kant's saying that "the moral law within me" for sublimity holds the balance with the "starry heavens above me." Hartmann comments that it is "incumbent upon us to hold the metaphysic of this great vision within strictly critical limits. It gives neither ontological priority to axiology nor primacy to the practical reason.

All that it really justifies is an axiological primacy of the ideal sphere, in contrast to the ontological primacy of the real sphere" (*Ethics,* vol. I, pp. 243–244. The italics are mine.). If this statement is a fair expression of Hartmann's view, it is easy to see the extent of the gap between being and value, between ontology and axiology, in his thought. It is my attempt to show that a far more nearly adequate metaphysical approach lies in investigating the problems of being and value simultaneously. Ultimately the justification for such an approach lies in the fact that any datum which falls under philosophical analysis has both an ontological and an axiological dimension. Hartmann himself in a very few instances seems to be aware of this principle, but his exclusive preoccupation with the realm of value evidently prevents him from addressing himself to the problems of being and value simultaneously. One such instance comes when he is delineating the human moral agent as a "carrier of values and disvalues," *i.e.,* as the instrument of introducing values into the realm of "actuality." Man "is himself at the same time an ontological and an axiological entity, a real self-existing being, and at the same time possessing in himself the higher, the distinctively moral values or their opposites" (*Ethics,* vol. I, p. 269). Another passage is even more explicit: "In a certain sense one may say that everything, which exists, somehow falls practically under the category of values, that everything in the world, even the most remote and indifferent, is in the perspective of positive or negative worth. The same universe, which in its totality underlies ontological phenomena, belongs also in precisely the same totality to ethical phenomena. It is no less a world of goods and evils than of things and their relations. At least it is as radically the former as it is the latter" (*Ethics,* vol. II, p. 24). It is to be regretted that Hartmann did not develop his analysis of the value problem in the light of this statement, rather than in the perspective of the isolated autonomy of value.

the major portion of his book to the "mapping" of what he calls "valuational space." He proceeds in the spirit of a speculative pioneer, and is most modest in his claims for the validity of his results. At the same time, his analyses of valuational structures tend to drive a wedge between the two philosophical spheres of ontology and axiology, between being and value, and the net result seems to produce a radical divorce between the two.

The divorce is emphasized by his continual insistence that the whole realm of ideal objective values possesses a status of absolute autonomy. Having isolated this realm, Hartmann assumes the role of an axiological cartographer, and, as J. H. Muirhead in his editor's introduction to the book points out, with considerable originality develops, under the heading of "The Antinomic of Values," "the modal, relational and the qualitative and quantitative polar opposites that are traceable in . . . 'valuational space.' "[29] These hypostatized values, under Hartmann's analysis, are carefully ordered into a hierarchy, with the higher, or more valuable, values dependent upon the lower, *i.e.,* less valuable, though more fundamental values. These latter have an independence of their own, and their own incontrovertible autonomy in their proper spheres.

As we follow Hartmann in his mapping exercise, we cannot escape the feeling that in many instances he is operating on a level of abstraction which has lost contact with the content and concrete data of human experience. This is not to say that as a man of moral sensibility he has not made many illuminating and perceptive observations, particularly with respect to the relation of values with one another, and with respect to the whole vexed question of the relation between the positive or "good'" value, and its "bad" opposite or disvalue. But the most unfortunate aspect of his thought results from his conviction that value is autonomous in the most absolute sense. Not only does this impede the effectiveness of establishing the relations between being (in his own sense or in the more conventional philosophical sense) and value, but also it precludes the possibility of postulating any type of theism, a consequence which many ethical thinkers would not accept. There is, in fact, no room for God or for so-called religious values in his system. The absolute autonomy of values needs no God as Creator or sanction.

The complete acceptance of autonomous values leads Hartmann, at one point when he is speaking of Plato, Aristotle, and the Stoics, into a

[29]*Ethics,* vol. I, p. 6.

bit of Procrustean philosophical criticism. Hartmann announces blandly that in the method of the ancients "there is everywhere a kernel of aprioristic research." There is no radical contrast between the Platonic and Aristotelian procedure, "between the pure intuition of the 'idea of the good,' and the careful detailed work in the fixing of the ἀνθρώπινον ἀγαθόν." Aristotle's concept of virtue does not come "from the empirical, but from the utterances of the moral judgment of values, from praise and blame, from respect and contempt, from love and hate; and his final views are purely idealistic: the measure (the 'mean'), energy, the καλόν, the ὡς δεῖ."[30] To show that this involves a metaphysical falsification of Aristotle's position, one needs only to recall his unwavering insistence that terms like the καλόν or the ὡς δεῖ (*i.e.,* the beautiful and the "ought") cannot point to something which has a separate or "ideal" existence.

No one can deny Hartmann's contention that Plato's Ideas are aprioristic, and indeed it is fair to say that Hartmann's values and Plato's Ideas of values are to all intents and purposes identical in so far as they are both ideal objects. Hartmann tends to see more apriorism in Stoicism than is actually there. Surely one of the major grounds for the Stoics' belief in the goodness of Nature, and the consequent exhortation to "follow Nature" rested on the empirical observation of cosmic regularity. Thus Hartmann goes too far when he says that to "follow Nature" means, "the inner pursuit of the final essence, wherein nature is identified with the absolute logos. 'Nature' is only an expression for the totality of eternal laws not made by man." Hartmann then proceeds to add Christian ethics to the group. It likewise shares, so he says, the apriorism of Plato, Aristotle, and the Stoics. He sees only a slight difference between the more Platonic aspect in Saint Augustine and the more Aristotelian among the Scholastics. That the moral claims in Christian ethics are "understood to be the will of God" makes no real difference, in Hartmann's thinking. "The will of God is only the vehicle of the values,

---

[30]These and the following paraphrase and quotations are to be found in *Ethics,* vol. I, pp. 202–203. It might be well to point out that my thesis endeavors to suggest the radical contrast between Plato and Aristotle in the field of value theory, and that only in a certain limited number of instances can Aristotle's thought in this field be called either aprioristic or "purely idealistic." In other words, Hartmann is attributing to Aristotle a coherence of thought in value theory which the text of Aristotle seems not to substantiate. In fact, in the light of Aristotle's rejection of Plato's Theory of Ideas, it is impossible for him to have a thoroughgoing aprioristic or idealistic theory of value at all.

just as 'nature' is with the Stoics," and he goes on to summarize his position thus, "For ethics it is a matter of indifference what metaphysical significance is given to the realm of values, what religious or philosophical view is taken as a background, however much the emphasis may be laid by individual thinkers upon the cosmic view. For ethics the only concern is the apriority of the values themselves."

Of the four views which Hartmann has brought together, Platonism is the only one which has not been critically distorted. No convinced Aristotelian would be satisfied with the version given. In fact it is the genuine thoroughgoing empiricism of Aristotle which attracts many of his adherents. The Stoic perhaps would be less unhappy, whereas the orthodox Christian would violently protest against the relation between God and values which Hartmann's remarks presuppose. To be sure, such comprehension of God as a Christian may possess has an aprioristic dimension to it, but that the will of that God is merely the "vehicle of the values" is a position which he would never accept. The point should now be clear that when Hartmann develops as an isolated principle the absolute autonomy of values, he is unable to do justice to those problems of philosophy with which in human experience the problem of value is inevitably related. Also, and in many ways no less important, so intense is Hartmann's concentration upon this principle of absolute autonomy that he forces preceding philosophies into the mold of his own thought, and is thus prevented either from understanding them as they are, or from grasping properly how in them the various aspects of philosophy are related to one another.

One further phase of Hartmann's thought needs to be mentioned, namely, his rejection of teleology, or, as he sometimes puts it, "finalistic determinism." Having postulated the self-dependent existence of "valuational structures" and man as the moral agent by whom values become actualized, Hartmann attributes to man a genuine freedom of will.[31] With this will man is able to choose from among the values (and

[31]It is worth noting that Hartmann does not believe that he has "proved" the freedom of the human will as he has "proved" the ideal existence of values. Yet, though he regards the freedom of the will as a highly probable hypothesis, he will not take as a ground for "proof" the consciousness of freedom. He remarks, ". . . real freedom of consciousness (that of the conscious will) never follows from the given consciousness of freedom, however unescapable and imperturbable this may be. The imperturbability might be the consequence of a necessary illusion" (*Ethics,* vol. III, p. 120). Perhaps with a certain amount of metaphysical subtlety apart, it is difficult to see how Hartmann on *a priori* grounds ac-

disvalues) and bring them into actuality in the real world. In Hartmann's view, this is possible only if teleology is eliminated. As has already been noted, God in effect has been dropped from the picture. Hartmann believes that, though no one can either prove or disprove the
existence of God, in any event so far as values are concerned, even if He
did exist, His presence or presumptive power is irrelevant to the ethical
situation, *i.e.,* the free choice of values by man as moral agent. Hartmann
admits quite frankly that the upshot of this position amounts to granting to man the attribute of Divinity, and thus the only teleology possible
is a teleology forged by man himself. Hartmann is quite vehement on
this point and here again those who would not accept a divorce of moral
values from religion can see an unfortunate consequence of his principle
of autonomous and isolated valuational structures.

The vehemence of Hartmann's view cannot be overlooked nor its
corollary of the absolute apotheosis of man. He writes, for example,
"The setting up of ends by man is a fact. Ethics does and must do what
in the eyes of the pious may be blasphemy; it gives to man an attribute
of Divinity. To him it restores what he, mistaking his own nature, discarded and ascribed to Divinity. Or, to express it differently, it allows
Divinity to step down from its cosmic throne and dwell in the will of
man. The metaphysical heritage of God falls to man."[32] Or again, "The
metaphysical humanization of the Absolute is the moral annulment
of man."[33] Man's Godhead is elsewhere described thus: "Through
man's purposive activity, that is, his categorially higher form of determination, which originates with him, he proves himself to be an entity
superior to the powers of Nature, a Being in whose hands forces blind
and aimless in themselves become means to ends discerned and posited
beforehand."[34] And finally Hartmann speaks in the strongest language
possible: "That anything whatsoever in heaven or on earth, even though
it be God himself, should take precedence of Man, would be ethically
perverted; it would not be moral; it would be treason to mankind,

---

cepts the absolute independence of values and at the same time will not accept as equally
valid the freedom of the will, for which virtually the same type of *a priori* evidence is
available.

[32]*Ethics,* vol. I, p. 282.

[33]*Ethics,* vol. I, p. 290.

[34]*Ethics,* vol. III, p. 80. Shades of Henley, "I am the master of my fate; I am the captain
of my soul"!

which must rely upon itself alone."[35] So far as Man's position in the universe is concerned, it would be hard to find a more extreme statement of Humanism, as we have described it.

In the light of this situation, it is easy to see why Hartmann will have nothing to do with "finalistic determinism" or any kind of cosmic or religious teleology. He can see only an absolute disjunction between freedom of the will and teleological determinism, and he can only deplore the persistence of the theory that such a teleology exists: "In a world determined finalistically throughout, such as the later metaphysics under the spell of a time honoured prejudice accepted almost unanimously, moral freedom is an impossibility. The categorial structure of the finalistic nexus bars it out. If a teleology of the existential process was ontologically fixed, there would be no place in the world for the existence of morality, and all ethical phenomena would be phantom appearances. Man already would be preordained in his will, in his spiritual attitude, indeed in all his behaviour; and all accountability, every feeling of responsibility would be an illusion—perhaps a gracious one, but just the same an illusion. There would be no room for a moral being. 'Man' is possible only in a world not teleologically determined."[36]

Hartmann in this way cuts the Gordian knot, and decides in favor of the freedom of the will as against finalistic determinism. This is clearly the rationalistic answer, essentially a simplist answer, and even in rationalistic terms is sound only if free will and finalistic determinism are really in a genuinely disjunctive relation. If they are not mutually exclusive (and indeed the central position of Christianity, for example, has never seen them as such)[37] then it may be that Hartmann should modify his conceptions of free will and finalistic determinism. In the case of free will, the simplism of his analysis appears when he says: "It is the nature of human volition that it never is directed towards anything contrary to value as such. That was the never-to-be-forgotten meaning of the Socratic ethics: no one does evil for evil's sake, it is always a good

[35]*Ethics,* vol. III, p. 264.

[36]*Ethics,* vol. III, pp. 71–72.

[37]Hartmann would no doubt call the attitude of Christianity on this point a signal instance of "time-honoured prejudice." Whether it is erroneous or not, I would venture to say that the simultaneous presence of free will and a divine or transcendental determinism of some sort is the implicit assumption underlying the view of human life shared by the creators of great epic and tragedy in the Western world.

(something valuable), which hovers before him."[38] Whatever may be the merits of the famous Socratic paradox that virtue equals knowledge (and there are obviously many), practically no one, not even Plato himself, would consider it to be an exhaustive analysis of the moral or of the volitional problem. The plain fact of the matter is that men on occasion actually "do evil for evil's sake," and consequently any theory of the freedom of the will must take this into account if it is to achieve any profundity.

As for teleology, according to Hartmann's philosophical assumptions, it is very difficult to see why he talks of finalistic determinism at all. In the first place, he is at pains to show that his autonomous values are absolutely independent of any deity. The divine is superfluous, for Man has become God. In this kind of context, to introduce a concept of finalistic determinism is indeed to set up a man of straw. Actually he is knocked down even before he is set up. Hartmann's reasoning must be something like this: if there were a supreme agent who could set in motion a finalistic determinism (and we know perfectly well on other grounds that there isn't), then this supposititious agent would be of such a sort as to determine and fix absolutely and in complete detail everything and every event in the world we know, in such a way as to reduce man to a complete state of automatism. Since the reduction of man to an automaton is unthinkable, there cannot be a supreme agent, and hence no finalistic determinism. Cosmic teleology, divine or finalistic determinism, however it may be designated, can be meaningful only if God, or the Supreme Agent is characterized in far different terms from those which the nature of Hartmann's philosophical position dictates that he must employ. God as a Creator of man and the universe, as a Being Who is infinitely good (a view of Him shared by the religion of Plato, Christianity, and other great religions) can be conceived as the controller of man and the cosmos, and at the same time without denying to man a genuine and valid freedom of will. Such a God would be the Creator and source of all values, but such an hypothesis obviously is contrary to Hartmann's position.

The whole matter may be summarized by observing that the absolute value philosophy promulgated by Hartmann has much of importance to say within the limits of value theory. In the same way as Ayer has a

[38]*Ethics*, vol. II, p. 46.

contribution to make to the investigation of that which constitutes a valid proposition, but is found unsatisfactory when the implications of his principles are developed in other areas, so the philosophy of Hartmann, limited as it is by the principle of the absolute autonomy of values, does less than justice to fields other than that of value. For example, both Naturalist and Theist would object almost with equal violence to the hypothesis that man is as God, or to the implicit optimism that man through his own efforts can and will resolve his problems. If the critiques of both Ayer and Hartmann are to any degree significant, it should follow that any philosophical analysis is foredoomed which drives into one single philosophical problem with the tacit assumption that it can validly be isolated and abstracted from the whole universe of philosophical discourse. The specialization may, indeed, and does contribute, particularly if the individual system is seen in the perspective of the entire history of philosophical thought. But one is constrained to wonder how much such contributions are worth when balanced against the distortions which emerge. The history of the race shows that men simply do not live in the value anarchy postulated by Ayer's system, quite irrespective of the naiveté or sophistication of their value thinking. And the same general kind of statement could be made about Hartmann, *mutatis mutandis*. Therefore it would seem to be axiomatic that no particularized or specialized philosophical inquiry should be undertaken without constant reference to the broad context of the whole of philosophy.

Such in fact may be an ideal impossible to actualize. Yet, however imperfectly it may be attained, it still should suffice to reduce the error of distortion, and at the same time to compel thinkers never to forget the undeniable fact that the complex data of philosophy are always copresent to the mind as a unified amalgam (or alternatively, that the human personality is one), and that it is the reason which breaks down these complex data into compartments, which in fact never do have an independent existence. Not only should this axiom apply to the original speculative thinker, but also it can serve as a test or touchstone to be applied as a standard to the various systems of thought of the past. If this axiom is truly valid, then the degree to which any philosopher evinces an awareness of it should be a true index of his greatness. Though the principle has been stated as having the widest possible application, it would appear to have peculiar cogency in the case of being and value, and their relation. To be sure, certain philosophers have concentrated specifically upon this problem, with some concluding that being and value are absolutely separated, whereas others have reached the opposite opinion. But still the fact remains that for the most part Western philosophers have tended to think of being and value as divorced.

The view of Saint Augustine on the problem is most relevant. He, almost more than any other great thinker of the West, kept all aspects of his thought simultaneously before him,[39] and as one result, he keeps being and value strictly together. His doctrine is to be found most explicitly in his famous treatise, *On Free Will*. As is always the case, Saint Augustine begins with God, as his well known "proof" for His existence makes perfectly clear. To review the argument briefly, Saint Augustine points to the fact that man, in his mind and through his reason, is aware of the existence of certain mathematical relations. Inevitably he is able to say that certain mathematical propositions are true, something which he would be unable to do, had he not within his mind a conception of truth. This immediately suggests absolute Truth, which in turn can be no different from God. Hence, Saint Augustine would contend that there is this Divine Illumination within man which enables him to build an epistemology which can be called an "inner empiricism." God, Whom man knows through Divine Illumination, is the Creator not only of man but of the whole physical universe. God is infinitely good, all wise, and omnipotent, and thus it is necessary that that which He creates will possess something of His goodness.

On these grounds, Saint Augustine puts forward his doctrine of "natures." Everything which God creates in the universe of space and time is a "nature," no matter whether it is to be found in the mere physical order, or in the order of plant and animal life, or in the human order. God has seen fit to arrange these "natures" in a hierarchy, so that the whole may represent a harmoniousness. These "natures" are not all of equal value or importance, for, Saint Augustine would contend, there would be no way by which a more important "nature" could be identified, unless there were present a less important "nature" with which it could be compared. But the important point is that a "nature," of whatever order, is, by virtue of its being a creature of God, good in some degree or other. As a creature it must reflect in some measure the goodness of its Creator. Hence, it is not possible to talk about the "being" or

[39]See the remarks on this point in the Introduction to my edition of *Basic Writings of Saint Augustine*, Random House, New York, 1948, pp. ix ff.

existence of a "nature" without taking into consideration its "value" or goodness. God's creation of it has bound together inextricably in it being and value. The epistemological method of inner empiricism leads man to this doctrine of God as the Creator of "natures," and hence man, in his ordinary empirical experience of objects external to himself in the universe of space and time, can see them as "natures," can be aware of them as units of being-and-value, and can see them properly in their relation to other "natures," as well as in their relation to their Creator.

This is not the place to go into Saint Augustine's theory of evil, which is based heavily upon Neo-Platonism, whereby he would attempt to explain the palpable flaws and defects in these created "natures." Nor in turn is it possible to argue here about the validity of Saint Augustine's so-called demonstration of God's existence, or the relation of these, his more philosophical, views to the data which derived from his religious faith. It is enough to cite Saint Augustine in his doctrine of "natures" as a clear instance of a thinker who was aware of the main problem which is before us, and who solved it in such a way as to recognize the deep association of being and value. Obviously the Augustinian solution will satisfy neither the Naturalist nor the Humanist, but still whether the approach be that of a Naturalist, Humanist, or Theist, there seems to be the obligation of the investigator to see being and value together, because that is the way they are related in actual human experience, which is after all the final court of appeal, no matter what type of philosophical systems may subsequently be developed. A. E. Taylor in his Gifford Lectures of 1926–1928 has devoted a long section to a discussion of the problem, and concludes that being, or as he calls it, "actuality," and value must be seen together.[40] With respect to the point that being and value are always copresent in human experience, Taylor writes that he refuses to admit the ultimate severance of value from existence, and goes on to say; "The point on which I would lay the chief stress is that such severance falsifies the facts of real life, where existence and value appear always as distinguishable, but always as conjoined."[41]

Now it would be safe to assume that, if this point is sound, those philosophies which see an ultimate severance of being and value, must do so upon the basis of some metaphysical prior assumption. If such an

[40]A. E. Taylor, *The Faith of a Moralist*, The Macmillan Company, Ltd., London, 1930, vol. I, pp. 24–66.
[41]*Ibid.*, vol. I, p. 55.

assumption leads to a genuine falsification of the "facts of real life," then the assumption, it goes without saying, is profoundly suspect. The whole point here is not to state in absolute terms what the solution of the problem of being and value should be. It can be, and, indeed, has been in the past resolved variously by the Naturalist, Humanist, and Theist. Solutions are possible in any of these three general modes of thought, but we should not forget that in a distressingly large number of instances, thinkers have neglected the basic datum which has been so clearly formulated by Taylor. What rather should be suggested is that a philosopher must in his thinking take this basic datum fully into account, and that the degree to which he has done so in his fully articulated system will constitute one of the tests whereby the system may be validly appraised.

The congenital fault, which has certainly tended to pervade Western philosophy, at least since the time of Descartes, lies in what can be called speculative "isolationism." Both Ayer and Hartmann, in their respective ways, reveal it to a high degree, and, indeed, we undertook the analyses of their positions in order to emphasize this point. But it should be readily clear that of all areas within the domain of philosophy, there is scarcely any one where indulgence in speculative "isolationism" can be more costly than in connection with the problem of being and value. Not only do being and value of themselves put into play the disciplines of ontology and axiology, but also and inevitably both logic and epistemology are involved. Hence there must be a quadripartite attack on the problem, or so it would seem, if any genuine fruitful results are to appear.

In considering the systems of Plato and Aristotle with reference to the problem of being and value, it is incumbent upon us, at least in brief, to make clear the metaphysical framework within which this consideration is to take place. One point should be stressed, *viz.,* the enterprise is at once philosophical and historical. The proposition that Aristotle's rejection of the Platonic Theory of Ideas had certain identifiable consequences for his system when we seek to discover the relation of being and value in it—this proposition is basically historical, and is susceptible of more or less conclusive historical documentation. But the task cannot stop at this point, for the general philosophical problem is raised: which of the two attitudes toward the problem of being and value is superior? Does Aristotle represent an advance over Plato in this area, as he does, let us say, in the descriptive area of biological science, or does Aristotle retrogress from a more enlightened Platonic position?

Now the answer to these questions cannot be fundamentally historical, but rather it must be philosophical. It is freely admitted that a certain view of both philosophy and history is implicit in the very fact that we are supposing that these are valid questions to ask. So far as history is concerned, it is presupposed that the events of history have meaning and significance, and that every historian, no matter how strongly he may deny it theoretically, does in fact discriminate among his various sources according to some conscious or unconscious criteria of significance. As for philosophy, it is presupposed that it is possible upon reasonable and philosophical grounds for men to say that System *A* is superior to System *B*. This may be difficult, and enormous errors may be perpetrated in the attempt, but still the possibility exists. Of course, there have been many philosophers, particularly those who propound some variant of relativism, who would insist that one can say only that *A* is different from *B*, but never better than *B*. But even this assertion, in and of itself, in reality argues for our presupposition. Does not the relativistic assertion which says that difference is determinable, but not superiority and inferiority, amount actually to an assertion that in an absolute sense the relativist hypothesis is better and more satisfactory than the hypothesis which maintains the possibility of validly discriminating between better and worse? In fact, has there ever been a case where a writer undertook to compose a philosophical work of any sort without at least the tacit assumption that somehow he would produce something better in some respect than had hitherto been in existence?

On these grounds, we are obliged to see the historical fact of the difference between Plato and Aristotle in the full light of its historico-philosophical significance. The philosophical point of view from which this whole complex problem is approached will not be acceptable to the Naturalist, though it might be hoped that he would feel the force of the argument for the copresence of being and value as basically in accord with the "facts of real life," in Taylor's phrase. Both Humanist and Theist should not find too much difficulty in agreeing with our general position, though, of course, there will be several individual points of divergence. In any event, a sketch of the position is offered here in order that the method of interpreting Plato and Aristotle may be better understood, and also in order to lay down the general lines along which an adequate theory of being and value may be developed. Naturally the full philosophical arguments for the position cannot be given here. That is a book in itself—a book, we might say, which has been written by many a Humanist and Theist author. However, the character of the position and many of the grounds for it have been expressed in the critique of Ayer, Hartmann, and Saint Augustine.

To characterize in summary the position from which my argument takes its start: it is based first on the conviction that it is valid epistemologically to assume in the process of "knowing" a relation between a human consciousness and objects of all sorts and orders[42] which are in fact external to the human consciousness.

Secondly, our hypothesis would assert that when the mind, or "knowing subject" becomes aware of any object, there is simultaneously an awareness of its existence and an appraisal of its value. Thus an evaluational aspect is part of the recognition of the existence of an object. Or, to put it in another way, "being appraised" is an inescapable concomitant of "being known" to human beings.

Among the various ways of interpreting this situation, there is the familiar method of "subjectivism." According to this view, evaluation comes after the complicated process of becoming aware of the object in question, and exists solely in the mind of the "knowing subject." The complex of characteristics and attributes and relations of the object are of a sort which leads the subject to engage in an evaluational judgment. But it follows that in no sense could value as such be said to inhere in the object. So far as value theory is concerned, the subjectivist hypothesis leads inevitably to some type of relativism. If there is no necessary connection between the object and the evaluation which a subject may place upon it, then the fact that there are many different appraisals of the same object becomes a matter of no real concern to the theorist. He can readily attribute the differences to the varying temperaments, environment, and views of the several subjects, and dismiss the whole problem by reaffirming the dictum, *de gustibus non est disputandum.*

A most serious objection to this "subjectivist" point of view may be expressed quite simply: the sum total of human experience indicates that

[42]The phraseology here is meant to include not only the objects of normal sense experience, but also other "nonempirical" objects, such as mathematical relations. In other words, the empirical realm is assumed to have much wider limits than the empiricism of sense.

there is far more agreement than disagreement among the myriad value judgments which men make. This appears to be certainly true in the case of the most fundamental moral values. It is surely safe to say that honesty and personal integrity are in one way or another universally approved. On the subjectivist hypothesis, this phenomenon can be explained only on the ground of some form of coincidence, an argument, to say the least, which is far from compelling. An alternative "objectivist" view appears to do more justice to the manifold of relevant evidence. If it is assumed that the value of an object is functionally related to its constitution or construction, or that it is as much "of the object" as is the very being of the object itself, then the value inherent in the object would be apprehended by the knowing subject along with its other constitutive factors. Since the "being-and-value" of the object would be apprehended with varying degrees of accuracy and completeness by the knowing subject, differences in value judgments of the same object can readily be explained. And, in turn, since the object (in itself and in its contextual relations) functions basically as a constant, we can account for the phenomenon that there is more universal agreement than disagreement among value judgments.[43]

The objectivist theory, as thus far described, would suggest as a consequence that *within the limits of the space-time universe* there are no independently existing values. Rather, the content of this universe is made up of things, *i.e.,* anything that can lay claim to be an existential status, each of which is a being-and-value. Hence neither ontology nor axiology can be regarded as an autonomous discipline. They are only

[43]It is fully realized that epistemologists might object to the somewhat old fashioned and simplified character of our analysis here, presupposing, as it does, the sharp distinction between subject and object. The simplified character is partly justified by the contention that the object must be viewed as "being-and-value," and partly by the fact that common human experience suggests such a relation between an interior mind and a world of facts and values external to it. The subtler epistemologies perhaps have developed under the impact of recent scientific developments. There it has been a matter of concern to point out certain conditions of scientific experiment wherein it is clear that the mind of the experimenter is as much a part of the experiment as are the data with which he deals. This problem is, of course, made all the more difficult when the philosopher of science tries to determine precisely the existential status of those conceptions which are employed in the analysis of the subatomic; that is, when he tries to answer with more philosophic than scientific precision such questions as, "What is a proton?", or "What are the waves of wave mechanics?", or "Where *are* the systematic or statistical laws of subatomic physics?" Since in the field of value theory the relation between subject and object is by no means identical with that between scientific experimenter and scientific data, the old fashioned distinction between subject and object may be validly maintained.

analytically distinct, and therefore any problem in the area of the two disciplines must be investigated in the full context of them both.

But as yet there has been no explanation offered to account for the fact that the object, as being-and-value, functions as a constant in the objectivist theory, with the result that the objective world, peopled as it is with knowing subjects, presents a picture of value order rather than value anarchy. In this respect the objectivist view in general terms would permit at least two alternative solutions. But, be it noted, the two solutions would have this much in common, that value criteria are "absolute," in the sense that they cannot in any way be modified by a knowing subject. And, in turn, this would suggest that both solutions would require a careful distinction between the thing valued, *i.e.,* a being-and-value, and the criterion or norm of value.

The two solutions differ according to their respective conceptions of Reality. If Reality, *i.e.,* all that is, is assumed to be coextensive with the universe of space and time, then the objects within it (each considered as a being-and-value) would reveal a value pattern which would be absolutely intrinsic in the structure and organization of things, and which could be grasped, with greater or less accuracy, by the knowing subject. And not least among objects would be the knowing subject himself who would have an awareness of himself, as object, *i.e.,* as a being-and-value.[44] From the subject's grasp of these varied objects he would be able to build up his understanding of the criteria of value, which would actually not have a separate existence, and he would thus be more competent when he engages in value judgments. In many ways ancient Stoicism may be taken as a good example of this view. In so far as it is "pantheistic" in the sense that the *"logos"* runs through the universe, or in so far as it bids men to live "according to Nature," it presupposes that value order is immanent in things, and that it is incumbent upon man to make the "proper use of his impressions" if he is either to act rightly or to achieve wisdom.

The other solution would postulate that Reality is not limited to the universe of space and time, but rather that above and beyond this universe is a transcendental and eternal realm in which above all are to be found the constitutive principles both of being and value in terms of which the objects of the world in space and time must be grasped and

---

[44]The fact of man's unique capacity to be conscious of himself has been frequently used, as is well known, as the starting point for many a Humanist and Theist metaphysic.

understood. In this view, norms or standards of value[45] would have their existence independent of the conditions of space and time, but yet would impinge upon the objects of space and time in such a way as to make it necessary for each of these objects to be treated as a being-and-value. Perhaps the greatest difficulty in this solution lies in the epistemological problem which it presents. How can the subject know the being-and-value object in space and time? How can he know the contents of the transcendental realm? What is the relation between space-time objects and the transcendental realm? Answers to these questions vary, and they characteristically have two aspects. One is empirical. Close and careful contact with the objects in space and time will permit the subject to "see through" them to the transcendental realm beyond. The other aspect may be called loosely *a priori*.

It is possible, so it is urged, that the subject can grasp via an intuitive process the contents of the transcendental realm. But never for the knowing subject can these two aspects be dissociated. In fact the process of knowing involves a continual and rapid oscillation between the empirical and the intuitive.

Plato, as is well known, was the first philosopher to work out in detail this second solution. The history of Western culture continually manifests the influence of Plato, and the Platonic view of value. Not only do we have the Neo-Platonists, and in more modern times the various forms of the idealist tradition down to Whitehead,[46] but also those various amalgamations of Platonism with Christianity, commencing with the Christian Platonists of Alexandria, and proceeding through Saint Augustine on down to contemporary Christian philosophy and theology. The attitude is by no means confined to the professional philosopher or theologian, for many poets and artists have given expression to it in its essence in their respective media. As an example, one can cite the view of Reality and the human predicament which underlies the great tragedies of Shakespeare, at least if we can trust the analysis of A. C. Bradley.[47]

[45]In pointing to the distinction between the "thing valued" and the "norm" of value, it should not be forgotten that in the transcendentalist theory, the so-called "norm" has a supreme ontological status as well.

[46]*E.g.*, his famous formula concerning the "ingredience of objects into events," where "objects" connotes the transcendental, and "events" that which is in space and time.

[47]*Cf.* his chapter on the nature of tragedy in A. C. Bradley, *Shakespearean Tragedy, Lectures on Hamlet, Othello, King Lear and Macbeth,* The Macmillan Company, Ltd., London, 1904.

According to Bradley, Shakespeare sees in Reality a transcendental Moral Order, which reacts violently against any human infractions thereof. The waste which results in terms of the loss of human potential lies at the base of tragedy.

If we can assume that the foregoing account of the objectivist theory is reasonably accurate, and that Plato may be regarded as its leading exponent, we should be in a position to consider Plato's theory of being and value and then turn to Aristotle to observe the consequences of his rejection of Plato, as he comes to grips with objects which, we have argued, combine being and value. But at this point one crucial fact should not be overlooked, and this is that the value theorist is faced at every turn with the humanly insurmountable problem of evil. *Unde Malum?* Why is it that with every positive value there is paired an opposite disvalue? The number of such difficult questions is legion. It has been remarked that, of all the perennial problems, philosophy has made the least "progress" in the face of the problem of evil. Consequently, the best that can be done is to be aware of the theories of evil held respectively by Plato and Aristotle, and to attempt *pari passu* to suggest as firm a working hypothesis as possible which will take into account the notion that the view of an object as being-and-value does involve a conception of disvalue.

But, while the problem of evil is indeed humanly insurmountable, still the view that Reality is marked by value order and not value chaos, indicates that there is a genuine teleology in Reality. This, however, can only be the case, if the subjectivist view and its attendant relativism are rejected. The objectivist theory, in contrast, does make possible not only cosmic teleology but also individual human teleology. Furthermore, the objectivist theory presupposes that man, as a knowing subject, can have a valid, though perhaps always imperfect, understanding of the realms of being-and-value, and that, as endowed with a freedom of will in some sense, he can direct his life and his value judgments accordingly.[48]

To summarize, then, the objectivist view and its various assumptions:

1) Man, as a knowing subject, has external to himself a realm or realms of objects.

2) Man's mind is finite, but at the same time he is able to grasp with a fundamental validity objects external to himself.

3) Valid evidence on the nature of Reality and his own predicament

---

[48]To this extent, Hartmann's view of man as a "carrier of moral values" is completely acceptable to the objectivist theory.

can come to man from the widest variety of sources, *viz.,* history, philosophy, religion, sense experience, as well as religious, esthetic, and moral experience.

4) Reality may not necessarily be coextensive with the universe of space and time. Indeed, more often than not, it is assumed that Reality has its spatiotemporal component and its nonspatio-nontemporal component.

5) On the basis of human experience, it is valid to consider objects as compounds of being and value.

6) Reality, so analyzed, has teleology within it.

7) Completely compatible with the objectivist view, though not absolutely essential to it, is Theism which holds that God, as Creator and Orderer of Reality, is the source of being and value, and the goal of teleology.

To set the stage for the discussion of Plato and Aristotle against the background of the objectivist theory, a remark of Werner Jaeger may be appropriately quoted: "When the Platonic theory of Forms was abandoned being and value fell apart, and dialectic thereby lost its direct significance for human life, which to Plato was an essential feature of it, the distinction between metaphysics and ethics became much sharper than before."[49]

He here appends a footnote which runs, "This is true of all specifically human values, but not of absolute value or good. Aristotle believed as much as Plato that being and value in the absolute sense coincide in the conception of God. In that respect he remained a Platonist to the day of his death. The highest being is also the highest good. At the point that is farthest removed from human affairs metaphysics penetrates into ethics and ethics into metaphysics." Jaeger is quite right in asserting that being and value fall apart for Aristotle with the rejection of the Theory of Ideas. Metaphysics and ethics lose their vital contact. But it may be questioned whether either Plato or Aristotle in the fullest sense saw being and value coincide in God. Did Aristotle in this respect remain "a Platonist until the day of his death"? In what sense is the highest being for Aristotle the highest good? What a strange place for ethics to be, in its consorting with metaphysics at a point "farthest removed from human affairs." Can ethics be ethics at that point? These, and many questions like them, must be faced in investigating the consequences of Aris-

[49]Werner Jaeger, *Aristotle, Fundamentals of the History of His Development,* translated by R. Robinson, Clarendon Press, Oxford, 1934, pp. 83–84.

totle's refusal to espouse the Platonic theory. The remarks of Jaeger indicate in some measure Aristotle's situation. So close was he to Plato that hardly a page of his does not bear some vestige of Platonic influence. This much of a Platonist he must always be. But he repudiates categorically the heart and soul of Platonism, the Theory of Ideas. This much of a Platonist he can never be. This is the Aristotelian dilemma: how to be a Platonic nonPlatonist. Nowhere do the consequences of this dilemma reveal themselves more clearly than in Aristotle's doctrines in the field of value.

Let us look a little further into the philosophical quarrel between Plato and Aristotle. First it may be convenient to examine the Theory of Ideas and its four functions. These are:

1) The logical function: here the Idea is the equivalent of a logical universal. Hence the Theory of Ideas can provide an explanation of the phenomena of predication.

2) The ontological function: here we are provided with a theory of reality and existence. For Plato, of course the Idea is the ultimately real; all else exists, but does not possess as much "reality" in Plato's sense.

3) The epistemological function: here we have a theory of knowing. Strictly speaking for Plato knowledge is of that which is ultimately real. We can only have opinions about that which is less real, *i.e.,* the phenomenal world.

4) The axiological function: here we have a theory of value. In the esthetic and ethical realm the Ideas provide nonspatial, nontemporal norms, criteria of value. Any entity in the phenomenal world is valuable in proportion to the degree to which it participates in, shares in, or imitates the Ideas. The theory works in similar ways when it is concerned not with the esthetic or ethical realm, but when it attempts to determine the value of objects or "things."

In his writings Plato now concentrates on one function, and now on another, according to the context raised by the particular problem which he is considering. Sometimes he invokes two or three of the functions simultaneously, as he does in the image of the Divided Line. But the interesting feature of the theory for our purpose is that in it reality and value are copresent. The more real a thing is the more valuable, and the converse, the more valuable a thing is the more real. Hence the Idea or Form, is that which is both ultimately real and ultimately valuable.

It is well known that Aristotle, though in very early life he was probably strongly in sympathy with Plato's position, was led to reject completely the Theory of Ideas. His objections, as they appear in the *Metaphysics,* may perhaps be briefly considered to fall under two heads:

1) There is the difficulty involved in the relation obtaining between Ideas and particulars. Aristotle dismisses the characteristic Platonic explanation of "participation" or of "imitation" as mere metaphor, empty verbiage, which leaves the essential question untouched.

2) There is the difficulty of efficiency. Aristotle asks: why talk of ideas if they cannot be shown to do anything? In effect, he maintains, the Ideas only serve to complicate the picture; there is enough in this world to puzzle us, and which needs explanation; why create a whole other realm of Ideas—quite gratuitously, in his opinion—which only doubles the things which have to be explained?

On these grounds, Aristotle refused to accept the Ideal theory, and therefore was forced to build for himself a new philosophical position. In the logical sphere, as we have already suggested, he maintained in general the Platonic system, but, of course, transformed the idea whose existence was apart, into the universal whose existence is "in" the particular object. Aristotle then constructs a new ontology and an appropriate epistemology; and, finally, according to our thesis, he never constructed a systematic axiology at all; or to put it another way, he never squarely faced the problem of the relation of Being and Value. Here it is important to remember that, while Aristotle's attack on the Ideas is at times on logical grounds (*e.g.,* when he uses the third man argument), most frequently he argues on ontological grounds, for example, when he seeks to equate the Platonic Idea with his own conception of substance. But Aristotle never seems to realize the axiological function of the Ideal theory, nor does he give any adequate evidence of any awareness that Plato himself had recognized, notably in the *Parmenides,* many of the difficulties pointed out by Aristotle. In fact, Aristotle never mentions explicitly the *Parmenides.* To repeat, the result then for Aristotle is this: signal achievement in the logical and the ontological spheres, difficulty in some degree in epistemology, and finally a considerable measure of confusion in axiology.

The fundamental principle of Aristotle's position is that the τόδε τι, the individual thing, the concrete σύνολον is that which is ultimately real, is οὐσία in its primary and ultimate sense. This root conviction makes it possible for him to achieve such notable success in logic, or in the development of his theory of the four causes, which is so illuminating when applied to certain specific kinds of particular entities, or in his scientific and biological works. In this respect Lucian satirizes him again in his *Sale of Creeds*. Hermes is auctioning off Aristotle to the highest bidder and recommends him thus:

Buyer: Eighty pounds is a long price.

Hermes: Not at all, my dear sir, not at all. You see there is some money with him, to all appearance. Snap him up before it is too late. Why, from him you will find out in no time how long a gnat lives, to how many fathom's depth the sunlight penetrates the sea, and what an oyster's soul is like.

Buyer: Heracles! nothing escapes him.

Hermes: Oh, these are trifles. You should hear some of his more abstruse speculations, concerning generation and birth and the development of the embryo; and his distinction between man the laughing creature, and the ass, which is neither a laughing, nor a carpentering, nor a shipping creature.

To suggest briefly the ways in which Aristotle deals with questions of value, let us consider first a less specifically philosophical work, the *Poetics*. If one tries to discover what are the criteria upon which he gives his value judgments here, he will find several. Sometimes Aristotle uses conventional Greek standards of value or worth. Objects of poetic imitation, he says, are actions with agents who are necessarily either good men or bad, since virtue and vice divide the whole of mankind. Homer's personages are better than we are; Cleophon's are on our level, while Hegemon's are below our level. Or, at times, reason leads him to other value criteria; for example, he asserts the superiority of πρᾶξις, action, which makes him determine that the plot is the most important element of tragedy. His criterion is similar when he argues that poetry is more philosophical than history. Or criteria are sometimes derived from pleasure, for example, when he says that both tragedy and epic must evoke each its own distinctive pleasure, and value is accordingly attributed to each on this ground. Or sometimes he relies on a human being's own intuitive value responses, for example, when developing the notion of the tragic hero, he rejects the situation of "a good man passing from happiness to misery, as not fear-inspiring or piteous, but simply odious to us."

In the *Metaphysics*, from the logical point of view, values may be said to fall under the category of quality, as Aristotle remarks in Chapter XIV of *Metaphysics* Δ, "Quality refers especially to 'good' and 'bad' in the case of living things, and of these especially in the case of such as possess choice." Here, and as is so frequently the case, value or values are attached to objects as qualities. In fact in Z, 1028 a 25, he says categorically that τὸ ἀγαθόν, good, has no meaning apart from something that is good, but he gives us no real clue as to how to identify what is good. Further in the *Metaphysics,* when we try to discover why Aristotle assigns a higher value to some things rather than to others, in most instances he does not seem to make the requisite distinction between the thing valued, on the one hand, and the criterion or sanction for the value so assigned, on the other. And so, as in the *Poetics,* we are faced with a puzzling situation. Frequently Aristotle relies on nature, φύσις, as a source of value, or as a legitimate starting point for a rational argument which will conclude either in a positive value judgment or else one which has in it clear axiological overtones. A fine example comes in the opening sentence of the *Metaphysics,* "All men by nature desire to know," which sanctions or legitimates the whole ensuing argument about knowledge and wisdom and their value. Or again how frequently he substantiates a value claim by saying, "Nature (φύσις) does nothing in vain."

To continue this summary sketch of Aristotle on value, when one considers his position concerning actuality and potentiality and how in *Metaphysics,* Θ, Chapter VIII, he argues to establish the priority of actuality over potentiality, reason seems to determine the greater value of actuality. Actuality carries with it always a positive value overtone, so that Aristotle can easily insist in the *Nicomachean Ethics* that virtuous activity is superior to the mere possession of the virtuous ἕξις or state. All this in turn is in full accord with the Aristotelian theory of evil when he insists that there is no evil principle in the world. Evil does not exist apart from particular things. As Sir David Ross has in substance pointed out, evil is not a necessary part of the world process, but it casually emerges as each individual tries to reach such perfection as is available to it. The individual fails either through matter or necessity. Matter has no predisposition toward evil, but being a potentiality of opposites, it is a potentiality of evil as well as of good.[50]

In other contexts, Aristotle appeals to the "normal" man, as the meas-

[50]W. D. Ross, *Aristotle,* Methuen, London, 1924, p. 186.

ure, reflecting the same attitude as he holds for the φρόνιμος or the σπουδαῖος in the *Nicomachean Ethics*. For example, in a passage in *Metaphysics* K, Chapter VI, Aristotle advises that, in a dispute between parties, one should never lend his support equally to each side, one party must be mistaken:

> For the same thing never appears sweet to some and bitter to others, unless in the one case the sense-organ which discriminates the aforesaid flavors has been perverted and injured. And if this is so, the one party must be taken to be the measure, and the other must not. And I say the same of good and bad, and beautiful and ugly, and all other such qualities.

Then again there is the continual tendency toward identifying the good and final cause. In setting up a perfection toward which each individual strives, it is usually described as *the good for the particular thing involved*. This whole tendency finally reaches its climax in the treatment of the unmoved mover in *Metaphysics, Λ,* where the final cause κινεῖ δὴ ὡς ἐρώμενον, "produces motion by being loved" and as such in this context is presented as the source of goodness in the world, in much the same way as he maintains in the opening section of Chapter X of *Metaphysics* Λ.

So briefly then for the question in the *Metaphysics,* whose major emphasis is ontological and where the axiological problem *per se* is perhaps less crucial. But when we move into the *Nicomachean Ethics,* the situation is naturally somewhat different. For example, we come face to face with the value problem, when Aristotle is talking about βούλησις, wish. He says that the object of βούλησις is the end. Then he asks whether it is the good or the apparent good. If the apparent good, we are led into a relativism that is untenable for Aristotle. So he is driven somewhat reluctantly to submit the σπουδαῖος as the norm: "Perhaps the good man differs from others most by seeing the truth in each class of things, being as it were the norm and measure of them."[51]

Of course, the prime example in the *Nicomachean Ethics* of this same type of argumentation comes in the famous definition of virtue, after happiness has been set up as the highest human good, and has been defined as an activity which is in accordance with virtue. And here Aristotle introduces the central principle or doctrine of the mean. The

[51]*Nicomachean Ethics,* 1113 a 29–31.

definition of virtue runs as follows: "Virtue, then, is a state of character concerned with choice, being in a mean which is relative to us, and which is determined by reason or that by which the φρόνιμος would define it."[52]

This, as everyone knows, is an extremely important sentence because so much of Aristotle's whole ethical doctrine is built from it. But for our purposes we must emphasize that the alternatives of γόγος, reason or rational principle, or φρόνιμος, the cultivated, sober, serious, good man, are submitted as the only final courts of appeal to give ultimate sanction to value judgments in the ethical realm.

Limitations of space prevent us from pointing to the innumerable instances where conventional value thinking operates in the *Nicomachean Ethics,* as is the case in almost every one of Aristotle's descriptions of the various types of men. One is tempted to say that Aristotle might not have been forced to go into such tremendous detail in each of these cases, if he had had a more nearly adequate theory of value upon which to rely. Nor have we time to consider the value implications in the knotty problem concerning the position of pleasure in the *Ethics.* But with all of this, we still have the tenth book with its definite theistic tone. We should not forget that he opens his general discussion in this book from a characteristic empirical point of view, an implication of which comes even when he says, "Those who object that that at which all things aim is not necessarily good are, we may surmise, talking nonsense. *For we say that that which every one thinks really is so;* and the man who attacks this belief will hardly have anything more credible to maintain instead."[53]

Then by gradual steps he works up to the assertion that νοῦς is the divinest element within us, that the life of θεωρία or contemplation is the best, and that it is the obligation of a man to make himself, in living this kind of life, as immortal as is possible for him. So again, as in *Metaphysics* Λ, God or the divine is postulated as a final sanction for values and evaluations, but it is extremely difficult to make this conception cohere or integrate with the ethical theory promulgated in the earlier books. Some have argued that Aristotle never finally fused the tenth book of the *Ethics* with his other theory, and it is surely hard to see how they do come together. So, let us attempt to draw some tentative

[52]*Nicomachean Ethics,* 1106 b 36–1107 a 2.
[53]*Nicomachean Ethics,* 1172 b 35–1173 a 2.

conclusions from these very puzzling data. If one remembers Aristotle's characteristic preoccupation with the individual thing, the particular, the real τόδε τι (and remember, this is strictly an ontological preoccupation) it would not be surprising if his value thinking were not a function of the particular context in which he is working at any given moment. In other words, having let being and value fall apart, he is reduced to an *ad hoc* system. That is, whatever value theory seems appropriate to the context is invoked. Hence then to venture a list of different types of value thinking in which he engaged, according to the various contexts in which he worked:

1) Conventional value thinking. For example, consider the rather crass and conventional list of goods in the sixth chapter of the *Rhetoric*, Book I.

2) Thinking of the good as the good for the thing itself in question; *i.e.,* good is to have its meaning for any particular thing in terms of the perfection it itself might possibly achieve.

3) The use of reason as the means of getting at and determining things which have value.

4) The use of the φρόνιμος or the σπουδαῖος as the person who can really tell what is valuable.

5) The use of a hedonistic value approach.

6) The presentation of a theism, from which all values derive, as is the case in *Metaphysics* Λ and the *Nicomachean Ethics*, Book X.

Now, for the reasons why this lack of coherence has emerged in Aristotle's thought, these preconditions may be suggested:

1) Under the drive of rational analysis, indeed by virtue of a kind of apotheosis of the reason, the analytical distinguishability of being and value became real in Aristotle's mind when he decided that "being" could be investigated in isolation.

2) As a result of this conviction, Aristotle maintained his belief that the τόδε τι, the individual particular thing, is that which is ultimately real.

3) There always remained in Aristotle certain vestiges of Platonic influence.

The compresence of vestigial Platonism and scientific empiricism in Aristotle creates a situation from which it was impossible for him to extricate himself when faced with the problem of value. Indeed, if one urges that Aristotle's God, Whose existence and nature as "contemplation of contemplation" were so characterized as a result of a severely rational process of argumentation, and is finally the ultimate sanction of values, this in fact does not seem to be the case in Aristotle's thought. For evidence, all one need cite is the *Nicomachean Ethics,* where no sufficiently explicit relation is established between God, *logos,* and the φρόνιμος.

A final and crucial point seems to be this: for all persons in whose thought there is a religious dimension, or for whom Reality is not coextensive with the universe of space and time, teleology must provide the answers to all questions of value; in other words, what is valuable for man is a function of the destiny of man. Now, Aristotle is normally regarded as a teleological thinker. Surely he sees reality as filled with particulars, each of which is struggling to reach its *telos.* Then there is the cosmic teleology, where the unmoved mover moves by being loved. But it may be fair to say that these two notions produce only a spurious teleology from the point of view of man. On the one hand, he sees myriads of particular teleologies going on, and on the other, he is invited to believe in the cosmic final cause, which has a kind of static universe forever and ever revolving about it. Is it unreasonable to suggest that it may not be possible to have a genuine teleology without a doctrine of creation and some kind of linear conception of time, with a concomitant conception of an end of time? It may be that the reason why Aristotle never felt it necessary to put forth a doctrine of creation (note, there is a quasidoctrine of creation in Plato's *Timaeus*) betrays the same quality of his position which reveals its inadequacy in the face of the problem of value. Or to put it in another way, any system without a genuine teleology, perhaps one could say, without a religious answer to the problem of the destiny of man involving a doctrine of creation, will tend to look at being and value apart from each other, and will tend to operate in the field of value either on the basis of some sort of relativism or with some degree of incoherence.

The discussion of Ayer, Hartmann, and Saint Augustine, and in particular the relation suggested between the positions of Aristotle and Plato so far as Being and Value are concerned, should, it is hoped, throw some light on the complex entities, objectively conceived, for which symbols of all sorts and orders stand. It seems impossible to avoid facing these fundamental metaphysical, philosophical, and ultimately religious problems concerning man's nature and destiny, if we are to understand with any degree of depth the relation of symbols to society and their function therein.

Comment by Howard L. Parsons:

It seems to me that Aristotle, particularly in the *Ethics,* does not so much isolate being from value ("existence," he says, "is good to the virtuous man") as he fails to refine, extend, and elaborate a certain objective, naturalistic, organismic concept of the good which is suggested in the *Ethics.*

Man's good is there defined as man's orderly and all round development, the harmonious fulfilment of his distinctive and individual capacities, the active realization of his normal (what does this mean but "basic" or "real"?) nature under the guidance of reason.

This good, I think, reveals "a value pattern which would be absolutely intrinsic in the structure and organization" of the organism and its activities—a pattern which is in modern times being "grasped, with greater or lesser accuracy," by biologists like D'Arcy Thompson, psychologists like Erich Fromm and Karen Horney, and philosophers like Whitehead. Aristotle, as ethicist and scientist, concentrated his attention on this value pattern as it is embodied in human beings, but an extension and generalizing of his approach to the other objects and processes in nature, and to the natural and historical contexts of events in which man is formed and transformed, would reveal, I believe, a comparable value pattern in the individual objects as well as in what Oates terms their "contextual relations."

The implications of a contextualistic analysis of value have already been explored in part by writers such as Pepper and Wieman, approaching in an empirical way the "value pattern" alluded to by Oates and continuing what Aristotle and the Stoics started.

CHAPTER XVI

The True Face of Our Country[1]

By JOHN LaFARGE, S.J.

IN ADDRESSING so distinguished and scholastic a gathering, I feel that you will appreciate my interest in learning that the people of York, Pennsylvania, have committed themselves municipally to the study of the French language. They are responding to the equally heroic resolve of the people of Arles in France to undertake a mass study of English. This is the second such twinned-cities enterprise undertaken under the auspices of an international project, entitled *Le Monde Bilingue,* or the bilingual world. Its projectors hope that ultimately people everywhere will learn a second great language, and so enable us all to talk to one another and thus create better international understanding. I am captivated by the idea that the people of Arles will pick up some of the time honored phrases of that grand old historic section of Pennsylvania.

I

Certainly we in this country are always glad to inform other peoples of our progress and accomplishments, even if we are a little puzzled at times as to just what items we should send over the Voice of America or relay through the more intimate channels of exchange visitors and students. At the present moment we wish to communicate to the entire world the news of our recent great liberating achievement: the unanimous decision of the Supreme Court of the United States on May seventeenth, outlawing the principle of racial segregation in the nation's public schools. We distributed the news at once by shortwave broadcast in thirty-four languages, and we want to continue telling of this event, because we believe it removes a painful blemish from the true face of our

[1]This article was originally presented as a Phi Beta Kappa Oration at Harvard University, June 14, 1954. Father LaFarge kindly consented to distribution of the paper by the Conference because of its relevance to the fourteenth meeting. The paper first appeared in *The American Scholar,* vol. 24, no. 1, Winter, 1954–1955, pp. 28–35, and is reprinted here by permission of the publishers, the United Chapters of Phi Beta Kappa.

country. This decisive step refutes the gross caricatures spread wide by Communist propaganda; it corrects unduly pessimistic ideas as to the racial situation in the United States which are currently accepted even in friendly nations abroad. It is quite characteristic that the Soviet press has abstained from mentioning it at all.

We want to do more than merely notify the globe of the event. There is a story in this business, the story of how a right principle does finally win out in a democracy, even though it may take a half-century to gain its point. For our friends we would like to trace the way in which each great political principle contains, as it were, the seeds of its successor and ultimate development. The framers of the Constitution compromised on slavery. But rooted as it were in our institutions, slavery could not resist the gradual, inevitable impact of our primary postulate that "all men are created equal." Similarly, when we adopted the Fourteenth Amendment in 1868 we embraced a right principle, "the equal protection of the laws," which in time would wipe out the last vestiges of slavery in the form of racial discrimination.

Such a development is an instance of what Cabot Lodge recently referred to as the irresistible onward march of the human race in the direction of increase of human rights and increased belief in the dignity of the individual. But the human race does not march forward by some blind impulse. It moves ahead because people will and choose for it to move ahead.

It is not enough for us to inform our bilingual friends about the fact of this forward march; we want also to give them some idea of how it came about. The Emancipation Proclamation that in 1865 destroyed slavery as a legalized institution, though technically the act of one great man, was in point of fact the collective deed of the American people. So, too, when on May seventeenth of this year the Court erased all legal respectability from the last vestiges of slavery, it was also the people of the United States speaking. A fair account of the events that led up to that decision would recite the bitter lessons we learned as to the price required for the continuation of racial disunity: the toll it has taken in social and political division, retarding the progress of our nation. We would speak of all that our people have learned through new contacts, new opportunities, as well as new threats to civic peace resulting from our enormous internal migrations from country to city, from South to North. And we would need to take ample reckoning of what war experiences have meant for our young people, as well as for our armed forces as such; for the recent decision was made against the background of complete racial integration in all three branches of the armed forces, completed only a couple of weeks before May seventeenth.

But the story I should like most to stress for our foreign friends and visitors is that of the great army of the forgotten or even unknown: dedicated people, who worked in obscurity for the education and the inner development of the racial minorities, particularly in the South: Negro educators who overcame extreme personal handicaps of poverty and timidity, who braved the pessimism of their own kith and kin and struggled to build something out of nothing. White men and women who faced violent disapproval, social ostracism, or even personal danger. We should include among them people who contributed their time, means, and talents to the express task of securing equal opportunity, who were not afraid to demand explicitly full equality for all in our American society, regardless of race, color, or creed. And finally the expert legal staff who actually prepared the decisive material, and the humble contributors who made their work possible.

Now my aim here is not to pronounce an Independence Day panegyric for all these good men and true, these heroes living and dead. Others can do that job more effectively than myself. I do want to emphasize their motives, the fact that these people, with no exceptions worth bothering about, acted from deep, intense conviction. They believed that certain things were right and certain things were wrong, with no if's or but's. They were liberals, yes; liberals in the most weighty sense of the word. As liberals, they believed that human rights inhered to the individual persons, and could not be entrusted to the whims of politicians or legislators. As liberals, they believed that it was a noble and a necessary thing for men to labor to secure these rights for their neighbor. Some of this action was highly reasoned, some of it instinctive, but in any case it was carried on by those who placed conviction before doubt. They were not people who put their faith in "steadfast" skepticism. They questioned popular errors and misconceptions, but were entirely positive when it came to those basic notions upon which we have built the structure of our nation. Such people are not the most interesting type of liberal; they do not breed aphorisms or soothe wounded feelings. But they get things done.

Moreover, a sizable proportion of this army of workers were religious.

people; persons who looked upon their striving for justice as the logical corollary of their own religious beliefs. They believed that religion itself speaks with the voice of freedom: not some elaborately rationalized interpretation of religion, but a simple faith in the teachings of the Bible as they knew it, in the Law of Moses or the Gospel of Jesus Christ. Their personal liberalism derived no nourishment from an attitude of religious skepticism, however refined.

I have spoken of the plainer people, but these remarks apply to the scholars as well. Popular enthusiasm would have failed of its goal without the patient research of our own American scholarship. Learned people of every section and race contributed. Honest scholarship has paid great dividends for the general welfare in the past forty or fifty years by demolishing ethnic racism, analyzing historical and psychological causes of our current tensions, studying the effect of separatism upon the character, especially of the young, assaying methods of intergroup personality, and, in more recent times, examining the working of racial integration in our schools and communities.

Here again the burden and the heat of the day were carried largely by scientists, historians, and sociologists who were not satisfied with endless processes of dissolution and criticism. Their work is distinguished by its positive note. Such a note characterizes one of the most monumental pieces of research, the *American Dilemma* of Gunnar Myrdal, as well as more modest but painstaking jobs, like that of Kenneth Clark and his wife, cited in the recent decision.

The Supreme Court has closed serious debate on the constitutional issue on which it passed verdict. The elimination of a false solution clears the way now for a nationwide debate on a vastly larger issue; the myriadfold question of how we shall learn to live together in peace in all our institutions and communities throughout the nation, and by the same token with all the peoples of the world. With a moot point of law cleared up, the moot of human coexistence itself remains to be examined. By postponing to later months the consideration of any practical implementation of its decision, the Court indicated now was the time to begin this discussion. Those of the minority group who were most successful in bringing out the verdict have wisely proposed that the discussion be conducted everywhere upon the local level. Back of that recommendation is the belief that the people themselves can find answers to the most vexing questions of group relationships, provided the people who are immediately concerned can converse among themselves in their own neighborhood, without throwing the burden of decision upon experts and agencies from afar. Implicit in that recommendation is the belief that free discussion is precisely the best plan. Let us solve these questions, Negro leaders declared at Atlanta, in the "atmosphere of give and take." It was through half a century of free discussion that we created a climate of opinion which made possible the decision of May seventeenth. In that same atmosphere we shall perfect a climate of opinion which will make possible newer and more positively constructive decisions in the future. Such decisions are particularly urgent as we are obliged to sleep on our arms, in the face of what Cardinal Spellman recently referred to as "the narrowing circle of freedom."

II

What, then, is the role of the scholar in this future period of general debate? Evidently he will need to collect and assess the lessons of the past and evaluate various techniques for developing mutual understanding. Immediate difficulties can be solved at the local level, and locally the different groups can learn to work together for the common good. But the question still remains as to the nature of that common good. People will not stay content merely with one another's peculiarities, or to labor conjointly for the more immediate needs of daily life. They will seek a wider and deeper basis of cooperation, they will seek to know what is the destiny of the nation itself. They will ask what are we, all of us, here on earth for anyhow. They will inquire as to whether we are anything but an inexplicable accident, or are we beings who can make free decisions based on a concept of life's ultimate goals, if life, they ask, has an ultimate goal. They will want to know if it is reasonable to talk of ultimates at all, and if so, how far is language a significant medium for such discussion. They will inquire about the meaning of men's dialog with one another, and whether all human dialog may not resolve itself in the last analysis into a dialog with the God Who put us here. Sooner or later they will inquire whether there may not be two participants to that dialog, whether it is all Job speaking to God, or whether God may not be saying something to Job.

This might sound as if I were expecting that the scholars' role in the coming discussion should be to pronounce upon matters of religious doctrine. I believe the theologians will have much to say in the future as they have had in the past, but my proposal is more elementary, one that I make as I see it, in the interests of true liberalism. Scholarship of the future, as concerned with the debates of the future, should feel free to study and reappraise the connection between religion—including organized, dogmatic religion—and a liberal policy of universal human rights. Is this proposal unreasonable? Are we obliged to pose the problem of liberalism as a choice between two extremes (I believe artificially assigned extremes): either as uneasy suspicion that some miching mallecho is brewing whenever the theologian enters the universe of discourse; or else paternally and piously to evade the pressing questions of the social community. It would seem reasonable for the genuine liberal to go still further, and to seek to explain historically some of the reluctances that certain large groups of our population show when asked to subscribe to liberal causes. Historical scholarship recalls, for instance, the days when the Irish immigrant and the Catholic citizen—immigrant or old-line American alike—were cruelly lampooned by the same broadminded elements who championed the cause of the ex-slave: the same broadminded elements who a decade or so later forgot all about the ex-slave, when it became convenient to conclude a business deal with the renascent South.

In short, I see no reason why the liberalminded scholar is obliged to assume that an organized or institutionalized religion is necessarily unrelated to a policy of human rights, whatever attitudes individuals may assume. If an eminent and much beloved liberalminded scholar, in his table talk, expresses just such a complete abhorrence of theology and theologians, I am not particularly surprised. After all, that is the climate of opinion in which he moves, and I am not aware of just what human or religious phenomena he may have encountered. We are all free to express our pet attractions and repulsions, and for all I know, he may be just spoofing. People moreover have committed sins under the sacred name of religion, as they have under the venerated egis of science and scientific investigation. But certainly out of its own tenets science never devised the cruelties of Dachau or Buchenwald. Those horrors were hatched in the minds of individuals who used a good and noble thing for their own evil and ignoble ends. So, too, what certain people may have derived from the misuse of religious doctrine is not necessarily to

be ascribed to the nature of religion itself, but rather to its use emotionally as a handy instrument.

III

Of late, critical historical scholarship seems more ready to upset certain
misconceptions of this type. As, for instance, in the case of my fellow
Rhode Islander, Roger Williams. Few, if any, in that terraqueous State
subscribe today to Williams's peculiar doctrinal tenets, and none, I assume, are attracted by his cantankerous character. Yet a coolheaded
scholar, Perry Miller, demonstrates that Roger Williams derived his
ideas on the treatment of people of various faiths, as well as his benign
attitude toward the Narragansett Indians, directly from his views on the
proximately unrealizable ideal religious commonwealth. The point of
the matter is not the validity of Williams's religious notions nor the
soundness of his historically famous conclusions, but simply the significant fact that the two sets of ideas were connected. He was not tolerant
in spite of his contempt for the New Jerusalem of the Massachusetts Bay
Colony, but palpably *because* of it.

Mention of Roger Williams recalls to me the very different and quite
benign person of another famous Rhode Islander, the Reverend
Thatcher Thayer, of Newport, who died when I was a boy of fifteen.
Visiting Europe around 1847 with the purpose of discovering, as he said,
the true nature of both Popery and Calvinism, the Dominie, as he was
called, reflected mournfully on Europe's social evils one lovely summer
day as he sat in front of a little Catholic chapel on the slopes of Mount
Chamonix, in Switzerland. He was annoyed by the opinion of one of
his Geneva colleagues, who argued that social backwardness was due to
religious superstitions, and he asked himself whether one might not
discover the remedy to these same grave social evils, if men were to
study, as he said, the social doctrine contained in both Protestantism
and Popery. If more men in Europe had shared the wisdom of Dominie
Thayer, it might have escaped the disastrous upheavals of the year 1848.
Europe might not have fallen into the disastrous nineteenth century
choice of economic, *laissez-faire* Liberalism, with a big "L," as the Common Good, in place of its direct opposite, the social liberalism taught by
certain great Christian theologians. Such men held that "government

must not be thought of as a mere guardian of law and of good order, but must rather put forth every effort so that through the entire scheme of laws and institutions . . . both public and individual well-being may develop spontaneously out of the very structure and administration of the State"; and that all citizens, without distinction, may have equal share in the goods of order, liberty, and opportunity.

These were a clergyman's speculations. But they also might have been the musings of a scientist as such. Some, of course will shy at any mention of causes or causation in these affairs; but as Gordon Allport remarks: "Methodologists who banish causation from the front door, often admit it surreptitiously at the back. . . . To my mind social science at its present stage of development will be concerned with causation, or else it will be concerned with nothing of consequence."[2] If this scientist today were a truly reflective man, not bound too tightly by the methodology and the limits of his own particular specialty, a man of somewhat larger view and wider consciousness of the many strictly factual elements in human life that nonetheless cannot be mathematically weighed and measured—he might also wish to examine more closely the roots of liberalism in certain Judeo-Christian doctrinal ideas. He might suspect—with the blessing of Dominie Thayer—that, after all, some help and light from on high, some divinely inspired graces are needed, if political liberalism is to pass effectively from mere theory to practice in this world of intense political passions and mass pressure on human freedoms. The very fact of that mass pressure might suggest some types of theological speculation.

He might go still further, and consider that the liberal's most difficult combat today is not so much with the selfishness of the reactionary as with the terror of the mass mind. Governor Talmadge in the flesh presents a sizable but limited difficulty. But Governor Talmadge photographically and electronically multiplied *ad infinitum* is something else again. The magnificent forces which man's mind has liberated so far seem to work as readily for man's enslavement as for his freedom. A universe conceived in nebulae and light-years can remain, of itself, blankly walled off from the spiritual infinitudes while the four walls of a contemplative's cell may open wide upon the vistas of eternity. On this crucial question as to how to free man's spirit from the crushing weight

[2]Gordon W. Allport, "Prejudice: A Problem in Psychological and Social Causation," *Journal of Social Issues,* Supplement Series, no. 4, November, 1950, p. 22.

of an unmanageable material liberation, the theologian has much to say. Whether we agree with his theory or not, it is not without pertinence to the practical problems of human freedom. Indeed, when the entire free world is caught in a stranglehold with an enemy who relentlessly contests the very groundwork of all free existence, it would seem rather difficult to shrug off all talk of ultimates as irrelevant mysticism.

IV

The experiences of the recent convulsed decades have made us cautious and skeptical. They have also increased our readiness to attribute objective worth to certain ancient landmarks of spiritual experience and philosophical thought. They make us also more ready to probe deeply into the age old, but ever new questions of reality and being; more anxious to find a bridge between the irreconcilable elements in our disparate universe—a bridge which will unite but will not confound. The unified field theory has given us the atomic and the hydrogen bomb. It has enriched us with resources of nuclear energy which may save man's existence upon this planet. But like Joseph Wood Krutch, I see no reason for bowing down to it as a god. Social sciences, he observes, "will never help to solve our problems as long as they continue to go on the assumption that whatever is true of a rat is true of a man."[3] We are by no means certain that such a restricted outlook will provide us with the key to permanent peace and freedom.

I believe that just as the great step taken by the Supreme Court has helped to reveal the true face of our country, so the growth in understanding which I expect to come out of these impending debates will express still more what the American people genuinely wish and feel; how they do business with one another and, I hope, eventually with the world. Precisely because of this belief on my part I take a more hopeful attitude than is frequently expressed toward the development of scholarship in the years immediately to come. Even from a purely pragmatic point of view, reasoned hope turns out to be stronger liberal medicine than does sustained and angry dissent.

That we are facing a certain wave of anti-intellectualism and pure utilitarianism is evident enough. But I do not see why this trend should necessarily develop into a tidal wave to engulf all free thought and free

[3] Joseph Wood Krutch, *The Measure of Man*, Bobbs-Merrill, New York, 1954, p. 195.

inquiry. I see grounds for such extreme anxiety only in the case of those who have allowed themselves to become fascinated by the intoxication of total doubt and a dogmatically negative attitude toward all normal human moral and religious values. Their hypercriticism earned for them, it now appears, some strange ideological bedfellows. The American people, from my own experience as a worker over the years for certain great principles of human rights, will listen and do listen to the voice of reason, when the arguments are presented intelligently and dispassionately. Prejudices may be inborn, a young African said to me the other day, as he was preparing to return to his native country, but in these matters, he insisted, people may be and frequently are born again. There may be giants in the path, but giants, too, are vulnerable, and sometimes flop helplessly in the face of a well aimed slingshot.

Says the biblical Wise Man in the Latin Vulgate version: *"os bilingue detestor,"* which may be rendered as: "I have no use for a face that talks with a double tongue." The *os bilingue,* the doubletalking face, has nothing in common with *le monde bilingue*—a world where men can talk straight to each other despite language barriers. It has also nothing in common with the traditional traits of the American people. Despite the clamor of many bitter and angry voices, our country, when it speaks for itself, does speak today, as it has in the past, with a tone of reverence for things holy and with humble respect for the needs of the least human being. I believe that scholarship will take increasing cognizance of this truth, and so play a powerful part in presenting to the world the true face of our country.

The southern globular cluster No. 55 in Messier's catalog (M 55) in the
constellation Sagittarius.

Messier 83, a spiral galaxy.

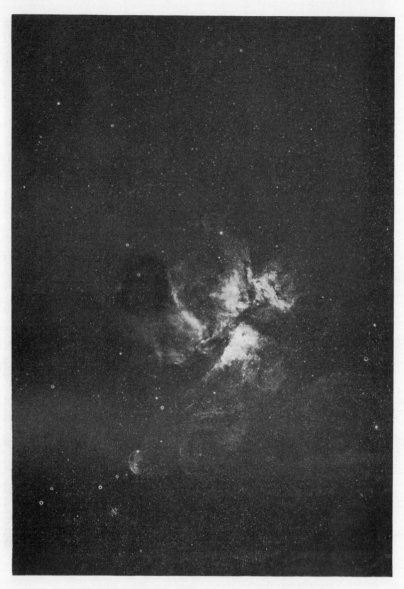

The bright, diffuse nebula surrounding Eta Carinae.

The 25-foot radio telescope of Harvard Observatory's George R. Agassiz Station at Harvard, Massachusetts.

Edge-on spiral galaxy.

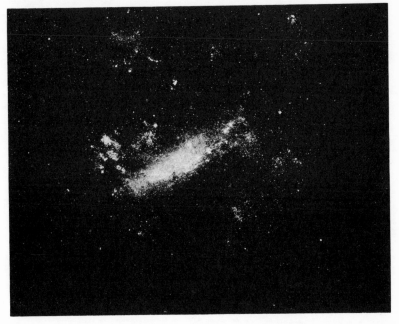

The Large Magellanic Cloud—an irregular galaxy.

APPENDIX I

First Conference on Science, Philosophy and Religion Lecture: Galaxies and Their Human Worth

By HARLOW SHAPLEY

AUGUST 31, 1954

Galaxies and Their Human Worth

By HARLOW SHAPLEY

WHEN FROM time to time we balance our ethical books in the hope of showing a morality profit, we should of course not only enter gross good and gross evil but for each item and act compute the net returns. For out of great good there is often counterbalancing sadness or defeat—the runnerup in the race or in the game that you win is envious and unhappy; joyous childbirth has its misery; the beautiful nightshade when misused is toxic; and, in general, there are often too many flies in the ointment.

And on the other side of the ethical ledger little virtues often go along with great evils. Bombing a city clears the slums. Burning of forests encourages the brilliant fireweed. Rolling a drunk diminishes his alcoholic intake. With the welter of radio's disgusting commercials and cheap comedy and song has also arisen a tribe of radio hams whose ingenuity can help no little in man's attempted conquest of the unknown—some good from evil, some advance to offset cultural degeneracy. For these radio wizards, with circuits and grids, backed by much erudite theory, have made new contacts with the outside universe and have expanded man's limited eyesight and limited hearing. They have given man what is in effect new organs of sight and new collections of data that inspire new hope for a net advance of the human body, mind, and spirit.

That remark provides me my cue. I now come on, and remark that the genius of the radio amateurs and professionals, who have grown in number and power because of the encouragement and commercial necessity of radio broadcasts and television, has transcended the needs of the temporarily glamorous stars of the theater and reached out to the eternally glamorous stars of remote galaxies. (In a close argument I would probably yield the concept of eternal stars, scarce knowing whether I should yield or stand, in view of our incomplete evidence on the death of radiation and on stellar destinies.)

My assigned subject is "Galaxies and Their Human Worth." The conjunction "and" does not imply equality of humanity with galaxies, and possibly we would not all agree as to which is primal, but from the standpoint of a student of galaxies the human valuation is irrelevant, and I feel justified in devoting the whole of this First Conference on Science, Philosophy and Religion Lecture to the galaxies. There may be a moment's time for a footnote on their human worth, or perhaps the question of values should be left to the auditors. Or possibly the human worth will be so deeply insinuated into the simple story of galaxies that nothing more need be said by the storyteller. No moral need be drawn. The stars themselves read the lesson. Forgetting the figures and charts and diagrams, you may want to join Walt Whitman, escaping from the solemnity of the astronomical lecture, who reported:

> Soon, unaccountable, I became tired and sick;
> Till rising and gliding out, I wandered off by myself
> In the mystical moist night air,
> And from time to time, looked up in perfect silence at the stars.

Historical Introduction

In a lecture series on *Cosmography—an Approach to Orientation,* which I give annually in Harvard University, I state that the only prerequisite for the course is a bit of spiritual courage and persistent curiosity. I can define courage as a willingness not to run away. The concept *spiritual* is somewhat fearful, and it is to me ambiguous in the light of recent advances in biochemistry, comparative neurology, and our embryonic psychologies. But I shall assume that we here are all mature, and brave in the light of the stars. Let us assume that we are objective scientists, and that along with many of the philosophers of the past and present we cheer for and live by the revelations of science. We are guided more by them than by the Revelations of Holy Writ. We shall take the new knowledge of the Universe as it comes, no matter how corroding it is to human pride or how inciting to human vanity.

A galaxy (Figure 1) is a system of stars of major dimensions and population, greater in both qualities than the well known clusters of stars like the Pleiades and the globular cluster M 55 in Sagittarius. (Figure 2) But *galaxy* was originally, by the earliest Greeks and their successors, applied to the Milky Way band of light that encircles the celestial sphere. Because of the milkiness of the *Via Lactea,* the term for milk was applied;

and the designation was not dropped when Galileo and his successors equipped with telescopes discovered that the milkiness resolved into individual stars.

The recognition that the Milky Way system of individual stars, with a slight admixture of star clusters and nebulosities, is discoidal in shape is properly accredited to Thomas Wright of Durham, England, and Immanuel Kant of Koenigsberg. In the middle of the eighteenth century they wrote on the nature of the sidereal universe. Thomas Wright mixed in with his proper deductions a lot of funny fancy and imaginative picturization, and Kant soberly depicted the wheelshaped form of the stellar system and made some shrewd intimations about sidereal evolution and the depths of space. He went so far as to suggest that our flattened Milky Way system is perhaps but one of many in unending space and that some of the hazy nebulosities, revealed by early telescopes, might be other galaxies. Both Wright and Kant recognized that the Milky Way band was but a projection, against the background of space, of the myriads of stars which we can see from our position near the central plane of the discoid.

Not until the middle of the following century did the concept of other galaxies impress itself upon observers of the universe, and even then the cautious scientists said little. The name and idea of external galaxy arose among the popular writers. There was an epoch around the beginning of the nineteenth century when the spiral galaxies were surmised to be forerunners of planetary systems like our own, and about thirty-five years ago brave speculators again suggested that the spirals are outside our own system. The evidence was not strong. My work and the work of others on the globular star clusters of our own galaxy gave a strong impetus to speculations of this sort, for, as mentioned later, the distances of globular star clusters turned out to be extraordinarily great—greater than we had supposed the radius of the whole measurable universe to be—and they led to the now accepted concept that the sun and naked-eye stars are far away from the center of our galaxy.

The work on the Magellanic Clouds at Harvard and the explorations with the large reflectors at Mount Wilson established definitely the outside character of spiral galaxies, such as the Andromeda Nebula. The researches of Hubble, chief among several, were epochal in our concept of the measurability of the outer universe. He made use of the same indirect but effective methods of measuring distances that had been used on the globular star clusters and on some of the remoter stars of our own Milky Way system. The Andromeda galaxy, brightest of those of the Northern Hemisphere, was soon estimated to be nearly a million light years away, and in many characteristics, such as size, population, and internal structure, it appeared to be much like the galaxy in which sun, earth, and human investigators are located.

Methods of Investigation

During the past twenty years much attention has been given to the structure of our own Milky Way system. Three important methods of investigation have been developed. One is the important analysis from analogy. Once we had got over the first jolt of finding ourselves peripherally located in a wheelshaped galaxy—and that galaxy only one of thousands that can be easily photographed with modest telescopes—we recognized that among the many types of galaxies ours was probably not peculiar in form and activity. We therefore began to study the motions and luminosities in and of the external spiral galaxies; while closely observing them, we fruitfully speculated about ourselves. Although we are located in the midst of chaotically moving stars and are surrounded by clouds of interstellar dust, and although we are located out toward the edge of our stellar system, we were soon able to detect that our galaxy had spiral arms, that it had a great massive nucleus of stars, a population in the billions, and so far as astrochemistry could be trusted, it had a stellar composition not unlike that of some of the other galaxies within the reach of our increasing telescopic power. The deductions from this analogical analysis have been fully supported by other approaches.

A second method of exploration depends on the counting of stars of all brightnesses, variously located, in the thick of the Milky Way, on its borders, and in its sparsely populated polar zones. From these star counts, carried on largely by American and Swedish astronomers, much progress has been made in locating the spiral arms of our galaxy and the clouds of interstellar dust that hide so much of the distant star fields from us. (Bart J. Bok of Harvard is the American leader in this research.) The amount of the material that hides the remoter stars can be deduced from star counts, from the colors of the stars, and from their spectra. Recently the astronomers at the Yerkes and Harvard observatories, and at some of the southern stations, have been able to locate the shining nonstellar gaseous masses that appear to be concentrated along the spiral arms of galaxies—masses like the Orion Nebula and the spectacular southern nebulosity surrounding Eta Carinae. (Figure 3) Thus from the gas and dust and stars themselves we are steadily making progress in depicting the structure of our spiral system. It has been a serious handicap to be located far from the center and near the galactic plane where the clouds of interstellar dust prevent quick and accurate measures of large stellar distances. The dark Rho Ophiuchi nebulosity conceals from us a hundred million stars. Fortunately this obscuring matter is thin in the direction of the polar zones of the galaxy, and therefore in those galactic latitudes we can reach far out into intergalactic space and register other galaxies by the thousands.

The red light that we get from the stars is less blocked by interstellar dust than is the short-wave blue, and therefore the longer the wave lengths we work with, the higher the transparency of dusty interstellar space. This situation leads us to a third, brand new, and highly important method for the study of the structure of galaxies. Although the ordinary stars radiate only weakly in long-wave red light, compared with the high intensity radiations in green, blue, and violet, nevertheless some radiation a thousand times the wave length of visual light is transmitted across space. And this long-wave length radiation comes in as short-wave radio. Our atmosphere is transparent to these radio waves, or it would be if it were not for two characteristics of its composition. One is that the normally transparent atmosphere of oxygen and nitrogen does contain also the molecules of water vapor, which block out large sections of the electromagnetic spectrum of the radiations from sun and stars. Also there are other molecular obstructors in our atmosphere. And, of more power in obstructing long-wave radiation from sun and stars, is the "radio roof"—layers in the upper atmosphere where sunlight has partly disrupted the dominant nitrogen and oxygen molecules. These ionized gases form an electric barrier to radio waves, both those coming in from radiating bodies outside and those waves that we ourselves send out under the name of radar. The ionospheric blockage is nearly complete for waves longer than ten yards, and the blockage is also nearly complete (by molecular absorption) for wave lengths less than one-tenth of an inch. But fortunately for the new science of radio astronomy there is a transparency, a sort of window, that permits our receipt of radiation with wave lengths greater than a tenth of an inch and less than ten yards. (Figure 4) In that interval there is of course some absorption, and it varies a bit with the time of day and with geographical position, but much radiant information can get through. We have new access to the universe. We have astronomical revelations provided as a byproduct of the skillful development of electronic instrumentation—a development of that scientific ingenuity that has made radio communication and radio entertainment major factors in our current culture.

Although three or four ingenious American engineers were pioneers in the development of radio astronomy, the leadership in this field was taken over at the close of the Second World War by Australians, Canadians, and Britons. They still dominate the field, although finally at Harvard, Ohio State, Cornell, and Stanford universities, and in two governmental scientific departments and at the Carnegie Institution of Washington, important progress and significant communications have been made.

Radio Astronomy

To many astronomers it begins to appear that contributions to knowledge through the radio "window" of our atmosphere may turn out to be as important as the age long researches through the red-to-violet visual window. Incidentally, at the other end of the spectrum, the ultraviolet end, we are also blocked by the molecules in our own atmosphere—chiefly by O_3, ozone. But way down in the sequence of radiation beyond the ultraviolet, beyond rays and gamma radiation, are the cosmic rays. They penetrate our atmosphere, considerably transformed but still of high significance, because a considerable part of the whole energy of the universe appears to be carried in these mysterious penetrating radiations for which we do not yet know certainly the origin.

Radio astronomy has in the past few years made an important contribution to our knowledge of the structure of our galaxy, in some ways more important than the knowledge we get from star counting or from analogical reasoning based on observations of similar galaxies far off in space. Let us look at some of the work of the radio astronomers. In the first place, the early pioneers (two decades ago) recorded with the early radio telescopes "noises" from the Milky Way, the greatest noise coming from the deepest part of the Milky Way—*i.e.,* from that section in the direction of Sagittarius where I located the galaxy center from the study of star clusters. Later came the discovery of "radio stars." They are localized spots in and outside the Milky Way whence come intense radio signals. As the equipment becomes more nearly precise, we find an increasing number of the radio sources. Some we can identify with specific objects, such as the Crab Nebula which is the remnant of a supernova explosion of 1054 A.D. (Actually the explosion was some thousands of years earlier, but 1054 was the year the message got to the earth's surface and was recorded by the Chinese and Japanese recorders of unusual celestial events.)

Another strong radio signal appears to come from the collision of two very distant faint galaxies seen through Cygnus, or possibly it is the collision actually of the gases (not stars) associated with those galaxies. Radio signals also come in from "hot spots" in the nearer galaxies, such as the Andromeda Nebula. After less than five years' work, more than two hundred such radio sources are now [August, 1954] on record, and the number will probably increase to a thousand or so within a year or so.

The radio telescopes locate the gas clouds of "neutral" (that is, un-ionized) hydrogen in the spiral arms of our Milky Way. They record shooting stars in our atmosphere more numerously than can the eye or the photographic plate, and register them night or day, cloudy or clear. They bounce radar off the moon, and diagnose solar disturbances, such as sunspots, solar prominences, and coronal flares. Individual galaxies, such as the two irregular Clouds of Magellan of the Southern Hemisphere, are found to be of great dimensions when their surrounding hydrogen gas is measured with the radio telescopes, much greater than recorded optically.

It is all a new science and very exciting. Although it requires mirrors of extraordinary size, they can be made of wire netting (which is cheap) and not of the expensive high quality Pyrex glass with which we make the great optical mirrors. Several of these radio telescopes are already larger in diameter than the famous 200-inch reflector on Palomar; and the largest radio telescope under construction, near Manchester, England, will have a diameter of 3,000 inches for its paraboloidal mirror or "dish." Dimensions of this sort, and electronic recorders of equally dramatic power, are necessary to handle these relatively long waves of radiation and correctly identify the sources.

Finally, in recent months, especially in Sydney, Australia, and Columbus, Ohio, serious studies of the structure of the Metagalaxy—of the overall system of all galaxies—are under way. Radio signals apparently are received from groups of distant galaxies, many of which are more than ten million light years away.

Although a new epoch is opening in the measurement of galaxies with the aid of the radio telescopes, we have already explored and will continue to probe with ordinary visual light deep into metagalactic space. The work is done through direct photography on commercial plates, or sometimes on specially sensitized plates. It is done also with the penetrating spectroscopes that analyze the chemical constitution of galaxies, as well as their speeds of recession and approach, and the character of their rotations. The remotest regions are also explored, dramatically and boldly, with cosmogonical theory, of which more later.

Nearby Galaxies

We shall now survey in some detail our galaxy and our nearest galactic neighbors. The greatest interest of course attaches to the spiral in which we are located. The measurement of its dimensions has been one of my principal interests. We now believe on the basis of analyses by four independent methods that the center is between 25,000 and 30,000 light years distant. Its overall diameter in the galactic plane is something like 100,000 light years. The sun and naked-eye stars are located in or near one of the faint spiral arms. For the past several years I have carried forward photographic investigations of variable stars and galaxies in the anti-center direction, in the direction, that is, toward the constellations of Taurus, Auriga, Gemini, and Orion. Using fairly simple methods, which need not be detailed in this place, we have been able to locate a good many members of our galaxy at distances even greater than our distance from the center of the Milky Way. But these most distant anti-center stars are not properly members of the galactic discoid. They seem to be a part of a corona or halo of stars, more or less spherical in dimensions, that surrounds our whole discoidal galaxy. We have measured some of these scarce distant objects far above and below the galactic plane. How did they get there? (Figure 5) Are they escapees from our flattened discoid, the victims of near collisions, or are they the remnants of an overall spherical system that has now condensed mostly but not

wholly into a wheelshaped central organization? We believe we see such
outlying stars around the Andromeda galaxy, and possibly around the
Magellanic Clouds. Here obviously is a field for studies in the higher
celestial mechanics, as well as for observational research. As it stands,
however, we can correctly say that our solar system is peripheral to the
great mass of stars of our galaxy, estimated at something like two hundred thousand million. Perhaps one per cent of its stars are more distant
from its center than we are.

Already the content of our majestically rotating system has been
mentioned—stars, star clusters, diffused gaseous nebulosities, dust clouds
that are both irregularly diffuse and all pervading. The average separation of stars in our part of the galaxy is a few light years; near the concentrated center in the direction of Sagittarius they are probably much
nearer together, but still so far apart that collisions must be exceedingly
uncommon. An average star like our sun has a diameter of a million
miles, and our nearest stellar neighbor, Alpha Centauri, is twenty-five
million million miles away. Very little danger, therefore, of a bump or
even of a near approach that might disturb the planets moving around
our sun. This point is of considerable significance. It reminds us of the
long interval of time in which the sun and the earth have undisturbedly
permitted the protoplasmic development that has culminated in the local
biological aspect of the universe. It tends to guarantee the even longer
interval that probably lies ahead for further progress. The land and the
sea, the earth's orbit and the sun's radiation, all appear propitious for
life. They will be sufficiently stable for millions of years, unlikely to be
disturbed by sidereal interference from without or exhaustion of energy
resources from within.

The rotation of our galaxy is assumed by everyone who examines the
spiral whirls of the analogous systems outside; but it took much skillful
work of observation, interpretation, and mathematical analysis to demonstrate that the part of the galactic system in which we are located does
a complete turn around the nucleus—completes one cosmic year—in
about two hundred million of our terrestrial years, notwithstanding the
speed of nearly two hundred miles a second, in our galactocentric orbit.
This long time is required for one revolution, since the distance trav-
elled is so long.

What lies in our galactic system beyond the obscuring dust clouds in
the direction of the center, will never be adequately known by us, al-

though red photography and microwave astronomy give us much richer information than we have heretofore obtained visually or by ordinary photographs. But reasoning from analogy, we would assume that the system is probably fairly symmetrically constructed, like the Andromeda galaxy. In the course of a cosmic year, if we were privileged to persist and record, we could know a good deal more about the other parts of the now hidden galactic star fields; regions nearer the center of our system revolve in shorter cosmic years, exposing to us other star fields, and those more distant more slowly, even as Mercury has an eighty-eight day year, being near the sun, and the outermost planet, Pluto, requires for its year two hundred and fifty of our earth-years.

We now leave the confines of our galaxy and take a quick look at our neighbors. According to present evidence, and it almost certainly is sufficient, the nearest external galaxies are the two Clouds of Magellan, much studied during the past two generations by the Harvard astronomers who have had the advantage of a station in the Southern Hemisphere, near Bloemfontein in the Orange Free State. These objects are irregular in form, although now we commonly suggest that the Large Cloud of Magellan is a somewhat aberrant barred spiral. That is, its center of mass is not in a concentrated nucleus, as in our system and in the Andromeda galaxy, but lies in an axis or bar. Perhaps time will smooth it out and we will have a typical barred spiral, or possibly it is "degenerating" toward greater chaos. Not long ago we customarily referred to the Clouds of Magellan as broken-off pieces of the southern Milky Way, although they are in fairly high galactic latitude (distant from the galactic circle). They look somewhat like the irregular star clouds of the Milky Way. But the researches on stellar distances, by way of the luminosities of the variable stars of the class of Delta Cephei, have gradually led us to recognize these star clouds as irregular external galaxies, of which there are many examples within a few million light years. I have specialized in studies, with several colleagues, on the variable stars and other features of the Magellanic Clouds. Our best estimate at present of the distances makes both of them about 170,000 light years away—about a tenth the distance to the Andromeda galaxy. Being so near, their individual stars can be easily photographed, even with moderate sized instruments—that is, their giant and supergiant stars can be photographed. The Irish-American instrument at Bloemfontein probes them deeply. It is much more difficult, however, with any available equipment to get down in faintness to the level of our sun. In fact, no individual stars in the Clouds as faint as ten times the brightness of our sun have yet been photographed, but we have not the slightest doubt but that such objects exist by the millions. Our researches show that the Clouds of Magellan are average galaxies, in dimensions and population, but less than ten per cent the size and population of the Andromeda galaxy and our own system, both of which are "supergiants."

Fainter than the Clouds of Magellan are large numbers of galaxies of which we have not known much until very recently. The Andromeda galaxy has two faint companions, much less massive and bright than the Clouds of Magellan. About fifteen years ago I found two exceedingly faint but large clusters of stars in the constellations of Sculptor and Fornax. Studies at Harvard and Mount Wilson proved them to be of galaxy size—not of star cluster size. Their distances were much greater than that of the Magellanic Clouds, and their total candle powers were only a few per cent as much as those of our nearest companions. In recent years a Palomar telescope has uncovered others of these dwarf systems, and now something like twenty are known to exist within two million light years of our galaxy.

We have tended to identify these nearby objects as members of a local family, but I think the designation is improper. There is a local family—a small group of seven or eight that are uncommonly close together compared with the general separation of galaxies throughout external space. The seven are the Andromeda Nebula and its two companions, the two Magellanic Clouds, another bright spiral called Messier 33, and our own galaxy. Possibly there may be another one or two lying behind the obscuring dust clouds of our Milky Way, unattainable by us with sufficient clarity (unless the radio telescopes eventually do the job) to give us the distances and dimensions.

All the faint "Sculptor-like" objects, some of which are spheroidal and some irregular, I take to be just general members of the substratum of galaxies throughout space. By making a complete survey of such systems out to four million light years, we would probably find eight times as many, because we would cover eight times as much volume. But even our biggest telescopes will have difficulty in recording these intrinsically faint dwarfish galaxies at distances greater than a few million light years. We can easily get thousands or millions of galaxies of brighter intrinsic luminosity and for them reach deep into space. The largest telescopes have already undoubtedly photographed supergiant galaxies of the dimensions and total luminosity of our own at distances greater than two billion light years.

The Metagalaxy

The foregoing remarks indicate that in any general survey of the metagalaxy we are going to do a much more penetrating census of the supergiant and giant galaxies than we are of the average and the dwarfish systems. If all galaxies were of the same size and luminosity, a sample would suffice to suggest the character of the metagalactic population; but because of the discovered spread in luminosities and sizes, we shall find it more difficult to talk about things like the bounds of space and the total masses of all stars in all galaxies. In fact, theories based on fundamental principles of space, time, and energy may give us a better picture of the structure of the metagalaxy than we shall be able to ascertain otherwise in the next several decades.

Incidentally, there is some indication that the big radio telescopes may be able to reach deeper into space than we can with the best of our optical power. Of course they will need to deal only with those galaxies in which there are objects (exploding stars or nebulosities) that emit radio signals which are detectable above the general background "noise" of intergalactic space and the noises of our instrumentation.

We turn now to explorations of the Metagalaxy. For the past two decades I have been making with modest equipment a general survey of the distribution of the million brightest galaxies. The job is too big to complete in detail, but all these million systems have been photographed both at northern and southern stations, and for several hundred thousand of them details of position or brightness or type have been deduced from the photographic plates. On the basis of this survey, and of the important work done at the Mount Wilson and Lick observatories in the same general field, we can now say something of 1) the apparent average separation of galaxies, 2) their numbers per cubic light year, and 3) the frequency of the various types. In a survey down to a given faintness we find that about three out of four of the galaxies are spiral in form, some twenty per cent are spheroidal without trace of spiral arms, and the remainder are irregular in structure. But if we recognize that spirality is generally associated, if not always, with large masses and luminosities, then it means that we have made a serious preferential selection of our material. We do not include many of the nonspiral dwarfs. The actual relative frequency of spirals, spheroidals, and irregulars is quite different if we examine all in a given volume of space. If we should deduce the true frequencies on the basis of the types of all galaxies within two million light years of our own, we would certainly conclude that perhaps only some twenty per cent are spirals and well over half of all are dwarf spheroidal and irregular galaxies. This is a technical point but is of high importance in considerations of the evolution of the material universe.

Out in space, away from the concentrated clusters such as our revised local family, the average separation of galaxies is something like a million light years. Between the galaxies of course is mostly emptiness, but throughout that emptiness there is undoubtedly a considerable amount of flying gas and dust which has been driven off from the surfaces of the stars, or remains there wandering, as debris left over from the evolution of stars out of the aboriginal clouds of dust and gas.

And here is an odd thought. Through every cubic inch of intergalactic space is passing continuously the dying radiation from nearly all the stars of the universe. Some speculators, interested in the cyclical nature of a universe that is permeated with energy radiating from the stars, like to believe that there is a process by which this ever present radiation may be "miraculously" reconstituted as atoms of matter. The machinery has not yet been discovered for such transformations in the coldness of nearly empty space; but we can after a fashion accomplish such transformations of energy into matter in our terrestrial atom-transforming laboratories.

Comments on Creation

The creation of matter, even in its simplest form, say, neutral hydrogen, which is composed of a single proton and a single electron, is a high reach for the imagination. If we (the Universe!) could create such material, out of which higher atoms, and dust particles, and eventually the stars are composed—create hydrogen out of nothing whatever (a still more miraculous performance than synthesizing matter from dying radiation)—then we might compensate in part or whole for the loss of matter that results from the ever expanding universe. Such is a part of the hypothesis that Bondi, Gold, Hoyle, and others have advanced, and many students of cosmogony are giving the strange suggestion very serious consideration. Theoretically it has something in its favor, observationally it has not yet much against it; but the testing is under way. The question is simply whether creation (material creation) is continuous, or did it happen at some one time in the past before the galaxies formed and began to scatter. Did all creation occur long ago miraculously, before the matter of the universe was explosively set agoing, and a group of natural laws took charge, managing the world from there out? Or is it going on now piecemeal and equally miraculous?

To contrast the "once only" and "continuous" theories of creation, we should back up a little and look at the alleged facts. We should go back to a most astonishing observation relative to external galaxies. Nearly forty years ago the spectroscopists at the Lowell Observatory in Arizona, commenced systematic observation on the spectra of the brighter galaxies. Individual stars in the galaxies could not be analyzed spectroscopically (they were too faint), but the total contribution of light from the millions of stars in the nucleus of a spiral or spheroidal galaxy would register faintly after a photographic exposure of several hours. An astonishing result was found. The absorption lines in the spectra of a few of the galaxies within the range of the available equipment were shifted toward the red end of the spectrum, and the shift was so considerable that, interpreted in the usual way on the Doppler principle, it meant velocities of several hundreds of miles per second. Individual stars and nebulosities do not move with such speeds with respect to the earth. Observations made at other observatories checked this result of a general red shift. It applied whatever the direction of the galaxy. The research was taken over by Milton Humason at the Mount Wilson Observatory, who has throughout the years with the Mount Wilson and Palomar telescopes measured the red shifts (and radial velocities) of several hundred galaxies. On the basis of these observations, and his own estimates of the distances of the individual galaxies, Edwin P. Hubble deduced a fundamental law of the cosmos. The red shift is now accepted generally as representing the expanding of the universe, and the astonishing part is that the more remote the object from the observer, the faster the expansion. The relation of speed to distance is linear — $s = Kd$, where K is a constant. It happens that this observation fits in very neatly with a prescription of the relativity theory. Other interpretations of the cosmic red shift are sought, and they should be sought, for those who are skeptical of velocities that are now measured as high as 40,000 miles a second.

The big telescopes have now reached out to distances where the speed of the receding galaxies is more than one-fifth the velocity of light, and no indication is found that the linear relation is changing. If we could get objects ten times as far away as the furthest now measured (and be sure of our distances which are very difficult to measure) then we would, unless an asymptotic situation set in, have velocities greater than the speed of light. This situation brings up some problems for the relativity theory, wherein speeds cannot be greater than the velocity of light; but that does not bother us as yet.

If objects in this expanding universe have crossed the barrier marked by the distance where the speed of recession would be greater than the speed of light, then those objects (galaxies) are lost to our observable universe. Their radiation cannot get back to us. The group of cosmogonists who propose the continuous creation theory would like to keep the average density of matter throughout space always the same. Therefore, to make up for the galaxies that for us escape "beyond the rim of the world," they need to create new matter. Hence the hypothesis mentioned above that new atoms appear out of nothing whatever. A strange conception, you may think, but is it easier for you to accept a creation occurring only once, a few thousand million years ago, or creation going on continuously? I see little choice, but I shall be happy to swing my sentiments in alignment with what the ingenious observations of the future suggest.

Let us look further at the conventional view of creation, remembering that such distant extrapolations are scarcely scientific. The observed rate of expansion of the universe is such that a few thousand million years ago all the observable galaxies (and we now estimate that there are two billion within two billion light years) were pretty close together. Canon Lemaître, in his famous "once only" cosmogony of twenty-five years ago, suggested that a few thousand (perhaps ten thousand) million years ago all the material of all the present stars of all the galaxies in the whole universe, and the interstellar dust and gas, was in one big chunk—the primitive atom. He suggests that it may have exploded violently. As the material receded, while stars and galaxies were forming, the average density of matter in space became less and less until gravitation lost control, cosmic repulsion took over, and the universe became hopelessly blown up, never to return into the primitive atom from which it was born. But the mathematical analyses by Robertson, Eddington, de Sitter, and others, have shown that there are alternatives. The mathematics is a bit too complicated to get exact solutions and the observational data that bear on the problem are too scarce or flimsy. We are obliged to make certain assumptions to solve the equations. According to the choice of assumptions, we can have something like a dozen different styles of behavior of the universe, two or three of which are close to the Lemaître-Eddington hypotheses. Some even are cyclic with the universe expanding as now observed and later contracting, only to expand again. Present observational data can eliminate three or four of the mathematical possibilities, such as the static universe, the high density universe, the empty universe, and the one that never existed, but they cannot establish which of the others is the correct one.

The continuous creation theory would suppose that the universe did not have a beginning but was eternal in the past and will be eternal, and in its totality unchanging, in the future. This supposition bypasses the observed continuous expanding; it accepts a continuous loss of matter over the "rim of the world" and interprets otherwise the current evidence that we approach the death of heat and infinite dissipation.

Evolution of Galaxies

I see that I have taken this inquiry on the galaxies beyond the realm of science into that of cosmology, and possibly to the edge of theology. I back out embarrassedly, and, in conclusion, comment on one other phase of the galactic problems.

We have myriads of galaxies that we can classify as irregular, spiral, and spheroidal, and we know that there are various degrees of irregularity, and various styles of spirality, and various forms of the spheroidal galaxies. Many years ago astronomers arranged them in a series and naturally wondered if one kind developed into another. For a good many years Sir James Jeans and less positively Hubble surmised that spheroidal galaxies, rotating, would sprout spiral arms and go through successive stages of tight, average (like ours), and open spirality, ending perhaps in the irregular chaotic form of the Magellanic Clouds.

There is no question but that such a sequence of types can be arranged, an evolutionary pattern, with the semblance of inescapable logic. But do the galaxies conform—know which way to go? There is a growing conviction that the evolution of a galaxy is in the other direction, that it goes from the irregular to the spiral forms, then on to and through the spheroidals, with increasing rotundity, and possibly all the way to the true globular type. I proposed that alternative evolutionary sequence on the basis of the obvious celestial dynamics, especially the shearing effect, such as that which must even now be taking the Hyades apart and bothering the Pleiades as the galaxy rotates at different speeds for different distances from the nucleus. On the basis of turbulence, as well as shearing effects, von Weizsaecker and others agree on the high probability of this direction in the evolution of galaxies.

Also there are arguments for such an evolutionary trend that can be based on the frequency of the supergiant stars. They are newly born and quickly die off as they rapidly radiate away their substance. They appear preferentially in the arms of spirals and not at all in the spheroidals. For a final answer we may need to wait around for two or three cosmic years; by then these majestic processes may have recorded themselves clearly on our photographs.

In Partial Summary of Galaxies and Their Human Worth

My study, I hope I have shown, is more than mildly interesting to the human kind. The galaxies appear to be "worthy" in their own right, as major parts of the universe, whatever their worth to terrestrial plants and animals. We have first defined a galaxy and located ourselves near the rim of one that seems to be of more than average size. We have analyzed its contents of stars, dust, and gas; we have located its center, timed its rotation, and gone out from it to inspect our nearest neighbors —the Small and Large Magellanic Clouds. (Figure 6) Naturally we attached special interest to these two nearby irregular galaxies that got into our literature permanently with the historical record made at the time Ferdinand Magellan attempted to circumnavigate this small planet. We looked then at the nearest of the true spirals, the Andromeda Nebula, and found that one of the best ways to study our own galaxy is through studying those that are, like us, well outside but not too far away. Such studies of our galaxy we can supplement by making a census of the galactic stars, by measuring motions with spectroscopes and otherwise, and by using the newly born techniques of radio astronomy. Outside, in metagalactic space, we find the galaxies abundantly, far beyond where our greatest telescopes can measure in detail. We have now reached to a depth of more than a thousand million light years. We have found that these galaxies are scattering from some unknown origin with enormous speeds, and rather promptly we are led into cosmogonical speculations on the nature of the origin, on the meaning of space, time, matter, and energy, on the direction and causes of the evolution of galaxies. Looking beyond our material fragility, beyond our peripheral and ephemeral position in the totality of nature, we end up nevertheless in being moderately proud of the terrestrial organism that has been able to unravel and reason about some of these facts and mysteries.

APPENDIX II

Some Considerations of Symbolization and Nervous Action: Inaugural Address of the Fourteenth Conference on Science, Philosophy and Religion

By HUDSON HOAGLAND

Natural scientists, of course, like everyone else, are concerned with symbols and are especially interested professionally in their manipulation. As a matter of fact they have greatly refined and extended their special use in mathematics and in modelmaking but they use symbols mainly as signs or as denotive symbols, in contrast to conative or evocative symbols with which we here have agreed to be concerned. The training of the scientist as scientist, as indeed the training of all scholars, tends to develop in some of us aversion for the emotionally charged evocative symbol. Too often such symbols are used for shortcircuiting reason and blowing the fuse of considered judgment in favor of anti-intellectualism and the destruction of truth. There are, of course, many illustrations of this. The swastika came to us to symbolize a perversion of truth in terms of racial and social pseudoscience. The hammer and sickle symbolize to us a rigid orthodoxy of perverse meanings, the degradation of the individual and the prostitution of free science as exemplified by the fate of Russian genetics. The burning of witches by the orthodox during the Inquisition was aided and abetted by the rich symbolism of the church. The evocative symbol has all too often been a tool in the hands of the powerful for exploitation, bigotry, and tyranny.

On the other hand, symbols are essential to the development and continuity of orderly social institutions. As Albert Salomon has written in his interesting chapter for this volume:

> Illusion is a constructive and beneficial constituent of the organization of social action. It enables men to reach for the impossible in order to

accomplish the possible. At the same time it enables men to endure the vicissitudes of life and to hope for a new beginning. Illusion is the trust in the truth of symbolic meanings. It is the very foundation of social conduct.[1]

All thinking and communication are in terms of symbols and the necessity of the symbolic process is embedded in our whole biological history as a property of the phylogenetic development of organized nervous systems.

In this connection I would like to take a few minutes to consider an aspect of symbolism that I believe has not been dealt with by others in these Conferences. By way of introduction I should say that I am a physiologist whose primary professional interest is in the mechanisms of brain action. It is an article of faith, or perhaps I should say a working hypothesis, for some of us to consider that all behavior, whether it be the reflex response to a pinprick or the composition of a Beethoven symphony, is mediated by the integrated action of the billions of cells that make up the nervous system. Work over the past few decades has shed new light on mechanisms of nervous action in relation to perception, learning, and memory, and has led to the view that the formation of symbols, particularly in the field of perceptual processes, is a correlate of the basic nature of the integrated behavior of organized nerve nets ranging all the way from worms to man. The brain is an enormously complicated electronic device continually active in patterned ways. Over its billions of fibers course kaleidoscopic, shifting patterns of electrical activity which can be recorded by the tools available in our laboratories. The brain is not just a resting telephone switchboard into which connections from the environment can be plugged by way of our sense organs to eventuate in motor responses by our muscles. It is rather a continuously active network of reverberating electrical circuits, active in complex patterns of messages both awake and asleep which appear to correspond symbolically to events in the world about us and to their correlates in consciousness. Electrical nerve messages from the sense organs modify these reverberating patterns and translate them into consciousness, and into conscious and unconscious drives. As Mueller pointed out 100 years ago, we experience not the direct world about us but only events in the nervous system which we assume reflect the world we live in. New concepts in recent years have emerged from studies of

[1]Albert Salomon, "Symbols and Images in the Constitution of Society," Chapter VI.

the brain, so that today we even speak of purposive mechanisms without contradiction of terms, for purpose can be defined in systems of communication such as nerve nets containing appropriate feedback.

As symbolization is a basic product of nervous action we might expect that certain disease conditions and a variety of chemical agents would modify the significance of symbols. The widespread mental disorder known as schizophrenia is characterized by, above all else, a distortion of one's ability to use symbols in a socially acceptable fashion. The schizophrenic has his own private set of symbols. It is interesting in this connection that some striking paintings have emerged from the brushes of schizophrenic patients; perhaps we appreciate them because we may all be a little schizophrenic. I might also add, that it seems to me some effective modern painters produce remarkable results by the use of schizophreniclike distortion of symbols in their pictures. But most symbolic productions of these patients are bizarre and quite meaningless to us although full of significance for them. I recall, for example, a patient who liked beefsteak but got little satisfaction out of eating it. His enjoyment came from drawing pictures of steak on paper and eating the paper. The language of the schizophrenic particularly reflects his disordered ability to deal with symbols. Words have quite different meanings for him than they do for us, but, despite this superficial meaninglessness, psychiatrists who study the language of a schizophrenic patient can often with patience and diligence learn a great deal about him.

It is a hypothesis on the part of some of us that these patients are suffering from a disease of internal chemical metabolic origin operating so as to disturb the circuits of transmission of nerve messages in the brain. The particular nature of the psychotic manifestations will, of course, depend upon the past conditioning history of the individual—his psychodynamics—but this in turn is dependent upon the patterns of action of nerve messages in his brain. These patients, I believe, are no less physically ill than are persons suffering from arthritis or cancer. We have simply not as yet been able to unravel the subtle chemical and physical disturbances of their tissues. But interesting advances are being made. For example, there are certain drugs which will produce psychoticlike behavior of short duration in normal human subjects. The most interesting of these substances is known as lysergic acid diethylamide, abbreviated—LSD. A 30-millionth part of a gram taken by mouth is sufficient to produce psychotic experiences in a normal individual lasting eight to ten hours and evidence suggests it probably does so by acting upon specific chemical receptors in cells of the brain. LSD is not produced in the body. It is of plant origin and has been synthesized in the laboratory, but within the past two or three years Canadian investigators have reported that a substance that structurally bears some resemblance to LSD and is active in producing psychotic symptoms when it is administered to normal persons in small doses, may possibly be formed in the body of some persons by aberrant metabolism of certain hormones. It has not yet been possible for technical reasons to demonstrate that this substance is produced more in psychotic patients and less in other persons and this particular lead may prove to be unfruitful, but work along these and related lines may lead ultimately to a better understanding of the chemical basis of schizophrenia and perhaps to its eventual chemotherapy.

I mention this example because it introduces the subject of psychopharmacology, a term for the study of the effect of drugs on psychological processes. In this connection I would like to call attention to a delightfully written little book by Aldous Huxley, called *The Doors of Perception,* in which he describes his own remarkable personal experience after taking a half gram of mescaline. This is the active principle of peyote—the desert cactus long used by the Indians of Mexico and the Southwest in their religious rites. The drug is harmless and nonhabitforming and produces profound alterations of consciousness. The world is transfigured with a strange beauty and inspiring significance. Huxley describes his remarkable perceptions in relation to aspects of religious experience, to art, and to problems of philosophy.

The field of psychopharmacology is relatively new, although some crude aspects of it are very old and it has at times been used for undesirable ends. Thus changes in personality brought about by alcohol have been employed by white traders to drive stiff bargains with Indians and other primitive peoples usually with a sorry backlash for all concerned. I have read that Oriental nations have plied neighboring states with opiates to reduce resistance to conquest. Drugs and conditioned reflex techniques have been used by the Communists and Fascists to break men and extract false confessions for political purposes. Just as gunpowder, the airplane, and nuclear energy can be misused, so can drugs in affecting men's ability to deal with symbols and values. The late Russian physiologist, I. P. Pavlov, I am told, was a gentle, kindly scholar, quite disinterested in politics. The procedures of brain-washing, using his conditioned reflex techniques developed from animal studies of brain function, seem as alien to his spirit as would be the destruction of Boston by a nuclear explosion to the spirit of Albert Einstein. On the other hand, many drugs, misused for political ends, particularly the barbiturates, have, in the hands of psychiatrists, enabled shattered neurotic patients to recall events and relive experiences producing beneficial therapy. This is especially the case with the war neuroses. These same drugs can give sleep to the sleepless and anesthesia to the suffering patient. With advances in our understanding of brain chemistry and physiology, it is not too much to expect that selective drugs and surgical procedures may be used to improve the lot of man more extensively. But the beginnings along these lines are modest and the dangers of misuse are great. Thus, the operation known as leucotomy, referred to by some as psychosurgery, severs nerve fibers to the frontal lobes of the brain. It often has dramatic effect in relieving the misery of depression and acute anxiety. The tortured psychotic may have his worries cut out by the surgeon's knife, as patients have themselves described the effects of this operation which unfortunately is not always successful in improving the patient's personality. Brain operations by neurophysiologists on animals, not yet successfully applied to man, have demonstrated that savage, aggressive, and thoroughly dangerous monkeys can be converted to friendly, cooperative, and even affectionate ones without apparent impairment of mental function by the destruction of small, specific areas of nerve cells. The brain is not one organ but a multitude of functionally interrelated organs composed of tissues with different chemical responsivities. It is not too much to hope that better understanding of this remarkable set of mechanisms may ultimately make possible the modification of pathological symbolization, whether it occurs in a psychotic patient or in a psychopath like Adolf Hitler.

To summarize then, the effect on a subject of evocative symbols depends basically on the physical chemistry and organization of action in the nerve cells of his brain and on chemical factors in the brain's internal environment. The patterns of physiological action within the brain corresponding to symbols are subject to direct modification not only by conditioning techniques but by chemical and surgical procedures. These procedures while crude now will surely improve in time and I have indicated a few of their present applications in medicine and to politics. Like all the discoveries of science, psychopharmacology may be exploited by the wrong people for the wrong ends and ethical problems raised by these approaches are extensive and complicated. Even in purely therapeutic procedures such as those of so-called psychosurgery, argument about the ethics of irreversibly changing a patient's personality, even for the better, has been the subject of controversy over the past decade.

APPENDIX III

Symbols and Symbolism[1]

(With particular reference to the religious symbol, especially as it appears in Judaism.)

By SIMON GREENBERG

I

Any phenomenon in so far as it rouses in consciousness an awareness of phenomena in addition to itself and/or stimulates in the observer a reaction appropriate to those phenomena, thereby functions as a symbol.[2]

Words spoken or written, are the most universal phenomena that serve primarily as symbols. Except for students of language, the sound represented by the letters *t a b l e* or the appearance of the written letters *per se,* interest very few people who speak, hear, write, or read the word. These letters or their sound ordinarily attract attention not to themselves but to a piece of furniture used for various well known purposes.

But while words spoken or written are the most ubiquitous symbols,

[1] The following pages represent an attempt to develop for myself at least the beginnings of a systematic understanding of this vast and complicated area of inquiry. The papers presented to the Thirteenth Conference, the seminar on the subject conducted by Lyman Bryson during the course of the past three years and the papers presented to this Conference, were so stimulating that they constituted a well nigh irresistible challenge to make this effort. The notes will refer primarily to papers presented to the Fourteenth Conference and included in this volume.

[2] John E. Burchard in his chapter on "Symbolism in Architecture—The Decline of the Monumental" suggests that "a symbol must be understandable without footnotes or scholarly exegesis by *some minimum number of people* before it can properly be called a symbol, and we might suppose that minimum number to be greater than one" (p. 403). That may be true for a phenomenon consciously employed by one individual as a symbol, in order to communicate with another individual. But one can create his own symbols for his own purposes only. Some modern poets and painters who are interested primarily in "expressing themselves," rather than in communicating with others, create symbols which are meaningful at times only to themselves. One can argue that such artists and poets are not properly fulfilling their functions. But we cannot deny that they create symbols.

every other phenomenon may at times function as a symbol, whether it be a gesture, a building, a drawing, or a mood, for in the human consciousness no phenomenon is completely isolated from all other phenomena. Through the basic psychological process of association of ideas,[3] anything we think of can at once bring to mind something else to which it is in some manner related. Hence anything can be used as a symbol for any one of a vast number of other things with which it has been or can conceivably be related. The more obvious and widely recognized the association, the more likely that one will be used as symbol for the other. In more sophisticated circles more subtle and esoteric associations will be recognized. The range of symbolism thus available to the poet, the artist, or the average citizen is infinite.

In the statement, "Man is a reed," the reed is symbolic of man, because both are related to the phenomenon of weakness and fragility. The Empire State Building is associated in our minds with America's tremendous industrial and engineering progress. Hence it can and undoubtedly has been used as a symbol for American civilization.[4] The number of illustrations readily available is infinite, for the association can be traceable either to correspondence between aspects of the form or quality of the symbol and its referent, or to some accidental, historical association or to a consciously planned association between the two, as the association between Paul Revere and community vigilance, the flag and the country, the red cross and the army nurse.

[3]The basic role of "association of ideas" in symbolism is comprehensively discussed in Alfred Schutz's, "Symbol, Reality, and Society," Chapter VII, and is indicated in many passages in William Y. Tindall's "The Literary Symbol," Chapter XI, especially pp. 358–361.

[4]Every artistic creation whether it be literary or architectural may be symbolic as a whole and symbolic in its details. "The literary symbol may be the work or one of its parts" (Tindall, p. 356). Modern architecture by eschewing the ornamental has practically eliminated that aspect of ancient and medieval architecture which contributed most to its symbolic or "monumental" significance. But as one modern architect has phrased it—"we have actually created monuments unconsciously, *and with them symbols,* as we have built our industrial society, our dams, bridges, and factories. . . . monuments often turn out to be different than expected by their builders. . . . the Romans may have expected to be remembered by their temples and law courts, and not the baths, roads, and aqueducts by which we actually remember them" (Burchard, p. 397).

II

To the best of our knowledge, man is the only creature upon earth who has the power to symbolize.[5]

The power to symbolize is dependent upon the power to differentiate a quality from an object which concretizes it, and an object from the other objects with which it is associated when it impinges upon the senses. This power to differentiate is rooted basically in self-consciousness, which is in essence a differentiation by the self of itself from all else that transpires outside itself or within itself. To the best of our knowledge, man alone "knows that he knows," and can distinguish between himself as knower and the objects he knows, and hence also between one object of knowledge and another.

III

The power to symbolize makes human thought, as we know it, possible.

We cannot think at all about anything for which we did not first create a symbol, whether it be visual, aural,[6] tactile, or olfactory. But no thinking on a level above the most elementary can be done without first creating symbols for phenomena, whether those symbols be primarily aural, visual, or tactile in nature. There is good reason to believe that thought and symbols are inseparable and that what one does not have a "symbol" for, he cannot think about.[7]

[5]"Not higher sensitivity, not longer memory or even quicker association sets man so far above other animals that he can regard them as denizens of a lower world: no, it is the power of using symbols—the power of *speech*—that makes him lord of the earth." Susanne K. Langer, *Philosophy in a New Key*, Penguin Books, Inc., New York, 1948, p. 20.

[6]Louis Finkelstein's "The Hebrew Text of the Bible: A Study of Its Cadence Symbols," Chapter XIII, is a most interesting discussion of the symbolic meaning imbedded in the sounds of words, and the cadences and intonations of words in sentences. His attempt to establish his feeling that Nathan rebuked David not in wrath but in kindness, by analyzing the sounds of the words used by Nathan, can perhaps be further substantiated by the fact that Nathan took a rather long time to make his point, in contrast to the abrupt, explosive manner in which Elijah rebuked Ahab. Indignation when not tempered by mercy, is not wont to clothe itself in telling folkloristic stories. Nathan, in contrast to Elijah, is interested not merely in denouncing David but in having him recognize for himself the wickedness of his deed. He appears in this story not so much as the angry prophet, but rather as the kindly teacher, *cf.* II Samuel 11, 12, and I Kings 21.

[7]The classic instance of the tactile symbol is of course the case of Helen Keller. The mov-

IV

While significant distinctions can be made among symbols, depending upon the purposes they serve, all attempts to make significant distinctions between signs and symbols have, it seems to me, taught us a good deal about the nature of symbols but have beyond that been little more than interesting exercises in semantics.

The fact of the matter seems to be that we have thus far used both words almost interchangeably. The dictionary defines *symbol* as a "visible *sign* of something invisible," and *sign* as "a conventional *symbol* representing an idea," etc.

Some have attempted to restrict the use of "sign" to phenomena which represent a one to one relationship between the phenomenon used as a sign and the phenomenon which it is intended to suggest. Thus the $+$ is a sign because it supposedly suggests only one thing, namely, that the phenomena on either side of it are to be added one to the other. But it has that limited meaning only when it appears in a mathematical equation. In different situations it can suggest other things. Teachers are in the habit of marking students as B$+$ or A$+$. In such a setting the $+$ no longer has a definite one to one relationship with any other phenomenon. In like manner the English word *road* when heard ordinarily indicates or signifies a highway leading from one place to another. But the same word heard by an American

ing account given by her of her discovery of the fact that things have names, that what she drank was identified by a certain sequence of tactile impressions, and what that meant for her consequent mental development is well known (Langer, *op. cit.*, pp. 50–51). It is for this reason I feel that the opening statement in F. S. C. Northrop's "Linguistic Symbols and Legal Norms," Chapter IV, while it seems self-evident, needs further elucidation. He states, "Undescribed experience came first. Expressed experience, and hence language, came afterwards." An "experience" which is "undescribed" is different in kind from an "experience" that is "expressed," for an "experience" which is "expressed" is one that has entered consciousness and has thereby been transformed from an "event" into an experience. But that which remains "undescribed" has never entered consciousness, for nothing which enters consciousness remains completely "undescribed" in some manner adequate for identification by the individual undergoing the experience, although the manner of identification may not be adequate for purposes of communicating the experience to others. Hence, to speak of "undescribed" and "expressed experience," as if the concept "experience" refers to the identical phenomenon in both instances, is misleading. In the one instance, consciousness is involved. In the other it is not. And whatever is touched by consciousness is at once transformed into a category different in essence from that which is not so touched.

in a foreign country may indicate or signify that someone who knows how to speak English is within hearing distance. Under other circumstances it may symbolize the song, "The Road to Mandalay," and thus almost *ad infinitum*. The fact of the matter seems to be that man's mental capacities are so constituted that he cannot, except by conscious determination limit the symbolic aspects of any phenomenon to only a one to one relationship. Through the inevitable process of association incessantly going on in the mind, the symbolic potentialities of every phenomenon are constantly being multiplied. All literary and artistic creativity is dependent upon it. It is undoubtedly true that the symbolic potentialities of some phenomena are more limited than those of other phenomena. But this limitation is as often due to the quality and range of the consciousness upon which the phenomenon impinges, as to the phenomenon itself.

Susanne K. Langer limits the use of "sign" to phenomena that produce a reaction to a referent without involving consciousness.[8] Thus defined, it would seem to me that *sign* is descriptive not of the phenomenon but of the subject upon whom the phenomenon impinges. Signs, thus defined, relate to the experiences of subhuman creatures or to man on the subconscious level. What appears to happen on that level is the identification of the sign with its referent. The dog hearing the bell acts as if the food were present. The bell is not known by the dog as an independent phenomenon. But on the human level every phenomenon is known in its own right, either before or after it is known as a sign or a symbol. Consciousness is never completely absent from the process which transforms a phenomenon into a symbol or sign. It may not always be present at the moment when a phenomenon is reacted to by the human being who encounters it. But at no time can a human being's reaction to a sign be equated with an animal's reaction to it, even though, technically speaking, we may say that the reaction in both instances did not involve consciousness. In the case of the human being such a reaction was on the subconscious level of habit which must have been preceded by a period of consciousness. However, in the animal's case the whole process occurred on the nonconscious level of instinct. The difference between the two is infinite.

Thus anyone can define sign or symbol as he prefers and use them

[8]*Ibid.*, p. 52

in accordance with his definition. But there is little in the uses to which these words have thus far been put in ordinary English usage which justifies any very clear and consistent distinction between them. One can speak of a sign as belonging to the species "symbol" or *vice versa,* with equal validity.[9]

V

The symbolic aspect of a phenomenon is not inherent in it, and hence it is not self-evident. Before a phenomenon can take on the character of a symbol a learning process must take place.

That is true even of the "natural" signs[10] such as clouds or thunder. A child who never saw snow fall will not associate clouds with snow the first time he finds himself in a temperate climate in the fall or winter. He must see the phenomenon first. Moreover, clouds do not always bring rain. Clouded heavens may have served as a sign that the Deity is displeased. Lightning is often seen without the accompaniment of claps of thunder. One must learn that the two are interrelated.

When we leave the area of "natural" symbols and enter the area of manmade symbols, the part that the learning process has in the creation of symbols becomes self-evident. There is nothing in the sound of the letters *t r e e* which when heard should rouse in consciousness the awareness of an object with roots, branches, and leaves. There is nothing inherent in the stones of the Lincoln or the Washington monuments, which makes their symbolic significance self-evident. *A phenomenon can, therefore, function as a symbol only in relation to phenomena which at one time or another are independently known by the observer, and then consciously or subconsciously related by him one to the other.*

The quality and the range of the symbolic aspects of any phenomenon depend, therefore, only secondarily upon the phenomenon itself,

[9]Among the papers presented to this Conference that by Alfred Schutz treats this subject most comprehensively. He makes a heroic effort to distinguish between "mark, indication, sign, and symbol." Whether his effort is also but another exercise in semantics, is, of course, a matter of opinion. See also the chapters by Tindall, pp. 338–340, Theodore M. Greene, pp. 230–236, and Robert Ulich, pp. 205–207.

[10]For an excellent discussion of "natural signs" see Ernest Nagel, "Symbolism and Science," *Symbols and Values: An Initial Study,* Chapter III, p. 39.

and primarily upon the quality and range of the learning process through which the observer of the phenomenon has passed.[11]

VI

In some areas of human activity the efficacy of a phenomenon as a symbol depends upon the consciously defined limitations that are set by us to its symbolic aspects. This is particularly the case with the scientific symbol.

In mathematics, in all the sciences, in the military pursuits of man, the symbolic aspects of phenomena must be meticulously circumscribed, so that the symbolic aspect once having been consciously learned, may become almost as completely identified with the phenomenon itself as was the sound of the bell with the food in the case of Pavlov's dog. But there is never complete identification. Phenomena used in mathematics, science, and by the military as symbols, such as $+$, H_2O, or the officers' epaulet, remain phenomena in themselves, which when encountered in nonmathematical or nonscientific or nonmilitary circumstances, continue to be of some interest, even though they may have shed their dominantly symbolic aspects completely. But in these areas of human activity wisdom requires that the symbols should be of such nature as to discourage to the maximum the mind's tendency to turn everything into a symbol for many various phenomena. Hence, whenever possible the symbol itself should be a phenomenon that has previously not been encountered at all by men, or one that we are not likely to encounter, except in well defined situations, such as in mathematical equations or in chemical formulas or in the military establishment. Hence the laws forbidding civilians to wear military uniforms and the indiscriminate use of the flag.

VII

In some areas of human activity the efficacy of a phenomenon as symbol depends upon the conscious and studied expansion of the range of phenomena which it summons into consciousness. This is particularly the case with group symbols.

[11]"How many Americans are aware that a gigantic symbol of Freedom rests at the peak of the national Capitol, or would be aware of the meaning of the 'delicate figure' if not suitably instructed?" (Burchard, p. 391).

The efficacy of a symbol as a unifying force in human society depends primarily upon the multiplicity of other phenomena which it is capable of mustering within the range of consciousness of its observers. It is this multiplicity of associations roused from the subconscious[12] by the symbol, which alone can achieve two results equally indispensable for the unification of large societies. On the one hand, the symbol binds the individual closer to itself by involving itself in the greatest possible number of his memories, emotions, and capacities. On the other hand, it attaches the greatest possible number of individuals to itself, each one of whom may be personally involved in only one or two of its many symbolic aspects.

Hence each group in human society, whether it be a religious sect, a political party, a state, or a social club, strives incessantly, if it is wise, to associate its symbols with the greatest possible number of other phenomena. Hence our efforts consciously to multiply the symbolic aspect of the word *America,* as we did in the popular *"Ballad for Americans"* during the Second World War. Hence, also, our most staple theme for school children's essays, "What America Means to Me."

The demagogue's chief task is to make a symbol mean not "All things to every *man*," but "All things to all men," *i.e.,* every man is to find in it the thing or things that he is seeking. Hence the demagogue is not concerned primarily that logical consistency characterize his program, but rather that it endow his emblem with maximum symbolic plenitude, so that each one may find in it what he seeks.

But most often the demagogue will not create his own new symbol, as under the best of circumstances the association of meaning with a group symbol involves a long and difficult process. He will prefer to attach himself and his particular purposes to a symbol which already

[12]The point made in Karl W. Deutsch's "Symbols of Political Community," Chapter III, that no one symbol, no matter how meaningful, can adequately serve the needs of any community, national or international, should here be noted. The studies referred to in the paper indicated that whenever in history there existed a "successful union, or even a successful pluralistic political community," there was always present "a *multiplicity* of unifying symbols." That does not contradict the point we wish to make, that a group's chief "unifying symbols" each tend to acquire a multiplicity of meaning or referents.

By saying that the symbol is to "rouse a multiplicity of associations from the subconscious" we mean to stress the same point that Deutsch stresses, namely, "the importance of the relatedness of the effective political symbols to the *previously acquired* memories" (p. 39).

has vast and effective associations with the individuals of the group he seeks to dominate.[13] An American listening to a speaker whose stand is decorated with an American flag must make a heroic effort to dissociate what the speaker is saying from the phenomena, conscious and emotional, which the flag *per se* stirs within him.

While, therefore, a phenomenon with a multiplicity of symbolic aspects, such as a flag, may be very effective as a force unifying different and often conflicting elements in a society, it is a most ineffective agent for exact communication. Two people can with equal vigor protest their loyalty to the flag of America, but can today associate it with altogether different phenomena. To the one the American flag as symbol may call the Marshall Plan into consciousness, to the other the McCarran immigration laws.

Hence the chief duty of the leaders of any group is not merely to multiply the symbolic aspects of the group's chief symbols, but to see to it that those aspects are not self-contradictory, that they are inherently consistent and make for a deepening and broadening of the group's highest moral and intellectual aspirations. That is the sacred and never ending obligation of the group's leader and teachers. *We cannot overemphasize the fact that the symbolic aspects of any phenomenon whether flag or map, word or gesture, are learned and that the learning process starts early and determines the meaning of the symbol.*[14] Waving the map of the United States will not bring the same reaction as waving the flag, not because the Stars and Stripes make a prettier picture than the map, but because a long learning process has taught us how to act when we see a piece of cloth colored in a given way waving from a pole, while a map recalls to consciousness either a teacher and a classroom or plans for a journey. There is no way other than that of the tireless, well planned educational process whereby we may avoid the dangers inherent in the fact that the chief symbols

[13]The Nazi movement created its own symbol, because at the time there was no national symbol, no flag, to which Nazis could attach themselves. The flag of the Weimar Republic was anathema to them, that of the old Reich was forbidden. Nor were they interested in restoring the old Reich. Hence a period of intensive propaganda was carried on by them to create a plenitude of association with their new symbol.

[14]On the characteristic desirable for the symbols of the group see Ulich's "Symbolism and the Education of Man" (p. 216). He is, moreover, entirely right in his emphasis upon the fact that "even the finest aspirational symbols have the charisma not in and by themselves, but only to the degree to which man understands their transparent character and uses them for directing his thought to the superior aspects of life" (p. 225).

of a group must have a multiplicity of symbolic aspects, if they are to serve as unifying factors in the group's life. Only thus can demagogues be prevented from corrupting the group's symbols with vehicles for their destructive, disruptive activities.

VIII

In some areas of human concern the efficacy of a phenomenon as symbol depends neither upon the limitation nor the comprehensiveness of its symbolic impact, but rather upon the poignancy with which it involves human aspirations, moods, or emotions. Literary and artistic creations are such phenomena.[15]

Literature and art are not concerned merely with symbolizing, phenomena other than themselves, but primarily with symbolizing them in such a manner as to involve the observers emotional and esthetic capacities, his power to experience love and hate, pity and indignation, joy and sorrow, and his ability to sense the beautiful and the ugly, the attractive and repulsive. Art and literature are not concerned with depicting circumstances and disseminating information which involves merely the intellect. The truly great artist, we believe, rouses hate in the observer for things that the intellect will adjudge as hateful and love for that which the intellect will adjudge as lovable, attachment to that which is truly beautiful and repulsion from that which is indeed ugly or evil. But whether his success as an artist depends primarily upon his ability to direct the emotions properly, or rather merely upon his ability to stir them into being, is one of the perennially debated questions touching the nature of art. Dante's delight in the suffering of the sinner may be repugnant to our moral sense. Should we, therefore, deny him a place among the world's great poets, or adjudge the

[15] There is practically unanimous agreement among the chapters that deal with the role of symbol in literature and art, that its characteristic, *if not its exclusive purpose,* is that of involving the feelings or the emotions of the observer. Even Greene who is most insistent upon maintaining the position that art is "neither hedonistic nor practical" and that it does not address itself "merely to the intellect or merely to the emotions, but to both in fruitful harmony," nevertheless also writes that, "It [art] exhibits a subject-matter of human concern, and it does so in such a way as to make evident the artist's *emotive* response to this concern and to evoke in the observer a corresponding *emotive* response" (p. 235).

Tindall, basing himself on Cassirer, writes, "whereas science builds it [the universe] of facts, art builds it of feelings, intuitions of quality and the other distractions of our inner life" (p. 340).

On the relations of architecture to the emotions, see Burchard's chapter, pp. 384, 386, 394–395, and in many other places.

particular passage in which this unworthy rejoicing is expressed as "artistically inferior" to the rest of the poem?

Most of us fortunately resist all attempts to divorce our ethical from our esthetic sensitivities, so that we welcome all philosophical efforts to identify the beautiful with the good, or the good with the beautiful. But philosophical niceties notwithstanding, the experience of any normal individual involves him in situations in which he finds his ethical judgments and his esthetic sensitivities not so much in conflict with one another as apparently unrelated to one another. Obviously the greater the perfection of the artistic creation, *i.e.,* the greater its power to involve our esthetic sensitivities, the more difficult does it become to judge it on any basis other than the esthetic. A sufficiently effective esthetic appeal can and has overcome ethical considerations[16] in the judgment of works of literature or art. Only those who had an unwavering loyalty to a moral doctrine which for them is the final arbiter of their opinions and tastes, have had the courage or temerity —depending upon one's point of view—to place or to urge the placing of works of widely acknowledged literary and artistic merit on a list of the condemned and forbidden.

As for the "liberals" who oppose indexes and censorship, only a handful are willing to follow their position to its logical conclusion of opposing all and any censorship. Almost all would agree that the work which both lacks artistic merit and advocates or represents a morality obnoxious to our "normative insights," should be legally banned from circulation. The question then arises as to the point at which a work's artistic merit makes its moral quality irrelevant. No universally accepted measuring rod has as yet been found by anyone.

A somewhat larger number will argue that the artist need be as little concerned with the moral implications of his creations as is the scientist with the ethical import of his discoveries or creations. Beauty being as ultimate as truth, Beauty for Beauty's sake has as much validity as Truth for Truth's sake.

Most of us, however, who would argue against indexes generally

[16]Greene would apparently deny to any work the claim to artistic merit if it does not offer what he designates as "normative enlightenment" (p. 235). He nowhere defines what he means by that. The great artists, he says, have in common "the effort to express their normative insights as precisely and eloquently as possible. . . ." But an artist's "normative insights" may do great violence to the "normative insights" of the generality of society. Does the merit of his work depend upon the quality of his "normative insights" or on the "significant form" in which those insights have been presented?

would most likely do so first for pragmatic reasons, namely, that in the long run the harm of censorship is greater than that of freedom. In addition, we would base our position on the belief that the mature individual can distinguish between the beautiful and the moral and that he can enjoy the beautiful without injury to his moral personality. Finally we would most likely express our conviction, all experience notwithstanding, that all "significant form" inevitably embodies overtones of significant moral quality. Our esthetic sensitivities cannot be poignantly involved without at the same time beneficently involving our ethical sensitivities. That argument is more an expression of hope than a description of reality. It is, nevertheless, an irrepressible argument and as such may indicate that it represents reality at least in part.

Moreover the literary and artistic symbol being concerned primarily with the involvement of mood, aspiration, and emotion, its quality as a symbol may be judged either by the profundity of the emotion or mood or by the multiplicity of emotions or moods which it involves. Each one of the tragedies of Shakespeare as complete works involves one great human emotion or mood. *Romeo and Juliet* involves the love of young lovers, *Othello* blind jealousy, *Macbeth* unbridled ambitions, *Hamlet* wavering resolution. These universal human emotions are symbolized in great variety of expression and embodiment. None can doubt the emotion which each play involves. *Othello* calls forth no mood of wavering resolution, nor *Hamlet* of jealousy, nor *Macbeth* of love. But just as often the great literary or artistic symbol is capable of symbolizing a vast variety of different and sometimes even conflicting moods and emotions. *Moby Dick, Ulysses, Peer Gynt* will continue to be subjects for wide differences of opinion among those who will seek to spell their symbolism out discursively, both in matters of detail and in matters of basic meaning.[17]

IX

In some areas of human concern the efficacy of a phenomenon as a symbol depends both upon the specificity of the phenomenon other than itself to which it refers and its capacity for bringing that phenomenon into consciousness in a manner that involves the aspirations,

[17] See Tindall, pp. 346 ff.

moods, emotions, and actions of the observer in a previously determined desirable manner.

Such in essence is the religious symbol.

The specific phenomenon to which all religious symbols refer *in so far as they are religious* is that which is considered as the fundamental all embracing ultimate reality.[18] In the religious tradition of the West the most common symbol for that ultimate reality is *God*. Hence the efficacy of the religious symbols in Western tradition is judged by their ability to involve man's emotional endowments and overt acts in a relationship of loyalty toward, dependence upon, hope in, obedience of, joy in, and love for, God. The symbol may involve the emotional endowments of the observer with an almost infinite number of specific phenomena other than God. But if it stops short of involving him finally with God, it may be one of a number of other types of symbols, national, personal, esthetic, or scientific, but it is not a religious symbol.

Like all other symbols, the religious symbol also tends inevitably to gather around it an increasing number of secondary significances, which constantly threaten to overshadow or crowd out its primary significance.[19] Thus the Hebrew Scripture designates a number of phenomena as "signs," among them being the Sabbath (Exodus 31, 17), the fringes in the corners of the four cornered outer garment (Numbers 15, 37-41), and circumcision (Genesis 17, 11). Over a period of some three thousand years of history, however, each one of these symbols took on meanings and referents neither mentioned nor envisioned by Scripture.

[18]See appendix by Paul J. Tillich and Greene to Greene's paper, p. 283.

[19]There is no religious symbol that has *only* religious significance, that is, one which involves the observer only in a relationship to God, without involving him in relationship with any other referent. Such a limited religious symbol is impossible because all religious symbols involve some kind of action, and all action involves associations with specific place and time, with objects and, above all, with other human beings. These associations inevitably acquire significance in their own right and may come to be valued in and by themselves, regardless of their relationship to any ultimate reality.

The question of priority in time between the primary religious significance of a symbol and its secondary sociological significance depends of course upon one's approach to the history of religion. If one rejects completely any kind of Revelation, then one argues that the secondary sociological significances of the Sabbath preceded its primary religious significance. But would one argue, for example, that for the Christian the sociological significances of the Cross preceded its religious significance, or that for the Jew the sociological significance of the *Mezzuzah* placed on the doorpost preceded its religious significance?

In the life of observant Jews the Sabbath rouses all the memories and emotions associated with family life, with mother kindling and blessing the Sabbath lights, with father pronouncing the *Kiddush* (the benediction sanctifying the Sabbath), with the father's blessing of the children, with the family in its best clothes gathering around the table for the festive meal of the week, and with any number of other deeply rooted emotional experiences. The Sabbath as a symbol has become a most effective instrument for galvanizing all the infinite strands of meaning and emotion associated with the intricate web of human relationships ever present in a normally functioning family. As such, the Sabbath has become for many for whom God no longer has any meaning, the symbol of Jewish family solidarity. Family solidarity undoubtedly is a most desirable virtue and activates a great number of desirable emotional experiences, such as love and loyalty. Scripture, however, declares the Sabbath to be "The sign between Me and the children of Israel forever that in six days the Lord made heaven and earth and on the seventh day He rested." Hence, if the Sabbath as symbol is limited only to the involvements implied by family solidarity, important and significant as these undoubtedly are, it ceases to be a religious symbol.

Scripture specifically designates the "commandments of the Lord" as the phenomenon which should be brought into the center of consciousness by the fringes in the corner of the outer garment. Note that it is to "the commandments of the Lord," that they are to direct attention and not simply to "commandments" issuing from folkways or group customs. Nor are they anywhere declared to be efficacious protectors against evil spirits or unfortunate mishaps. When viewed purely on the folkloristic or magical level the fringes cease to be a religious symbol. They become instead either a charm or an anachronistic group custom.

Finally, circumcision is enjoined by Scripture as a sign of the covenant between God and Abraham and his descendants. As such, it is to be performed at a specified time and in a specified manner. Hence, if performed as a health measure even in the specified manner and time, it loses its character not merely as a religious symbol but as symbol *per se;* for that which is done because in itself it is good for one's physical health, has no symbolic import to the actor. To the observer it may be symbolic of the value that man places on health, in that he is willing to subject an infant to great pain merely in the hope that it will be good for his health even though an infinite number of males have lived long healthy lives without being circumcised. But surely circumcision used as symbol of man's concern with health has little or no symbolic meaning to anyone.

The religious symbols of Judaism, as of all great world religions, have constantly been exposed, therefore, to these three abuses. 1) Those charged with significant, desirable personal or group experience have been divorced from their religious moorings and associated with purely sociological and humanistic referents. 2) Many have been divorced from their symbolic character by being transformed into interesting folkways, important national bonds, or magically effective rites. 3) Some have lost their symbolic meaning by being emptied of all significance other than the desirable results inherently flowing from them to him who is immediately affected by them.

X

The Relationship of the Symbol to its Referent

Since the symbol is the fundamental, and probably the only vehicle of conscious human thought, the problem of the relationship of the symbol to its referent, *i.e.,* of one phenomenon to another phenomenon which it calls into the center of consciousness, is in a way but the old epistemological problem of the relationship between our ideas and the world which we know or believe to be independent of and different from us or our ideas. But the two problems are not identical, and we shall not discuss the purely epistemological aspects of our problem. We are concerned with investigating the differences, if any, between the relationship of the scientific symbol to its referent and that of the artistic and religious symbols to their referents.

1. *The scientific symbol and its referent.*

Until comparatively recently it was universally accepted that the distinction of the scientific symbol consisted in this: that its referent was always in some manner directly or indirectly accessible to one or more of the five senses. Hence, the existence of the referent as independent from its symbol[20] was believed to be empirically demonstrable. Moreover, a scientific symbol whether it be a one word concept like "the field," or a more elaborately formulated law like $E = mc^2$, was viewed as having a "one-to-one relationship" with its referent which could be demonstrated by ordering the referent in a pattern suggested by the scientific symbol and then actually observing that it behaved in the manner indicated by the symbol. Hence the validity of a scientific symbol depended upon its formal correspondence to a pattern formed by sensibly observable phenomena.

Scientists have been making great efforts to remain loyal to this conception of the scientific symbol. But they have repeatedly gone beyond the limits thus indicated, and used symbols whose referents were by no means empirically demonstrable. These deviations from the norm are most often due not to intellectual carelessness or willfulness but rather to intellectual necessity. Parts cannot be constructively studied without relating them to the whole and the whole which in this instance is the universe, can never be known directly through the senses. When, therefore, science creates for the whole a symbol which it validates to its own satisfaction on the basis of the evidence it gathers from the empirically accessible parts, it is no longer scientific.

Religion's profoundest differences with science occur in the area in which science employs such nonscientific symbols, as, for example, the "wound up clock" as "scientific" symbol for the universe. The wisest among the scientists always were conscious of the nonscientific character of these symbols, and distinguished between them and other scientific symbols by referring to them as tentative or working hypotheses. Nevertheless, they felt in duty bound vigorously to defend their

[20]Albert Hofstadter's very keen analysis of "The Scientific and Literary Uses of Language" takes as one of its main theses the proposition that "in science language is an external means—a means of expression which is not itself an element in the expressed content—in literature language is an internal means [if "means" is the right word here]—a mode of expression which is itself an element in the expressed content" (p. 294). What is true of language as symbol both in science and literature is true of all kinds of symbols when used for scientific or artistic purposes.

A. J. Ayer's version of Logical Positivism which would apply the test of possible empirical verification to establish the validity or "sense" of all symbols, is excellently discussed by Whitney J. Oates in his paper, "Being and Value" (pp. 462 ff.). A fuller analysis of that position and an attempted refutation of it, is presented by Wilbur M. Urban in his *Language and Reality*, The Macmillan Company, New York, 1939, see index under Positivism (Logical).

scientific character since they appeared to be the "coimplicates"[21] indispensable to the rational organization of all the other empirically validated scientific symbols. At this moment science seems to be in an era of bewilderment, precisely because the more recently empirically validated symbols of parts of the universe, such as the "nuclear particles" and the "quantum" do not as yet point to a "coimplicate," which would organize all the available scientific symbols into an acceptably rational system.

But these aspects of the problem take us beyond our immediate concern, to define the character of the scientific symbol. The scientific symbol then has two basic characteristics. 1) It is a phenomenon that is consciously and carefully limited in its capacity to bring to the awareness of its observer phenomena other than itself. The ideal scientific concept is one that has only a one-to-one relationship between itself and its referent. 2) The observer of the scientific symbol can verify empirically that the referent exists independent of its symbol and validate the truth or efficacy of the symbol through empirically establishing the *formal* relationship between symbol and referent.

2. *The literary and artistic symbol and its referent*

The literary and artistic symbol is not pointed primarily toward an empirically verifiable referent but toward stimulating the emotional and esthetic sensitivities of its human observer. These sensitivities are intertwined with the basic instincts of sex, hunger, fear, and play. These instincts are basically self-activating. But they can also be stimulated into action. On the exclusively animal level they are to the best of our knowledge stimulated only by phenomena that impinge from without directly upon the animal's senses. On the human level they are stimulated both by phenomena that impinge directly on the senses and by phenomena that exist only in the human imagination. A human mind suffering from hallucinations induces emotional reactions in the body of its possessor that are completely unrelated to the phenomena immediately impinging upon the individual's senses. To the best of our knowledge, animals may go "mad" because of a

---

[21]The role of "necessary coimplicates" in all our thinking and symbolizations, whether it be scientific, artistic, or religious, is elaborately presented by Urban, *op. cit.,* see index "Coimplicates" (of Experience).

complete breakdown of their nervous systems resulting in the utter collapse of their powers of muscular coordination, but they are not subject to observable extended periods of hallucination. Artistic and literary symbols feed the human imagination and stimulate our emotional sensitivities with a power at times approaching the power of the stimulus occasioned by the referent itself. Since the literary and artistic symbol impinges upon the emotional sensitivities of the observer primarily through his imagination, its referent need not be a phenomenon whose being or existence could be empirically experienced. Hence the referents of literature and art need in no way be "scientific" facts. It is sufficient that they be "figments of the imagination" with which we can temporarily indentify ourselves sympathetically. I stress the word "temporarily," because a more permanent self-identification with a figment of the imagination is among the most patent symptoms of a diseased human mind. Kafka's cockroach struggling to get out of bed was never seen by anyone. But the reader of that story can sympathetically emotionally identify himself with that struggle and thus in part with the cockroach itself. The emotional satisfaction produced by that story depends entirely upon its power to stimulate the emotions of the reader through leading him into a temporary self-identification with the cockroach. If even while reading the story the reader is not conscious of the fact that this is not the story of a cockroach that ever was, or that there is no real identification between himself and the cockroach, his emotional experience will be profounder. But it also may be very harmful to him, as was the identification of many a young reader with the inner struggles of Goethe's young Werther, leading in a number of instances to actual suicide.[22]

The literary and artistic symbol in so far as its efficacy is concerned, belongs therefore, to a category altogether different from that of the scientific symbol. The efficacy of the scientific symbol depends upon the observer's ability to observe and manipulate phenomena outside himself, in accordance with the pattern suggested by the symbol, and arrive at predictable results. The efficacy of literary and artistic symbols depends upon their ability to move an observer to experience emotional states appropriate to the phenomena, that *for the moment* are in

[22]See Greene's discussion of Bullough's principle of "psychic distance" as indispensable to profound and mature appreciation of the arts (p. 253).

possession of his imagination. The scientific symbol reflects objective truth and reality, in so far as it directs the senses to phenomena outside themselves. The literary and artistic symbol reflects objective truth and reality, in so far as it directs the emotions to phenomena other than themselves which have power to affect them. "A figment of the imagination" may not be real scientifically, *i.e.,* it may not be validated by the senses, but it is very real esthetically, *i.e.,* it is validated by the emotions.

Whether on the highest level the esthetically real must also be at least the conceivably scientifically real, depends upon one's opinion regarding the manner in which the artistic creation is to be approached by the observer. For those who would completely divorce the intellect from esthetic experience there is no relationship whatsoever between one realm of reality and another. They are the counterpart of the mystic in religion who claims all attempts to "know God" through the intellect to be not only futile but blasphemous. But those who believe that music is not only to be listened to, paintings and architecture not only to be viewed, poetry or novels not only to be read, *but also understood,* would maintain that on the highest level no artistic symbol has a scientifically inconceivable referent. One listening to a symphony does not necessarily have to put his mind and imagination to sleep, keeping only his emotions exposed to the sound emanating from the orchestra. On the contrary, his emotional response may be all the more profound precisely because his mind and imagination are involved on an equally high level—in translating what he hears into terms equally amenable to sight, smell, touch, or motion. Music does not make its impact upon us only through the ears,[23] any more than a painting impinges merely upon our sight. Through the imagination, what is heard by the ears is transformed into a phenomenon delightful to the eyes or the touch, and what is seen by the eyes the imagination transforms into phenomena delighting the ears or the nose. Hence literary or artistic symbols whose referents are inconceivable are either essentially religious symbols in so far as they incline man's mind to contemplation of the Ultimate or his emotions to involvement in some appropriate relationship to the Ultimate, or else they have "meaning" only so far as they refer to disembodied ideas. Man's noblest nonreligious artistic and literary symbols have, however, always had referents

[23]See preceding reference to Greene's paper.

that may not have been historically real, but were either believed to be real or were at least conceived as scientifically possible.

To be sure, there never was a Hamlet who actually spoke to the ghost of his foully murdered father. But except for that one incident, which in Shakespeare's day was believed to be altogether scientifically conceivable, there is nothing that Hamlet says or does which might not have been said or done by a "real" person. Had Shakespeare depicted in Hamlet an "unreal" person, Hamlet could never have become the great literary symbol that he is. But conceivable scientific reality alone would not be enough to make him a literary symbol. To those aspects of Hamlet which are conceivably empirically approachable, Shakespeare added aspects which while beyond the reach of the senses were completely within the grasp of the emotions—the Hamlet of deep mourning, of unfulfilled love, but, above and beyond all, the Hamlet of indecision, of resolution repeatedly thwarted by the "pale hue of thought." To establish the reality of this esthetically and emotionally real Hamlet, it is sufficient to have not an actual, historically real Hamlet but a conceivably real Hamlet.

The literary and artistic symbol, therefore, has the following characteristics: 1) Its referent need not be "scientifically real" but should be "conceivably scientifically real." 2) Its referent should be capable of sensitizing the emotional capacities of the observer—preferably without doing violence to his intellectual capacities or ethical sensitivities.

3) *The Religious Symbol and its Referent*

We said above that the fundamental characteristic of the religious symbol is that its ultimate referent is God. None of the Western religions have many symbols that refer exclusively to God. Judaism has none but the unpronounced and unpronounceable Tetragrammaton. All other symbols in Judaism refer to God only through the mediation of another phenomenon referred to by the symbol. It is in this other phenomenon that God's presence is involved. The Sabbath symbolizes first a created universe and only secondarily Him Who created it. The fringes directly symbolize the Commandments that are to be remembered and only secondarily Him Who is the author of the Commandments. Circumcision symbolizes directly the covenant between God and Abraham and only indirectly the God with Whom the covenant is thus renewed in every generation.

a) *The scientific aspects of the religious symbol*

The religious symbol partakes of the nature of a scientific symbol in the fact that its referents on both levels are specific, *viz.*, the universe and God—the law and God—the covenant and God. But that is where the similitude between the two types of symbols ceases, and the conflict between them begins.

In so far as the religious symbol refers exclusively to God or to those manifestations of God that have thus far remained completely beyond empirical verification, the religious symbols resemble the "pseudo-scientific" symbols of science, such as the wound up clock discussed above. The "created universe" symbolized by the Sabbath is as "scientific" as the universe symbolized by the machine or the clock. The differences between these "universal" symbols of religion and science derive in part from the differences in phenomena with which both are primarily concerned. For science derives its hypotheses or "necessary coimplicates" from the phenomena which are made available to it by the five senses, namely, the physical universe, while religion derives its "necessary coimplicates" primarily, though not exclusively, from phenomena which are not subject to direct or conceivable empirical examination, namely, the moral and ethical conscience of man, his innate sense of responsibility and guilt, his sense of awe and wonder. But in part these differences are due to the temperament of the individual investigator, for there are many today who after examining the same phenomena arrive at different conclusions regarding the nature of the "necessary coimplicates." On this level the profoundest conflicts and reconciliations between science and religion have repeatedly occurred from the days of Philo to our own.

But the conflicts between science and religion which take place on what we designated as the secondary level of reference, of the religious symbol, are in many ways more damaging to religion and raise some fundamental issues regarding the nature of the relationship between the religious symbol and its referent. The relationship between the fringes and the Law which they symbolize is as clearly established as the relationship between the scientific symbol E and the actual physical energy which it symbolizes. The Law is there to be seen and read. Moreover, the fringes are, by Rabbinic legislation, so intertwined as to form a pattern corresponding to the number 613 which is the traditional number of Commandments in the Torah. But these fringes are to remind us also of the divine origin of the Law. In the passage discussing the fringes, nothing specific is said about the manner in which the Law was given to Israel. But it is minutely described in Exodus 19. If then one is to recall when he looks upon the fringes the events described in that chapter, events which reportedly occurred in historic time and mundane space, is he called upon to apply to the fringes the same test that he applies to a scientific symbol, namely, to see if its referent is subject to or conceivably subject to independent empirical verification? Or is the religious symbol's validity to be compared rather to the validity of the literary and artistic symbol, namely, by its power to involve the emotions of the observer in an acceptable manner rather than by our ability to check its correspondence with its referent?

Since the days of Philo there have always been many who would validate the religious symbol by treating it as a "pseudoscientific" symbol on its primary level, namely, in so far as it refers directly to God, and as a literary or artistic symbol, or "myth," on its secondary level, namely, in so far as it refers directly to phenomena associated with time and space, and, therefore, actually or conceivably subject to independent verification by the senses. On this secondary level they stress the religious symbol's power to involve the emotions and actions in an acceptable manner, rather than its reference to phenomena other than itself which were or are empirically approachable. I doubt whether this method can successfully preserve the efficacy of the religious symbol to involve even the emotions, let alone the actions of their observers over an extended period of time. The referent of the religious symbol on this secondary level must have more than mere artistic or literary character if the symbol is to maintain its religious efficacy.

The present crisis in religion is due, it seems to me, not so much to the "pseudoscientific" aspects of our religious symbols as to those of their aspects which originated as scientific symbols and now can be accepted by many as little more than literary or artistic symbols. As such they can be and in altogether too many instances are, accepted because they furnish pleasant *temporary* emotional involvements even as do literary and artistic symbols. But they do not have the power to sustain over extended periods of time those desirable actions which inferentially should follow upon the intellectual and emotional involvements stimulated by the effective religious symbol. Efforts to preserve the religious symbol by transforming it into a national, sociological, or artistic symbol have indeed helped to preserve it as a symbol, but have not been too helpful in preserving it as a religious symbol. Religious symbols must, therefore, on the primary level be "pseudoscientific" in the nonderogatory sense in which we use that term in this paper; and scientific on the secondary level, if they are to be both effective and religious. They cannot on either level be primarily literary or artistic.

But having said that, we hasten to add that, just as the great literary and artistic symbols are enhanced by their conformity or conceivable conformity to referents that have an existence independent of the symbols, so the great scientific or pseudoscientific religious symbols are enhanced when their expression involves great literary and artistic symbolism. The artistic, literary, and sociological expressions that have become part of the Sabbath enhanced its efficacy as symbol of God the Creator. The efficacy of the Scroll of the Torah as symbol of God's self-revelation to man is enhanced by the manner in which it is written and chanted and by the artistic beauty of the Ark in which it is kept in the synagogue. The Jewish High Holidays—New Year's Day and the Day of Atonement—as symbols of man's responsibility toward his Creator, are the more effective because of the liturgy, the chants, and the elaborate synagogue ritual enacted on those days. But if Judaism is to remain a religion, these artistic and literary addenda dare never replace the substance. Examples without number to illustrate this predicament can be readily adduced from the experiences of all Western religions. What is happening to Christmas in America, is probably the best illustration of the danger to religion when its symbols begin to have nonreligious referents which in number and immediate appeal overshadow its distinctly religious referents.

The case is somewhat different where the religious symbol is one like *Kol Nidre,* the legal formula for the annulment of vows, impressively chanted in all traditional synagogues immediately before the services on the eve of the Day of Atonement. The *Kol Nidre* has become for many the symbol of Jewish martyrdom for the faith, because of its association particularly with incidents that are believed to have occurred during the Spanish Inquisition and Expulsion. Assuming that the association of *Kol Nidre* with the Spanish Inquisition or any other particular historic event is not "scientific," the loyalty of many Jews to their faith under persecution *is* a scientifically established fact. Moreover, knowing as we do that the *Kol Nidre* when first composed had no relationship whatsoever to loyalty to one's faith under persecution, the gradual development of *Kol Nidre* as the symbol of this particular historic group experience, is nevertheless altogether valid. One can try to explain this development by examining the content or the melody of *Kol Nidre*. There undoubtedly must be something in both the words and the chant, as well as in the association of these words and chant with certain historic experiences of the group. But all of these may not be absolutely scientifically established. It is enough in this instance for *Kol Nidre* to serve even as an *arbitrarily chosen artistic symbol of an actual historic experience*. Its efficacy as a religious symbol then depends completely upon its innate power to involve the emotions of the congregant in a manner that would incline him to be loyal to the faith. The validity of the scientifically established larger experience of the group as a whole which *Kol Nidre* symbolizes is sufficient to validate the symbol, since the symbol itself is not dependent upon scientifically historic validation.

A group may thus arbitrarily bestow upon an actual phenomenon, in this instance the *Kol Nidre,* the status of a religious symbol, a status which is inherently valid because it is based on historic associations. But in such an instance it must be obvious that the association between the symbol and its referent is only a little more inherent than that between *table* and its referent. Such religious symbols retain their efficacy only if they possess inherent artistic or literary power to focus attention on the referent as long as the referent continues to be poignant and meaningful. If the referent remains significant while the symbol's artistic or literary expression loses its power to focus attention, the referent "will seek" another symbol. If the referent ceases to be significant while the symbol retains its artistic power, it "will seek" another referent. Should the "search" in either instance fail, the surviving member of this "phenomenon of pairing or coupling"[24] will also perish. For just as no "event" can become an experience without first acquiring unto itself a symbol, and just as no experience can con-

24Schutz, p. 143.

tinue to be significant when its symbol loses the power to attract attention to it, thus also can no symbol continue to hold interest if its referent ceases to be of significance. Referents may discard old symbols and take on new ones. Symbols may detach themselves from old referents and attach themselves to new ones. But neither can long maintain a solitary existence. Like a cut flower, either may live on for a while, but the end is inevitable. In every generation there have been old referents looking for new symbols and old symbols looking for new referents. When this search goes unrewarded, religions die and civilizations disintegrate.

Comment on Papers of John E. Burchard, Theodore M. Greene, Albert Hofstadter, and William Y. Tindall

By M. L. ROSENTHAL

I

THE THEME of the present Conference is "symbols and society." It may therefore be useful to approach these distinguished papers with a view to their direct relevance to this theme.

In doing so, I wish first to call attention to two other papers, prepared for the Thirteenth Conference: Harold D. Lasswell's "Key Symbols, Signs and Icons"[1] and Richard McKeon's "Symbols, Myths, and Arguments."[2] Both these essays seek, as McKeon puts it, to "isolate the social use of symbols" and therefore may provide at least a tentative "practical" frame of reference for the discussion in the Fine Arts section.

McKeon distinguishes two kinds of socially active symbols. Symbols of *external* communication express the "intention, attitude, desire, or expectation of one person or group to others." And symbols of *internal* values, "bonds of community and stimuli to action," are attached directly to basic institutions—"my family, my church, or my country."

External symbols—the atom bomb, for instance, or the forced labor camp—are easy to identify but hard to use: "In all negotiations, one side can profit by ambiguity while the other side must, unless it finds an alternative symbol practicable in the situation, remove ambiguity by action. . . . There is a region of necessary and fruitful ambiguity in all communications designed to lead to action, precisely because symbolic communication is necessary only when both parties are in

[1] Harold D. Lasswell, "Key Symbols, Signs and Icons," *Symbols and Values: An Initial Study,* Chapter XIII, pp. 199–204.
[2] Richard McKeon, "Symbols, Myths and Arguments," *ibid.,* Chapter II, pp. 13–38.

agreement on the problem that calls for action but not on principles and purposes."

"Primary" *internal* symbols, such as the hearth or the Cross or the Crescent, elicit an immediate response within the group, of a kind which neither myth nor argument have the ability, by force of content alone, to bring about. Their impact alone will summon up that unquestioning "sense of rightness" which governs our action with regard to others. Myth and argument—"the epic or origins of the institutions, the creed or principles that animate it, the gospel or purposes it fulfils"—do, it is true, serve as "secondary" symbols here. "The development of human conscience and sensitivity to values is precisely the history of the operation of symbols which in their fullest statement in art, philosophy, and religion are subject to repeated and divergent interpretation."

These two kinds of symbols, we are told, "are interrelated since the symbols that unite a group determine the significance of the symbols that set forth its intended actions." McKeon tells us, finally, that we have adequate symbols for unity "in overt conflict and war," but that such a basis is "almost totally lacking or is inoperative in the absence of hostile symbols employed in action or in the presence of hostile symbols ambiguously preparing for action." For primary symbols of the desperately needed "concord and agreement" of mankind at large, we must turn after all to the philosophers, poets, and prophets.

Both kinds of symbols, presumably, would be included under what Lasswell calls "key signs": "the most important and frequently repeated components" of the "pattern of standardized interpretations" of "symbol events" and "the related patterns of signs." These key signs or symbols, it must be remembered, tend to be fairly rigid in themselves. Even the "secondary symbols" of McKeon—among them the Homeric epics, the sacred Books of Jew and Christian and Moslem, and the writings of Marx—have served their social purpose less through literal content, as he shows, than through the "impulse" they provide "to a common life and to common actions."

". . . the principal fact about key signs," Lasswell writes, "appears to be the conservative, standardizing role that they play in society. They are cues to collective action and occasions of unifying common experience. It is true that the common experience may thrust beyond the confines of any locality and foster the occurrence or spread of great transformations. On the other hand, the standardization of perception may falsify the intelligence function in a given society and put a barrier in the path of acting integratively in the presence of new conditions. The specific signs that come to play an outstanding role owe something to the arrangement of component elements (style). The principal factors, however, appear to be the condensation of salient allusions to a crucial context. The context may be the configuration of incidents in a crisis" (as the Crucifixion provides the important context for the Cross as symbol, or "events connected with the historic founder of the religion" for the Tree in the Buddhist world), or it may be "the fundamental values and practices of a society" (*Lares* and *Penates,* for example). "Although some light can be shed by examining the *formal characteristics* (style) of signs, it appears more probable that *critical contexts are more important determinants.* The critical context, for instance, refers to such fundamental events in the development of a culture (or subculture) as the happenings during the formative period."

How relevant are these formulations to the approaches adopted in the papers for the art section? How important are they in the consideration of symbols of art and their relation to society?

Without here going into the substance of the matter, I must suggest that the very posing of these questions is a reminder of the general neglect by scholarship and criticism of the relation between the arts at their best (the kind of art that we acknowledge produces masterpieces), and popular forms and works of art, as well as of the somewhat ambiguous status of drama in our day. What symbols emerge in popular art-forms? In what sense do some characteristic works of this kind constitute symbolic wholes? What social motives and perspectives do they reveal, and how do these compare with what the "higher" forms reveal? What similarities and differences are inherent in the symbolic operation of works at these different levels? I propose these questions, without further reference to them now, for possible exploration in the sectional meetings.

II

Theodore M. Greene's "normative symbols," since their primary function is "To serve as vehicles for many different kinds of evaluation," since rhetorical efficacy is among their major powers, and since emotion plays an "essential but limited role" in their operation, are clearly subject to the social uses which McKeon distinguishes. These normative symbols are conceived as consolidators of group unity, and as Greene's argument works up from lower types to art at its highest and the Absolute, his program becomes almost identical with McKeon's.

It is significant that both writers stress the difficulty of the task. "Normative symbols are of use only to those who can and will use them," writes Greene. "Indeed, a culture with a limited sense of values will neglect most of the first rate symbols at its disposal, and incur more and more cheap vehicles . . . of the superficial values which it in fact cherishes." And McKeon: "These symbols will not themselves be widely effective . . . for a long time."

"Widely effective," however, the symbolism of a rich and complex art cannot be, unless some great change in social attitudes comes into existence and makes it possible for art itself, and particularly certain great works, to arouse that immediate emotional and attitudinal communion needed to draw a group's ranks in close together. And, indeed, if we study the conception of "pure" esthetic symbolism in modern writers on art, we cannot help being struck by the emergence of a veritable religion of art—a mystical idealization of the mystery-laden, virtually untranslatable artistic symbol and its formal vehicles as at once dramatically compelling in their sensuous, concentrated intensity and richly multiple in their suggestiveness:

> As the feeling in the symbol is more important than our emotional response, so the symbol is more important than what, by virtual analogy, it suggests. Lacking embodiment and the semblance of actuality, what it suggests turns back to its source to recapture a body and enlarge it. The symbol is not there like a sign to point to something else, to take the place of something else, or even to stand for it, but to display itself with all it has created and welcomed home (William Y. Tindall, Chapter XI, p. 350).

> Literature does not make men respond to the qualities and values of things in one way or another; it gives them those qualities and values, and they respond in accordance with their interests and bents (Albert Hofstadter, Chapter X, p. 333).

> The symbols which our period is forming I call "anonymous symbols" as they are attached to no religious faith or political system but they

are direct projections for what is going on in the human soul (Sigfried Giedion, quoted in John Ely Burchard, Chapter XII, p. 383).[3]

Monumentality consists in the eternal need of the people to create symbols revealing their inner life, their religious and political aspiration (*loc. cit.,* p. 384).

. . . esthetically satisfying form is a very mysterious thing. . . . It is *sui generis* and therefore not reducible to, or definable in terms of, anything else; it is not intellectually demonstrable by reference to any principles or laws. . . . In short, it is, like all irreducible ultimates in human experience, *ineffable* (Theodore M. Greene, Chapter IX, p. 246).[4]

In selecting the passages just quoted, I have admittedly cut across the considerable differences of specific subject and viewpoint among these distinguished and original papers: the contrasts drawn between poetic and scientific discourse by Greene and Hofstadter, the former tending to identify the motives of art and religion with one another, the latter those of art and rhetoric; the rather skeptical inquiry into the possibilities for a new symbolism in modern architecture by Burchard; and the exhaustive review of definitions of the symbol and its manifestations and functions in modern literature by Tindall. These very differences in perspective, however, make all the more striking the almost unanimous apotheosis of the symbol, or at least of whatever it is that brings the symbol into being—whether the symbol is discovered as one element of a work or as the whole work itself.

One way of accounting for this apotheosis is by reference to the well known romantic repossession, in the past century—deliberately accelerated by the French Symbolists—of certain "religious" aims: to induce a state of spiritual exaltation, to suggest experience beyond sense-perception, and to locate value beyond the reach of the worldly philistine. A powerful tendency in modern literature has sustained this development in many ways, often subjecting traditional religious symbols themselves to the strain of concerns apparently alien or hostile

[3]Burchard does not dispute the sentiments of Giedion expressed in this quotation and the succeeding one. Indeed he seems to approve of their spirit, while doubting their further applicability.

[4]It is true that on pages 270–271 Greene attacks a different kind of "religion of art"— that which exploits it for the sake of aims extraneous to its nature—social prestige, cultural veneer, professional obscurantism. Such exploitation cannot always be distinguished from the more soundly motivated forms. What may appear merely precious and decadent estheticism *can* turn out very differently. In any case, I heartily agree with the program suggested in the next paragraph (p. 271).

to them: the pagan revisionism of Lawrence's *The Man Who Died,* the caste-mysticism of Yeats's *Purgatory,* the cyclical vision of Yeats's *The Resurrection,* the "blasphemous" estheticism of Joyce's *Portrait of the Artist as a Young Man* with its protagonist's avowed aim of bringing into being, through art, the "uncreated conscience of my race," the daring use of Holy Family imagery throughout Faulkner's *As I Lay Dying*—an imagery at the heart of its symbolic design. It is, in fact, a literature of salvation, corresponding in character to the definition by Greene and Tillich, of "implicitly religious" art (p. 283).

The modern artistic sensibility, seeking salvation from supposedly devitalized institutions, is less fearful of science and technology than of being invaded and destroyed by the ever growing system of uniformities in a highly organized but spiritually limited society. If we are going to talk of artistic symbols and society, therefore, from the point of view of what motives and attitudes these symbols reveal, we shall have to remember that this sensibility, of the artist himself, is a chief symbolic ingredient. (Witness Hofstadter's quotations from Matisse, Proust, Poe, and James, on pages 308–312 of his essay.)

To return to Greene's argument, what exactly is the "normative" symbolism of this pervasive sensibility? Is the artist not speaking, often, for and to a beleaguered minority of people more or less like himself? At the very least, when he says, "See these intensely experienced relationships, this dynamic manifestation of things hitherto unperceived," does he not also imply criticism of a life of unrealized potentialities and of those who are opposed or dead to those potentialities? Is Picasso's *Guernica,* described by Greene and Tillich as implicitly "profoundly religious . . . because it expresses so honestly and powerfully modern man's anguished search for ultimate meaning and his passionate revolt against cruelty and hatred" (p. 283) really an expression for *all* "modern men"? Of course, all men, once their right sensibilities are aroused, *will* be passionately moved by these symbolic "statements," we think. But so will all Russians who respond "appropriately" to the American flag. "Normative symbols are of use only to those who can and will use them."

We often hear the phrase "struggle for the minds and hearts of men," but we never seem to apply it to the *interests* of artist, intellectual, and teacher. Yet it seems that the meaning of art to these groups is both deeply conservative of values and uninhibitedly exploratory—a symbol with power, to repeat Lasswell's language again, to guide "the common experience" so that it "may thrust beyond the confines of any locality and foster the occurrence or spread of great transformations." Is the religion of art, and its recurring symbolism of sacrifice and rebirth, not simultaneously one of those ambiguous power-symbols McKeon describes as "externals" and an "internal," rank-closing value-bearer for those who must wage the long struggle to win acceptance for the "higher normative symbols"? When the struggle is won, no doubt, *all* can identify the "critical context" of the successful symbol. Before then, it will seem to the "outsider" presumptuous, self-contradictory, and blasphemous (as Blake's poem "London" must have appeared to many, despite the passionate concern for love, religion, and his fellow countrymen that underlay the merciless if tragic bitterness of its tone and imagery).

It is, of course, great good fortune that the "enemy" is so often converted unawares by the impact of art, or at least by the double impact of art first experienced naively and then brought into focus through explication. But the initial conversion is too rarely sufficiently bolstered by repetitions of the experience in new ways. As "important and frequently repeated components" of the social pattern of "standardized interpretations," I suppose the symbols of great art are statistically negligible. Though rarely providing the sunny shallows of "standardized interpretation," however, each art has its special kinds of triumphant achievement and moments of epiphany which bring the thrill of recognition and deepening of affection to its audience. Once the ability to respond to genuine art in its own terms has been cultivated, the emotional responsiveness to cruder types of symbol is considerably weakened.[5]

I note the significance of Greene's assertion, in two separate places, first that "the arts are, *par excellence,* the symbols of religious apprehension and religious worship" (p. 237) and then that they are "the vehicle, *par excellence,* of our cultural values" (p. 261)—"the unique expression," in either case, "of authentic normative insight via the artistic organization of an artistic medium" (p. 247). While these as-

---

[5]In his otherwise convincing observations on the comparative "presentational immediacy" of literature and other arts (p. 255), Greene does not seem to take into account the immediacy of drama and film, though these forms would seem to have a special interest from the standpoint of "normative interpretation."

sertions are true, and convincingly demonstrated, it does seem to me that we here approach the point at which science, criticism, and religion of "the daylight regime" must all pause for station announcements. The trained and courageous sensibility of the future, conditioned and sophisticated by exposure to all the influences to which an open intelligence can be submitted, will perhaps one day be able to interpret this particular critical stage in its own development. At present, it seems possible at least to say of the great literary work as a symbol that its rhetoric and structure emerge into affirmation by way of a struggle to reconcile suffering with faith in the possibility of love and meaning. Through evocation, through incantation, through devices of paradox and the dialectical encompassing of opposites, through voices and modulations of tone set against one another, through movement from one stage of insight or tension to the next and always toward the final moment of equilibrium or assertion, this reconciliation takes place. When it does, the triumph is of the candid, passionate, and resurgent poetic imagination rather than of any particular creed or ideology.

III

A further assumption in all four of these papers is that artistic symbols bear a decisive relationship to the realities of human experience and behavior. They can perhaps be manipulated like other symbols—interpreted and used in various ways to serve particular ends—but their true *force* will be as dependent on their faithfulness to motivating reality as on the readiness of "the world" to respond to them. Hofstadter, in developing his conception of the "rhetorical order of literature," employs terminology apparently intended to transcend the conventional distinctions in critical writing between a work of art considered as an independent entity unique in structure and in its organic internal relationships and the work considered in terms of its effect.

> A rhetorical ordering of materials is an ordering of them in such a way as to result in the building of a whole for an experiencer, a whole which becomes intrinsically impressive and interesting to the experiencer and in which the parts, acting and reacting upon each other, repelling and attracting each other, gain a salient relevance to each other, give to each other and the whole, . . . their own interest within that whole.

More shortly, we may define a rhetorical ordering of materials as one in which a) they produce an effect, and b) the effect is intrinsically *interesting, impressive, arresting,* or *vital* (*loc. cit.,* p. 307).

But what is the source, the vital transcending motivation informing this otherwise incomprehensible "intrinsic interest"? It is the reordering of elements of reality by the artist in such a way as to create a new vision of them, a vision prior to any quest for an effect on an audience. Note that the quotations furnished by Hofstadter from Matisse, Proust, and James all relate the creative process to the world of nature, time, etc., in this way; even Poe's audacious propaganda on behalf of one of the most self-caricaturing poems ever written cannot conceal the *a priori* romantic assumptions concerning the elements and relationships that make for a "beautiful" reality in this poet's view (though vulgarized by Poe, who seems here and elsewhere to be carried away by his otherwise laudable interest in *technique* as a value in itself).

The quotations by Matisse and Proust speak to us of values which nature and our own sensibilities make available to us. Without going into the further implications of this "message"—the affirmation of possibility implicit in the creative act, the concern for love and happiness that can go into even an art of sustained revulsion and bitterness, the uses of irony, and the paradoxical insights into history and the life-cycle afforded by art—this one value of intense realization is enough to tie the purest esthetic vision to ordinary reality.

Actually, Hofstadter is saying the same thing, more economically, when he asserts that "in literature language is . . . a mode of expression which is itself an element in the expressed content" (p. 294). Tindall repeats an anecdote in his book *James Joyce* which provides a perfect example; Joyce, we are informed,

> once told Frank Budgen that he had been working all day at two sentences of *Ulysses:* "Perfume of embraces all him assailed. With hungered flesh obscurely, he mutely craved to adore." When asked if he was seeking the *mot juste,* Joyce replied that he had the words already. What he wanted was a suitable order.[6]

Or again, as Hofstadter puts it, "A single act of consciousness holds its varied materials together in an act of immediacy, and is able to do

[6]William Y. Tindall, *James Joyce: His Way of Interpreting the Modern World,* Charles Scribner's Sons, New York, 1950, p. 96.

so because they 'fit' together to make a unified object of mind" (p. 315). From the Joyce quotation, of course, we learn that the "act" may —despite its later impact as something performed in a flash—take a long time; it consists, after all, in discovering an order, and the relationships within that order.

In "The Literary Symbol," Tindall quotes approvingly an unpublished definition of Susanne K. Langer: A work of art is an "unassigned syntactical symbol." He adds: "At once assigned and unassigned, literature troubles esthetic philosophers and moralists alike." But it intrigues and attracts them even more, satisfying their demand for mystery in the lion's den itself of the freely ranging intelligence. It is *their* symbol as well as the artist's. A work of art is an "abstraction" in concrete sense-terms from the realities behind its production: traditions, traits of the culture, confrontations of apparently approved value within the culture and between it and others (oppositions seeking a relationship, as the sexes, religionists and pragmatists, capital and labor, laughtermakers and solemnizers, armies at war), the artist's own life —the work's whole "background." In formal criticism we reduce direct consideration of these source-realities as much as possible; but a work of genuine artistry does encompass and even exploit their emotional potential. It transcends their particular content, however, replacing it by a structure capable of many other kinds of "application" to reality in situations the artist himself could never have dreamed of. And this is the kind of symbol we do want to help us open our minds and spirits to the complexities of reality and the enormous possibilities for transformation of self and society it promises. The "internal means" employed by the arts, to rephrase Hofstadter, are *all* "modes of expression which are themselves elements in the expressed content." Words, and all other sense-vehicles of impression, thought, and feeling capable of being organized in esthetically significant contexts, are the counters of unrealized potentialities; when actually so organized, they make patterns for actual realization.[7]

Hofstadter's comment on the lines by Nash might be expanded from this point of view. Nowhere in these lines (the one that follows— "Dust hath closed Helen's eye"—should be added for the full effect of

---

[7]See Kenneth Burke, "Fact, Inference, and Proof in the Analysis of Literary Symbolism," *Symbols and Values: An Initial Study,* Chapter XIX, pp. 283–306, for a full length examination of this process—and also of the way symbolic "embodiment" takes on its "body."

the passage) does the poet state explicitly his melancholy underlying theme that death must come to all things, even the most beautiful. It is the unusual, brilliant effect of the first line that especially takes the imagination. The notion is so unexpected that at first we may get the *wrong* impression, an impression of heavenly brightness descending and illuminating us—a happy and blessed picture. Then the true picture takes shape, of bright daylight that disappears and leaves the air dark, dull, and cold. The shock of this belated realization adds to its power and intensity, to the effect of irredeemable loss. And finally, therefore, aided by the lines that follow, "Brightness falls from the air," we will think of the universal fact of death, applicable to all things however glorious and lovely.

Supporting this striking image that so takes us unaware, we have first the simple pathos—half folk wisdom and half a "truth" of fairy-tale lore—of "Queens have died young and fair." The fresh, naive direct-ness of the statement saves it from triteness and provides an emotional frame for the preceding line. And afterward, the full elegiac note of sadness is struck in the reminder of the death of Helen of Troy, the great popularly accepted symbol of erotic feminine beauty in all ages since Homer. It is hard to think of Helen *dead,* and the somewhat surprising use of her name with all its evocative power in this way helps give the passage its reverberating richness. The second and third lines lend to the extraordinary image, they follow the quality of a traditional symbol, for they bring to it their own connotations of fallen brightness from mythology and popular legendry.

If only the *whole* poem, "A Litany in Time of Pestilence," had the unexpectedness and brilliance of these lines, its very conventional lamentation, acceptance, and prayer would be transformed thereby into the same kind of "vital realization" they possess. A poet using a traditional theme and symbol will indeed often elaborate on it by add-ing details of action, atmosphere, and sense-impression which convey his own response to it. He hopes thus to gain from its initial advan-tages and at the same time to re-create it into something newly dis-covered. Milton's *Lycidas* gives a striking example in lines 115-131 of how a writer of great power can transmute what would, in weaker hands, be merely trite, simply by force of his own intensely conceived realistic details. The "blind mouths" and "scrannel pipes of wretched straw" (this for its scratchy authenticity of sound especially) and sheep "swoln with wind" that "rot inwardly," are so alive with their disgust that they re-define the traditional associations of pastoral poetry as well as of the relation of the clerical pastor and his flock.

The relation between "reality" and symbolic vision *is* organic, I think, in two senses (not however in the sense rejected by Hofstadter on page 320). It is first of all essential to the *life* of the artist's work. And, secondly, it is essential to its growth as an esthetic structure, the movement organized within it of unrelated or limitedly suggestive elements to its most highly concentrated, multiply supported, and reverberating emotional and moral insight.

IV

Burchard's paper posits a plight of architecture today from the standpoint of the social uses of symbolism we have been considering. Quoting W. G. Constable on the effect of the modern conception of a work of art as "primarily a means" of expression for its maker, and only secondarily "a means of communication to other people," he goes on to account for this development as linked to the rise of logic and science—the organization of social communication around "shared perceptions" rather than around physical or verbal symbols.

It must be admitted that if the sensibility of the artist, encompassing his sense of realities and his vision of a satisfying order, is conceived as a sacred ingredient in the esthetic symbol, and if one use of this conception is the rallying of a struggling potential elite (though this is not quite the right word) to the work of educating an indifferent or hostile society—then the architect would seem to be in an exceptionally weak position. As an artist he cannot *simply* accept and communicate the diluted values which he senses all around him; nor will society pay for his necessarily self-expressive experimentations with what it shortsightedly considers irrelevant or inimical to its needs. Particularly when the "monumental" is in question[8]—created by the eternal need of men for symbols by which to realize their own highest aspirations for ideals and for communion (Giedion); testifying to the future (Hitchcock); providing a new, flexible pattern for higher civic

---

[8]The statements that follow in this sentence concerning the supposed aims of monumental architecture are paraphrased from quotations given by Burchard on pages 383–384, 394–395, and 399.

life (Gropius); declaring love and admiration for these high social purposes (Mumford)—does his dilemma seem sharpest.

But suppose the architect does reject the popular values embodied (or, as he thinks, *buried*) in contemporary institutions? If he does really believe in communion, the future, the higher civic life, etc., there is certainly an area within which the outward *pretensions* of our institutions provide opportunity for him to press forward meaningfully in his work. Has this not been done, as Burchard implies when he cites George H. Nelson as saying that "we have actually created monuments unconsciously, and with them symbols, as we have built our industrial society, our dams, bridges, and factories"? Is not the repression of overt symbolism in architecture, and the emphasis (as suggested in Mendelsohn's essay for the Thirteenth Conference)[9] on materials and structure more than a mere stripping away of the overornamentation of the still recent past? To triumph over nature by her own means—to bridge over, dam up, redirect the power of great rivers, for instance, through structural materials and methods that express our growing knowledge of nature itself—is this not, literally, a *value?* But there is another, related problem. Modern man is certainly conditioned to be powerfully moved by each new conquest of nature, scientific and technical. The thought alone of such conquest thrills him, and evokes varied emotion from purest joy to trembling foreboding. But is he similarly ready to be thrilled by the very idea itself of a United Nations building, good or bad—and behind it by the whole risk of the United Nations undertaking itself?

Such problems are pointers toward value and symbolism in architecture. I do not know whether they indicate conclusively the answer to whether monumentality is necessary or desirable for it today. But certainly the notion held by some people that monumental landmarks are inimical to democracy is a naive one. It is like saying that the once aristocratic virtues—or moral prerogatives—of graciousness, elegance, generosity, and disinterested responsibility to society at large are undemocratic.[10] Why should not the dignity, grandeur, and lavish-

---

[9]Eric Mendelsohn, "The Three Dimensions of Architecture—Their Symbolic Significance," *Symbols and Values: An Initial Study,* Chapter XVII, pp. 235–254.

[10]We have heard this kind of objection launched against Yeats, for instance—in part for his supposed overvaluing these virtues for themselves (which he translates esthetically in "passion," "precision," "ceremony of innocence," etc.) and in part for his attribution of them to the Irish aristocracy.

ness of the monument be part of the common heritage? Be *made* part of it, one should say—and here we are back to the long range perspectives of Greene and McKeon. Why, for that matter, should not the whole past be the heritage of everyone, and the repossession of that heritage lead to the values of the future? As Burchard himself says, "The building as symbol reaches its apogee when . . . combined with sculpture and painting, in an inextricable whole"—because art itself is a valued symbol carrier. People must *look* at and get the sense of the buildings built, be absorbed by the act of doing so; as they must be got to *read* the poetry, and pronounce it, for that matter. The tendency not to *care* what is said, written, played, built, what is thought out, what has happened, is as destructive of the other arts as of architecture—but destructive of logic, rhetoric, and creative science also. It is mere drifting with power, not interest in the possibilities of power, that is to be feared.

Concerning Burchard's six "unanswered questions," I should like to hear his own answers in the light of his quotation from Whitehead (p. 402). We all believe in reconciling "the symbolic code" with "fearless revision" in the interests of "an enlightened reason." I think, too, that we should probably all agree that modern communications and rates of technological change are such that the slow accretion of symbols in a fairly stable context—their "natural" growth—is rarely any longer possible in its original forms. Whitehead's program is like Greene's and McKeon's in one respect at least: it implies not an "unconscious" process of symbolizing (symbols, it may very well be, were *never* the product of an entirely unconscious process[11]) but a purposeful one, involving thought, analysis, teaching, encouragement of artistic experimentation. "Good" symbols, new or old, are too easy to exploit for short term power-aims—*unless* the scholar, the critic, the teacher, and the enlightened journalist does his work conscientiously and well. What we are quite likely to be unconscious of, since we shall be in the midst of things, is the particular symbol; and the particular artistic masterpieces which will help produce it. In *What Is a Classic?*, Sainte-Beuve tells us that Molière and La Fontaine, both

---

[11]See Lasswell, *op. cit.*, p. 203:

> *The deliberate elaboration* of key signs plays an unmistakable role in the development of the configurations of historic record. Even the evolution of patterns in folk societies does not proceed wholly free from conscious elaboration, if we are to judge from fragmentary insight into some specific cases of manipulation.

working in an intellectually self-conscious milieu, were "apparently the least classical" of the great poets of their age. Yet: "With regard to classics, the least expected prove the best and greatest: seek them rather in the vigorous genius born; immortal and flourishing forever. . . . Observe after two centuries what is the result for both, . . . now unanimously considered to possess in the highest degree the characteristics of an all embracing morality."

I have already mentioned some of Tindall's ideas earlier in this comment. His general approach to literary symbolism, particularly in modern literature, is close to my own critical interests, and I find myself nodding admiringly and voting affirmatively almost all along the way. Doubtless some of my observations on this unfamiliar subject of the social uses of literary symbolism derive from assumptions like those which he develops. At this late point, therefore, I shall merely comment on two passages in "The Literary Symbol," in his essay.

1) On page 342, the subject is broached of the context of a work as a symbolic whole. I have made some suggestions on this subject in commenting on the relation of art and "reality" as viewed in these papers. But the problem is narrowed down here to "immediate" context: "the constituent image has immediate literary context and the work has not. . . . This lack is more or less supplied by the greater richness and complexity of the internal relationships that, providing control and enhancement, compose the whole" (pp. 342–343). Is not this explanation all the more true inasmuch as "the work as a whole" is the *reciprocal* relation or harmony of the moments and elements within it—and this relation shifts depending on the point we have reached in our experience and identification of it? If we are at the "final impression," for instance, everything that has gone before is the context. If we return to an earlier stage, our having experienced the whole growth or structure of the work presents it in another contextual light. The work spins its own "critical context" as it grows, and in the self-contained reality of its vision throws unexpected light on the reader's vision of ordinary reality. (For active symbols do, in their own turn, provide a context for private experience.)

2) Another way (in addition to that offered by Tindall) of looking at the symbolic structure of "Who Goes with Fergus" (p. 364) is to note that, in the passage where supposedly there is presented "peace, all passions put aside," the imagery has a more "disturbed" character than in the opening stanza. The "white breast of the dim sea" may suggest "the

comforts of mother," but it also suggests, as does the closing line, "love's bitter mystery" itself, though the young man and the maid have been promised it will trouble them no more.

There is characteristic romantic irony in the suggestion that the pure, untrammeled peace promised in the dreams of other-worldly joy preserved in myth and folklore is really self-deception—irony such as we find more explicitly expressed in "The Love Song of J. Alfred Prufrock." But the poem's theme and structure recall more nearly Blake's "Ah! Sunflower," in which "that sweet golden clime" of the sun is denied in succession to the sunflower, to the youth and maid dying of frustrated desire, and to the same lovers *even beyond the grave,* where they can still only "aspire." The theme of "Who Goes with Fergus" recalls, also, that of the next poem in Yeats's *Collected Poems,* "The Man Who Dreamed of Faeryland"—another complaint against that dream of perfect happiness which in life *and* death, harasses men who might otherwise have gained *some* real satisfaction from *this* life.

The whole body of Yeats's poetry, in fact, explores the dialectical interpenetrating relation of such opposites—"here" and "there," Self and Soul, the world of sensual experience and the world of imaginative creativity, the secular and the spiritual. Greene's term "normative" is particularly useful in a review of this aspect of his symbolic constructions.

3) Reverting for a moment to the idea of art as "unassigned syntactical symbol," we might also recall a wise saw of Kenneth Burke: "Free speculative tinkering with terms is the birthright of man, as the symbolusing species." The essay "Freedom and Authority in the Realm of the Poetic Imagination,"[12] in which this assertion appears, argues on behalf of "a many-termed view of motives" which will permit international communication to go beyond the limits of standardized attitudes. Does not art provide us, to borrow from Greene again, with the vehicle *par excellence* for communication of this sort? Not only is one of the prime functions of artistic symbolism the reconciling of opposites through transcendence in structure; but the apparent openness to interpretation and the vulnerability freely exposed in the social motives implied are

[12]Kenneth Burke, "Freedom and Authority in the Realm of the Poetic Imagination," *Freedom and Authority in Our Time,* edited by Lyman Bryson, Louis Finkelstein, R. M. MacIver, and Richard P. McKeon, Conference on Science, Philosophy and Religion in Their Relation to the Democratic Way of Life, New York, 1953, Chapter XXXII, pp. 365–375.

disarming and can transcend the narrow political determinism that keeps bedeviling individual nations and the whole world. In fact, the art which most cruelly exposes the agony of spiritual condition of a people is often the most decisive factor in endearing them to other peoples. It reveals perforce their essential, overriding humanity—their vitality and resilience of spirit, and perhaps their saving grace of a high comic sense also.

APPENDIX V

Report on the Conference on Science, Philosophy and Religion

DURING THE Fourteenth Conference at the regular business meeting, revision of the by-laws was announced whereby an Executive Committee has been substituted for the Board of Directors. The new Executive Committee includes:

Lyman Bryson	R. M. MacIver
Thurston N. Davis, S.J.	Richard P. McKeon, Chairman
Louis Finkelstein	I. I. Rabi
Hudson Hoagland	Harlow Shapley
F. Ernest Johnson	Wendell M. Stanley
John LaFarge, S.J.	Ordway Tead

M. L. Wilson

The Conference officers are:

Louis Finkelstein, President	R. M. MacIver, Vice President
Lyman Bryson, First Vice President	Richard P. McKeon, Chairman, Executive Committee of the Fellows
John LaFarge, S.J., Vice President	Hudson Hoagland, Vice President

Jessica Feingold, Executive Secretary

At the Eleventh Conference, the committee headed by Harry J. Carman reported on suggestions for reorganization of the Conference, looking toward its establishment on a permanent basis. Members agreed that a first step should be organization of a group of Conference Fellows, in addition to the members of the Board of Directors. The group of Fellows now includes:

William F. Albright	Stewart G. Cole
Van Wyck Brooks	William G. Constable
Lyman Bryson	Norman Cousins
Harry J. Carman	Thurston N. Davis, S.J.

Karl W. Deutsch

Irwin Edman (deceased)

Hoxie N. Fairchild

Clarence H. Faust

Louis Finkelstein

Lawrence K. Frank

Philipp G. Frank

Simon Greenberg

Caryl P. Haskins

Charles W. Hendel

Hudson Hoagland

Charles S. Johnson

F. Ernest Johnson

Clyde Kluckhohn

John LaFarge, S.J.

Harold D. Lasswell

Robert H. Lowie

R. M. MacIver

Jacques Maritain

Richard P. McKeon

Margaret Mead

Henry A. Murray

John Courtney Murray, S.J.

John U. Nef

F. S. C. Northrop

J. Robert Oppenheimer

Harry A. Overstreet

Anton C. Pegis

Gerald B. Phelan

I. I. Rabi

Roy W. Sellars

Harlow Shapley

George N. Shuster

Wendell M. Stanley

Donald C. Stone

Ordway Tead

M. L. Wilson

The Fifteenth Conference will discuss "The Concept of the Postulates of Equality of Opportunity" in 1956. A preliminary meeting of Conference Fellows and paper writers is to be held from August 29 to September 1, 1955, at The Men's Faculty Club of Columbia University.

The group that met at Amherst in 1944 and at Lake Mohonk in 1946, 1948, 1949, 1950, 1951, and April, 1952, again assembled there in November, 1952, in June and December, 1953, in April and November, 1954, and in May, 1955, for discussion of a number of suggestions that had been submitted to the Council of the Conference of which Harlow Shapley served as president. Other proposals and criticisms of the activities of the Conference generally will be welcome.

CONTRIBUTORS TO "SYMBOLS AND SOCIETY"*

THOMAS RITCHIE ADAM, *New York University*, professor of political science; author, *The Civic Value of Museums, Museums and Popular Culture, Education for International Understanding*

SWAMI AKHILANANDA, *Ramakrishna Vedanta Society*, Boston

ROBERT E. BASS, *Department of Physics, University of Toledo*

DAVID BIDNEY, *Indiana University*, associate professor of anthropology and philosophy; author, *The Psychology and Ethics of Spinoza, Theoretical Anthropology*

R. S. BRUMBAUGH, author, *Plato's Mathematical Imagination, The Scope of Philosophy*, and others

LYMAN BRYSON, *Teachers College, Columbia University*, professor emeritus of education; Conference on Science, Philosophy and Religion, first vice president; author, *The Next America, The Drive Toward Reason*, and others; editor, *The People's Library, The Communication of Ideas;* co-editor, 2nd, 3rd, 4th, 5th, 6th, 7th, 8th, 9th, 10th, 11th, 12th, 13th, and 14th Conference symposia

JOHN ELY BURCHARD, *School of Humanities and Social Studies, Massachusetts Institute of Technology*, dean; *American Academy of Arts and Sciences*, president; co-author, *The Evolving House* (3 vols. with A. F. Bemis), author, *QED, A History of MIT during World War II, Mid-Century, The Social Implications of Scientific Progress*, and others, together with numerous essays on architectural subjects

STEWART G. COLE, author (with Mildred W. Cole), *Minorities and the American Promise*

JAMES COLLINS, *St. Louis University*

MARTIN C. D'ARCY, S.J., *English Province of Society of Jesus*, Provincial, 1945–1950; author, *Mirage and Truth, The Problem of Evil, The Mind and Heart of Love*, and others

KARL W. DEUTSCH, *Massachusetts Institute of Technology*, professor of history and political science; Guggenheim Fellow, 1954–1955; Conference on Science, Philosophy and Religion, Fellow; author, *Nationalism and Social Communication, Political Community at the International Level*

FRANCIS FERGUSSON, *Rutgers University*, professor of comparative literature; author, *The Idea of a Theatre, Plays of Molière, Critical Introduction, Dante's Drama of the Mind*

LOUIS FINKELSTEIN, *The Jewish Theological Seminary of America*, chancellor and Solomon Schechter professor of theology; Conference on Science, Philosophy and Religion, president; author, *Akiba—Scholar, Saint and Martyr, The Pharisees: The Sociological Background of Their Faith*, and others; editor, *American Spiritual Autobiographies, Thirteen Americans, The Jews: Their History, Culture, and Religion;* co-editor, 2nd, 3rd, 4th, 5th, 6th, 7th, 8th, 9th, 10th, 11th, 12th, 13th, and 14th Conference symposia

FREDERIC B. FITCH, *Department of Philosophy, Yale University*

PHILIPP G. FRANK, *Institute for the Unity of Science*, president; Conference on Science, Philosophy and Religion, Fellow; author, *Foundations of Physics, Einstein: His Life and Times*, and others

JOHN H. E. FRIED, *New York University*

SIMON GREENBERG, *The Jewish Theological Seminary of America*, vice chancellor and professor of homiletics; Conference on Science, Philosophy and Religion, Fellow; author, *Ideas and Ideals in the Jewish Prayer Book, The First Year in the Hebrew School: A Teachers Guide*

THEODORE M. GREENE, *Yale University*, professor of philosophy; author, *The Arts and the Art of Criticism*, and others; editor (with others), *Liberal Education Re-examined: Its*

*Positions based on list of September, 1954.

Role in a Democracy, and others; translator (with H. H. Hudson) *Kant's Religion Within the Limits of Reason Alone*

HUDSON HOAGLAND, *Worcester Foundation for Experimental Biology,* executive director; *Boston University Graduate School,* research professor of physiology; 1954 Conference on Science, Philosophy and Religion, chairman; author, scientific papers on the nervous system and on endocrinology

ALBERT HOFSTADTER, *Columbia University,* professor of philosophy

STANLEY EDGAR HYMAN, *"The New Yorker,"* staff writer; author, *The Armed Vision: a Study of the Methods of Modern Literary Criticism*

DAVID NORIMATO IINO, *International Christian University,* Tokyo

MORDECAI M. KAPLAN, *The Jewish Theological Seminary of America,* professor of philosophies of religion; author, *Judaism in Transition, The Meaning of God in Modern Jewish Religion, The Future of the American Jew,* and others

JIRI KOLAJA, *Talledega College*

JOHN LAFARGE, S.J., *"America,"* associate editor; Conference on Science, Philosophy and Religion, vice president; author, *Interracial Justice, The Race Question and the Negro, No Postponement, The Manner is Ordinary,* and others

DANIEL LERNER, *Massachusetts Institute of Technology,* professor of sociology; *Center for International Studies (M.I.T.),* research associate; author, *Sykewar: Psychological Warfare Against Germany, Propaganda in War and Crisis* (with Harold D. Lasswell), *The Policy Sciences,* and others

WILLIAM F. LYNCH, S.J., *"Thought," Fordham University,* editor

R. M. MACIVER, *Columbia University,* Lieber professor emeritus of political philosophy and sociology; Conference on Science, Philosophy and Religion, vice president; author, *The Web of Government, The More Perfect Union, The Ramparts We Guard, Democracy and the Economic Challenge,* and others; editor, *Group Relations and Group Antagonisms, Civilization and Group Relationships, Unity and Difference in American Life, Discrimination and National Welfare, Great Expressions of Human Rights, Conflict of Loyalties, Moments of Personal Discovery, The Hour of Insight, New Horizons in Creative Thinking: A Survey and Forecast;* co-editor, 4th, 5th, 6th, 7th, 8th, 9th, 10th, 11th, 12th, 13th and 14th Conference symposia

CHARLES MORRIS, *The University of Chicago,* lecturer in philosophy

HAJIME NAKAMURA, *University of Tokyo,* professor of Indian philosophy

F. S. C. NORTHROP, *Yale University,* Sterling professor of philosophy and law; Conference on Science, Philosophy and Religion, Fellow; author, *Science and First Principles, The Meeting of East and West, The Logic of the Sciences and the Humanities*

WHITNEY J. OATES, *Princeton University,* professor of classics; author, *The Influence of Simonides of Ceos upon Horace;* editor, *The Basic Writings of St. Augustine,* and others

HOWARD L. PARSONS, *Department of Philosophy and Psychology, University of Tennessee*

M. L. ROSENTHAL, *Washington Square College, New York University,* assistant professor of English; contributor to literary journals; author, textbooks on poetry and reading analysis

ALBERT SALOMON, *The Graduate Faculty, The New School for Social Research,* professor of sociology; author, *The Tyranny of Progress,* articles on sociology, political theory, and intellectual history in modern society

ALFRED SCHUTZ, *The Graduate Faculty of Political and Social Science, The New School for Social Research,* professor of philosophy and sociology; author, books and articles in these fields

ROY W. SELLARS, *University of Michigan,* professor emeritus of philosophy; Conference on Science, Philosophy and Religion, Fellow; author, *Principles and Problems of Philosophy, Religion Coming of Age, The Philosophy of Physical Realism,* and others

HARLOW SHAPLEY, *Harvard University*, Paine professor of practical astronomy and lecturer on cosmography; Conference on Science, Philosophy and Religion, Fellow and member, executive committee of board of directors; First Conference on Science, Philosophy and Religion Lecturer

WILLIAM Y. TINDALL, *Columbia University*, professor of English; Guggenheim Fellow, 1954; author, *D. H. Lawrence and Susan His Cow, Forces in Modern British Literature, James Joyce*, and others

ROBERT ULICH, *Graduate School of Education, Harvard University*, James Bryant Conant professor of education; author, *Crisis and Hope in American Education, The Human Career: A Philosophy of Self-Transcendence*, and others

JOSHUA WHATMOUGH, *Harvard University*, professor of comparative philology; author, *Dialects of Ancient Gaul*, and others

Program

"SYMBOLS AND SOCIETY"

FOURTEENTH CONFERENCE ON SCIENCE, PHILOSOPHY AND RELIGION IN THEIR RELATION TO THE DEMOCRATIC WAY OF LIFE

HUDSON HOAGLAND, Chairman, 1954 Conference
M. L. WILSON, Vice-Chairman

MONDAY, TUESDAY, WEDNESDAY, and THURSDAY
AUGUST 30 and 31, SEPTEMBER 1 and 2, 1954
HARVARD UNIVERSITY
CAMBRIDGE, MASSACHUSETTS

All sessions (with the exception of the First Conference on Science, Philosophy and Religion Lecture) will be held on the Fifth Level of the Lamont Library, Harvard College, Harvard University

MONDAY, AUGUST 30th

6:00 p.m.

Dinner meeting of Conference Fellows, the Chairmen and Co-chairmen
Hotel Commander

8:30 p.m.

SECTIONAL MEETINGS[1]

THE FINE ARTS

Contributors

LYMAN BRYSON, *Chairman*
JOHN E. BURCHARD
WILLIAM G. CONSTABLE
NORMAN COUSINS
THEODORE M. GREENE
ALBERT HOFSTADTER
STANLEY EDGAR HYMAN
M. L. ROSENTHAL
WILLIAM Y. TINDALL

Smoking Room

POLITICAL AND SOCIAL ORGANIZATION

Contributors

R. M. MacIver, *Chairman*
Thomas Ritchie Adam
Henry D. Aiken[2]
Lyman Bryson[3]
Ralph W. Burhoe
Stewart G. Cole
Karl W. Deutsch
Philipp G. Frank
John W. Gardner
Hudson Hoagland
Charles S. Johnson
Daniel Lerner
Irving D. Lorge[2]
William Malamud
Margaret Mead
F. S. C. Northrop
I. I. Rabi
Albert Salomon
Alfred Schutz
Roy W. Sellars
Harlow Shapley
Robert Ulich
Rupert B. Vance
Joshua Whatmough
M. L. Wilson

Woodberry Poetry Room

PHILOSOPHY AND RELIGION

Contributors

Clarence H. Faust, *Chairman*
Swami Akhilananda
David W. Barry
Thurston N. Davis, S.J.
Nels F. S. Ferré
Louis Finkelstein
Simon Greenberg
John LaFarge, S.J.
William F. Lynch, S.J.

Richard P. McKeon[2]
Whitney J. Oates
Gerald B. Phelan

Farnsworth Room

TUESDAY, AUGUST 31st

10:00 a.m.

SECTIONAL MEETINGS (Continued)

2:30 p.m.

GENERAL SESSION

Formal Inauguration of the 14th Conference on
Science, Philosophy and Religion

Hudson Hoagland, *Chairman*

Discussion of[1]

THE FINE ARTS

Lyman Bryson, *Chairman*

based on papers by

John E. Burchard
Theodore M. Greene
Albert Hofstadter
William Y. Tindall

Prepared discussants

William G. Constable
Norman Cousins
Stanley Edgar Hyman
M. L. Rosenthal

Forum Room

8:30 p.m.

FIRST CONFERENCE ON SCIENCE, PHILOSOPHY AND RELIGION LECTURE

"Galaxies and Their Human Worth"
by
Harlow Shapley

Greetings from Harvard University, McGeorge Bundy

Louis Finkelstein, *Chairman*

Littauer Auditorium,
Graduate School of
Public Administration

WEDNESDAY, SEPTEMBER 1st

8:30 a.m.

Breakfast business meeting of the members of the Conference on Science, Philosophy and Religion, to transact necessary business of the corporation, including election of officers.

Hotel Commander

10:30 a.m.

GENERAL SESSION

R. M. MacIver, *Chairman*

Discussion of[1]

POLITICAL AND SOCIAL ORGANIZATION

based on papers by

THOMAS RITCHIE ADAM
HENRY D. AIKEN[2]
LYMAN BRYSON
KARL W. DEUTSCH
PHILIPP G. FRANK
IRVING D. LORGE[2]
F. S. C. NORTHROP
ALBERT SALOMON
ALFRED SCHUTZ
ROBERT ULICH

Prepared discussants

RALPH W. BURHOE
STEWART G. COLE
JOHN W. GARDNER
HUDSON HOAGLAND
CHARLES S. JOHNSON
DANIEL LERNER
WILLIAM MALAMUD
MARGARET MEAD
I. I. RABI
ROY W. SELLARS
HARLOW SHAPLEY
RUPERT B. VANCE
JOSHUA WHATMOUGH
M. L. WILSON

Forum Room

8:30 p.m.

GENERAL SESSION

CLARENCE H. FAUST, *Chairman*

Discussion of[1]

PHILOSOPHY AND RELIGION

based on papers by

LOUIS FINKELSTEIN
WILLIAM F. LYNCH, S.J.
RICHARD P. McKEON[2]
WHITNEY J. OATES

Prepared discussants

SWAMI AKHILANANDA
DAVID W. BARRY
THURSTON N. DAVIS, S.J.
NELS F. S. FERRÉ
SIMON GREENBERG
JOHN LaFARGE, S.J.
GERALD B. PHELAN

Forum Room

THURSDAY, SEPTEMBER 2nd

10:00 a.m.

CRITIQUE OF THE CONFERENCE ON SCIENCE, PHILOSO-
PHY AND RELIGION, with special reference to the fourteenth meeting and plans for the future.

M. L. WILSON, *Chairman*

Forum Room

12:00 noon

Luncheon meeting of the Council.

Hotel Commander

---

[1]Papers available in mimeographed form. All oral discussion off the record.
[2]Text not received before program in press.
[3]Paper to serve as basis for discussion.

PARTICIPANTS IN PROGRAM*

Thomas Ritchie Adam, *New York University*
Henry D. Aiken, *Harvard University*
Swami Akhilananda, *Ramakrishna Vedanta Society, Boston*
David W. Barry, *The National Council of the Churches of Christ in the United States of America*
Robert W. Bass, *University of Toledo*
David Bidney, *Indiana University*
Russell T. Blackwood, III, *Hood College*
R. J. Blakely, *The Fund for Adult Education*
Stephen Borsody, *Pennsylvania College for Women*
Lyman Bryson, *Teachers College, Columbia University*
McGeorge Bundy, *Harvard University*
John E. Burchard, *Massachusetts Institute of Technology*
Ralph W. Burhoe, *American Academy of Arts and Sciences*
José Maria Chaves, *Embajada de Colombia*
Stewart G. Cole
James Collins, *St. Louis University*
William G. Constable, *Museum of Fine Arts, Boston*
Norman Cousins, *"Saturday Review"*
W. J. Crozier, *Harvard University*
Thurston N. Davis, S.J., *"America"*
William R. Dennes, *Graduate School, University of California*
Karl W. Deutsch, *Massachusetts Institute of Technology*
Ralph I. Dorfman, *Worcester Foundation for Experimental Biology*
Fred Elmadjian, *Worcester Foundation for Experimental Biology*
Clarence H. Faust, *Fund for the Advancement of Education, Ford Foundation*
Francis Fergusson, *Rutgers University*
Nels F. S. Ferré, *School of Religion, Vanderbilt University*
Louis Finkelstein, *The Jewish Theological Seminary of America*
Sister Mary Francis, *College of Mount Saint Vincent*
Philipp G. Frank, *Institute for the Unity of Science*
John H. E. Fried
William G. Friedrich
Royal M. Frye, *Simmons College*
John W. Gardner, *Carnegie Corporation of New York*
R. W. Gerard, *College of Medicine, University of Illinois*
Marija Gimbutas, *Peabody Museum, Harvard University*
William J. Grede, *National Association of Manufacturers*
Simon Greenberg, *The Jewish Theological Seminary of America*
Theodore M. Greene, *Yale University*
Leo Gross, *Fletcher School of Law and International Relations*
Marvin P. Halverson, *The National Council of the Churches of Christ in the United States of America*
Erving P. Hayes, *Dennison Manufacturing Company*
Charles W. Hendel, *Yale University*
Hudson Hoagland, *Worcester Foundation for Experimental Biology*
Richard Hocking, *Emory University*
Albert Hofstadter, *Columbia University*
Gerald J. Holton, *Harvard University*
R. Gordon Hoxie, *College of Liberal Arts and Sciences, Long Island University*
William H. Huggins, *Massachusetts Institute of Technology*

Arno G. Huth, *The New School for Social Research*
Stanley Edgar Hyman
Blanche F. Ittleson
Lucie J. N. Jessner, *Harvard University*
Charles S. Johnson, *Fisk University*
Mordecai M. Kaplan, *The Jewish Theological Seminary of America*
Hans Kohn, *The College of the City of New York*
Jiri Kolaja, *Talledega College*
Lawrence Krader
John LaFarge, S.J., *"America"*
Philippe LeCorbeiller, *Harvard University*
Daniel Lerner, *Massachusetts Institute of Technology*
Joseph R. Levenson, *University of California*
Clem C. Linnenberg, Jr.
Irving D. Lorge, *Teachers College, Columbia University*
Lewis L. Lorwin
William F. Lynch, S.J., *"Thought," Fordham University*
R. M. MacIver, *Columbia University*
William Malamud, *Boston University*
Maurice Mandelbaum, *Dartmouth College*
Simon Marcson, *Brooklyn College*
Sydney G. Margolin, *New York Psychoanalytic Institute*
Eugene J. McCarthy, *Congress of the United States, House of Representatives*
Warren S. McCulloch, *Research Laboratory of Electronics, Massachusetts Institute of Technology*
Richard P. McKeon, *The University of Chicago*
Margaret Mead, *The American Museum of Natural History*
Henry A. Murray, *Harvard University*
F. S. C. Northrop, *Yale University*
Whitney J. Oates, *Princeton University*
Glenn A. Olds, *Cornell University*
John Osman, *The Fund for Adult Education*
Ralph T. Overman, *Oak Ridge Institute of Nuclear Studies*
Alan Burr Overstreet, *Smith College*
Howard L. Parsons, *University of Tennessee*
Anton C. Pegis, *Pontifical Institute of Mediaeval Studies, Toronto*
Gerald B. Phelan, *St. Michael's College, Toronto*
Paul Pigors, *Massachusetts Institute of Technology*
Ithiel de Sola Pool, *Massachusetts Institute of Technology*
I. I. Rabi, *Columbia University*
Walter A. Rosenblith, *Massachusetts Institute of Technology*
M. L. Rosenthal, *Washington Square College, New York University*
Joseph S. Roucek, *University of Bridgeport*
Albert Salomon, *The Graduate Faculty, The New School for Social Research*
Harold K. Schilling, *Graduate School, The Pennsylvania State College*
Alfred Schutz, *The New School for Social Research*
Roy W. Sellars, *University of Michigan*
Harlow Shapley, *Harvard University*
Helen Silving, *Office of Alien Property, United States Department of Justice*
Robert J. Slavin, O.P., *Providence College*
T. V. Smith, *Syracuse University*

Mark Starr, *International Ladies' Garment Workers' Union*
Kenneth W. Thompson, *Northwestern University*
William Y. Tindall, *Columbia University*
Robert Ulich, *Graduate School of Education, Harvard University*
Rupert B. Vance, *University of North Carolina*
Joshua Whatmough, *Harvard University*
Jerome B. Wiesner, *Massachusetts Institute of Technology*
M. L. Wilson
Max Wolff
Louise L. Wright, *Institute for International Education*

*Writers of papers and comments, and those expected to attend, as of August 17th.

Index

Abraham, 416, 420-421, 548, 555
Absolom, Absolom, 365-367
Abstract art, 251, 263
Abstraction, 263
Abstract symbols, 38
Académie Française, 210
Achievement, rewards of, 81
Adam and Eve, 415
Adam, Thomas Ritchie, 9-22, 581, 586, 588, 590
Advertising, high pressure, 270
Afrikaners, 16
Aggression, legitimate outlets for, 45
Agnostic, 464-465
Ahab, King, 414, 537
Aiken, Henry D., 586, 588, 590
Akhilananda, Swami, 581, 586, 589, 590
  comments by, 423, 450-452
Albright, William F., 579
Alcohol, personality changes and, 532
Allport, Gordon, 506
Alpha Centauri, 519
Amalie, Princess, of Prussia, 213
America:
  as symbol, 542-544
  life in, 79
  prestige changes in, 92-101
American Dilemma, 502
American Revolution, 39, 40
Analytical proposition, 325-326
Anaxagoras, 3
Ancestor worship, 105, 108
Andromeda Nebula, 513, 514, 517, 520, 521, 527
Angel and devil, 216
Animals:
  brain operations on, 533
  experimentation with, 220-221
Anthropology, historical and philosophical, 221
Anti-intellectualism, 507
Apollo, 446
Apperception, analogical, 143
Apperceptional scheme, 147, 174
  relative irrelevance of vehicle, 151-153
Apprehension, 264-265
Appresentation:
  concept of, 143-146

Appresentation (*Cont.*)
  orders involved in, 146-148
  symbolic (*see* Symbolic appresentation)
Appresentational references, dependence on social environment, 193-197
Appresentational relations:
  figurative transference, 153
  intersubjective world, 159-175
  structural changes, 151
Appresentational scheme, 148, 174
Aquinas, Thomas, 220
Arab countries, 30
Aragon, oath of, 109
Architecture, 251, 254-256, 572-574
  Egyptian, 371, 377
  Gothic, 377-379
  Greek, 371, 376, 377, 398
  inferior, imitative, 271
  in totalitarian states, 398
  mechanization and, 390
  mid-twentieth century, 379-381
  modern revolution in, 396-397
  monumental:
    decline of, 381-396
    need for, 397-400
  of earlier periods, 371-372
  painting and, 372-373
  problem of scale, 391
  Roman, 400
  Russian, 391
  symbolism in, 371-418
    symbols, 400-404
  the dome in, 376
Architectural Review, 382, 384, 386, 391, 392-395
Aretino, 121
Aristocracy in England and France, 88-92
Aristotle, 5, 140, 220, 321, 334, 453, 455, 469, 470, 472, 473
  rejection of Plato, 487, 488-490
  value theory of, 456, 457, 473, 474
  value thinking, types of, 495
Armed forces, racial integration in, 501
Army as symbol, 104
Art and the arts, 341
  artistic appraisal, levels of, 259-260
  as normative vehicle, 261-275
  basic components of, 258-259